WEST ACADEMIC
EMERITUS ADV

PRINCIPLES OF ANTITRUST

Second Edition

Herbert Hovenkamp

James G. Dinan University Professor
Penn Law and the Wharton School
University of Pennsylvania

CONCISE HORNBOOK SERIES™

© 2017 LEG, Inc. d/b/a West Academic
© 2021 LEG, Inc. d/b/a West Academic
    444 Cedar Street, Suite 700
    St. Paul, MN 55101
    1-877-888-1330

Printed in the United States of America

ISBN: 978-1-68467-436-7

To Arie, Erik, and Mira

Summary of Contents

Table of Contents

PRINCIPLES OF ANTITRUST

Second Edition

Chapter 1

THE BASIC ECONOMICS OF ANTITRUST

Table of Sections

§ 1.1 Price Theory: Economic Behavior and Perfect Competition

Market economies are dedicated to the principle that in the first instance people are responsible for their own welfare. Further, they are best off if they can make voluntary exchanges of goods and services in competitive markets. If all exchanges are voluntary, each person will continue to exchange goods and services until she can make herself no better off by a further exchange. If all exchanges occur at competitive prices, society as a whole is wealthier than if some occur at a higher or lower price. An important goal of antitrust

1

law—arguably its only goal—is to ensure that markets are competitive.

1.1a.   The Perfectly Competitive Market

A competitive market is one in which 1) every good is priced at the cost of producing it, giving the producers and sellers only enough profit to maintain investment in the industry; and 2) every person willing to pay this price will be able to buy it.

The conditions most conducive to competition, and which obtain perfectly in an economic model of "perfect competition," are: 1) All sellers make an homogenous product, so that customers are indifferent as to which seller they purchase from, provided that the price is the same; 2) each seller in the market is so small in proportion to the entire market that the seller's increase or decrease in output, or even its exit from the market, will not affect the decisions of other sellers in that market; 3) all resources are completely mobile, or alternatively, all sellers have the same access to needed inputs; 4) all participants in the market have good knowledge about price, output and other information about the market. As a general rule, the closer a market comes to fulfilling these conditions, the more competitively it will perform.

The perfect competition model generally assumes "constant returns to scale"—that is, that costs of production per unit remain constant at all practical rates of output. As we shall see in § 1.4, the presence of substantial economies of scale—that is, of per unit costs that decrease as output increases—can undermine the perfect competition model if a firm must acquire a large market share in order to take advantage of these scale economies.

The most important rule governing price is the law of supply and demand. Price setting in any market is a function of the relationship between the amount of a product available and the amount that consumers, at the margin, are willing to pay. The market allocates goods to customers based on their individual willingness to pay. For example, if all the world's steel mills produced only 1000 pounds of steel per year, customers would likely bid a very high price for the steel, which would naturally be sold to the highest bidder. The price would be determined by the marginal customer's willingness to pay—that is, by the amount that some buyer would be willing to pay for the 1000th pound. Perhaps orthodontists, who put one half ounce of steel in a set of $2000 braces, would be willing to buy all the steel at $3000 per pound. In that case no steel would be sold at a lower price. If the supply of steel increased 1000-fold, however, there might be far more steel than orthodontists could use at a price of $3000 per pound.

The price of steel would drop so that the market could take in additional customers also who place a high value on steel but are not willing to pay $3000 per pound.

As more and more steel is produced, the market price must drop further in order to reach customers who have a lower "reservation" price, which is the highest amount that a consumer is willing to pay for a product. As the price of steel drops those customers with very high reservation prices, such as the orthodontists, can also buy steel at the lower price. In the perfect competition model all sales tend to be made at the same price, even though different groups of consumers have vastly different reservation prices. If the seller attempted to charge orthodontists $3000 per pound but automakers $3 per pound, the seller's plan would be frustrated by "arbitrage." That is, automakers would buy steel at $3.00 per pound and resell some steel to orthodontists at a price higher than $3.00 per pound but lower than $3000 per pound. If all buyers have complete information about the market, all of them will pay the same price, regardless of their reservation prices. When a market reaches this condition, it is said to be in "equilibrium."[1]

Assume that the market contains 100 sellers of steel. Each seller wants to make as much as possible, and every buyer (regardless of his reservation price) wants to purchase at the lowest possible price. How much steel will be produced in the market and what will be its price?

Figure 1 illustrates how a perfectly competitive market arrives at equilibrium, where supply and demand are perfectly balanced and will not change unless the market is disturbed. The figure illustrates the market demand curve (D) and the market supply curve (S) for a single product. Since both price and output are generally positive numbers, it is common to display only the upper right quadrant of the standard two-axis graph. The vertical axis represents price, which increases from 0 as one moves upward. The horizontal axis represents output (or quantity), which increases from 0 as one moves from the origin to the right.

---

[1]   In real world markets, however, price discrimination, or obtaining higher profits from one set of customers than from another set, is both possible and common. See §§ 14.1–14.3.

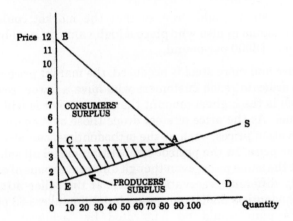

Figure 1

The graph shows that at low levels of output the market price is quite high. Since few units are being produced, the good is sold only to customers who have very high reservation prices. Sellers will be earning enormous profits on their output. Profit, which is revenue (or price times quantity sold) minus cost, is measured by the vertical distance between the supply curve and the demand curve at any point. The supply curve itself includes "competitive" or "normal" profits. Any vertical distance between the supply curve and the demand curve is referred to as "economic" or "monopoly" profits. These are profits in excess of those earned by a competitive industry, and in excess of the amount needed to maintain investment in the industry.

If profits per unit of output are extremely high, as they are when output is very low, two things will happen. First, existing sellers will be encouraged by the very high profits to increase their output. Suppose current output is twenty units, the cost of production is approximately $2.00, but the price is on the order of $10.00. Each additional unit that the firm produces will give it economic profits of $8.00. Secondly, and for the same reason, new firms will come into the market. People with money to invest invariably seek opportunities where the expected return is highest.

The figure shows an upward sloping supply curve. A horizontal supply curve would imply that the costs of producing additional units are the same at all levels of market output. However, this is commonly not the case. The new production must make use of increasingly marginal (less attractive) resources. The first units of steel, for example, will be produced from the iron ore that is the cheapest to obtain and refine. As output increases, however, these firms must turn to more marginal ore. Likewise, as new steel producers enter the market they will buy up the best remaining ore reserves, and firms that come in later will have to take more marginal reserves. As the market grows, increasingly marginal materials will be used and the cost of producing steel will rise.[2]

As output increases, the market price will fall as customers with lower and lower reservation prices must be drawn in. The market will finally stabilize at point A. At any point on the supply curve to the left of A, an increase in output of one unit will generate positive economic profits—that is, more in revenue than the cost of producing that unit. At least one firm will increase its output or at least one new firm will enter the market and start producing. This process will continue until the supply curve and demand curve intersect. The market constantly moves toward this "equilibrium."

As noted above, in a competitive market all buyers pay the market price, even if their individual reservation prices are higher. The difference between the buyers' reservation prices and the price they actually pay is called "consumers' surplus." The size of the consumers' surplus in Figure 1 is represented by triangle ABC. A competitive market tends to maximize the size of the consumers' surplus: the consumers' surplus cannot be larger than ABC without at least one sale being unprofitable.

Some firms in the market are likely to have lower costs than others. They may have the richest veins of ore or the lowest energy, labor, or distribution costs. Cross-hatched triangle ACE represents "producers' surplus:" the difference between total revenue at the competitive price and the sum of the producers' costs. Only at the margin does a firm earn zero profits. Such a marginal firm is the one with the highest costs that is still capable of earning a competitive rate of return when the product is sold at a competitive price. If the market shifts in a way that is unfavorable to sellers, this marginal firm is likely to be the first, or one of the first, to go out of business.

The supply and demand curves in Figure 1 can assume many shapes. The figure shows them as straight lines, suggesting that the quantity demanded increases at a uniform rate as price falls, and that production costs rise at a uniform rate as output increases. But in most markets the two lines are non-linear. Drawing them as straight lines is a useful analytic device, however, that often does not affect analysis.

---

[2] If these costs differences result from new entry by additional firms, they are usually diagrammed by a supply curve that shifts to reflect higher costs. If they are the increasing costs of a single firm or group of firms, they are generally diagrammed by a curve that has an upward slope, as in Figure 1.

Elasticity of *supply* is a relationship between changes in the price of a product and the amount produced. As the price of a product rises, more of it will be produced because existing firms will increase their output or new firms will enter the market and start producing. The elasticity of supply is measured by the percentage change in the amount supplied that results from a certain percentage change in price. For example, if a 10% price increase yields a 30% increase in supply, the elasticity of supply in the market is 3. If a 30% price increase yields a 15% supply increase, the market's elasticity of supply is .5. Elasticity of supply is a positive number.

For antitrust policy one must consider not only the absolute elasticity of supply, but also the amount of time it takes for supply to increase in response to a price increase. Suppose that the elasticity of supply in a market is 3, which is very high. If price goes up by 10%, the quantity supplied to the market will increase by 30%. But suppose that the construction of the additional plants that account for the 30% supply increase takes 10 years. A seller attempting to raise its price to a monopoly level will eventually lose sales to this increased output by competitors. But during the ten year construction period the seller will earn monopoly profits. Further, the expense and time required to build a competing plant may enable the incumbent to engage in certain "strategic" behavior. For example, if prospective competitors know that the incumbent has substantial excess capacity and can increase output and drop price at will, the large investment and long wait for an uncertain return may look unprofitable.

The importance of time in antitrust analysis results from the fact that the policy maker is necessarily concerned with *short*-run dislocations in the market. Even if all markets would eventually become competitive, antitrust is properly concerned with ensuring that this occurs sooner rather than later. The concern is not unique to antitrust. For example, we would not need contract law in competitive markets if our only concern was with the long run. Firms who break their contracts would be shunned by buyers and sellers who have other alternatives. Likewise, in the long run all of us will be dead. But that fact does not undermine the state's concern to protect us from murderers or see to it that we are provided with nutrition and health care.

The previous discussion of the relationship between supply and demand assumes that the market is unaffected by changes imposed from outside. If relative consumer income rises or falls, new technology makes a product obsolete or the country goes to war, however, demand for any good may rise or fall regardless of available supply or costs of production. In such cases we talk, not about changes *along* a demand (or supply) curve, but about *shifts* in the curve. For example, the invention of the electronic calculator had no effect on the cost of production of a slide rule or on the capacity of slide rule factories. Nevertheless, when the electronic calculator was invented the demand for slide rules dropped precipitously.

Supply curves may shift just as demand curves do. The invention of the microprocessor in a silicon chip reduced the cost of building computers by a factor of hundreds. The result is that the new supply curve for computers in the 1990's is much lower than the supply curve of the 1960's, and equilibrium output is much higher.

1.1b.   Behavior of the Competitive Firm

We have considered the competitive, multi-firm market, and can now examine the behavior of the individual firm in that market. We assume a market with a large number of sellers, into which entry is relatively easy and can be accomplished in a short time. How will an individual firm in that market decide how much to produce and what price to charge?

Even though the steel market's equilibrium price is $3.00 per pound, there are still individual buyers, such as the orthodontists, whose reservation price is far higher than $3.00. Suppose that the individual firm attempts to charge a higher price than $3.00— perhaps $4.00—for a pound of steel. The orthodontists are certainly willing to pay $4.00, but if they can buy for $3.00 they will do so. When one firm in a 100-firm market attempts to charge $4.00, a buyer who knows that the "going" price is $3.00 will look for a different seller. In a perfectly competitive market in which all buyers have complete price information, all the sellers will be "price takers"—they must simply accept the market price as given. No single firm is large enough to influence either the total amount produced or the market price. As a result, the individual firm can sell as little or as much as it pleases at the market price, but it will lose all sales if it attempts to charge more.

The situation facing the perfect competitor can be described in two ways. First, the firm faces a perfectly horizontal demand curve, as is illustrated in Figure 2. For the perfect competitor the market price is the same at all rates of output. Alternatively, the individual competitor faces extremely high firm elasticities of supply and demand. In response to a very small price increase, alternative suppliers will immediately offer substitute products to the price raiser's customers, and all customers will switch to those substitutes. The firm will lose all of its sales.

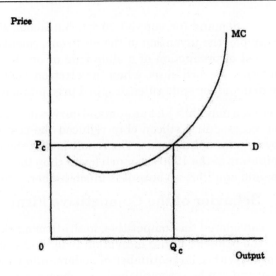

Figure 2

One must therefore distinguish between *market* elasticities of supply and demand, and individual *firm* elasticities of supply and demand. Except for the pure monopolist (whose output is the same as the output of the entire market) the individual firm faces higher elasticities of supply and demand than does the market as a whole. If the market contains 100 producers of identical steel, then A's steel is indistinguishable from B's steel, which is indistinguishable from C's, and so on. The fact that customers are indifferent as to whose steel they buy means that they will switch immediately to B or C if A attempts to increase price; conversely, B or C will happily provide the steel.

The firms in a perfectly competitive market have little discretion about what price to charge. They do make individual decisions, however, about the amount to produce. Even in a perfectly competitive market with an established single market price, different firms are of different sizes and produce differing amounts.

The individual competitor's output decision is a function of its marginal costs. Marginal cost is the additional cost that a firm incurs in the production of one additional unit of output. The best way to understand marginal cost is to consider several related cost curves. A firm's costs can be divided into two broad categories, fixed and variable. Fixed costs are those costs that do not change with output over the short-run, which is some finite period of time, usually less than the lifetime of the plant. Land costs, property taxes, management salaries, plant and durable equipment all generally fall into the category of fixed costs. Once the money for fixed cost items is invested it must be paid whether or not the plant produces anything, and the costs do not vary with the amount the plant produces.

Variable costs, by contrast, are costs that change with output. For the steel mill, the costs of iron ore and other raw materials are variable costs, as are fuel to burn in the refining furnaces, hourly wages, and transportation. If a firm increases its output by, say 10%, the cost of all these things rises because the firm must purchase more. The cost of the plant, durable equipment and the president's salary are likely to stay the same. Over the long-run, however, even these "fixed" costs must be considered variable. Eventually plant and durable equipment will have to be replaced. The firm will then decide whether to increase capacity, decrease it, or perhaps even go out of business.

Both fixed and variable costs are generally expressed as costs per unit of output. These are illustrated in Figure 3. "Average fixed cost" (AFC) is the amount of fixed cost divided by the amount of output. Since total fixed costs remain constant, average fixed costs decline as output increases. "Average variable cost" (AVC) is total variable cost divided by the amount of output the firm produces. The behavior of the average variable cost curve is more complex. Every established plant has some particular range of output in which it is most efficient. For example, a plant properly designed to produce 80–100 units per year will perform at lowest cost when output is in that range. If output drops to 50 the plant will perform less efficiently and per unit costs will rise. Thus the AVC curve shows higher than minimum AVC at low outputs. Blast furnaces, to give just one example, cost the same amount to heat whether they are used at capacity or only at half capacity. The same thing generally holds true for output that exceeds the plant's "optimal capacity." For example, a plant and work force designed to produce 80 units per week may be able to increase output to 100 units per week only if workers are paid overtime wages, which may be twice their normal wages, or if equipment is used at a level at which its breakdown rate is high. Thus, the AVC curve increases to the right of the minimum point as output increases.

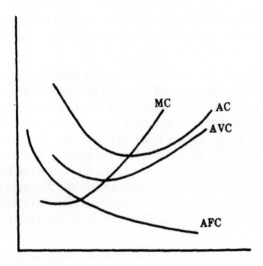

Figure 3

The average variable cost curve (AVC) of the plant tends to be U-shaped. AVC is at the lowest point when the plant is producing the optimal output for which it was designed, and increases when the plant's output exceeds optimal capacity. The AVC curve often has a relatively flat bottom, because many plants are efficient over a fairly broad range of output.

Just above the AVC curve in Figure 3 is the average total cost curve (AC), usually called the average cost curve, which is nothing more than the *sum* of all fixed and variable costs divided by output. Since all costs are either fixed or variable, the AC curve represents the total costs that a firm incurs. As a result, the AC curve is important in determining the firm's profitability. In order to be profitable the firm must obtain an average price per unit equal to or greater than AC. The AC curve is shaped roughly like the AVC curve, except that the two converge as output increases.[3]

Once again, *marginal* cost is the additional cost that a firm incurs in producing one additional unit of output.[4] Since a firm incurs no increased *fixed* costs in expanding output in the short run, marginal cost is a function of variable costs alone. The marginal cost curve (MC) falls and rises more dramatically than the average variable cost curve does, because the marginal cost curve considers

---

[3] The AC and AVC curves converge because AC is equal to the vertical sum of AVC and AFC; as output increases AFC continually decreases, approaching zero.

[4] Or, $MC = AC_j - AC_i$, where the difference between output i and output j at any level is one unit. In the short run, it is also true that $MC = AVC_j - AVC_i$; that is, short-run marginal cost is a function of variable costs alone.

merely the additional costs of one added unit of output. By contrast, the AVC curve averages that difference over the entire output being produced.[5] Importantly, the marginal cost curve always intersects the AVC curve at its lowest point. A minute's reflection about averages will tell you why. Suppose that you are averaging the height of United States Supreme Court Justices and you have managed to gather eight of them, and have computed their average height as 6'0". Now the ninth Justice walks in the door and happens to be 5'3" tall. The average height will decline. But if the ninth Justice happens to be 6'7" the average will increase. Whether the average falls or rises is a function of the height of the "marginal" Justice. As long as the marginal Justice is below the average, the average will be declining; as soon as the marginal Justice is above the average, the average will be increasing.

How will the competitive firm make its output decision? Suppose the market price is $100.00 per unit. At its current rate of production the firm has marginal costs of only $60.00 per unit. That is, if it produced one additional unit it would incur $60.00 in additional costs but would earn $40 in profits upon sale. A profit-maximizing firm will increase production by one additional unit. However, suppose that the firm's marginal cost at its current rate of output is $120.00. If it produced one fewer unit it would spend $120.00 less. In that case the production of the last unit is generating $20.00 in losses: the firm could make $20.00 more by producing one unit less.

Look back at Figure 2 to see the relationship between the competitive firm's marginal cost curve and the demand curve that it faces. The firm will always try to produce at a rate of output at which its marginal cost equals the market price. If it is producing more than that, it can increase profits by decreasing production. If it is producing less it can increase profits by increasing production. The competitive rate of output in Figure 2 is Q_c.

Although the market price might be less than a firm's average total cost at any output level, the firm will not necessarily cease production. The fixed costs may have been "sunk"—that is, the firm may not be able to recover them if it goes out of business. Further, the fixed costs must be paid whether or not the plant produces. As a general rule, the firm will be able to cut its losses as long as the market price is above its average variable costs, and it will continue to produce. However, when the plant wears out and needs to be

---

[5]   For example, suppose that AVC for 100 units is 3, and at that point marginal cost is 6. When unit 101 is produced, marginal cost is 6, but AVC would rise only to 306/101, or 3.029.

replaced, the firm may then decide to go out of business, or else to build a more efficient plant.

Perfectly competitive markets are generally thought to be "efficient" because they do the best job of providing consumers with goods at the cost of producing them. As a result, competition maximizes the total value of goods produced in society. In a competitive market no single firm has the power to reduce the available supply of goods, and no firm has the power to increase the price above the market level.

The world contains no perfectly competitive markets, and many markets do not even come close. Firms often differentiate their products from other firms; as a result, customers are no longer indifferent to the particular brand or identity of the seller. Information about market conditions is always less than perfect; as a result many transactions take place at some price other than the market price, and some socially valuable transactions never occur at all.[6] "Economies of scale"—the ability of larger firms to produce at a lower cost than smaller firms—may result in markets that have fewer than the number of sellers required for perfect competition to occur.[7] In short, like all scientific models, the model of perfect competition applies only imperfectly in the real world; nevertheless it can be of great service to the antitrust policy maker in predicting the consequences of a certain action or legal rule.

§ 1.2   Monopoly

1.2a.   Price and Output of the Protected Monopolist

The monopolist—the only firm selling in a particular market—faces a different array of price and output decisions than those that confront the perfect competitor. For this formal analysis we assume that the market contains only one firm, whose demand curve is therefore identical with the market demand curve. Second, the formal monopolist does not need to worry about new entry by a competitor. These assumptions often will not apply to the *de facto* "monopolist" that exists in most antitrust litigation. The antitrust "monopolist" is a dominant firm, but the market may contain a

---

6   In general, the more expensive it is for consumers to search out relevant information about prices and markets, the more likely they will make a less than optimal transaction. As a result, prices tend to vary more in markets where search costs are high in relation to the value of the product. See George J. Stigler, The Economics of Information, 69 J. Pol. Econ. 213 (1961).

7   See § 1.4a.

competitive "fringe" of smaller competitors.[8] Third, the antitrust monopolist ordinarily has no legal protection from competitive entry. If either formal assumption is relaxed the monopolist will face a certain amount of competition and will vary its behavior accordingly.[9] Assuming, however, that the monopolist has a 100% share of a market and no concern about entry by a competitor, how much will it sell and what price will it charge?

The monopolist has one power that the perfect competitor does not have. If the monopolist reduces output, total market output will decline, for the monopolist is the only producer in the market. As total market output goes down, the market-clearing price goes up. As a result, the monopolist, unlike the competitor, can obtain a higher price per unit by producing less.

However, the monopolist will not be able to charge an infinite price for its product. Even the orthodontists may be unwilling to pay more than $3000 per pound for steel; if the price goes higher they will change to silver or some other alternative.

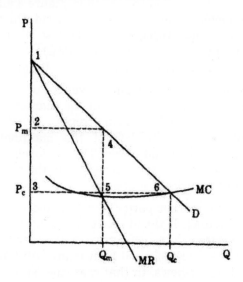

Figure 4

Figure 4 introduces the marginal revenue curve (MR), which represents the additional revenue that the monopolist obtains when it produces one additional unit of output. As Figure 4 shows, the

---

[8]   Economists generally speak of such firms not as "monopolists," but rather as "dominant firms."

[9]   For example, it may charge a lower, or "limit" price, calculated to make entry by outsiders less attractive. See § 8.3b.

marginal revenue curve facing the monopolist is steeper than the demand curve. This is because the monopolist must sell all units of output at the same price. Thus the marginal revenue curve shows not only that increases in market output reduce the market clearing price (which is what the demand curve shows), but also that less revenue is obtained from sales of all units, not just the incremental unit. This is easy to see in Table B. At output of one unit, the price is $20 and the seller's marginal revenue—the difference between the amount it obtains from one unit and the amount it obtains from zero units—is also $20. When output increases to 2 units, price drops to $18. However, the monopolist must sell both the first and the second units for $18.00. While the price drops by $2.00, marginal revenue drops by $4.00—$2.00 for each of the two units. This process continues and yields the MR curve in Figure 4.

The profit-maximizing monopolist, just as the profit-maximizing competitor, will expand production to the point that one additional unit will produce greater additional costs than additional revenues. It will produce at point Q_m on the graph in Figure 4 and charge price P_m. If the monopolist expands output beyond Q_m the additional revenue, shown by the MR curve, will be less than the additional costs, shown by the marginal cost curve (MC). P_m is known as the "monopoly price," or as the monopolist's "profit-maximizing price."

For the competitor, the marginal revenue curve is identical with the demand curve, and therefore with the market price.[10] For the monopolist, by contrast, the marginal revenue curve and marginal cost curve intersect to the left of the marginal cost curve's intersection with the demand curve. The monopolist produces at a lower rate than would a perfect competitor in the same market, and its profit-maximizing price is higher.

A monopolist's market power is a function of the elasticity of demand for its product. If the elasticity of demand for pistachios at the competitive price is high, consumers will be sensitive to changes in the price. If the price goes too high many will buy a substitute, such as almonds or cashews. In that case, the "spread" between the competitive price and the monopolist's profit-maximizing price will be relatively small. However, if the elasticity of demand is low, then consumers view the product as having few good substitutes. The monopolist will be able to extract a much higher price without losing too many sales.

---

[10]   This is so because the competitive price remains constant at all rates of output. For example, if price is $20, each additional sale at any output level the competitive firm chooses will generate an additional $20, and marginal revenue will remain constant at $20.

Market power can also be computed directly from a firm's price elasticity of demand. The formulas are also discussed in § 3.1. The formulas also offer several insights about the relevant variables in market power measurement.

1.2b.   Monopsony; Output Effects; Policy Implications

The mirror image of monopoly is "monopsony." A monopsonist is a monopoly buyer rather than seller. Although most antitrust litigation of market power offenses has involved monopoly sellers rather than buyers, monopsony can impose social costs on society similar to those caused by monopoly.[11]

By reducing its demand for a product, a monopsonist can force suppliers to sell to it at a lower price than would prevail in a competitive market. Some people are skeptical about this conclusion. No supplier would stay in business if it were forced to sell to the monopsonist at a price lower than its average costs, and price would tend toward average cost in a competitive market. Can a monopsonist actually force suppliers to engage in continuous loss selling?

The important policy implication of monopsony is that it often *reduces* rather than increases output in the monopsonized market. Some judges have failed to see this. The consumer welfare principle in antitrust, or the notion that the central goal of antitrust policy should be low prices,[12] seems to suggest that monopsony is not all that important an antitrust policy concern. For example, in *Balmoral* the court faced an agreement among theater operators not to bid against each other for motion pictures.[13] As a result, the prices they paid for the pictures were lower than if they had bid competitively. The court suggested that such an agreement could result in lower prices to consumers and concluded that the agreement might "serve rather than undermine consumer welfare."[14] Likewise, in the *Kartell* case, the First Circuit refused to condemn as monopolistic a health insurer's policy of setting the maximum price it was willing to pay for health care services used by its insureds.[15] The court noted that "the prices at issue here are low prices, not high prices * * *. [T]he

---

[11]   For a thorough, readable study of the law and economics of monopsony, see Roger D. Blair & Jeffrey L. Harrison, Monopsony: Antitrust Law & Economics (2d 2010). On the law and economics of buying cartels, see 12 Antitrust Law ¶¶ 2010–2015 (4th ed. 2019).

[12]   See §§ 2.2–2.3. On the correct meaning of "consumer welfare," see § 2.2d.

[13]   Balmoral Cinema v. Allied Artists Pictures Corp., 885 F.2d 313 (6th Cir. 1989).

[14]   Id. at 317. The court approved the lower court's instruction to the jury to apply the rule of reason, and its subsequent judgment for the defendants.

[15]   Kartell v. Blue Shield (Mass.), 749 F.2d 922 (1st Cir. 1984), cert. denied, 471 U.S. 1029, 105 S.Ct. 2040 (1985).

Congress that enacted the Sherman Act saw it as a way of protecting consumers against prices that were too *high*, not too low."[16]

These decisions apparently assume that monopsony buyers will generally pass their lower costs on to their consumers. But that is not necessarily the case. The monopsonist reduces its buying price by *reducing* the amount of some input that it purchases. If the input is used in the output in fixed proportions, then the output must be reduced is well. This suggests two things: (1) the monopsony buyer that resells in a competitive market will charge the same price, but its output will be lower than if it were a competitive purchaser; (2) the monopsony buyer (or cartel) that resells in a monopolized (or cartelized) market will actually charge a *higher* price than if it were a competitive purchaser.

Consider this illustration. A monopoly manufacturer of aluminum is also a monopsony purchaser of bauxite. Bauxite is an ingredient in aluminum, and one ton of bauxite, when mixed with other ingredients, yields two tons of aluminum. In a competitive market bauxite sells for $25 per ton and the producer would purchase 1000 tons, which it would then use to make 2000 tons of aluminum. The aluminum would be sold at the monopoly price of $80 per ton. In the monopsonized bauxite market, however, the monopsonist/ monopolist reduces its purchases of bauxite to 700 tons, which it purchases at $20 per ton. If it uses bauxite and other ingredients in fixed proportions of one ton of bauxite to two tons of aluminum, then it must also reduce the output of aluminum to 1400 tons. In that case, the market clearing price of the aluminum will rise to, say, $105.00. In sum, even though the monopsonist/monopolist buys an input at a lower price, the lower output entails a higher, not a lower, resale price. If the monopsonist/monopolist can change the proportion of bauxite in its aluminum the story becomes more complicated. But in general two things will be true. First, the price of aluminum will not go down and will almost always go up anyway. Second, consumers will not get the aluminum alloy that they would have gotten in a competitive market.[17]

The foregoing suggests that monopsony is an important antitrust concern and is just as inconsistent with consumer welfare as monopoly is. Indeed, one should not presume that the lower prices paid by a monopsonist are passed on to consumers as lower resale prices. Second, however, the antitrust policy maker must distinguish between lower buying prices that result from reduced transaction

---

[16] Id. at 930–931.

[17] For a more technical explanation, see Roger D. Blair & Jeffrey L. Harrison, Monopsony in Law and Economics, Ch. 3 (2d ed. 2010).

costs or the elimination of upstream market power, and lower buying prices that result from monopsony. If a large buyer is able to obtain lower prices by reducing transaction costs, the buyer will generally buy *more* rather than less.[18] The result will be lower resale prices, even if the large buyer resells in a monopolized market. Most of these conceptual problems can be avoided if we define consumer welfare in terms of output rather than price. The consumer welfare goal is maximum output consistent with sustainable competition. Articulated that way, it protects against both sell side and buy side monopoly.[19]

A principal difficulty of antitrust policy toward monopsony is distinguishing between the efficient low purchase prices that result from reduced transaction costs or elimination of upstream monopoly, and the inefficient low purchase prices that result from monopsony. Perhaps the most problematic area is joint purchasing arrangements, which create a significant potential for cost savings but may also facilitate buyer price fixing.[20] The decision maker must determine whether the defendants' managers are encouraging members to purchase as much as possible, which is generally inconsistent with buyer price-fixing; or encouraging them to suppress their buying, which is highly suspicious. Another area is so-called predatory buying, which occurs when a firm that is dominant in its buying market increases its purchase price in order to drive less pecunious rival purchasers out of the market. In *Weyerhaueser* the Supreme Court held that the same tests that govern the law of predatory pricing, namely prices below cost and a reasonable prospect that predation costs could later be recouped during a prolonged period of monopsony returns, apply to predatory buying.[21]

Currently, although belatedly, antitrust writers are examining labor market monopsony—or the result of employer power that suppresses wages. The problem is a real one: wages have not come close to keeping up with returns to capital. As a result, workers are receiving an ever smaller share of the benefits of economic growth. This makes it doubly important for antitrust policy makers to pay close attention to restraints that operate so as to suppress wages.[22]

---

[18]   See, for example, Northwest Wholesale Stationers v. Pacific Stationery & Printing Co., 472 U.S. 284, 105 S.Ct. 2613 (1985), where the Supreme Court noted that joint buying is most generally efficient—a claim that the courts can test by assessing the venturers' market share of the market in which they buy.

[19]   See § 2.2d.

[20]   See § 4.1d. See also 13 *Antitrust Law* ¶ 2135 (4th ed. 2019).

[21]   Weyerhaeuser Co. v. Ross-Simmons Hardwood Lumber Co., Inc., 549 U.S. 312, 127 S.Ct. 1069 (2007). The decision is discussed in § 8.10.

[22]   See Ioana Marinescu & Herbert Hovenkamp, Anticompetitive Mergers in Labor Markets, 94 Ind. L.J. 1031 (2019); Suresh Naidu, Eric A. Posner & Glen Weyl,

1.2c.   The *De Facto* Monopolist

The analysis of monopoly in this section was predicated on two assumptions—namely, that the monopolist had 100% of its market and that new entry was impossible. Such monopolies do exist in the real world, but most of them are price-regulated public utilities, such as electric companies. The rationale for the legal recognition of such "natural monopolies" is discussed below in § 1.4. Most antitrust policy concerning monopolies is directed at the *de facto* monopolist, which has no such legal protection. The *de facto* monopolist most generally does not have 100% of its relevant market, although the percentage may be close. Furthermore, the *de facto* monopolist must consider the possibility of entry by new firms.

Once these two assumptions of pure monopoly are relaxed, analyzing the monopolist's output and price decisions becomes more difficult. The *de facto* monopolist behaves strategically. In making a price or output decision it must either take the current output of competitors into account, or else it must try to anticipate responses by small competitors or potential competitors. It may also strategize a price or output decision designed to eliminate a competitor or potential competitor from the market. Much of antitrust law is concerned with the strategic decisions of the *de facto* monopolist trying to enlarge or protect its monopoly position.

Whichever decision the firm makes, it will likely be attempting to maximize its profits. That is to say, a firm's monopoly profits are a function not only of their magnitude at any instant, but also of their duration. Thus we speak of a "short run" profit-maximizing price, determined by the intersection of marginal cost and marginal revenue, which maximizes the monopolist's profits in the immediate instant. But we can also speak of a "long run" profit-maximizing price that takes the duration of monopoly profits into account as well. The latter price will often be significantly lower than the former.

§ 1.3   Antitrust Policy and the Social Cost of Monopoly

1.3a.   Monopoly as a Status; Monopolization as a Process

A *social cost* is a net loss that society suffers as a result of a particular transaction. A *social benefit* is a net gain. If A gives B $100, B is $100 richer and A is $100 poorer. Disregarding the costs of the

---

Antitrust Remedies for Labor Market Power, 132 Harv. L. Rev. 536 (2018). On the economics, see David Autor, et al., Concentrating on the Fall of the Labor Share, 107 Am. Econ. Rev. (Papers & Proc.) 180 (2017).

transaction itself, such "transfer payments" produce neither a social cost nor a social benefit. By contrast, if A produces for $100 a widget that B values at $150, society may become $50 richer. B might pay $150 for the widget. In that case B will be neither better nor worse off, for he valued the widget by just what he paid for it. But A will be $50 richer, for his costs were only $100. Alternatively, if A sells the widget at $100, A will be neither better nor worse off, but B will be $50 better off.

If A holds out for a price of $150 and B is willing to pay only $140, however, the transaction will not occur. In that case no one will be better off. B may then enter into a transaction with C and purchase a substitute that B values at perhaps $130, and which costs C, say, $110. The price will be between $110 and $130. Even if that alternative transaction occurs, however, society will be only $20 better off. The substitute transaction is less favorable to both B and society as a whole than B's preferred transaction would have been.

Social costs can also result when transactions injure someone who was not a party to the transaction. For example, the builder of a factory may not bother to negotiate with neighbors for the right to pollute their air, particularly if he thinks the neighbors have no legal right to protect their air from pollution. However, the neighbors are worse off. The common law of nuisance and the National Environmental Policy Act are both attempts to force the factory to "internalize" and pay at least a part of this cost.[23]

For antitrust purposes, the *social cost* of monopoly is equal to the loss produced by monopoly pricing and monopoly behavior, minus any social gains that monopoly produces. *Monopolization*—or the antitrust offense of creating or maintaining a monopoly by means of anticompetitive exclusionary practices—is a process rather than merely an outcome. We sometimes distinguish the two when we call the outcome "monopoly," and the process by which it is created by a term such as "monopolization," or "rent seeking." For any antitrust policy concerned with minimizing the social cost of harmful activity, both the process and the outcome are properly counted as a part of the activity's social cost, and part of the reasons for prevention. This is generally true of the economic theory of criminal behavior. For example, the social cost of theft is not merely the money value of the stolen object—indeed, the theft itself is only a wealth transfer. The social cost must also include the collateral damage that the thief

---

[23]   See 42 U.S.C.A. §§ 4321–47; and see Ronald H. Coase, The Problem of Social Cost, 3 J.L. & Econ. 1 (1960). On the history of these changes, see Herbert Hovenkamp, The Opening of American Law: Neoclassical Legal Thought, 1870–1970, Epilogue (2015).

inflicts on society, as well as the costs of the elaborate mechanisms that we use to deter theft.[24]

To be sure, some of the processes that create monopoly are efficient. For example, monopoly can be created by research and development. So we must have rules that distinguish harmful from beneficial practices that create monopoly. But this problem of definition or characterization is quite different from the question whether losses caused by harmful exclusionary practices should be counted as part of monopoly's social costs.

Antitrust law's concern with this *process* of monopolization, rather than merely with the outcome, is quite apparent from the statutory scheme. The law of monopolization requires not only a monopoly position, but also the commission of one or more anticompetitive "exclusionary practices," thus signaling that the process by which monopoly is to be created determines its legality.[25] We condemn collusion, attempts and conspiracies to monopolize, tying arrangements, exclusive dealing, mergers and other practices only because we believe that these tend to facilitate the creation of monopoly. We may sometimes be wrong about our underlying facts or even about the economic theories we employ, but the basic premise remains the same: the principal target of the antitrust laws is not static monopoly as such, but rather the manifold mechanisms by which monopoly is created or preserved. Indeed, there is no law of "no fault" monopoly; the innocent monopolist does not violate the antitrust laws simply by charging its profit-maximizing price.[26]

1.3b.   The Deadweight Loss Caused by Monopoly

Because the monopolist reduces output, it forces some people to forego the transaction that was their first choice and would have produced the largest benefit. Rather, they either buy nothing or else take their second choice, which produces a smaller benefit. Importantly, the monopolist makes no revenue from unmade sales either. This traditional "deadweight loss" of monopoly does not derive from the fact that consumers pay higher prices. Within the pure monopoly model that loss to consumers is offset by an equal gain to the monopolist and from an efficiency standpoint is a "neutral" transfer of wealth. The deadweight loss arises because the monopoly encourages some customers not to purchase the monopolized product at all. A monopoly in the brick market may force a builder to switch

---

[24]   See Gary S. Becker, Crime and Punishment: An Economic Approach, 76 J. Pol. Econ. 169 (1968).

[25]   See Chs. 6–8.

[26]   See 3 Antitrust Law ¶¶ 630–650 (4th ed. 2015).

to aluminum siding, even though it preferred bricks and was willing to pay the competitive price for them.

1.3c.   The Social Cost of Monopoly: Rent-Seeking

The *de facto* monopolist—the firm that does not have legal protection from new entry—must continually exclude competitors, who would increase output and drive prices down to the competitive level. In fact, the more profitable the monopoly, the more that potential entrants will be willing to spend in order to enter the market, and the more the monopolist will spend to keep them out.

As the previous section observed, one way the monopolist might deter competition is by charging a price lower than its short-run profit-maximizing price. Although full analysis of such entry-deterring pricing is complex,[27] the short-run consequence is to make both the "wealth transfer" and the "deadweight loss" smaller than they would be under short-run profit-maximizing pricing. Whether such entry-deterring pricing reduces the social cost of monopoly in the long run, however, depends on the effect of the pricing on the duration of the monopoly.

A firm might also deter new entry by spending part of its monopoly profits in research and development (R & D), thus keeping ahead of its industry and making it more difficult for competitors to keep up. Throughout the 1970's, for example, IBM Corp. probably retained a dominant position in the computer market by being an aggressive innovator.[28] R & D may reduce the net deadweight loss of monopoly if society values the product of the R & D by an amount that exceeds its costs plus the increased social costs of any additional monopoly power that the R & D creates. Nevertheless, effective R & D also makes new entry by competitors more difficult.

The relationship between R & D expenditures and monopoly is controversial, and has produced a significant economic debate. At one end is Joseph Schumpeter's argument that since research is both expensive and risky, firms in competition will not be able to afford it. A large amount of money spent without an assured return may be enough to deter a competitive firm from innovating.[29] At the other is Kenneth J. Arrow's critique arguing that a monopolist with an established investment in a particular technology will be less likely to conduct innovation designed to displace it. Further, the monopolist

---

[27]   See § 8.3b.

[28]   See Franklin M. Fisher, et al., Folded, Spindled and Mutilated: Economic Analysis and U.S. v. IBM (1985).

[29]   See Joseph A. Schumpeter, Capitalism, Socialism, and Democracy 106 (3d ed. 1950).

has no need to worry about innovations from rivals because it has none. By contrast, competitors are earning only competitive returns and are continuously threatened with ouster by the innovations of others. As a result, on balance a competitor has a greater incentive to innovate than a monopolist does.[30] The many manifestations of this debate have produced a very considerable literature.[31] Today there is a broad consensus with some support in both theoretical and empirical economics that the "innovation-concentration" curve is shaped like an inverted "U." At one extreme, truly monopolized markets do not exhibit great amounts of innovation; at the other extreme, neither do highly competitive markets with many tiny firms. Most innovation goes on in moderately concentrated markets.[32]

The ambiguous relationship between monopoly and innovation has been apparent in the case law since soon after the Sherman Act was passed. In the *American Can* case,[33] the court faced the defense that a monopoly created by merger should be preserved because the monopolist could afford research and development activities that had not occurred before the monopoly came into existence. The judge was "reluctant to destroy so finely adjusted an industrial machine * * *." Thirty years later Judge Learned Hand wrote that monopoly was bad because it "deadens initiative * * * and depresses energy," and because "immunity from competition is a narcotic, and rivalry is a stimulant, to industrial progress." In the very same opinion, however, Judge Hand found that Alcoa had illegally monopolized the market because it aggressively "embrace[d] each new opportunity as it opened" and faced "every newcomer with new capacity already geared into a great organization, having the advantage of experience, trade connections and the elite of personnel."[34]

Before criticizing judges for being unclear about the relationship between monopolization and innovation, however, one should note

---

[30]   Kenneth J. Arrow, Economic Welfare and the Allocation of Resources for Invention, in Essays in the Theory of Risk-Bearing 144, 157 (1962; 3d ed. 1976).

[31]   See, e.g., Christina Bohannan & Herbert Hovenkamp, Creation Without Restraint: Promoting Liberty and Rivalry in Innovation, ch. 1 (2012); Michael A. Carrier, Innovation for the 21st Century: Harnessing the Power of Intellectual Property and Antitrust Law 298–299 (2009); Richard Gilbert, Looking for Mr. Schumpeter: Where Are We in the Competition-Innovation Debate?, in 6 Innovation Policy and the Economy 159, 165 (Adam B. Jaffe et al. eds., 2006).

[32]   See Bohannan & Hovenkamp, id.; Jonathan Baker, Beyond Schumpeter and Arrow: How Antitrust Fosters Innovation, 74 Antitrust L.J. 575, 586 (2007).

[33]   United States v. American Can Co., 230 Fed. 859, 903 (D.Md.1916), appeal dismissed, 256 U.S. 706, 41 S.Ct. 624 (1921). See 11 Antitrust Law ¶ 1801a (4th ed. 2019).

[34]   United States v. Aluminum Co. of Am. (Alcoa), 148 F.2d 416, 427 (2d Cir. 1945).

that economists have not done much better. Even today there is widespread disagreement about whether monopoly encourages or discourages research and development and, if monopoly encourages R & D, whether that fact increases or decreases the social costs of monopoly.[35] At least equal controversy exists about the patent system. Today many people argue that the system often stifles innovation through overissuance of ambiguously drafted patents and excessive enforcement. Others disagree.[36]

The monopolist threatened with new entry may also spend part of its monopoly returns in less ambiguous entry-deterring practices which increase the social costs of monopoly. Properly defined predatory pricing,[37] sabotage, espionage, fraudulent or recklessly brought litigation,[38] false and misleading advertising can all have the effect of prolonging the period during which a *de facto* monopoly exists and thereby increase the social cost of the monopoly.

§ 1.4   Industrial Organization Theory and Economies of Scale

The field of economics known as Industrial Organization ("IO") performs two important functions in antitrust analysis.[39] First, it can help us decide whether the perfect competition model is optimal for a particular market. Second, industrial organization can help us understand whether a particular firm's activities that affect market structure are efficient and should be encouraged, or inefficient and ought to be condemned. Indeed, the field of industrial organization developed in response to increasing policy concerns about the rise of "big business" in the late nineteenth century, and the resulting debate among lawyers concerning when antitrust condemnation is in order. Many of the basic doctrines of industrial organization theory

---

[35]   One study finding that firms become less efficient internally as the industries in which they operate become more oligopolistic is Richard E. Caves & David R. Barton, Efficiency in U.S. Manufacturing Industries (1990).

[36]   The issues are discussed in Herbert Hovenkamp, Antitrust and the Patent System: A Reexamination, 76 Ohio St. L. J. 467 (2015).

[37]   See ch. 8.

[38]   See ch. 18.

[39]   The classic text on industrial organization is Edward A.G. Robinson's The Structure of Competitive Industry (rev. ed. 1958). Very useful and comprehensive contemporary texts are Lynne Pepall, et. al., Industrial Organization: Contemporary Theory and Empirical Applications (2014); Dennis W. Carlton & Jeffrey M. Perloff, Modern Industrial Organization (4th ed. 2004).

were suggested first by lawyers in the context of litigation, and later adopted and formalized by economists.[40]

Many real world markets do not come very close to the classical model of perfect competition. In some markets this failure is an antitrust problem: the market would perform more efficiently if the firms behaved more competitively. In other markets, competition among large numbers of incumbents producing undifferentiated products is simply not the optimal structure.

1.4a.   The General Case of Economies of Scale

One of the most important factors undermining perfect competition is economies of scale. The model of perfect competition is premised on the notion of a market containing many equally efficient firms, each indifferent to the output decisions of others. Within this model, firm size is not a factor in competitor decisions, because the model assumes constant returns to scale: production and distribution costs do not vary with size. A small firm can thus compete quite effectively with a large one. Suppose, however, that one firm develops a new process that enables it to produce the product at substantially lower cost. In order to take advantage of this new process, however, the firm must build a plant capable of serving one half of the existing market. Now incumbent firms can no longer be indifferent to the price and output decisions of the innovator.

Most economies of scale are not as dramatic as the illustration suggests. However, economies of scale obtain in most industries, and they range from the trivial to the very substantial. Technically, an economy of scale exists whenever the costs per unit of some input decrease as volume increases.[41] The following examples illustrate the manifold presence of scale economies in a wide variety of industries.

> 1)   To drive a truck from point A to point B costs $100, whether the truck is full or half empty. As a result, the full truck can transport its cargo at a lower cost per pound than the half empty truck.

---

[40]   See Herbert Hovenkamp, Enterprise and American Law, 1836–1937 at chs. 22–25 (1991). On the postwar period, see Herbert Hovenkamp, The Opening of American Law: Neoclassical Legal Thought, 1870–1970, chs. 11–12 (2015).

[41]   By contrast, an economy of *scope* exists when there are economies to performing two different economic activities together. For example, if corn starch and corn flakes are separate products from a kernel of corn, a company that produced both products simultaneously in the same plant might have lower costs than individual companies that produced each in separate plants. For a brief technical discussion, see John C. Panzar & Robert D. Willig, Economies of Scope, 71 Am. Econ. Rev. Pap. & Proc. 268 (1981).

2) A 30-second television commercial advertising automobiles costs $100,000, whether the manufacturer has 4,000 dealerships across the country and produces 10,000,000 cars per year, or has 300 dealerships and produces 90,000 cars per year.

3) To set up an automatic metal lathe to turn out a particular machine part costs $100 in labor. Once the lathe is set up, the costs of turning out the parts is $1.00 each. If the lathe is set up to turn out a single part, its cost will be $101.00. If the lathe is set up to turn out 10,000 parts, their cost will be $1.01 each.

4) A procurement department and legal staff spend $2000 to negotiate and draft a contract to purchase an essential raw material, whether the company is buying 50 units of the material or 5000 units.

5) A manufacturer of essential medical or industrial supplies must always keep one production machine in reserve, so that a breakdown will not interrupt production. If it produces with a single machine operating at a time, it must therefore maintain capacity equal to twice its actual output. If it produces with eight machines, however, it needs to maintain only nine machines, a capacity equal to 12% more than output.

6) A production process requires 40 discrete functions. If a firm has ten employees, each must perform, on average, four different functions. If the firm has 4000 employees, no single employee will have to perform more than one function, in which she will be a specialist. If she becomes ill, another specialist in the same function will replace her.

7) The transaction costs of borrowing money (or raising equity capital) are 2% for blocks of $1,000,000; 1% for blocks of $10,000,000; or .5% for blocks of $100,000,000.

8) The development of a new manufacturing process reduces the cost of manufacturing widgets by 50¢ per unit. The research and development costs for inventing the new process are $1,000,000, regardless of the amount of production to which the process is applied. If the firm produces 1,000,000 units per year, the new process will pay for itself in 2 years and thereafter the firm will save $500,000 per year. If the firm produces 12,000,000 units per

year the new process will pay for itself in two months and thereafter the firm will save $6,000,000 per year.

This list is only a tiny sampling of the economies of scale that can exist.[42] Traditionally atomized industries, such as farming, are no exception. An automatic milking machine may greatly reduce the cost of milking dairy cows, but the basic cost of the machine is such that the farmer will not reach the "break-even" point unless he milks at least 100 cows.

Economies of scale are largely a function of technology, which both creates and destroys economies of scale. The invention of the milking machine meant that the large farmer could obtain a cost advantage over the farmer too small to use the machine profitably. As a result, dairy farms tended to become larger. By contrast, the invention of the microprocessor (the tiny silicone chip that is the heart of the modern computer) made it possible for much smaller firms to manufacture computers efficiently.

The above list also reflects that not all economies of scale need to be attained within a single plant. Certain "multi-plant" economies can also give a cost advantage to the operator of multiple plants. Other economies, such as advertising, may obtain as output increases, whether or not the output comes from a single plant. As a result, it is often impossible to determine the most efficient minimum size of a single plant and conclude that a firm that operates such a plant has attained all available economies of scale. A firm that operates two or more such plants may have even lower costs.

The term Minimum Efficient Scale (MES) refers to the smallest production unit capable of achieving all relevant economies of scale. If a firm or plant operates at MES, no other firm or plant can be more efficient because of its scale of operation (although it may be more efficient for other reasons; for example, it may have better management).

In a competitive market firms will gravitate toward MES, perhaps through trial and error. One firm will grow to a larger size or begin performing for itself a service that it previously purchased in the market. If the change creates no economies, the balance of the market will remain unaffected. If the change gives the firm lower costs, however, the firm will likely expand output and increase its market share at the expense of competitors. These competitors will then be forced to achieve these economies for themselves or eventually be forced out of business. By making a few qualifying

---

[42] For a fuller discussion, see Frederic M. Scherer & David Ross, Industrial Market Structure and Economic Performance 97–141 (3d ed. 1990).

assumptions, economists have been able to guess MES in certain industries by a rule of "natural selection": firms that have attained all important economies of scale tend to survive; those that fail to attain important economies tend not to.[43]

If the market is monopolized or cartelized, some fringe firms may be able to survive even if they are not of MES. For example, suppose that MES in a particular industry is 20% of the market, and an MES firm can produce widgets for $1.00 each. A firm with 10% of the market has costs of $1.20. But what if three firms, each with 30% of the market, are engaged in price fixing and charging $1.30? The inefficiently small firm will find it quite easy to survive, because the cartel has created a price "umbrella" which protects the small firm from its inefficiency. If the cartel ever falls apart the small firm may be in trouble. That same thing is true of oligopoly, or tacit collusion. Among the relatively few beneficiaries of collusion and oligopoly are fringe competitors.

What role does the notion of economies of scale play in antitrust? First, it suggests that much of antitrust's historic preoccupation with bigness *per se* was ill-advised, at least if low prices are an important goal of antitrust policy. Firms frequently become big because large firms are more efficient than small firms. The unfortunate result, of course, is that the small firms become unprofitable and are forced either to become big themselves or else to exit the market. Invariably, the minimum efficient *size* of firms in a particular market dictates the optimal maximum *number* of firms in the market. If MES is 25% of the market, the market will not have room for more than four MES firms. High market concentration, with all its possible attendant evils, is often a function of economies of scale.

Second, knowledge of economies of scale in a market can help a policy maker evaluate the consequences of certain practices alleged to be monopolistic. Many such practices, such as vertical integration, may be nothing more than a means of attaining economies. Likewise, knowledge of scale economies may help predict the consequences of mergers.

Third, knowledge of scale economies and optimal market structure can help a policy maker determine the appropriateness of "structural" relief in certain cases. When a firm has been found guilty of monopolization or illegal merger, should the court respond by ordering divestiture—judicially enforced break-up of the defendant into two or more smaller firms? What if the new firms are too small

---

[43]   See George J. Stigler, The Economies of Scale, 1 J.L. & Econ. 54 (1958); Leonard W. Weiss, The Survival Technique and the Extent of Suboptimal Capacity, 72 J.Pol.Econ. 246 (1964).

to achieve important economies of scale? The result might be that prices would be higher in the new "competitive" market than they were in the old "monopolized" market. In such cases a more efficient solution may be to tolerate the highly concentrated, "oligopoly" market and use the antitrust laws to force the firms to compete with each other as much as possible.[44]

1.4b.   Two-Sided Platforms

A two-sided platform, or two-sided market, is a business that depends on relationships between two noncompeting but interdependent groups of participants.[45] A traditional example is the printed periodical, such as a newspaper, which earns revenue by selling both advertising and subscriptions to the paper itself. Depending on the chosen business model, such a periodical might obtain very different mixtures of advertising and subscriber revenue. At one extreme, *Consumer Reports* does not sell advertising but derives its revenue entirely from subscriptions and donations. At the other extreme, the local neighborhood shopping flier might be distributed free to customers, with its production and distribution supported entirely by advertising revenues. The manager of a two-sided platform maximizes profits by coming up with the optimal balance of participation and revenue on the two sides.

Two-sided platform sellers can be harmed by feedback effects if they make the wrong choice on one side of their platform. For example, a magazine might keep its user subscription price low by relying on more advertising, but the excessive advertising may repel customers. The trick for the magazine is to find the "sweet spot" that optimizes revenue between paid subscribers and paid advertisers. Such an optimized allocation is a consequence not merely of the price level on the two sides of the platform, but also appropriate participation balancing.[46] This spot, once achieved, is also an equilibrium for that firm. That is, it has no reason to change the

---

[44]   The problems of high concentration and oligopoly pricing are discussed in § 4.4a.

[45]   The classic treatment of two-sided markets is Jean-Charles Rochet & Jean Tirole, Platform Competition in Two-Sided Markets, 1 J. Eur. Econ. Ass'n 990 (2003). On definitional problems, see generally Herbert Hovenkamp, Antitrust and Platform Monopoly, ___ Yale L.J. ___ (2021) (forthcoming), available at https://papers.ssrn.com/sol3/papers.cfm?abstract_id=3639142; Michael Katz & Jonathan Sallet, Multisided Platforms and Antitrust Enforcement, 127 Yale L.J. 2142 (2018).

[46]   See Erik Hovenkamp, Platform Antitrust, 44 J. Corp. L. 713 (2019). See also Dennis W. Carlton, The Anticompetitive Effects of Vertical Most-Favored-Nation Restraints and the Error of Amex, 2019 Colum. Bus. L. Rev. 93, 96 (2019) ("The insight of Rochet and Tirole is that a two-sided market has the property that the price to each side of the market matters separately. That is, it is not only the sum of the prices that matters but also the relative prices on each side of the market.")

balance as long as circumstances remain the same. Of course, if something changes that balance—such as a large postage rate increase for magazine subscribers—then the firm may have to seek out a new equilibrium. Significantly, not only the aggregate level of fees, but also their balance determines the point that maximizes the platform operator's profits.

In the platform literature, the term "indirect" network effects describes situations in which the value of the platform to one side depends on either the revenue generated or the number of users on the other side.[47] For example, ride-hailing platforms such as Uber can succeed only if they have a critical volume of drivers on one side and a critical number of passengers on the other side. If fares are set too high, the number of passengers will fall off. If they are set too low, the number of drivers will fall off.

The fact that a platform has two sides does not necessarily mean that both sides are positive contributors of revenue. It is important to distinguish between the revenue *level*, which is the aggregate price, and the revenue *distribution*, which is how the price is divided up among participants on the two sides. Sometimes the price to users on one side of the platform is zero, as it is for consumer web search engines, such as Google Search, Bing, and Yahoo, and social networking sites such as Facebook. These services are generally free to users, but are supported by advertising revenue. Nevertheless, those advertising revenues still depend on the number of users or the number of page views.

In some cases the revenue from one side can be negative.[48] Credit card companies routinely charge merchants acceptance fees for the use of the cards, while the cost to customers can be zero or even negative depending on the terms of customer card ownership.[49] A typical card might charge no annual fee to customers, and no usage fees other than interest on unpaid balances or penalties for late payments. In addition, the card may award "perks" or other inducements that make the cost of the credit card negative to the consumer. These can include favorable treatment such as airline travel miles, extended warranties on products purchased with the card, or increased insurance protection for vehicles rented on the card.

---

[47]   See DAVID S. EVANS & RICHARD SCHMALENSEE, MATCHMAKERS: THE NEW ECONOMICS OF MULTISIDED PLATFORMS 25 (2016).

[48]   E.g., Ohio v. American Express, 138 S.Ct. at 2274, 2281 (2018). See the District Court's opinion, 88 F.Supp.3d 143, 203 n. 36 (E.D.N.Y. 2015).

[49]   Ohio v. American Express, *supra*.

Assessing the antitrust legality of a practice on a two-sided platform typically requires the tribunal to look at effects on both sides. This is clearly true if the claim is something like predatory pricing: we cannot determine whether a price is below cost, as the law of predatory pricing requires, without aggregating costs and revenue on both sides. For example, a computer search engine that is free to users is not being priced at below cost unless the sum of revenues from all sides of the market, including advertising, is too low.

This principle can lead to incorrect results if it is not used carefully. In particular, exclusionary practices do not necessarily cause harm on one side of the platform and benefits on the other side. Often they produce harms (or benefits) on both sides. This tripped up the Supreme Court majority in the *American Express* case.[50] At issue was an "anti-steering rule" that prevented a merchant from offering a customer a discount for using a different card. Amex's fees were higher than those charged by other cards, such as Visa. If a large transaction incurred a $30 fee on Amex but only $20 if the customer used a Visa card, the merchant had an incentive to offer the customer a lower price for using the cheaper card. The anti-steering rule that the Court majority approved prevented such offers. The Court reasoned that the only way to examine this restraint was to define a relevant market that included both sides, even though they were not competing, and then net out costs and benefits on the two sides. As noted later, this approach did considerable damage to rational conceptions of market definition and in the process approved a practice that caused consumer harm each and every time it prevented a customer from using a cheaper card.[51]

If the Court had examined the transaction more closely it would also have seen that there was no harm on one side offset by a benefit on the other side. The Amex customer who would have preferred to switch but was denied the opportunity by the no switching rule was injured, but so were both the merchant and the competing card issuer—the first because it was denied the opportunity to use a lower cost card, and the second because it lost the opportunity to make that sale. In sum, there was no harm to one side to be offset by benefits to the other side. Rather, harm accrued to both sides of the market. The only benefit accrued to AmEx, which was able to obtain a transaction at a price greater than the value that anyone placed on it. Higher profits from a practice that restrains trade is hardly a defense.

---

[50]   Ohio v. American Express, 138 S.Ct. at 2274, 2281 (2018); and see Erik N. Hovenkamp, Platform Antitrust, *supra.*

[51]   See § 3.3b3.

§ 1.5   Less-than-Perfect Competition

Antitrust economics is "applied" economics, which means that it must accept real world markets as given and consider any deviations from the perfect competition model. The imperfections described below can often help explain the motive or effect of certain litigated practices.

Several economic theories have been applied to observed deviations from perfect competition in real world markets. These generally fall under the heading of "oligopoly," "imperfect competition"[52] and "monopolistic competition."[53] All can be relevant to antitrust policy in a variety of situations.

1.5a.   Product Differentiation and Monopolistic Competition

Many products in markets that appear competitive are nevertheless differentiated from one another. Although Ford and Chrysler automobiles compete, some buyers prefer one to the other and are willing to pay more for their first choice. To the extent this is true the manufacturer faces a slightly downward sloping demand curve and may charge a price higher than marginal cost. The result is greater variety but possibly lower output. In the 1930s Edward Chamberlin modeled such markets on an assumption that entry was easy but that firms had unlimited power to vary their products.[54] This theory, which Chamberlin termed "monopolistic competition," has had a powerful influence on industrial economics, and monopolistic competition models are commonly used today to describe markets for manufactured, differentiated products. In the 1950s critics, particularly from the Chicago School, faulted monopolistic competition theory for not being testable.[55] Today it seems clear, however, that not only is the theory testable but it is more robust empirically than theories of perfect competition. Monopolistic competition theory predicts higher price cost margins in product differentiated markets, a great deal of investment in differentiation itself, and a proposition now widely applied in merger

---

[52]   See Joan Robinson, The Economics of Imperfect Competition (1933).

[53]   See Edward H. Chamberlin, The Theory of Monopolistic Competition (1933). On the historical influence of these theories on antitrust policy, see Herbert Hovenkamp, The Opening of American Law: Neoclassical Legal Thought, 1870–1970, chs. 11–12 (2015).

[54]   Edward H. Chamberlin, The Theory of Monopolistic Competition (1933).

[55]   E.g., Milton Friedman, The Methodology of Positive Economics 2–43, in Essays in Positive Economics (1953).

law that two firms who are very close to one another in product space compete more than those that are further apart.

Product differentiation plays a complex role in modern antitrust economics, however. One the one hand, it can make collusion and some kinds of oligopoly more difficult.[56] Sellers find it harder to agree on price and output when they do not produce precisely the same product, or they have different costs.

But the more pronounced effect of monopolistic competition is to limit the degree of head-to-head competition among firms. For example, a firm facing an efficient rival making an identical product could either cut its price to the bone in order to compete strictly on price, or else it could figure out a way to differentiate its product in order to make it distinguishable from its rival. Importantly, the decision to design a unique product is ordinarily unilateral and usually unreachable under the antitrust laws. Further, consumers typically prefer product variety. Nevertheless, the result is also higher margins and lower output than occurs under perfect competition.

A variation on monopolistic competition theory is implicitly incorporated into the Government's analysis of "unilateral effects" mergers.[57] In general, however, a firm's decision to diversify its product from those of rivals is not presumptively anticompetitive and, except for a few brief flirtations,[58] has not been considered an antitrust violation. Product differentiation itself also serves to explain many vertical restrictions on distribution, tying arrangements, exclusive dealing and other practices that may sometimes be anticompetitive. Finally, the theory of monopolistic competition has had a considerable role to play in antitrust assessments of market power, particularly the extent to which competitive diversity or intellectual property rights enhance single-firm power.[59]

1.5b.   Price Discrimination

In the perfect competition model systematic price discrimination is impossible. In the real world it occurs daily. The two imperfections that facilitate most price discrimination are information costs and transportation costs. If one group of buyers does not know enough

---

[56]   See § 4.1a.

[57]   See §§ 12.3d, 12.5.

[58]   For example, in the 1970s the FTC flirted with the idea of making periodic design style changes an exclusionary practice, under the rubric of "excessive" product differentiation. See Herbert Hovenkamp, United States Competition Policy in Crisis: 1890–1955, 94 Minn. L. Rev. 311, 339–340 (2009).

[59]   These issues are taken up in Ch. 3.

about market conditions or about the contents of the product, they may pay a higher price than more knowledgeable buyers. Likewise, high transportation costs make it possible for firms to earn higher profits from near-by "captive" purchasers than from more remote purchasers.

Relatively small amounts of market power can facilitate price discrimination, and it is more widespread in product differentiated markets. It is particularly common in markets for intellectual property, such as franchising and patent licensing. Most price discrimination is not illegal, and it generally benefits rather than harms consumers in the aggregate.

1.5c.   Oligopoly

When markets are highly concentrated, because of economies of scale or for other reasons, a firm cannot reasonably ignore the price and output decisions of competitors. Ford Motor Co., for example, would be unwise *not* to respond to General Motors' price reduction or output increase.[60]

Oligopoly has become a major concern of American antitrust policy. The laws against price fixing, expressed mainly in § 1 of the Sherman Act, have generally proved ineffectual.[61] So the focus has shifted to merger policy, an important goal of which is to prevent mergers that may facilitate various kinds of oligopoly pricing.[62]

§ 1.6   Barriers to Entry

For antitrust purposes, a barrier to entry is some factor in a market that permits firms already in the market to earn monopoly profits, while deterring outsiders from coming in.[63] More formally, entry barriers measure "the extent to which, in the long run, established firms can elevate their selling prices above the minimal average costs of production and distribution" without "inducing potential entrants to enter the industry."[64]

Economists have not been unanimous in accepting the foregoing definition of entry barriers, which is sometimes called "Bainian" after the economist Joe S. Bain who developed it. Some prefer the "Stiglerian" definition that entry barriers are costs that a prospective

---

[60]   See § 4.2.

[61]   See §§ 4.4, 4.6.

[62]   See Ch. 12.

[63]   Joe S. Bain, Barriers to New Competition: Their Character and Consequences in Manufacturing Industries (1962). See 2A Antitrust Law, Ch. 4C (4th ed. 2014).

[64]   Joe S. Bain, Industrial Organization 252 (1968). Others have suggested that marginal cost rather than minimum average cost should be the correct measure.

entrant must incur at or after entry, that those already in the market did not have to incur when they entered. More technically, an entry barrier under this definition is "a cost of producing (at some or every rate of output) which must be borne by a firm which seeks to enter an industry but is not borne by firms already in the industry."[65]

The difference between the two definitions of entry barriers can be quite substantial. For example, under the Bainian definition economies of scale is a qualifying barrier to entry. If scale economies are significant, then incumbent firms with established markets may have a large advantage over any new entrant, who will enter the market at a low rate of output. As a result, scale economies can permit incumbent firms to earn monopoly returns up to a certain point without encouraging new entry.

By contrast, scale economies are not a qualifying entry barrier under the Stiglerian definition. Both incumbent firms and new entrants had to deal with them at the time of entry; so scale economies are not a cost that applies only to new entrants.

The Stiglerian conception of entry barriers is based on the premise that entry barrier analysis should distinguish desirable from undesirable entry. If prospective entrants face precisely the same costs that incumbents faced but still find entry unprofitable, then this market has probably already attained the appropriate number of players, even though monopoly profits are being earned. For example, suppose that minimum efficient scale (MES) in a market requires a 30% market share. Such a market has room for only three MES firms—and a three-firm market is quite likely to perform oligopolistically or else be conducive to collusion. The Stiglerian approach to entry barriers would say that, although monopoly profits are being earned in the industry, entry barriers should not be counted as high because entry by a fourth firm is not socially desirable. Additional entry would force at least one firm to be of suboptimal size, and eventually one of the four would probably exit the market.[66] The socially desirable solution to the problem of oligopoly performance in this market is *not* to force entry of a fourth, inefficiently small firm; but rather to look for alternative measures that make collusion more difficult.

Nevertheless, antitrust analysis has mainly used the Bainian rather than the Stiglerian definition of entry barriers. The Bainian definition is written into the 2010 Horizontal Merger Guidelines

---

[65]   George J. Stigler, The Organization of Industry 67 (1968).

[66]   See Harold Demsetz, Barriers to Entry, 72 Am. Econ. Rev. 47 (Mar. 1982); Harold Demsetz, Industry Structure, Market Rivalry, and Public Policy, 16 J.L. & Econ. 1 (1973).

promulgated by the Justice Department's Antitrust Division and the Federal Trade Commission (FTC).[67]

For example, suppose the relevant question is whether a market structure is sufficiently conducive to oligopoly behavior that we should be concerned about a merger that further reduces the number of firms in the market. The Stiglerian approach provides no basis for distinguishing markets in which oligopoly behavior is likely to be successful from those in which it is not. Markets that have high entry barriers in the Bainian sense but not the Stiglerian sense, such as those with substantial scale economies, could nevertheless be quite susceptible to coordination of prices. The Bainian approach goes straight to the question whether attempts to raise price above the competitive level will be disciplined by new entry into the market. If the answer is no, the merger is a matter for antitrust scrutiny. Of course, we may still wish to conclude that the merger is necessary to enable the firms involved to achieve scale economies, but that is a different matter.

Numerous things have been suggested as entry barriers in antitrust cases. Among these are scale economies, product differentiation, high initial investment, risk, cost of capital, advertising, extent of vertical integration or vertical contracting, and government regulation. The case for treating each of these as a qualifying barrier to entry is considered later.[68]

Barriers to entry can also be classified by their height and source. On the question of height, "blockaded" entry occurs when the firm or firms in a market are able to charge their short-run profit-maximizing price without concern about new entry. Suppose an incumbent monopolist has marginal costs of $1.00, a profit-maximizing price of $1.50, and that new entry will not occur unless the entrant anticipates post-entry prices of $1.55 or higher. In that case the monopolist could freely charge $1.50 without concern about new entry. Since post-entry prices will be lower than current prices, the prospective entrant will see that entry is unprofitable.

As the illustration suggests, firms contemplating entry must base their calculations on *post*-entry rather than *pre*-entry prices. The firm needs to know whether it will make a profit after its own output has been added to the output of firms already in the market, taking into account any adjustments in output that incumbent firms might make in response to entry.

---

[67] On entry barriers under the 2010 Merger Guidelines, see § 12.6d. For more detail, see § 12.6; and Herbert Hovenkamp, Antitrust and the Costs of Movement, 78 Antitrust L.J. 67 (2012).

[68] See § 12.6.

The optimal strategy in some markets may be for firms to permit a certain amount of entry to occur. This is likely to be the case when prospective entrants have upward sloping cost curves. That is, the new entrants can get into the market and produce on a small scale rather cheaply, but entry at a larger scale very quickly becomes more expensive.[69] In that case the dominant firm will compute its profit-maximizing price by determining its "residual" demand, or demand after the fringe firms have served a small portion of the market. The most profitable strategy may be to permit a small amount of entry.[70]

---

[69] Alternatively, there may be pockets of customers who can be served by fringe sellers, but these sellers could not expand their sales without incurring substantially higher costs.

[70] See § 3.5a, which diagrams this problem in the context of the domestic firm's decision whether to exclude or permit foreign imports.

Chapter 2

HISTORY AND IDEOLOGY
IN ANTITRUST POLICY

Table of Sections

§ 2.1   The Development of American Antitrust Policy

2.1a.   The Goals of the Sherman Act: Efficiency and Interest Group Explanations

Few elements of statutory interpretation are more frustrating than the study of legislative history to determine a statute's meaning. The debates and compromises leading to a statute's passage often contain conflicting statements, made by persons who were elected by disparate interest groups, who had different motives and different perceptions about what a statute would do. Sometimes legislative committees achieve compromises by making statutory language intentionally ambiguous, leaving to the courts to decide later which interpretation should prevail.

One solution to this problem is to ignore legislative history and look only to the plain language of the statute.[1] But the antitrust laws

---

[1]   E.g., Public Citizen v. U.S. Dep't of Justice, 491 U.S. 440, 479, 109 S.Ct. 2558, 2579 (1989); EEOC v. Arabian Am. Oil Co., 499 U.S. 244, 247, 111 S.Ct. 1227, 1230 (1991) (construing plain language of statute rather than its legislative history).

are not conducive to such an approach because their language is so spare and malleable. For example, the Sherman Act condemns "every contract, combination * * * or conspiracy in restraint of trade," or every person who shall "monopolize," without giving a clue about what those phrases mean.[2] The meaning must be discerned from collateral sources.

The legislative histories of the federal antitrust laws are not always that helpful. Their ambiguous language has produced considerable scholarly dispute over Congressional intent. This is particularly true of the Sherman Act, whose expansive text has always been the driving force in American antitrust policy. Some scholars have argued that the framers of the Sherman Act were concerned almost exclusively with allocative efficiency as measured by modern economics.[3] Others have concluded that Congress has often expressed concern with "justice" or fairness in business behavior, but has never articulated any concept of efficiency as such, not even in the antitrust laws.[4] Still others have argued that Congress' chief concern was to arrest wealth transfers away from consumers and toward price fixers or monopolists.[5] Finally, others have argued that the Sherman Act was passed at the behest of particular non-consumer interests groups, such as small firms[6] or farmers.[7] These divergent, conflicting theories of the Sherman Act reflect underlying ideologies about the nature of legislation generally, or the nature of the relationship between the Sherman Act and the common law.[8]

The Chicago School of antitrust analysis,[9] which dominated antitrust thinking during the final decades of the twentieth century, believed that preserving economic efficiency was the dominant concern of the antitrust laws. This Congressional concern was said to

---

[2]   15 U.S.C.A. §§ 1, 2.

[3]   For example, Robert H. Bork, Legislative Intent and the Policy of the Sherman Act, 9 J.L. & Econ. (1966).

[4]   For example, Louis B. Schwartz, "Justice" and other Non-Economic Goals of Antitrust, 127 U.Pa.L.Rev. 1076 (1979).

[5]   Robert H. Lande, Wealth Transfers as the Original and Primary Concern of Antitrust: the Efficiency Interpretation Challenged, 34 Hastings L.J. 65 (1982).

[6]   See George J. Stigler, The Origin of the Sherman Act, 14 J. Legal Stud. 1 (1985); Thomas J. DiLorenzo, The Origins of Antitrust: An Interest-Group Perspective, 5 Int'l. Rev. L. & Econ. 73 (1985).

[7]   See William F. Shughart, Antitrust Policy and Interest Group Politics 11–12 (1990).

[8]   See Daniel A. Crane, Antitrust's Unconventional Politics, 104 Va. L. Rev. Online 118 (2018). For the great ideological diversity, both at the time the Sherman Act was passed and during its first century of enforcement, see Herbert Hovenkamp, The Opening of American Law, chs. 11 & 12 (2015).

[9]   See § 2.2b.

have been undermined, however, by judicial interpretations and legislation subsequent to the Sherman Act, particularly the Robinson-Patman Act and the Celler-Kefauver amendments to the merger law.[10] The Chicago School scholars who initially did this writing were uninterested in Public Choice theory, something that later members of the School embraced with more enthusiasm.[11] Under Public Choice theory, or interest group analysis, the efficiency position gave way to the idea that the legislative intent of those passing the antitrust laws has never been economic efficiency. Rather, the Sherman Act was special interest legislation, and the principal protected class was small business.[12]

To be sure, the Sherman Act's framers could have had a conception of efficiency in mind. A great deal of writing in the classical economic tradition defended competitive markets on what we today would call "efficiency" grounds. However, only a few statements in the debates leading up to the Sherman Act sound even remotely like efficiency arguments. Most of these statements concern the impact of monopoly on consumer prices, or a desire to protect consumers from high prices. As a result, the statements may suggest that the primary intent of the Sherman Act's framers was not economic efficiency at all, but rather the distributive goal of preventing monopolists from transferring wealth away from consumers.[13]

Most of the substantive federal antitrust laws were passed in four years: 1890, 1914, 1936, and 1950.[14] The legislative history of the Sherman Act of 1890 contains the best case for the "efficiency" view: that Congress intended the antitrust laws to protect consumers from the high prices and reduced output caused by monopolies and cartels. The legislative history of the Federal Trade Commission Act and Clayton Act of 1914 is somewhat more concerned with the protection of small businesses from the unfair or "exclusionary" practices of bigger firms. The legislative history of the Robinson-Patman Act in 1936,[15] and the Celler-Kefauver Amendments to the

---

[10] For example, Robert H. Bork, The Antitrust Paradox: A Policy at War With Itself (1978; rev. ed. 1993).

[11] On public choice theory and antitrust, see § 2.2c.

[12] Stigler, The Origin of the Sherman Act (1985); and The Causes and Consequences of Antitrust: the Public Choice Perspective (Fred S. McChesney & William F. Shughart, eds. 1994).

[13] Robert H. Lande, Wealth Transfers as the Original and Primary Concern of Antitrust: the Efficiency Interpretation Challenged, 34 Hastings L.J. 65 (1982).

[14] 1890: Sherman Act; 1914: Clayton and Federal Trade Commission Acts; 1936: Robinson-Patman Act; 1950: Cellar-Kefauver Amendments to Clayton Act.

[15] See 14 Antitrust Law ¶ 2303 (4th ed. 2019); Hugh C. Hansen, Robinson-Patman Law: A Review and Analysis, 51 Fordham L.Rev. 1113 (1983). See § 14.6a.

antimerger provisions of the Clayton Act in 1950,[16] depart much more decisively from any consumer welfare model. In both 1936 and 1950 Congress was concerned chiefly with protecting small businesses from larger competitors who faced lower costs, even though the result of such protection would be lower total output and higher consumer prices.

A theory with more explanatory power is that the Sherman Act was passed at the behest of small businesses who had been injured by the formation of larger, more efficient firms. This was the one group of people who were injured, were well organized, and had long been effective in making their case to legislative bodies. Among the most effective lobbying organizations of the day were various associations of independent and small businesses, whose positions were threatened by large vertically integrated firms. Senator Sherman himself may have been acting at the behest of independent oil producers in Ohio, who wanted protection from the Standard Oil Company and the railroads. Various labor organizations also lobbied Congress, but their principal concern seems to have been that new technology would steal jobs.[17] Although the Sherman Act included provisions for private lawsuits, nearly everyone who spoke on the issue believed that *consumer* lawsuits would be ineffectual. When the Congressmen spoke of private lawsuits, they were thinking of competitor suits.[18]

An alternative explanation that is perhaps more consistent with historical American ideology generally, is that the antitrust laws were passed out of a pervasive fear of private "bigness" and the political power that it engendered. The nineteenth century American rhetoric on monopoly is concerned at least as much with bigness *per se* as it is with monopoly prices. Further, the American ideal was a market economy into which any entrepreneur could enter and compete on the merits—that was the American worker's escape from the sweatshop. Big firms such as Standard Oil or Carnegie Steel threatened that ideal by signaling that only big firms could survive. If one looks at the ideology of nineteenth century Americans, rather than at the interest groups that may have contributed to the

---

[16]   See 4 Antitrust Law ¶¶ 901–904 (4th ed. 2016); Derek C. Bok, Section 7 of the Clayton Act and the Merging of Law and Economics, 74 Harv.L.Rev. 226 (1960); Herbert Hovenkamp, Derek Bok and the Merger of Law and Economics, 21 J. L. Reform 515 (1988). See § 12.2.

[17]   See Hovenkamp, Enterprise at 246–247.

[18]   See Herbert Hovenkamp, Antitrust's Protected Classes, 88 Mich. L. Rev. 1, 25–27 (1989).

Sherman Act's formation, the anti-bigness rationale seems to be very important.[19]

2.1b.   The Common Law and the Federal Antitrust Laws

One solution to the problem of ambiguous statutory language and legislative history is to assume that antitrust violations are a kind of "common law" offense, where judicial precedent defines the substance of the legal rules to be applied. Many of the practices challenged under the Sherman Act had previously been addressed under common law rules.[20] The framers of the Sherman Act believed that they were simply "federalizing" the common law of trade restraints, making the common law more effective by creating a forum with jurisdiction over monopolies or cartels that operated in more than a single state.[21] The earliest Sherman Act decisions construed the statute in that way: they generally decided cases by reference to common law precedents.[22]

The federal antitrust laws differed from the common law in at least one important respect, however. At common law most of the agreements addressed under § 1 of the Sherman Act were unenforceable but not affirmatively illegal. For example, contracts in restraint of trade could not be enforced by one participant against another. However, a consumer or competitor of the contracting parties was generally not permitted either to enjoin the contract or to obtain damages for injuries.[23] By contrast, § 7 of the original Sherman Act (and later §§ 4 and 16 of the Clayton Act) gave *non*participants in Sherman Act contracts, combinations or conspiracies a right to challenge such practices and obtain either damages or an injunction.

---

[19]   For an argument that the proper target of antitrust policy should be bigness and consolidated power, see Lina M. Khan, Amazon's Antitrust Paradox, 126 Yale L.J. 710 (2017).

[20]   For a survey of the nineteenth century common law decisions, see 1 Antitrust Law ¶ 104 (5th ed. 2020); Herbert Hovenkamp, The Sherman Act and the Classical Theory of Competition, 74 Iowa L. Rev. 1019 (1989).

[21]   Senator Sherman described his bill as setting "out in the most specific language the rule of the common law which prevails in England and this country * * *." 20 Cong.Rec. 1167 (1889); see Donald Dewey, The Common-Law Background of Antitrust Policy, 41 Va.L.Rev. 759 (1955); Hovenkamp, *Sherman Act, supra*.

[22]   For example, United States v. Addyston Pipe & Steel Co., 85 Fed. 271, 278–291 (6th Cir. 1898), affirmed, 175 U.S. 211, 20 S.Ct. 96 (1899).

[23]   See Cent. Shade-Roller Co. v. Cushman, 143 Mass. 353, 363–364, 9 N.E. 629, 631 (1887); Perkin v. Lyman, 9 Mass. 522, 530 (1813); and see Albert Stickney, State Control of Trade and Commerce by National or State Authority 157 (1897); Hovenkamp, *Sherman Act, supra*, at 1026–1027.

As Sherman Act precedent began to accumulate, the courts began to diverge from the nineteenth century common law. The federal antitrust laws took on a life of their own. In short, the Sherman Act can be regarded as "enabling" legislation—an invitation to the federal courts to learn how businesses and markets work and formulate a set of rules that will make them work in socially efficient ways. The standards to be applied always have and probably always will shift as theory, technology and the American economy changes.[24]

Federal courts have always interpreted the antitrust statutes in a common law fashion,[25] and the result is a substantial divergence between statutory language and judicial decision. For example, the language of the antitrust statutes does not contain anything resembling the distinction between the *per se* rule and the rule of reason, the market power requirement for monopolization cases, or the "indirect purchaser" rule.

Nevertheless, the most famous "common law" interpretation of the Sherman Act actually distorted the common law so badly that it effectively cut the knot between common law and antitrust approaches to combinations in restraint of trade. Judge Taft's opinion in United States v. Addyston Pipe & Steel Co.[26] has often been praised for its expression of the relationship between the Sherman Act and the common law. The great brilliance of the opinion, its admirers have argued, is that Taft was able to show that the common law had always condemned anticompetitive price fixing agreements, while it had approved efficiency creating joint ventures.[27] Under Taft's rule, "naked" restraints such as price fixing were condemned automatically, under a *per se* analysis, while restraints that were legitimately "ancillary" to an efficiency creating joint venture were approved.[28]

In fact, Judge Taft's vision was based on a distorted view of the common law.[29] The cases that Judge Taft cited for the reasonableness of ancillary restraints actually involved covenants not to compete contained in employment agreements or agreements for the sale of property. Although they were subject to a rule of reason, the content

---

[24]   See William H. Page, Ideological Conflict and the Origins of Antitrust Policy, 66 Tul.L.Rev. 1, 36 (1991).

[25]   For example, see the discussion in Apex Hosiery Co. v. Leader, 310 U.S. 469, 497–99, 60 S.Ct. 982, 994–996 (1940). See Daniel A. Crane, Antitrust and the Judicial Virtues, 2013 Colum. Bus. L. Rev. 1 (2013).

[26]   85 Fed. 271 (6th Cir. 1898), affirmed, 175 U.S. 211, 20 S.Ct. 96 (1899).

[27]   See, for example, Robert H. Bork, The Antitrust Paradox: A Policy at War With Itself 26–30 (1978; rev. ed. 1993).

[28]   On cartels, joint ventures, and the rule of reason, see Chs. 4 & 5.

[29]   See 1 Antitrust Law, id. at ¶ 104d.

of that rule was generally nothing more than consideration of whether the noncompetition agreement was limited in duration and confined to a fairly narrow geographic area. The relationship between approval of such agreements and their underlying efficiency is no more than haphazard.

At the same time, Taft painted an impressionistic, noninterpretivist picture of the law of cartels and contracts in restraint of Trade. His *Addyston Pipe* opinion was as important for its disingenuousness as for its brilliance. He ignored or misconstrued common law and even Sherman Act decisions that had unambiguously approved naked price-fixing.[30] He cited half the opinions in order to explain why they were wrong.[31] Some of the cases he cited for the common law position on trade restraints actually relied on statutes that deviated from the common law.[32] Some of the opinions he cited as condemning "naked" restraints in fact condemned joint ventures with great efficiency-creating potential.

Nonetheless, one of the great accomplishments of Taft's *Addyston Pipe* opinion was to fuse the emerging economic model of competition with the traditional legal doctrine of combinations in restraint of trade. In the process Judge Taft created the illusion that the law of combinations in restraint of trade had always been concerned with competition as economically defined. The result was a Sherman Act whose ideology was much more economic than that reflected in either the common law or the Congressional history. Congress' own notion that the Sherman Act simply federalized the common law cut the courts free from the Act's legislative history, but Taft's *Addyston Pipe* decision effectively freed the courts from the substance of the historical common law. From that point on, federal courts forged their own set of antitrust rules through an essentially common law process in which only Sherman (and later Clayton) Act precedents counted. Common law precedents were mainly, although not entirely, ignored.

---

[30] For example, United States v. Nelson, 52 Fed. 646, 647 (D.Minn.1892) (upholding collusion under Sherman Act); Dolph v. Troy Laundry Mach. Co., 28 Fed. 553, 555–556 (C.C.N.D.N.Y.1886), reversed, 138 U.S. 617, 11 S.Ct. 412 (1891) (upholding price fixing under common law).

[31] For example, Gloucester Isinglass & Glue Co. v. Russia Cement Co., 154 Mass. 92, 27 N.E. 1005 (1891) (upholding combination in restraint of trade because it did not involve a necessity of life) Other cases are discussed in Herbert Hovenkamp, The Sherman Act and the Classical Theory of Competition, 74 Iowa L. Rev. 1019, 1043 (1989).

[32] Gibbs v. Consolidated Gas Co. of Balt., 130 U.S. 396, 9 S.Ct. 553 (1889) (relying on statute that prohibited a gas company from combining with another gas company); Ford v. Chicago Milk Shippers' Ass'n, 155 Ill. 166, 39 N.E. 651 (1895) (relying on statute forbidding combinations by trust).

2.1c.   A Thumbnail History of Federal Antitrust Policy

The history of American antitrust policy has been told many times, at varying levels of detail and sophistication. The following is an extremely brief overview, with citations to other historical works.[33]

Most early enforcement of the Sherman Act was by the federal government, and its main target was cartels and the array of tighter combinations then known as "trusts." Many of the earliest attempts foundered, because the federal courts interpreted the Act under the general common law rules that (1) agreements to increase price not accompanied by any coercive actions against third parties were not illegal; and (2) cartels were generally not illegal unless they controlled virtually all of the affected market.[34] Equally pessimistic was the first Supreme Court decision interpreting the Sherman Act, the *E. C. Knight* case of 1895, which held that the Act did not reach a combination of sugar producers because the combination mainly affected manufacturing, and manufacturing itself was not interstate commerce. As a result, the indictment was outside the federal government's jurisdictional reach under the commerce clause.[35]

Blame for the early failures of the Sherman Act is sometimes laid at the feet of Richard Olney, President Cleveland's Attorney General, who was not an enthusiastic trustbuster. But an alternative view of Olney is that he was highly restrained because he predicted— correctly, it turned out—that the courts were unlikely to cooperate in any attempt to use the Sherman Act expansively.[36] The one place the Sherman Act did find aggressive use, much to the horror of some of its early supporters, was as a tool against labor union organizing. Indeed, twelve out of the first thirteen Sherman Act convictions,

---

[33]   The classic, highly factual account is Hans B. Thorelli, The Federal Antitrust Policy: Origination of an American Tradition (1955). A few of the others are Rudolph J.R. Peritz, Competition Policy in America, 1888–1992: History, Rhetoric, Law (1996); William Letwin, Law and Economic Policy in America: The Evolution of the Sherman Antitrust Act (1981); Herbert Hovenkamp, The Opening of American Law: Neoclassical Legal Thought, 1870–1970, chs. 11–12 (2015). The legislative history of the antitrust laws is collected in Earl W. Kintner, The Legislative History of the Antitrust Laws (1978). On the history of antitrust policy toward distribution restraints, see Laura Phillips Sawyer, American Fair Trade: Proprietary Capitalism, Corporatism, and the "New Competition, 1890–1940 (2017).

[34]   See for example In re Greene, 52 Fed. 104, 114 (C.C.S.D.Ohio 1892) (merger of distillers intending to control entire market not illegal where the acquisition agreements did not prevent sellers from re-entering).

[35]   United States v. E.C. Knight Co., 156 U.S. 1, 15 S.Ct. 249 (1895). See Herbert Hovenkamp, Enterprise and American Law: 1836–1937 (1991), at 241–245.

[36]   Letwin, Law and Economic Policy in America, *supra*, at 117–118.

obtained between 1890 and 1897, were against labor unions.[37] Congress eventually responded to labor's concerns by exempting most labor organizing from the antitrust laws, first in § 6 of the Clayton Act,[38] and later in the Norris-LaGuardia Act.[39]

The federal government's first major Sherman Act successes were against railroad cartels operating mainly in the Midwest,[40] and in 1904 against a railroad merger.[41] By the turn of the century the government's win record in cases against capitalists rather than labor began to improve, with victories against cartels,[42] and major convictions against the Standard Oil Company and the tobacco trust in 1911 for monopolization by predatory practices and merger to monopoly.[43]

The period 1895–1905 witnessed an enormous wave of mergers, caused in part by the Sherman Act itself. Many entrepreneurs believed that the Act would prohibit cartels but be quite tolerant of tighter combinations involving asset acquisitions or holding companies.[44] At any rate, following the great merger wave, the United States became deeply involved in merger policy—a concern that has not subsided to the present day.

Two things account for the great interest in antitrust during the 1912 Presidential election. One was the great merger wave noted above. The other was the development of the "rule of reason" in the *Standard Oil* and *American Tobacco* decisions of 1911.[45] Notwithstanding the convictions in those cases, many Progressive Era liberals believed that the rule of reason would greatly weaken the Sherman Act, a position reinforced by rulings such as Henry v. A.B. Dick & Co.[46] that tying arrangements should be considered reasonable under the Sherman Act. The new Wilson administration

---

[37]   Hovenkamp, *Enterprise, supra* at 229.

[38]   15 U.S.C.A. § 16, passed in 1914.

[39]   29 U.S.C.A. §§ 101–110, 113–115, passed in 1932. On antitrust's labor exemption today, see § 19.7b, *infra*; and 1A Antitrust Law ¶¶ 255–257 (5th ed. 2020).

[40]   United States v. Trans-Missouri Freight Ass'n, 166 U.S. 290, 17 S.Ct. 540 (1897); United States v. Joint-Traffic Ass'n, 171 U.S. 505, 19 S.Ct. 25 (1898).

[41]   Northern Sec. Co. v. United States, 193 U.S. 197, 24 S.Ct. 436 (1904).

[42]   For example, United States v. Addyston Pipe & Steel Co., 85 Fed. 271, 278–291 (6th Cir. 1898), affirmed, 175 U.S. 211, 20 S.Ct. 96 (1899)

[43]   Standard Oil Co. (N.J.) v. United States, 221 U.S. 1, 31 S.Ct. 502 (1911); United States v. Am. Tobacco Co., 221 U.S. 106, 31 S.Ct. 632 (1911).

[44]   See Herbert Hovenkamp, Enterprise and American Law: 1836–1937 (1991), at ch. 20.

[45]   Standard Oil Co. (N.J.), 221 U.S. 1, 31 S.Ct. 502 (1911); Am. Tobacco Co., 221 U.S. 106 (1911). See the excellent symposium "100 Years of Standard Oil," 85 S.Cal.L.Rev. 429 (2012) (Barak Orbach & D. Daniel Sokol, eds.); and Herbert Hovenkamp, The Rule of Reason, 70 Fla. L. Rev. 81 (2018).

[46]   224 U.S. 1, 32 S.Ct. 364 (1912).

responded with the Clayton Act[47] and the Federal Trade Commission Act.[48] The Clayton Act explicitly condemned anticompetitive price discrimination, tying and exclusive dealing, expanded private enforcement, created an early but rather ineffectual exemption for labor organizing,[49] and condemned mergers on a far more aggressive standard than the Sherman Act had done. The FTC Act created the Federal Trade Commission, an administrative body that could summon expertise unavailable to the courts,[50] and also created a more expansive basis for liability, namely § 5 of the FTC Act, which condemned unfair methods of competition. Under that statute, as eventually interpreted, the FTC could go after practices it deemed anticompetitive, but which did not violate one of the other antitrust laws.[51]

The period from the end of the Progressive Era, through World War One and up to the New Deal is generally characterized by a very moderate merger policy[52] and greatly increased attention to joint ventures and trade associations.[53] The government also became heavily involved in enforcing the law against resale price maintenance, which had been condemned by the Supreme Court in 1911,[54] and of exclusive dealing, which was condemned when anticompetitive by the Clayton Act.[55]

The 1930's was a turbulent and contradictory period for both economic theory and antitrust policy. On one side were those who believed that price competition was unworkable and inefficient, and

---

[47]   15 U.S.C.A. §§ 12 et seq.

[48]   15 U.S.C.A. §§ 41 et seq.

[49]   See Hovenkamp, *Enterprise, supra* at ch. 19.

[50]   See Daniel A. Crane, The Institutional Structure of Antitrust Enforcement, *passim* (2011). For a good but detailed and dated history see Gerard C. Henderson, The Federal Trade Commission: A Study in Administrative Law and Procedure (1924).

[51]   See FTC v. Brown Shoe Co., 384 U.S. 316, 86 S.Ct. 1501 (1966); FTC v. Sperry & Hutchinson Co., 405 U.S. 233, 92 S.Ct. 898 (1972).

[52]   For example, United States v. United Shoe Mach. Co., 247 U.S. 32, 38 S.Ct. 473 (1918); United States v. United States Steel Corp., 251 U.S. 417, 40 S.Ct. 293 (1920); United States v. S. Pac. Co., 259 U.S. 214, 42 S.Ct. 496 (1922).

[53]   For example, Board of Trade of City of Chi. v. United States, 246 U.S. 231, 38 S.Ct. 242 (1918); Am. Column & Lumber Co. v. United States, 257 U.S. 377, 42 S.Ct. 114 (1921); Maple Flooring Mfrs'. Ass'n v. United States, 268 U.S. 563, 45 S.Ct. 578 (1925).

[54]   Dr. Miles Med. Co. v. John D. Park & Sons Co., 220 U.S. 373, 31 S.Ct. 376 (1911), overruled by Leegin Creative Leather Products, Inc. v. PSKS, Inc., 551 U.S. 877, 127 S.Ct. 2705 (2007). United States v. Colgate & Co., 250 U.S. 300, 39 S.Ct. 465 (1919); United States v. A. Schrader's Son, Inc., 252 U.S. 85, 40 S.Ct. 251 (1920); FTC v. Beech-Nut Packing Co., 257 U.S. 441, 42 S.Ct. 150 (1922); and numerous others.

[55]   For example, FTC v. Sinclair Refining Co., 261 U.S. 463, 43 S.Ct. 450 (1923). On other early decisions, see 11 Herbert Hovenkamp, Antitrust Law ¶ 1801 (4th ed. 2019).

who advocated broad freedom from antitrust prosecution for joint ventures, trade associations or other group activities thought to increase efficiency.[56] On the other were those who insisted on aggressive antitrust enforcement against all combinations. The first group temporarily won out during the First New Deal, when Roosevelt's "Codes of Fair Competition" virtually legalized various forms of collusion. But after the National Recovery Administration was struck down by the Supreme Court, Roosevelt changed course. He made Thurman Arnold head of the antitrust division. Until World War II intervened, Arnold pursued vertical integration,[57] collusion and, for the first time, oligopoly aggressively, going after obvious collusion facilitators such as price-posting as well as tacit agreements. Finally, he launched a major campaign against perceived abuses of intellectual property rights, particularly patents.[58] He also greatly expanded the use of antitrust consent decrees as a mechanism for obtaining government relief faster and more predictably than more protracted litigation would produce. At the same time, Congress expanded § 2 of the Clayton Act by passing the Robinson-Patman Act,[59] which greatly limited the ability of firms to charge lower prices to large customers than they did to smaller ones. With that statute, the government enforcement agencies embarked on the highly anticompetitive policy of trying to protect small business from more efficient, larger firms.[60]

Undoubtedly the most lasting legacy of the problems attending the New Deal and the recovery was the increasing attempt by antitrust policy makers after World War II to take efficiency concerns more seriously, and to recognize that bigness and even a certain amount of oligopoly were a fact of life.[61] This required a more

---

[56] See generally Ellis W. Hawley, The New Deal and the Problem of Monopoly (1974); Ellis W. Hawley, Herbert Hoover and the Sherman Act, 1921–1933: An Early Phase of a Continuing Issue, 74 Iowa L. Rev. 1067 (1989); Robert F. Himmelberg, The Origins of the National Recovery Administration, Business, Government, and the Trade Association Issue, 1921–1933 (1976).

[57] For example, United States v. Paramount Pictures, Inc., 334 U.S. 131, 68 S.Ct. 915 (1948); United States v. Pullman Co., 330 U.S. 806, 67 S.Ct. 1078 (1947).

[58] See Herbert Hovenkamp, The Opening of American Law: Neoclassical Legal Thought, chs. 11–12 (2015); Spencer Weber Waller, Thurman Arnold: A Biography (2005). For example, American Tobacco Co. v. United States, 328 U.S. 781, 66 S.Ct. 1125 (1946); United States v. Socony-Vacuum Oil Co., 310 U.S. 150, 60 S.Ct. 811 (1940). See also Sugar Inst. v. United States, 297 U.S. 553, 56 S.Ct. 629 (1936); Interstate Circuit, Inc. v. United States, 306 U.S. 208, 59 S.Ct. 467 (1939).

[59] See ch. 14.

[60] See 14 Antitrust Law, ch. 23 (4th ed. 2019).

[61] For example, John Maurice Clark, Toward a Concept of Workable Competition, 30 Am. Econ. Rev. 243 (1940).

sophisticated dialogue between antitrust and economic theory.[62] The economic theory of the day placed a heavy emphasis on structural issues. Concern for concentration, entry barriers, and the linkage between structure and oligopoly dominated the post-war period.[63] At the same time American enforcement agencies became highly concerned—in fact, almost paranoid—about vertical practices that were thought to increase entry barriers, facilitate collusion, or enable firms to leverage additional monopoly profits out of secondary markets. The result was continued aggressive enforcement of the laws against resale price maintenance, new attention to vertical nonprice restraints, and numerous challenges to tying arrangements, exclusive dealing and vertical mergers.[64]

The most prominent antitrust policy document of the period was the *Report* of the Attorney General's National Committee to Study the Antitrust Laws (1955), which was mildly expansionary by the standards of that time. The report advocated stricter merger standards that relied heavily on structural factors but generally disregarded the efficiencies that could result from mergers. Even Carl Kaysen's and Donald F. Turner's *Antitrust Policy*,[65] which was more rigorous economically, identified the promotion of "fair" conduct and the limiting of growth of big business as desirable antitrust goals.[66] Indeed, they even suggested that a legitimate goal of antitrust policy is the equitable distribution of income.[67] Much of the foundational analysis for this thinking, but without the explicit normative concerns, was contained in Harvard economist Joe S. Bain's 1950's work on barriers to entry, industry structure, and oligopoly. His work, more than that of many contemporaries, clearly showed a concern with high prices.[68]

By 1950, when the Celler-Kefauver amendments to § 7 of the Clayton Act were passed, concern with market imperfections had

---

[62] See Herbert Hovenkamp, United States Competition Policy in Crisis, 1890–1955, 94 Minn.L.Rev. 311 (2009); Hovenkamp, Opening, ch. 11.

[63] For example United States v. Aluminum Co. of Am., 148 F.2d 416 (2d Cir. 1945); United States v. Columbia Steel Co., 334 U.S. 495, 68 S.Ct. 1107 (1948).

[64] Among the long list of examples are United States v. Yellow Cab Co., 332 U.S. 218, 67 S.Ct. 1560 (1947); Int'l Salt Co. v. United States, 332 U.S. 392, 68 S.Ct. 12 (1947); United States v. Griffith, 334 U.S. 100, 68 S.Ct. 941 (1948); Standard Oil Co. of Cal. v. United States, 337 U.S. 293, 69 S.Ct. 1051 (1949).

[65] Carl Kaysen & Donald F. Turner, Antitrust Policy: An Economic and Legal Analysis (1959).

[66] Id. at 11–17.

[67] Id. at 11: ("[E]quitable distribution of income" is a "desirable economic result," against which antitrust policy should be tested.).

[68] See Joe S. Bain, Barriers to New Competition: The Character and Consequences in Manufacturing Industries (1956). See Herbert Hovenkamp, Antitrust and the Costs of Movement, 78 Antitrust L.J. 67 (2012).

become much more pronounced. Further, Congress may have been overly responsive to lobbying organizations of small businesses who were injured by the efficient practices of larger firms. The culmination of this thinking was a 1960's antitrust policy that was often hostile toward innovation[69] and that became a zealous protector of the right of small business to operate independently.[70]

The literature criticizing 1960's antitrust policy for its excesses routinely blames the Warren Court. But the first party to blame is the enforcement agencies of the government. The great majority of Warren era decisions that are characterized today as overly aggressive came in suits brought by the government, in which the Court did precisely what the government asked it to do.[71] For this reason arguments such as those analyzed in § 2.2c below that competitors are inferior plaintiffs, or that most antitrust litigation should be pursued by the government, must be seen in historical perspective. Over the 120 year history of the antitrust laws most of the zealotry and expansiveness in doctrine has been requested by the government itself. Aggressive private plaintiffs did no more than pick up where the government left off. Today the tables are turned, and the private plaintiff is generally viewed as the enforcer who pushes antitrust to its limits. But these are contingent rather than eternal positions, and they could change once again.

This brief history concludes here, with the end of the Warren Era. The Chicago School, which was in large part energized by the expansive antitrust policy of the 1950s and 1960s and eventually fell victim to its own failures, is discussed below.

§ 2.2   On the Role of Economics in Antitrust

2.2a.   Antitrust and Economics Before 1960

Antitrust has always been closely tied to prevailing economic doctrine. To be sure, antitrust policy makers sometimes applied economics ineptly, sometimes gravitated toward the fringes of economic theory rather than the center, and sometimes pushed good points too far. But even the common law was driven largely by the then-prevailing rules of classical political economy concerning the

---

[69]   It was particularly hostile toward innovations in distribution systems that tended to replace small, independent entrepreneurs.

[70]   For example, Brown Shoe Co. v. United States, 370 U.S. 294, 82 S.Ct. 1502 (1962).

[71]   For example, *Brown Shoe*; United States v. Von's Grocery Co., 384 U.S. 270, 86 S.Ct. 1478 (1966); FTC v. Procter & Gamble Co., 386 U.S. 568, 87 S.Ct. 1224 (1967); United States v. Arnold, Schwinn & Co., 388 U.S. 365, 87 S.Ct. 1856 (1967); FTC v. Consol. Foods Corp., 380 U.S. 592, 85 S.Ct. 1220 (1965). See Herbert Hovenkamp, The Antitrust Enterprise: Principle and Execution, Ch. 9 (2005).

nature of competition and the efficiency consequences of various anticompetitive practices.[72] With the rise of neoclassicism in the 1870's and 1880's (best identified with the development of the marginal cost and marginal revenue curves), the analysis became more subtle and economists became increasingly aware of market imperfections that might allow various anticompetitive practices.[73] Antitrust policy was not far behind.

The New Deal period saw substantial inroads of economic theory into antitrust policy. But at that time the dominant economic ideology was also quite suspicious of unregulated markets and inclined to believe that government regulation would work better. Beginning after 1935 or so, American antitrust policy became increasingly aggressive against mergers and various vertical practices. Once again, the change did not occur in spite of prevailing economic doctrine. On the contrary, it was driven by economic theories such as those developed in Edward Chamberlin's theory of monopolistic competition, a New Deal classic that emphasized the role of imperfections such as product differentiation in American markets.[74] Within this framework competition was regarded as a fragile state of affairs that could be maintained only by constant antitrust supervision. The reaction to this New Deal ideology led directly to the concept of "workable competition," which was extremely influential in the 1940's and 1950's.[75] That theory was incorporated into the 1955 *Report* of the Attorney General on antitrust policy, which attempted to develop an antitrust policy based on industrial organization theory.[76] Competition was seen not as something inherent in many American industries, but rather as something that could be made workable, even in highly imperfect markets, provided that the government was willing to intervene and challenge anticompetitive practices.

The economic theory that prevailed in the 1960's was quite different from the economics of the 1980's, and economists of the earlier period were much more suspicious of the unregulated market. For example, Joe S. Bain, probably the most influential antitrust

---

[72]   See Herbert Hovenkamp, The Sherman Act and the Classical Theory of Competition, 74 Iowa L. Rev. 1019 (1989).

[73]   See Herbert Hovenkamp, The Opening of American Law: Neoclassical Legal Thought, 1870–1970 (2015).

[74]   Edward H. Chamberlin, The Theory of Monopolistic Competition (1933). See Herbert Hovenkamp, United States Competition Policy in Crisis, 1890–1955, 94 Minn.L.Rev. 311 (2009).

[75]   See John M. Clark, Toward a Concept of Workable Competition, 30 Am. Econ. Rev. 241 (1940).

[76]   Report of the Attorney General's National Committee to Study the Antitrust Laws (1955).

economist of the day, based his relatively interventionist theories on three important economic premises. The first was that economies of scale were not substantial in most markets and dictated truly anticompetitive concentration levels in only a small number of industries.[77] As a result, many industries contained larger firms and were more concentrated than necessary to achieve optimal productive efficiency.[78] The second theory was that barriers to entry by new firms were very high and could easily be manipulated by dominant firms.[79] The third was that the noncompetitive performance (monopoly pricing) associated with oligopoly began to occur at relatively low concentration levels.[80] The combination of these views created an antitrust policy that was quite concerned with deconcentrating oligopolistic markets and, to a degree, with protecting small firms from larger rivals.[81]

2.2b.   The Chicago School and Its Aftermath

The revolution in market economics that took place at the University of Chicago in the 1950's and after was a full assault on the New Deal/Chamberlain/Bain conception of the frailty of markets and the appropriate scope of antitrust intervention.[82]

The Chicago School has traditionally stood for the following propositions:

(1)   Economic efficiency, the pursuit of which should be the exclusive goal of the antitrust laws, consists of two relevant parts: productive efficiency and allocative efficiency. *Productive* efficiency is a fraction in which the value of a firm's output is the numerator and the value of its inputs is

---

[77]   See Joe S. Bain, Economies of Scale, Concentration, and the Condition of Entry in Twenty Manufacturing Industries, 44 Am. Econ. Rev. 15, 38 (1954).

[78]   Joe S. Bain, Barriers to New Competition: Their Character and Consequences in Manufacturing Industries 53–113 (1956); Joe S. Bain, Relation of Profit Rate to Industry Concentration: American Manufacturing, 1936–1940, 65 Q.J.Econ. 293 (1951).

[79]   Bain, *Barriers, supra* at 1–42, 114–43.

[80]   Ibid. On oligopoly, see ch. 4.

[81]   The concerns were exacerbated by the fact that the first post-war census appeared to show rapidly increasing industrial concentration. The data are discussed in the second edition of Frederic M. Scherer, Industrial Market Structure and Economic Performance, ch. 3 (2d ed. 1980).

[82]   On the development of the Chicago School generally and in antitrust see Edmund W. Kitch, The Fire of Truth: A Remembrance of Law and Economics at Chicago, 1932–70, 26 J.L. & Econ. 163 (1983); Richard A. Posner, The Chicago School of Antitrust Analysis, 127 U.Pa.L.Rev. 925 (1979). More critical is Herbert Hovenkamp & Fiona Scott Morton, Framing the Chicago School of Antitrust Analysis, ___ Univ. Penn. L. Rev. ___ (2020), currently available at https://papers.ssrn.com/sol3/papers. cfm?abstract_id=3481388. See also Herbert Hovenkamp, The Antitrust Enterprise: Principle and Execution, ch. 2 (2005).

the denominator; the higher this ratio, the more efficient the firm. *Allocative* efficiency refers to the general efficiency of markets, generally measured by the Pareto criterion.[83] As a general matter, markets attain optimal allocative efficiency when they are competitive—that is, when price equals marginal cost. Because monopoly profits provide an important incentive to research and development, however, increases in productive efficiency often operate to reduce the market's allocative efficiency. For example, construction of a large plant and acquisition of a large market share may increase a firm's productive efficiency by enabling it to achieve economies of scale; however, these actions may simultaneously reduce allocative efficiency by facilitating monopoly pricing. A properly defined antitrust policy will attempt to maximize *net* efficiency gains.[84]

(2) Most markets are competitive, even if they contain relatively few sellers. Even if firms in concentrated markets are able to coordinate prices, they will continue to compete in other ways, such as by increasing customer services. It is very difficult for oligopolies or cartels to close off every possible avenue of competition. Further, product differentiation tends to undermine competition far less than was formerly presumed, and it makes collusion far more difficult to maintain. As a result, neither high market concentration nor product differentiation are the anticompetitive problems earlier oligopoly theorists believed them to be.[85]

(3) Resources tend to move freely from lower value to higher value uses; as a result, monopoly tends to be self-correcting; that is, the monopolist's higher profits generally attract new entry into the monopolist's market with the result that the monopolist's position is quickly eroded. About the best that the judicial process can do is hasten the correction process.[86]

---

[83] A situation is Pareto optimal when no person can be made better off without making someone else worse off.

[84] For example, Robert H. Bork, The Antitrust Paradox: A Policy at War with Itself 91 (1978; rev. ed. 1993): "[t]he whole task of antitrust can be summed up as the effort to improve allocative efficiency without impairing productive efficiency so greatly as to produce either no gain or a net loss in consumer welfare."

[85] See, for example, Yale Brozen, Concentration, Mergers and Public Policy (1982); John S. McGee, In Defense of Industrial Concentration (1971).

[86] For example, Frank H. Easterbrook, The Limits of Antitrust, 63 Texas L. Rev. 1, 2 (1984) (in the long-run markets become competitive; the goal of antitrust is merely to "speed up the arrival of the long run."). See Herbert Hovenkamp, Antitrust and the

(4) "Natural" barriers to entry are more imagined than real. As a general rule, investment will flow freely from points of lower to points of higher return. The one significant exception consists of barriers to entry that are not natural—that is, barriers that are created by government itself. In most markets society would be best off if the government left entry and exit unregulated.[87]

(5) Economies of scale are far more pervasive than economists once believed, partly because earlier economists looked only at intra-plant or production economies, and neglected economies of distribution or transacting.[88] While the vast majority of business practices are driven by a quest for efficiency, in most cases efficiencies cannot be measured.

(6) A firm generally maximizes its own profits when downstream and upstream firms behave competitively; so it has no incentive to facilitate monopoly in vertically related markets. Further, a monopolist cannot possibly "leverage" additional monopoly profits by using its monopoly position in one market to earned increased returns in vertically related markets.[89] As a result, virtually all instances of vertical integration, including tying arrangements, resale price maintenance and vertical nonprice restraints, are efficient.[90]

(7) Business firms are profit maximizers. That is, their managers generally make decisions that they anticipate will make the firm more profitable than any alternative. The model would not be undermined, however, if it should turn out that many firms are not profit maximizers but are motivated by some alternative goal, such as revenue maximization, sales maximization, or "satisficing."[91] The

---

Costs of Movement, 78 Antitrust L.J. 67 (2012); George L. Priest, The Limits of Antitrust and the Chicago School Tradition, 6 J.Comp. L. & Econ. 1 (2010).

[87]   For example, Harold Demsetz, Barriers to Entry, 72 Am. Econ. Rev. 47 (1982).

[88]   See the debate between John S. McGee (Chicago School) and Frederic M. Scherer (critic), in Industrial Concentration: The New Learning 15–113 (Harvey J. Goldschmid, H. Michael Mann & J. Fred Weston, eds. 1974).

[89]   E.g., Ward S. Bowman, Jr., Tying Arrangements and the Leverage Problem, 67 Yale L.J. 19 (1957).

[90]   Lester G. Telser, Why Should Manufacturers Want Fair Trade? 3 J.L. & Econ. 86 (1960); Robert H. Bork, The Rule of Reason and the Per Se Concept: Price Fixing and Market Division (part 2), 75 Yale L.J. 373 (1966); Richard A. Posner, The Rule of Reason and the Economic Approach: Reflections on The Sylvania Decision, 45 U.Chi.L.Rev. 1 (1977).

[91]   A firm "satisfices" when its management adopts a certain goal for profits, sales, or market share and then tries to meet the goal but not necessarily to exceed it. Under the theory, management will not be inclined to set an extremely high goal, because

integrity of the market efficiency model requires only that a few firms be profit-maximizers. In that case, the profits and market shares of these firms will grow at the expense of the non-profit-maximizers.

(8) Antitrust enforcement should be designed in such a way as to penalize conduct precisely to the point that it is inefficient, but to tolerate or encourage it when it is efficient.[92] Further, competitors in a market are generally benefitted by collusive practices and injured by efficient practices; as a result, they have precisely the wrong set of incentives to sue. Most competitor lawsuits for alleged antitrust violations should be thrown out, and private enforcement limited to consumers.

(9) Models of imperfect or monopolistic competition—the two most commonly presented alternatives to perfect competition—are either severe exaggerations from reality or else are simply wrong.[93] Economists would do better to begin with perfect competition as a starting point, and then try to explain why there are individual deviations. Even if markets are imperfect, government intervention is justified only if the result is an improvement, taking the costs of intervention into account. It is highly presumptuous to think that State-administered relief will yield more efficient outcomes than natural market processes.[94] A corollary of this position is the Chicago School belief that "error costs" are asymmetric. The cost of a "type 1" error, or recognizing a monopoly problem that does not exist, is to interfere with the market's natural movement toward a competitive equilibrium. This cost is much higher than that of a "type 2" error, which is failure to recognize a monopoly problem that does exist. In the latter case natural market

---

they do not want to be viewed later as failing. The theory of satisficing is part of a more general theory of the firm, emphasizing the separation of ownership and control, suggesting that managers and stock holders often have different motives, and that these interfere with profit maximization. See, for example, Adolph A. Berle, Jr. and Gardiner C. Means, The Modern Corporation and Private Property (1932). For a firm rejection, see Frank H. Easterbrook & Daniel R. Fischel, The Economic Structure of Corporate Law (1991).

[92]   William M. Landes, Optimal Sanctions for Antitrust Violations, 50 U.Chi.L.Rev. 652 (1983). On the "optimal deterrence model," see §§ 17.1–17.2.

[93]   For example, Robert Bork believed that oligopoly existed only in economics textbooks. See Robert H. Bork, The Antitrust Paradox: A Policy at War With Itself 221 (1978).

[94]   See, for example, Frank H. Easterbrook, Ignorance and Antitrust 119, in Antitrust, Innovation, and Competitiveness (Thomas M. Jorde & David J. Teece, eds., 1992); Frank H. Easterbrook, Workable Antitrust Policy, 84 Mich. L. Rev. 1696 (1986).

forces can be trusted to set things right. We are better off with an underdeterrent antitrust policy because under-acknowledgement of monopoly problems tends to be self correcting, while over-acknowledgement tends not to be.

(10) The decision to make this market efficiency model the exclusive guide for antitrust policy is nonpolitical. That is, it is adopted without regard for the way that wealth or entitlements are distributed in society, but only so as to maximize society's overall wealth.[95] Thus if a practice produces greater gains to business than losses to consumers, it is efficient and should not be illegal under the antitrust laws. But the same should be said about practices that produce larger gains to consumers than losses to business. The member of the Chicago School can thus argue that he is not taking sides in any political dispute about how wealth or entitlements ought to be distributed among conflicting interest groups. Such things should always go where they do the most net good.

Some of these principles are empirically robust and have become all but uncontroversial in antitrust writing. Others have little more than ideology to support them.

2.2c.   Error Cost Analysis; Competitor v. Consumer Suits; Private v. Public Suits

The Chicago School generally assumed that competitive markets are robust, while alternatives are fragile. As a result, markets are naturally "self correcting," so we would do well to be skeptical about the appropriateness of government intervention. But the last few decades have produced a significant amount of economic scholarship that has substantially undermined this position. For example, against the perfect competition models that dominated the Chicago School, today we are more likely to see product differentiation as substantial and profitable. Monopolistic competition, which the Chicago School once took great pains to discredit, came roaring back and a variation on it is particularly prominent in merger policy involving "unilateral" effects.[96] The "free rider" explanation of resale price maintenance (RPM) was a good one, but it probably applies to

---

[95]   For example, Robert H. Bork, The Antitrust Paradox: A Policy at War with Itself 90 (1978; rev. ed. 1993): "Antitrust * * * has nothing to say about the ways prosperity is distributed or used." For critiques, see Herbert Hovenkamp, Distributive Justice and the Antitrust Laws, 51 Geo. Wash. L. Rev. 1, 16–26 (1982); Jonathan B. Baker & Steven C. Salop, Antitrust, Competition Policy, and Inequality, 104 Geo. L.J. Online 1 (2015).

[96]   See § 12.3.

only a small percentage of RPM situations.[97] The Chicago models showing vertical integration to be invariably efficient rested on very simple assumptions. When these are relaxed the conclusion is much more ambiguous.[98] Strategic behavior, which appears in a variety of disguises, is both plausible and anticompetitive under a host of situations that standard Chicago scholarship failed to acknowledge.[99] The Chicago theory that market power is a relative rarity has given way to numerous econometric procedures for measuring market power with greater precision than we have had in the past. These procedures indicate that significant market power is not all that rare, even in markets that do not have dominant firms.[100]

Also significant is the fact that the old structuralist school, widely associated with Harvard economics in the 1930s through the 1950s, has given way to thinking about antitrust that has moved significantly to the right. Indeed, the two schools are often thought to be close to indistinguishable on many issues.[101] Writing in 1979 then Professor Richard A. Posner concluded that in "a number of areas" the two schools had "overlapped, converged, or crossed over."[102]

The Chicago School view was that markets tend to self-correct towards a competitive equilibrium. As a result, failure to recognize a monopoly problem, a type 2 error, simply lets market forces do their work of restoring competition. By contrast, a type 1 error falsely sees a monopoly problem when none exists, thus interfering with natural market forces. As a result, the social cost of type 1 errors is greater than that of type 2 errors and a cost minimizing approach to errors should trend toward underdeterrence.[103]

This argument very likely originated with George H. Stigler. He viewed oligopoly and monopolistic competition as limited qualifications of the model of perfect competition, with firms constantly trying to figure out ways to compete.[104] Within that

---

[97] See §§ 11.2–11.3.

[98] See §§ 9.2–9.3.

[99] See generally Jean M. Tirole, The Theory of Industrial Organization (1988).

[100] See Ch. 3.

[101] See, e.g., William E. Kovacic, The Intellectual DNA of Modern U.S. Competition Law for Dominant Firm Conduct: The Chicago/Harvard Double Helix, 2007 Colum. Bus. L. Rev. 1, 43–71 (speaking mainly of exclusionary pricing).

[102] Richard A. Posner, The Chicago School of Antitrust Analysis, 127 Univ. Pa.L.Rev. 925 (1979).

[103] Frank H. Easterbrook, The Limits of Antitrust, 63 Tex. L. Rev. 1 (1984). For excellent critiques, see Jonathan B. Baker, Taking the Error out of "Error Cost" Analysis, 80 Antitrust L.J. 1 (2015); C. Frederick Beckner & Steven C. Salop, Decision Theory and Antitrust Rules, 67 Antitrust L.J. 41 (1999).

[104] George J. Stigler, A Theory of Oligopoly, 72 Pol. Econ. 44 (1964).

framework markets tended to be regarded as inherently self-correcting, and departures as anomalous and temporary, provided that they were left to themselves.

But a half century of subsequent economics has strongly indicated the contrary. Oligopoly, monopolistic competition and their variations seem to be highly durable, and competition appears to be more fragile than Stigler believed. In most empirical economic analysis today various models of imperfect or monopolistic competition perform much better than models of perfect competition. As a result, a good case can be made that the error cost framework should be flipped: false negatives are more costly than false positives. This does not mean that antitrust law should leap to irrational theories of competitive harm, as it has sometimes done in the past. Nevertheless, there are tweaks that would improve error cost analysis. One is to make the plaintiffs burden in a rule of reason case lighter. In a rule of reason antitrust case the plaintiff must typically show power and make out a prima facie case of competitive effects sufficient to require the defendant to provide an explanation. At that time the burden of proof shifts to the defendant to justify its action. Recent Supreme Court decisions have made the plaintiff's prima facie case unreasonably difficult to prove.[105]

The Chicago School's biggest success in antitrust policy occurred in the late 1970s and 1980s when there was a great deal of low hanging fruit in the form of aggressive antitrust doctrines that were difficult to justify economically. However, the Supreme Court became more conservative on antitrust issues and mainstream economics moved on, rejecting models based on perfect competition in favor of models emphasizing market imperfections and that were empirically more robust. The result has been to make the Chicago School sound somewhat outdated and even reactionary. Its biggest source of support today comes from businesses who profit from limitations on antitrust liability.[106] Competition is a public good. Its beneficiaries are numerous but small and diverse. If markets are left to themselves too little competition will be produced.

One Chicago School position that deserves mention is that competitor standing to bring antitrust actions should be greatly restricted or perhaps eliminated.[107] According to this position,

---

[105]   See § 5.6.

[106]   Hovenkamp & Morton, *supra.*

[107]   For example, Edward A. Snyder & Thomas E. Kauper, Misuse of the Antitrust Laws: The Competitor Plaintiff, 90 Mich. L. Rev. 551 (1991); for responses, see Daniel A. Crane, Optimizing Private Antitrust Enforcement, 63 Vand.L.Rev. 675 (2010); William H. Page & Roger D. Blair, Controlling the Competitor Plaintiff in Antitrust Litigation, 91 Mich. L.Rev. 111 (1992).

consumers have the correct incentives while competitors do not. Consumers are injured by monopoly overcharges, but competitors are injured most often by the increased efficiency of the firms whose conduct is being challenged.

Competitors are simultaneously the worst and best of antitrust plaintiffs. First, their incentives are almost always questionable. Although competitors are injured by monopolistic exclusionary practices, they are also injured by increased efficiency. Since competitors, just as any private party, sue to vindicate private rights they cannot be expected to distinguish efficient from inefficient practices. They will sue if they have a cause of action and the value of the expected remedy exceeds the cost of suit.

But competitors are also the best antitrust plaintiffs. Competitors are knowledgeable participants in a market, who generally know about an anticompetitive practice long before consumers do, assuming that consumers find out at all. Competitors are well placed to pursue an antitrust violation before it produces monopoly, or at a much earlier stage. Remember, the social cost of monopoly is a function not only of its size but also of its duration.[108] Likewise, competitors generally feel the injury in much more perceptible ways. An exclusionary practice may create a monopoly that raises the price of photocopying by one cent per page. But the same practice may drive a rival out of business. This gives the rival an incentive to sue that consumers often lack.

Limiting standing to consumers would reduce the *number* of antitrust suits. But there is no good reason for thinking that those eliminated would be the nonmeritorious suits, while the meritorious suits would survive. Rather, the number of suits would be reduced simply because information costs are much higher for consumer groups, because consumer groups are much less well organized than competitors are, and because individual consumer injuries tend to be much smaller. These reasons presumably cut across all antitrust challenges, both meritorious and nonmeritorious.

A better way to reduce the number of nonmeritorious antitrust suits is to develop substantive and procedural rules that distinguish good lawsuits from bad. For example, the cure for excessive predatory pricing suits is not the elimination of the competitor plaintiff, whose early challenge can be far more effective than the later challenge of any consumer group. The cure is rigorous use of market structure and market share thresholds that will enable us to determine

---

[108]   See § 1.3.

whether predatory pricing is a plausible monopolistic strategy;[109] and close attention to price-cost relationships to help us determine whether prices were indeed predatory. More generally, the law must continue to develop a rigorous conception of "antitrust injury" to enable it to distinguish competitive from anticompetitive uses of the antitrust laws.[110]

Finally, any argument that private antitrust enforcement should generally yield to public enforcement aborts in the face of one powerful historical fact: over time, the government has not done much better. The truly scandalous decisions in the Chicago School lexicon are cases such as *Brown Shoe, Von's Grocery, Procter & Gamble,* and *Schwinn.*[111] But the plaintiff in *Von's Grocery* was Sally's Family Foods, or in *Schwinn* was Pop's Bike & Trike. Most of the overdeterrent antitrust law based on innovative or even crackpot economic theories was made in cases brought by the United States Department of Justice and the Federal Trade Commission. At least private plaintiffs are consistent about one thing: they sue in order to further their own interests. Courts can begin with that premise and limit standing or remedies accordingly. When the government sues, it may be difficult to tell what interest is being vindicated. To be sure, the record of government enforcement today is considerably different than the record in the 1960's, but the historical record is there just the same, and the fault cannot be lain entirely at the feet of a liberal judiciary unable to understand economics. To be sure, the Warren Court decided the four antitrust decisions listed above. But they did no more than give the Executive Branch what it asked for. If history has taught us anything, it is that government plaintiffs are not invariably better than private parties in identifying meritorious suits.

2.2d.   The Consumer Welfare Principle: Theory and Measurement

The discussion in these last two chapters should give you some idea about the meaning of antitrust's consumer welfare principle. Although traditionally defined in terms of low prices, which is certainly important, it is helpful to think of consumer welfare as maximized by the largest *output* that is consistent with sustainable competition. High output and low prices go together. Defining

---

[109]   As, for example, in Brooke Group Ltd. v. Brown & Williamson Tobacco Corp., 509 U.S. 209, 113 S.Ct. 2578 (1993). See § 8.8.

[110]   On antitrust injury, see § 16.3.

[111]   Brown Shoe Co. v. United States, 370 U.S. 294, 344, 82 S.Ct. 1502, 1534 (1962); United States v. Von's Grocery Co., 384 U.S. 270, 86 S.Ct. 1478 (1966); FTC v. Procter & Gamble Co., 386 U.S. 568, 579, 87 S.Ct. 1224, 1230 (1967); United States v. Arnold, Schwinn & Co., 388 U.S. 365, 87 S.Ct. 1856 (1967).

consumer welfare this way emphasizes not only that consumers benefit from low prices, but sell-side participants benefit as well. Input suppliers, manufacturers, dealers or retailers, and labor are all best off when output is maximized.

While measuring consumer welfare effects in particular cases can be complex, most of the time we can draw reasonable inferences. The easiest cases are ones that show individualized consumer harm from specific unlawful transactions. For example, price fixing is easy, because each sale raises consumer prices by the amount of the overcharge. The "anti-steering" rule in the *AmEx* case, discussed later,[112] should also have been easy. Each time the defendant's anti-steering rule was enforced, requiring a merchant to take a higher priced credit card, the consumer making that transaction was injured. Further, the merchant was also injured, as well as the lower priced rival that was excluded. The same thing is true of "pay-for-delay" settlements in pharmaceutical markets, which were the subject of the *Actavis* decision.[113] Each such settlement imposed higher prices on consumers by delaying the production of generic competitors.

In other cases, consumer harm must either be inferred from lower output, or lower output itself must be inferred from other market factors. These include an increased likelihood of collusion or foreclosure of a rival. That is true of many exclusionary practices,[114] as well as most mergers.[115] However, if these practices are correctly identified the inferences are robust, because they are driven by the fact that market wide output reductions cause competitive harm to participants on both sides of the market.

---

[112] See § 10.9.

[113] FTC v. Actavis, Inc., 570 U.S. 136, 133 S.Ct. 136 (2013). See § 5.5c3.

[114] See, e.g., Chs. 7–8 (monopolization and exclusionary pricing); §§ 10–11 (vertical restraints).

[115] See Ch. 12.

Chapter 3

MARKET POWER AND MARKET DEFINITION

Table of Sections

§ 3.1   Introduction

Market power is a firm's ability to profit by reducing output and charging more than a competitive price for its product. In the *du Pont* (cellophane) case the Supreme Court defined market power as "the power to control prices or exclude competition."[1] But that definition is both imprecise and incomplete. Market power itself is not an "exclusionary" practice: in fact, the exercise of market power—the sale of products at a supracompetitive price—generally attracts new sellers into the market. While exclusion of competitors is not market power, it is an important mechanism by which a firm obtains or maintains market power. Further, the ability to hold market power for a significant period of time is always important to antitrust policy makers, who must weigh the costs of limiting market power against the potential for gain. The more durable market power appears to be,

---

[1]   United States v. E.I. du Pont de Nemours & Co., 351 U.S. 377, 391–92, 76 S.Ct. 994, 1005 (1956).

the greater its social cost, and thus the greater the gains from getting rid of it.

Further, to say that market power is the power to "control" prices is not particularly descriptive. Any firm will begin to lose sales when it raises the price of a product. More appropriately, market power is the power to raise prices above competitive levels without losing so many sales that the price increase is unprofitable.[2] A firm that can make more money by selling its output at a higher-than-competitive price has a certain amount of market power.

Many antitrust violations require the plaintiff to show that the defendant[3] has some market power. For example, illegal monopolization under § 2 of the Sherman Act requires that the defendant have monopoly power, which is a high degree of market power.[4] The offense of attempt to monopolize has a somewhat more ambiguous market power requirement depending on the nature of the activity that is alleged to be an illegal attempt.[5] At the very least, however, the defendant must be shown to have a dangerous probability of acquiring substantial market power.[6] Establishment of an illegal tying arrangement under § 1 of the Sherman Act and generally under § 3 of the Clayton Act[7] requires a showing that the defendant has a certain amount of market power in the market for the tying product.[8] Today most courts require a showing of market power in cases alleging unlawful vertical restrictions or dealer terminations, including resale price maintenance.[9] The law of mergers under § 7 of the Clayton Act[10] does not generally require a showing that either of the merging firms has present market power. Mergers are condemned in part, however, because of their propensity to create market power. As a result, a power assessment is essential in merger cases. Finally, although market power is not a requirement

---

[2]   Rebel Oil Co., Inc. v. Atlantic Richfield Co., 51 F.3d 1421, 1434 (9th Cir.), cert. denied, 516 U.S. 987, 116 S.Ct. 515 (1995).

[3]   Or group of defendants acting in concert. The term "defendant" is often used in this book to describe the firm whose activity is being evaluated, even though it has not been sued or is purely hypothetical.

[4]   15 U.S.C.A. § 2; see Chs. 6–8.

[5]   See § 6.5.

[6]   Spectrum Sports v. McQuillan, 506 U.S. 447, 455–6, 113 S.Ct. 884, 892 (1993), remanded, 23 F.3d 1531 (9th Cir. 1994); Tops Mkts., Inc. v. Quality Mkts., Inc., 142 F.3d 90, 100 (2d Cir. 1998).

[7]   15 U.S.C.A. §§ 1, 14.

[8]   See ch. 10. On whether a tying arrangement can be condemned under the Clayton Act without market power in the tying product, see § 10.3.

[9]   E.g., PSKS, Inc. v. Leegin Creative Leather Products, Inc., 615 F.3d 412 (5th Cir. 2010) (dismissing complaint of resale price maintenance where defendant was not shown to have significant market power). See ch. 11.

[10]   15 U.S.C.A. § 18. See chs. 9, 12 & 13.

in most *per se* cases, such as price fixing, a consumer plaintiff seeking damages must generally show that there has been an "overcharge," which may require a showing of the defendants' collective market power.[11]

3.1a.   Market Power Technically Defined

Market power is a firm's ability to deviate profitably from marginal cost pricing. Further, marginal cost, or competitive, pricing is an important goal of the antitrust laws. Marginal cost is therefore a useful base from which to measure market power: the greater the ratio of a firm's profit-maximizing price to its marginal cost, the more market power the firm has. The Lerner Index is one attempt to quantify market power in terms of marginal cost. Its simplest formulation is:[12]

$$\frac{P - MC}{P}$$

Where,

P   =   the firm's price at its profit-maximizing level of output; and

MC =   the firm's marginal cost at the profit-maximizing level of output.

Under perfect competition, where price equals marginal cost, the index gives a reading of zero. As P approaches infinity, or as marginal cost approaches zero, the Index value approaches one. If a firm maximizes its profits at a price double its marginal cost, its market power measured by the Lerner Index would be $(2X - X)/2X$, or .5. If a firm maximizes its profits at a price 20% above its marginal cost, its Lerner Index number would be $(1.2X - X)/1.2X$, or .167. The simplicity of Lerner's formula is misleading. If we knew the elasticity of demand facing any firm we could plug it into the formula and immediately know the ratio of that firm's monopoly price to its competitive price. From such data we could develop some presumptive legal rules about how high a reading would be necessary to make a merger illegal, or to establish one of the requirements for illegal monopolization. Unfortunately, our economic tools do not permit such simple measurement.

---

[11]   See ch. 17.

[12]   For more technical variations, see William M. Landes & Richard A. Posner, Market Power in Antitrust Cases, 94 Harv.L.Rev. 937, 940–941 (1981).

3.1b. Market Share as a Surrogate for Market Power

Direct measurement of marginal cost and firm elasticity of demand can be difficult, and adequate data are not always available. Courts often rely on the fact that there is a positive correlation between market *share* and market power. Suppose that the market for widgets is shared by 10 firms, each with 10% of the market. The marginal cost (and competitive price) of widgets is $1.00. If firm A attempts to raise its price to $1.25, A's customers will look to A's competitors for widgets at the old price. If each of the other nine firms can increase its own output by a little over 10%, A will lose all of its sales.

By contrast, if A has 90% of the market for widgets, A's price increase is much more likely to be profitable. A's customers will still look to A's rivals for lower-priced widgets, but now the rivals will have to increase their own output substantially in order to steal a large percentage of A's customers. For example, suppose that A reduces its output from 90 units to 80 units in order to raise the price from $1.00 to $1.25. If A's competitors, who make the remaining 10 units, are to raise output back to the competitive level, each will have to double its output. To be sure, over the long run A's monopoly profits will encourage the existing rivals to increase their production and new firms to enter the widget market. Eventually A's market share will erode, unless A devises some scheme for excluding its rivals.

All other things being equal, a firm with a large market share has a greater ability to increase price profitably than a firm with a smaller share. When A's market share is 10%, the effect of A's unilateral price increase would likely be the *immediate* loss of most sales. When A's market share is 80%, however, A may be able to make sales at the higher price for quite some time. This correlation of market power and market share has permitted courts to use market share as a qualified proxy for market power in antitrust cases.

The word "qualified" is important. Market share is an incomplete proxy for market power. The correlation between market share and market power can be rigorously expressed in a formula. However, the formula contains *three* variables: market share, market demand elasticity, and the elasticity of supply of fringe firms. If the two elasticity variables remain constant, then market power would be proportional to market share. In the real world, however, market elasticities vary from one market to another. Thus in order to estimate a firm's market power we must gather some information not only about a firm's market share, but also about the demand and supply conditions that it faces.[13]

3.1c. Market Share as More than a Surrogate; Independent Relevance of Market Share

The underlying evil that antitrust addresses is the power to raise price profitably above marginal cost. But antitrust itself is concerned with the *process* by which market power is created or maintained. This process question forces the tribunal to consider whether some practice is likely to be anticompetitive. The answer often depends, not on the firm's abstract ability to raise price above marginal cost, but on its ability to restrict the entry or output of rivals.

For example, many monopolization cases involve "exclusionary" practices that are plausible only because the defendant occupies a large portion of the relevant market in question. This is certainly true of predatory pricing, where the relative costs of predation are a function of the predator's market share. But the same thing is true of the various "foreclosure" offenses, whether under § 2 of the Sherman Act (monopolization and attempt), § 1 of that statute (vertical agreements), § 3 of the Clayton Act (tying and exclusive dealing), or Clayton Act § 7 (vertical and some other mergers). In each of these cases the claimed harm to competition results, not from the defendant's ability to raise price above marginal cost, but rather from its ability to cut rivals off from sources of supply, distribution outlets and the like. The real "power" basis of the offense, then, is market share, not market power as such. To be sure, antitrust's central concern is increased market power. But when we consider the threat and basic plausibility of the alleged offense we are examining means, not ends.

3.1d. The Relevant Antitrust Market

In antitrust cases that require proof of market power the court traditionally queries whether some "relevant market" exists in which the legally necessary market power requirement can be inferred. In order to do this, the court usually 1) determines a relevant product market, 2) determines a relevant geographic market, and 3) computes the defendant's percentage of the output in the relevant market thus defined. Section 2 of the Sherman Act and § 7 of the Clayton Act, the two statutes that most often require analysis of market power, both hint at this approach. Section 2 of the Sherman Act condemns monopolization of "any part of * * * trade or commerce

---

[13]   See the discussion of elasticities of supply and demand in § 1.1.

* * *."[14] Section 7 of the Clayton Act makes mergers illegal if they tend to lessen competition "in any line of commerce in any section of the country."[15] The court must identify some part or "line" of commerce in which injury to competition is threatened.

If market power or a proof of a relevant market are essential to the plaintiff's antitrust cause of action, then the relevant market must be alleged in the complaint together with the reasons supporting that allegation.[16]

§ 3.2   Estimating the Relevant Market; the SSNIP and the "Hypothetical Monopolist"

A firm with a large share of a properly defined relevant market likely has market power. Markets do not define themselves, however. The passenger car division of Ford Motor Company makes "Ford cars," "American passenger cars," "passenger cars," "passenger vehicles," and "vehicles." Which of these is a relevant market for antitrust purposes? If the first, Ford Motor Company's share of the relevant market is 100%. If the last, it is small, probably less than 1%.

For most antitrust purposes, a relevant market is the smallest grouping of sales for which the elasticity of demand and supply are sufficiently low that a "hypothetical monopolist" with 100% of that grouping could profitably reduce output and increase price substantially above marginal cost. The "hypothetical monopolist" query is the same thing as asking whether a cartel whose members accounted for this output would be able to raise price significantly above the competitive level.[17] The price increase need not be large but it must be more than trivial and also durable—that is, we do not want to bring antitrust's cumbersome machinery into operation for a price increase that will be immediately dissipated by customer defections or new entry. This hypothetical price increase has

---

14   15 U.S.C.A. § 2.

15   15 U.S.C.A. § 18.

16   See 2B Antitrust Law ¶ 531f (4th ed. 2014); Simpson v. Sanderson Farms, Inc., 744 F.3d 702, 710–711 (11th Cir. 2014) (rule-of-reason antitrust plaintiffs must always "present enough information in their complaint to plausibly suggest the contours of the relevant geographic . . . market[ ]"); Hicks v. PGA Tour, Inc., 897 F.3d 1109 (9th Cir. 2018) (pleading of "contorted" relevant market of "in action" advertising to golf fans failed to meet Twombly pleading standards; claim was of advertising on caddies' bibs or part of the uniform covering the torso).

17   See Malcolm B. Coate, A Practical Guide to the Hypothetical Monopolist Test for Market Definition, 4 J.Comp. L. & Econ. 1031 (2008). The methodology of starting out with a very small grouping of sales and drawing ever larger circles until the test is satisfied is sometimes called the "circle principle." See Bryan Keating, Jonathan Orszag, & Robert Willig, The Role of the Circle Principle in Market Definition, 17 Antitrust Source 1 (Apr. 2018).

acquired the name SSNIP, or "small but significant and nontransitory increase in price."[18]

Consider first the possibility that the relevant market is "Ford cars." What would happen if Ford raised the price of its cars by, say, $1,000 each. Customers would turn away from Ford cars in droves and go to General Motors, Chrysler, Toyota or some other automobile manufacturer instead. The likely result of Ford's unilateral $1,000 price increase would be that Ford would lose much of its business. In that case "Ford cars" is not a relevant antitrust market.

Consider next the market for "American passenger cars." Suppose that a single firm made 100% of American passenger cars, and increased the price by $1,000. Once again, many customers would probably attempt to buy Japanese, German or other foreign cars instead. This time we may be a little less certain that these firms will be able to increase their output or imports enough to satisfy this new demand. If they can, however, our "market" is still too small to be a relevant antitrust market.

Now consider the market for "passenger cars." Suppose that a single firm manufactured all the world's passenger cars and increased the price by $1,000. This time it would seem that the elasticity of the market on the *demand* side is rather low. Many automobile customers would probably switch from American to foreign cars if the price difference were great enough. But if the price of *all* passenger cars went up, they would have to switch to trucks, bicycles, horses, or simply do without cars. A far higher percentage of consumers would simply pay the higher price.

How about the supply side? If the passenger car monopolist raised its price by $1,000, the passenger car market would become very attractive to firms in related industries, such as tractor manufacturers, and they might switch to production of cars. Eventually enough new firms would enter the passenger car industry to deprive the monopolist of its monopoly profits. However, switching takes time, depending on how specialized the tractor producing equipment and plants are, and how long it takes tractor manufacturers to develop a system for distributing their new automobiles. This could be three or four years or even more. During that time the $1,000 price increase might be very profitable. "Passenger cars" is probably a relevant market.

---

[18]   See, e.g., In re Southeastern Milk Antitrust Litig., 739 F.3d 262, 277–278 (6th Cir. 2014), cert. denied, 574 U.S. 1011, 135 S.Ct. 676 (2014) (recognizing SSNIP test); IGT v. Alliance Gaming Corp., 702 F.3d 1338, 1345–1346) (Fed. Cir. 2012) (same); FTC v. Whole Foods Market, Inc., 548 F.3d 1028, 1038 (D.C.Cir. 2008) (same).

Having determined the smallest relevant market, now we must calculate Ford's share of it.[19] In this case it appears that Ford is not a monopolist. Its share of the world passenger car market is less than 10%.

As the above illustration indicates, a grouping of sales is not a relevant market unless *both* the elasticity of demand and the elasticity of supply are sufficiently low. This is simply another way of saying that (1) customers must not be able to find adequate substitutes easily in response to the price increase; and (2) other firms must not be able to enter the market in question or change their own production so as to compete with the price increaser's sales.

The basic framework for delineating markets outlined above suggests a few additional issues, to which we now turn.

3.2a.   Size of Hypothesized Price Increase

In the example concerning Ford automobiles we spoke of estimating the supply and demand responses to a hypothesized price increase of $1000. Clearly, however, if the hypothesized price increase had been only $1.00, the supply and demand shifts would have been far less dramatic. By contrast, if the increase had been $10,000 they would have been much more dramatic, probably reducing Ford's output to zero. Which number should we use?

The size of the price increase presents a question of policy, not one of economics *per se*. It all depends on how much market power we want to squeeze out of markets, given our capabilities and the costs of antitrust enforcement. In a world of differentiated and branded goods many manufacturers have at least a small ability to profit by raising price above marginal cost. Other imperfections in markets, such as information failures, transaction costs, intellectual property rights, and small geographic market size, or high transportation costs, imply the same result. Market power that results in profit-maximizing prices somewhat above marginal cost seems to be ubiquitous and may even be desirable. Further, the institutional costs of reducing market power are high. Market power is difficult to measure. When courts do measure it, they are prone to make errors, and as they try to make increasingly fine judgments the error rate will rise. Further, if numerous sellers have sufficient market power, then the volume of litigation would be extremely large.

At least presumptively, it seems that 10% above the competitive level (generally marginal cost) is about the correct hypothesized price

---

[19]   On calculating market share, see § 3.7.

increase for antitrust market delineation.[20] A smaller number encourages us to pursue market power that is not worth the costs of correction. A larger number might seem appropriate, particularly in product differentiated markets. But there are some reasons for adhering to a 10% figure. First of all, the ability to set price at 10% above marginal cost could represent the ability to earn *double* the competitive profit rate in a particular industry. Suppose that when a particular market is behaving competitively, it produces 8% in accounting profits—a typical number. For example, the firm might earn 8 cents in accounting profits on an item priced at $1.00. In this case, a 10% price increase above marginal cost represents an accounting profit increase from 8 cents to 18 cents per unit; however, one would have to subtract from this the monopoly output reduction, on which the monopolist earns no profits at all. The net increase could quite easily double the monopolist's profits.[21] Of course, eliminating high profits is not a goal of the antitrust laws, but exclusionary practices and cartelization are profitable precisely to the extent that they increase profits. The chance to double one's profits could represent a major incentive to engage in anticompetitive practices. We do not abhor the profits, but we do abhor the exclusionary practices that the opportunity to earn them invites.

The hypothesized price increase must be computed from the *competitive* level, which is not necessarily the current level.[22] For example, the 2010 Horizontal Merger Guidelines, which are discussed in § 3.8, most typically use a 5% price increase. However, in the concentration ranges where horizontal mergers become a matter of concern, prices are typically already somewhat above the competitive level.

3.2b.   The "Profit-Maximizing" Increase; Critical Loss Analysis

Given our decision to hypothesize price increases in the range of 10% above the competitive level, the question that we ask is whether the profit-maximizing price increase is *10% or more*. We do *not* ask whether a 10% price increase would be profitable. This difference

---

[20]   Also advocating a 10% rule is Lawrence J. White, Antitrust and Merger Policy: Review and Critique, 1 J. Econ. Perspectives 13, 15 (1987).

[21]   For example, suppose that at a marginal cost price of $1.00 accounting profits are 8per unit and output is 100. Accounting profits would be $8.00. In response to a 10% price increase, demand falls by 5% to 95 (a not atypical elasticity of demand in markets for which an additional price increase would be profitable). At the new price and output the firm will earn 18 multiplied by 95 units, or $17.10. Even if the elasticity of demand were one, post-increase profits would be 18 multiplied by 90 units, or $16.20.

[22]   This problem is discussed in § 3.4.

may seem subtle, but it can be very important. Suppose firms A, B & C make widgets. Another group of firms, D, E & F, make gidgets, which are an imperfect substitute for widgets. Customers are grouped into two classes. One is a "low elasticity" class which must have widgets and are willing to pay much more than the competitive price for them. The other is a "high elasticity" class which is quite sensitive to price and will quickly substitute to gidgets if the widget price goes up. The first class collectively purchases 80 units and the second class collectively purchases 20 units, for a total of 100 units. The current price of widgets is $1.00. We also assume that costs are zero.[23]

Suppose that the firm raises its price from $1.00 to $1.10 and the high elasticity class immediately substitutes to gidgets. The result is that the firm sells 80 units at $1.10, for revenues of $88. Since revenues before the price increase were $100, the 10% price increase is probably unprofitable. That would suggest that the market for "widgets" is too small, and should be drawn larger to include at least "widgets plus gidgets."

But now suppose that in response to a 60% price increase precisely the same thing happens—that is, the 20 high elasticity sales are lost, but the 80 low elasticity sales are maintained. In that case total revenue is $1.60 multiplied by 80 units, or $128. This price increase is highly profitable and suggests that the market should be drawn as widgets alone.

The second answer is the correct one. It would be anomalous to draw a market in such a fashion that a 10% price increase were unprofitable but a price increase by some greater amount were profitable. So the relevant question is whether the profit-maximizing price increase would be 10% *or more*. A profit-maximizing firm in the above market would charge at least $1.60, and it might charge more.

By the same token, we do not ask whether a 10% price increase would be profitable. In some circumstances a 10% price increase might be profitable, but a 4% price increase would be more profitable.[24] In that case, the profit-maximizing firm (or cartel) will increase price by only 4%, and this would not meet our market

---

[23]   Alternative cost assumptions will not change the analysis, but they will make it more complex.

[24]   For example, a firm might lose almost no sales in response to a 4% price increase, but 20% of its sales in response to a 10% price increase. In that case the smaller increase is probably more profitable. See F.T.C. v. Whole Foods Market, Inc., 548 F.3d 1028 (D.C.Cir. 2008) (applying such analysis to conclude that a relevant market could exist for premium natural and organic supermarkets).

definition test. In sum, the relevant question is whether the *profit-maximizing* price increase is 10% or more.

A methodology used by economists known as "critical loss analysis" considers what percentage of sales a firm would have to lose in order to make a price increase of a given magnitude unprofitable. If the predicted loss in sales that is likely to result from a price increase exceeds the critical loss, then that particular price increase will be unprofitable. One advantage of critical loss analysis is its verisimilitude; firms making differentiated products use this kind of analysis all the time in order to determine whether a contemplated price increase would be profitable. The 2010 Horizontal Merger Guidelines issued by the Antitrust Division of the Justice Department and the Federal Trade Commission state that the agencies will use this methodology to evaluate markets in merger cases:

> When the necessary data are available, the Agencies also may consider a "critical loss analysis" to assess the extent to which it corroborates inferences drawn from the evidence noted above. Critical loss analysis asks whether imposing at least a SSNIP on one or more products in a candidate market would raise or lower the hypothetical monopolist's profits. . . . A price increase raises profits on sales made at the higher price, but this will be offset to the extent customers substitute away from products in the candidate market. Critical loss analysis compares the magnitude of these two offsetting effects resulting from the price increase. The "critical loss" is defined as the number of lost unit sales that would leave profits unchanged. The "predicted loss" is defined as the number of unit sales that the hypothetical monopolist is predicted to lose due to the price increase. The price increase raises the hypothetical monopolist's profits if the predicted loss is less than the critical loss.[25]

Measuring the predicted loss can be difficult and technically demanding, particularly when products are imperfect substitutes as it often the case in merger analysis.[26] In cases where sufficient data

---

[25]   United States Dept. of Justice and FTC, Horizontal Merger Guidelines, § 4.1.3 (Aug. 19, 2010), available at https://www.ftc.gov/sites/default/files/attachments/merger-review/100819hmg.pdf. For helpful discussion addressed to non-economists, see Shen Li, Christine Meyer, and Gabriella Monahova, Unpacking the Economic Toolbox: How to Make Sense of your Economic Expert's Analysis, 32 Antitrust 24 (Spg., 2018). On the 2010 Guidelines' approach to market delineation, see § 3.8.

[26]   On technical methodologies, see Joseph Farrell & Carl Shapiro, Recapture, Pass-Through, and Market Definition, 76 Antitrust L.J. 585 (2010); Daniel A. Crane, Market Power Without Market Definition, 90 Notre Dame L.Rev. 31 (2014).

are not available economists can use a technique to measure Upward Pricing Pressure (UPP), which relies on the theory of monopolistic competition but requires a knowledge only of margins and the extent of diversion in response to an increase. Further, it does not require a market definition.[27]

3.2c.   Broader and Narrower Markets; General Irrelevance of Submarkets[28]

The fact that "motor vehicles" is a relevant market does not entail that a sub-grouping such as "four-wheel-drive motor vehicles" or "diesel fueled vehicles" could not be a relevant market as well. Further, we would employ *precisely the same criteria* in determining whether one of these sub-groupings is a relevant market. That is, we would ask whether on the demand side consumers would be willing to pay an above-cost price before they would switch—for example, from four-wheel-drive to two-wheel-drive vehicles; or from diesel to gasoline powered vehicles. Maybe they would or maybe they would not, but one could certainly surmise that customers who buy four-wheel-drive or diesel fueled vehicles value these alternatives highly. On the supply side, one would ask whether people who do not make four-wheel-drive vehicles or diesel fueled vehicles could readily do so in response to a non-cost-justified price increase.

As a result, this grouping of markets might look like the figure below:

---

[27]   Joseph Farrell & Carl Shapiro, Antitrust Evaluation of Horizontal Mergers: An Economic Alternative to Market Definition, 10 B.E. J. Theoretical Econ. 1 (2010). For further discussion and a response to critics, see Joseph Farrell & Carl Shapiro, Upward Pricing Pressure and Critical Loss Analysis: Response, CPI Antitrust Journal 1 (2010), available at https://www.competitionpolicyinternational.com/upward-pricing-pressure-and-critical-loss-analysis-response-3/.

[28]   On submarkets, see 2A Antitrust Law ¶ 533 (4th ed. 2014).

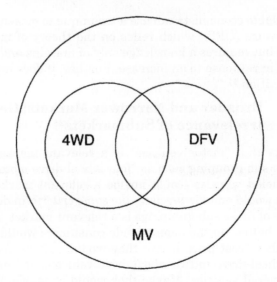

The large circle represents the market for motor vehicles (MV) generally. The two smaller circles indicate relevant markets for four-wheel-drive (4WD) and diesel fueled vehicles (DFV), and the overlap indicates that some vehicles are both four-wheel-drive and diesel fueled.

If an antitrust enforcer were to consider a merger or claims of monopolization in a motor vehicle market, any one of these circles could be a relevant market—*provided* that it met the usual criteria for market definition. For example, if the Antitrust Division feared that a merger threatened higher prices in the market for "four-wheel-drive" vehicles, it would have to show that this particular grouping of sales constituted a relevant market.

This reasoning illustrates the general uselessness of the term "*sub*market." Since the 1950's, the Supreme Court has held that relevant antitrust markets might contain one or more "submarkets" in which the challenged practice should be analyzed. The Supreme Court noted in *Brown Shoe*:

> The outer boundaries of a product market are determined by the reasonable interchangeability of use or the cross-elasticity of demand between the product itself and substitutes for it. However, within this broad market, well-defined submarkets may exist which, in themselves, constitute product markets for antitrust purposes. The boundaries of such a submarket may be determined by examining such practical indicia as industry or public recognition of the submarket as a separate economic entity,

the product's peculiar characteristics and uses, unique production facilities, distinct customers, distinct prices, sensitivity to price changes, and specialized vendors.[29]

This language, which has since been used by courts in market power analysis under both the Sherman and Clayton Acts,[30] often suggests things that make little sense. Did the Supreme Court mean to say that one uses ordinary economic criteria in defining a market, but then uses something other than economic criteria in defining a submarket? If so, then the purpose of submarkets is not to identify groupings of transactions where there is a genuine possibility of monopoly. They must be for some other purpose.

Why, then, the concept of submarkets? In general, submarkets have been used to take several possibilities into account. Among them are product differentiation, price discrimination, differences in physical characteristics, manufacturing in different plants, and different distribution networks. In some of these cases, the term "submarket" states only that the smaller grouping of sales is in fact a relevant market. For example, suppose a seller of widgets discriminates in price among three groups of buyers, A, B and C. Further, buyers in the A group are charged a price that is at least ten percent higher in relation to costs than B and C buyers pay. This tells us that the sale of widgets to buyers in A defines a relevant market. With respect to that particular grouping of sales, a price increase to 10% above the competitive level is profitable. If we then analyze the impact of an alleged antitrust violation in a market of "widgets sold to A buyers," it becomes totally irrelevant that there might be a larger grouping of sales that is also a relevant market. That is, the A grouping is not a "submarket," but a market.[31]

§ 3.3 The Product Market; General Considerations

In one sense the problem of product market definition is less tractable than that of geographic market definition. Often geographic market definition is a function of cost of transportation, and this is an objective number that can be measured. By contrast, product market definition is often a function of consumer taste, and taste cannot be measured so easily. To be sure, there are exceptions on both sides. In some geographic markets, such as the market for movie exhibition, consumers go to the theater, and consumer willingness to

[29] Brown Shoe Co. v. United States, 370 U.S. 294, 325, 82 S.Ct. 1502, 1524 (1962).

[30] See Newcal Indus., Inc. v. Ikon Office Solution, 513 F.3d 1038 (9th Cir. 2008) (permitting a plaintiff to proceed on the basis of a single brand submarket), cert. denied, 557 U.S. 903 (2009).

[31] See 2A Antitrust Law ¶ 533 (4th ed. 2014).

travel is a function of taste or preference as well as objectively measurable cost. Likewise, many products are used by businesses as intermediate inputs, and substitutability is largely a function of technology and cost.

But over a broad range of cases, product definition depends on substitutability in consumers' eyes, and since consumer utility cannot be measured by some easily identified criterion, such as cost of transportation, the market definition question can become complex. We can measure consumer responses directly by looking at substitution rates, or elasticities. For example, if 50% of consumers are observed to shift from widgets to gidgets in response to a 10% widget price increase, that may give us enough information to conclude that widget sales do not define a relevant market. But such methodologies depend on the existence of good data, and these are not always available.

In all events, we should never group two things into the same market simply because the same customers buy both. The Supreme Court made this error in *Alcoa (Rome Cable)*, which involved a merger between Alcoa, which made bare and insulated aluminum electric conductor, and Rome, which made bare and insulated conductor of both aluminum and copper.[32] The Supreme Court concluded that a single market existed for bare and insulated aluminum conductor, but cited only the fact that both were used for the same purpose (conducting electricity) and sold to the same customers.[33] Whether or not the Court was factually correct, those facts alone were insufficient to establish a single market. One could say the same thing about electric dish washers and dish cloths. The fact that they are used for the same purpose and that the same customers buy both does not establish a relevant "dish washer/dish cloth" market.

When there are no obvious differences in the cost of production[34] and consumer substitutability is high, the inference is strong that the

---

[32]   United States v. Aluminum Co. (*Rome Cable*), 377 U.S. 271, 84 S.Ct. 1283, rehearing denied, 377 U.S. 1010, 84 S.Ct. 1903 (1964).

[33]   Id. at 277, 84 S.Ct. at 1287.

[34]   Even complete functional substitutability does not indicate a relevant market when production costs differences are substantial. Consider Consolidated Gas Co. v. City Gas Co., 665 F.Supp. 1493, 1517 (S.D.Fla.1987), aff'd, 880 F.2d 297 (11th Cir. 1989), reinstated on rehearing, 912 F.2d 1262 (11th Cir. 1990), vacated as moot, 499 U.S. 915, 111 S.Ct. 1300 (1991). The court correctly refused to place natural gas and propane (LP gas) in the same relevant market because, although they performed the same functions, the cost of producing the latter was far higher than the cost of producing the former. Propane was generally purchased by rural customers who were out of reach of a natural gas utility. Given the production cost differential, buyers of natural gas would pay a large monopoly markup before they would substitute to propane.

two alternatives should be in the same relevant product market.[35] By contrast, products that do not compete in the eyes of consumers should not be regarded as in the same market.[36] For example, in *NCAA* the Supreme Court concluded that the audience for televised NCAA football games was sufficiently differentiated from the television audience for other sporting events. Indeed, advertisers were willing to pay a premium for spots on college football games. As a result, televised college football was a relevant market.[37]

3.3a. Markets and Brands; "Lock-In"

3.3a1. Single Brand Ordinarily Not a Relevant Market; Kodak; Patented Pharmaceuticals

Suppose the biggest difference between alternative products is not technological. Rather, the offerings are distinct brands, which may or may not exhibit significant technological differences as well. For example, Maytag washing machines may be technologically different from General Electric washing machines; however, the differences are likely to be small in relation to the total cost of producing the product. In such cases most courts refuse to find single brand relevant markets.[38] A few courts disagree, however. Today, one of the strongest cases for single-brand markets is pharmaceuticals, where pioneer drugs are often patented discrete molecules.[39]

Our analysis should start with a few premises. *First*, patents, trademarks and copyrights standing alone very rarely confer substantial market power, although a few patents that control the

---

[35] For example, Little Rock Cardiology Clinic, PA v. Baptist Health, 591 F.3d 591 (8th Cir. 2009), cert. denied, 561 U.S. 1026, 130 S.Ct. 3506 (2010) (grouping hospital patients using private insurance and other hospital patients into same market); Morgan, Strand, Wheeler & Biggs v. Radiology, Ltd., 924 F.2d 1484, 1489 (9th Cir. 1991) (grouping university and osteopathic radiologists into the same market as radiologists in private practice).

[36] Omni Outdoor Adver., Inc. v. Columbia Outdoor Adver., Inc., 891 F.2d 1127 (4th Cir. 1989), rev'd on other grounds, 499 U.S. 365, 111 S.Ct. 1344 (1991) (billboard advertising and advertising in newspapers or radio not in the same product market, because customers did not view them as substitutes). See § 3.5.

[37] Board of Regents of the Univ. of Okla. v. NCAA, 546 F.Supp. 1276 (W.D.Okl.1982), aff'd in part, rev'd in part, and remanded, 707 F.2d 1147 (10th Cir. 1983), aff'd, 468 U.S. 85, 111–112, 104 S.Ct. 2948 (1984).

[38] See Universal Avionics Sys. v. Rockwell Int'l Corp., 184 F.Supp.2d 947 (D.Ariz. 2001), aff'd, 52 Fed. Appx. 897, 2002 WL 31748602 (9th Cir. 2002) (defendant's own brand of avionics not a relevant market); Tunis Bros. Co. v. Ford Motor Co., 952 F.2d 715 (3d Cir. 1991), cert. denied 505 U.S. 1221, 112 S.Ct. 3034 (1992) (plaintiff did not meet burden of showing that Ford tractors were distinct market from tractors in general).

[39] In re Aggrenox Antitrust Litig., 11 F.Supp.3d 1342 (Mem), 2015 WL 1311352 (D. Conn. March 23, 2015); In re Nexium (Esomeprazole) Antitrust Litig., 968 F.Supp.2d 367 (D. Mass. 2013).

entire product, such as pharmaceutical drugs, might be an exception.[40] Copyrighted code for market dominant software might be another one. *Second*, sometimes brand differences reflect very substantial technological differences, or differences in both cost of production and consumer appeal, and sometimes they do not. The case for narrower markets becomes stronger as these differences become more pronounced. For example, the case for placing aspartame ("Nutrasweet"), an artificial sweetener, in a distinct market is stronger than the case for placing Band-Aid plastic bandages and Buy-Rite plastic bandages in separate markets. *Third*, in a few extreme cases customers may become "locked in" to a particular brand, and this fact may justify a narrower market definition.

The lock-in problem arises this way. Although Chrysler automobiles are sold in competition with Chevrolets, Fords, Toyotas and many others, many of the repair parts for Chryslers are unique. For example, when the Chrysler owner's transmission fails, she will not be able to purchase a Ford or Toyota transmission as a substitute. So the person who has made a relatively major investment in a Chrysler automobile has been "locked in" to Chrysler repair parts. The relevant antitrust question is whether this lock-in enables Chrysler to somehow take advantage of its own automobile owners, and if any such advantage amounts to "monopoly."

In a well functioning market where customers have adequate information, such lock-in is unlikely. Suppose that automobiles last ten years but their transmissions last only two years. Further, automobiles are sold in a competitive market, where costs for new automobiles are $30,000 and for replacement transmissions are $1000. Consumers generally know these facts. Can Chrysler seriously "monopolize" this market by selling automobiles for the going price of $30,000, but then charge buyers $3000 for subsequent transmission replacements? Probably not. The customer is interested in the package of automobile-plus-subsequent-maintenance, and the overcharge for subsequent transmissions will show up in her calculus as nothing other than an increase in the price of the package. She will go to another seller who behaves competitively.

But the real world is a less tidy place where the initial competition is imperfect, costs of subsequent repairs are uncertain (some Chryslers need a new transmission after two years; others never need one) and are probably unknown to the consumer. Presumably the customer who knows the current price and is highly uncertain about the price of future repairs discounts the latter and

---

[40]   See § 3.9d.

considers mainly the former. Further, sometimes anticipated repairs will be only a small fraction of the original package price. Finally, some sellers may find it advantageous to change their policies when they withdraw from a market. For example, suppose Maytag has decided to abandon the washing machine business (or has already abandoned it). Now it can double the price of replacement parts, knowing that previous customers have no alternative. It does not have to worry about the impact on future sales, for there will not be any.

This range of concerns quickly shades from "antitrust" to "consumer protection." As a general premise, the goal of the antitrust laws is competitive pricing and output consistent with the nature and (legal) structure of the market at hand. Competition in concentrated markets for durable goods is inherently imperfect, however, and so the policy question becomes one of degree: how many and what kinds of deviations should be tolerated?

In Eastman Kodak Co. v. Image Technical Services, Inc.,[41] the Supreme Court held that a manufacturer of photocopiers might have substantial market power in the market for its own replacement parts, notwithstanding that it lacked market power in the market for the photocopiers themselves. Kodak sold photocopiers in competition with several other firms, and had a market share of about 20 to 23 percent.[42] Most courts require market shares far larger than this to support market power claims of any sort, including tying claims.[43] Although Kodak repaired many of its own machines, numerous independent service organizations (ISOs) repaired them as well. The antitrust dispute arose when Kodak refused to sell parts to Kodak machine users unless they had their machines serviced with Kodak as well. This effectively denied several ISOs an opportunity to service Kodak's machines.[44] They alleged that Kodak had illegally tied Kodak service to the replacement parts for Kodak machines, and that Kodak was attempting to monopolize the market for its own replacement parts, as well as service.

Both the tying claim and the attempt claim required a showing of at least some market power in the market for Kodak replacement parts. Kodak's defense was that, given its competitive position in the primary market, it followed as a matter of law that Kodak could not

---

[41]   504 U.S. 451, 112 S.Ct. 2072 (1992). See Herbert Hovenkamp, Post-Chicago Antitrust: A Review and Critique, 2001 Col. Bus. L. Rev. 257 (2001).

[42]   See the Ninth Circuit's opinion. 903 F.2d 612, 616 & n. 3 (9th Cir. 1990).

[43]   For example, Jefferson Parish Hosp. Dist. No. 2. v. Hyde, 466 U.S. 2, 104 S.Ct. 1551 (1984) (tying; 30% insufficient). See generally §§ 6.2, 6.5b, & 10.3; and 10 Antitrust Law ¶ 1740 (4th ed. 2018).

[44]   504 U.S. at 459, 112 S.Ct. at 2078.

have market power in the market for its own replacement parts. To hold to the contrary would make every manufacturer of durable equipment with brand-specific replacement parts into a monopolist for antitrust purposes.

3.3a2.   Lower Court Decisions Limiting Kodak

The lower court decisions on *Kodak* have been quite critical. The courts have found various ways of limiting *Kodak*'s lock-in theory so as not to make monopoly power so easy to prove that almost every seller in a moderately concentrated market is found to have it.

The first significant limitation is that relevant lock-in can occur only if the "locked-in" product is purchased subsequent to purchase of the primary product. Suppose, for example, that a firm with a nondominant share of the computer market sells a computer and requires buyers to take its operating system as well. We cannot say that buyers are "locked-in" to the defendant's operating system, thus justifying a smaller relevant market limited to that seller's brand, because the buyer makes the decision to purchase the computer and the operating system at the same time. The *PSI* decision so held, distinguishing the *Kodak* situation where the defendant supposedly changed its policy "after its customers were 'locked-in,'" thus taking advantage "of the fact that its customers lacked the information to anticipate this change."[45]

By the same token, even if the aftermarket parts are sold in a later transaction, most courts have required plaintiffs to be able to point to a *change* in the defendant's policy respecting tied aftermarket parts.[46] A customer can legitimately be said to be "locked in" if aftermarket parts were one price when she purchased the machine, but were increased afterward. Further, the change must be one that adversely affected consumers. For that reason one court denied relief when the plaintiff repair organization complained that the defendant prospectively changed its warranty from one year to three.[47] The court noted that pre-existing customers were not affected at all by the change, and new customers knew of the extended warranty when they first bought their computer. Suppose, however, that the defendant had retroactively extended its warranty

---

[45]   PSI Repair Servs. v. Honeywell, 104 F.3d 811, 821 (6th Cir. 1997), cert. denied, 520 U.S. 1265, 117 S.Ct. 2434 (1997).

[46]   See DSM Desotech, Inc. v. 3D Sys. Corp., 749 F.3d 1332, 1346 (Fed. Cir. 2014); Harrison Aire, Inc. v. Aerostar Intl., Inc., 423 F.3d 374 (3d Cir. 2005), cert. denied, 547 U.S. 1020, 126 S.Ct. 1581 (2006) (balloon manufacturer's own replacement fabric not a relevant market when defendant had never changed its pricing or availability policy).

[47]   SMS Sys. Maint. Servs. v. Digital Equip. Corp., 188 F.3d 11 (1st Cir. 1999), cert. denied, 528 U.S. 1188, 120 S.Ct. 1241 (2000).

to three years. This change would undoubtedly injure independent service organizations who would be denied lucrative repair work—but it would also benefit pre-existing customers, who are getting something for free. It would be hard to find antitrust injury in such a claim.

Finally, no one is locked in if other companies make equally suitable repair parts. For example, while Chrysler makes gaskets or axle joints that fit only Chrysler automobiles, no one could be locked in if several other firms are also in the business of making parts that, while not bearing Chrysler's brand, fit and work just as well.[48]

3.3b.   Substitutes v. Complements; Cluster Markets and Two-Sided Platforms

3.3b1.   *Relevant Market Consists of Substitutes*

A relevant market consists of goods that are effective *substitutes* for each other. For example, we place all canned tomatoes in a single relevant market because the Del Monte brand competes with the General Foods brand, which in turn competes with Trader Joe's house brand, and so on.[49] This definition of a market is fundamental, but a few courts have gotten it wrong. In the *Kodak* case after remand from the Supreme Court, for example, the Ninth Circuit confused substitutes and complements, concluding that there was a single relevant market for all Kodak photocopier parts because a machine user or repairer needs "all the parts" in order to make the machine function properly.[50] The court cited a "commercial reality" that a service provider "must have ready access to all parts."

While factually true, that is hardly the rationale for placing goods in the same relevant market. People need both cars and gas to operate an automobile, both a toaster and bread to make toast, or both a racquet and a ball to play tennis. But these facts hardly establish a single "car/gas," "toaster/bread," or "racquet/ball" market. The relationship that exists between these pairings is that they are complements, not substitutes. Placing complements into a "relevant market" ignores the fact that a market must be a set of sales that *compete* with each other. For example, when we place the four

---

48   Tarrant Serv. Agency v. American Standard, 12 F.3d 609 (6th Cir. 1993), cert. denied, 512 U.S. 1221, 114 S.Ct. 2709 (1994) (several firms made "generic" parts that fit defendants equipment; judgment as a matter of law).

49   See 2A Antitrust Law ¶ 565 (4th ed. 2014); United States v. Bazaarvoice, Inc., 2014 WL 203966 (N.D.Cal. 2014) (excluding certain services from relevant market because they functioned as complements rather than substitutes).

50   Eastman Kodak Co. v. Image Technical Servs., Inc., 504 U.S. 451, 462, 112 S.Ct. 2072 (1992), remanded, 125 F.3d 1195, 1203 (9th Cir. 1997), cert. denied, 523 U.S. 1094, 118 S.Ct. 1560 (1998).

gasoline stations at the same intersection into a single relevant market, it is manifestly not because a customer needs to go to all of them. The four stations are in the same relevant market because the customer does *not* need to go to all of them; as a result, the firms must compete with one another for sales.

One critical reason for not placing complements in the same relevant market is that the price of complements in demand actually move in *opposite* directions. By contrast, the prices of goods in the same market tend to move together. To illustrate, if gasoline prices rise significantly people will respond by driving less, thus reducing the demand for cars. Another reason for not placing complements in the same market is that the extent of monopoly in one typically provides no useful information about the other. For example, it is quite plausible that toasters are made by a toaster monopolist, while bread is sold in a fiercely competitive market. The list of 5000 parts that went into a Kodak photocopier included a patented image loop and several other patented parts in which Kodak may have had some power. But it also included thousands of nuts, bolts, screws, belts, springs and switches that were sold off-the-shelf by numerous manufacturers; and things such as a flat glass plate and metal doors that could readily be made to size specifications by any glass cutter or machine shop. Once the court grouped all of these things into a single "relevant market" it lost control of the power issue altogether, for there is no way of looking at this grouping in the aggregate and saying that Kodak did or did not have market power in any relevant grouping of sales.

3.3b2. The Limited Rationale for Finding "Cluster" Markets

Sometimes courts must consider whether a grouping of products is a relevant market even though each individual product or service in the group might not be. For example, in the *Philadelphia Bank* case the court found a "cluster" of commercial banking services to be a relevant market.[51] For some of these services, such as business checking accounts, the banks had few competitors. For others, such as savings deposits and small loans, banks faced competition from savings and loan associations and small loan companies. Problematically, checking accounts and consumer loans are not *competing* products at all.

---

[51]   United States v. Philadelphia Nat'l Bank, 374 U.S. 321, 356–357, 83 S.Ct. 1715, 1737–1738 (1963). See also Brown Shoe Co. v. United States, 370 U.S. 294, 327–328, 82 S.Ct. 1502 (1962) (clustering men's, women's, and children's shoes). Cf. Comcast Corp. v. Behrend, 569 U.S. 27, 133 S.Ct. 1426 (2013) (observing that relevant market was claimed to be a cluster of CATV services, but not deciding issue).

Clusters of complementary products are sometimes grouped into a relevant market if there are substantial economies of joint provision, sometimes called economies of scope. While an economy of scale is an economy that results from doing more of one thing, an economy of scope results from doing two things together more cheaply than each can be done separately.[52] A good example is the "cluster" of services supplied by a typical hospital. [53]

One word of warning: an economy of scope does not justify a cluster market definition unless other firms face barriers to attaining the same economies of joint provision. Suppose the first retailer to cluster electrical, plumbing and building supplies under one roof discovers substantial cost savings. But existing plumbing stores, electric supply stores and lumberyards can easily expand and do exactly the same thing. In this case, the only entry requirement might be the construction or enlargement of a cheaply built, general purpose building. In that case any monopoly pricing in the clustered "market" will not last long.

The government's Horizontal Merger Guidelines generally avoid clustering, at least in cases that do not involve hospitals. They generally define markets with reference to each product of each of the merging firms.[54]

3.3b3.   Assessing Market Power on Two-Sided Platforms

A two-sided platform intermediates between two complementary groups in order to determine the optimal mixture of price, quantity or quality.[55] For example, the Uber ride platform must balance the demands of riders against the willingness of drivers to sell their services. If the platform sets the price for drivers too high there will be plenty of drivers but too few customers. If the price is too low, there will be plenty of customers but two few drivers. The two sides are complements in production. That is, the two parts, driver and rider, are produced together. In general, one cannot assess

---

[52]   See Alfred D. Chandler, Scale and Scope: Dynamics of Industrial Capitalism, chs. 5 & 6 (1990), who offers a rich history of the way American firms achieved economies of scope through diversification.

[53]   E.g., ProMedica Health Sys., Inc. v. FTC, 749 F.3d 559, 556 (6th Cir. 2014), cert. denied, 135 S.Ct. 2049 (2015) (finding a cluster of hospital services where they were delivered out of the same facility and the players had similar market shares in the services).

[54]   See § 3.8. See, e.g., Fruehauf Corp. v. FTC, 603 F.2d 345 (2d Cir. 1979) (considering separately the markets for shock absorbers, wheels and brakes, in which the merging firms operated).

[55]   On two-sided platforms, see §§ 1.4c, 10.9. See also Erik Hovenkamp, Platform Antitrust, 44 J. Corp. L.713. (2019); Herbert Hovenkamp, Antitrust and Platform Monopoly, ___ Yale L.J. ___ (2021) (forthcoming), available at https://papers.ssrn.com/sol3/papers.cfm?abstract_id=3639142.

effects on one side without also considering the "feedback" effects that occur on the other side.

In the *American Express* decision the Supreme Court held that determining market definition in a two-sided market required grouping the two sides together into a single "market."[56] That decision does very considerable harm to the concept of a "relevant market," which only makes sense if we think of a market as a group of substitutes that vie with one another for trade. The Court reasoned that looking at one side exclusively could provide an incomplete picture unless offsetting effects on the other side were included as well. That is certainly true as a matter of fact, but courts routinely take such extra-market considerations into account when assessing power.

Further, the court assumed that harms on one side must be offset against benefits on the other side, but in this case the anti-steering rule caused harm on both side of the market,[57] so there was no tradeoff.

The Court's insistence on this incoherent market definition was entirely a result of its conclusion that a market had to be defined at all. In fact, the government had sought to measure power directly, which would not require a market definition.[58] Why the court assessed this requirement is unclear, but the conclusion is regressive given that the tools for direct measurement are consistently improving and were readily applicable in this case. Direct proof provides a better estimate of the defendant's power when there are different factors pulling in different directions.

One particular dictum in the Supreme Court's decision could be catastrophic for rational analysis of market power offenses. That was the Court's statement that as a matter of law a two-sided platform competes only with other two-sided platforms.[59] That decision has already produced the bizarre conclusion that a merger between two airline reservation firms did not involve competitors, because one was a two-sided platform while the other was not.[60] The Supreme Court's statement was not necessary to its decision, which involved competition among different two-sided credit card platforms.

---

[56]   Ohio v. Am. Express Co., 138 S.Ct. 2274, 2287 (2018). For a critique, see Herbert Hovenkamp, Platforms and the Rule of Reason: the American Express Case, 2019 Col. Bus.L. Rev. 35.

[57]   See § 10.9.

[58]   See § 3.9e.

[59]   *Amex*, 138 S.Ct. at 2287 ("only other two-sided platforms can compete with a two-sided platform for transactions").

[60]   United States v. Sabre Corp., 452 F.Supp.3d 97 (D.Del. 2020), vacated on other grounds, 2020 WL 4915824 (3d Cir. July 20, 2020).

Further, it was completely inconsistent with one of the most fundamental principles of antitrust that issues about the extent of competition present questions of fact, to be verified or falsified by evidence, and not simply to be declared as a matter of law.

§ 3.4 Product Differentiation and the "Cellophane" Fallacy

3.4a. Cross-Price Elasticities and Their Meaning

When the price of a product rises, some buyers substitute away. A cross-elasticity (or cross-price elasticity, in economic jargon) is a measure of the rate at which buyers substitute to some product B in response to a price increase in product A. For example, if wheat and corn are close substitutes for many uses when both are sold at a competitive price, a small increase in the price of wheat will encourage many wheat customers to buy corn instead. In that case we would say that the cross-elasticity of demand between wheat and corn is quite high. For antitrust purposes the two may be in the same relevant market.

Used properly, cross-elasticity measures should help the fact-finder assemble into a single relevant market products that are close substitutes when each is sold at a competitive price. For example, if Ford Motor Company was accused of monopolizing the market for Ford automobiles, the fact-finder should consider whether Chevrolet automobiles, Chrysler automobiles or others ought to be included in the relevant product market. The fact-finder would probably decide that when Fords, Chevrolets and Chryslers are sold at cost many customers regard them as competitive with each other. If the price of Fords increased, these customers would switch to Chevrolets or Chryslers. As a result the relevant product market is "automobiles" and not "Fords."

What if the fact-finder were asked to include bicycles and horses in this same relevant market? The effect would be to reduce Ford's share of the "market" even further. In that case the fact-finder would have to make some estimate about the degree to which the demand for horses and bicycles would change in response to a price change in the automobile market. When automobiles and bicycles or horses are all being sold at the competitive price, the cross-elasticity of demand between them is probably not very high. Not many prospective automobile purchasers would regard a horse or bicycle as a good substitute unless the price of automobiles increased by a very large amount. The fact-finder would probably conclude that bicycles or horses should not be included in the relevant market.

3.4b. Cross-Elasticity of Demand in the du Pont (Cellophane) Case

Judges have often misused the concept of cross-elasticity of demand because they have not understood its limitations. The problem is particularly serious in product differentiated markets. In thinking about the assessment of market power in significantly differentiated markets, one must always begin with one sobering proposition. Market definition in differentiated markets is always "wrong," in the sense that it is either over- or under-inclusive. For example, should automobiles and pickup trucks be placed in the same relevant market? Clearly, sometimes they are used for the same purposes. You can use either for grocery shopping or picking up your child from school. Placing them in the same market implies that they are *perfect* competitors, however, a conclusion that significantly exaggerates the degree of competition between them. Many users have strong preferences for one over the other. On the other hand, placing them in different markets suggests that they do not compete at all, a conclusion that is equally false. Here, direct measurement has a distinct advantage because it is not purely binary: it can measure degrees of substitutability, rather than taking an all-or-nothing approach.[61]

In United States v. E.I. du Pont de Nemours & Co.[62] the defendant was alleged to have monopolized the market for cellophane. du Pont produced about 75% of the cellophane sold in the United States. du Pont argued that the relevant market was not cellophane, but "flexible packaging materials," which included not only cellophane but also aluminum foil, glassine, pliofilm, greaseproof paper and waxed paper. While these products served the same purpose for many buyers, they used different inputs and different manufacturing technologies. For example, a maker of aluminum foil could not readily convert to producing cellophane, or vice-versa.

Some forms of flexible packaging materials, such as glassine, were cheaper than cellophane. Others, such as polyethylene, were much more expensive. Different wrapping materials had various degrees of acceptance among different buyers, and some buyers were far more cost-conscious than others. For example, virtually all grocery store meats and vegetables had to be wrapped in transparent materials in order to attract grocery consumers. Cellophane occupied about 35% of the market for retail meat wrapping and about half of the market for retail vegetable wrapping. By contrast, bread was

---

[61]   See § 3.9.

[62]   351 U.S. 377, 76 S.Ct. 994 (1956).

commonly wrapped in opaque paper, and cellophane furnished only 7% of the bakery products market. When a product was expensive in proportion to the amount of wrapping material it needed, cellophane obtained an advantage over cheaper, less transparent packaging materials. For example, 75%–80% of all cigarettes were wrapped in cellophane.[63] However, the court refused to hold that "cellophane for cigarettes" constituted a relevant market, even though cigarette manufacturers would have been willing to pay a monopoly price before substituting to an alternative flexible wrap.

The Supreme Court concluded that the relevant market must include "products that have reasonable interchangeability for the purposes for which they are produced. That was the entire market for flexible packaging materials.[64]

The court's definition of the relevant market was probably wrong. A simple example will illustrate. Suppose that widgets are sold in a competitive market for $1.00, which is also their marginal cost of production. Suppose that A invents the gizmo, which performs the same functions as a widget but can be manufactured for 80 cents. A is the only producer of gizmos.

Now suppose A is charged with illegal monopolization. A defends by arguing that he has no market power because the relevant market is not gizmos (in which A's market share is 100%) but rather gizmos plus widgets (in which A's market share is lower). A supports this market definition by providing evidence he is currently charging 99 cents for gizmos, while the market price of widgets is $1.00. At those prices there is a high cross-elasticity of demand between gizmos and widgets. In fact, if A attempts to raise his price by as little as 1% (1 cent), A will lose large numbers of customers to widgets.

Is A's defense good? Clearly not. To be sure, cross-elasticity of demand between gizmos and widgets at the *current price* is very high. It is not high because A lacks market power in gizmos, however, but because A has market power in widgets *and is already exercising that power*. Every seller, whether monopolist or competitor, sells its output in the high elasticity region of its demand curve. That is to say, every seller sets as high a price as it can without losing so many customers that the price increase is unprofitable. To say it another way, the monopolist that is not pricing at a level where the elasticity of demand is high is probably not maximizing its profits, and we would ordinarily regard such behavior as irrational. High cross-

---

[63] Id. at 399–400, 76 S.Ct. at 1009–10.

[64] Id. at 404, 76 S.Ct. at 1012. The decision is criticized in Donald F. Turner, Antitrust Policy and the *Cellophane* Case, 70 Harv.L.Rev. 281 (1956).

elasticity of demand at the current market price is simply evidence that the seller could not profitably charge an even higher price.[65]

The Horizontal Merger Guidelines use an approach that may understate the size of markets if market power is already being exercised at the time of analysis; however, it is also the case that the questions asked in a merger case are somewhat different from those asked in a case involving unilateral exercises of market power.

3.4c.   Correcting for the "Cellophane" Fallacy

The Cellophane analysis exposes a dilemma for antitrust market definition in differentiated markets. The concept of cross-elasticity of demand is useful for establishing whether two products are close substitutes when both are sold at the *competitive* price. If two things appear to be close substitutes when both are sold at marginal cost, then the two should be included in the same product market. But how do we know if the current price is competitive?

The impact of the *Cellophane* fallacy depends on the question one is asking. Suppose that a manufacturer of paper cartons wants to acquire a manufacturer of plastic cartons. A merger between two firms selling in the same relevant market is termed "horizontal" and is subject to a rather strict legal standard. A merger between two firms selling in different markets, however, is a "conglomerate" or "potential competition" merger, and is subject to a much more lenient standard.[66]

Suppose that the paper carton manufacturer is in competition with five other carton manufacturers, and that its own share of those sales is 20%. The plastic carton manufacturer is in competition with eight other plastic carton manufacturers, and its share of plastic carton sales is 10%. For nearly all uses plastic cartons and paper cartons compete intensely with each other. In the past customers of paper cartons have responded to a small price increase by switching in large numbers to plastic cartons, and vice-versa.

In this case the high cross-elasticity of demand at current market prices tells us quite reliably that paper and plastic cartons ought to be included in the same product market. The small market shares and relatively large numbers of firms *within* each fungible product category suggest that both kinds of cartons are currently being sold at or near a competitive price. The sensitivity of each to a price change in the other indicates that cross-elasticity of demand between the two is high even at this price. As a result, the presence

---

[65]   See 2A Antitrust Law ¶ 539 (4th ed. 2014).

[66]   See chs. 12 & 13.

of the plastic carton manufacturers tends to hold paper carton manufacturers to the competitive price, and vice-versa. The merger should be treated as horizontal.[67]

Much more difficult is the monopolization case such as *du Pont*. When the defendant is accused of being a monopolist, we must assume that its current price is *not* the competitive price, and we would ordinarily expect cross-elasticity of demand to be high at current prices.

One good corrective for the Cellophane fallacy is more direct measurement of market power that does not depend on market definition. Direct measures have the advantage that they can assess the competitive distance between differentiated products. These methodologies are commonly used in "unilateral effects" merger cases today.[68] The principal deficiency of direct measurement is that the data needed to use it may not always be available.

A related possibility is to examine changes in demand in response to changes in price for one particular variation of a product. For example, the evidence in the *American Express* case indicated that that AmEx was able to increase its merchant fees repeatedly without losing significant business to rival credit cards.[69] A perfect competitor would lose all its business in response to a unique price increase, but differentiated markets present a different situation. Then the questions become how much of a price increase is enough, and how durable must it be. The fact that a firm can exact a significant non-cost-justified price increase without losing so many sales to rivals that the price increase is unprofitable indicates that this firm and its rivals are in distinct markets. Of course, AmEx's price increases may have been a consequence of cost changes on the other side of the platform, as would occur if AmEx increased its perks, but that itself is a testable proposition.

§ 3.5   Supply Elasticities; Foreign Imports

Elasticity of supply has been an implicit part of judicial market definition for many years.[70] A firm with a large share of a proposed

---

[67]   See United States v. Aluminum Co. of Am., 377 U.S. 271, 84 S.Ct. 1283 (1964); United States v. Continental Can Co., 378 U.S. 441, 84 S.Ct. 1738 (1964).

[68]   See § 12.3d.

[69]   Ohio v. American Express Co., 138 S.Ct. 2274, 2293 (2018). The district court observed that "The record demonstrates, in fact, that Defendants have the power to repeatedly and profitably raise their merchant prices without worrying about significant merchant attrition." 88 F.Supp.3d 143, 151 (E.D.N.Y. 2015).

[70]   However, see United States v. Columbia Steel Co., 334 U.S. 495, 510, 68 S.Ct. 1107, 1116 (1948), a merger case in which one issue was whether steel plates and shapes should be included in the same product market as other rolled steel products. The Court concluded:

market will have little power to increase prices if other firms can immediately flood this market with their own output. Courts often refer to this as supply "substitutability."

One significant source of high supply elasticity is the divertible production or excess capacity of competing firms. Divertible production refers to the output of rivals or potential rivals that is currently not sold in the defendant's geographic market, but could come in if the price rose. Excess capacity generally refers to unused plant capacity that can be brought into production at a cost no higher than current production costs.

3.5a.   Foreign Imports and the Alcoa Case

In *Alcoa*[71] Judge Learned Hand attempted to determine whether Alcoa had a monopoly in the production of aluminum. Alcoa's market share of virgin aluminum produced in the United States was 100%. Its market share dropped to 90% when Judge Hand included aluminum that was manufactured abroad but imported into the United States. Judge Hand refused to include either (1) foreign aluminum sold elsewhere or (2) the additional plant capacity of the foreign aluminum producers. Clearly, however, the fact that some aluminum was coming into the United States indicated that foreign aluminum could be sold profitably here. What would have happened if Alcoa had attempted to raise the price of aluminum? The foreign producers could have diverted some aluminum destined for other markets into the now more profitable American market. Alternatively, they could have produced more aluminum and shipped it into the United States.[72] Assuming that foreign aluminum shipped into the United States and Alcoa's aluminum were price competitive, Judge Hand was wrong to include only foreign aluminum actually imported into the United States in the relevant market.

If rolled steel producers can make other products as easily as plates and shapes, then the effect of the removal of Consolidated's demand for plates and shapes must be measured not against the market for plates and shapes alone, but for all comparable rolled products. The record suggests * * * that rolled steel producers can make other products interchangeably with shapes and plates * * *.

The Court therefore included both in the relevant market.

[71]   United States v. Aluminum Co. of Am., 148 F.2d 416, 424 (2d Cir. 1945).

[72]   Judge Hand supposed as much:

While the record is silent, we may therefore assume—the plaintiff having the burden—that, had "Alcoa" raised its prices, more ingot would have been imported. Thus there is a distinction between domestic and foreign competition: the first is limited in quantity, and can increase only by an increase in plant and personnel; the second is of producers who, we must assume, produce much more than they import and whom a rise in price will presumably induce immediately to divert to the American market what they had been selling elsewhere. 148 F.2d at 426.

Does this analysis ignore the error that the Supreme Court made in the *Cellophane* case?[73] Perhaps foreign aluminum was entering the United States market because Alcoa was already charging a monopoly price. However, the fact that *some* aluminum was coming into the United States suggests that Alcoa was unable to exclude the foreign production completely.

The "foreign" producer problem is pervasive. Most of the analysis applies not only to the imports of foreign firms, but also to imports from remote geographic areas domestically. For example, if a firm were accused of monopolizing the retail market for gasoline in Delaware County, one should consider the actual imports, divertible output and excess capacity of firms in other counties that could ship into Delaware County. The analysis would not be materially different than that in the *Alcoa* case.

3.5b.   Other Decisions Addressing (or Failing to Address) Supply Issues

When judges measure market power, they often ignore elasticity of supply[74] or else they have difficulty in stating the relevant concerns. For example, in Telex Corp. v. IBM Corp.,[75] the issue was whether IBM had monopolized the market for "plug-compatible peripherals." A peripheral is a unit such as a printer, monitor, or disk drive that is attached to the central data processing part of a computer. Historically, peripherals were designed to work with a particular central processing unit (CPU). An IBM "plug-compatible" peripheral is one that is capable of easy attachment and use with an IBM CPU. Telex and other plaintiffs alleged that IBM monopolized the market for peripherals that were plug-compatible with its own CPUs. IBM's share of the market for IBM plug-compatible peripherals was quite large. But if *all* peripherals were included in the market, IBM's share was fairly small.

The district judge found that IBM plug-compatible peripherals were a relevant market because the elasticity of demand was low: customers who already owned IBM CPUs could not use peripherals unless they were compatible.[76] In reversing, the circuit court noted

---

[73]   See § 3.4b.

[74]   For example, see Fineman v. Armstrong World Indus., 980 F.2d 171 (3d Cir. 1992), cert. denied, 507 U.S. 921, 113 S.Ct. 1285 (1993), concluding that video tape "magazines" of floor coverings were a relevant market because linoleum sellers wishing to purchase such videos would not find other kinds of videos a substitute; but totally ignoring the fact that someone with the equipment needed to videotape floor coverings could probably videotape refrigerators, sofas or farm animals, or vice-versa, with little additional investment.

[75]   510 F.2d 894 (10th Cir.), cert. dismissed, 423 U.S. 802, 96 S.Ct. 8 (1975).

[76]   367 F.Supp. at 280–82.

two things: first, a producer of IBM non-plug-compatible peripherals could easily and cheaply switch to producing plug-compatible peripherals; secondly, by the use of an inexpensive "interface," which cost as little as $100, a non-compatible peripheral could often be made compatible with the IBM. This degree of "substitutability of production" convinced the circuit court that the relevant market should include all peripherals, and not merely those plug-compatible with IBM central processing units.[77] Likewise, *Rebel Oil* concluded that there was no relevant market for self-service gasoline; if the price of self-service gas rose to monopoly levels, providers of full-service gas could almost instantaneously switch to self-service.[78]

A recurring problem in addressing supply concerns is the relevant weight that should be given to technological as opposed to behavioral considerations. For example, suppose the evidence in the *Telex*[79] case, discussed above, revealed (1) that non-IBM plug compatible peripherals could be redesigned so as to be plug compatible for a cost as little as 1% of their value; but (2) customers greatly preferred to purchase CPUs and peripherals from the same seller. For example, if something went wrong with the computer, the customer did not want to get involved in a finger-pointing game where the CPU seller blamed the disk drive seller and the disk drive seller blamed the problem on the CPU. Clearly, *relevant* elasticity of supply is the rate at which potential competitors will actually steal sales from the price-increasing monopolist, and this question is not fully addressed by considering only the costs of developing the necessary technology or building the plant. By the same token, an array of patents or software copyrights can serve to reduce the elasticity of supply into a market that might otherwise be quite easy to enter, as Judge Bryson pointed out in his dissent in the *IGT* gaming case.[80]

Where the technological cost of redesigning is indeed very low, the best rule seems to be a presumptive conclusion that the firm capable of doing the redesigning should be included in the market; but this evidence could then be rebutted by evidence that consumer resistance to the redesigned product would be substantial.

---

[77]   510 F.2d at 919.

[78]   Rebel Oil Co. v. Atlantic Richfield Co., 51 F.3d 1421 (9th Cir.), cert. denied, 516 U.S. 987, 116 S.Ct. 515 (1995).

[79]   Telex Corp. v. IBM, 510 F. 2d 894 (10th Cir.), cert. dismissed, 423 U.S. 802 (1975).

[80]   IGT v. Alliance Gaming Corp., 702 F.3d 1338, 1350 (Fed. Cir. 2012).

§ 3.6   The Geographic Market

Someone who has market power does not generally have it everywhere. A relevant market for antitrust purposes includes both a product market and a geographic market.[81] Firms that produce products that are not substitutes do not compete with each other. Neither do firms that sell the same product in mutually exclusive geographic areas. The size of the geographic market depends on the nature of the product and of the people who buy and sell it. The relevant geographic market for Alcoa's aluminum, for example, was the entire United States. By contrast, the owner of the only movie theater in Ozona, Texas, may have substantial market power in Ozona, but virtually none 50 miles away.

Elasticity of demand and supply are important to determining the proper geographic market, and the discussion in the preceding sections applies to geographic as well as product markets. For example, assume that widgets are manufactured in Chicago and St. Louis. The owner of Chicago's only widget factory may have no market power if all its customers can costlessly shift their purchases to the St. Louis manufacturers. Likewise, the Chicago widget manufacturer will have no market power in Chicago if the St. Louis manufacturers can flood the Chicago outlets at a price close to the Chicago manufacturer's costs.

The relevant geographic market for antitrust purposes is some geographic area in which a firm can increase its price without 1) large numbers of its customers quickly turning to alternative supply sources outside the area; or 2) producers outside the area quickly flooding the area with substitute products. In the first case elasticity of demand is high; in the second elasticity of supply is high. If either of these things happens when the firm attempts to charge a supracompetitive price, then the estimated geographic market has been drawn too narrowly and a larger market must be drawn to include these outside suppliers.[82]

A final introductory warning is that the *"Cellophane"* fallacy, discussed in § 3.4 applies as much to geographic market definition as

---

[81]   Determination of a relevant product market and of a relevant geographic market both address the same question: is there a grouping of sales in which the defendant has market power? As a result the distinction made between the two markets in antitrust case law is exaggerated. Economists often note that "From the standpoint of economic analysis the distinction between product and geographic markets is not particularly useful." Janusz A. Ordover & Robert D. Willig, The 1982 Department of Justice Merger Guidelines: An Economic Assessment, 71 Calif.L.Rev. 535, 543 (1983).

[82]   See 2A Antitrust Law, Ch. 5C-2 (4th ed. 2014); William M. Landes & Richard A. Posner, Market Power in Antitrust Cases, 94 Harv.L.Rev. 937, 963–972 (1981).

it does to product market definition. For example, suppose that the only movie theater in a small town charges $15.00 per seat, and many local residents travel to the movies in towns ten or fifteen miles away. Including the theaters in these other towns in the geographic market may overstate the market's size if these customers are traveling in order to avoid the monopoly prices that the local theater is already charging. Drawing a larger market to include the remote theaters on the basis of observed competition at current prices, would serve to understate the market power of the local firm.

3.6a.   Shipped Goods; Minimum Geographic Market

For many manufactured products the size of the geographic market boils down to transportation costs. For example, the facts that automobile plants are scattered about the country and most of these plants ship automobiles nationwide suggest at least a national market. In general, the size of the geographic market for shipped products is a function of three things: (a) shipping costs, (b) the value of the product, and (c) the size of the hypothesized price increase that expresses our degree of concern about monopoly power. Suppose the production cost of a product is $50, shipping costs are $1 per one hundred miles, and we hypothesize a 10% price increase above the competitive level for purposes of market delineation. These numbers suggest that the *minimum* geographic market is a circle with a radius of 500 miles. That is, any firm within 500 miles, or $5 in transportation costs, would be able to respond to a 10% price increase by shipping its own product to the same customer at a profitable price.

3.6b.   Stationary Goods and Services

Geographic markets may be smaller and also more difficult to measure if the customers, rather than the goods or the suppliers, do the traveling. This is particularly true if the customers are end use consumers rather than business firms. As a result some goods are quite mobile in the wholesale market but stationary in the retail market. For example, although grocery items are wholesaled in large, often national or even international markets, they are retailed over a much smaller geographic range. The average grocery store customer may not want to drive more than 12 or 15 miles to buy groceries.[83] On the supply side, however, competition might cover a wider region than customer willingness to travel suggests, particularly if the competitors are chains that operate in several

---

[83]   See United States v. Von's Grocery Co., 384 U.S. 270, 296, 86 S.Ct. 1478, 1492 (1966).

states. For example, if grocery chains A & B both operate in California and chain A has a store in Sacramento which is earning monopoly profits, chain B will likely regard the Sacramento market as attractive for entry. Ordinarily, we would not take this fact into account by placing the entire area where the two chains operate in the same geographic market. Rather, we would say that entry barriers in Sacramento are low, given the likelihood that chain B will enter.

The Supreme Court must have had such considerations in mind when it decided that the merger in United States v. Von's Grocery Co.,[84] was one between competitors, and therefore should be treated as horizontal. The merger united two grocery store chains, Von's, Inc. and Shopping Bag, Inc., that operated in the Los Angeles area. The Von's stores were located in the southwest part of the city, however, and the Shopping Bag stores were located in the northeast part.[85] Except for a few pairs of stores in the middle of the city, the Von's stores did not compete on the demand side with the Shopping Bag stores. Few consumers would drive half way across Los Angeles to buy groceries. By contrast, analysis of supply elasticities might indicate that the market was indeed citywide. Von's could probably supply any location in the city from its existing warehouses. As a result, if there were supracompetitive profits to be earned in the northeast part of the city, Von's could easily have responded by building its own stores there.[86]

The geographic market definition in United States v. Grinnell Corp.,[87] was more problematic. The Supreme Court decided that the defendant had monopolized the business of providing accredited central station protective services, and that the relevant market was the entire United States. An accredited central station protective service involved an electronic hook-up between a building to be protected and a central station that monitored the building for break-ins, fires, or other threatening events. "Accredited" services were approved by insurers and qualified the subscriber for lower premiums. The nature of the central station system meant that people who owned buildings in Chicago had to purchase their services from the Chicago station, people in St. Louis from the St. Louis station, etc. On the demand side the market was quite clearly local, since the service itself could be transmitted only a relatively small

---

[84] Id.

[85] Id. at 295, 86 S.Ct. at 1492 (Stewart, J., dissenting).

[86] In merger cases courts have generally regarded high elasticity of supply as evidence of "potential" rather than actual competition. See ch. 13.

[87] 384 U.S. 563, 86 S.Ct. 1698 (1966). Product market definition in this case is discussed in § 3.3b.

distance. Of course, the defendant could build additional central stations in new areas.

In explaining why it accepted a nationwide market, rather than a set of individual markets, the Supreme Court observed that the defendant had a "national schedule of prices, rates, and terms, though the rates may be varied to meet local conditions."[88] This is merely another way of saying that the defendant charged its profit-maximizing price in each city. Where it faced competition that price was generally lower than it was in cities where it had a monopoly. But these facts tend to establish that the local areas rather than the entire nation were the correct geographic markets.

On the supply side, however, ADT may have been able to exercise market power on a nationwide basis. For example, it might have used below-cost pricing in one city to "signal" its willingness to engage in predatory pricing to competitors located in many cities.[89] However, the court did not cite any evidence that the defendant was actually engaged in such practices, or even that it was capable of doing so. There was also some evidence that ADT faced intense competition from local companies,[90] and this suggests a local rather than national market.

The Court ordered Grinnell to divest its stations in some cities.[91] This order is consistent with the decision that the market was nationwide and not citywide. But if the Court's market definition was incorrect and the defendant really had a large number of citywide monopolies, then the only effect of the divestiture was to give the defendant a smaller number of monopolies than it had before, and to transfer the other monopolies to one or more additional firms. Consumers may have been no better off.

Finally, the mobility of labor shares some of the same characteristics as consumer mobility. In general, lower wage workers will commute only relatively small distances for work and are recruited locally. By contrast, high salary professionals may be recruited over a much greater distance. A great deal of recent empirical work indicates that we have consistently underestimated

---

[88]   384 U.S. at 575, 86 S.Ct. at 1706. The district court had found that customers of a particular station were located within 25 miles of the station. It nevertheless concluded that the relevant market was national because "financing, selling, advertising, purchasing of equipment, process of management, and over-all planning" were conducted by central company headquarters on a national scale. 236 F.Supp. at 253.

[89]   See Steven C. Salop, Strategic Entry Deterrence, 69 Amer.Econ.Rev. 335 (1979).

[90]   See 384 U.S. at 575, 86 S.Ct. at 1706 (Fortas, J., dissenting).

[91]   384 U.S. at 577–79, 86 S.Ct. at 1707–08.

the amount of power that employers have over labor by exaggerating commuting or recruiting distances.[92] The new perspective should result in more aggressive antitrust policies against collusion or mergers in concentrated labor markets.

3.6c.   Price Movements and Shipping Patterns

3.6c1.   Price Movements Generally; Asymmetry

A study of price movements in two different areas will often help a court determine whether they should be included in the same geographic market. For example, if over a certain period a price decrease in area A is always followed by a price decrease in area B, and vice-versa, A and B are likely to be in the same geographic market. Likewise, if producers in A make sales in both areas A and B, the two are likely a single geographic market.[93] Thus in Tampa Electric Co. v. Nashville Coal Co.,[94] the Supreme Court decided that the petitioner did not have monopsony power in the market for coal sold in Florida, because coal producers as far away as western Kentucky were eager to sell coal at the competitive price in the Florida market. This suggested to the court that not only the Kentucky producers of coal, but all coal producers closer to Florida than the Kentucky producers should be included in the relevant geographic market.

Once we have determined that a remote plant in Kentucky can provide coal to the Florida market at the competitive price, we should include the entire divertible output of the Kentucky plant, and not merely the amount that it is currently shipping into the Florida market. If the Kentucky plant can profitably sell *any* of its coal into the Florida market, then it will probably be able to respond to a price increase in the Florida market by selling even more coal there.

Determining a relevant geographic market means identifying some area such that the firm or firms inside the area have a cost advantage over firms not inside the area. In that case the favored firms will be able to raise the price as much as the cost advantage permits. Frequently the local firms' cost advantage results from transportation costs. For example, if Dallas and Denver firms can both make widgets at a cost of $1.00, but it costs 25 cents to ship

---

[92]   José Azar, Ioana Marinescu, Marshall Steinbaum & Bledi Taska, Concentration in US Labor Markets: Evidence From Online Vacancy Data (Nat'l Bureau of Econ. Research, Working Paper No. 24395, 2018); Suresh Naidu, Eric A. Posner & Glen Weyl, Antitrust Remedies for Labor Market Power, 132 Harv. L. Rev. 536 (2018); Ioana Marinescu & Herbert Hovenkamp, Anticompetitive Mergers in Labor Markets, 94 Ind. L. J. 1031 (2019).

[93]   See 2A Antitrust Law ¶¶ 550–552 (4th ed. 2014).

[94]   365 U.S. 320, 81 S.Ct. 623 (1961).

widgets from Dallas to Denver, then a Denver monopolist could charge any price up to $1.25 in the Denver market without worrying about competition from Dallas. The size of the geographic market depends heavily on the relationship between the value of the product and the costs of shipping. Certain products such as cement and gravel have very high transportation costs in proportion to their value. A Denver producer of cement would probably not worry about competition from Dallas producers. By contrast, the transportation costs of mink coats may be trivial in comparison to their value, and a Dallas manufacturer could respond quickly to a price increase in the Denver market.

A good illustration of use of shipping information is the Seventh Circuit's *A.A. Poultry* decision.[95] The court held that the state of Indiana could not be a relevant market for eggs. The defendant itself shipped eggs more than 500 miles to Buffalo, N.Y., and there was ample evidence that egg processors turned to suppliers over a 500 mile radius.

Suppose that there were no actual 500 mile shipments to observe. Would a 500 mile market still be a possibility? Yes, if the markets were competitive on both the selling and buying side and there was a local equilibrium, then any shipping costs proportional to distance would tend to confine transactions over a small range. Shipments would extend over a larger range only if an area produced more than was locally consumed.[96]

Geographic markets are often asymmetrical. Suppose that A Co. and B Co., which make chocolate cream pies in Manhattan, plan to merge. Each company sells 15% of the pies sold in Manhattan. There are 15 producers of pies in Manhattan, and there is no evidence that they are colluding. However, there are a large number of pie makers in nearby Brooklyn, who have lower labor costs and can produce equally good pies at a lower price. Currently many of the pies retailed in Manhattan are baked and shipped from the Brooklyn companies.

In this case the Manhattan pie makers operate at a cost disadvantage with respect to the Brooklyn companies. Any attempt by the Manhattan pie makers to charge a supracompetitive price will flood the market with Brooklyn pies. Therefore the divertible output of the Brooklyn pie makers must be included in the relevant market.

---

[95]   A.A. Poultry Farms v. Rose Acre Farms, 881 F.2d 1396 (7th Cir. 1989), cert. denied, 494 U.S. 1019, 110 S.Ct. 1326 (1990).

[96]   See Baxley-DeLamar Monuments, Inc. v. American Cemetery Ass'n, 938 F.2d 846, 851 (8th Cir. 1991) ("[T]he fact that a party does all its business in a certain geographic area does not necessarily mean that that area constitutes the relevant geographic market.").

The market shares of A Co. and B Co. may be substantially lower as a result.

It would not follow, however, that Manhattan must be included in the relevant market if two Brooklyn companies planned to merge. In fact, on the above facts it is clear that the Manhattan pie makers will not be able to compete effectively with the Brooklyn pie makers in Brooklyn unless the Brooklyn price rises substantially above the competitive level. In a merger case involving two Brooklyn pie makers, Manhattan should not be included in the relevant geographic market.

3.6c2.   The Elzinga-Hogarty Test

In 1973[97] Elzinga and Hogarty proposed that an area could not be a well defined market if (1) more than 25% of the product produced in the area was sold outside,[98] or (2) if buyers inside purchased more than 25% from outside.[99] In a later article the authors revised their proposal and suggested that an area was a relevant geographic market if the average of production inside the area shipped outside, and of production outside the area consumed inside, was less than 10%.[100] Today some courts speak of the 25% rule as defining a "weak" market, and the 10% rule as defining a "strong" market.[101] Numerous decisions have cited this test for geographic markets.[102] But many have also been critical. As the cited cases indicated, the Elzinga-Hogarty test has had its biggest impact in health care markets, particularly in challenges to hospital mergers.

One complaint about the Elzinga-Hogarty formulation is that it provides an instantaneous snapshot of what buyers and sellers are doing in the current situation; but it does not address the question that is more relevant in antitrust: what *would* buyers and sellers do in response to a future price increase.[103] While true, this criticism may go too far. *All* of our data about markets is historical, in the sense

---

[97]   Kenneth G. Elzinga & Thomas F. Hogarty, The Problem of Geographic Market Delineation in Antimerger Suits, 18 Antitrust Bull. 45 (1973). See 2A Antitrust Law ¶ 550b3 (4th ed. 2014).

[98]   This is sometimes called "little out from inside," or LOFI.

[99]   This is sometimes called "little in from outside," or LIFO.

[100]   Kenneth G. Elzinga & Thomas F. Hogarty, The Problem of Geographic Market Delineation Revisited: The Case of Coal, 23 Antitrust Bull. 1 (1978).

[101]   See FTC v. Freeman Hosp., 911 F.Supp. 1213 (W.D.Mo.1995), aff'd 69 F.3d 260 (8th Cir. 1995); FTC v. Butterworth Health Corp., 946 F.Supp. 1285 (W.D.Mi.1996), aff'd, 121 F.3d 708 (6th Cir. 1997).

[102]   Nilavar v. Mercy Health System, 244 Fed. Appx. 690, 2007 WL 2264439, 2007–2 Trade Cas. ¶ 75,897 (6th Cir. 2007, unpublished); United States v. Rockford Mem'l Corp., 717 F.Supp. 1251, 1266–75 (N.D.Ill.1989), aff'd, 898 F.2d 1278 (7th Cir.), cert. denied, 498 U.S. 920, 111 S.Ct. 295 (1990).

[103]   See Freeman Hospital, note 158, 69 F.3d at 269.

that it measures what was happening at the time the measurement was taken. A rule that firmly required "evidence" of what people would do in response to a price increase that has not been experienced would make relevant markets virtually impossible to prove.

Another critique of Elzinga-Hogarty, which has more traction, is that it defines markets too broadly. Several courts have observed this in cases involving hospital mergers.[104] The problem is particularly severe in situations where price discrimination is possible. Suppose that patient data show that 20% of the people in a town go elsewhere for surgery, and this number is sufficient to suggest that the local municipality is not a geographic market. However, further inquiry reveals that all of these 20% are patients who need cosmetic or other elective surgery that can be scheduled in advance. In this case a local hospital might very well have the power to charge monopoly prices for people who are not getting elective surgery, because they are not in as good a position to travel or shop for alternatives.[105]

3.6d.   Price Discrimination[106]

True geographic price discrimination occurs when differences in a firm's prices as between two areas do not reflect differences in costs. Price discrimination indicates that the firm has market power in at least some geographic areas.[107] For example, if a firm charges $4.00 in Milwaukee and St. Paul, and $3.00 in Dubuque, while its costs appear to be the same, then presumptively it has a certain amount of market power in Milwaukee and St. Paul, assuming the price in Dubuque is competitive. If a relevant market is defined in terms of ability to raise price 10% above cost, the area including Milwaukee and St. Paul over which prices are $4.00 would appear to be a relevant market.

Used in this fashion, price discrimination really operates as a limited surrogate for the defendant's marginal cost. That is, assuming we can measure the price discrimination, which requires us to observe both prices and cost differentials, then the percentage

---

[104]   FTC v. Penn State Hershey Med. Ctr., 838 F.3d 327 (3d Cir. 2016); FTC v. Advocate Health Care Network, 841 F.3d 460 (7th Cir. 2016).

[105]   As a result, several decisions have concluded that the Elzinga-Hogarty test defines markets too broadly in hospital merger cases. See, e.g., FTC v. Penn State Hershey Medical Center, 838 F.3d 327, 340–341 (3d Cir. 2016); FTC v. Advocate Health Care Network, 841 F.3d 460, 464 (7th Cir. 2016).

[106]   See 2A Antitrust Law ¶ 517 (4th ed. 2014).

[107]   Technically, a firm price discriminates when it has different ratios of price to marginal cost. If the price to "favored" purchasers is equal to marginal cost, then the price to "disfavored" purchasers must reflect a certain amount of market power. See § 14.1.

amount of price discrimination provides us a minimum percentage of the defendant's ability to raise price above marginal cost in the high priced area. Of course, the low priced area might already be priced above marginal cost, so the price in the high priced area reflects even greater market power than the price difference suggests. The only exception to this rule would be where the price in the low priced area is less than marginal cost—as, for example, if the defendant were practicing predatory pricing in that area. But predatory pricing can never be assumed and is presumably rare.[108]

While price discrimination is evidence of market power, it rarely provides useful information about the amount of power that a firm has. For example, product differentiation can make price discrimination possible even when it confers only modest power on individual firms. For example, relatively minor scholarly journals might charge higher prices to institutional buyers such as libraries, and lower prices to individuals. The library must attempt to carry a full set of journals, while the individual always has the option of going to the library. So the library can be made to pay more.[109] In addition, price discrimination may simply reflect different amount of risk that accompany different transactions. For example, firms may be willing to sell at a lower price under long term-term contracts that provide stable, guaranteed markets. Or firms with high fixed costs, such as airlines, my use price discrimination in order to fill their aircraft by offering lower prices to more price sensitive buyers. Even small airlines that clearly lack significant power use price discrimination in this fashion.[110]

§ 3.7   Computation and Interpretation of Market Shares

After a relevant product and geographic market have been delineated, the market share must be computed. Monopolization, attempt, tying, exclusive dealing and vertical restraints cases ordinarily require computation of the market share of the

---

[108] See Ch. 8.

[109] See Brand Name Prescription Drugs Antitrust Litig., 186 F.3d 781, 786–87 (7th Cir. 1999) (price discrimination in differentiated markets such as pharmaceuticals often practiced by firms lacking significant power; here, pharmacies were expected to carry a full range of drugs, and thus could be forced to pay more than managed care providers, who could pre-select the particular variations that they would prescribe to their patients).

[110] See 2A Antitrust Law ¶ 517 (4th ed. 2014). See Jonathan B. Baker, Competitive Price Discrimination: The Exercise of Market Power Without Anticompetitive Effects, 70 Antitrust L.J. 643 (2003); Benjamin Klein & John Shepard Wiley, Jr., Market Power in Economics and in Antitrust: Reply to Baker, 70 Antitrust L.J. 655 (2003).

defendant.[111] Merger cases analyzed under the Herfindahl index theoretically require one to compute the market share of every firm in the market.[112] Restraints analyzed under the rule of reason may require computation of the market share of the collected participants in the restraint.[113]

Conceptually, computing market share seems easy. The fact finder sums total market output and places it in the denominator of the fraction, with the output of the firm under consideration in the numerator. The resulting fraction, expressed as a percentage, gives the firm's market share. But the difficult issue is deciding which numbers to use in the fraction: revenue, units of output manufactured, units of output sold, capacity, or perhaps some other number reflecting an amalgam of these.

The easiest case for computing market share involves the group of firms selling a fungible product at the same price and are operating at full capacity. In that case measures based on revenue, units produced or capacity will all give the same percentage. But product differentiation accompanied by price differences complicates the problem. Suppose we conclude that Marantz stereos and Panasonic stereos are in the same relevant product, but the typical Marantz sells for $1200, while the typical Panasonic with the same features sells for $600. During the period in question each company has produced 10,000 units. Market share numbers based on units produced give us a 50% share for each firm; market share numbers based on revenue suggest that Marantz's share is 66.7%, while Panasonic's is 33.3%. Using the first number, Marantz is probably not capable of being charged with monopolization. Using the second number, it probably is.

3.7a.   Revenue v. Units

In most cases, market share is based on either revenue or the number of units produced. One clear advantage of these numbers is that they are often readily available. When products are fungible, the two numbers are the same. That is also largely true of products that are only modestly differentiated. For example, the ready-to-eat breakfast cereal industry exhibits significant brand differentiation (Wheaties, Trix, Captain Crunch, Raisin Bran, and hundreds of others) but a relatively small amount of price difference among offerings. The market shares of the producers probably would not

---

[111]   See Chs. 6 & 10.

[112]   See § 12.4a.

[113]   See § 5.2.

vary much if we moved from computations based on revenue to computations based on units produced.

Even when products are differentiated substantially, it is important not to exaggerate the impact of differentiation on market share measurements. The Marantz/Panasonic example given above assumed that one firm's product sold for double the price of the other firm's. But such extreme price variations usually indicate that the two brands are not in the same relevant market at all.

Technically speaking, units rather than revenue seems to be the best measure of market share for most, but not all, purposes. For example, if Marantz is accused of monopolization, the relevant question is to what extent Panasonic, its rival, will be able to satisfy customers when Marantz reduces its output. Presumably, the customer will purchase either *one* $1200 Marantz or *one* $600 Panasonic. The substitution takes place unit-by-unit rather than dollar-by-dollar. The person who switches to Panasonic steals one sale from Marantz for each unit of Panasonic.

When units are used, is the correct number units manufactured or units sold? Once again, large differences between these two numbers should not be common. Apparent differences may result from looking at too short a time period.[114] In a given three month period a firm might produce much more or much less than it sells during that same period, but very few firms would do this over a time period of, say, two or three years. In all events, the *ability to produce* is most generally the best estimate of a rival's ability to steal customers from a price-increasing firm. A firm with an accumulated inventory of non-perishable goods may have even a greater ability and desire to steal sales than does a firm that is currently selling all it produces. As a general matter, production figures are better than sales figures.

3.7b.   Output v. Capacity

A theoretical case can easily be made that the denominator of the market share fraction should include (1) the output of the firm or firms whose market power is being assessed; and (2) the capacity of rival firms.[115] The argument is simply that, when the ability of a firm

---

[114]   See, for example, Associated Radio Serv. Co. v. Page Airways, 624 F.2d 1342, 1352 (5th Cir. 1980), cert. denied, 450 U.S. 1030, 101 S.Ct. 1740 (1981), where the relevant market, avionics systems in a particular brand of aircraft, had produced only 20 sales over a nine or ten year period.

[115]   We use the output of the firm or firms under investigation because their *own* excess capacity cannot be used to defeat their price increase. As an illustration: suppose a market contained firms A, B, C, D & E. Each currently produces 10 widgets, but each has 5 units of excess capacity. A's market share as measured by capacity would be its own output divided by the sum of its own output plus the capacity of B—

to increase price above the competitive level is assessed, we wish to know the ability of rivals to fill in the gap by increasing their own output. A rival with excess capacity can increase its output without making an expensive and perhaps irreversible investment in additional productive capacity. Indeed, the rival with substantial excess capacity might be able to increase output on very short notice and deprive the putative monopolist from any possible gains.

But the theoretical case for capacity measures of rival firms runs into numerous practical problems.[116] *First,* almost any firm can increase its output if cost of production is not a factor. Properly measured excess capacity includes capacity where average variable cost of production does not significantly exceed current costs. But this constraint can make excess capacity very difficult to measure.[117] *Second,* properly defined capacity must include not only the capacity to produce an extra unit, but also the capacity to distribute it to the consumer. In some cases distribution of additional output is easy, but in others it may be very difficult. *Third,* even the capacity to produce an extra unit depends on more than the existence of unused equipment in a plant. For example, new personnel may have to be brought in and trained, and this itself could be an irreversible investment and a time-consuming activity. *Fourth,* use of capacity measures may greatly increase the cost of litigation since production and revenue figures are readily available, while capacity figures often are not.

In most cases, therefore, the output rather than the capacity of rivals is the better measure, although there are some exceptions.[118] If there is excess capacity that can obviously be brought into a market at very low additional cost, it should be counted. For example, suppose an airline's rival is flying the same route with a 200 seat airplane currently carrying only 50 passengers. The marginal cost of adding additional passengers is extremely low, and the distribution network for tickets is presumably already in place. The 200 figure seems a much better estimate than the 50 figure of the rival's ability to restrain future monopoly pricing.

E. This would be 10/70, or about 14%. A's market share based strictly on output would be 20%.

[116]   William M. Landes & Richard A. Posner, Market Power in Antitrust Cases, 94 Harv. L.Rev. 937, 949–950 (1981), generally prefer capacity measures.

[117]   See generally George J. Stigler, The Theory of Price 156–158 (3d ed. 1966).

[118]   A few courts have used capacity measures. See FTC v. Bass Bros. Enters., 1984–1 Trade Cas. (CCH) ¶ 66041 at 68, 610, 1984 WL 355 (N.D.Ohio 1984) (suggesting that capacity is better measure of future competition).

§ 3.8   Market Definition in the Justice Department Merger Guidelines

In 2010 the Antitrust Division of the Justice Department and the Federal Trade Commission jointly issued revised merger Guidelines for assessing horizontal mergers. Their approach to market definition has attained considerable acceptance by the courts.

The Merger Guidelines state the Agencies' principal purpose in delineating markets for evaluating mergers is to "identify one or more relevant markets in which the merger may substantially lessen competition."[119] In addition, market definition is necessary to enable the Agencies to identify the relevant market participants. The Guidelines also make clear that the Agency will not rely exclusively on market definition in order to assess a merger's anticompetitive effects. In particular, "[w]here analysis suggests alternative and reasonably plausible candidate markets, and where the resulting market shares lead to very different inferences regarding competitive effects, it is particularly valuable to examine more direct forms of evidence concerning those effects."[120] The merger statute expressly requires a showing of probable anticompetitive effects in some "line of commerce" and some "section of the country."[121] However, this language could certainly refer to something less technical than a "relevant market" as we use the term today.

The Guidelines note that its market delineation methodology "focuses solely on demand substitution factors." While supply substitutability is equally important the Guidelines address these factors in their process of identifying the market participants and barriers to entry.[122] In sum, the question "what are the boundaries of the market" is generally addressed by looking at demand; the question of "which firms should be counted as market participants" is answered by looking additionally to the ease with which they can reposition themselves into this market.

---

[119]   2010 Merger Guidelines, § 4.

[120]   Ibid.

[121]   15 U.S.C.A. § 18 (2006).

[122]   Gregory J. Werden, Market Delineation and the Justice Department's Merger Guidelines, 1983 Duke L.J. 514, which gives step-by-step instructions for defining a market under the 1982 guidelines.

3.8a.   Product Market Delineation in the 2010 Guidelines

The Guidelines employ the "hypothetical monopolist" test[123] in order to determine whether a group of products constitutes a relevant product market:

> Specifically, the test requires that a hypothetical profit-maximizing firm, not subject to price regulation, that was the only present and future seller of those products ("hypothetical monopolist") likely would impose at least a small but significant and non-transitory increase in price ("SSNIP") on at least one product in the market, including at least one product sold by one of the merging firms. For the purpose of analyzing this issue, the terms of sale of products outside the candidate market are held constant. The SSNIP is employed solely as a methodological tool for performing the hypothetical monopolist test; it is not a tolerance level for price increases resulting from a merger.[124]

In measuring the SSNIP, the Agencies ordinarily start with prevailing prices, or the prices that are assumed to prevail absent the merger. This will "most often" be an increase of five percent, but that number could vary depending on nature of the industry and the relative positions of the merging firms.[125] The Agency then employs econometric techniques to determine whether such a price increase would be profitable by estimating the number of sales that would be lost in response to such a price increase. In making this estimate the Agency will look at historical evidence, such as how customers have shifted their purchases in the past in response to a price change, information from buyers themselves, objective information concerning the costs of switching for various types of products and consumers, evidence from other sellers, and legal and regulatory limitations.[126] In making this assessment the Guidelines state that the Agency may employ critical loss analysis, as described above.[127]

The Guidelines also note the possibility of a narrower market if there is a recognizable subset of "targeted customers" who might be particularly vulnerable to a price increase.[128] This is another way of

---

[123] See § 3.2.

[124] Id. at § 4.1.1.

[125] Guidelines, § 4.1.2.

[126] Id., § 4.1.3.

[127] See § 3.2b. For a fuller description of how critical loss analysis works in merger analysis, see § 12.3d.

[128] Guidelines, § 4.1.4.

saying that the Guidelines may define a smaller relevant market in instances when the seller is able to price discriminate. They give this example:

> Glass containers have many uses. In response to a price increase for glass containers, some users would substitute substantially to plastic or metal containers, but baby food manufacturers would not. If a hypothetical monopolist could price separately and limit arbitrage, baby food manufacturers would be vulnerable to a targeted increase in the price of glass containers. The Agencies could define a distinct market for glass containers used to package baby food.[129]

The Guidelines do not speak of "submarkets."[130]

The supply side analysis in the Guidelines is not a part of market definition but rather part of the Guidelines' identification of the firms who are counted as "in the market" once it is defined. This includes all firms that are currently earning revenues in the market, including vertically integrated firms that might be producing although not selling. For example, if an automobile manufacturer produces its own gaskets exclusively for use in the automobiles that it manufacturers that firm must be counted as in the gasket market; each gasket that it uses in its own production displaces and thus competes with a gasket sold by an independent gasket manufacturer.[131] In addition so-called "rapid entrants," which are firms that are committed to entering in the near future, are also included. Such firms are ones that can get into the market without incurring significant "sunk" costs, or costs that they could not recover in the event of failure. The Guidelines note:

> Firms that clearly possess the necessary assets to supply into the relevant market rapidly may also be rapid entrants. In markets for relatively homogeneous goods where a supplier's ability to compete depends predominantly on its costs and its capacity, and not on other factors such as experience or reputation in the relevant market, a supplier with efficient idle capacity, or readily available "swing" capacity currently used in adjacent markets that can easily and profitably be shifted to serve the relevant market, may be a rapid entrant. However, idle

---

[129]   Ibid., Example 11.

[130]   However, the Agencies have continued to use "submarkets" in litigation, even since the 1982/84 Guidelines apparently abandoned them. See FTC v. Whole Foods Market, Inc., 548 F.3d 1028 (D.C. Cir. 2008).

[131]   See 2010 Guidelines, § 5.1.

capacity may be inefficient, and capacity used in adjacent markets may not be available, so a firm's possession of idle or swing capacity alone does not make that firm a rapid entrant.[132]

3.8b.   Geographic Market Definition Under the 2010 Guidelines

Geographic market definition under the Guidelines follows principles similar to those laid out for product market definition. One important factor is transportation costs, but in addition the Guidelines cite "language, regulation, tariff and non-tariff trade barriers, custom and familiarity, reputation, and service availability" as relevant to the quality of long distance transactions. Further, a firm's ability to price discriminate based on customer location may justify the recognition of smaller markets.[133] Once again, the Agency employs the hypothetical monopolist test, and it divides its analysis into two parts—first is market delineation based on the locations of suppliers; second, is market delineation based on the locations of customers. On the first,

> The hypothetical monopolist test requires that a hypothetical profit-maximizing firm that was the only present or future producer of the relevant product(s) located in the region would impose at least a SSNIP from at least one location, including at least one location of one of the merging firms. In this exercise the terms of sale for all products produced elsewhere are held constant. A single firm may operate in a number of different geographic markets, even for a single product. When the geographic market is defined based on supplier locations, sales made by suppliers located in the geographic market are counted, regardless of the location of the customer making the purchase.[134]

In making this assessment, the Guidelines state that the Agencies will consider these factors:

- how customers have shifted purchases in the past between different geographic locations in response to relative changes in price or other terms and conditions;

---

[132]   Ibid.

[133]   Id., § 4.2.

[134]   Guidelines, § 4.2.1.

- the cost and difficulty of transporting the product (or the cost and difficulty of a customer traveling to a seller's location), in relation to its price;

- whether suppliers need a presence near customers to provide service or support;

- evidence on whether sellers base business decisions on the prospect of customers switching between geographic locations in response to relative changes in price or other competitive variables;

- the costs and delays of switching from suppliers in the candidate geographic market to suppliers outside the candidate geographic market; and

- the influence of downstream competition faced by customers in their output markets.[135]

3.8c. Calculation of Market Shares Under the 2010 Merger Guidelines

The 2010 Horizontal Merger Guidelines state that the Agencies will usually use historical evidence to estimate market shares, except where "recent or ongoing changes in market conditions" suggest that the current share either overstate or understates "future competitive significance."[136] For example, if other firms in a market have attained a new technology that is not available to the firm being examined one might predict that its market share will fall.

On the issue of revenues as opposed to units of output the Guidelines state:

> In most contexts, the Agencies measure each firm's market share based on its actual or projected revenues in the relevant market. Revenues in the relevant market tend to be the best measure of attractiveness to customers, since they reflect the real-world ability of firms to surmount all of the obstacles necessary to offer products on terms and conditions that are attractive to customers. In cases where one unit of a low-priced product can substitute for one unit of a higher-priced product, unit sales may measure competitive significance better than revenues. For example, a new, much less expensive product may have great competitive significance if it substantially erodes the revenues earned by older, higher-priced products, even if it

---

[135]   Ibid.
[136]   Guidelines, § 5.2.

earns relatively few revenues. In cases where customers sign long-term contracts, face switching costs, or tend to re-evaluate their suppliers only occasionally, revenues earned from recently acquired customers may better reflect the competitive significance of suppliers than do total revenues.[137]

And on the issue of capacity:

In markets for homogeneous products, a firm's competitive significance may derive principally from its ability and incentive to rapidly expand production in the relevant market in response to a price increase or output reduction by others in that market. In such markets, capacities or reserves may better reflect the future competitive significance of suppliers than revenues. . . .[138]

3.8d. Conclusion; the Guidelines as a Policy Statement

The Horizontal Merger Guidelines convey an impression of considerable precision in market definition. Nevertheless, the degree of uncertainty remains large. The process of hypothesizing a "small but significant and non-transitory" price increase in a fluctuating market, and then considering how neighboring firms will respond, requires predictive abilities not demanded by the old analysis of current prices and shipments. Furthermore, the predictions must be made in situations where the variables are manifold and complex. The HHI concentration index, discussed in Chapter 12,[139] is critically sensitive to the accuracy of market definition. In sum, the 2010 Merger Guidelines have advanced antitrust analysis of mergers very considerably, but they have not yet turned it into an exact science.[140]

§ 3.9 Alternative Methods of Establishing Market Power

As previous sections of this chapter indicate, computation of a firm's market share involves a plethora of uncertainties. Often market share analysis fails to produce a reliable measure of a firm's market power. The exercise of the power to raise prices by reducing output leaves other traces, however, and these can sometimes be used as evidence of market power.

---

[137] Ibid.

[138] Ibid.

[139] See § 12.4.

[140] See Carl Shapiro, The 2010 Horizontal Merger Guidelines: from Hedgehog to Fox in Forty years, 77 Antitrust L.J. 49 (2010).

As our measurement tools have improved, these "direct" measures have become more prominent, particularly in merger cases. As noted in § 3.4b, traditional market share measurements are always "wrong" in differentiated markets, which are the focus of the great majority of antitrust litigation. Excluding the differentiated product exaggerates the power of the firm in question. However, including it treats the two as if they were perfect competitors. A direct econometric measure may enable us to measure substitution rates as between two differentiated but competing products and produce a more accurate picture of power. It is worth noting that when economists measure market power for their own purposes (not merely when testifying in court), they usually do not define a market. Indeed, some even go so far as to say that the notion of a relevant market does not exist in industrial economics.[141]

3.9a.   Measuring Residual Demand Directly

"Residual" demand, or residual demand elasticity, refers to the demand for a particular firm's product after the sales of competitors have been taken into account. Thus we can say that a true monopolist's residual demand curve is equal to the market demand curve. By contrast, a perfect competitor's residual demand curve is horizontal, reflecting the fact that the competitor will lose all sales if it attempts to charge more than the going price.[142]

The Lerner Index is one measure of a firm's residual demand.[143] Using empirical data about the firm's marginal cost and its current price, the Index measures the demand elasticity facing a firm; but the Index is difficult to use because marginal cost is so difficult to measure.

Residual demand can also be measured directly if one knows the market share, the market elasticity of demand, and the elasticity of supply of competing firms. But market elasticity of demand and the elasticity of supply of competing firms are not always easy to compute either. Further, this method requires defining a market and computing a market share. Thus, although it is useful for clarifying the meaning of market shares once a market share of a properly defined relevant market is known, it cannot be used as an alternative to market definition.

---

[141]   See Louis Kaplow, Market Definition: Impossible and Counterproductive, 79 Antitrust L.J. 361 (2013); Franklin M. Fisher, Economic Analysis and "Bright-Line" Tests, 4 J. Comp. L. & Econ. 129 (2008).

[142]   See § 1.1.

[143]   See § 3.1a.

It would be far more useful to estimate residual demand directly without the need of market definition.[144] This is particularly true in product differentiated markets, where some competitors compete with the principal firm much more strenuously than others, but classical market definition does not generally permit us to take these differences into account. That is, we have the choice of defining the other firms as inside or outside the market, but not as something in between.

The 2010 Horizontal Merger Guidelines permit the agencies to use econometric techniques to delineate markets for the purposes of merger analysis. However, this is a somewhat different query than estimating the market power of a single firm. In any event, estimating residual demand is a technical process, which usually requires the use of regression analysis and ample data about how changes in a firm's costs affect changes in its prices.

3.9b.   Persistent Price Discrimination[145]

Not all purchasers of widgets place the same value on them. Suppose that the marginal cost of producing a widget is $1.00. Some buyers will be willing to pay exactly $1.00 for them, others $1.25, others $1.50. A seller can maximize its profits by selling every widget to a customer for the largest price that particular customer is willing to pay. Competition prevents such persistent price discrimination from occurring, however. Even though a particular customer is willing to pay $1.50 for a widget, the customer would prefer to pay $1.00 and will do so if it can find a willing seller. Competition tends to drive all sales to the competitive price.

The monopolist has the power to discriminate, however, provided that it can identify and segregate groups of customers who place different values on the monopolist's product. Not all sellers with market power can engage in price discrimination. For example, arbitrage occurs when the buyers who pay a low price resell the product to buyers asked to pay a high price. If the monopolist cannot prevent arbitrage, then price discrimination may not work. So the absence of price discrimination does not necessarily show the absence of market power.

Only "persistent" price discrimination is evidence of market power. Price discrimination is a common occurrence, even in the most competitive of markets. Prices fluctuate daily as markets are continually shocked by new information and changing supply and demand conditions. Price discrimination is good evidence of market

---

[144]   See § 3.5a.

[145]   For a more complete discussion of price discrimination, see ch. 14.

power only when a particular seller is able systematically to achieve a higher rate of return from one group of customers than it does from another.[146]

While price discrimination evidence is of limited utility in measuring market power directly, it can be an aid in delineating markets under more conventional measures. For example, suppose we have established the threshold of our market power concern as the ability to raise price above cost by 10%. We now observe that a seller of widgets has segregated two groups of buyers, whether by geography or by configuration of the product. Costs of serving the buyers appear to be the same, but one group of buyers pays $1.00 per widget while the other group pays $1.15.

We do not know the seller's marginal cost, but we assume that the $1.00 price is equal to marginal cost. It might exceed marginal cost, but that only increases the seller's total market power. Assuming the low price equals marginal cost, the high priced sales must be 15% higher than marginal cost. With this information we can conclude either (a) that the grouping of sales to the high priced buyers constitutes a relevant market; or (b) that with respect to the high priced buyers the market power requirement has been met, without the need to define a relevant market.

3.9c.   Persistent Monopoly Profits; High Margins; Exclusion Payments

Courts have frequently acknowledged high profits as evidence that a firm has market power, or absence of high profits as evidence that it does not.[147] Such evidence comes with enormous, potentially disabling qualifications, however. First, accounting profits are not the same thing as economic profits. Second, the fact-finder must be able to distinguish between monopoly profits and "rents." In nearly all cases price-cost margins represent a superior mechanism for assessing power.

---

[146] Price discrimination may sometimes be evidence that the market contains one or more powerful, monopsony buyers, rather than a monopoly seller. A monopsonist may be able to reduce its demand for a product and buy at a lower price. A seller who deals with the monopsonist as well as other buyers may be price discriminating even though it has no market power. See 12 Antitrust Law ¶ 2011 (4th ed. 2018).

[147] In United States v. E.I. du Pont de Nemours & Co. (*Cellophane*), 351 U.S. 377, 76 S.Ct. 994 (1956), discussed in § 3.4b, the evidence indicated that du Pont had an extraordinarily high rate of return on cellophane: 31% before taxes. 351 U.S. at 420, 76 S.Ct. at 1020 (Warren, C.J., dissenting). In other markets, such as rayon, du Pont's rate of return was much lower. Id. at 420–421 n. 15, 76 S.Ct. at 1020. See Robert Pitofsky, New Definitions of Relevant Market and the Assault on Antitrust, 90 Col.L.Rev. 1805, 1846–1847 (1990).

3.9c1.   Monopoly Profits v. Accounting Profits

Economic profits are profits in excess of the amount that is necessary to sustain investment in the industry. Thus a firm that is earning "zero profits" may still be paying its expenses and providing a dividend to its shareholders. It will simply be earning a competitive return. By contrast, "accounting profits" refers to a collection of conventions used by accountants for reporting the difference between a firm's revenues and its expenses during a given time period. The differences between the two concepts of profit are significant.[148]

The difference between economic profit, which is the true measure of market power, and accounting profit, is not merely a question of data. There are important conceptual differences. Accountants generally divide the world into finite time periods, such as years or quarters, and consider "profits" earned over those periods. By contrast, the economist's measure of profits looks at an investment over its lifetime, from development, through marketing and sales, until it is closed out. Second, accounting profits reflect the way durable equipment is depreciated, and the rate of depreciation may bear little relation to the useful life of the asset—as, for example, when depreciation at a certain rate is required by the tax laws. Third, accounting data is generally aggregated over a firm, a plant or a division. By contrast, economists generally consider the profitability of each product separately.

Perhaps most importantly, economic profits include the opportunity costs of capital, while accounting profits do not. This has various implications. First, the opportunity cost of capital itself shows up as a profit in the accountant's ledger. For the economist, by contrast, capital that is earning only its opportunity cost, or a "reasonable" rate of return, is not earning profits at all; economic profits are only those profits earned *in excess of* the opportunity cost of the capital supplied. So a firm earning zero in economic profits is nevertheless paying its investors the opportunity cost of their capital—or the same rate that they could get in an alternative competitive investment of equivalent risk.

In other ways, accounting data considers opportunity costs only sporadically. For example, suppose a firm needs a large building for storage purposes. If the firm rents the building for $5000 monthly, the accountant will carry the building as a cost. By contrast, if the building is owned and has already been depreciated, the accountant will likely attribute no cost to the building itself, other than

---

[148] For example, Franklin M. Fisher & John J. McGowan, On the Misuse of Accounting Rates of Return to Infer Monopoly Profits, 73 Am. Econ. Rev. 82 (March 1983); 74 Am. Econ. Rev. 492 (June 1984).

maintenance, taxes and the like. But the value of the building is an opportunity cost of capital whether or not the building is owned. That is, the firm could either sell the building or rent it to someone else for $5000 a month, if it were not using the building itself. By not showing this opportunity cost, accounting data tends to show a "profit" rate higher than true economic profits.

More useful conclusions can be drawn from accounting data if we can adjust them to consider the true cost of a firm's capital, including the opportunity costs, or estimated market value, of owned assets that are fully depreciated.[149] In particular a firm's margins, or difference between cost and price, can provide useful information about the amount of market power it has.[150]

3.9c2.   *Power Inferred from Exclusion Payments:* Actavis *Decision*

A competitive producer could not pay a rival a large sum to stay out of the market. First of all, it would not have the margins to afford such a payment. Secondly, getting one rival out of a competitive market would do the payor no good. Other competitors would quickly expand their output. Rather, a large payment to another to stay out of a market is more typical of collusion, and the payment either reflects or is intended to create power. Following this logic, the Supreme Court held in *Actavis* that market power could be inferred from a pharmaceutical manufacturer's large payment to a generic rival to stay out of its market.[151]

The Court is clearly correct, provided that the payment is actually for exclusion. One might object that the payor could have high fixed costs and may not earn high profits in spite of its high margins. But that argument proves far too much. *All* of the methodologies for assessing power presented in this chapter pay relatively little attention to fixed costs; their focus is on "mobility" of assets in some relatively short run where fixed costs do not matter. Further, even firms with high fixed costs are not entitled to the full cartel value of their product, but this is what an exclusion payment in a two-firm market would yield. In any event, the power question addresses only power and nothing more. To be sure, high fixed costs may sometimes justify collaborative practices, mainly ones that

---

[149]   See 2A Antitrust Law ¶ 516 (4th ed. 2014).

[150]   E.g., McWane, Inc. v. FTC, 783 F.3d 814, 829–32 (11th Cir. 2015) (fact that firm was able to exclude rivals while maintaining high margins evidenced market power). See Herbert Hovenkamp & Carl Shapiro, Horizontal Mergers, Market Structure, and Burdens of Proof, 127 Yale L.J. 1996 (2018).

[151]   FTC v. Actavis, Inc., 570 U.S. 136, 133 S.Ct. 2223 (2013). For further discussion, see 2A Antitrust Law ¶ 520b (4th ed. 2014).

involve sharing of resources. But that issue needs to be addressed under the rule of reason directly, not avoided by an incorrect conclusion that the defendant lacks market power.

3.9d.   Market Power and Intellectual Property

For many years courts in tying arrangement cases had indulged a presumption that market power in the tying product can be presumed if the tying product is patented.[152] Other courts have extended the presumption to copyrights and occasionally even to trademarks.[153] As a general matter these presumptions had not been extended to other antitrust violations, such as monopolization or attempt. Indeed, in *Walker Process*, an attempt to monopolize case, the Supreme Court agreed in principle that fraudulent procurement of a patent could be a violation, but it remanded for a determination whether the patent created any market power.[154]

The entire notion that an intellectual property right creates market power is belied by one simple fact: such rights are very easy to obtain. In the case of a copyright, one need only write down a few words and mail a copy with the required fee to the copyright office. Getting a trademark is not much more difficult. Obtaining a patent is a little harder, because the patent application must provide evidence that the device or process for which a patent is sought is new, useful and nonobvious. Once again, however, patents are rather easily granted, and most of them have no commercial value.

In its *Illinois Tool Works* decision the Supreme Court discarded the presumption, holding that in a case where the defendant tied a specialized printer to ink power in the printer market could not be presumed merely because the printer was protected by some patents.[155] The Court observed that the presumption had grown out of a period in which antitrust jurisprudence was extremely hostile toward tying arrangements, believing that they were nearly always anticompetitive. It also noted that in 1988 Congress had amended the Patent Act to provide that one could not be guilty of patent "misuse"—an offense that closely tracks antitrust principles—unless the patentee had market power in the patented product, clearly

---

[152]   For example, see the dicta in Jefferson Parish Hosp. Dist. No. 2 v. Hyde, 466 U.S. 2, 16–17, 104 S.Ct. 1551, 1560–1561 (1984). See § 10.3c; and 2A Antitrust Law ¶ 518 (4th ed. 2014).

[153]   See generally, § 10.3c, which summarizes the case law.

[154]   Walker Process Equip., Inc. v. Food Mach. & Chem. Corp., 382 U.S. 172, 86 S.Ct. 347 (1965).

[155]   Illinois Tool Works, Inc. v. Independent Ink, Inc., 547 U.S. 28, 126 S.Ct. 1281, 1292 (2006).

implying that power could not be inferred from the patent itself.[156] The Court then concluded that in all antitrust cases including tying cases market power "must be supported by proof of power in the relevant market rather than by a mere presumption thereof."[157]

Intellectual property rights are a fact of life in modern markets, where each firm seeks product differentiation in the eyes of consumers. Toasters, cameras, small computers, lamps and laundry detergents are all protected by patent rights, but all are sold in markets that range from moderately to robustly competitive. Likewise, fast food restaurants, grocery stores, clothing stores and banks have copyrights or trademarks protecting their various products, slogans, symbols, or advertisements. All of these markets are competitive—some, such as grocery stores, are intensely competitive. In many, entry is quite easy and the market shares of most individual firms quite small. Putting it bluntly, to presume market power in a product simply because it is protected by intellectual property is nonsense.

Does this mean that the presence of intellectual property rights is irrelevant to market power questions? Hardly. On the demand side, one can seldom infer that an intellectual property right so strengthens customer appeal that they are willing to pay a monopoly price rather than substitute. But on the supply side, intellectual property rights can restrict entry. This is particularly true of patents.[158]

Suppose a paint manufacturer develops a process that makes its paint more durable than the paint of competitors, without increasing the cost. Customers prefer this 12-year paint to the 8-year paint offered by rivals, and they are willing to pay more if no one else manufacturers the superior paint as well. Now the scope of the patent right may be able to tell us something about the nature and duration of the monopoly in question. If the patented process is really needed to make the better paint, then the patent operates as an entry deterrence device. If, as a result, the paint manufacturer can reduce the output of the better paint and raise its price for a substantial length of time, the better paint defines a relevant market.

---

[156] Illinois Tool Works, 547 U.S. at 41, 126 S.Ct. at 1290, referring to the Patent Misuse Reform Act, 35 U.S.C. § 271(d).

[157] Id. at 1291.

[158] See, e.g., Broadcom Corp. v. Qualcomm, Inc., 501 F.3d 297, 314 (3d Cir. 2007) (once patent became incorporated into an industry standard and was thus "essential" to operating in a market it could be sufficient to confer market power). See also Herbert Hovenkamp, FRAND and Antitrust, ___ Corn. L. Rev. ___ (2020), available at https://papers.ssrn.com/sol3/papers.cfm?abstract_id=3420925.

Finally, as some courts have observed, the owner of "standards essential" patents, which are patents that have been declared to be an integral part of a network or other market wide standard, can exert significant power unless their obligation to license at reasonable rates is taken seriously.[159]

3.9e.   Assessing Market Power for Vertical Restraints

As noted earlier, defining a relevant market and estimating share is not the only way of assessing market power, and in many situations it is not the best way. In its *American Express* decision, however, a closely divided Court held that a relevant market must be defined in a case alleging an unlawful vertical restraint. The Court's reasoning is unclear, and amounts to little more than an unsupported assertion that market power cannot be assessed in such cases without a market definition.[160] The holding is particularly problematic in that decision because all of the relevant credit card transactions in the market at issue were digitized and recorded, thus making direct measurement quite feasible. While the Court's conclusion is incorrect as a matter of economics and seems unwise as a matter of antitrust policy, it is the law today.

The Court did not justify its conclusion that traditional market share approaches would be superior to direct measurement in a vertical case involving a two-sided platform. To the contrary, direct measure would very likely be superior even on two sided platform markets, and even on the assumption that harms on one side will be offset by benefits on the other. For example, the *Amex* dissenters observed some twenty instances in which the defendant increased its merchant acceptance fees.[161] Whether these were exercises of market power or simply reflections of increased benefits on the other side is

---

[159]   See, e.g., Microsoft Corp. v. Motorola, Inc., 696 F.3d 872, 876 (9th Cir. 2012) ("standards threaten to endow holders of standard-essential patents with disproportionate market power").

[160]   Ohio v. American Express Co., 138 S.Ct. 2274, 2285 n. 7 (2018). The Court's full statement is:

> The plaintiffs argue that we need not define the relevant market in this case because they have offered actual evidence of adverse effects on competition—namely, increased merchant fees. We disagree. The cases that the plaintiffs cite for this proposition evaluated whether horizontal restraints had an adverse effect on competition.... Given that horizontal restraints involve agreements between competitors not to compete in some way, this Court concluded that it did not need to precisely define the relevant market to conclude that these agreements were anticompetitive.... But vertical restraints are different. Vertical restraints often pose no risk to competition unless the entity imposing them has market power, which cannot be evaluated unless the Court first defines the relevant market.

[161]   *Amex*, 138 S.Ct. at 2294.

a testable proposition, and direct measurement's more quantitative approach makes it easier to test than does a market definition approach to power. The relevant question would be whether the price increases were offset by increased card holder benefits or other cost increases on the other side of the platform.

In most cases, the effects of the Supreme Court's decision requiring a market definition in vertical cases can be limited, however. A conclusion drawn from direct measurement can readily be turned into a statement about a relevant market. Recall that a relevant market is a grouping of sales over which the exercise of market power is plausible. For example, suppose that direct measurement such as the Supreme Court approved in the *Actavis* case suggests that a firm has significant power in its particular pharmaceutical drug.[162] The direct evidence that this particular drug enjoys significant power is sufficient to warrant the conclusion that sales of the drug also define a relevant market. In the *American Express* case the record showed that AmEx was able to increase its price to merchants several times without losing significant business or increasing the costs of its customer perks.[163] Assuming these increases were not justified by cost increases on either side of the platform, this firm's sales constitute a relevant market.

The one discomfort of this approach is that it may lead to narrow or even single-brand relevant markets in the presence of product differentiation. This simply reflects the fact that direct measures work better in product differentiated markets, where it is well known that relevant market definitions that group differentiated producers together necessarily define markets too broadly. The problem is closely related to the one exposed by the *Cellophane* fallacy discussed previously.[164]

---

[162]   FTC v. Actavis, Inc., 570 U.S. 136, 133 S.Ct. 2223 (2013). See § 3.9c4.

[163]   See § 3.4c.

[164]   See § 3.4c.

Chapter 4

ANTITRUST POLICY TOWARD COLLUSION AND OLIGOPOLY

Table of Sections

§ 4.1 Introduction: The Basic Economics of Price Fixing

A cartel is an agreement among otherwise competing firms to reduce their output to agreed upon levels, or sell at an agreed upon price. The firms acting in concert can earn monopoly profits just as a single-firm monopolist.[1] Price fixing is said to be "naked" when it involves no more than an agreement to restrict output or raise price, with no collateral agreements organizing production or distribution.[2] In that case, the agreement is profitable only if the firms jointly have the power to raise market prices by reducing output.[3] Naked price fixing is not only illegal *per se*, it can also be a felony.[4]

In general, joint conduct of competitors warrants closer antitrust scrutiny and more severe rules than those that apply to single firm conduct.[5] This is true even though cartels are inherently more volatile than single-firm monopolists. They can come into existence far more easily. The formation of a monopoly may take many years of mergers, superior research and development, marketing, predation or simply good luck. By contrast, a cartel can be created overnight.

At the same time, however, the cartel is inherently more fragile than the monopolist. The interests of the cartel as a whole often diverge substantially from the interests of individual participants. The nature of a cartel is to invite cheating by members. Often cleverly disguised cheating can impose rather small losses on the cartel as a whole, but give large gains to the individual cheater. If enough cartel members cheat, however, the cartel will fall apart. As a result, many cartels go to extraordinary lengths to reduce the opportunities for cheating.

In order for a cartel to succeed for any length of time, six conditions must exist:

(1) The product or service to be cartelized must define a relevant market with sufficiently high barriers to entry that newcomers cannot undermine the cartel's pricing decisions.[6]

(2) The cartel members must produce a sufficiently large share of the product or service that their decisions are not

---

[1]   On price and output of the monopolist, see § 1.2. Two or more firms bargaining together will maximize joint profits, which in the case of a perfect cartel occurs when its price and output are equal to that of a monopolist. See 12 Antitrust Law ¶ 2002b (4th ed. 2019); Ronald H. Coase, The Problem of Social Cost, 3 J.L. & Econ. 1 (1960).

[2]   In fact, however, almost any output restriction agreement "allocates" output and creates at least the potential for realizing some production efficiencies.

[3]   On this definition of "naked" restraints, see § 5.1; for elaboration, see 11 Antitrust Law ¶ 1906 (4th ed. 2018).

[4]   See § 15.1a.

[5]   On the rationale for treating multilateral conduct more severely than unilateral conduct, see § 5.1b.

[6]   On market definition and entry barriers, see ch. 3 and §§ 1.6, 12.6.

undermined by existing rivals who are not cartel members; further, these nonmembers must be unable or unwilling to expand their own output rapidly.

(3) The cartel members must be able to arrive at an agreement about the output that each cartel member will produce—in most cases the important decision variable is *output*, not price.[7]

(4) The cartel must be able to detect cheating on the cartel by cartel members.

(5) The cartel must be able to punish cheating effectively when it is detected.

(6) The cartel must be able to do all these things without being detected by public enforcers or injured victims.[8]

The perfect cartel would contain relatively few members who collectively account for 100% of production in a market. All members would be the same size and equally efficient, and they would produce an identical product. The product would be sold by sealed auction bids made by the sellers in a market containing many, relatively small purchasers, and the winning bids publicly announced.

The cartel would have the most success in raising price by reducing output if it included all competitors in the market. If they were equally efficient and produced identical products, they would all have the same profit-maximizing price and would agree quite easily about a price. If they were the same size they would have little trouble allocating the output reduction among members. If the cartel had relatively few members, made its sales by sealed auction bids with publicly announced results, and sold to a large number of small buyers, there would be little opportunity for cheating.[9]

Few cartels satisfy all of these conditions. The products of different competing firms often differ from each other, and the firms vary even more. Few markets make their sales by simple auction bidding. The variations from one market to another are considerable.

---

[7]   See, e.g., United States v. Andreas, 216 F.3d 645 (7th Cir. 2000) (Lysine cartel regulated volume rather than price). See Joseph E. Harrington, How do Cartels Operate? 6–30 (2006).

[8]   See Christopher R. Leslie & Herbert Hovenkamp, The Firm as Cartel Manager, 64 Vand.L.Rev. 813 (2011).

[9]   For evidence that cartels are most successful in such situations see Joseph E. Harrington, How Do Cartels Operate (2006). In the great majority of cases involving large numbers a trade association was used as the cartel facilitator. George A. Hay & Daniel Kelley, An Empirical Survey of Price Fixing Conspiracies, 17 J.L. & Econ. 13, 21 (1974).

As a result, some markets are more conducive to cartelization than others, and in some markets effective cartelization is impossible.

Theoretically, the cartel would determine its profit-maximizing price just as a single-firm monopoly does. For example, if the cartel controlled 100% of the market and new entry was blockaded or relatively slow,[10] the cartel price would be determined by the intersection of the market's marginal revenue curve with the cartel's supply curve—effectively, the marginal cost curve of the cartel as a whole.[11] The cartel faces problems that the monopolist does not, however, because individual members of the cartel generally have different costs: some are more efficient than others; different firms may operate on different portions of their average cost curves (for example, some may have excess capacity while others do not); some may produce slightly different products, which cost either a little less or a little more than the product sold by other cartel members.

4.1a.   The (Virtual) Universality of Cartel Cheating

Incentives to cheat are present even in the most homogeneous of cartels. They are merely exacerbated by heterogeneity. If the cartel is successful each member will be selling its output at a price such that its own individual marginal revenues exceed its marginal costs. If a member can secretly make sales at a lower price, it can enlarge its own profits, either by attracting buyers unwilling to pay the cartel price but willing to pay the "shaved" price, or else by stealing buyers from other cartel members.

4.1a1.   *Divergence Between Cartel and Single Firm Profit Maximization*

The optimal cartel sets output the way a monopolist would, which is to equate *cartel-wide* marginal revenue with marginal cost. But for each individual cartel member, the marginal revenue obtained from a sale is significantly higher than the firm's marginal cost because the cartel member absorbs only a fraction of the price reduction that accompanies an output increase. For example, when a monopolist increases output from 100 units to 101 units, it must consider that the price for all 101 units will be lower as a result of the output increase.[12] When one member of an identical-firm ten-member cartel increases output by one unit, the market price of all

---

[10]   On entry barriers, see § 1.6.

[11]   If the monopolist or cartel controlled less than 100% of the market, or if entry at the monopoly price was likely, the profit-maximizing price would be lower, lest market share would erode too quickly. See § 1.2c.

[12]   See § 1.2a.

units drops by the same amount, but the cartel member experiences these losses only for the ten units that it is producing.

The individual cheater's decision is unprofitable for the remaining non-cheaters. Their output remains constant at ten units, but their price drops Note that this incentive to cheat is totally independent of entry barriers, product differentiation, differences in levels of efficiency, in firm size and so on. Thus even the "perfect" cartel must regard cheating as a problem.

Cheating is particularly profitable in industries that have relatively high fixed costs. In the railroad industry, for example, short-run marginal costs (the costs of shipping one extra package on a partially loaded train that is already scheduled) are quite small in comparison with the total costs of operating a railroad. As a result the cartel price, which covers total costs plus monopoly profits, will be much higher than the lowest price that is profitable to the railroad. The railroad could give a substantial secret price reduction and still make large profits from the transaction.[13]

4.1a2.   Cartel Cheating Strategies

A cartel member would not likely be able to make all its sales at a price less than the agreed cartel price. Such pervasive cheating would be quickly detected. Often it is more profitable and less risky for the cartel member to honor the cartel price as a general rule, but look for opportunities to make large, secret sales at a lower price.

Cheating by secret price discrimination has been rampant in many cartels.[14] The chance of detection increases with the number of sales, so it is important that the sales be large. The terms of the sale will usually be disguised in some way. For example, in the 1911 *Standard Oil* case the defendant was accused of monopolizing the oil market by obtaining "secret rebates" from railroads in exchange for its trade. The secret rebates were used to explain how Standard could undersell its competitors and drive them out of business. In fact, the railroads were engaged in price fixing, and the secret rebates enabled

---

[13]   See Herbert Hovenkamp, Enterprise and American Law, 1836–1937, at chs. 12 & 13 (1991); Christopher R. Leslie, Trust, Distrust, and Antitrust, 82 Tex.L.Rev. 515, 624 (2004). See also George L. Priest, Rethinking the Economic Basis of the Standard Oil Refining Monopoly: Dominance Against Competing Cartels, 85 S.Cal.L.Rev. 499 (2012).

[14]   For example, see the discussion of the *Addyston Pipe* cartel in 2 Simon N. Whitney, Antitrust Policies: American Experience in Twenty Industries 5 (1958); United States v. Addyston Pipe & Steel Co., 85 Fed. 271 (6th Cir. 1898), modified and aff'd, 175 U.S. 211, 20 S.Ct. 96 (1899). If the cartel is legal, it might enlist the help of the government in prosecuting cheating.

a cheating railroad to make a large sale to Standard at a profitable price.[15]

Often the effect of a price fixing agreement is merely to change the nature of the competition among the cartel members. Before the cartel was formed they competed in price. After they compete by throwing more and more services into the bargain until their marginal costs rise to the cartel price.[16] The cartel members then end up with no more than a competitive return. Customers take the services whether or not they would have been willing to pay their market value in a competitive market. Several empirical studies of unlawful cartels conclude that their members often earn no more than the competitive rate of return.[17]

4.1a3. *Detecting and Punishing Cheating; Cartel "Amnesty"*

The ease of cheating varies considerably with the type of market. Cheating is most difficult (and cartels therefore most successful) in auction markets where sales are large, relatively infrequent, and determined by secret bids with publicly announced results. In such a market the cartel members will merely pick the "winning" bidder for each prospective sale and determine the bid price. All other members agree to bid a higher price. If a different member wins the bid, the cartel members will know immediately.[18] A famous cartel involving 29 American companies in the market for large electrical equipment used such schemes.[19]

By contrast, if sales are individually negotiated with specifications and terms that vary from one transaction to the next and not publicly disclosed, cheating will be far more difficult to

---

[15]   See Standard Oil Co. v. United States, 221 U.S. 1, 32–33, 31 S.Ct. 502, 505 (1911), charging Standard with obtaining "large preferential rates and rebates in many and devious ways over [its] competitors from various railroad companies, and * * * by means of the advantage thus obtained many, if not virtually all, competitors were forced either to become members of the combination or were driven out of business * * *."

[16]   See Douglas H. Ginsburg, Nonprice Competition, 38 Antitrust Bull. 83 (1993).

[17]   See Peter Asch & Joseph J. Seneca, Is Collusion Profitable?, 58 Rev. Econ. & Stat. 1 (1976). However, see Dick, Stable Contracts, 39 J. L. & Econ. at 243–244, who argues that such studies skew the data by looking at condemned or challenged cartels, in which cartel enforcement costs are presumably higher because the cartel is illegal and the risk of detection requires elaborate precautions.

[18]   As a result, statutes regulating government procurement which require secret competitive bidding and public announcement of the winning bid can actually facilitate cartelization. See Jon M. Joyce, The Effect of Firm Organizational Structures on the Incentives to Engage in Price Fixing, 7 Contemp. Pol'y Issues 19 (1989) (importance of auction markets as facilitating collusion).

[19]   See Richard A. Smith, The Incredible Electrical Conspiracy, *Fortune* 224 (May 1961).

detect. Cheating is also easy to conceal if buyers and the cartel members deal with each other outside the cartelized market. For example, if a manufacturer of widgets and gidgets is involved in a widget cartel, it might cheat by selling widgets to a firm at the cartel price but giving a compensating price reduction in gidgets.

Sometimes cartels can reduce cheating by using alternatives to the simple fixing of prices. For example, some industries may be more conducive to output restriction agreements, in which the members decide how much each should produce and sell. The market itself determines the price. This kind of agreement generally works well in industries where the government requires detailed reporting of output, or where output or number of units sold is easy to verify.

An alternative to the output reduction agreement is the agreement on market share, with penalties for firms that exceed their assigned shares.[20] Each member promises to reduce its output by an agreed-upon percentage. The result is that the market shares of the respective firms remain constant, although each produces less than it would under competition. Price will rise to reach a new equilibrium with output. Such an agreement can be more flexible than a strict output reduction agreement, because it enables the parties to deal with sudden changes in demand for the product without consulting each other. In general, market share agreements discourage firms from bidding aggressively for new customers, or from trying to use low bids to steal customers away from other cartel members.

Horizontal market division can be an effective method of cartelization, although it may not work in as many markets.[21] Naked market division agreements come in three general kinds. Under horizontal territorial division, firms divide the map and agree that each one will obtain exclusive sale rights in a designated area. In a horizontal product division agreement the firms agree that each will avoid production or sale of a designated product produced by a rival.[22]

---

[20]   See George J. Stigler, The Organization of Industry 42–43 (1983). E.g., United States v. Andreas, 39 F.Supp.2d 1048 (N.D.Ill.1998), aff'd, 216 F.3d 645 (7th Cir.), cert. denied, 531 U.S. 1014, 121 S.Ct. 573 (2000) (cartel assigned market share to each member). See 12 Antitrust Law ¶ 2030 (4th ed. 2019).

[21]   Cartelization by territorial division works only if the members are able to divide a relevant market into sections such that each is a monopolist in its own section. An alternative is horizontal customer division, in which the firms agree that each will deal exclusively with certain groups of customers. See David Boies, Courting Justice 233 (2004) (on customer division agreements in the vitamin cartels).

[22]   For example, Microsoft proposed to Netscape that Microsoft would design and sell its web browser, Internet Explorer, only for Windows machines, and Netscape would service only non-Windows machines. See United States v. Microsoft Corp., 253 F.3d 34, 80 (D.C. Cir. 2001). If Netscape had accepted the proposal the result would

In a customer division agreement the firms agree not to compete for one another's pre-assigned customers.[23]

For example, four widget manufacturers may divide the country into exclusive zones. Once each firm has an exclusive territory it is free to estimate its own monopoly price and make its own output decisions. As a result, the cartel may circumvent many of the problems attending a compromise agreement on price and output. Horizontal market division robs the firms of an opportunity to cheat simply by cutting price. Indeed, one important difference between price fixing and territorial division is that within a territory each firm equates its own marginal cost and marginal revenue, and thus has no incentive to cheat.[24] While firms can still cheat by making secret sales to customers in the territory of another cartel member, these may be easier to detect, particularly if the firms are fully integrated to the retail level.

Detecting cheating by cartel members is one thing. Punishing it is quite another. Most importantly, cartels are illegal, and the members of a cartel cannot take cheaters to court. They must devise ways to punish cheaters that simultaneously (a) make cheating unprofitable without (b) causing public discovery of the cartel. Even if cheating can be punished, the punishment will not be effective unless its expected costs exceed the value of cheating. As a result, it is also important that cheating be detected quickly.

Among the most successful and credible punishments for cheating is for the non-cheating cartel members to lower their price to the competitive level.[25] If cheating could be detected immediately and punished without exception, it would become unprofitable. For example, if each cartel member knew that in response to a single cheating sale it would earn only competitive returns for a subsequent month, no one would cheat. In order for such a strategy to work perfectly, however, the cheating would have to be detected almost immediately. If a firm can cheat for an extensive period of time

---

very likely have been a per se unlawful market division agreement, but because Netscape declined there was no agreement, which § 1 of the Sherman Act requires.

[23]   On the three types of market division, see 12 Antitrust Law ¶¶ 2030–2033 (4th ed. 2019). See also Palmer v. BRG of Ga., 498 U.S. 46, 111 S.Ct. 401 (1990) (per curiam; condemning horizontal territorial division under per se rule); United States v. Brown, 936 F.2d 1042 (9th Cir. 1991) (rivals divide market for billboard sites and agree not to compete for one another's cites; affirming criminal conviction); United States v. Suntar Roofing, 897 F.2d 469 (10th Cir. 1990) (horizontal customer allocation among roofers; unlawful per se; criminal conviction upheld).

[24]   On this problem under price fixing, see § 4.1a1.

[25]   See Martin J. Osborne & Carolyn Pitchik, Cartels, Profits and Excess Capacity, 28 Int'l Econ. Rev. 413 (1987).

without detection, then it will trade the gains from cheating against the costs of punishment and the cheating may be profitable.[26]

In general, too much democracy is the enemy of cartel stability. Cartels in which each cartel member has a voice in daily administration can in fact be quite unwieldy.[27] Cartel stability often requires that the managerial role be given to one or two ringleaders or an organization with centralized decision making authority.[28]

4.1b.   Competitive Fringe Firms

The thorn in every cartel's flesh is the firm that refuses to participate. Conversely, the outsider in a cartelized market has the best of all possible situations. First, it suffers no risk of antitrust liability.[29] Second, it can ride on the cartel's price increases without reducing its own output. In fact, it can increase output and sell all it wishes at a large profit by charging only slightly less than the cartelized price.[30]

A nonmember who increases output substantially can destroy a cartel by depriving it of sufficient demand to obtain supracompetitive returns. Cartel members often find it necessary to put various forms of pressure on competitors who refuse to join. Many private actions alleging illegal predatory pricing, concerted refusals to deal or a variety of business torts have been based on the theory that the defendants were attempting to cartelize the market, and that the plaintiff was a competitor who refused to participate.[31] While

---

[26]   As a result, such punishment is credible only if cartel members maintain sufficient excess capacity that they can easily and quickly increase their output in response to the cheater's additional sales. For an argument focusing on the single dominant firm rather than the cartel, see Garth Saloner, Excess Capacity as a Policing Device, 18 Econ. Letters 83 (1985).

[27]   See Margaret C. Levenstein and Valerie Y. Suslow, Breaking Up is Hard to Do: Determinants of Cartel Duration, 54 J.L. & Econ. 455 (2010); Christopher R. Leslie, Cartels, Agency Costs and Finding Virtue in Faithless Agents, 49 Wm. and Mary L. Rev. 1621 (2008). See also Joseph E. Harrington, Jr., How do Cartels Operate?, 2 Foundations and Trends in Microeconomics 1 (2006); Thomas G. Krattenmaker and Steven C. Salop, Antitrust Exclusion: Raising Rivals' Costs to Achieve Power over Price, 96 Yale L.J. 209, 238–40 (1986) (describing role of cartel "ringmaster").

[28]   See George Baker, Robert Gibbons, and Kevin J. Murphy, Relational Contracts and the Theory of the Firm, 117 Q.J. Econ. 39 (2002).

[29]   However, a few plaintiffs have attempted to obtain damages from an illegal cartel for overcharges they paid in purchases from a nonmember. See § 16.6e.

[30]   See Charles Van Cott, Standing at the Fringe: Antitrust Damage and the Fringe Producers, 35 Stan.L.Rev. 763, 770 (1983); William H. Page, Optimal Antitrust Penalties and Competitors' Injury, 88 Mich.L.Rev. 2151, 2155 (1990).

[31]   For example, Utah Pie Co. v. Continental Baking Co., 386 U.S. 685, 87 S.Ct. 1326, reh'g denied, 387 U.S. 949, 87 S.Ct. 2071 (1967) (allegations of collusive predatory pricing); and see Matsushita Elec. Indus. Co. v. Zenith Radio Corp., 475 U.S. 574, 106 S.Ct. 1348 (1986) (alleged predatory pricing by cartel); Eastern States Retail

predatory pricing to discipline a cartel cheater may not seem very plausible, predatory pricing or concerted refusals to deal may be an effective way of dealing with fringe competitors, depending on the underlying market structure.

4.1c.   Internal Efficiencies of the Cartel

Suppose that a half dozen manufacturers of heavy pipe are involved in price fixing. The firms generally deliver the pipe to construction sites, and contractors generally select a seller by taking competitive bids. Different cartel members will be located different distances from any particular construction site, and a competitive market would naturally favor the closest firm. If the firms have equal production costs, the closest firm to the site can deliver the pipe for the lowest total price for pipe plus freight. Even a monopolist who owned all six plants would, other things being equal, deliver the pipe from the plant closest to the delivery point.

A simple price fixing agreement among the pipe manufacturers would destroy the natural advantage of the closest firm. For example, if the contractor received six identical bids for delivered pipe he would have little incentive to select the closest firm. He might choose a firm he has dealt with before, or one that a different contractor has reported to be good. If transportation costs are a high percentage of total costs, a substantial part of the monopoly overcharge would go, not to the cartel members, but to the railroad or trucking company that delivered the order.

Sometimes cartels preserve efficiency by holding out a fixed price to customers but engaging in internal competition for the right to make the sale. The cartel condemned by the Supreme Court in United States v. Addyston Pipe & Steel Co.[32] used a complex internal bidding arrangement to award the right to sell. First the companies agreed about a bid price that would be presented to the customer as the competitive bid. Then the cartel members bid against each other to see who would transfer the largest amount of the bid price as a "bonus" to the cartel as a whole. Presumably, that would be the firm capable of performing the job at the lowest cost. The winning member would keep the bid price less the bonus; the bonus would be divided among the cartel members in proportion to size.

In spite of all these efforts, naked cartels are generally not able to operate as efficiently as single-firm monopolists. First of all, the

Lumber Dealers' Ass'n v. United States, 234 U.S. 600, 34 S.Ct. 951 (1914) (boycott orchestrated by lumber dealers against "obnoxious" lumber wholesalers who had entered retailing themselves).

[32]   United States v. Addyston Pipe & Steel Co., 85 Fed. 271, 280 (6th Cir. 1898), modified and affirmed, 175 U.S. 211, 20 S.Ct. 96 (1899).

cartel must sustain the transaction costs of bargaining, coordinating activities, and investigating and punishing cheating among its own members. To be sure, the monopolist must coordinate as well. However, the costs of such coordination are higher for the cartel, because each member's interests are different. The primary interest of each member is to maximize its own, not the cartel's, profit. Since each member knows that the other members have monopoly profits to look forward to, they will probably be willing to spend much time and resources in bargaining. This generally means a great deal of posturing—threats to pull out of the cartel, to report it to the Justice Department, to exceed quotas, etc. Some public cartels that are not reachable by the antitrust laws, such as OPEC, have been unable to arrive at agreements that the members can accept and live with for prolonged periods. For illegal cartels, whose negotiations must be secret and infrequent, the problems are even greater.

Cartels may also have less flexibility than monopolists in coordinating overall production. For example, the monopolist who has five plants and wishes to cut production to 80% of capacity has the option of closing the least efficient plant and running the other four at optimal capacity. A cartel of five firms, each having one plant, may not have that option. The cartel will probably have to settle on some compromise scheme for allocating production among the members, even though the result is not optimal.

Notwithstanding these difficulties, there is good reason for thinking that the social cost of cartels is quite high, notwithstanding the inability of many of them to lower market output substantially or earn supracompetitive returns for lengthy periods of time. As long as firms are tempted to fix prices, the strong policy against cartels in the American antitrust laws is a good one.

One particular type of cartel involving buyers rather than sellers is employer agreements suppressing wages and salaries. A naked anti-poaching agreement, in which two or more firms simply agree not to hire one another's employees, is unlawful per se, even if the defendants are not competitors in the product market.[33] More problematic are intra-franchise agreements. Suppose, for example, that a fast food franchisor such as McDonald's puts the same language into each of its many franchise agreements, forbidding the individual franchises from hiring one another's employees. In form the agreements appear to be vertical, but operationally they seem

---

[33]   E.g., California v. eBay, Inc., 2014 WL 4273888 (N.D.Cal. Aug. 29, 2014). See Todd v. Exxon Corp., 275 F.3d 191 (2d Cir. 2001). On mergers that facilitate labor market collusion, see Ioana Marinescu and Herbert Hovenkamp, Anticompetitive Mergers in Labor Markets, 94 Ind. L.J.1031 (2019).

more like horizontal no-poaching agreements.[34] For example, some of the agreements have third-party beneficiary provisions that enable one franchisee to enforce the no-hire provision against other franchises.[35] The courts that have confronted such arrangement have expressed understandable concern over their anticompetitive potential.[36]

§ 4.2   Imperfect Competition

One of the most complex and frustrating issues in competition policy is dealing with the widely acknowledged, empirically robust ways that multiple firms can achieve noncompetitive prices without engaging in detectable, explicit agreements. Both the case law and the economic analysis of this issue stretch back eighty or more years, but the bottom line is that antitrust has not developed particularly effective tools for disciplining such behavior. Most decisions are willing to condemn such conduct only if they find an actual communication among the parties that can be reasonably characterized as an "agreement."

Section 1 of the Sherman Act is addressed to "contracts," "combinations," or "conspiracies" in restraint of trade. This language requires the plaintiff or prosecutor to prove an "agreement" among two or more firms to fix prices or reduce output. In determining whether such an agreement exists, courts have relied heavily on common law contract formulations, such as "meeting of the minds" or "mutual assent."

By contrast, § 2 of the Sherman Act generally applies to conduct by the single firm acting alone.[37] Concerted conduct is inherently suspicious; single-firm conduct is not. As a result the law of § 2 applies to a relatively narrow range of circumstances. For example, § 2 generally requires a showing either that the defendant is a monopolist, or else that there is a dangerous probability it will become one.

---

[34]   Deslandes v. McDonald's USA, LLC, 2018 WL 3105955, 2018-1 Trade Cas. ¶ 80,435 (N.D. Ill. June 25, 2018) (agreements between McDonald's and its franchisees forbidding them from hiring away one another's employees: " . . . the restraint has vertical elements, but the agreement is also a horizontal restraint. It restrains competition for employees among horizontal competitors: the franchisees . . . ."; court employed "quick look" analysis).

[35]   Butler v. Jimmy John's Franchise, LLC, 331 F. Supp. 3d 786 (S.D. Ill. July 31, 2018).

[36]   See Herbert Hovenkamp, Competition Policy for Labour Markets (OECD, May, 2019), available at https://papers.ssrn.com/sol3/papers.cfm?abstract_id=34210 36.

[37]   See Chs. 6–8.

Some conduct falls through a fairly wide crack in the Sherman Act. Although anticompetitive, there is no evidence that it resulted from agreement among competitors. Nor is it the unilateral conduct of a firm that has or threatens to have monopoly power. Since early in the nineteenth century economists have argued that firms in concentrated markets can increase their prices above the competitive level without expressly communicating with one another, and certainly without the need for anything resembling a "conspiracy" or agreement among the parties. Today the theoretical and empirical literature on oligopoly is enormous and complex.[38] Although wide disagreement exists about details, as well as the ubiquity and extent of oligopoly behavior in the American economy, there is general agreement that it exists. Further, the resulting social loss (as compared to competitive behavior by firms with the same costs) seems to be quite substantial.

One disconcerting conclusion for antitrust policy is that oligopoly strategies can be more stable and free from incentives to cheat than are cartel strategies. Further, the more stable strategies are often those that come furthest from satisfying the agreement requirement of § 1 of the Sherman Act, because in such markets the firms do not *need* to engage in the kinds of explicit communication that the law tends to regard as a "contract" or agreement. One appellate decision was very candid about this state of affairs:

> In non-oligopolistic markets, "[p]arallel behavior among competitors is especially probative of price fixing because it is the sine qua non of a price fixing conspiracy." But in an oligopolistic market, parallel behavior "can be a necessary fact of life," and "[a]ccordingly, evidence of conscious parallelism cannot alone create a reasonable inference of a conspiracy." Therefore, to prove an oligopolistic conspiracy with proof of parallel behavior, that evidence "must go beyond mere interdependence" and "be so unusual that in the absence of an advance agreement, no reasonable firm would have engaged in it."[39]

A related, equally disturbing conclusion is that the agreement requirement obliges antitrust enforcers to put their limited resources in the wrong place. Since the antitrust laws require "agreement," enforcement money is generally spent in areas where an agreement can be proven. But only the least stable situations require a

---

[38]   For good discussions see Louis Kaplow, Competition Policy and Price Fixing 174–215 (2013); W. Kip Viscusi, Joseph E. Harrington, Jr., & David E.M. Sappington, Economics of Regulation and Antitrust, Ch. 5 (5th ed. 2018).

[39]   Valspar Corp. v. E.I. Du Pont De Nemours & Co., 873 F.3d 185, 193 (3d Cir. 2017) (quoting other decisions).

qualifying antitrust agreement. In those areas where cooperative interaction among firms is likely to do the most damage, no "agreement" is required.[40]

Apart from variations in oligopoly, other imperfect competition models are based on theories of monopolistic competition. One important difference between oligopoly and monopolistic competition is that oligopoly tends to emphasize how firms coordinate with one another, while the theory of monopolistic competition is more concerned with individual strategies for limiting competition by differentiating one's own product.[41] As a result, monopolistic competition has a smaller role in the antitrust analysis of collusion than do theories of oligopoly. It does have a large role to play in merger policy, however. Somewhat oversimplified, "coordinated effects" challenges to merger are driven manly by theories of collusion or oligopoly, while "unilateral effects" merger challenges more closely resemble monopolistic competition theories.[42]

4.2a.   Non-Cooperative Cournot Oligopoly

The most important historical model of non-cooperative oligopoly came from Augustin Cournot and is nearly two centuries old.[43] In some ways the model seems quite crude and counter-intuitive. Nonetheless, it remains highly influential and forms the basis of many more complex variations. Furthermore, its simplicity may not be crudeness at all, but an important insight into the kinds of simplifying assumptions that firms make when the information they have is imperfect.

Cournot assumed that firms in concentrated markets choose output rather than price as the relevant decision variable; that is, they select an output, and then attempt to sell that output at whatever price the market will bear. In case that strategy strikes you as unrealistic, keep in mind that it is the same as the choice made by the perfect competitor, who has no control over price but can produce as much or as little as it pleases. The farmer planting corn at the beginning of the season asks "How much shall I plant?" not "What price shall I charge?" Second, Cournot presumed that each firm

---

[40]   See Richard A. Posner, Antitrust Law 51–192 (2d ed. 2001). See also Howard P. Marvel, Jeffrey M. Netter & Anthony M. Robinson, Price Fixing and Civil Damages: An Economic Analysis, 40 Stan. L. Rev. 561 (1988), noting that many criminal price fixing cases fail to produce subsequent private damages actions, presumably because the defendants—although they "fixed" prices—were unable to sustain supracompetitive prices for any length of time.

[41]   See § 1.5a.

[42]   The two approaches mergers are discussed in §§ 12.3, 12.4.

[43]   A. Augustin Cournot, Studies in the Mathematical Principles of the Theory of Wealth (1838; English translation by Nathaniel T. Bacon, 1897).

would set its output on the assumption that others would hold their output constant; that is, they would not respond to the actor's output decision by adjusting their own output. Once again, the competitor makes the same assumption.

The process by which a Cournot equilibrium is reached in a duopoly, or two-firm market, goes like this. The first firm sets its output as if it were a monopolist, by equating its marginal cost and marginal revenue. That is, it simply assumes that the other firm will produce zero. The second firm then takes the *residual* demand—the demand that is left over after the first firm has set its price and output[44]—and equates its own marginal cost and marginal revenue. The first firm will then need to revise its price downward, or it will lose too many sales to the second firm; so it will equate its marginal cost and marginal revenue once again, using the residual demand curve left by the output of the second firm. The second firm will respond to this revised output by the first firm, and so on. They will finally reach an equilibrium point where each is equalizing its own marginal cost and marginal revenue. If the two firms are the same size and have identical marginal cost curves, they will end up with the same output as well. Each will produce two-thirds of the monopoly output; so total output will be 1.333 times the monopoly output.[45] As the number of firms in a Cournot oligopoly increases, total market output increases as well, and the price is correspondingly lower.

The basic Cournot theory is an oversimplification of reality. But just as the theory of perfect competition, it seems quite vigorous and every text on industrial organization discusses it. Alternatives and more sophisticated approaches designed to take market complexities into account have been developed as well.[46] These alternatives consider markets with a threat of entry, markets where firms are of different sizes or are not equally efficient or produce differentiated products, and firms that are presumed to be capable of more complex strategic behavior. The models generally try to identify a "Cournot-Nash equilibrium,"[47] which is a situation in which no firm can profit

---

[44]   On residual demand, see Jonathan B. Baker, Estimating the Residual Demand Curve Facing a Single Firm, 6 Int'l J. Ind. Org. 283 (1988).

[45]   For simple explications, W. Kip Viscusi, Joseph E. Harrington, Jr., & David E.M. Sappington, Economics of Regulation and Antitrust, Ch. 5 (5th ed. 2018); Roger D. Blair & David L. Kaserman, Antitrust Economics 225–230 (2d ed. 2008).

[46]   For surveys and critiques, see Shapiro, *supra* at 336; and Frederic M. Scherer & David Ross, Industrial Market Structure and Economic Performance, chs. 6–8 (3d ed. 1990); and see generally Jean M. Tirole, The Theory of Industrial Organization (1988).

[47]   Named after Cournot and John F. Nash, Jr. who formalized the concept. See John F. Nash, Jr., Noncooperative Games, 54 Annals of Mathematics 286 (1951).

from deviating (such as by price cutting), provided the other firms stay put as well. To this extent a Cournot-Nash equilibrium is self enforcing. By contrast, in a classical cartel by agreement each firm could earn more by surreptitiously cutting its price and producing more. As a result, the cartel requires an enforcer.

4.2b.   Oligopoly Strategies

Cooperative strategies are devices that enable firms to reach the same levels of price and output that would be produced by a profit-maximizing monopolist or a perfectly functioning explicit cartel. Presumably, cooperative strategies will be employed by firms who believe they can obtain higher returns than non-cooperative, Cournot behavior will yield. As the previous section notes, although Cournot strategies may theoretically be more stable than cartel strategies, they are also less profitable. For example, in the simplest Cournot model, an oligopoly of five equal sized firms has an output of about 83% of the competitive output. This would likely yield price increases in the range of 10% to 30% above the competitive level, depending on the market elasticity of demand. A perfect cartel could do much better, perhaps achieving prices 50% or more above the competitive level.

§ 4.3   Antitrust Policy Toward Oligopoly and Tacit Collusion

One reason antitrust law has had so little success with oligopoly is its continued adherence to a common law concept of "agreement" that makes little sense in the context of strategic behavior among competing firms. This agreement requirement frequently targets the wrong set of practices. *Non-cooperative* oligopoly situations are often more stable, and thus more easily sustained, than cooperative ones.

Under Sherman Act analysis, the collusion question has generally reduced to consideration of whether there is sufficient agreement-like behavior that one can say a "contract," "combination" or "conspiracy" existed among the parties. Historically, this kind of question caused a great deal of difficulty in the common law of contracts. By its language, Sherman § 1 invited the same problems into antitrust analysis of concerted behavior. Many Sherman § 1 decisions hold that the statute requires an explicit agreement, although evidence of the agreement may sometimes be circumstantial.[48] Much § 1 case law is preoccupied, not with the

---

[48]   See First Nat'l Bank of Ariz. v. Cities Serv. Co., 391 U.S. 253, 88 S.Ct. 1575 (1968) (conspiracy could be inferred from fact that conduct was parallel, and that an agreement would have been beneficial to the defendants by giving them higher prices);

defendant's conduct as such, but with whether that conduct was undertaken pursuant to such an agreement. This unfortunate bit of formalism has been the major impediment to effective antitrust action against poor economic performance in oligopoly markets.

4.3a. Attacking Oligopoly; the Turner-Posner Debate

The emphasis of Sherman § 1 case law on "agreement" has led some to think that oligopoly is effectively out of reach of the antitrust laws. In an important article written in 1962, Professor Donald Turner argued that such behavior was beyond the reach of the Sherman Act for an additional reason: it is rational and virtually inevitable, given the structure of the market.[49] Each firm in an oligopoly market is forced by circumstance to consider its own profit-maximizing rate of output, given the output of rivals and their anticipated responses to its own price and output decisions. To ignore these issues would be completely irrational. Furthermore, no court could draft a decree that would force the firms to "ignore" each other in their market decision-making. The only solution, Turner concluded, was structural relief: persistent, poor economic performance in highly concentrated markets should warrant a court decree breaking the firms into smaller units that would give the market a more competitive structure. Turner believed that such an approach would require new legislation.

Turner's critics emphasized that the term "agreement" makes more sense when one thinks of oligopoly as a kind of "tacit" collusion. In a response to Turner, Professor (later Judge) Posner emphasized the similarities rather than the differences between cartel and oligopoly behavior.[50] Whether firms in a concentrated market act in response to an express agreement or simply have read the market's clear signals in the same way should be a mere detail. Under this approach to oligopoly analysis, explicit cartel agreements are referred to as "express collusion," while oligopolistic, interdependent behavior is called "tacit collusion." This term is designed to draw attention to the fact that there is a certain "meeting of minds" of

---

Theatre Enters., Inc. v. Paramount Film Distrib. Corp., 346 U.S. 537, 74 S.Ct. 257 (1954) (discussed in § 4.5); and see 6 Antitrust Law ¶ 1400 (4th ed. 2017).

[49] Donald F. Turner, The Definition of Agreement Under the Sherman Act: Conscious Parallelism and Refusals to Deal, 75 Harv.L.Rev. 655 (1962); see also Carl Kaysen & Donald F. Turner, Antitrust Policy 110–119, 266–272 (1959). On the role of this structural approach in the antitrust policy of this era, see Herbert Hovenkamp, United States Competition Policy in Crisis, 1890–1955, 94 Minn.L.Rev. 311 (2009).

[50] Richard A. Posner, Oligopoly and the Antitrust Laws: A Suggested Approach, 21 Stan.L.Rev. 1562 (1969). Judge Posner updated and restated his position in Richard A. Posner, Antitrust Law 51–100 (2d ed. 2001).

competitors in at least some oligopolistic markets, even though the firms do not formally communicate with each other.

4.3b. Identifying Tacit Collusion and Facilitators; Policy Options

The term "tacit collusion" does not seem to fit very well with the traditional Cournot model of oligopoly, which is not cooperative at all. However, the term does fit quite well with two situations: (1) price fixing when the terms are communicated by informal or non-verbal means; (2) cooperative behavior that consists in a serious of repeated actions and reactions until the parties settle upon an equilibrium price or output level. Most importantly, firms may be able to facilitate the Cournot or cartel outcome by changing the way information is communicated in the market, the way that transactions take place, or the terms of those transactions. This raises some possibilities for antitrust policy. We must be able to identify oligopoly performance when we see it. Then, however, we may be able to direct antitrust at market conditions or practices that make oligopoly outcomes more likely. The principal weapon here is merger policy, but it is preventive rather than corrective.[51] Alternatively, we may challenge various facilitating practices themselves.[52]

Oligopoly pricing is aided by a market that is highly concentrated on the selling side, but it should also be rather diffuse on the buying side. If the market contains a small number of large and knowledgeable firms on the buying side, they may be able to force the sellers to bid against each other and offer concessions, particularly if the terms of individual sales are kept secret. If the market contains numerous small buyers, then prices may have to be advertised or publicly posted in a way that makes them apply equally to all customers. In that case, the oligopolist may be able to cut price substantially only by giving all buyers the same cut. The Cournot oligopolist will have no incentive to cut prices, assuming it was equating marginal cost and marginal revenue to begin with.

Likewise, oligopoly pricing just as much as express price fixing can be frustrated by easy entry or output increases from fringe firms. The lower the market share of fringe firms on the "edge" of the market, and the more difficult and time-consuming entry is, the greater will be the returns from tacit collusion.

Both oligopoly pricing and collusion are less successful if the firms in the market are not equally efficient or produce distinguishable products. In addition, however, as the number of

---

[51]   See § 12.1b.

[52]   See § 4.6; Louis Kaplow Competition Policy and Price Fixing, *passim* (2013).

firms in a market increases, or if one of the above impediments to collusion exists, tacit collusion becomes ineffectual more quickly than express collusion.

Firms in oligopoly markets often develop certain "facilitating devices" that make tacit collusion easier by reducing the benefits of cheating, making price discrimination more difficult, or by increasing the likelihood of detection or the costs of punishment. For example, if all firms produce uniform products, offer similar terms or conditions of sale, and make all transactions public, they can make the market more conducive to oligopoly or collusive results. If the facilitating device results from an express agreement, it may receive rule of reason treatment under the antitrust laws, because it does not explicitly affect price. For example, an agreement that all firms will produce "standardized" products may appear to be efficiency creating if it lowers customer search costs.[53] Further, the facilitating devices themselves often result from tacit agreement. The firms never formally communicate with each other but simply reach a shared perception about how to maximize joint monopoly profits.

One of the most controversial questions in antitrust policy is how courts and enforcers should deal with the problem of poor economic performance in concentrated markets when there is no evidence of express collusion. The Turner proposal favoring structural relief[54] (that is, judicially mandated dissolution of the firms in the market) was predicated on the premise that monopoly pricing was inevitable in oligopoly markets. The poor performance was perfectly rational, profit-maximizing behavior dictated by the environment in which the oligopoly firm found itself. Marginal cost pricing, by contrast, was irrational.

Even if courts could administer the restructuring of an entire industry, however, it is by no means clear that consumers would benefit. Absent unusual deterrents to competitive entry, markets are generally concentrated because operation at minimum efficient scale (MES) requires a firm with a relatively large share of the market.[55] For example, if MES in the widget industry requires an output level equal to 30% of market demand at the competitive price, the market in equilibrium is likely to have three or fewer firms. Smaller firms would either combine by merger, increase their own market share by driving other firms out of business, or else go out of business themselves. A program of combatting oligopoly by breaking the

---

[53]   See 12 Antitrust Law ¶ 2136 (4th ed. 2019).

[54]   Donald F. Turner, The Definition of Agreement Under the Sherman Act: Conscious Parallelism and Refusals to Deal, 75 Harv.L.Rev. 655 (1962).

[55]   See § 1.4a.

market into a dozen firms would deprive all or most of MES, and the costs of the loss in productive efficiency might well exceed the social loss caused by oligopoly performance.

So the consequences of severe structural change in most industries are difficult to predict, and the litigation process is certainly not well designed to make such predictions. Break-up of oligopoly firms will certainly yield an industry with more firms, and they will likely price their output closer to their costs, but their costs could be higher. *Ex ante*, it may be difficult to say whether the structural change will yield a price increase or a price decrease. Once we include the large administrative costs of predicting when such relief would be appropriate, and the costs of administering such relief, it is doubtful that the result of structural reorganization of oligopoly industries would be efficient.

There are some reasons for believing that the social costs of oligopoly behavior, at least of the noncooperative kind, are small compared to the costs of denying firms the chance to achieve their most efficient rate of output.[56] If that is the case, consumers may be best off if firms are permitted to attain minimum optimal scale, even at the expense of some high concentration, with the antitrust laws used to make both non-cooperative and cooperative price coordination as difficult as possible.

In practice, this has meant that plaintiffs and prosecutors hobbled by § 1's "agreement" requirement have attempted to do three different things. First, they have tried to loosen up the evidentiary standards for proving a combination or conspiracy, or to convince courts that certain kinds of understandings should be interpreted as "agreements" for antitrust purposes, even though they do not seem to fit the common law understanding. This effort is directed largely at cooperative forms of oligopoly behavior, or at explicit price-fixing for which there is insufficient direct evidence of a classical "agreement."[57]

Second, antitrust enforcers have tried to convince the courts that certain kinds of conspicuously parallel behavior should be condemned whether or not there is evidence of an underlying

---

[56]   See Sam Peltzman, The Gains and Losses from Industrial Concentration, 20 J.L. & Econ. 229 (1977); John S. McGee, In Defense of Industrial Concentration (1971).

[57]   On the definition of "direct" evidence, see Champagne Metals v. Ken-Mac Metals, Inc., 458 F.3d 1073, 1083 (10th Cir. 2006) ("Direct evidence in a Section 1 conspiracy "must be evidence that is explicit and requires no inferences to establish the proposition or conclusion being asserted. . . . [W]ith direct evidence the fact finder is not required to make inferences to establish facts."); accord In re Publication Paper Antitrust Litig., 690 F.3d 51, 63 (2d Cir. 2012), cert. denied, 568 U.S. 1123, 133 S.Ct. 940 (2014).

agreement about price or output. In particular, the Federal Trade Commission has tried to employ § 5 of the FTC Act, which does not require proof of an agreement. Unfortunately, its record is not particularly promising.[58]

Third, those bringing antitrust cases have challenged certain "facilitating" practices because they tend to make both cooperative and non-cooperative behavior more likely. In some cases these practices result from agreement among firms; in other cases they appear to be unilateral but widespread across the industry. These facilitating practices are treated mainly in § 4.6, although we return to the issue in the next chapter, since the presence of such practices plays an important role in determining the legality of joint ventures.

Finally, the Federal Trade Commission should issue guidelines describing the types of behavior that should cross the line from unilateral to improper interactive conduct when challenged under the FTC Act. There are good institutional as well as practical reasons for doing. First, § 5's "unfair methods of competition" language does not by its terms require an agreement, and this could remove the bias excluding nearly everything but traditional "contracts" or "conspiracies" from liability.[59] Second, the courts seem to be more willing to go along with the Agencies when they state their enforcement objectives in a set of general Guidelines instead of briefs drafted in the course of particular litigation. The D.C. Circuit Court of Appeals brought this out in 2019, when it dismissed a government complaint challenging a vertical merger and in the process observed that the agencies had not produced any Guidelines on vertical mergers in more than three decades.[60] Guidelines have more credibility to the extent that they are focused on general policy concerns rather than specific lawsuits, where the Agencies are more likely to do what they need to do in order to win a case. Third, the FTC Act cannot be enforced by private parties. In order to raise the likelihood of private enforcement the FTC would have to state that it is applying Sherman Act standards. That would tend to limit private enforcement to situations where a more traditional agreement could be shown, reducing concerns about overdeterrence of more ambiguous conduct.

---

[58]   See § 4.6d.

[59]   On the use of § 5 of the FTC Act to challenge collusion, see *infra* § 4.6d.

[60]   United States v. AT&T, 916 F.3d 1029, 1037 (D.C. Cir. 2019); see § 9.4.

§ 4.4   Proving a Price or Output "Agreement" from Indirect or Circumstantial Evidence; Hub-and-Spoke Conspiracies

Occasionally the Supreme Court has condemned practices as collusive without direct evidence of explicit collusion. In Interstate Circuit, Inc. v. United States,[61] the defendants were a group of eight distributors and several exhibitors of motion pictures. The distributors controlled about 75% of "first-class feature films exhibited in the United States." One of the largest exhibitors sent a letter to the eight distributors suggesting that each insert two clauses in future exhibition contracts with theaters: 1) a clause requiring the theatre to charge at least 40 cents admission for first-run films, and 25 cents admission for subsequent-run films; 2) a clause prohibiting the theaters from exhibiting first-run films with other films as double features. Subsequently the eight distributors incorporated these clauses into many of their contracts. There was no evidence, other than the fact that all eight had received the letter, that the distributors had agreed among themselves.

It is easy to see why an exhibitor would want such clauses in its contracts and those of its competitors: the "price maintenance" clause effectively prevented the theaters served by these distributors from price competition with each other. One common cartel facilitator is dealers' collective inducement of resale price maintenance clauses from their supplier.[62] The clause restricting double features prevented the theaters from competing by increasing the amount of entertainment they would provide at the maintained price.

If each of these restrictions had been imposed unilaterally by a distributor on an exhibitor, they would probably have been legal. They were not illegal vertical price maintenance because the films were not sold to the exhibitors, but merely licensed to them. The Supreme Court had not yet dealt with vertically imposed nonprice restraints, so the status of a purely vertical clause prohibiting double features was uncertain.[63]

The use of the clauses was clearly illegal, however, if the eight distributors had agreed *among themselves* to place them in every exhibitor's license agreements. In that case there would have been an agreement among competitors which effectively reduced output: fewer people would have attended movies because the price was higher, and those who did attend would have seen fewer movies for

---

61   306 U.S. 208, 59 S.Ct. 467 (1939).

62   On dealers' use of RPM to facilitate collusion, see § 11.5a.

63   On such restrictions, see ch. 11.

their admission price. Often the best way for a cartel to enforce its terms is to find a vertically related firm to do it for them, since such a firm deals with all of them directly. Further, the vertically related firm can sometimes force unwilling competitors to participate. In effect, Interstate Circuit was asking the distributors to make exhibitor collusion enforceable by means of vertical contracts.

The Supreme Court held that the offer given to the eight distributors, plus their nearly unanimous acceptance, was sufficient evidence from which the district court could infer the existence of an agreement among them. As the Court noted:

> Each [distributor] was aware that all were in active competition and that without substantially unanimous action with respect to the restrictions * * * there was risk of a substantial loss of the business and good will of the * * * exhibitors, but that with it there was the prospect of increased profits.[64]

As the Court saw it, each distributor's apparently unilateral decision to impose resale price and double feature restrictions was irrational given the presumption of competition: a theatre that did not wish to be bound by the restrictions would have sought out a different distributor. In a competitive market, a distributor that could profitably increase its market share by eliminating the restrictions would do so.

The Court characterized the case not as using the antitrust laws to reach tacit collusion, but as using circumstantial evidence to infer the existence of express collusion. There was an explicit "offer." Although there may not have been an explicit "acceptance," acceptance could nonetheless be inferred from the evidence.

A rigorous use of such an approach suggests the following: (1) because the proof is not available, many antitrust conspiracies cannot be established by "direct" evidence, such as written agreements, tape recordings, or testimony of offer and acceptance.[65] As a result, *some* kind of circumstantial proof must be accepted. However, (2) the mere fact that the firms had an opportunity to collude, or that collusion would appear to be profitable to them, is not sufficient to prove collusion;[66] and (3) the plaintiff relying on

---

[64]   306 U.S. at 222, 59 S.Ct. at 472.

[65]   See Todorov v. DCH Healthcare Auth., 921 F.2d 1438, 1456 (11th Cir. 1991) (evidence of explicit agreements found "only in rare cases"); accord Petroleum Prods. Antitrust Litig., 906 F.2d 432, 439 (9th Cir. 1990).

[66]   See, e.g., Blomkest Fertilizer v. Potash Corp. of Saskatchewan, 203 F.3d 1028, 1036 (8th Cir. 2000, en banc), cert. denied, 531 U.S. 815, 121 S.Ct. 50 (2000) (mere meetings not enough; however, court did not pay sufficient attention to the fact that

circumstantial evidence must show in addition to (2) that the defendants' actions were rational (with rational generally meaning profit-increasing) only if they were undertaken with the understanding that other firms would modify their behavior in a similar fashion.

The fact that defendants had the opportunity to conspire is particularly unhelpful if regular meetings are part of the ordinary business of the firms at issue. For example, one should not infer price fixing merely from the fact that competitors had an opportunity to meet at trade association conventions, and that one of the items on the agenda was declining market conditions.[67] Likewise, the fact that competitors occasionally socialize is insufficient.[68] Of course, if there is some evidence that these meetings included discussions of price fixing, or the carrying out of plans to exclude a rival, the evidence is ordinarily admissible and may establish a qualifying agreement, but then we would be back in the territory of establishing an agreement by explicit evidence.[69]

As a general proposition, decisions made by trade associations must be regarded as an "agreement" of their members, and trade associations have a history of involvement in collusion.[70] At the same time, of course, the mere fact that participants in a trade association discuss price or output does not mean that they are agreeing to fix price or reduce marketwide output.

Courts often say that parallel behavior alone does not establish an agreement unless the plaintiff can also show the presence of certain "plus factors" making the inference of agreement stronger. Relevant plus factors include such things as an oligopolistic market structure, advance posting of parallel prices, a history of price fixing or exchange of price information.[71] Alternatively, as in *Interstate*

---

much more than meetings was going on). Other decisions are discussed in 6 Antitrust Law ¶ 1417 (4th ed. 2017).

[67]   See Kelsey v. NFL, 757 Fed. Appx. 524 (9th Cir. 2018) (fact that NFL teams met on numerous occasions showed neither conspiratorial intent nor actual agreement to refrain from poaching or to fix cheerleaders' wages).

[68]   Souza v. Estate of Bishop, 821 F.2d 1332 (9th Cir. 1987) (extensive social contacts among land owning families insufficient to establish agreement to restrict output, particularly where the lease-only land policies being challenged seemed to be independently rational).

[69]   ES Dev., Inc. v. RWM Enters., Inc., 939 F.2d 547 (8th Cir. 1991), cert. denied, 502 U.S. 1097, 112 S.Ct. 1176 (1992) (meeting to discuss tactics for excluding a rival tended to establish a conspiracy).

[70]   See, e.g., Simon N. Whitney, Trade Associations and Industrial Control (1934).

[71]   For a more detailed account, see 6 Antitrust Law ¶¶ 1433–1434 (4th ed. 2017); William E. Kovacic, The Identification and Proof of Horizontal Agreements under the Antitrust Laws, 38 Antitrust Bull. 5 (1993).

Circuit,[72] the plaintiff must show that the actions were contrary to the individual self-interest of the actors, and can be explained as rational behavior only on the premise that they were undertaken in concert.[73] Most courts thus disagree with the conclusion expressed in *Petroleum Products* that "parallel pricing alone" may be sufficient to establish agreement in a highly concentrated market.[74] One would ordinarily expect parallel pricing in such a market, particularly if it is sequential—that is, if each firm is able to observe the prices of others before setting its own price. If prices are quoted simultaneously, as in a sealed bid auction, then identical prices become far more suspicious, depending on the circumstances. For example, a court should have little difficulty inferring an agreement in the circumstances of the *Cement Institute* decision, in which ten of the Institute's members once bid $3.286854 per barrel of cement—that is, supposedly secret bids were identical to the 1/10,000 of one cent.[75]

Price leadership is also more consistent with collusion when it is "perilous"—that is, when reversing a price change is impossible or costly to the presumed leader. In that case, it would not risk a change unless it believed that rivals would follow.[76]

In sum, parallel behavior in a concentrated market may establish an agreement, depending on how transactions in the

---

[72]   Interstate Circuit, Inc. v. United States, 306 U.S. 208, 59 S.Ct. 467 (1939).

[73]   For example, see In re Beef Indus. Antitrust Litig., 713 F.Supp. 971, 974 (N.D.Tex.1988), aff'd, 907 F.2d 510 (5th Cir. 1990):

[a] plaintiff relying on a theory of conscious parallelism must show two things: (1) that the defendants engaged in consciously parallel action, and (2) that this parallel action was contrary to their economic self-interest so as not to amount to a good-faith business judgment. To avoid summary judgment under this theory, Plaintiffs cannot rely on proof of parallel behavior alone. Significant probative evidence of conscious parallelism is required, with some "plus factor" tending to exclude the possibility that the packers' behavior was unilateral.

See also Anderson News, LLC v. American Media, 899 F.3d 87 (2d Cir. 2018), cert. denied, 139 S.Ct. 1375 (2019) (bankrupt wholesaler of single-copy magazines inadequately alleged conspiracy among magazine publishers and distributors to drive it out of business; the conspiracy was economically implausible, because plaintiff did not show how defendants could have benefitted from it; the more likely explanation is that each defendant independently decided that dealing with single-copy magazines was not profitable).

[74]   *Petrol. Prods.*, 906 F.2d at 445 n. 9. Cf. the Ninth Circuit's subsequent decision in Citric Acid Antitrust Litig., 191 F.3d 1090 (9th Cir. 1999), cert. denied, 529 U.S. 1037, 120 S.Ct. 1531 (2000) (parallel pricing standing alone not a sufficient plus factor).

[75]   FTC v. Cement Inst., 333 U.S. 683, 713 & n. 15, 68 S.Ct. 793 (1948). All the bids also offered a 10per barrel discount for payment within 15 days. The Court noted that there were many such situations.

[76]   See 6 Antitrust Law ¶ 1425d (4th ed. 2017); and see Kleen Prods., LLC v. Georgia-Pacific, LLD, 910 F.3d 927, 937–938 (7th Cir. 2018) (finding that the price leadership in this case was not perilous).

market are designed and information is ordered. If the nature of the market requires all prices and terms to be publicized, then no agreement can be inferred. For example, in the passenger airline industry we can assume that (1) price and service information is communicated to customers through shared computer reservation systems, the internet, and public advertising; and (2) large numbers of customers are indifferent to which carrier they choose, provided that price is the same. The same assumptions would generally apply to, say, the retail sale of gasoline. In such cases a firm that fails to follow a price cutter will face immediate loss of market share. As a result, mere parallel behavior does not create an inference of agreement. By contrast, if one or more important terms of sale are negotiated individually and not publicly disclosed, then parallel behavior in the oligopolistic market creates a much stronger presumption of mutual forbearance, from which an "agreement" can be inferred without stretching § 1 requirements unreasonably far.

In addition, parallel pricing decisions that are made simultaneously, excluding the possibility of follow-the-leader behavior, suggest secret collusion. Mere sequential following of prices does not. For example, in its original *Text Messaging* decision, the Seventh Circuit sustained a complaint alleging that parallel changes in prices were simultaneous.[77] However, the district court subsequently gave summary judgment to the defendants when the evidence showed that the price changes were in fact sequential over a period of several months. This time the Seventh Circuit affirmed, concluding that there was no direct evidence of price fixing and the circumstantial evidence was inadequate to support a different inference.[78]

Finally, even invited common action fails to establish an agreement if the actors had perfectly rational reasons for engaging in the practice, whether or not they had agreed with others. The relevant question is whether for each individual a particular act would be profit-maximizing whether or not others did the same thing. For example, in *Interstate Circuit* the distributors were invited to adopt uniform contracts forbidding double features of first run films. An affirmative response would be proof of agreement if it would have been foolish for a distributor to do so unilaterally. For example, if the structure and nature of the market made clear that any distributor who unilaterally eliminated double features would simply lose market share to other distributors who did not, then the conduct was rational only in the presence of an agreement. The affirmative

---

[77]   In re Text Messaging Antitrust Litig., 630 F.3d 622 (7th Cir. 2010).

[78]   In re Text Messaging Antitrust Litig., 782 F.3d 867 (7th Cir. 2015).

responses themselves indicate an understanding that all would do the same thing.

One potentially complex set of situations involve so-called "hub-and-spoke" conspiracies. In a pure hub-and-spoke conspiracy the conspirators communicate with a central organizer, or "hub," but they do not communicate with one another directly. Often the "hub" is a manufacturer or franchisor, while the "spokes" are individual dealers or franchisees. This naturally invites the question whether the arrangement is a horizontal agreement at all, or rather a set of vertical agreements. In the absence of any communication among the "spokes," courts have been inclined toward the vertical agreement interpretation.[79] *Interstate Circuit*[80] is a clear exception. There the "hub," communicated with each "spoke" and each knew about the communications, but they did not communicate with each other.[81] There was no explicit evidence of *either* a horizontal conspiracy or even a set of vertical conspiracies, because the theaters never communicated acceptance of Interstate Circuit's offer, either individually or collectively.

On the other hand, if there is significant communication among the "spokes," as there was in the *Apple* eBooks case, then the courts have little difficulty finding a horizontal agreement.[82] Apple orchestrated a cartel of publishers to collectively impose higher resale prices for ebooks on Amazon, but in the process of forming and carrying out the conspiracy the publishers exchanged numerous emails discussing the terms of their arrangement.

§ 4.5   Reaching Oligopoly Behavior on Less Explicit Evidence of Agreement

This section deals with two different issues that are directed at the same result. The first is the use of the antitrust laws to go after conspicuously parallel and apparently anticompetitive behavior on the basis of slight evidence of an agreement. The second is antitrust's success in going after "facilitating" practices, that may or may not be

---

[79]   E.g., Nexium (Esomeprazole) Antitrust Litig., 42 F.Supp.3d 231, 255 (D.Ma. 2014), aff'd, 842 F.3d 34 (1st Cir. 2016) (there must be "agreement or connection between the spokes") See 6 Antitrust Law ¶ 1402 (4th ed. 2017).

[80]   Interstate Circuit v. United States, 306 U.S. 208 (1939). See also Toys "R" Us, Inc., 126 F.T.C. 415, 574–75 (1998), aff'd, 221 F.3d 928 (7th Cir. 2000) (large toy retailer communicated its wish that toy manufacturers discriminate against big box stores and all followed; affirming FTC's finding of horizontal agreement even though toy manufacturer were not shown to have communicated with one another).

[81]   See Barak Orbach, Hub-and-Spoke Conspiracies, 12 Antitrust Source 1 (Apr 2015).

[82]   United States v. Apple, Inc., 952 F. Supp.2d 638, 706–707 (S.D.N.Y. 2013), aff'd, 791 F.3d 290 (2d Cir. 2015).

the product of an agreement among firms, but which are believed to make collusion or oligopoly behavior more likely to occur. Although the questions are analytically distinct, most decisions that deal with either issue at any length involve both, and their discussion often mixes the two.

4.5a.   Introduction; Incomplete Agreements

In *Interstate Circuit*[83] the Supreme Court relied on circumstantial evidence that the distributor's responses were inconsistent with profit-maximization unless there had been an understanding, or agreement, among the firms. However, in often-quoted dicta the Supreme Court added the following:

> While the District Court's finding of an agreement of the distributors among themselves is supported by the evidence, we think that in the circumstances of this case such agreement * * * was not a prerequisite to an unlawful conspiracy. It was enough that, knowing that concerted action was contemplated and invited, the distributors gave their adherence to the scheme and participated in it.[84]

Whether the Court really meant that an agreement was not required seems unclear. The most reasonable meaning is that a "conspiracy" for antitrust purposes could be inferred from conduct that manifested some, but not all, of the attributes of an agreement.

All contracts are "incomplete," in the sense that they do not specify every contingency that may occur. Even common law courts routinely "filled in the gaps" by completing terms that the parties left unsaid.[85] Of course, most contracts are between vertically related firms—i.e., buyers and sellers. Filling the gaps in a contract among competitors is a somewhat different exercise than filling the gaps in a contract between a buyer and a seller.

Filling in contractual gaps is largely a matter of objective reconstruction from the circumstances. Relatively determinate blanks are filled in while more ambiguous ones are not. For example, the Uniform Commercial Code permits a court to fill in a missing price term with a "reasonable" price, but not a missing quantity term.[86] Those rules makes sense because price can often be

---

[83]   Interstate Circuit, Inc. v. United States, 306 U.S. 208, 59 S.Ct. 467 (1939).

[84]   306 U.S. at 226, 59 S.Ct. at 474.

[85]   A classic example is Carlill v. Carbolic Smoke Ball Co., 1 Q.B. 256 (1893), which held that a printed offer and a silent acceptance constituted an agreement.

[86]   U.C.C. § 2–305(1) (if the price is "not settled" in the contract it will be "a reasonable price at the time for delivery. . . ."). Contrast U.C.C. § 2–201 (a "contract . . . is not enforceable . . . beyond the quantity of goods shown. . . ."). See Jessen Bros. v. Ashland Recreation Ass'n, 204 Neb. 19, 281 N.W.2d 210 (1979) (contract for sod

reconstructed from objective market factors, but quantity typically cannot be. For example, if the price of corn on a given day in late 2020 is $2.30/bu. we can expect that most sales will occur close to that price. Quantity is a different matter. One buyer may take 500 bushels, another 5000, and another 50,000. The court fills the gap, not by looking for the intent of the parties, but rather by asking what a reasonable (i.e., profit-maximizing) buyer and seller would likely have agreed about when bargaining for a good with an objectively identifiable price.

Cartel contracts are likely to be incomplete for the simple reason that they are illegal. While firms go to great lengths to preserve evidence of their legally enforceable agreements, they go to equally great lengths to avoid an evidentiary trail of unlawful ones. Further, when we move from buyer-seller relationships to relationships among competitors, *both* price and quantity can become relatively determinate numbers, particularly if the market contains few sellers. To be sure, the terms are not always as definite as the price term in a contract for the sale of corn on a given day, but they are much more determinate than the missing quantity term in that same agreement. The criteria that courts use to fill the gaps in incomplete buyer-seller contracts could be tailored to apply to competitor agreements and the result would be increased willingness to infer Sherman Act conspiracies from purely objective evidence.

There is one other important difference between buy-sell and cartel agreements. In the former case the purpose of filling in gaps is to enforce the contract, which the court cannot do without reconstructing the terms with a fair degree of confidence. By contrast, in the cartel case the court is seeking to identify an agreement only for the purposes of condemning it. The amount of information one needs to enforce an agreement is considerably greater than the amount one needs to strike it down. The former requires a basis for establishing the precise terms, while the latter requires only a sufficient basis for concluding that an agreement exists. Further, as Judge Posner has put it, the more conducive the market is to collusion, the less evidence a plaintiff need produce to show that collusion is occurring.[87]

---

unenforceable for lack of specific quantity term). See Herbert Hovenkamp, The Antitrust Enterprise: Principle and Execution, ch. 6 (2005).

[87]   High Fructose Corn Syrup Antitrust Litig., 295 F.3d 651, 661 (7th Cir. 2002), cert. denied, 537 U.S. 1188, 123 S.Ct. 1251 (2003) ("More evidence is required the less plausible the charge of collusive conduct."). Accord Flat Glass Antitrust Litig., 385 F.3d 350 (3d Cir. 2004), reh'g denied, 2004 WL 2454008 (3d Cir. 2004).

4.5b.   Challenging Facilitators Established by Agreement

Firms may agree among themselves, either explicitly or tacitly, to engage in certain practices that will make collusion easier. In all such cases it is important to distinguish the agreement to engage in the practice from the agreement to fix prices.[88] Agreements to exchange price information or to standardize products are clearly agreements, and they may facilitate the maintenance of prices at supracompetitive levels. But in and of themselves such agreements are not price-fixing and may be quite pro-competitive.

One of the most obvious of these facilitating agreements is exchanges of price information. Nothing makes monitoring of market prices easier than an agreement that every firm will disclose its sale prices to competitors. Like many suspicious nonprice agreements, however, information exchanges can also make a market perform more competitively. Their relative merits are discussed in the next chapter.

Agreements among competitors to standardize products or terms of sale fall into the same ambiguous category. Such standardization can substantially reduce customer information costs and make the market operate more efficiently; if "number two plywood" or "grade A eggs" mean exactly the same thing to all sellers and buyers in a market, customers can determine what they are buying far more easily and the market will perform more efficiently. However, in a concentrated industry, product standardization can facilitate express or tacit collusion because it enables each firm more effectively to monitor the pricing of another firm. It may make noncooperative oligopoly behavior more successful as well.

Courts have seldom condemned simple product standardization by agreement among competitors.[89] However, they have been very strict about any agreed standardization of price or other transaction terms. For example, in Sugar Institute, Inc. v. United States[90] the Supreme Court condemned a trade association rule that required the Institute members to publicize their prices in advance and forbad deviation from those prices, price discrimination, or giving secret discounts or other price concessions. The industry was highly concentrated, and the rules may have

---

[88]   See id., ¶ 1409.

[89]   But see § 5.4c, on standard setting coupled with refusals to deal; and C-O-Two Fire Equip. Co. v. United States, 197 F.2d 489 (9th Cir.), cert. denied, 344 U.S. 892, 73 S.Ct. 211 (1952) (condemning collusion facilitated by an agreement to manufacture standardized fire extinguishers); see 12 Antitrust Law ¶ 2136b (4th ed. 2019).

[90]   297 U.S. 553, 56 S.Ct. 629 (1936).

permitted sugar manufacturers to achieve cartel-like prices.[91] In
Catalano,[92] the Supreme Court condemned an agreement among
beer wholesalers to eliminate a short term trade credit that many of
them had formerly given to retailers. Under the agreement the
wholesalers would sell only if the buyer paid before or at delivery.
The effect of the agreement was to standardize the price terms and
make a firm's sale prices easier to monitor. For example, a price of
$6.00 per case, payable 180 days after delivery is lower than a price
of $6.00 per case payable immediately upon delivery. The Supreme
Court treated the agreement as little more than a variant of price
fixing and condemned it under the *per se* rule.

The problem with so many facilitators established by agreement
is that, while they may facilitate collusion, they may also make
production or distribution work more efficiently. Information
exchanges, product standardization and testing, agreements creating
markets, regulating them, and standardizing transactions all fall
within this category. They are treated in the subsequent chapter on
joint ventures.

4.5c. "Unilateral" Facilitators; Basing-Point Pricing Schemes

The case for bringing facilitating practices within § 1 of the
Sherman Act becomes more difficult when the facilitators themselves
seem to be unilateral—that is, when there is inadequate evidence
that the firms agreed among each other to use them.

A variety of practices can facilitate collusion, even though the
practices themselves are unilateral. Some of the practices may be
independently efficient, and thus firms may employ them without
regard for their ability to facilitate collusion. For example, industry-
wide vertical integration and resale price maintenance can facilitate
cartel behavior even as they improve the efficiency of a firm's
distribution network.[93] At the same time, they can enable firms to
monitor one another's final output prices. If manufacturers deal with

---

[91] The *Sugar Institute* case revealed a pattern of price leadership much like that
used in the airline industry today. A dominant firm in one area would announce a price
increase well in advance of the effective date. If other firms went along, the increase
would stick. If the other firms did not, it would be rescinded. The Court noted that a
"move," or price increase "takes place only if all refiners follow a similar course. If any
one fails to follow with a like announcement, the others must withdraw their advance,
since sugar is a completely standardized commodity." 297 U.S. at 580, 56 S.Ct. at 634.
"Often, too, the advance [that is, price increase] would be withdrawn because one
refiner would refrain from following the announcement. Except in a few instances, a
decline announcement was followed by all." Ibid.

[92] Catalano, Inc. v. Target Sales, Inc., 446 U.S. 643, 100 S.Ct. 1925 (1980). See
12 Antitrust Law ¶ 2022 (4th ed. 2019).

[93] See generally ch. 11.

large distributors, their sales are likely to be infrequent, covering large amounts of merchandise, and having individually and privately negotiated terms. In such cases both express and tacit collusion will be difficult to maintain. However, if all sales are small, with publicly announced prices and terms, then price cutting will be detected far more quickly.[94] But in any event, today it seems clear that only a small percentage of RPM or vertical nonprice restraints are in fact used to facilitate horizontal conclusion.[95] As a result, proving the vertical restraint in no way establishes a horizontal agreement.

Facilitators of price discrimination are particularly interesting. Price discrimination occurs whenever a seller has two different rates of return on different sales of the same product.[96] Assuming that the lower price sale is competitive, the higher price sale must give the seller some monopoly profits. Persistent price discrimination of a fungible product[97] is inconsistent with competition: customers asked to pay the discriminatorily high price will seek out a different seller, and in a competitive market there will always be a seller willing to make the sale at marginal cost. The existence of persistent price discrimination is therefore evidence that the market is not performing competitively.

Among the most revealing collusion cases involving price discrimination are the delivered pricing cases, particularly those involving basing point pricing. Delivered pricing schemes have been common in industries in which transportation costs are high in proportion to the value of the commodity sold. Such schemes involve a certain amount of price discrimination. As a result, their existence alone may be enough to create an inference of express or tacit collusion. Like information exchanges, agreements to standardize products and terms, or vertical integration, delivered pricing schemes can enable firms to monitor each other's prices and respond to changes more effectively.[98]

Suppose that a single firm sells to three customers located 10, 100 and 400 miles away from the seller. All three buyers place the same value on the product, $100, and the seller sells the product to each of them at that price, which includes delivery. If delivery costs

---

[94]   Likewise, vertical integration by price or territorial restrictions may facilitate cartelization at the *retail* level. See § 11.2b.

[95]   See Pauline M. Ippolito, Resale Price Maintenance: Empirical Evidence from Litigation, 34 J.L. & Econ. 263 (1991).

[96]   See § 14.1.

[97]   On differentiated products, see the discussion of Brand Name Prescription Drugs Antitrust Litig., 186 F.3d 781 (7th Cir. 1999), cert. denied, 528 U.S. 1181, 120 S.Ct. 1220 (2000).

[98]   See 12 Antitrust Law ¶ 2025 (4th ed. 2019).

are proportional to distance and the sale to the most remote buyer is profitable, the sales to the closer buyers will give the seller a monopoly profit. In this case the seller clearly is engaging in price discrimination.

In a perfectly competitive market, the two buyers who were 10 and 100 miles from the seller would have found a seller willing to charge a lower delivered price. Competition tends to drive prices to actual costs and favors the "best placed" or closest seller to any particular buyer, particularly if transportation costs are substantial in relation to the value of the product.

A cartel will often want to eliminate this "placement" competition. If price fixers merely set a price, to which actual freight costs are added, the firms may continue to compete by establishing a proliferation of "shipping points" close to customers. The firms can then cheat on the cartel by billing a lower freight rate from one of these shipping points, even though the shipment actually originated somewhere else. Further, demand in the industry may shift geographically from one period to the next, and the current sales of individual sellers in a competitive market will reflect these cycles. By contrast, most cartels would prefer that market shares of their members be relatively stable from one period to the next.

Finally, complicated shipping tariffs make policing of the cartel very difficult.[99] If every member of a cartel adds actual freight costs to the cartel price in order to produce a delivered price, final output prices will vary considerably from one transaction to the next. For one firm to monitor the prices of other firms in the cartel would be very difficult.

In order to solve all these problems many cartels have not only fixed the price of the commodity itself, but they have also "fixed" the freight rates. One of the most effective mechanisms for eliminating all placement competition and producing uniform delivered prices across the entire cartel is basing point pricing. In basing point pricing systems the sellers identify some central point as the "basing point." All quoted prices then add freight charges measured from the basing point to the buyer's delivery point, even though the product was in fact shipped from somewhere else. For example, under the "Pittsburgh Plus" formula once used in the steel industry, steel mills located across the northeastern and north central United States

---

[99]   This appears to be the explanation for delivered pricing in the *du Pont (Ethyl)* case, 101 F.T.C. 425 (1983), rev'd sub nom. E.I. Du Pont De Nemours & Co. v. FTC, 729 F.2d 128 (2d Cir. 1984). The Commission noted the great difficulty that the participants would have had tracking each other's prices in the absence of such a scheme. 101 F.T.C. at 637.

billed all customers for freight computed from Pittsburgh to the delivery destination.[100] If the price of the steel were fixed, the buyer would receive identical bids for delivered steel. In this way the basing point system facilitates collusion, for each firm finds it fairly easy to track the actual price of steel in the market.[101]

When the evidence indicated an agreement among competitors to engage in basing point pricing, the courts have consistently condemned it.[102] More controversial, however, has been judicial treatment of industry-wide basing point pricing when there is no evidence that the sellers agreed to engage in the practice. In Triangle Conduit and Cable Co. v. FTC[103] the Court upheld the FTC's condemnation of market-wide basing point pricing on two different theories: first, that the firms had agreed with each other to engage in basing point pricing; second, that the mere "concurrent use of a formula" in making delivered price bids, with the knowledge that other firms did the same thing, violated § 5 of the FTC Act. The Court affirmed the FTC's finding of a conspiracy, but also approved the second theory, noting that even absent express agreement,

> each conduit seller knows that each of the other sellers is using the basing point formula; each knows that by using it he will be able to quote identical delivered prices and thus present a condition of matched prices under which purchasers are isolated and deprived of choice among sellers so far as price advantage is concerned * * *. [W]e cannot say that the Commission was wrong in concluding that the individual use of the basing point method as here used does constitute an unfair method of competition.

---

[100]   See United States Steel Corp., 8 F.T.C. 1 (1924); FTC v. Cement Inst., 333 U.S. 683, 714, 68 S.Ct. 793 (1948). For a more detailed economic analysis of basing point pricing see George J. Stigler, The Organization of Industry 147–164 (1983).

[101]   Lastly, basing point pricing schemes can give cartels a mechanism for punishing cheaters: they can make the cheaters' location an involuntary basing point for a fixed period of time. During that period the cheater can compete for sales only by cutting its sale prices or absorbing some of its actual freight costs. See Cement Institute, 333 U.S. at 683, which describes use of this method of discipline.

[102]   Cement Institute, 333 U.S. at 683, condemned basing point pricing under § 5 of the FTC Act. There was no direct evidence of explicit agreement among the firms; however, firms in the industry were notorious for submitting identical competitive bids for projects. The Court held that the Commission could infer a conspiracy, whether "express or implied," from these facts. Basing point pricing has also been condemned as illegal price discrimination under the Robinson-Patman Act. Corn Prods. Ref. Co. v. FTC, 324 U.S. 726, 65 S.Ct. 961 (1945). See 14 Antitrust Law ¶ 2321 (4th ed. 2019).

[103]   168 F.2d 175, 181 (7th Cir. 1948), aff'd sub nom. Clayton Mark & Co. v. FTC, 336 U.S. 956, 69 S.Ct. 888 (1949).

In Boise Cascade Corp. v. FTC[104] the Ninth Circuit called the
Triangle Conduit decision into question, refusing to condemn
industry-wide basing point pricing when there was no evidence of an
agreement among the firms to engage in the practice. The Court
concluded that § 5 of the Federal Trade Commission Act requires the
Commission to show *either* an "overt agreement" among the firms to
engage in basing point pricing or else that the practice "actually had
the effect of fixing or stabilizing prices." The Fifth Circuit condemned
the same practice under § 1 of the Sherman Act, however, by
affirming a jury verdict that the practice did have an effect on prices
and that the plaintiffs had been injured as a result. There was also
evidence of communication among the parties from which the jury
could have inferred an explicit agreement.[105]

4.5d.   Other Facilitators, Including Algorithms; § 5 of Federal Trade Commission Act

The "contract," "combination" or "conspiracy" requirement has
frustrated judicial efforts to use § 1 of the Sherman Act to reach poor
performance in concentrated markets without some evidence of
express collusion. The Federal Trade Commission has tried
repeatedly to take advantage of the broader language of § 5 of the
FTC Act, which condemns "unfair methods of competition," to attack
apparent tacit collusion. That statute's language does not explicitly
require an agreement. Its efforts have not been encouraging. In Ethyl
Corp.[106] the FTC relied on § 5 to condemn several sales practices of
the four firms that manufactured gasoline antiknock compounds. The
practices, all undertaken uniformly but without apparent agreement
among the four firms, included 1) a policy of announcing price
changes 30 days in advance; 2) "most-favored-nation" clauses in sales
contracts, which promised that the buyer would receive the full
benefit of any subsequent price reduction for a certain specified
period; and 3) uniform delivered prices.

The Commission placed great emphasis on the fact that FTCA
§ 5, unlike § 1 of the Sherman Act, does not require proof of
agreement among the firms. If a practice both affects competition
adversely *and* violates the "basic legislative goals of the Sherman
Act," then it could be reached under § 5 even though it might fall
outside the Sherman Act. The Commission evaluated the market and
found all the indicators of tacit collusion: very high concentration and

---

[104]   637 F.2d 573 (9th Cir. 1980).

[105]   In re Plywood Antitrust Litig., 655 F.2d 627, 634 (5th Cir. 1981), cert.
dismissed, 462 U.S. 1125, 103 S.Ct. 3100 (1983).

[106]   *du Pont (Ethyl)*, 101 F.T.C. 425 (1983), rev'd sub nom. E.I. Du Pont De Nemours
& Co. v. FTC, 729 F.2d 128 (2d Cir. 1984).

firms with roughly equal costs; high entry barriers compounded by extensive government regulations; inelastic demand; a generally homogenous and undifferentiated product; and finally, a net rate of return 50% higher than the rate earned by most producers of chemicals.[107]

In such a market any of the alleged practices could have facilitated tacit collusion. The policy of announcing price changes 30 days in advance would enable firms to monitor and respond to the price decisions of the other firms. In this case, two smaller firms in the market generally followed the price leadership of the two larger firms.

Price protection clauses and price matching guarantees are somewhat more ambiguous. In the first of these, the seller retroactively promises the buyer that it will match a competitor's lower price. A matching price guarantee is usually a sellers promise that it will match any advertised price offered by a competitor.

Buyers may think price protection clauses protect *them* from subsequent price reductions that might be given to other firms. If A buys today at a price of $50, and tomorrow the seller sells to B at a price of $45, A will be entitled to a refund of $5. Nonetheless, such clauses are often a sign not of hard customer bargaining but of tacit seller collusion. The clauses effectively make discriminatory price reductions very expensive and easy to detect, and give the cartel a new set of policemen: customers. If the seller attempts to cheat by giving B a $5 reduction in price, A will demand similar treatment under its price protection clause.[108]

Price protection clauses and similar price matching guarantees can operate as cartel facilitators. If A and B agreed that each would match the other's prices, we would have a cartel. But if A and B individually agree with customers that each will match the other's prices, we have two vertical agreements that look superficially pro-competitive, but could have precisely the same anticompetitive result.[109] We sometimes think that the Wal-Marts of the world are doing us a favor by advertising that they will match any competitors' price. In fact, they could simply be making advertised low prices less attractive to competitors. As low price advertising becomes less

---

[107]   On the use of accounting data to infer monopoly profits, see § 3.9c.

[108]   For further explication, see Aaron S. Edlin, Do Guaranteed-Low-Price Policies Guarantee High Prices, and Can Antitrust Rise to the Challenge, 111 Harv. L. Rev. 528 (1997).

[109]   See Joseph J. Simons, Fixing Price With Your Victim: Efficiency and Collusion with Competitor-Based Formula Pricing Clauses, 17 Hofstra L. Rev. 599 (1989).

attractive, it will also become less frequent and the result could be an oligopoly structure with the large "discount" store as price leader.[110]

The Second Circuit was not impressed by any of the Commission's theories of tacit collusion. The court vacated the Commission's decision, expressly refusing to hold that § 5 could be "violated by non-collusive, non-predatory and independent conduct of a non-artificial nature," even when the conduct *results* in a substantial lessening of competition. Rather, the Commission would have to show either "(1) evidence of anticompetitive intent or purpose on the part of the producer charged, or (2) the absence of an independent legitimate business reason for its conduct."[111] The court opined that oligopoly is a market "condition," not a "method" of avoiding competition. This characterization would appear to be a reference to Professor Turner's observation that poor economic performance is inherent in oligopoly, and marginal cost pricing would be irrational. But as § 4.4a notes, the observation ignores the fact that *discriminatory* price cuts, given to some buyers but not others, can undermine oligopoly and restore competitive prices. Defendants have often deceived courts by fly-specking the evidence to show that collusive schemes were not perfect. In fact no scheme, including competitive ones, is perfect.

The court did not rule out any possibility that § 5 could be used in the future to pursue facilitating devices in oligopoly markets. However, it held that the FTC "owes a duty to define the conditions under which conduct claimed to facilitate price uniformity would be unfair," so that firms would be able to predict what they could legally do and what they could not.

A troublesome part of the Second Circuit's reversal is that it failed to consider the limited remedies available to the FTC, which make the social cost of overdeterrence in FTC actions smaller than it would be in cases brought by the Justice Department or private plaintiffs under the Sherman Act. The fact that FTC remedies are both prospective and limited to injunctive relief justifies broader standards of liability under the FTC Act than under the Sherman Act. In this particular case, even if the FTC were wrong and the practices at issue were not intended to facilitate tacit collusion, the social cost of enjoining the practices would not be high, for there was no convincing evidence that the practices were efficiency creating either. In a concentrated market, easily conducive to collusion, a little overdeterrence in cases involving ambiguous practices can be a good thing, provided that the practices have little obvious social value.

---

[110]   See 6 Antitrust Law ¶ 1435 (4th ed. 2017).

[111]   E.I. Du Pont De Nemours & Co. v. FTC, 729 F.2d 128, 139 (2d Cir. 1984).

As noted earlier,[112] one way to address this problem could be for the FTC to produce Guidelines describing how its jurisdiction over "unfair methods of competition" could be extended to cartel-like behavior where Sherman Act agreement requirements cannot be met. Courts such as those in *Ethyl* and *Kellogg*, which were reluctant to step too far beyond Sherman Act case law, might be more willing if they were following positions that were not drafted with particular litigation in mind.

The use of computerized pricing algorithms has provoked a great deal of recent debate but so far not much antitrust litigation. An algorithm is nothing more than a set of instructions, often digital, to some decision maker to respond in a certain way to a specified event. At that level of generality even a computerized algorithm can cover a large host of things that have nothing to do with antitrust policy. But many do. Suppose, for example, that an online seller programs its computer to search competitors' prices and continuously match the lowest (or highest) discovered price; or to meet any advertised term. More complex algorithms might play economic games with price matching, even to the point of "punishing" rivals for certain behaviors.[113]

Clearly, an agreement among a group of firms to use the same algorithm could operate as nothing more than a mechanism for naked price fixing, and should be treated accordingly.[114] Even agreed upon algorithms can be economically beneficial in certain joint ventures, however. For example, UBER uses a computer algorithm that continuously monitors the supply and demand for drivers and potential riders and adjusts the price accordingly. As a result, an UBER ride costs more during rush hour when demand is high.[115]

---

[112]   See § 4.4b.

[113]   See Ariel Ezrachi and Maurice E. Stucke, Virtual Competition: The Promise and Perils of the Algorithm-Driven Economy (2016); Ai Deng, What Do we Know About Algorithmic Tacit Colusion 33 Antitrust (fall 2018); Anita Banicevic, et al, Algorithms: Challenges and Opportunities for Antitrust Compliance (ABA Antitrust Section Fall, 2018).

[114]   In 2015 the Antitrust Division obtained a criminal indictment and plea agreement against wall poster retailers who sold through Amazon Marketplace and agreed to use the same algorithm to set prices. "According to the charge, [The] co-conspirators discussed the prices of certain posters sold in the United States through Amazon Marketplace and agreed to adopt specific pricing algorithms for the sale of certain posters, with the goal of offering online shoppers the same price for the same product and coordinating changes to their respective prices. See https://www.justice.gov/opa/pr/e-commerce-exec-and-online-retailer-charged-price-fixing-wall-posters.

[115]   See Salil K. Mehra, Antitrust and the Robo-Seller: Competition in the Time of Algorithms, 100 Minn. L. Rev. 1323, 1323–1324 (2016). See also Meyer v. Kalanick, 174 F.Supp.3d 817 (S.D.N.Y. 2016) (dubious conclusion that UBER's algorithm might constitute per se unlawful antitrust conspiracy).

If each firm makes a unilateral decision whether or not to employ an algorithm and which one to employ, then the antitrust law is currently not much further along than it is with respect to conscious parallelism and tacit collusion generally. Nevertheless, algorithms can quickly become another important way that firms in concentrated industries reduce the costs of monitoring and coordinating prices without the need to form a traditional agreement. This is another area where § 5 of the FTC Act could be of use.

4.5e. Motions to Dismiss and Summary Judgment in Conspiracy Cases; Courts' General Adherence to Traditional Conspiracy Requirements

In *Twombly* the Supreme Court considerably heightened the pleading requirements in actions under § 1 of the Sherman Act, although *Twombly* now applies to nonantitrust actions in the federal courts as well.[116] The Court held that a conspiracy could not be inferred from allegations that for several years the regional telephone companies had the legal right to enter one another's geographic territories but had declined to do so. In addition was an alleged statement from one corporate officer to the effect that competitive entry would not have been good for business.

Clearly plaintiffs claiming antitrust conspiracies must do more than allege an agreement with a couple of assertions about when and where. They must also provide sufficient specificity to create a "plausible" inference of concerted as opposed to independent action. The Court was concerned about the considerable cost of antitrust discovery, particularly in cases involving allegations of far-flung, ambiguously defined conspiracies. *Twombly* has led to dozens of dismissals of antitrust complaints that were found to be too thin under its standards.[117] At the same time, there is a growing recognition that *Twombly* can be unduly harsh on plaintiffs when the important evidence of conspiracy is controlled by the defendants. In

---

[116]   Bell Atlantic Corp. v. Twombly, 550 U.S. 544, 127 S.Ct. 1955 (2007), See also Ashcroft v. Iqbal, 556 U.S. 662, 129 S.Ct. 1937 (2009) (extending Twombly to nonantitrust cases).

[117]   For the numerous decisions, see 2A Antitrust Law ¶ 307 (4th ed. 2014). For critiques see Herbert Hovenkamp, The Pleading Problem in Antitrust Cases and Beyond, 95 Iowa L.Rev. Bull. 55 (2010); Adam N. Steinman, The Pleading Problem, 62 Stan.L.Rev. 1293 (2010) ("potential to upend civil litigation as we know it"); Kevin M. Clermont & Stephen C. Yeazell, Inventing Tests, Destablizing Systems, 95 Iowa L. Rev. 821 (2010) (similar); Richard A. Epstein, Bell Atlantic v. Twombly: How Motions to Dismiss Become (Disguised) Summary Judgments, 25 Wash. U. J.L. & Pol'y 61 (2007); Scott Dodson, New Pleading, New Discovery, 109 Mich.L.Rev. 53 (2010).

that case perhaps plaintiffs who have alleged all they can should have at least limited discovery on the agreement issue.[118]

Already twenty years earlier the Supreme Court had applied much stricter standards for summary judgment in antitrust conspiracy cases in its *Matsushita* decision.[119] *Matsushita* has had a tremendous influence on federal litigation, and it ranks as the third most cited Supreme Court decision of all time.[120] In fact, in part as a result of *Matsushita* as well as *Twombly* antitrust trials have become relatively infrequent.[121]

§ 4.6   Intraenterprise Conspiracy

For a half century the courts were plagued by questions about whether firms related by ownership, such as a parent and its wholly owned subsidiary, can "conspire" within the meaning of the Sherman Act.[122] In Copperweld Corp. v. Independence Tube Corp. the Supreme Court gave a definite answer, at least with respect to one version of the question: a parent and its wholly owned but separately incorporated subsidiary should be treated as a single firm; they cannot be considered "conspiring entities" for the purposes of § 1.[123] The Court concluded that just as the "officers of a single firm" are not separate economic actors for the purposes of § 1 of the Sherman Act, so too a parent and its wholly owned subsidiary "have a complete unity of interest."[124] A corporation's decision whether to create an unincorporated division or an incorporated subsidiary turns almost entirely on tax consequences or questions of law unrelated to competition. A firm cannot enhance its market power simply by separately incorporating a division.

The basic question exposes a tension between the law of § 1 conspiracies and the law of monopolization under § 2. Antitrust is generally more hostile to inter-firm agreements than to alleged

---

[118]   See, e.g., Evergreen Partnering Group, Inc. v. Pactiv Corp., 720 F.3d 33 (1st Cir. 2013).

[119]   Matsushita Elec. Indus. Co. v. Zenith Radio Corp., 475 U.S. 574, 106 S.Ct. 1348 (1986).

[120]   See Steinman, The Pleading Problem, *supra* at 1357.

[121]   On the impact of Matsushita, see § 16.8b. For a fuller discussion of decisions, see 2A Antitrust Law ¶ 308 (4th ed. 2014).

[122]   For example, United States v. Yellow Cab Co., 332 U.S. 218, 67 S.Ct. 1560 (1947); Kiefer-Stewart Co. v. Joseph E. Seagram & Sons, 340 U.S. 211, 71 S.Ct. 259 (1951); Timken Roller Bearing Co. v. United States, 341 U.S. 593, 71 S.Ct. 971 (1951); Perma Life Mufflers v. Int'l Parts Corp., 392 U.S. 134, 88 S.Ct. 1981 (1968). In each case, the Court used broad dicta stating approval of an intra-enterprise conspiracy doctrine, but in each there were alternate grounds for the decision. See 6 Antitrust Law ¶ 1463 (4th ed. 2017).

[123]   467 U.S. 752, 104 S.Ct. 2731 (1984).

[124]   467 U.S. at 771, 104 S.Ct. at 2741–42.

exclusionary practices by the single firm. But this extra deterrence gives plaintiffs an incentive to try to turn single-firm conduct into a conspiracy or combination. If Kodak's practice can be characterized as a conspiracy between its president and vice president; or if General Motors' policies can be characterized as a conspiracy among Chevrolet and Buick (both wholly owned subsidiaries), then the plaintiff can take advantage of § 1's more expansive reach. He might even be able to turn price setting by the single firm, a completely legal act, into a *per se* illegal price fixing conspiracy.

In light of these possibilities, the *Copperweld* doctrine is clearly important to the rational administration of the antitrust laws. The question is how far to push the point. When the firm is unmistakably a single profit-maximizing entity and has always been so, it makes no sense to find a Sherman Act "conspiracy" among any of its personnel, divisions, subsidiaries or other subordinate organizations. But the rationale of *Copperweld* becomes more strained in two different circumstances: (a) where ownership is less than completely unified; and (b) where one or more agents of the firm has a separate profit-making interest that is different than the interests of the principal firm.

Suppose that a parent company has an ownership interest in two subsidiaries, but the interest is less than 100%. The two extremes seem rather easy. If the parent owns a controlling interest in each subsidiary and effectively makes all of their decisions, then the firms should be treated as part of a single entity and *Copperweld* should apply. By contrast, if the "parent" owns a trivially small share in one or both subsidiaries, and has little legal or practical influence on their decision-making, then the subsidiaries are separate profit-maximizing entities, responsible to largely different sets of stockholders. *Copperweld* should not apply.

One helpful way to think about the problem is to look back at the analysis of cartel cheating, discussed in § 4.1. Cartels fail to behave like single profit-maximizing entities, because individual members have both the inclination and the power to cheat on the agreement by making secret price concessions. Although cheating benefits the cheater, it injures the cartel as a whole. If these same incentives to cheat remain when a parent and, say, a partially owned subsidiary jointly commit themselves to a policy, then presumptively they are independent actors with conspiratorial capacity. In the case of a wholly owned subsidiary such an incentive to cheat should ordinarily not be present, for the subsidiary's ledger sheet is simply a page of the parent's ledger; any additional profits that the subsidiary makes by cheating would be more than offset by losses that accrued to the parent, and *all* relevant owners would treat that as a loss.[125]

By contrast, when the subsidiary is only partially owned there may be a divergence of interest among the owners. Those owners who are able to control the decisions of one subsidiary may be able to profit by cheating on the agreement. This analysis suggests that legal control should be decisive against conspiratorial capacity. If a controlling interest of alleged cartel members is held by common owners, then the firm will already behave as a single profit-maximizing entity absent the challenged agreement. Conspiratorial capacity is lacking.

In its *American Needle* decision the Supreme Court looked at the obverse of the *Copperweld* issue—in this case at a group of entities that were in fact separately owned but whose licensing practices were tightly controlled by a central organization.[126] The Court unanimously held that a decision by the National Football League to refuse to license the intellectual property of individual NFL teams, who were its members, should be treated as an agreement among the teams, not as the unilateral conduct of the NFL. However, the Court also held that the legality of this act, while concerted, should be assessed under the rule of reason.[127] The NFL is itself an unincorporated association whose membership includes 32 separately owned and separately incorporated football teams. Each team owns its own intellectual property rights, primarily in trademarks covering their names, colors and insignia. Prior to 1963 the individual teams had licensed these rights individually, often to outside manufacturers for use on authorized clothing such as caps and jerseys. In that year the NFL created National Football League Properties (NFLP) as a common entity to assist the teams in developing and marketing their IP rights. During that time NFLP granted numerous nonexclusive licenses to various manufacturers, including the plaintiff American Needle. In 2000, however, it began to adopt a policy of licensing exclusively and granted Reebok, a

---

[125]   However, the suggestion may not work if the managers of individual subsidiaries are not profit-maximizers. For example, if they are awarded on the basis of sales or output, they may do things that increase the sale or output of their own subsidiary while injuring the firm as a whole. Likewise, if their actions are evaluated only with respect to their effect on the subsidiary's profits, rather than the profits of the parent, the subsidiary's actions may be inconsistent with the parent's interests.

[126]   A related but distinguishable issue can arise when multiple large shareholders, such as fund managers, own shares in the same stock and may be in a position to facilitate cartel-like behavior among the companies. See Fiona Scott Morton & Herbert Hovenkamp, Horizontal Shareholding and Antitrust Policy, 127 Yale L.J. 2026 (2018).

[127]   American Needle, Inc. v. National Football League, 560 U.S. 183, 130 S.Ct. 2201 (2010). On the rule of reason for joint venture conduct, see § 5.6.

manufacturer in competition with the plaintiff, an exclusive license to manufacture NFL logoed headware for a ten year period. This contract was not only exclusive as to Reebok, it also covered the IP rights to all of the NFL teams.

The exclusivity provision in that contract, which ousted American Needle from the manufacturing of licensed, NFL logoed headware, provoked the lawsuit. American Needle alleged that the exclusivity provision should be treated as a concerted refusal to deal under § 1 of the Sherman Act, given that the NFL team members whose individual IP rights were being licensed were all separately owned corporate entities. The district court granted the NFL summary judgment on the conspiracy issue, holding that the teams had "so integrated their operations" with respect to this facet of their conduct that they should be "deemed a single entity rather than joint venture. . . ."[128] The Seventh Circuit affirmed, following its own precedent.[129] As the Supreme Court characterized the Seventh Circuit's opinion, it "discounted the significance of potential competition among the teams regarding the use of their intellectual property" because the teams "can function only as one source of economic power when collectively producing NFL football."[130]

The Court noted that not every agreement between two individuals should be counted as a conspiracy. Rather, the defining characteristic of conspiracy is that the general organization controls the separate or potential separate business of the individual members. Thus the important thing in this case was not that the shareholders in NFL Properties were independent teams, but rather than NFL Properties controlled the separate business interests of the individual teams in their own trademarks. That is, the more important question is not who controls, but rather who *is* *controlled*.[131] The specific question the Court asked is whether "the agreement "deprives the marketplace of independent centers of

---

[128]   American Needle, Inc. v. New Orleans La. Saints, 496 F.Supp.2d 941, 943 (N.D. Ill. 2007).

[129]   538 F.3d 736, 741 (7th Cir. 2008), rev'd, 560 U.S. 183 (2010). The Supreme Court did not cite Chicago Professional Sports Ltd. Partnership v. NBA, 95 F.3d 593 (7th Cir. 1996), which had established the single entity status for a similar professional sports organization in Seventh Circuit law. However, the facts differed, as we discuss later. See 7 Antitrust Law ¶ 1478d3 (4th ed. 2017).

[130]   *American Needle*, 130 S.Ct. at 2208, quoting the Seventh Circuit's opinion, 538 F.3d at 742–743.

[131]   See Christopher Leslie & Herbert Hovenkamp, The Firm as Cartel Manager, 64 Vand.L.Rev. 813 (2011).

decisionmaking," and therefore of "diversity of entrepreneurial interests" and "thus of actual or potential competition."[132]

As the court observed, "Agreements made within a firm can constitute concerted action covered by § 1 when the parties to the agreement act on interests separate from those of the firm itself." In such cases the intra firm agreement "may simply be a formalistic shell for ongoing concerted action."[133] In this case,

> decisions by the NFLP regarding the teams' separately owned intellectual property constitute concerted action. Thirty-two teams operating independently through the vehicle of the NFLP are not like the components of a single firm that act to maximize the firm's profits. The teams remain separately controlled, potential competitors with economic interests that are distinct from NFLP's financial well-being. Unlike typical decisions by corporate shareholders, NFLP licensing decisions effectively require the assent of more than a mere majority of shareholders. And each team's decision reflects not only an interest in NFLP's profits but also an interest in the team's individual profits.[134]

Indeed, "If the fact that potential competitors shared in profits or losses from a venture meant that the venture was immune from § 1, then any cartel "could evade the antitrust law simply by creating a 'joint venture' to serve as the exclusive seller of their competing products."[135]

Finally, the Court concluded that while the NFL's conduct satisfied § 1's agreement requirement it should be addressed under the rule of reason. "When 'restraints on competition are essential if the product is to be available at all,' *per se* rules of illegality are inapplicable, and instead the restraint must be judged according to

---

[132] *American Needle*, 130 S.Ct. at 2212. This makes reorganization and transfer of decision making power to participants a promising remedy against platform monopoly. See Herbert Hovenkamp, Antitrust and Platform Monopoly, 130 Yale L.J. ___ (2021) (forthcoming).

[133] Id. at 2215, citing United States v. Topco Associates, Inc., 405 U.S. 596, 609, 92 S.Ct. 1126 (1972); United States v. Sealy, Inc., 388 U.S. 350, 352–354, 87 S.Ct. 1847 (1967). On this point, see Christopher Leslie and Herbert Hovenkamp, The Firm as Cartel Manager, 64 Vand. L.Rev. 813 (2011). See also Laumann v. National Hockey League, 907 F.Supp.2d 465 (S.D.N.Y. 2012) (following American Needle).

[134] American Needle, 130 S.Ct. at 2215, citing Herbert Hovenkamp, Exclusive Joint Ventures and Antitrust Policy, 1995 Colum. Bus. L. Rev. 1, 52–61 (1995).

[135] American Needle, 130 S.Ct. 2215, quoting Major League Baseball Properties, Inc. v. Salvino, Inc., 542 F.3d 290, 335 (2d Cir. 2008).

the flexible Rule of Reason."[136] The Court found that "other features of the NFL" might serve to save such agreements from antitrust attack, even though they do not justify treating it as a single entity. However, it remanded for the lower courts to deal with what factors should go into the rule of reason determination.

When does finding multilateral as opposed to unilateral conduct make a difference? The Sherman Act case law as historically developed makes two important distinctions. *First*, exclusionary conduct, or conduct that is thought to be anticompetitive because it excludes rivals from the market, may be assessed under a different standard depending on whether it is unilateral or multilateral. The most extreme case is the simple refusal to deal, which is very close to per se lawful when the conduct is "unilateral," even by a monopolist,[137] and particularly in a case such as this one where American Needle and the NFL are not even competitors.[138] It can be per se unlawful, however, if the refusal is characterized as a naked boycott. *American Needle* was not such a case; the challenged conduct was an output contract, akin to exclusive dealing. *Second*, the historical concern of § 1 of the Sherman Act is collusion, or coordinated reductions in output that result in higher prices for consumers. Once again, a "naked" cartel is unlawful per se. At the other extreme, however, under United States a law a monopolist may set any price and output that it pleases, so its own unilateral price increase is legal per se. A single entity conclusion in *American Needle* would have given the teams free reign to engage in collusion while having relatively little impact on exclusionary practices.

Respecting collusion, a finding of separate entities enables us to pursue harmful collusive behavior while a single entity finding makes an output reduction in and of itself unreachable. We should not lose sight of the fact that the property interests in *American Needle* were team trademarks, a product that, unlike a jointly developed patent, is by nature exclusive to each team. There is no obvious reason why a group of football teams should be permitted to cartelize the licensing of their marks any more than a group of competing restaurants should be, and if a procompetitive rationale should emerge, the rule of reason should be quite sufficient to handle it.

---

[136]   American Needle, 130 S.Ct. at 2216, quoting NCAA, 468 U.S. at 101, 117, 104 S.Ct. 2948.

[137]   See, e.g., Verizon Communications, Inc. v. Law Offices of Curtis V. Trinko, LLP, 540 U.S. 398, 124 S.Ct. 872 (2004); and see 3B Phillip E. Areeda & Herbert Hovenkamp, Antitrust Law ¶¶ 771–774 (4th ed. 2015).

[138]   Courts routinely deny standing to noncompetitors in unilateral refusal to deal cases. See ¶ 774d.

Chapter 5

JOINT VENTURES OF COMPETITORS, CONCERTED REFUSALS, PATENT LICENSING, AND THE RULE OF REASON

Table of Sections

---

§ 5.1 Introduction: Naked and Ancillary Agreements Among Competitors

Agreements among competitors are not necessarily monopolistic or harmful to consumers. An agreement can enable a group of firms to carry on an activity at a more efficient scale, reduce information or transaction costs, or eliminate free rider problems. Antitrust policy must distinguish those agreements that pose significant anticompetitive threats from those that do not.

One of antitrust's more difficult tasks is to evaluate the relevant economic costs and benefits of the wide variety of agreements among competitors. Further, antitrust must be able to do this by means that are both relatively inexpensive and tolerably accurate. In a world of perfect and costless information, we could learn everything there is to know about a restraint before deciding whether to condemn it. But the actual world is full of ambiguities, and obtaining reliable information is typically costly.

The most important shortcut is the (rough) classification of restraints that determines the kind and amount of proof that is necessary for illegality, and the kinds of defenses that are permitted.[1] At one extreme, a "naked" restraint is one that is thought to have little potential for social benefit, and thus can be condemned under a "*per se*" rule, which requires little or no inquiry into market power or actual anticompetitive effects. At the other extreme, an "ancillary" restraint is one that arguably serves a legitimate and socially beneficial purpose. Such restraints are analyzed under a "rule of reason," which means that they can be condemned only after a relatively elaborate inquiry into power and likely anticompetitive effects. Further, a broader range of defenses are considered. One of the most important items on the antitrust agenda today is to devise more manageable approaches to the rule of reason that can ease the plaintiff's burden and in the process require the defendant to be more forthcoming about its defenses.

The widespread application of the *per se* rule to price-fixing agreements has often obscured the underlying complexities of joint arrangements involving competitors. For example, it is not generally a defense to a price fixing charge that the cartel members did not hold enough market power to reduce output profitably. If a town contains ten similar grocers, and three of them jointly run a newspaper advertisement quoting retail prices, the arrangement would reduce advertising costs for each of the three. Furthermore, three grocers out of ten would find it difficult to fix prices. Customers would buy from the other seven. The inference that the arrangement reduces costs is strong, while the inference of anticompetitive price fixing seems weak. Nevertheless, a court is likely to hold that the *per se* rule prevents it from considering both the argument that the defendants had no market power and that their agreement produced cost reductions that benefit consumers.[2]

---

1   See 11 Antitrust Law ¶¶ 1910–1912 (4th ed. 2018).

2   See, for example, United States v. Pittsburgh Area Pontiac Dealers, 1978–2 Trade Cas. ¶ 62,233, 1978 WL 1398 (W.D.Pa.1978) (consent decree prohibiting defendants from "adopting, participating in or adhering to any plan, practice or

5.1a. Distinguishing Naked from Ancillary Restraints; Question of Law

A restraint is "naked" if it is formed with the objectively intended purpose or likely effect of increasing price or decreasing output in the short run, with output measured by quantity or quality.[3] By contrast, a restraint is ancillary if its objectively intended purpose or likely effect is lower prices or increased output.[4] A useful way to determine whether a restraint is naked or ancillary is to listen to the proffered explanation and then ask: Would this restraint work if the participants collectively held a nondominant position in the market? For example, suppose that the only five physicians in town jointly purchase expensive radiological equipment and operate it as a joint venture. When this basic venture is challenged as facilitating price fixing, they answer that the fixed costs of this equipment is very high and one set of it is sufficient for all five physicians. At that point, the antitrust decision maker might consider whether this explanation would work if the market contained 100 physicians and these five had purchased the same equipment. The answer is clearly yes. Cost reduction is profitable even in a highly competitive market, and these five physicians could profitably share such equipment in the same way that two farmers might share an infrequently used machine or several firms might jointly set up a specialized firm to dispose of their hazardous waste. To be sure, the physicians might be lying about their reasons, or we might ultimately conclude that the threat of price fixing outweighed any efficiency gains from joint provision. But the physicians have at least made a prima facie claim for rule of reason treatment.

By contrast, consider the agreement at issue in the *Engineers* case, where members of a professional association of consulting engineers agreed not to bid competitively for jobs and would not even discuss fees until after they had been selected.[5] Their offered rationale was that competitive bidding would force engineers to cut corners because the resulting prices would be too low to enable them to do an adequate job. Now ask yourself, suppose that five New York City engineers refused to take competitive bids while NYC's

---

program, the purpose or effect of which is to advertise the sale price of a Pontiac automobile or fix the advertised price of a Pontiac automobile. . . .").

[3] On the meaning of relevant "output," see 11 Antitrust Law ¶ 1901d (4th ed. 2018).

[4] See Polk Brothers v. Forest City Enters., 776 F.2d 185, 190 (7th Cir. 1985) ("The reason for distinguishing between 'ancillary' and 'naked' restraints is to determine whether the agreement is part of a cooperative venture with prospects for increasing output. If it is, it should not be condemned per se.").

[5] National Society of Professional Engineers v. United States, 435 U.S. 679, 98 S.Ct. 1355 (1978).

remaining 2000 engineers did. Clearly, the restraint would not work. The agreement was necessary in the first place only because a significant number of customers *wanted* engineers to bid competitively. Further, the proffered justification admitted that prices would be higher under the rule than without it. Thus the engineers' restraint was naked.

In the *California Dental* case a dental association defended its limitations on dentists' advertising by arguing that they were necessary to prevent misleading or deceptive claims.[6] But the limitations were so severe that they effectively prohibited almost any price advertising at all, and virtually all quality claims. The claim that advertising restrictions reduce deception suggests rule of reason treatment, because even a trade association without market power could profit by guaranteeing nondeceptive advertising, thus raising consumer confidence. By contrast, the four dissenters saw the restraint as likely to eliminate all or most price advertising altogether. *That* restraint would be naked: a group of firms lacking power could not profit by agreeing not to advertise their prices or services, assuming that their rivals did advertise and consumers valued advertising.

While the question whether a restraint is naked or ancillary is a mixed one of law and fact, the question whether the per se rule or the rule of reason applies is clearly one of law.[7] The premise of the per se rule is that *judicial* experience with a certain class of restraints justifies more expedited treatment.[8] Jurors lack not only judicial experience, but typically have no experience at all in the matter. Further, the source material to which a court looks in determining the rule to be applied is prior opinions, mainly from the Supreme Court but also from the lower federal courts, making the question inappropriate for the jury.

5.1b.   Why Multilateral Activity Deserves Closer Antitrust Scrutiny[9]

Under the antitrust laws unilateral conduct receives the lowest level of antitrust scrutiny. Purely unilateral actions are unlawful only if they fall into the general classifications of monopolization or

---

6   California Dental Assn. v. FTC, 526 U.S. 756, 119 S.Ct. 1604 (1999). See 7 Antitrust Law ¶ 1511e (4th ed. 2017).

7   See Arizona v. Maricopa County Medical Society, 457 U.S. 332, 337 n. 3, 102 S.Ct. 2466 (1982).

8   See National Collegiate Athletic Association v. Board of Regents (*NCAA*), 468 U.S. 85, 100–101, 104 S.Ct. 2948 (1984) ("judicial experience" determines when per se rule should be applied).

9   See 11 Antitrust Law ¶¶ 1902b, 1903 (4th ed. 2018); and 13 id. at ¶ 2221d (4th ed. 2019).

attempt to monopolize, and both the conduct and the power requirements are quite severe.[10] Occasionally someone argues that the level of antitrust scrutiny given to joint ventures should be no higher than that given to single firms.[11] According to this argument, stricter scrutiny will condemn or at least put a chill on joint activity that is on balance procompetitive but that an antitrust court might not sufficiently understand.

But there are many good reasons for closer antitrust scrutiny of joint activity. *First*, of course, is the structure of the Sherman Act. Section 1 condemns any agreement of competitors that is in "restraint of trade," while § 2 condemns unilateral conduct only when it "monopolizes" or threatens to do so. While these statutory terms are hardly self-defining, a restraint of trade both historically and in the modern era can amount to very much less than a monopoly.

Second, the economic arguments for closer scrutiny of joint activity than of unilateral activity are powerful. The participants in joint ventures are private actors seeking private gains. The gains from joint ventures come from two sources: efficiency gains, which result from reduced costs or improved products; and market power gains, which result from the fact that the venture has sufficient power to cause market wide output reductions and price increases. One important reason for looking more closely at joint activity is that agreements creating significant market power can be formed very quickly. Most firms do not become monopolists overnight. For a single firm to acquire monopoly power ordinarily takes many years of innovation and aggressive production and marketing. Rivals can generally be expected to resist a single firm's attempts to dominate its market. Although monopolies can be created by anticompetitive acts, most such attempts are unsuccessful. It is usually very difficult for a nondominant firm to become dominant *simply* by doing anticompetitive things. In most cases such firms also have superior products or lower costs than their rivals, at least during the period when their monopoly is developing.

In sharp contrast, monopoly power can be created by agreement in a very short time and with little resistance. All it takes is firms who collectively dominate a market and agree to do something jointly. Resistance is much less because the agreement creates market power by bringing firms *into* the venture rather than excluding them from the market. As a result, *either* the opportunity

---

[10]   See generally Chs. 6–8.

[11]   See, e.g., Howard H. Chang, David S. Evans & Richard Schmalensee, Some Economic Principles for Guiding Antitrust Policy Towards Joint Ventures, 1998 Colum. Bus. L. Rev. 223.

to reduce costs or the opportunity to exercise market power can explain the formation of a joint venture. Without conducting any analysis it is hard to say which reason dominates.

A *third* reason for applying a more aggressive antitrust standard to joint activity than unilateral conduct harkens back to the "restraint of trade" standard stated in § 1 of the Sherman Act. Conduct restrains trade when it results in lower market output—measured by quantity or quality—and thus higher prices than competition would produce. By contrast, efficient conduct results in higher output and thus lower prices. Antitrust tries to determine the classification in which a particular venture rule belongs. By contrast, the antitrust laws do not recognize an offense of merely "being a monopoly." A firm with monopoly power is free to set its monopoly price, and is thus also free to reduce its output accordingly. Because most dominant firms are the result of either historical accident or a long period of growth resulting from efficiency, we ordinarily leave the dominant firm alone as long as it does not engage in anticompetitive exclusionary practices designed to perpetuate or strengthen its monopoly position. But the joint venture enjoys no such presumption. We permit competitors to join together *only* because we expect the result to be a better product, higher output, or lower prices. If they cannot produce these results then there is little reason to tolerate them as long as the threat to competition is significant. In sum, the mere exercise of market power by means of an output reduction or price increase is lawful for the monopolist, but appropriately unlawful for the joint venture.

A *fourth* reason for applying a different standard to joint ventures has to do with courts' ability to fashion appropriate relief.[12] Judicial relief ordering a monopolist to behave competitively threatens to turn that firm into a regulated utility. By contrast, judicial relief against a joint venture typically involves little more than an injunction against the harmful conduct. Consider a single pair of examples in two different contexts, price fixing and refusal to deal. American Express is a single firm that issues a "unitary" general purpose credit card. By contrast, Visa, Inc., which issues a competing general purpose credit card, was historically a joint venture of some 6000 banks and other financial institutions. Suppose that in different courts these two organizations are accused of two different things and found guilty: (1) fixing supracompetitive consumer interest rates and (2) refusing to share their card processing facilities with a rival card issuer.

---

[12]   See 11 Antitrust Law ¶ 1903 (4th ed. 2018).

On the interest rate claim, an injunction against American Express would not be able simply to order AmEx to set a "competitive" interest rate. Rather, it would have to develop some criteria by which the competitive interest rate is determined, and this rate might change as markets change. An interest rate order directed against a single firm effectively regulates its prices—an activity for which federal courts are not well suited and which in any event seems quite contrary to the general antitrust goal of facilitating competition rather than regulation. By contrast, an interest rate injunction against the Visa venture requires no more than is required in any cartel case: an order prohibiting the Visa members from fixing an interest rate. After that, competition among the 6000 Visa issuing banks would probably produce the appropriate rate. Thus, for example, a court order forbidding the NCAA from fixing the maximum price of basketball coaches need do no more than enjoin the fix, letting competition determine the proper salaries.[13] By contrast, assuming that General Motors had market power in the hiring of automotive engineers, an antitrust decree against allegedly low salaries would have to substitute the judgment of the court for the judgment of the market about what appropriate salaries should be.

Largely the same thing applies to the refusal to deal claim. Suppose that a court were to order AmEx to share its card processing facilities with a rival. Whatever one thinks of the wisdom of such relief, granting it requires a significant regulatory effort. The price of sharing and all of the numerous terms will have to be set, just as they would be for a regulated utility required to interconnect with a rival. By contrast, the refusal-to-deal claim in the Visa case arises from a joint venture rule forbidding member banks from issuing a competing card. A judicial decree need not "force" sharing at all; it need only enjoin enforcement of the rule. After that, competition among the 6000 banks, who are now free to issue a competitor's card if they wish, will determine whether and how many rivals' cards will be distributed through banks.[14]

In sum, antitrust relief against multilateral activity is or can be made to be consistent with the general antitrust goal of permitting competitive markets. This does not mean that such relief is always appropriate, but it does suggest that antitrust solutions can be

---

[13]   Law v. NCAA, 134 F.3d 1010 (10th Cir.), cert. denied, 525 U.S. 822, 119 S.Ct. 65 (1998).

[14]   See United States v. VISA U.S.A., Inc., 344 F.3d 229 (2d Cir. 2003), cert. denied, 543 U.S. 811, 125 S.Ct. 45 (2004), which approved such an order.

brought to bear more effectively against multilateral than unilateral conduct.

5.1c.   Partial Condemnation; Less Restrictive Alternatives

Some so-called "joint ventures" are nothing more than fronts for naked restraints.[15] In such cases the courts can condemn them with confidence that they are not disturbing socially valuable relationships. But often the defendants' overall arrangement or venture is clearly efficient or harmless and only one particular rule seems offensive. Further, a court order forbidding enforcement of the anticompetitive rule will not necessarily impair the operation of the venture. For example, courts have condemned NCAA rules that both limited the number of times an NCAA football team could have its games televised[16] and that fixed the maximum salaries of certain basketball coaches.[17] However, no one suggested that the antitrust laws required that the NCAA athletic joint venture of more than 1200 colleges be dissolved. Likewise, although courts have condemned the engineers' ban on competitive bidding,[18] the AMA's professional rules excluding chiropractors,[19] and the Indiana Federation of Dentists' collective refusal to submit x-ray data to an insurer,[20] none of these actions dissolved the trade associations that made these anticompetitive rules.

Indeed, many restraints are "naked" even though contained in elaborate joint ventures that were not being challenged and were almost certainly socially beneficial. For example, while the NCAA is a socially beneficial athletic venture involving colleges and universities, both its rule limiting televised football games and the rule fixing maximum coaching salaries were properly characterized by the courts as "naked" restraints on price or output.

---

[15]   See, e.g., United States v. Romer, 148 F.3d 359 (4th Cir. 1998), cert. denied, 525 U.S. 1141, 119 S.Ct. 1032 (1999) (rejecting argument that bid-rigging agreement was in fact a "joint venture").

[16]   National Collegiate Athletic Ass'n (*NCAA*) v. Board of Regents of the Univ. of Oklahoma, 468 U.S. 85, 104 S.Ct. 2948 (1984); Herbert Hovenkamp, The Rule of Reason, 70 Fla. L. Rev. 81 (2018).

[17]   *Law*, 134 F.3d at 1010. Cf. Deppe v. NCAA, 893 F.3d 498 (7th Cir. 2018) (NCAA rule requiring transfer athletes to have a year in residence was a presumptively procompetitive eligibility rule).

[18]   National Society of Professional Engineers v. United States, 435 U.S. 679, 98 S.Ct. 1355 (1978).

[19]   Wilk v. American Medical Association, 671 F.Supp. 1465 (N.D.Ill.1987), affirmed, 895 F.2d 352 (7th Cir.), cert. denied, 496 U.S. 927, 110 S.Ct. 2621 (1990).

[20]   FTC v. Indiana Federation of Dentists, 476 U.S. 447, 106 S.Ct. 2009 (1986).

The more difficult question is just how high must be the plaintiff's initial burden to show a prima facie anticompetitive restraint? Here, the plaintiff relies mainly on market evidence or that which is obtainable from public information or discovery; the most efficient way to manage decision making is to require the plaintiff simply to show a restraint that requires an explanation. At that point, the defendant should have a more specific burden to show that the restraint is justifiable under the circumstances. The defendant is the author of its own restraint and in a better position than anyone else to understand its purpose and effects.

§ 5.2   Joint Ventures: An Overview

5.2a.   Potential Harms and Benefits

A joint venture of competitors reached the Supreme Court in the very first antitrust case the Court decided on the merits, United States v. Trans-Missouri Freight Ass'n.[21] The Association was a consortium of eighteen railroad companies that formed a joint running agreement. Under the agreement the members coordinated schedules, transfer of cargo, and freight rates. Both the trial court and the federal court of appeals upheld the arrangement, emphasizing its efficiency-creating potential. As the circuit court observed,

> The fact that the business of railway companies is irretrievably interwoven, that they interchange cars and traffic, that they act as agents for each other in the delivery and receipt of freight and in paying and collecting freight charges, and that commodities received for transportation generally pass through the hands of several carriers, renders it of vital importance to the public that uniform rules and regulations governing railway traffic should be framed by those who have a practical acquaintance with the subject * * *.[22]

In the 1890's most railroads were small, located entirely within a single state. The Supreme Court had held that states had no power to regulate interstate railway traffic,[23] and it had substantially denied such regulatory power to the Interstate Commerce Commission.[24] The circuit court noted that a package shipped several

---

[21]   166 U.S. 290, 17 S.Ct. 540 (1897).

[22]   United States v. Trans-Missouri Freight Ass'n, 58 Fed. 58, 79–80 (8th Cir. 1893), reversed, 166 U.S. 290, 17 S.Ct. 540 (1897).

[23]   Wabash, St. Louis & Pac. Rwy. Co. v. Illinois, 118 U.S. 557, 7 S.Ct. 4 (1886).

[24]   Cincinnati, New Orleans & Tex. Pac. Ry. Co. v. I.C.C., 162 U.S. 184, 16 S.Ct. 700 (1896). The Interstate Commerce Commission apparently approved of the joint

hundred miles would probably be handled by several different railroads. Absent rule making by a government agency, the railroads needed an agreement among themselves concerning how such packages or cars should be transferred from one line to the next. Such transfers would naturally be facilitated by coordinated scheduling. The freight bill had to be collected either by the railroad that started the package on its route, or else by the railroad that delivered it to its final destination. The money must then be divided up among the participating railroads according to some formula—perhaps in proportion to the number of miles that each line carried the package.

The railroad industry may be unique, but the joint venture at issue in the *Trans-Missouri* case shared two common elements with many such agreements. First, it permitted the participants to operate more efficiently by eliminating much of the chaos that would exist in a market full of small, unregulated railroads. Second, the Association gave the member railroads the power to agree about rates.

Joint ventures can also reduce a firm's marketing costs, or enable it to take advantage of new marketing opportunities. Suppose that three growers of California kiwi berries want to introduce their product to New York. None of the three has output large enough to justify paying a full-time sales agent, but the three operating together could send an agent, each paying one third of the cost. If the product is fungible—that is, if customers cannot distinguish A's kiwi berries from B's kiwi berries—the agent will probably have to charge the same price for all berries of a certain grade or size.[25] So the use of the joint selling agency for fungible products may require a certain amount of "price fixing." However, that information alone does not suggest that the growers are reducing output or charging a supracompetitive price for their product. It merely suggests that a common price may be a necessary element of some market facilitating joint ventures.[26]

The Supreme Court approved a joint sales agency agreement in Appalachian Coals, Inc. v. United States.[27] The defendants were 137 coal producers who created an exclusive joint selling agency that

---

running agreement at issue in the *Trans-Missouri* case. See 12 ICC Ann.Rep. 10–16 (1898); and Herbert Hovenkamp, Enterprise and American Law, 1836–1937, chs. 12, 13 (1991).

[25]   If the product of the three farmers was perfectly fungible but the agent charged different prices for the output of the three farmers, buyers would buy all the lowest priced berries first, then all the next lowest, and finally the highest. If the product were not fungible but brand specific, such as televisions, automobiles, or personal computers, then the three producers could each set their own price and customers buying through the agent could compare the merits of each brand, including price.

[26]   See 13 Antitrust Law ¶ 2132 (4th ed. 2019).

[27]   288 U.S. 344, 53 S.Ct. 471 (1933).

classified the coal, marketed it, and distributed the proceeds to the participants. Since coal is fungible, the agent had to sell all coal of a certain grade and size at the same price. The Court's decision upholding the agency agreement has been criticized as a relic of the New Deal's distrust of competition and the antitrust laws. At the very least, however, the decision deserves further study, particularly in light of modern rules for measuring market power.[28] The defendants collectively controlled about 12% of coal production east of the Mississippi River, or about 55% of relevant production in the greater Appalachian region, which was not the region in which the coal was marketed. The market contained a great deal of excess capacity, however, and even these figures seriously overstated the agency's market power.

Courts have generally approved joint sales agreements, provided they found at least some integration of promotion, advertising or other activities among the participants.[29] A few exclusive joint sales arrangements have been condemned.[30] Joint purchasing agreements have been treated with even greater tolerance. For example, in *All Care Nursing* the Eleventh Circuit approved an arrangement under which a group of hospitals took bids for nursing services to be their preferred providers.[31] The court held that the rule of reason must be employed, and dismissed the plaintiff's case for failing to show market power.

Every joint venture is "exclusive" in the sense that it cannot offer an infinite number or volume of products. But many joint ventures are also exclusive in two other important senses that may have antitrust significance. *First,* they may limit the joint venture's membership, thus excluding others who might wish to join. *Second,* they might limit the right of existing members to engage in certain non-venture business, particularly if that business competes with the venture.

Limitations on joint venture membership are generally thought necessary to keep the costs of operating the venture manageable. It is one thing for two firms to join together to manufacture a product; it is quite another for twenty firms to do so, particularly if they have unique interests. Then the costs of negotiating product design, settling on the appropriate size plant, its location, and so on, can

---

[28]   See Ch. 3.

[29]   E.g., Broadcast Music, Inc. v. CBS, Inc., 441 U.S. 1, 99 S.Ct. 1551 (1979).

[30]   Virginia Excelsior Mills v. FTC, 256 F.2d 538 (4th Cir. 1958) (applying per se rule to joint selling of shredded wood packing material). Other decisions are discussed in 13 Antitrust Law ¶ 2137 (4th ed. 2019).

[31]   All Care Nursing Service v. High Tech Staffing Services, 135 F.3d 740 (11th Cir. 1998), cert. denied, 526 U.S. 1016, 119 S.Ct. 1250 (1999).

become quite unmanageable. Or in a different context, a sports league of ten or even twenty teams might readily manage a season schedule and conduct playoffs to pick a champion. But management would become far more difficult if the league had 1000 members or even 100. Thus all sports leagues have rules that limit the number of teams that can participate or place stringent limitations on new entry. As we shall see later, these problems are more significant in some joint ventures than others, and many ventures become more profitable as their membership increases. Such ventures typically have open membership policies.[32]

The two types of exclusion noted above may both be necessary to help the venture avoid free-rider problems, which make it impossible for the venture to capitalize on its own investment and risk-taking. For example, most joint ventures are closed to new members because the risk-to-reward ratio changes as the venture progresses. When a research joint venture is first formed the potential for success may be rather limited while the risks attached to the upfront investment are substantial. Three years later, however, when the venture has made important breakthroughs, it may be a much more attractive proposition and others might wish to join in. But a rule permitting them to join would encourage people to wait rather than invest up front.

A similar rationale may explain limitations on non-venture business. For example, consider the law firm rule forbidding partners from practicing law outside the partnership. Within the firm, each partner probably contributes a percentage of her receipts to the firm to account for operating costs and the payments of non-partners. But if the partner engages in "outside" practice she may be able to keep 100% of what she earns and may even be able to draw on the law firm's reputation, library, office equipment and the like. As a result, partners would be tempted to practice outside more and more, for their individual earnings would be higher. In the process they would cannibalize the firm.

Unfortunately, exclusivity has a serious downside as well: in the presence of market power, it makes anticompetitive results much more likely. Recall from Chapters 1 and 4 that a monopoly or cartel succeeds only by reducing market output. When a joint venture comes to dominate a relevant market, it may threaten a market wide output reduction. However, output will not be reduced as long as the venture is unable to exclude. Further, exclusion entails two quite different things. First, the venture must be able to succeed in reducing output within the venture, with output measured by either

---

[32]   See § 5.4b2.

quantity or quality. Second, the venture must be able to reduce non-venture output in the same market.[33]

For example, suppose a group of physicians organize a health maintenance organization (HMO) and agree to cover all of a patient's medical needs for a fixed fee per month. Currently 90% of the community's physicians are in this venture, but (1) the venture permits any new physician who wishes to join in, provided his credentials are in order; and (2) physicians are permitted to engage in unlimited fee-for-service practice outside the venture, or even participate in other HMOs. While the 90% market share is a danger signal suggesting possible collusion, the non-exclusivity of the venture largely ensures that price-fixing will not occur. Thus non-exclusivity often serves to mitigate our fears about joint venture exercises of market power. By contrast, exclusivity may be necessary to create the proper incentives to make a joint venture run properly, but if the venture has a dominant position in its market, then exclusivity rules have to be justified. The combination of market power and exclusivity rules makes anticompetitive outcomes plausible.

5.2b.   Ventures Facilitating R & D, Advertising and Promotion; Ancillary Market Divisions

5.2b1.   Free Rider Problems

Research and development (R & D) and advertising are two areas in which free rider problems are significant. For example, many of the results of expensive R & D cannot be patented or, even if patented, cannot effectively be excluded from appropriation by others. If one firm spends vast sums in R & D, a competing firm might be able to reap the benefits without having to pay the high costs. A firm in competition, facing the likelihood that a particular research project will cost a substantial amount but will benefit all firms in the market, will forego the project. It cannot afford to subsidize its competitors. A research joint venture will benefit all the firms in the market, however, and force all to share in the costs. Such joint ventures are relatively common in certain industries.[34] In the *PolyGram* "Three Tenors" case,[35] however, the FTC rejected a free rider defense to a joint venture agreement that suppressed the individual competing CD recordings of the venturers. In this case the

---

[33]   See 11 Antitrust Law ¶ 1908h (4th ed. 2018); and 13 id. ¶ 2104 (4th ed. 2018).

[34]   See Christina Bohannan & Herbert Hovenkamp, Creation without Restraint: Promoting Liberty and Rivalry in Innovation, Ch. 8 (2011).

[35]   Polygram Holding, Inc., 2003 WL 21770765 (F.T.C. 2003), aff'd, 416 F.3d 29 (D.C. Cir. 2005).

free rider threat was that the new CD would take a free ride on the promotion that the firms had previously made of their individually produced CDs. But the firms were suppressing the individually produced CDs, not the new one, so the free rider claim flowed in the wrong direction.

5.2b2.   Ancillary and Naked Agreements Pertaining to Advertising[36]

Joint advertising agreements pose some of the same concerns as joint research agreements, although there is some justification for treating them more harshly. First, joint advertising is much more explicitly involved with "sales" than is joint research and development, and quite naturally steps into the area of price setting. Second, scale economies and free rider problems may not loom as large in advertising as in R & D.

Nevertheless, joint advertising arrangements are often efficient, depending on the circumstance. For example, if Farmer Brown advertises the merits of Farmer Brown's Potatoes, she might discover that many customers think potatoes are potatoes. Farmer Brown's advertisement may increase potato sales, but they will be distributed over all potato producers in the advertising market.

In a competitive market Farmer Brown cannot afford to pay for advertising that benefits all local producers of potatoes. She will not advertise at all, even though the effect of the advertising would be to give consumers better information. However, the farmers collectively could increase their joint welfare, as well as that of consumers, if they organized a potato growers association, and each paid a proportionate share of the costs of the advertising. In that case both the benefit and the cost would be shared by all growers.

Most of the decisions condemning joint advertising involve not merely the agreement to advertise jointly, but also some other restraint. For example, in *Serta* the defendants not only advertised jointly, they also agreed not to engage in comparative advertising with other firms in the venture.[37] And in *Detroit Auto Dealers* the defendants jointly advertised that all their showrooms would be closing at 6 P.M.[38] In that case the restraint was not the joint

---

[36]   See 12 Antitrust Law ¶ 2023 (4th ed. 2019).

[37]   United States v. Serta Assocs., 296 F.Supp. 1121, 1125–26 (N.D.Ill.1968), affirmed per curiam, 393 U.S. 534, 89 S.Ct. 870 (1969) (joint price advertising and agreement to limit comparative advertising among Serta mattress dealers unlawful per se).

[38]   Detroit Auto Dealers Assn., 111 F.T.C. 417 (1989), affirmed, 955 F.2d 457 (6th Cir.), cert. denied, 506 U.S. 973, 113 S.Ct. 461 (1992).

advertising, but rather the agreement to shorten business hours, which was an output reduction.

Also suspicious are agreements *not* to advertise. Advertising is a valuable way of communicating information to consumers, and price advertising is particularly valuable because it is often costly for consumers to compare prices.[39] To be sure, advertising is often misleading or even fraudulent, and consumer confidence in a market might be strengthened if advertising were policed more rigorously. But the sellers themselves are generally the wrong policemen, for they are injured not only by the misleading advertising of their rivals but also by rivals' aggressive but essentially truthful advertising. Nonetheless, in its problematic *California Dental* decision the Supreme Court concluded that a professional association's advertising restraints must be addressed under the rule of reason.[40] The five-member majority saw a sufficient potential that the restraints were sufficiently well designed to prohibit only deceptive advertising, and thus might increase consumer confidence in dental services. Justice Breyer wrote for four dissenters who emphasized the apparently excessive nature of the restrictions, which often operated to prohibit all advertising whatsoever.[41]

When deception or fraud are not in issue, competitor initiated restraints on advertising are highly dubious. They have been used to facilitate market divisions,[42] to make it more difficult for consumers to engage in price comparison,[43] or to ward off the threat posed by

---

[39]   Cf. Bates v. State Bar of Arizona, 433 U.S. 350, 377–378, 97 S.Ct. 2691 (1977) (limits on price advertising increase consumer search costs); Virginia State Board of Pharmacy v. Virginia Citizens Consumer Council, 425 U.S. 748, 765, 96 S.Ct. 1817 (1976) (truthful advertising informs consumers about "who is producing and selling what product, for what reason, and at what price.").

[40]   California Dental Assn. v. FTC, 526 U.S. 756, 119 S.Ct. 1604 (1999).

[41]   The dissent noted that while nominally designed to prevent deceptive advertising, "[a]s implemented, the ethical rule reached beyond its nominal target, to prevent truthful and nondeceptive advertising." 526 U.S. at 782, 119 S.Ct. at 1618. Judge Posner was quite critical. See Richard A. Posner, Antitrust Law 30 (2d ed. 2001):

The [dentists'] trade association was obviously trying to reduce competition among its members. Any misleading advertising by dentists belonging to the association could be dealt with directly by the agencies charged with protecting the public from misleading advertising. It was not a case in which the benefits of collusion were so palpable in relation to the probable costs that a "benign cartel" defense should have been allowed.

[42]   Blackburn v. Sweeney, 53 F.3d 825, 827 (7th Cir. 1995) (agreement between lawyers that they would not advertise in one another's territories illegal per se).

[43]   E.g., Massachusetts Board of Registration in Optometry, 110 F.T.C. 549, 605 (1988) (striking down ban on all advertising, even if truthful). See also the following consent decrees: American Inst. of Certified Public Accountants, 113 F.T.C. 698 (1990) (prohibiting ban on truthful advertising); United States v. Gasoline Retailers Assn., 285 F.2d 688, 691 (7th Cir. 1961) (criminal case; per se unlawful for gasoline retailers

lower cost distribution methods or more aggressive rivals. In 2018 the FTC condemned an agreement among contact lens sellers that they would not name one another's brands in advertising.[44] The parties had been involved in a trademark infringement lawsuit and relied on a single district court decision that denied summary judgment on a claim that use of a rival's trademark in an advertisement could constitute trademark infringement.[45]

5.2b3.   *Ancillary Market Divisions and Noncompetition Agreements*

A market division is an agreement among firms that each will stay out of some portion of the market occupied by the others. Markets can be divided by *geography* (I'll sell only west of the Mississippi and you only east); by *product* (I'll sell only the electric version of this appliance and you agree to sell only the gas version), or by *customer* (I'll sell only to restaurants and you only to hospitals). A naked market division is simply a form of collusion,[46] is illegal per se,[47] and can be a criminal offense.[48] In 2014 the Eighth Circuit held that an asset swap between two wholesale grocers, plus an alleged agreement not to compete in one another's territories after the swap, could have been unlawful per se.[49] While the written agreement did not forbid the parties from competing for future customers in one another's territories, they had not done so and messages exchanged between them indicated a likely noncompetition agreement.

But market division agreements ancillary to other joint activity can increase output by reducing free rider problems, thus giving each

---

to agree not to advertise their gasoline prices except by posting it directly on the pump).

[44]   1-800-Contacts, Inc., 2018 WL 6201693, 2018-2 Trade Reg. Rep. ¶ 80,586 (F.T.C. Nov. 7, 2018), app. docketed, 2d Cir. (2019).

[45]   Soilworks, LLC v. Midwest Indus. Supply, Inc., 575 F. Supp. 2d 1118, 1129 (D. Ariz. 2008).

[46]   See, e.g., Blue Cross & Blue Shield United of Wisconsin v. Marshfield Clinic, 65 F.3d 1406, 1415 (7th Cir. 1995), cert. denied, 516 U.S. 1184, 116 S.Ct. 1288 (1996):

The analogy between price fixing and division of markets is compelling. It would be a strange interpretation of antitrust law that forbade competitors to agree on what price to charge, thus eliminating price competition among them but allowing them to divide markets, thus eliminating all competition among them.

[47]   E.g., Palmer v. BRG of Georgia, 498 U.S. 46, 111 S.Ct. 401 (1990) (per curiam) (geographic market division of bar review offers unlawful per se).

[48]   United States v. Andreas, 216 F.3d 645 (7th Cir. 2000) (worldwide market division of lysine); United States v. Brown, 936 F.2d 1042 (9th Cir. 1991) (affirming criminal conviction of rivals who divided market for billboard sites); United States v. Suntar Roofing, 897 F.2d 469 (10th Cir. 1990) (horizontal customer allocation among roofers; unlawful per se; criminal conviction).

[49]   In re Wholesale Grocery Prods. Antitrust Litig., 752 F.3d 728 (8th Cir. 2014) (denying summary judgment on per se claim).

firm an incentive to promote more aggressively. Nevertheless, the Supreme Court has been intolerant of horizontal agreements to use territorial division to overcome free rider problems. In the leading case, United States v. Topco Associates, Inc.,[50] the Court condemned an arrangement involving about 25 small grocery chains. Under the agreement the stores marketed their products separately and did not set or advertise prices jointly or pool earnings. The association created by the agreement bought grocery items in large quantities and redistributed them to members. Its most distinctive contribution was a jointly held "Topco" trademark that appeared on many of its grocery products, and which had acquired large consumer appeal. Under the agreement, each member promised to sell Topco brand merchandise only in its own assigned marketing territory. The member was free to open stores in another territory, but these stores could not display or sell the Topco brand. Thus each member had an exclusive area in which it could market Topco brand products.

The government challenged the market division scheme as a cartel, claiming that it operated "to prohibit competition in Topco-brand products among grocery chains engaged in retail operations." But the record revealed that each member's share of the grocery market within its assigned territory averaged about 6%. Further, entry into the retail grocery business was quite easy. The market division in the *Topco* case could not plausibly have turned the defendants into monopolists.

Why would a group of grocery chains producing under a common trademark divide territories if they could not earn monopoly profits as a result? In *Topco*, the defendants were trying to compete more effectively against larger grocery chains. A nationally recognized "Topco" brand could be created only by advertising. If two or more competing chains sold Topco brands in the same market area, however, all chains would benefit from the brand advertising of one. As a result, none of the stores would advertise. The territorial division scheme gave each member the exclusive right to sell the Topco brand in a territory, and thus the incentive to advertise the brand there. As the Supreme Court would recognize five years later in a vertical restraints case,[51] the territorial division arguably lessened "intrabrand" competition—that is, competition among

---

[50]　405 U.S. 596, 92 S.Ct. 1126 (1972). See also United States v. Sealy, Inc., 388 U.S. 350, 87 S.Ct. 1847 (1967), which struck down a territorial division agreement among mattress manufacturers that owned the Sealy trademark in common.

[51]　Continental T.V., Inc. v. GTE Sylvania, Inc., 433 U.S. 36, 97 S.Ct. 2549 (1977), on remand, 461 F.Supp. 1046 (N.D.Cal.1978), affirmed, 694 F.2d 1132 (9th Cir. 1982).

different stores selling Topco brand products.[52] However, it very likely increased "interbrand" competition—competition between stores selling Topco brand products and those selling other brands of the same products. The territorial division scheme enabled the consortium of small chain stores to compete more effectively with the large chain groceries that could afford to produce and advertise their own exclusive labels.

Topco has been widely criticized for ignoring the distinction between naked and ancillary horizontal market division schemes. While some market division is nothing more than a form of price fixing, the *Topco* arrangement was almost certainly efficient. In that case we must consider whether the division agreement reduced costs or gave the participants an incentive to invest that they would not otherwise have had. If so, rule of reason application would be called for. At that point the defendants' small market shares should have been decisive.[53] The Topco decision has been widely criticized but never explicitly overruled.

Noncompetition covenants are ubiquitous in both employment agreements and deeds, leases, or other agreements covering business property. They generally have the same economic effect as ancillary market division agreements. For example, one physician may sell her pediatrics practice in Bryan, Texas, to another physician and promise not to practice pediatrics in Bryan for five years following the sale.

Noncompetition covenants are typically regarded as "ancillary" restraints because they usually are contained in agreements providing for the sale of a business, the start of employment, or perhaps the beginning of a broader ongoing contractual relationship. They may be collateral to ongoing joint-venture agreements but they need not be. For example, the owner of a shoe store on Blackacre may sell Whiteacre across the street subject to a covenant that no shoes be sold on Whiteacre. In that case there is no obvious integration of entrepreneurial activities by the parties. Nonetheless, the trend is to treat such covenants under the rule of reason.

As the Supreme Court made clear in *Palmer*, however, not all noncompetition covenants are to be analyzed under the rule of reason.[54] That decision applied the *per se* rule to a horizontal territorial division scheme created when one offeror of a bar review course in Athens, Georgia, sold another firm the right to use its materials in Athens and promised not to offer a competing course in

---

[52]   However, for a critique of the concept of "lessening" intrabrand competition, see § 11.6a.

[53]   See § 5.6.

[54]   Palmer v. BRG of Georgia, 498 U.S. 46, 111 S.Ct. 401 (1990).

the Athens market. In return, the licensee of the materials promised
not to offer bar review courses anywhere else in the United States.
The immediate result was a dramatic increase in bar review fees for
University of Georgia Law School graduates. The Supreme Court
treated the case as nothing more than a naked territorial division
scheme. But noncompetition covenants attending the sale of
businesses are both common and not typically suspect unless the
acquiring firm ends up with significant market power.[55] In *Palmer*
the licensee's promise not to offer bar review courses in the rest of the
United States was clearly excessive, but that was not the covenant
that caused the Athens price to rise. The price increase was a
consequence of the licensor's promise to stay out of Athens—a quite
common form of ancillary noncompetition agreement. The
arrangement should probably have been treated as a merger to
monopoly, but that analysis would have required that a relevant
market be determined.[56] Another problematic use of noncompetition
covenants occurs when each of the stores in a franchise, such as
McDonald's, enter into noncompetition agreements with the
franchisor promising not to hire one another's employees. Should
such agreements be treated as a series of vertical agreements
between the franchisor and each franchisee, or else as a disguised
horizontal agreement among the franchisees?[57] At this writing that
issue remains unresolved.

If a horizontal territorial or customer division is found to be
reasonably ancillary to a joint venture, several circuit courts have
applied the rule of reason, virtually ignoring *Topco*. In *Polk* the
Seventh Circuit upheld a lease covenant between two stores
occupying the same building that one would not sell appliances in
competition with the other.[58] In approving this agreement, Judge

---

[55]   See 13 Antitrust Law ¶ 2134d (4th ed. 2019); and see LDDS Communs. v.
Automated Communs., 35 F.3d 198, 199 (5th Cir. 1994) (approving noncompetition
covenant attending sale of business assets between providers of long distance
telephone service).

[56]   On mergers to monopoly, see § 12.3b.

[57]   Deslandes v. McDonald's USA, LLC, 2018 WL 3105955 (N.D.Il. June 25, 2018)
(agreement between franchisor and each franchisee forbidding the latter from
"poaching" one another's employees; refusing to dismiss claim under Illinois Antitrust
Act). See Herbert Hovenkamp, Competition Policy for Labour Markets (OECD
working paper, 17 May 2019), available at https://papers.ssrn.com/sol3/papers.cfm?
abstract_id=3421036. See also Suresh Naidu, Eric A. Posner, & Glen Weyl, Antitrust
Remedies for Labor Market Power, 132 Harv. L. Rev. 536, 598 (2019) (suggesting that
such agreements be treated as cartels of the franchisees).

[58]   Polk Brothers, Inc. v. Forest City Enterprises, Inc., 776 F.2d 185 (7th Cir.
1985). See also Eichorn v. AT & T Corp., 248 F.3d 131 (3d Cir.), cert. denied, 534 U.S.
1014, 122 S.Ct. 506 (2001) (applying rule of reason and approving employee
noncompetition covenant preventing employees from transferring from spun-off
subsidiary back to parent).

Easterbrook observed that it was ancillary to the lease and that a noncompetition agreement covering a single building in an urban area lacked anything resembling market power.

Likewise, in *Rothery* the court refused to condemn an agreement among independent moving firms operated as franchisees to Atlas, a national branded moving company. The firms agreed not to use Atlas' name, goodwill or other services for any form of carriage made outside of the franchise arrangement, for which Atlas as franchisor was not compensated. As the court put it,

> A carrier agent can attract customers because of Atlas' "national image" and can use Atlas' equipment and order forms when undertaking carriage for its own account. To the degree that a carrier agent uses Atlas' reputation, equipment, facilities, and services in conducting business for its own profit, the agent enjoys a free ride at Atlas' expense. The problem is that the van line's incentive to spend for reputation, equipment, facilities and services declines as it receives less of the benefit from them. * * *[59]

5.2c.   Transactional Efficiencies Justifying Joint Venture Price Setting

Certain joint ventures of competitors are valuable because they reduce transaction costs so substantially that they virtually create a new market or make a market much larger than it had been before. Justice Brandeis characterized the agreement in Chicago Board of Trade v. United States[60] this way. At issue was the "call" rule adopted by the Board, which was the world's leading market for grain. During regular trading sessions from 9:30 a.m. to 1:15 p.m. the Board operated as one of the most efficient markets that can be found: hundreds of buyers and sellers of grain met on the floor and made transactions by public bids. Current price information was made available to both buyers and sellers, as fast as it could be displayed on the chalk boards. Under the "call" rule, Board members were permitted to trade after the close of the regular session only at the session's closing price. For example, if wheat closed at $1.00 per bushel at the end of the regular Wednesday session, all transactions by Board members after closing until the opening of the Thursday session had to be made at that price. A new price would be established competitively when the Thursday session opened.

---

[59]   Rothery Storage & Van Co. v. Atlas Van Lines, 792 F.2d 210, 221 (D.C.Cir. 1986), cert. denied, 479 U.S. 1033, 107 S.Ct. 880 (1987).

[60]   246 U.S. 231, 38 S.Ct. 242 (1918).

In challenging the call rule, the government made no attempt to show that it generated an output restriction or enabled the Board members to increase price. They argued simply that the rule "fixed" prices and was therefore illegal. In rejecting that proposition, Justice Brandeis noted that the call rule "created" a public market for grain scheduled to arrive. The market, after all, is not where the transaction is consummated but where the price is determined. Under the "call" rule all price determination was made under the most public and competitive of circumstances, with no buyer or seller in a position to take advantage of another party's ignorance. Finding no plausible way that the rule could disguise price fixing, the Court unanimously ordered the complaint dismissed.

A dramatic example of a market facilitating agreement was the blanket licensing arrangement at issue in Broadcast Music, Inc. v. Columbia Broadcasting System, Inc. (BMI).[61] BMI was an association made up of thousands of composers, publishers and others who owned the performance rights to musical compositions. A performance right gives its holder the exclusive right to perform a composition or license the right of performance to others. The market for such performance rights is vast: tens of thousands of radio stations, television stations, movie producers, and high school glee clubs may need to purchase a performance right before they can perform a musical composition publicly for profit. Theft can be a substantial problem for the owners of intellectual property. If someone 1000 miles away performs a song to which you have the exclusive right, you will not notice that any of it is missing; nevertheless you have been robbed.[62]

BMI sold "blanket licenses," which permitted the licensee to perform everything in BMI's library. The library consisted of performance rights to compositions owned by its members, who had given nonexclusive rights to BMI. The licensees paid a charge that varied with their revenues. The performance right holder received income that varied with the amount that his compositions were used. BMI also enforced its members' rights by the relatively inexpensive process of listening for the broadcasting of anything in its library by someone who had not purchased a blanket license.

The blanket license arrangement saved untold millions of dollars in transactions costs. Few radio stations could afford to negotiate individually for the right to perform every piece of music they played on the air. If they did, advertising costs would soar and

---

[61]   441 U.S. 1, 99 S.Ct. 1551 (1979).

[62]   See Edmund W. Kitch, The Law & Economics of Rights in Valuable Information, 9 J.Leg.Stud. 683 (1980).

the amount of music played would drop. In fact, if the market had operated on an individual contract per performance basis, the costs of the transactions would often have dwarfed the price of the performance right itself. Furthermore, the "shelf life" of many popular songs is rather short. The performance right might become worthless while the station was negotiating for the right to play it. The single blanket license, however, substituted for thousands of individual transactions and gave licensees immediate access to anything in BMI's library.[63]

More generally, transactional efficiencies justify joint ventures when firms must make costly, irreversible investments in risky markets whose output can efficiently be shared. Intellectual property rights are the prime example. Developing a new chemical or machine may be costly and the investment will be lost if the project fails; however, if it succeeds the new technology can be licensed to all venture participants as well as the venturers themselves.[64]

5.2d.　　The Relation Between Joint Venture Analysis and Merger Analysis

Virtually any efficiency that firms can achieve through a joint venture could also be achieved by a merger. This has suggested different things to different courts. In *Addyston Pipe* Judge Taft noted that a merger of the firms accused of fixing prices would probably have been legal; the "price fixing" that resulted would be an essential consequence of the union of firms.[65] However, the price fixing agreement in the actual case before the court was not ancillary to anything, and thus deserved to be condemned.[66] By contrast, in *Appalachian Coals*, which upheld a joint sales venture, Chief Justice Hughes reasoned that the coal companies involved in the venture could lawfully have merged; so why shouldn't they be able to accomplish the same goal by agreement?[67]

---

[63]　See 13 Antitrust Law ¶ 2132 (4th ed. 2019).

[64]　On transaction cost economics and antitrust, see § 1.8. See also Christina Bohannan & Herbert Hovenkamp, Creation Without Restraint: Promoting Liberty and Rivalry in Innovation, Ch. 8 (2011).

[65]　United States v. Addyston Pipe & Steel Co., 85 Fed. 271, 280 (6th Cir. 1898), modified and affirmed, 175 U.S. 211, 20 S.Ct. 96 (1899) (" * * * [W]hen two men become partners in a business, although their union might reduce competition, this effect was only an incident to the main purpose of a union of their capital enterprise * * * and * * * useful to the community."). Indeed, after the price-fixing agreement was condemned the defendants merged and the government did not object. See 2 Simon N. Whitney, Antitrust Policies: American Experience in Twenty Industries 7 (1958).

[66]　On *Addyston Pipe*, see §§ 2.1b, 4.1.

[67]　Appalachian Coals, Inc. v. United States, 288 U.S. 344, 376, 53 S.Ct. 471, 480 (1933).

Asking whether a merger among the same firms would be lawful is often irrelevant to the legality of a venture. When a joint venture simultaneously permits the parties to coordinate price or output *and* has the clear potential to produce substantial economies, then we must consider further whether the competitive risks outweigh the potential rewards. In that case a structural analysis similar to that undertaken in mergers is wholly appropriate.

Nevertheless, the analysis is very different to the extent that the joint venture (1) does not restrain the firms' non-merger output; and (2) actually expands production. To illustrate, consider the joint venture between GM and Toyota to build a new plant to produce small cars in Freemont, California.[68] Assume at the time that GM and Toyota each accounted for 20% of automobile production in the relevant market. A merger between the two firms would almost certainly be challenged. Significantly, however, the venture places no restraint whatsoever on the two firms' ability to produce cars at all of their other plants around the world and in competition with each other. Further, assuming they have not agreed to shut other plants down, the venture actually expands market capacity by resulting in the creation of a new plant. Clearly the anticompetitive potential of this joint venture is far less than the anticompetitive potential of a merger between the same two firms.[69]

In *Dagher* the Supreme Court was presented with a joint venture that came very close to being a merger in the territory where it operated.[70] Oil producers Shell and Texaco pooled all of their production resources in the western United States and produced gasoline in a joint facility called Equilon. The gasoline was then sold by Equilon to Shell and Texaco gasoline stations and marketed under their respective brand names. The antitrust dispute was a challenge to Equilon's decision to charge the same price to the Shell and Texaco dealers. The ninth Circuit condemned this price fixing agreement under § 1. In reversing, the Supreme Court's found the price agreement to amount to

> little more than price setting by a single entity—albeit within the context of a joint venture—and not a pricing

---

[68]   See General Motors Corp., 103 F.T.C. at 374.

[69]   See Texaco, Inc. v. Dagher, 547 U.S. 1, 126 S.Ct. 1276 (2006), discussed *infra*, where the joint venture united production between two gasoline refiners but did not place restrictions on the members' nonventure output. 13 Antitrust Law ¶ 2121c (4th ed. 2019). Contrast the FTC decision in Polygram Holding, Inc., 2003 WL 21770765 (F.T.C. 2003), aff'd, 416 F.3d 29 (D.C. Cir. 2005), which condemned a venture where the parties did put restraints on individual nonventure production.

[70]   Texaco, Inc. v. Dagher, 547 U.S. 1, 126 S.Ct. 1276 (2006).

agreement between competing entities with respect to their competing products.[71]

Dagher stands for the proposition that when firms participate in a traditional production joint venture that produces an essentially undifferentiated product, the venture cannot be condemned categorically simply because it sells its output at the same price, even if part of the output is allocated to one joint venture participant, part to another, and so on. Such an agreement must be analyzed under antitrust's rule of reason.

§ 5.3   Competitor Exchanges of Price or Output Information; Posting Agreements

The nature and extent of price information available to buyers and sellers varies considerably from one market to another. For example, current prices of every stock listed by the major stock exchanges are printed in daily newspapers. By contrast, in markets for rare works of art prices are often kept secret from everyone except the parties to the transaction.

If neither buyer nor seller has information about the market price, the market will probably not function very well. The seller can never be sure that he is asking the most the buyer will pay, and the customer can never be sure that she is paying the least the seller will take. The seller will probably begin negotiations by asking an inflated price, and the buyer is sure to respond by making a low-ball counteroffer. Each party has an incentive to negotiate as long as he perceives that the other party's position is "soft"—that further negotiations will yield a change in the price. It is not uncommon for the sale of a unique, expensive piece of property, such as a mansion or rare painting, to be negotiated for weeks or even months before the sale is made. It is also common that, after a substantial investment in negotiation, the parties finally decide that they cannot agree on a price.

At the other extreme is a commodity market with a large number of buyers and sellers with full knowledge about current prices. In such a market price negotiations are extremely limited. Every seller knows that if he asks more than the prevailing price the buyer will not even bother with a counteroffer, but will go to a competitor. Every buyer knows that the price is competitive and that each seller can clear the market at the current price. Transactions will take place at the published market price and someone unwilling to pay that price will never enter the market.

---

[71]   Id. at 6.

5.3a.   Industry-Wide Dissemination of Price and Output Information

The Supreme Court's approach to industry wide exchanges of price information was first developed in two cases from the 1920's, involving trade associations in the hardwood industry. In American Column & Lumber Co. v. United States[72] the Supreme Court condemned a price information exchange program under which each member manufacturer furnished the trade association with detailed reports showing the price of each sale and the purchaser's name, the member's rate of production and inventory on hand, plus an estimate of future production. This information was organized around uniform classifications of hardwood sizes and types adopted by the association. The association was clearly concerned about "overproduction," and the members occasionally met to urge members to hold back on output. These discussions convinced the Court that the information exchange was really a plan to raise prices.

However, the association contained 365 producers who collectively controlled only one-third of American hardwood production. Even assuming an explicit price fixing agreement, it is difficult to see how a cartel with that many members, controlling only one-third of the market, could have a substantial effect on prices.[73] Indeed, one frequently overlooked but very important issue in data dissemination cases is the relationship between the domain over which information is exchanged and the scope of the relevant market. For example, the Delaware County Pork Producers Association may collect information from its members about their output and pricing of hogs. But if hogs are sold in a nationwide market, one county's collection of such data is not likely to facilitate price-fixing.

If collusion was not the motive, why did the hardwood producers exchange such detailed information? Justice Brandeis's dissent suggested some reasons: the hardwood manufacturers were small, generally isolated, located in the forests that provided their essential material. No public agency gathered data about production in the industry,[74] and the isolated producers knew very little about market conditions. Furthermore, many of the direct purchasers were very large and presumably had good information about their demand. The

---

[72]   257 U.S. 377, 42 S.Ct. 114 (1921).

[73]   See Richard A. Posner, Antitrust Law 159–171 (2d ed. 2001).

[74]   Justice Brandeis's dissent noted, however, that all information gathered by the defendants was public and open to everyone, and copies of all reports were filed with the Department of Justice and the Federal Trade Commission, 257 U.S. at 414–15, 42 S.Ct. at 122.

exchange may simply have served to equalize information between buyers and sellers.

The more realistic competitive threat posed by the *American Column* data dissemination scheme was probably not its publication of market wide output and price data, but the detailed production, inventory and pricing information concerning individual members of the Association.[75] The Court offered almost no analysis of the relevant market other than to assume that it was hardwood and apparently nationwide. But hardwood was shipped mainly by rail and transportation costs were a significant component of value. Each hardwood mill competed mostly with fairly nearby mills and much less intensely with more remote mills.[76] As a result, a particular mill desiring to win the bid of a customer was concerned mainly with the inventory, output and pricing policies of a few nearby mills. The detailed data probably permitted such a firm to bid aggressively when it knew that its rivals had ample stock or excess production, but to bid more conservatively if it thought its rivals were already producing and selling all they could handle.

Four years later, in Maple Flooring Mfrs' Ass'n v. United States[77] the Court approved a program for the exchange of price information among the producers of hardwood flooring, again undertaken through a trade association. The Court distinguished *American Column* by emphasizing that the flooring manufacturers did not give the names of customers and that they reported only completed, past transactions instead of current prices. Why these differences made cartelization less likely the Court did not explain. The Court all but overlooked other facts that distinguished *Maple Flooring*: this time there were only 22 producers instead of 365, and they collectively controlled 70% of the market. Further, the information items that the Court stressed were relatively inconsequential: average figures will do as well as specific individual prices for establishing a cartel price, and the names of buyers are not essential. Most likely the Association distributed the information as it did because it had been organized about the time of the Supreme Court's *American Column* decision. It tailored its information exchanges around the language of that opinion.

---

[75]   See American Column, 257 U.S. at 396, 42 S.Ct. at 116 (detailed reporting requirements included size and price of specific transactions).

[76]   See id. at 415–416, 42 S.Ct. at 122–123 (Brandeis, J., dissenting).

[77]   268 U.S. 563, 45 S.Ct. 578 (1925).

5.3b.   Direct Competitor Exchange of Price Information

In United States v. Container Corp. of America[78] the Supreme Court faced an entirely different type of information exchange. The defendant manufacturers of pasteboard boxes agreed that one could call another and obtain price information for some upcoming transaction. For example, Firm A, preparing a bid for a buyer, might call Firm B to ask what B charged for the same product to the same customer. While there was an industry wide understanding that firms would supply each other with the requested information,[79] that fact would not serve to make the case resemble the industry wide dissemination cases. Direct competitor exchange of price information offers none of the informational benefits of industry wide promulgation. Indeed, its most likely and in most cases only reasonable purpose is the fixing of prices. Nevertheless, Justice Douglas opinion regarded the *Container* agreement as "analogous" to the one *American Column*,[80] and the two types of cases have largely been lumped together ever since.

Container Corp. concluded that direct competitor exchanges of price information are likely to be harmless in competitive markets. However, if concentration is high the exchange is more likely to affect price, and any interference "with the setting of price by free market forces" is illegal. The Court concluded that the information exchange in this case caused prices to "stabilize * * *, though at a downward level." The practical effect of the exchanges was that a prospective seller who knew a competitor's price would try to match it. However, these observations are as consistent with healthy competition in a properly informed market as they are with collusion. Given the tenuousness of any empirical conclusion about the reason for changes in price, the Court would have done well to avoid a rule that required a trial court to determine how a particular information exchange program affected the market price.

Further, the focus on overall industry concentration probably missed the real competitive danger of direct exchanges.[81] Even in relatively unconcentrated markets, product or spatial differentiation may give some firms advantages over others in bidding for a particular customer. For example, even if the container market has 100 sellers, high transportation costs may give sellers A and B a price

---

[78]   393 U.S. 333, 89 S.Ct. 510 (1969).

[79]   See *Container*, 393 U.S. at 335, 89 S.Ct. at 511.

[80]   393 U.S. at 337, 89 S.Ct. at 512, citing American Column, 257 U.S. at 396, 42 S.Ct. at 116; and Linseed, 262 U.S. at 371, 43 S.Ct. at 607.

[81]   See 13 Antitrust Law ¶ 2113 (4th ed. 2019).

advantage vis-a-vis customer X. A rule permitting a direct exchange of information between A and B can operate to create a kind of "mini-cartel" with respect to that particular customer.[82]

Under the rule of reason applied in *Container*, if the market in which the price information exchange occurred is concentrated, if the product is fungible so that price is the predominant element in competition, and if demand at the competitive price is inelastic, the exchange is virtually certain to be condemned, particularly if the court finds *any* relationship, downward or upward, between the information exchange and the market price.[83]

As the subject of the exchanged information wanders further from price and output, courts are less likely to condemn the exchange. For example, exchanges of credit information on customers, or the histories of customer dealings, are generally legal.[84] Such information is itself valuable intellectual property and expensive to produce; significant economies could result from joint provision. Exchanges of information totally unrelated to price or output generally raise no antitrust issues.

5.3c.   Agreements to Post or to Post and Adhere

Many firms post their prices periodically, perhaps by faxing or sending a price list to their regular accounts, or making them available on a website. Such price lists are valuable because buyers can compute their own costs readily without having to call for a quote. A firm's unilateral decision to post its price is legal. However, there is little competitive justification for competitors to agree with *each other* to post their prices. If posting is valuable to buyers, each firm has an incentive to do it unilaterally. Agreed posting is a strong inducement to price fixing.[85] Even more suspicious is an agreement among firms that they will post their prices monthly and then adhere to the posted prices during that month. In *Sugar Institute* the Supreme Court rejected the defense that an agreement to post and adhere to the posted prices was necessary to prevent secret discounts, which the participants regarded as "unethical."[86] But ethical or not,

---

[82]   The impact is not unlike that of a merger between adjacent or similar firms in a product differentiated market, thus facilitating a unilateral price increase. See § 12.3d.

[83]   393 U.S. at 337, 89 S.Ct. at 512. The Supreme Court did not clearly characterize Container as a rule of reason decision until United States v. Citizens & Southern Nat. Bank, 422 U.S. 86, 113, 95 S.Ct. 2099, 2115 (1975).

[84]   Zoslaw v. MCA Distrib. Corp., 693 F.2d 870 (9th Cir. 1982), cert. denied, 460 U.S. 1085, 103 S.Ct. 1777 (1983) (approving exchanges of credit histories and information on credit balances).

[85]   See 12 Antitrust Law ¶ 2024 (4th ed. 2019).

[86]   Sugar Institute v. United States, 297 U.S. 553, 56 S.Ct. 629 (1936).

secret discounting is the means by which a cartel or oligopoly can be undermined. The courts generally conclude that such agreements are unlawful *per se*.[87]

5.3d. Agreements of Wage and Salary Information; "Anti-Poaching" Agreements

In Todd v. Exxon, then Circuit judge Sotomayor sustained a complaint that agreements among petroleum companies exchanging information on salaries violated the Sherman Act when the complaint also alleged that the employers had an understanding that the information would be used to set new salaries.[88] The court also held that the rule of reason applied because the agreements did not literally fix prices. By contrast, a 2012 district court held that an "anti-poaching" agreement among Silicon Valley employees stated a claim for a per se violation,[89] and a 2014 decision approved a consent decree involving an agreement between eBay and Intuit.[90] This was not simply an exchange of information, but in effect a market division agreement. The case is interesting because eBay, an online auctioneer, and Intuit, a producer of business software, did not engage in substantial competition in the product markets where they sold. However, they did compete in the hiring of software engineers. The important thing for any type of buyer price fixing, including anti-poaching agreements, is to look to the market in which the firms purchase (or hire), which can be quite different from the market in which they sell.[91]

To be sure, employee free riding might be a problem. That is, after an employee has been fully trained by Alpha Company it might be tempted to take a better offer from Beta Company. But ordinarily this can be accomplished by means of a purely vertical noncompetition covenant. In this particular case, however, state law

---

[87] E.g., Miller v. Hedlund, 813 F.2d 1344 (9th Cir. 1987), cert. denied, 484 U.S. 1061, 108 S.Ct. 1018 (1988) (per se). See also United States v. United Liquors Corp., 149 F.Supp. 609 (W.D.Tenn.1956), aff'd per curiam, 352 U.S. 991, 77 S.Ct. 557 (1957) (condemning detailed agreement requiring posting of liquor prices and elimination of quantity discounts).

[88] Todd v. Exxon Corp., 275 F.3d 191 (2d Cir. 2001).

[89] In re High Tech. Employee Antitrust Litigation, 856 F.Supp.2d 1103 (N.D.Cal. 2012).

[90] California v. eBay, Inc., 2014 WL 4273888 (N.D.Cal. Aug. 29, 2014).

[91] For further discussion, see Herbert Hovenkamp, Competition Policy for Labour Markets (OECD working paper, 17 May 2019), available at https://papers.ssrn.com/sol3/papers.cfm?abstract_id=3421036.

(California) had generally been hostile toward employee noncompetition agreements.[92]

§ 5.4   Concerted Refusals to Deal, Joint Venture Membership Restrictions, and Standard Setting

5.4a.   Harms and Benefits; Appropriate Antitrust Standard

In most antitrust litigation involving refusals to deal the refusal itself is not the violation. Many antitrust complaints brought by victims of refusals to deal allege that the defendants were involved in illegal monopolization, tying, price fixing, resale price maintenance or vertical nonprice restraints, or an illegal merger. Other complaints do not explicitly allege a secondary violation, but the theory of the complaint makes sense only on the premise that the defendant was committing a secondary violation. If this "supporting" antitrust violation is not apparent, often the plaintiff is unable to offer any explanation why the refusal to deal is anticompetitive.

So the refusal to deal might more appropriately be considered a type of antitrust harm rather than a substantive violation. For example, if a firm engaging in resale price maintenance refuses to sell to a noncomplying retailer, the alleged antitrust violation is the attempt to control resale prices.[93]

The refusal to deal can perform two important functions in antitrust law, even when it is not a separate violation. First, it gives a cause of action to a set of plaintiffs who have good knowledge about a market and are highly motivated to sue. A high percentage of private antitrust filings come from people who have been excluded from a market by the collective decisions of others.

Second, the presence or absence of a refusal to deal often helps a court evaluate activities such as joint ventures that are arguably both efficient and anticompetitive. No court can quantify efficiency and injury to competition and balance one against the other, particularly in close cases. This complicates legal analysis of joint ventures that have a potential to be both anticompetitive and efficient. But often all the efficiencies could be attained without the refusal to deal. That is, although the joint venture might be competitive, an anticompetitive motive best explains the refusal to

---

[92]   See Edwards II v. Arthur Andersen LLP, 44 Cal.4th 937 (2008); Muggill v. Reuben H. Donnelley Corp., 62 Cal.2d 239 (1965).

[93]   See § 11.5.

deal. For example, Appalachian Coals, Inc. v. United States[94] involved a joint selling agency created by a group of competing coal producers. The agency almost certainly marketed coal more efficiently than the members did separately. Because coal is fungible, however, the agency charged the same price for all deliveries of a particular grade of coal. Therefore producers had to agree about price or the mechanism by which the price was to be set. But members were required to sell their coal exclusively through the agency. A member of the venture would have refused to deal with anyone who tried to buy coal from it directly. Even assuming that the sales agency was efficient, no reasonable explanation was offered why the agreement required exclusivity. One explanation is that the defendants were fixing prices and wanted to prevent members from making noncartel sales.

5.4a1.   A Rule of Reason, with Exceptions

It was once commonly said that concerted refusals to deal were illegal *per se*, but this rule is subject to so many exceptions that the presumption must be turned around. Today, most concerted refusals to deal, even those involving competitors, are evaluated under a rule of reason. As a general matter, concerted refusals should be treated as devices for making joint ventures or other associations of competitors operate more efficiently. This does not make them legal *per se*, but it means that most of the time *per se* illegality is inappropriate. The *per se* rule is reserved for so-called *naked* boycotts—that is concerted refusals of competitors to deal with another competitor, customer or supplier when no case can be made that the refusal is ancillary to any legitimate joint activity.

To be sure, naked boycotts abound in antitrust history. In W.W. Montague & Co. v. Lowry the Supreme Court first held that a competitors' concerted refusal was illegal.[95] The defendants, who were members of a trade association, agreed with each other not to sell their products to non-member dealers. The Court condemned the refusal using common law restraint of trade language, but nothing approaching the modern *per se* rule. A more categorical *per se* approach had to wait another decade. In Eastern States Retail Lumber Dealers' Ass'n v. United States[96] the Supreme Court decided that, although a firm acting alone may refuse to deal with anyone, an agreement among competitors not to deal with certain persons acts as a clog on the market and hinders competition. *Eastern States* involved an agreement among lumber retailers to identify lumber

---

94   288 U.S. 344, 53 S.Ct. 471 (1933). See § 5.2a.

95   193 U.S. 38, 24 S.Ct. 307 (1904).

96   234 U.S. 600, 34 S.Ct. 951 (1914).

wholesalers who were dealing directly with consumers. If a wholesaler was found to be retailing directly, the wholesaler's name was put on a "blacklist" and the retailers refused to purchase at wholesale from him.

The lumber retailers might have wanted wholesalers to stay out of retailing for two reasons. First, by eliminating one firm in the distribution chain, the wholesalers may have been more efficient retailers than the unintegrated retailers themselves.[97] By refusing to deal with wholesalers engaged in such vertical integration, the independent retailers may have tried to prevent the wholesalers' entry into retail markets. If vertical integration to retailing reduced the lumber wholesalers' costs, however, the boycott by the independent retailers would probably only delay, not prevent, the vertical integration. Some wholesalers would establish retail outlets and retail *all* their lumber through them. Then they would be immune from the boycott.

The second possibility is that the lumber retailers were fixing prices. The retailers' mark-up is the wholesalers' cost of distribution, and the wholesalers would naturally prefer to keep that cost as low as possible. If the retailers were engaged in price fixing the wholesalers would lose volume to the cartel's output reduction, but all the monopoly profits would go to the retailers. The wholesalers might try to protect their own interests by finding retailers who were not members of the cartel or else by retailing the lumber themselves. The concerted refusal to deal may have been a cartel's effort to prevent loss of sales because of competitive entry by the wholesalers.

In 1990 the Supreme Court reaffirmed that concerted refusals are illegal *per se* when their only purpose is to facilitate collusion. *Superior Court Trial Lawyers* condemned a boycott organized by trial lawyers against the City of Washington, D.C.[98] The lawyers were in the business of representing indigent criminal defendants, and received payment directly from the government. They believed that the rates the government paid were too low, and collectively withheld their services until the government agreed to pay more. The Court rejected, as it always has, the argument that the boycott should be legal because the old rates were too low; unrestrained markets should determine the rates.

In *Northwest Wholesale Stationers* the Court suggested that the *per se* rule be reserved for "joint efforts by a firm or firms to disadvantage competitors by 'either directly denying or persuading or coercing suppliers or customers to deny relationships the

---

[97] See the discussion of vertical integration in § 9.2.

[98] FTC v. Superior Ct. Trial Lawyers Assn., 493 U.S. 411, 110 S.Ct. 768 (1990).

competitors need in the competitive struggle.' " Such activities would
have to fall into the set of practices "likely to have predominantly
anticompetitive effects."[99] A year later in the *Indiana Dentists*
decision, also discussed below, the Court limited the *per se*
classification to "cases in which firms with market power boycott
suppliers or customers in order to discourage them from doing
business with a competitor."[100] Or as the Seventh Circuit has put it,
"boycotts are illegal per se only if used to enforce agreements that are
themselves illegal per se—for example price fixing agreements."[101]

Even the Supreme Court's earlier and expansive application of
the *per se* rule in Klor's, Inc. v. Broadway-Hale Stores, Inc.[102] is
consistent with the proposition that only concerted refusals
facilitating collusion or collusion-like behavior are illegal *per se*. The
allegations in *Klor's* were somewhat dubious. The plaintiff was a
retailer in kitchen appliances. One defendant, Broadway-Hale, was
a competing, although larger, retailer. The other defendants were
major manufacturers and distributors of kitchen appliances. Klor's
claimed that Broadway-Hale conspired with these distributors and
manufacturers to refuse to supply Klor's with appliances, or else to
supply them only at discriminatorily high prices and unfavorable
terms.

Assuming that Broadway-Hale had a motive for driving its
competitor out of business, why would the major appliance
manufacturers agree with *each other* to participate in this scheme?
The plaintiff alleged that Broadway-Hale used its "monopolistic"
buying power to force manufacturer agreement. That allegation is
plausible only on the assumption that Broadway-Hale had market
power in its local retail market, and Klor's was underselling its
monopoly price. However, the large appliance manufacturers would
be best off if their retailers were behaving as competitively as
possible, and Broadway-Hale's monopoly mark-up would make them
worse off.

There is a more plausible explanation: Klor's was a free rider
and Broadway-Hale complained to the manufacturers. The
manufacturers wanted their retailers to spend substantial resources
displaying and servicing their merchandise and providing
information to customers. If Broadway-Hale performed these

---

[99]　Northwest Wholesale Stationers v. Pacific Stationery & Printing Co., 472 U.S.
284, 298, 105 S.Ct. 2613, 2621 (1985).

[100]　FTC v. Indiana Federation of Dentists, 476 U.S. 447, 458, 106 S.Ct. 2009, 2018
(1986).

[101]　Collins v. Associated Pathologists, 844 F.2d 473 (7th Cir. 1988), cert. denied,
488 U.S. 852, 109 S.Ct. 137 (1988).

[102]　359 U.S. 207, 79 S.Ct. 705 (1959).

services but Klor's did not, Klor's would be able to charge a lower price. Furthermore, customers would be tempted to take a free ride on Broadway-Hale's services. They might go to Broadway-Hale and obtain all essential information about appliances, but then purchase at Klor's. A manufacturer might eliminate free riding either by giving its retailers exclusive territories, or else by resale price maintenance.[103] When *Klor's* was decided, the status of the first practice was undetermined, but the second was *per se* illegal. That would give each manufacturer an *independent* motive for excluding Klor's, although no reason to agree with each other.

Somewhat more difficult to characterize than *Klor's* is Fashion Originators' Guild of Amer. v. FTC[104] (FOGA). Garment designers and manufacturers agreed not to sell their "original creations" to retailers who also purchased garments from "pirates"— manufacturers who allegedly copied the designs of FOGA members and sold the garments at a lower price. As a defense, the FOGA members offered to show that the boycott was reasonable because manufacturers, laborers, retailers and consumers needed protection from the pirates. However, the garment designs could not themselves be copyrighted or patented. Two decades earlier, in International News Service v. Associated Press,[105] the Supreme Court had decided that Associated Press had a property right in its uncopyrighted news stories and could enjoin a competitor from paraphrasing them. However, in Cheney Bros. v. Doris Silk Corp.[106] Judge Learned Hand decided that the *International News* protection did not extend to clothing design piracy.

The patent and copyright laws encourage innovation by giving a limited legal power to exclude to the developer of a new invention, composition or design. The kind of innovation that qualifies for such protection has always been a subject of intensive legislative and judicial regulation. Both Congress and the courts had agreed that clothing designers did not merit such protection. The members of FOGA were effectively trying to give themselves the monopoly protection that the legislative and judicial branches had denied them. Justice Black concluded that it was not error for the FTC to refuse to

---

[103]　See §§ 11.5–11.6.

[104]　312 U.S. 457, 61 S.Ct. 703 (1941).

[105]　248 U.S. 215, 39 S.Ct. 68 (1918).

[106]　35 F.2d 279 (2d Cir. 1929), cert. denied, 281 U.S. 728, 50 S.Ct. 245 (1930). See Douglas G. Baird, Common Law Intellectual Property and the Legacy of International News Service v. Assoc. Press, 50 U.Chi.L.Rev. 411 (1983).

consider FOGA's defense that many constituents needed protection from style pirates.[107]

The "piracy" claim makes *FOGA* difficult to characterize. Lack of copyright or patent protection notwithstanding, the members of FOGA had a substantial free rider problem. If one group of manufacturers spends money developing new fashion designs, but another group is entitled to copy the designs at no charge, the result might be that creating original designs will become unprofitable and no one will do it. In that case the Guild was correct and consumers are better off if the free riders can be controlled. Nevertheless, the concerted refusal to deal employed by the defendants has a large potential to cover price fixing or concerted restraints on innovation. If the free rider problem in this instance is serious enough to have a solution, it should come from Congress.

In *Hartford* the Supreme Court gave the term "boycott" a narrow definition that may exclude at least some of the previously discussed cases.[108] Five members of the Court distinguished "concerted agreements on contract terms" from "boycotts." If a group of firms simply refuses to sell except at an agreed upon price, their action is not a boycott but merely a cartel.[109] Likewise, if a group of firms agrees to sell only a particular quality of product—as for example, if insurers should agree only to offer certain kinds of coverage—their agreement is a cartel but not a boycott. The latter term applies only when those negotiating a contract with another make concerted demands that are unrelated to the subject matter of that particular contract. For example, in the labor context a "boycott" is not merely an agreement by workers to withhold their labor, it occurs only when the workers make collateral demands unrelated to the labor contract at issue.

But this distinction is formalistic, finely drawn, and often impossible to apply. For example, in *FOGA* the defendants refused to sell clothing to retailers who also dealt with design pirates. The Court used the term "boycott" to describe this agreement,[110] and it certainly

---

[107]   312 U.S. at 468, 61 S.Ct. at 708. Some states have tried to give designs greater protection than is offered by federal law. In Sears, Roebuck & Co. v. Stiffel Co., 376 U.S. 225, 84 S.Ct. 784 (1964), the Supreme Court declared one such attempt to be preempted by federal patent and antitrust law.

[108]   Hartford Fire Ins. Co. v. California, 509 U.S. 764, 113 S.Ct. 2891 (1993).

[109]   In the ordinary Sherman Act case this distinction would be irrelevant, for both the cartel and the boycott would be illegal. But in *Hartford* the court was interpreting the boycott exception to the McCarran-Ferguson Act, a statute that permits insurance cartels but condemns "boycotts." For further discussion, see § 16.3c. The term "boycott," however, presumably had the same meaning under McCarran as under the antitrust laws generally.

[110]   See *FOGA*, 312 U.S. at 461, 465, 467, 61 S.Ct. at 337–338.

seems apt. But the *Hartford* opinion apparently (but ambiguously) refused to permit the term "boycott" to be applied to an agreement among reinsurers[111] and the defendant group of primary insurers that the reinsurers would not sell insurance to a second group of primary insurers unless the latter eliminated certain forms of coverage from their policies.[112] Clearly, the defendant primary insurers could negotiate any contract they pleased with the reinsurers with respect to their own reinsurance coverage. But could they negotiate the reinsurers' refusal to deal with the non-conspiring primary insurers as well? How this case should be distinguished from *FOGA*, which the Court appeared to approve, is difficult to say.

5.4a2.   Special Treatment for the Learned Professions?

Historically, the Supreme Court purported to apply the rule of reason to a boycott if the boycotters were members of the learned professions. In *Indiana Dentists* it considered an agreement among dentists to withhold X-Rays from a health insurer, who was purchasing dental services on behalf of its insureds.[113] The Court used the same kinds of sweeping statements that it would have applied in a *per se* decision—for example,

> "[a] concerted and effective effort to withhold (or make more costly) information desired by consumers for the purpose of determining whether a particular purchase is cost justified is likely enough to disrupt the proper function of the price-setting mechanism of the market that it may be condemned even absent proof that it resulted in higher prices. * * *"[114]

However, the Court then observed that it had always been reluctant to apply the *per se* rule to the collective decisions of professional associations.[115] Nonetheless, the Court condemned the agreement, noting that determination of a relevant market and a comprehensive market analysis were not necessary where there was clear evidence of actual anticompetitive effects.[116] Four years later in the *Trial*

---

[111]   Reinsurers are companies that sell insurance to primary insurance companies, permitting the latter to reduce the risk of catastrophic losses.

[112]   For more details, see § 16.3c.

[113]   FTC v. Indiana Federation of Dentists, 476 U.S. 447, 106 S.Ct. 2009 (1986). On restraints within the learned professions or other markets exhibiting unusual informational asymmetries, see 12 Antitrust Law ¶ 2008 (4th ed. 2019).

[114]   Id. at 461, 106 S.Ct. at 2019.

[115]   Id. at 458, 106 S.Ct. at 2018, citing National Society of Professional Engineers v. United States, 435 U.S. 679, 98 S.Ct. 1355 (1978). An earlier decision containing similar statements is Goldfarb v. Virginia State Bar, 421 U.S. 773, 778 & n. 17, 95 S.Ct. 2004, 2008 & n. 17 (1975).

[116]   Id. at 457, 106 S.Ct. at 2017.

Lawyers' decision the Court seemed quite willing to apply the *per se* rule.

Although the Court claimed to be applying a rule of reason in *Indiana Dentists*, the analysis in fact looked *per se*. *Trial Lawyers'* failure even to discuss the topic suggests that any notion that there is a substantial difference in the treatment of restraints among the learned professions has been abandoned.

A better way to view the whole problem is to begin with the premise that the learned professions trade heavily in information and expertise, areas prone to free-riding as well as other kinds of abuse. As a result, the scope of efficiency-creating joint practices may be somewhat larger in the learned professions than it is in, say, ordinary manufacturing. But the issues raised by *Indiana Dentists* and *Trial Lawyers* are in substance no different than those raised in many ordinary cases involving cartels and boycotts designed to facilitate collusion. Respecting such refusals to deal, the learned professions need be treated no differently.

The Supreme Court returned to the issue in the *California Dental* case, which involved a professional association's restraints on advertising rather than a concerted refusal to deal.[117] However, that distinction is largely semantic: if the plaintiff had been a dentist expelled for violating the advertising rules rather than the FTC, the complaint would have sounded in boycott. The challenged rules purported to control deceptive advertising, but in fact were so broad that they served to restrain much non-deceptive advertising as well. Nevertheless, the five-member majority insisted that the rule of reason be applied, emphasizing imperfections in the market for professional services.

California Dental seems to say that more suspicious restraints will be tolerated in complex markets where consumers are more likely to be misled. But the conclusion hardly follows from the premise. Indeed, we think that markets in which consumers are easily mislead are *more* rather than less conducive to collusion.[118] The less information a consumer has about price and quality, the easier it is for sellers to charge higher prices or provide inferior quality. Indeed, when consumer information is very poor one can have a "competitively structured" market with numerous service

---

[117]   California Dental Assn. v. FTC, 526 U.S. 756, 119 S.Ct. 1604 (1999).

[118]   See 12 Antitrust Law ¶ 2008c (4th ed. 2019); Aaron Edlin and Rebecca Haw, Cartels by Another Name: Should Licensed Occupations Face Antitrust Scrutiny?, 126 U. Pa. L. Rev. 1093 (2014).

providers but noncompetitive pricing.[119] The consumer tends not to know whether the dentist he has selected is offering competitive price and quality, but once the commitment is made the cost of switching to a different dentist can be high and the consumer cannot readily gauge whether the switch will make him better or worse off. Ordinarily, such markets are improved by more rather than less price and quality information, for the information enables the consumer to make comparisons *before* he or she selects a particular dentist.

Finally, in the *North Carolina Board of Dental Examiners* case, the Supreme Court agreed with the lower court and the Federal Trade Commission that the dentists' conduct was not immune under the "state action" doctrine.[120] Although the Supreme Court never discussed the standard of illegality, it refused review of the conclusion of both the FTC and the Fourth Circuit that either the rule of reason or a "quick look" applied to the dentists' rule that forbad teeth whitening by non-dentists. In ordinary production an agreement among firms to exclude a group of competitors might be unlawful per se, but the power of professional groups to set standards must also be acknowledged.

5.4b.   Efficient Joint Ventures and Refusals to Deal

5.4b1.   Closed-Membership and Other Traditional Joint Ventures

Many joint ventures involving refusals to deal are efficient— they enable the participating firms to operate at lower cost. As a result, a court evaluating a refusal to deal that accompanies a joint venture must ask two questions. First, is the joint venture itself competitive or anticompetitive? Second, if the venture is competitive, what policy is furthered by the refusal to deal? A refusal to deal might injure competition even if it is attached to a joint venture which is, on balance, socially beneficial.

The clearly anticompetitive joint venture presents the simplest case. If the only plausible motive for the joint activity is price fixing or delay of competitive entry, as it was in the *Eastern States* case,[121] both the joint venture and the refusal to deal are illegal.

---

[119]   See George J. Stigler, The Economics of Information, 69 J. Pol. Econ. 213 (1961).

[120]   North Carolina State Bd. Of Dental Examiners v. F.T.C., 574 U.S. 494, 135 S.Ct. 1101 (2015). On this decision and the "state action" doctrine, see § 20.5.

[121]   See § 5.4a1.

At the other extreme is the joint venture whose capacity for efficiency is large and whose danger to competition is very small. Consider a decision by three small firms in an unconcentrated market to undertake jointly a risky, expensive, but potentially profitable project. For any firm acting alone, the risk in proportion to the cost would make the venture unpromising. For three working together, however, the investment is far more attractive.[122] A fourth firm in the market is invited to participate but refuses. The project is developed, succeeds, and the new product or process is profitable. Now the fourth firm changes its mind and asks to "buy in." The three participants refuse.[123]

In this example any question about the competitive effects of the joint venture can be answered by looking at one fact: the participants collectively appear to have no market power. Three firms in an unconcentrated market could not likely reduce output or injure competition in some other way. They did not combine to fix prices but to reduce their costs.[124]

5.4b2.   Open-Membership Ventures; Positive Network Externalities

The traditional joint venture is "closed" in the sense that its membership is determined when it is first created and no one else is subsequently invited to join. For example, when Toyota and General Motors decided to join in the production of subcompact cars in Freemont, California, they probably never intended to invite Ford or Chrysler to join later. Further, as the previous section notes, there are good reasons why antitrust would not want to force Toyota/GM to open the venture to latecomers.

But many joint ventures are designed at the outset to take new members on an ongoing basis. For example, real estate multiple listing services, which permit competing brokers to sell one another's properties or split transactions, generally accept any licensed real estate broker.[125] Likewise, any new bank that qualifies for federal

---

[122] This is particularly true of research and development joint ventures. A three-way joint venture to develop a patentable product or process will cost each firm one-third as much as individual development would. However, the process, once developed, can be duplicated by all three firms. Each one will receive as great a benefit as if it had developed the patented product or process alone (ignoring monopoly profits that might be obtained by an individual developer but not by each of three competing developers).

[123] See 13 Antitrust Law ¶¶ 2200–2213 (4th ed. 2019).

[124] See Northwest Wholesale Stationers v. Pacific Stationery & Printing Co., 472 U.S. 284, 105 S.Ct. 2613 (1985) (joint venture's expulsion of member not illegal per se in absence of market power).

[125] See, e.g., United States v. Realty Multi-List, Inc., 629 F.2d 1351 (5th Cir. 1980) (condemning restrictive membership rules established by a multiple-listing service for real estate brokers).

deposit insurance may become a participant in joint ventures that issue general purpose charge cards such as Visa or MasterCard, or that facilitate electronic fund transfers through ATM machines.[126] Or any newly licensed lawyer or physician may join the ABA or the AMA.

Depending on the advantages they confer, open membership ventures can readily take up the entire relevant market. This places them in a position to use their membership rules anticompetitively. Furthermore, the latecomer argument for limiting free riders does not apply—everyone except the original members is a latecomer to one degree or another. To the extent that the original owners have intellectual property rights or are otherwise entitled to compensation for their risk, they generally do so through membership fees.

Open membership joint ventures often have important interests in intellectual property rights that may be subject to free riding, and this entitles the venture to make rules about how members might compete with the venture. For example, the Atlas moving joint venture at issue in the *Rothery* case enabled numerous local moving companies to participate in a nationwide joint venture facilitating the loading and shipment of goods across the country.[127] However, the Atlas members also engaged in local moving, which the joint venture permitted, but only on the condition that the member not use the Atlas name for business in which other joint venture members did not participate in the profits. This rule seems well designed both to protect the joint venture's intellectual property interests while minimizing the impact of any market power that the venture members might have.

By contrast, in the *Visa* case the Second Circuit struck down a rule that prohibited the 14,000 banks that issued a Visa or MasterCard from issuing any competitors' charge card.[128] The Visa and MasterCard ventures are open to any bank qualifying for federal deposit insurance, and new members are accepted on an ongoing basis. Further, every significant bank in the country issues Visa or MasterCard, thus effectively denying bank access to any competing charge card issuer, such as American Express, Discover, or a new entrant.

---

[126] See United States v. VISA U.S.A., Inc., 344 F.3d 229 (2d Cir. 2003), cert. denied, 543 U.S. 811, 125 S.Ct. 45 (2004); SCFC ILC v. VISA USA, 36 F.3d 958, 961 (10th Cir. 1994), cert. denied, 515 U.S. 1152, 115 S.Ct. 2600 (1995).

[127] Rothery Storage & Van Co. v. Atlas Van Lines, 792 F.2d 210, 214–16 (D.C.Cir. 1986), cert. denied, 479 U.S. 1033, 107 S.Ct. 880 (1987).

[128] See United States v. VISA U.S.A., Inc., 344 F.3d 229 (2d Cir. 2003), cert. denied, 543 U.S. 811, 125 S.Ct. 45 (2004).

Visa offered a free-rider defense—namely, that if the banks issued the cards of rivals they would be able to obtain confidential information that Visa had developed for its own use. The court found this claim to be unsupported by the evidence. Indeed, the Visa by-laws had an exception that permitted its members to issue rival MasterCard's general purpose cards, and MasterCard had the same exception in reverse. There was no reason to think that American Express, Discover, or some other issuer should be treated any differently.

While free-rider claims must always be taken seriously, the *Visa* case illustrates that it has been overused as a defense. Properly defined free riding is an output reducing strategy. That is, it undermines the primary firm's incentive to invest in a valuable asset, with the result that less of the asset is produced. But free rider problems do not exist every time they are asserted. *First*, not every instance of one firm's trading on another firm's investment is the kind of free riding that presents a policy concern. Many instances are simply product complementarity, and they typically increase rather than decrease output. For example, Ford profits greatly from the fact that Standard Oil, Exxon, and numerous others have developed a convenient network for the distribution of gasoline. If gasoline were hard to find, automobiles would be much less attractive. In this case, however, automobile makers and gasoline producers are "free riding" on each other, in a sense—that is, each profits because the other exists. Likewise, a bank that currently issued a Visa but wished to add American Express might be able to develop a Visa/AmEx package that is particularly valuable to consumers. But the result would be that *both* the Visa card and the American Express card would be sold in larger numbers.

Second, free riding is not a problem if the investor can capture the return on its investment by other means, such as an admission charge. Often the founding members in an open membership joint venture such as FTD, a joint venture of florists who will deliver flowers across the country, have intellectual property rights such as trademarks. But the value of these is readily captured by a membership or user fee.[129]

But even if price fixing is unlikely, open membership joint ventures can engage in anticompetitive exclusion of innovators that threaten the market share of the venture's existing members. The *Allied Tube* decision involved a standard setting joint venture that

---

[129]   See, e.g., Chicago Professional Sports Limited Partnership & WGN v. National Basketball Assn., 961 F.2d 667, 675 (7th Cir.), cert. denied, 506 U.S. 954, 113 S.Ct. 409 (1992) (NBA could capture value of its name and other intellectual property by charging a fee when its games were televised).

was open to a wide variety of manufacturers, insurers and other firms involved in the design, manufacturing and evaluation of electrical components used in buildings.[130] Approval by the venture was essential to market success, because the venture's proposals were typically incorporated without change into local building codes. The defendants were firms that manufactured metal electrical conduit and felt their market shares threatened by the plaintiff, whose plastic conduit was cheaper, easier to install, and safer than metal. The defendants then "packed" a standard setting meeting and managed to get a rule adopted that disapproved the plastic conduit and effectively kept it off the market for several years.

In such a case the competitive harm does not result from the fixing of prices, but rather from the restraint on innovation. Even if the steel conduit makers were competing vigorously with one another and earning only competitive returns, they would still be severely injured by an innovation that threatened to make their own product obsolete and idle their capacity. The result of the exclusion, however, was to deny consumers the benefit of a product that they would have preferred and that a competitive market would have given them.

The same analysis generally applies to industries subject to positive network externalities. In such industries being connected to or compatible with the network is valuable in and of itself, without regard to the absolute quality of the plaintiff's product.[131] For example, the best telephone in the world is not worth much if it cannot be connected into the telephone system. Those controlling the system are likely to have significant market power, but they also have a significant investment in their own technologies. As a result, a joint venture rule excluding a telephone instrument, switching device, or other component that seems to be superior and might threaten the investments of incumbents would have to be justified, and less restrictive alternatives examined.

One important case involving a refusal to deal by an open membership joint venture is Associated Press v. United States.[132] Associated Press (AP) was a joint venture whose members were about 1,200 newspapers. AP gathered, drafted and disseminated news. Part of the work was done by employees who worked for AP, and part by reporters that AP borrowed from member newspapers. When the AP correspondent gathered news and wrote a news story in, say,

---

[130] Allied Tube & Conduit Corp. v. Indian Head, 486 U.S. 492, 108 S.Ct. 1931 (1988); see 13 Antitrust Law ¶ 2220b (4th ed. 2019).

[131] See Richard A. Posner, Antitrust Law 245–258 (2d ed. 2001); Herbert Hovenkamp, The Antitrust Enterprise: Principle and Execution, ch. 12 (2005); 13 Antitrust Law ¶ 2220 (4th ed. 2019).

[132] 326 U.S. 1, 65 S.Ct. 1416 (1945).

Washington, D.C., all member newspapers were entitled to a copy of the story. In effect, AP enabled a single reporter to gather news that would be reported by each of the 1,200 member newspapers.

The joint venture itself was conceded to be very efficient. But the government challenged various by-laws adopted for AP by its members. The members were prohibited from selling news to non-members, and AP took several steps to insure that non-AP newspapers had no access to AP-gathered news until after it was published. AP's board of directors could freely elect new members unless the applicant competed with a newspaper that was already an AP member. In that case, if the competing member objected the new member had to pay a large fee and receive a majority vote of existing AP members. The Supreme Court held that these provisions on their face violated the Sherman Act.

5.4c.   Standard Setting and Rule Enforcement in Private Entrepreneurial and Professional Associations

Concerted refusals are an important mechanism by which trade associations, privately run markets, cooperatives and professional associations enforce rules and standards governing product or service quality. Disciplining violators most generally takes the form of excluding a firm from membership or penalizing it in some way that restricts its access to the market. Overwhelmingly, challenges to such discipline are evaluated as concerted refusals to deal under the rule of reason.[133]

Both standard setting and rule making are generally in the best interests of consumers, because they substantially reduce information costs, and therefore consumer search costs.[134] The labels "approved by United Testing Laboratories," "number two plywood," or "board certified operator" all convey information to consumers about the products or services they are purchasing.

An inevitable result of any meaningful standard-setting procedure is that some do not meet the standard and are excluded from the business association or even the market. This becomes an antitrust problem when the persons making and enforcing the standards are competitors of the person or firm who is excluded by them. At the same time, the providers of certain products or services

---

[133]   Herbert Hovenkamp, Standards Ownership and Competition Policy, 48 Boston Col.L.Rev. 87 (2007). On standard setting in high technology markets, see Christina Bohannan & Herbert Hovenkamp, Creation Without Restraint: Promoting Liberty and Rivalry in Innovation, Ch. 8 (2011).

[134]   See Herbert Hovenkamp, et al., IP and Antitrust: An Analysis of Antitrust Principles Applied to Intellectual Property Law, ch. 35 (3d ed. 2017).

are experts, and often are in a better position than anyone else to evaluate the quality of a competitor's product. For example, a patient would have a difficult time determining whether a particular surgeon is competent, unless perhaps she knows several people who have been under the surgeon's scalpel. Those in the best position to make this judgment are fellow surgeons familiar with the same area of practice. For this reason most medical institutions have peer review boards, composed largely of doctors, which evaluate the performance of other doctors. If the board members act in good faith, consumers are better off. If they act in bad faith, consumers suffer.

The problem of professional and product standard setting by private organizations is closely akin to that of refusals to deal by open membership joint ventures.[135] The fact that membership is desirable or even legally essential for market access effectively turns these organizations into market gatekeepers. While such organizations have the capacity to do much good, we cannot ignore the potential for competitive harm.

Radiant Burners, Inc. v. Peoples Gas Light & Coke Co.[136] involved an association of gas heater manufacturers, pipeline companies and utilities which evaluated products that burned natural gas and placed a "seal of approval" on products judged to be safe. If a product was judged unsafe, the association not only refused its seal of approval, but the utility companies in the association refused to provide gas to a home or business containing the disapproved product. The plaintiff manufacturer claimed that its Radiant Burner had been disapproved by the association, and that the standards used to evaluate the Burner were arbitrary and capricious, largely because the burner was evaluated by the manufacturers of competing gas burners. In a *per curiam* opinion the Supreme Court concluded that the allegations stated a cause of action for a *per se* violation of the Sherman Act, citing Klor's, Inc. v. Broadway-Hale Stores.[137]

The plaintiff's complaint in *Radiant Burner* contained two important allegations, both of which may be necessary to bring the concerted refusal by competitors under the *per se* rule: 1) that the plaintiff's product was not evaluated objectively, but in a capricious

---

[135]   See § 5.4b2.

[136]   364 U.S. 656, 81 S.Ct. 365 (1961).

[137]   359 U.S. 207, 79 S.Ct. 705 (1959), discussed earlier. See also American Medical Association v. United States, 317 U.S. 519, 63 S.Ct. 326 (1943) (accreditation association may not dismiss or discipline a member simply because she is a price cutter); United States v. ABA, 60 Fed. Reg. 39,421 (1995) (consent decree forbidding ABA from tying law school accreditation to faculty compensation); E Thomas Sullivan, The Transformation of the Legal Profession and Legal Education, 46 Ind. L. Rev. 145 (2013).

way by competitors who had a vested interest in disapproving the product; 2) that the defendants actually forced customers not to buy the disapproved product, or in some way prevented it from entering the market. Courts have been reluctant to apply the *per se* rule when one of these elements was present but not the other. They have usually approved the activity when neither was present.

Even a coercive refusal is unlikely to be anticompetitive if those making the adverse decision are not in competition with the firm whose product or service is rejected. For example, in *Radiant Burners* the defendant gas utilities might have justified their refusal to provide gas to installations using the Radiant Burner on the grounds that the product could injure the utility companies' lines or increase their insurance risks.[138] Often standard setting claims can be dismissed by the simple observation that those setting the standards are not in competition with the firm or person who is excluded. For example, if an anesthesiologist is denied staff privileges at a hospital by a board composed of rival anesthesiologists, an anticompetitive explanation is plausible. But the hospital itself, its surgeons, and physicians in non-competing areas of practice generally cannot profit by excluding a price-cutting or unusually innovative anesthesiologist. In fact, many of them would be benefitted. For example, both the hospital and its surgeons would be better off if the anesthesiologist charged lower prices or used an innovative procedure that had positive results.[139]

A requirement that the standards by which a product is evaluated be reasonable and applied in a nondiscriminatory way is important if a court is to avoid considering subjective intent.[140] To be sure, the protection offered by such a legal requirement is not perfect.

---

[138] The gas companies were not required to justify their refusal because the district court dismissed the complaint for failure to state a claim, and the Seventh Circuit affirmed. Radiant Burners, Inc. v. Peoples Gas, Light & Coke Co., 273 F.2d 196 (7th Cir. 1959).

[139] See Abraham & Veneklasen Joint Venture v. American Quarter Horse Ass'n, 776 F.3d 321 (5th Cir. 2015) (where association did not itself own quarter horses, standard that precluded cloned horses could not be shown to be anticompetitive); Super Sulky v. United States Trotting Assn., 174 F.3d 733 (6th Cir.), cert. denied, 528 U.S. 871, 120 S.Ct. 172 (1999) (association of drivers and race associations would not have incentive to disapprove plaintiff's racing sulky design if it really were superior); Moore v. Boating Industry Assoc., 819 F.2d 693 (7th Cir.), cert. denied, 484 U.S. 854, 108 S.Ct. 160 (1987) (association of boat trailer manufacturers did not violate antitrust laws by disapproving plaintiff's trailer light; they would stand to benefit from low cost high quality lights).

[140] Simple statements of disapproval, with no attempt at forced removal from the market, are typically approved. See 13 Antitrust Law ¶ 2232e (4th ed. 2019); and Schachar v. American Academy of Ophthalmology, 870 F.2d 397 (7th Cir. 1989) (no violation where defendant Academy had simply labeled plaintiff's procedure "experimental").

Often, however, it is the only means by which an outsider can assess the true effect of what purports to be a disciplinary act.

For example, in Silver v. New York Stock Exchange (NYSE)[141] a stockbroker complained that the Exchange members denied him access to the private telephone connections necessary to monitor and execute stock transactions on the exchange. Without such lines a stockbroker is generally unable to carry on its business. The NYSE refused to provide any explanation why Silver's communication was cut off, telling him only that "it was the policy of the Exchange not to disclose the reasons for such action." When Silver charged the Exchange members with violating the Sherman Act, they answered that under the Securities Exchange Act of 1934 the members were authorized to pass and enforce their own rules and regulations governing broker activity. As a result the termination was exempt from antitrust scrutiny.

The Supreme Court did not deny that the Securities Exchange Act gave members the authority to make and enforce their own business rules. However, "nothing built into the regulatory scheme * * * performs the antitrust function of insuring that an exchange will not in some cases apply its rules so as to do injury to competition which cannot be justified as furthering legitimate self-regulatory ends." At the time *Silver* was decided, brokerage commissions on the NYSE were fixed. The purpose of fixed commissions was arguably to force brokers to provide the optimal number of customer services. However, the members may have reached an "understanding" about the number of services they would give. A disruptive broker who provided more services could do substantial damage to such a service cartel. The defense asserted in *Silver* would effectively have given the NYSE members the power to cartelize all aspects of the stock brokerage market.[142]

The Supreme Court took a step back from *Silver* in the *Northwest Wholesale Stationers* decision.[143] The plaintiff stationery retailer had been expelled from a cooperative that wholesaled products to member retailers. Further, the record (of both the cooperative proceedings and the subsequent litigation) gave no explanation why the plaintiff had been expelled. The Supreme Court

---

[141]   373 U.S. 341, 83 S.Ct. 1246 (1963).

[142]   There was some history of the NYSE warning or disciplining members for competing too intensely. Brief for United States as Amicus Curiae 37–41, Silver v. NYSE, Oct. Term 1962.

[143]   Northwest Wholesale Stationers v. Pacific Stationery & Printing Co., 472 U.S. 284, 105 S.Ct. 2613 (1985). See also Gregory v. Fort Bridger Rendezvous Ass'n, 448 F.3d 1195 (10th Cir. 2006) (rule of reason applied to association's exclusion of plaintiff, a dealer who had participated in association-sponsored markets).

held that the lower court had incorrectly applied the *per se* rule. The activities of a wholesale cooperative that bought stationery supplies and resold them to members clearly represented substantial integration of the distribution process; so this was not a "naked" refusal to deal. As a result, the expulsion could not be condemned without a showing that the cooperative had "market power or unique access to a business element necessary for effective competition."[144]

Northwest substantially increases the plaintiff's burden in cases involving an association's refusal to deal. Under *Silver* the defendants had to provide minimal due process and an explanation for the discipline. Under *Northwest*, the defendant apparently need provide nothing at all unless the plaintiff shows market power. Or to say it another way, the mere fact that an expulsion from a joint venture is unexplained does not mean that it is unreasonable in the antitrust sense. The plaintiff has the initial obligation to allege and show that an expulsion *either* (1) facilitates a naked restraint such as price-fixing; or (2) is "unreasonable," with reasonableness measured in the antitrust sense of facilitating the exercise of market power, and not in the lay person's more general sense which might conclude that any unexplained or certainly any arbitrary expulsion is "unreasonable." Unexplained exclusions are more likely to raise the fact finder's suspicions.[145]

Finally, a great deal of standard setting occurs in the context of patent licensing, particularly when standards require patented technology. In that case participants may agree to license their patents on "Fair, Reasonable, and Non-Discriminatory" (FRAND) terms. Antitrust disputes involving these arrangements are discussed below in § 5.5c6.

5.4d. Agreements Involving Non-Competitors

The *Klor's* case[146] involved allegations that a group of appliance manufacturers conspired with each other and a competing appliance store to boycott the plaintiff's store. Whatever one might think of the factual plausibility of that claim, the allegation that a group of competing appliance sellers conspired with *each other* was essential to the Supreme Court's conclusion that the complaint alleged a per se violation. The Court made this clear in its *NYNEX* decision, which involved an agreement not to deal between a single purchaser and a single seller.[147] The plaintiff Discon sold removal services of obsolete

---

[144] Id. at 298, 105 S.Ct. at 2621.

[145] See 13 Antitrust Law ¶ 2214 (4th ed. 2019).

[146] See Klor's, Inc. v. Broadway-Hale Stores, Inc., 359 U.S. 207, 79 S.Ct. 705 (1959).

[147] NYNEX v. Discon, Inc., 525 U.S. 128, 119 S.Ct. 493 (1998).

telephone equipment. Defendant NYNEX, the local phone company for New York, entered into an agreement with a rival under which (1) the rival agreed to supply all of NYNEX's removal services; (2) the "public" price of these services would be inflated, thus going into NYNEX's regulated rate base and producing higher telephone rates; but (3) the rival would pay NYNEX a secret year-end rebate for this right.

The Supreme Court was willing to concede the plaintiff's claim:

that the petitioners' behavior hurt consumers by raising telephone service rates. But that consumer injury naturally flowed not so much from a less competitive market for removal services, as from the exercise of market power that is lawfully in the hands of a monopolist, namely, New York Telephone, combined with a deception worked upon the regulatory agency that prevented the agency from controlling New York Telephone's exercise of its monopoly power.[148]

Applying the per se rule in such a case:

would transform cases involving business behavior that is improper for various reasons, say, cases involving nepotism or personal pique, into treble-damages antitrust cases. And that per se rule would discourage firms from changing suppliers—even where the competitive process itself does not suffer harm.[149]

NYNEX makes clear that when two vertically related firms refuse to deal that refusal must be treated as a type of vertical restraint, so far as antitrust is concerned.[150] To be sure, it could also be fraud or some other legal violation. But antitrust treats vertical agreements not to deal under highly focused inquiries that generally prevent any broad per se rule even when the restraint is harmful on its face.

---

[148]   525 U.S. at 136, 119 S.Ct. at 498.

[149]   525 U.S. at 137, 119 S.Ct. at 498.

[150]   See, e.g., Total Benefits Planning Agency, Inc. v. Anthem Blue Cross & Blue Shield, 552 F.3d 430 (6th Cir. 2008) (agreement between insurance company and its agents purely vertical and covered by rule of reason; no claim that agents were conspiring with each other); Expert Masonry, Inc. v. Boone County, Ky., 440 F.3d 336 (6th Cir. 2006) (similar).

§ 5.5   Agreements Governing the Licensing and Use of Patents and Other Intellectual Property

5.5a.   Introduction; Basic Issues

This section discusses licensing and similar agreements among multiple actors that involve patents. In addition, unreasonably exclusionary patent practices are discussed in § 7.11, and tying and related patent practices throughout Chapter 10.

Three facts complicate antitrust analysis of agreements governing the use of patents and other intellectual property. First, problems of free-riding and economies of scale are substantial. The free rider problem derives from the fact that intellectual property rights can easily be appropriated if they are not given greater legal protection than is given to more tangible property rights. If the innovator cannot effectively exclude others from copying the innovation, then many of the returns to innovation will be lost and we can expect less innovation to occur.

Economies of scale exist because the costs of *duplicating* products or processes protected by intellectual property are so much lower than the cost of initial development. For example, if Chrysler develops a better airbag to protect automobile passengers and uses the patent only on its own automobiles, the development costs must be divided over its own limited output. But if Chrysler can license the patents to all other interested automobile manufacturers, the development costs can be spread over a much larger output. Of course, the licensing agreement would be a contract among competitors, and it may affect the price or output of automobiles—in sum, it may raise some of the flags that usually signal antitrust concern.

Second, intellectual property rights are by nature "nonrivalrous," which means that one person's use of an IP right does not inherently deprive someone else of that right, although competition may make the rights less value. This nonrivalrous nature makes IP rights inherently easier to share than rivalrous rights. For example, if two farmers operating independently decide to share a field, one can plant more only if the other plants less, assuming the field is being used to capacity. By contrast, if two manufacturers share a patented process each can produce as much as it pleases without taking any right to produce away from the other.[151]

The third complicating factor is that patents, as well as copyrights and trademarks, are governed by detailed federal statutes that create numerous potential conflicts with antitrust policy.[152] As a result, the antitrust laws and the federal intellectual property laws must be interpreted so as to accommodate one another. Importantly, the United States has both a patent policy and an antitrust policy, and neither should be interpreted in such a way as to disregard the other. One may therefore dispute the *SCM Corp.* conclusion that if a "patent has been lawfully acquired, subsequent conduct permissible under the patent laws cannot trigger any liability under the antitrust laws."[153] Simple legality under the patent laws cannot be decisive of an antitrust question, although *clear authorization* under the patent laws generally is decisive. Most of the discussion that follows is directed at the problem of patents. Although copyrights and trademarks raise similar concerns, these are not as well developed in the antitrust literature or the case law.[154]

5.5b.   The Scope of the Patent Misuse Doctrine, Antitrust and Beyond

Article I, Section 8, clause 8 of the Constitution grants Congress the power to "promote the Progress of Science and useful Arts" by "securing for limited Times to Authors and Inventors the exclusive Right to their respective Writings and Discoveries." This authorization is not limited by the commerce clause or other considerations of federalism, and thus gives Congress full authority over patents and copyrights. At the same time, however, it does not by its terms create a property interest, but rather an "exclusive right" such as might be contained in an exclusive contract.

Since the 1940s antitrust policy concerning patent licensing was closely tied to the patent law's doctrine of "misuse," although the doctrine is now in steep decline. The concept of patent misuse is

---

[151] See Christina Bohannan & Herbert Hovenkamp, Creation Without Restraint: Promoting Liberty and Rivalry in Innovation, ch. 8 (2011).

[152] See Herbert Hovenkamp, et al., IP and Antitrust: An Analysis of Antitrust Principles Applied to Intellectual Property Law (3d ed. 2017); William M. Landes & Richard A. Posner, The Economic Structure of Intellectual Property Law (2003); Herbert Hovenkamp, Antitrust and the Patent System: A Reexamination, 76 OSU L.Rev. 467 (2015).

[153] SCM Corp. v. Xerox Corp., 645 F.2d 1195, 1206 (2d Cir. 1981), cert. denied, 455 U.S. 1016, 102 S.Ct. 1708 (1982).

[154] For fuller treatment, see Hovenkamp, et al., *IP and Antitrust, supra*; and 10 Antitrust Law, Ch. 17G (4th ed. 2018) (vertical arrangements likened to tying); and 12 id. Ch. 20E (4th ed. 2019) (horizontal arrangements).

broad, and misuse can be found not only in licensing agreements, but also in the patentee's infringement suits directed at non-licensees (so-called contributory infringement).[155] The misuse claim typically arises when the patent holder sues another firm, claiming that its patent rights or contract rights under a licensing agreement have been violated. The defense raised is that the patent has been "misused," which is tantamount to a defense that the way the patent's owner used the patent violates patent law, antitrust law, or perhaps some less clearly articulated legal policy. If the misuse defense prevails, the patent is generally held to be unenforceable until the misuse is "purged."[156]

"Misuse" typically arises because, in the court's view, the patent is being used inconsistently with the policy of the IP laws or competition policy. This naturally invites the question of what the source of law is, given that most of these practices are not explicitly forbidden by the IP laws themselves. As a general matter the courts have readily found misuse in the case of well established antitrust violations. Many, but not all, instances of patent misuse are practices analogous to unlawful tying arrangements, which are taken up in Chapter 10. Clayton Act § 3, which was intended to be applied to tying and exclusive dealing, applies its proscriptions to all goods and commodities, "whether patented or unpatented."[157] In general, a "tie" of two products, or refusal to sell separately, is unlawful only if the seller has market power in the tying product or substantial anticompetitive effects result from the requirement. Indirectly, by admitting various defenses, many courts effectively assess both of these requirements.[158] By contrast, ties have been found to be patent misuse even though neither requirement was shown.

In *Motion Picture Patents* the court invalidated a license restriction printed on a motion picture projector that only movies leased from the patent owner could be shown with the projector. The patentee, a group controlled by Thomas A. Edison as licensor, had brought an infringement action against film distributors that violated the restriction by supplying films not leased by the patentee itself. In invalidating this restriction, the Court did not rely on the

---

[155]   See Mercoid Corp. v. Mid-Continent Investment Co., 320 U.S. 661, 64 S.Ct. 268 (1944) (*Mercoid I*) (applying the doctrine); Morton Salt Co. v. G.S. Suppiger Co., 314 U.S. 488, 62 S.Ct. 402 (1942) (same; patentee who was engaged in unlawful tying could not bring infringement claim against rival).

[156]   E.g., *Morton Salt, supra.*

[157]   15 U.S.C.A. § 14.

[158]   See §§ 10.3–10.5.

antitrust laws, but rather a general patent policy against using tying requirements to extend the scope of the patent monopoly.[159]

Likewise, in *Morton Salt* the patent holder had tied the lease of its patented salt injecting machines to the purchase of unpatented salt tablets.[160] The Court held that this tying arrangement constituted misuse of the patent and refused to enforce the patent against an admitted infringer. In the process, the Court held that it was "unnecessary to decide whether [the patent owner] has violated the Clayton Act," because enforcement of the tying arrangement under these circumstances was "contrary to public policy."[161] This holding suggested that the patent misuse defense permitted the alleged infringer to raise "antitrust-like" defenses and prevail even though the challenged practice was not literally an antitrust violation.[162]

Legislation passed in 1988 addresses, but does not resolve, the question whether a patent can be "misused" when there is no antitrust violation. The Patent Misuse Reform Act[163] provides that a claim of patent infringement cannot be resisted simply because the patentee tied patented and unpatented goods unless the patent owner has market power "in the relevant market for the patent or patented product on which the license or sale is conditioned." This provision does not require that patent misuse and unlawful tying be identical—but it does add to the patent misuse doctrine the economically reasonable requirement applied in the law of tying

---

[159] "[T]o enforce [this monopoly] would be to create a monopoly in the manufacture and use of moving picture films, wholly outside of the patent in suit and of the patent law as we have interpreted it." Id. at 518. For an extensive discussion of the case and its economic background, see 9 Antitrust Law ¶ 1701b (4th ed. 2018).

[160] Morton Salt Co. v. G.S. Suppiger Co., 314 U.S. 488, 62 S.Ct. 402 (1942).

[161] Id. at 494, 62 S.Ct. at 406.

[162] Accord Leitch Mfg. Co. v. Barber Co., 302 U.S. 458, 463, 58 S.Ct. 288, 291 (1938) ("Every use of a patent as a means of obtaining a limited monopoly of unpatented material is prohibited.").

[163] 35 U.S.C.A. § 271(d):

(d) No patent owner otherwise entitled to relief for infringement or contributory infringement of a patent shall be denied relief or deemed guilty of misuse or illegal extension of the patent right by reason of his having done one or more of the following: ... (3) sought to enforce his patent rights against infringement or contributory infringement; (4) refused to license or use any rights to the patent; or (5) conditioned the license of any rights to the patent or the sale of the patented product on the acquisition of a license to rights in another patent or purchase of a separate product, unless, in view of the circumstances, the patent owner has market power in the relevant market for the patent or patented product on which the license or sale is conditioned.

. . .

arrangements—namely, market power in the market for the tying product in those cases where tying is the gist of the misuse claim.[164]

As historically stated in *Morton Salt*, the patent misuse doctrine seems precisely wrong. The clear implication was that patents were a kind of "suspect class," and that arrangements involving patents were to be treated with greater hostility than would be applied to similar practices not involving patents. In fact, the opposite is generally true. Patent licensing is most generally efficient and should be encouraged. Concerns that the patent holder could "leverage" additional monopoly profits by combining its rights under the patent with contract requirements governing unpatented goods are either fanciful or greatly exaggerated.[165]

Claims of patent misuse might initially be tested by antitrust principles, but that cannot be the end of the story. After all, "misuse" is a creature of IP law, which protects values that are distinct from the competition values protected by antitrust. One value is protection of access to the public domain. Another is protection against practices that serve to restrain rather than promote innovation, even though they may not be technical antitrust violations.[166] The Supreme Court acknowledged the independent *patent law* relevance of misuse doctrine in the *Marvel* "Spiderman" decision. The Court adhered to a half century old rule that an agreement requiring royalties based on sales made after a patent expires is unenforceable per se.[167] That rule, the Supreme Court observed, emanated from patent law, not antitrust law. While antitrust analysis might have compelled a different outcome, such as treatment under the rule of reason, in this case *stare decisis* counseled for adherence. Three dissenting Justices (Alito, Thomas, and Chief Justice Roberts) protested that not only did antitrust policy not compel the rule against post-expiration royalty payment extensions, but nothing in the Patent Act did so either. In any event, a simple contract calling for royalty payments would rarely violate the antitrust laws, but the *Brulotte/Marvel* rule is per se, making it a significant expansion beyond antitrust.

---

[164]   See § 10.3.

[165]   On the "leverage" theory, see §§ 7.9, 10.6a, 13.3b. In the patent context, see 2 Erik N. Hovenkamp & Herbert Hovenkamp, "Tying Arrangements," 329–350, in Oxford Handbook of International Antitrust Economics (2015).

[166]   See Christina Bohannan, IP Misuse as Foreclosure, 96 Iowa L.Rev. 475 (2010). Cf. Thomas F. Cotter, Four Questionable Rationales for the Patent Misuse Doctrine 12 Minn. J.L. Sci. & Tech. 457 (2011) (arguing for limitation to antitrust principles).

[167]   Kimble v. Marvel Ent't, 576 U.S. 446, 135 S.Ct. 2401 (2015), adhering Brulotte v. Thys (1964) on grounds of stare decisis. See Herbert Hovenkamp, Brulotte's Web, 11 J. Comp. L. & Econ. (2015), available at http://papers.ssrn.com/sol3/papers.cfm?abstract_id=2626758.

5.5c.   Patent Licensing; the "Scope of the Patent" Rule

Historically, the courts often analyzed potentially anticompetitive licensing rules under a "scope of the patent" test: a restriction was permissible if it did reach further than the boundaries that the patent already gave to the patentee. For example, product price fixing contained within a patent license was thought to be within the "scope of the patent," because a patentee who made all of the patented goods itself could set the price.[168] By contrast, tying of patented and unpatented goods was thought to go beyond the "scope of the patent" by extending the patent "monopoly" to the unpatented goods. In the horizontal collusion context, the principal recognized exception to the "scope of the patent" rule was for very weak or invalid patents, where the patent might serve as nothing more than a cover for collusion.[169]

In the *Actavis* decision, discussed later, the Supreme Court majority rejected the "scope of the patent" test on the facts of that case, while three dissenters would have applied it.[170] Further, the Court held that patent validity or scope was not necessarily a defense to an anticompetitive agreement involving a patent.

One case that severely tests the scope of the "patent" doctrine is the settlement in *1-800-Contacts*, on appeal at this writing, which is actually a trademark dispute.[171] The parties were contact lens manufacturers who settled trademark infringement litigation with an agreement that they would not use one another's names in comparative advertising. The case stretches the "scope of the IP right" very far because the settlement relied on a single poorly reasoned decision denying summary judgment on a claim that use of another brand's name in comparative advertising amounts to trademark infringement.[172] For example, if Chrysler should advertise "our model is cheaper than an equivalent Ford," the use of the word "Ford" in that advertisement, which is clearly a "use" of a rival's trademark in commerce, could be trademark infringement. The settlement is within the scope of the IP right only if this one anticompetitive decision is correct while many others are wrong.

---

[168]   United States v. General Electric Co., 272 U.S. 476, 485 (1926) (patentee acts unlawfully only when "he steps out of the scope of his patent rights. . . .").

[169]   E.g., Asahi Glass Co. v. Pentech Pharm., Inc., 289 F. Supp. 2d 986, 992 (N.D. Ill. 2003).

[170]   FTC v. Actavis, Inc., 570 U.S. 136, 133 S.Ct. 2223 (2013).

[171]   1-800-Contacts, Inc., 2018 WL 6201693, 2018-2 Trade Reg. Rep. ¶ 80,586 (F.T.C. Nov. 7, 2018), app. docketed, 2d Cir.

[172]   Soilworks, LLC v. Midwest Indus. Supply, Inc., 575 F. Supp. 2d 1118, 1129 (D. Ariz. 2008).

Otherwise this is a simple case of an agreement among firms not to engage in comparative advertising.

A better way of assessing anticompetitive agreements involving patents is to consider first whether the practice in question is expressly permitted under the Patent Act. For example, the Act permits exclusive licenses and even domestic territorial restrictions,[173] but it never authorizes product price fixing or market division agreements unrelated to licensed production. When authorization is absent, then antitrust law rather than patent law should control the analysis. This does not mean that the practice is unlawful, but only that antitrust rules can be brought to bear.

5.5c1.   Price Fixing; Output Restrictions; Royalty Rates; Exclusivity

In *General Electric* the Supreme Court held that a firm could license technology to a competitor with the provision that the product manufactured by the licensee be sold at a price stipulated by the licensor.[174] The Court reasoned that General Electric could have kept the right to manufacture its light bulbs to itself, in which case it would have charged the monopoly price. As a result, the agreement did not reach beyond the scope of GE's patent. The Court did not observe that General Electric could have reached the same result by setting a license fee equal to the monopoly markup. That is, if the patented lamps cost $1.00 to make but General Electric maximized its profits at a price of $1.50, it could have charged Westinghouse, the licensee, a 50 cent per lamp license fee. But Westinghouse would have resisted this if the patent were worth much less. In sharp contrast, the opportunity to fix light bulb prices was valuable to both parties. The courts have also generally found that the licensor of a patent may limit the quantity of the patented product produced by the licensee.

General Electric has never been explicitly overruled,[175] but it is subject to some exceptions. First, the price fixing provision may not be extended to unpatented goods or processes—this would reach beyond the scope of the patent.[176] Second, the *General Electric*

---

[173]   Both in 35 U.S.C. § 261.

[174]   United States v. General Electric Co., 272 U.S. 476, 47 S.Ct. 192 (1926).

[175]   In 1965 a divided Supreme Court declined to overrule it. United States v. Huck Manufacturing Co., 382 U.S. 197, 86 S.Ct. 385 (1965). However, see Asahi Glass Co., Ltd. v. Pentech Pharmaceuticals, Inc., 289 F.Supp.2d 986, 992 (N.D.Ill. 2003) (Judge Posner, suggesting that *GE* would no longer be followed today); and see William M. Landes & Richard A. Posner, The Economic Structure of Intellectual Property Law 382–384 (2003).

[176]   Cummer-Graham Co. v. Straight Side Basket Corp., 142 F.2d 646, 647 (5th Cir.), cert. denied, 323 U.S. 726, 65 S.Ct. 60 (1944).

doctrine extends to the price initially charged by the licensee, but not to the resale price: that is, the licensor may not engage in a form of resale price maintenance in which it regulates the price charged at resale by those who purchase from the licensee.[177] This rule flows not from any articulated patent policy, but simply from the fact that resale price maintenance was illegal *per se* at the time.[178] Third, if patents are "cross-licensed"—that is, re-licensed from the original licensee to a second, or sub-licensee, the latter licensing agreement may not fix the price.[179] Finally, several decisions have suggested that while *GE* permits a single patentee to fix the price with a single licensee, it does not apply to agreements involving multiple patentees or a patentee and several licensees.[180]

The government has never concealed its disdain for the *GE* rule and has attempted repeatedly to have it overruled.[181] Its 2017 Antitrust Guidelines for IP licensing never discuss the rule and take the position that horizontal price restraints with efficiency prospects will be evaluated under the rule of reason, while the per se rule will be applied to naked restraints.[182] That approach is clearly preferable to the *GE* rule, which is not an antitrust rule of reason at all but rather an ill-conceived blanket immunity for price-fixing that falls within its realm.

Several courts have condemned license agreements that require the licensee to continue to pay royalties after the patent has expired. In *Kimble* the Supreme Court adhered to this rule on grounds of *stare decisis*.[183] The given rationale is another variation of the "scope of the patent" theory used to condemn ties of patented and unpatented products—in this case, that the patent holder is trying to take advantage of its monopoly power in the patented product to leverage additional monopoly profits from post-expiration sales.

Finally, a patent licensing agreement is lawful even if it is exclusive. In an exclusive patent license, the patent holder promises

---

[177] United States v. Univis Lens Co., 316 U.S. 241, 243–251, 62 S.Ct. 1088, 1090–1094 (1942); Ethyl Gasoline Corp. v. United States, 309 U.S. 436, 446–457, 60 S.Ct. 618, 620–626 (1940).

[178] On resale price maintenance, see § 11.5. Maximum RPM is governed by the rule of reason; presumably, a maximum price agreement in a patent license would receive the same treatment. See § 11.5c.

[179] United States v. Line Material Co., 333 U.S. 287, 293–315, 68 S.Ct. 550, 553–564 (1948).

[180] *Line Material*, id. at 314–315.

[181] For a list of the decisions, see 12 Antitrust Law ¶ 2041d (4th ed. 2019).

[182] See U.S. Dep't of Justice & Fed. Trade Comm'n, Antitrust Guidelines for the Licensing of Intellectual Property § 5 (2017), available at https://www.justice.gov/atr/IPguidelines/download.

[183] Kimble v. Marvel Ent't, 576 U.S. 446, 135 S.Ct. 2401 (2015).

not to license the patent to others. Often the licensor promises not to practice the patent itself as well. Even the latter agreement is no more than a transfer of the right to use a patent from one firm to another, something that does not ordinarily raise competitive concerns. Section two of the Sherman Act may be implicated, however, if a firm has a practice of acquiring exclusive licenses in an area and then not practicing the patents under these licenses.[184] Likewise, except in the context of a joint venture, competitors may not lawfully agree with each other not to license their patents.[185]

5.5c2. Horizontal Territorial and Other Market Division Agreements

The Patent Act expressly permits the patentee to grant exclusive rights "to the whole or any specified part of the United States."[186] Thus a patent holder may legally restrict its licensee's sales to a given territory, even if the patent holder and the licensee are competitors.[187] A naked territorial division agreement between competitors is ordinarily illegal *per se*.[188]

Patent licensing arrangements between competitors are often a form of joint venture in which multiple firms share a technology. The patent owner has every right to manufacture the product itself without licensing to anyone. But it may wish to grant others the right to produce in a given geographic area because barriers to new entry in that area are high, the market already has sufficient basic capacity, or the licensee has goodwill or intellectual property that can be used to advantage. In such cases the effect of the geographically restricted licensing agreement is to *increase* total output under the patent. That is, the patented product will be produced in the new area under the arrangement, while it would probably not be produced there at all, or at least in a smaller amount, if the arrangement were unlawful. By the same reasoning, courts generally uphold patent

---

[184] See § 7.11.

[185] Blount Mfg. Co. v. Yale & Towne Mfg. Co., 166 Fed. 555 (D. Mass. 1909).

[186] 35 U.S.C. § 261. See E. Bement & Sons v. National Harrow Co., 186 U.S. 70, 92–93, 22 S.Ct. 747 (1902) (upholding territorial restrictions in license agreement to make agricultural harrows); Brownell v. Ketcham Wire & Mfg. Co., 211 F.2d 121, 128 (9th Cir. 1954) ("owner of a patent may license another and prescribe territorial limitations.").

[187] Ethyl Gasoline Corp. v. United States, 309 U.S. 436, 456, 60 S.Ct. 618, 625 (1940).

[188] See § 5.2.

licensing agreements that restrict sales to specified classes of customers.[189]

An important exception to this rule is that the "licensing agreement" may not be merely a sham to cover naked territorial division. For example, firms cartelizing a market may agree to use a licensing agreement to give effect to a territorial division scheme, with the agreement covering a patent of dubious validity or a patent whose value is very small.[190] Palmer v. BRG of Georgia,[191] condemned such an agreement under the *per se* rule even though the territorial division at issue involved a licensing agreement for copyrighted materials.

Also generally legal under the antitrust laws are so-called "field of use" restrictions, under which the patentee restricts the range of products or uses to which a patent license can be applied. The field of use restriction can thus operate as a kind of product division scheme. For example, in *General Talking Pictures* the Court approved an arrangement under which the patent owner used the patent in manufacturing it own amplifiers for theaters, but authorized a licensee to use the same patent for making radio receivers.[192] The same arguments for territorial restrictions generally apply to field of use restrictions. For example, suppose a manufacturer of airplanes patents a navigation device that is useful in both aircraft and boats. The patent owner does not wish to license another aircraft manufacturer to use the patented device, and the law does not require it to do so. But boats do not compete with aircraft, and the world would be a better place if boats as well as aircraft could take advantage of the new device. The owner of the patent could use the patented device in its own aircraft but license boat manufacturers, restricting them to making the device only for boats.

---

[189] See In re Yarn Processing Patent Validity Litig., 541 F.2d 1127, 1135 (5th Cir. 1976), cert. denied, 433 U.S. 910, 97 S.Ct. 2976 (1977) (upholding agreement restricting sales to other licensees of patentee).

[190] See Timken Roller Bearing Co. v. United States, 341 U.S. 593, 598–599, 71 S.Ct. 971, 975 (1951) (court believed that intellectual property license was simply a device for suppressing competition, notwithstanding common ownership of participants); United States v. Crown Zellerbach Corp., 141 F.Supp. 118, 126 (N.D. Ill.1956).

[191] 498 U.S. 46, 111 S.Ct. 401 (1990).

[192] General Talking Pictures Corp. v. Western Electric Co., 304 U.S. 175, 58 S.Ct. 849, on rehearing, 305 U.S. 124, 59 S.Ct. 116 (1938). Accord Benger Laboratories v. R.K. Laros Co., 209 F.Supp. 639 (E.D.Pa.1962), affirmed per curiam, 317 F.2d 455 (3d Cir.), cert. denied, 375 U.S. 833, 84 S.Ct. 69 (1963). If a field of use restriction conditions the patent license on limitations on the use of *un*patented products, the restriction may be illegal. See Robintech, Inc. v. Chemidus Wavin, Ltd., 628 F.2d 142, 146–149 (D.C.Cir. 1980).

5.5c3.   *Pay-for-Delay Settlements of Pharmaceutical Patent Disputes;* Actavis

Patent "settlements" are agreements by which firms agree to resolve litigation over patent infringement or licensing. A settlement that simply authorizes someone else to practice a patent in exchange for a specified royalty does not ordinarily raise antitrust concerns. For example, Alpha may sue Beta for patent infringement. The two parties settle their dispute by an agreement that Beta may go ahead with its plans but pay Alpha a royalty. The license agreement itself is not subject to antitrust challenge, and the fact that it is a settlement cannot make it any worse. In general, the courts treat settlement agreements deferentially. Patents enjoy a presumption of validity (although not of infringement or high value) and determining their boundaries can be very difficult. So patent settlement agreements are often approved even if they are competitively suspicious.[193] The courts become most concerned when settlements fix product prices, divide product markets, or exclude rivals by means of practices that are both anticompetitive and not authorized by the Patent Act.

One problematic class of settlement agreements involve so-called "pay-for-delay" settlements, in which a patent infringement plaintiff pays an infringement defendant to stay out of the market. A naked payment to a competitor to stay out of the payor's market is a *per se* antitrust violation, and in these cases there is no joint production or other activity among the two parties. Indeed, a pay-for-delay settlement is not a license at all, but rather a payment to a rival not to produce. As a result, any deference due to a settlement license agreement does not obtain. Further, pay-for-delay exclusions are not authorized by the Patent Act.

Pay-for-delay patent settlements were unheard of prior to passage of the Hatch-Waxman Act, which was intended to encourage the entry of generic drugs manufacturers upon the expiration of the "pioneer" drug maker's patent or a declaration that it is invalid.[194] Under the Act a generic firm commits patent infringement when it files an abbreviated new drug application (ANDA) for a biological equivalent to a pioneer drug and the relevant patent has not yet expired. The significance of the "abbreviated" application is that, because the drug is bioequivalent to a drug that has already

---

[193]   See 12 Antitrust Law ¶ 2046 (4th ed. 2019) (collecting decisions).

[194]   Drug Price Competition and Patent Term Restoration (Hatch-Waxman) Act, Pub. L. No. 98–417, 98 Stat. 1585 (1984) (codified as amended in scattered sections of 15, 21, 28, and 35 U.S.C.A.). On the absence of pay-for-delay patent settlements prior to this Act, see Herbert Hovenkamp, Anticompetitive Patent Settlements and the Supreme Court's *Actavis* Decision, 15 Minn. J.L.Sci. & Tech. 3, 15–16 (2014).

undergone comprehensive FDA testing, most of that testing need not be repeated. At that time the pioneer patent holder can either acquiesce and permit the generic to produce or else file a patent infringement action. The Act provides that once the generic begins producing under this ANDA, it will have a 180 day period of exclusivity, during which time no other generics can enter the market.[195]

Congress did not foresee that this procedure creates a little bilateral monopoly between the pioneer and the ANDA-filing generic, allowing them to delay the generic's production date and split the patent's proceeds for that term. During this period no other generic firm can challenge the patent. This is particularly important because as many as 90% of large pay-for-delay settlements involve "secondary" patents on new dosages or uses for a drug, and these patents are invalid a high percentage of the time.[196] The size of the payment for delay reflects the parties' views about the strength of the patent: a very large payment is a sign that the parties do not believe the patent is very strong, and many of the payments in these cases run to several hundred million dollars. In general, a property owner has a right to exclude others and need not pay potential trespassers a great deal to say away. Thus the high payments reflect considerable suspicion about the patents in question.

By the time of *Actavis* several federal courts had approved pay-for-delay settlements under a "scope of the patent" test, which would generally exonerate any agreement that did not delay generic entry beyond the nominal expiration date of the patent.[197] Justice Breyer's opinion for the Court correctly rejected that test, however, emphasizing rather that the agreement in question had clear anticompetitive potential and was not authorized by the Patent Act. Further, questions about either patent scope or validity need not control the antitrust question whether the agreement restrained trade unlawfully. That point has been controversial, but it is essential to any form of ex ante analysis in which the parties'

---

[195] See 21 U.S.C. § 355(j)(5)(B)(iv) (2012). The Supreme Court described the process briefly in FTC v. Actavis, Inc., 570 U.S. 163, 133 S.Ct. 2223, 2228 (2013). See also 12 Herbert Hovenkamp, Antitrust Law ¶ 2046c (4th ed. 2019).

[196] See C. Scott Hemphill & Bhaven N. Sampat, Drug Patents at the Supreme Court, 339 Sci. 1386, 1386 (2013) (89 percent of large pay-for-delay settlements involved secondary drugs).

[197] FTC v. Watson Pharma., Inc., 677 F.3d 1298, 1311 (11th Cir. 2012) ("scope of the exclusionary potential of the patent"); Arkansas Carpenters Health and Welfare Fund v. Bayer AG, 604 F.3d 98 (2d Cir. 2010) (question is "whether patent settlements in which the generic firm agrees to delay entry into the market in exchange for payment fall within the scope of the patent holder's property rights"); In re Ciprofloxacin Hydrochloride Antitrust Litig., 544 F.3d 1323, 1332–1333 (Fed. Cir. 2008).

reasonable expectations rather than ex post realities must govern the antitrust analysis. Deterrence based theories must be tied to the point in time when decisions are made. Thus in a case applying state law similar to federal law the California Supreme Court properly held that the patent's "expected life" at the time that the agreement was negotiated was the controlling question.[198] That term refers to the nominal remaining duration of the patent, discounted by the percentage likelihood of invalidity.

At the same time the Court rejected the FTC's proposed "quick look" analysis and indicated that antitrust rule of reason should be applied, but under a "sliding scale" approach that did not require the lower courts to "litigate the patent's validity, empirically demonstrate the virtues or vices of the patent system, present every possible supporting fact or refute every possible pro-defense theory. . . ."[199] He also indicated that market power for rule of reason purposes could be inferred from the large payment itself,[200] and that even anticompetitive effects could be inferred from a large payment. On the question of how large is "large," the Court suggested that a payment equal to reasonably anticipated litigation costs would be reasonable, as well as compensation for the fair market value of any services that the generic firm performed.[201]

5.5c4.   *Package Licenses*

A package license covers more than one patent. Package licenses are ubiquitous and reduce transaction costs substantially if a single process is covered by many patents, each of which covers a small part of the process, or if there is uncertainty about whether particular patents cover the licensee's technology. For example, the old fashioned stapler sitting on the author's desk—hardly a piece of high technology—is covered by seven listed patents. Were the owner of these patents to license another firm to manufacture the stapler, it might well draft a single licensing agreement covering all. Package licensing of patents reduces the transaction costs of individual negotiations much like blanket licensing of numerous copyrights reduced transaction costs in the *Broadcast Music* case.[202]

Package licensing is generally legal,[203] although it is sometimes thought to be anticompetitive when a patent holder with market

---

[198]   In re Cipro Cases I & II, 348 P.3d 845, 61 Cal.4th 116 (May 7, 2015).

[199]   FTC v. Actavis, Inc., 570 U.S. 136, 159, 133 S.Ct. 2223, 2237–2238 (2013).

[200]   Id. at 2236.

[201]   Id. at 2237.

[202]   Broadcast Music v. CBS, 441 U.S. 1, 99 S.Ct. 1551 (1979). See § 5.2c.

[203]   Automatic Radio Manufacturing Co. v. Hazeltine Research, 339 U.S. 827, 70 S.Ct. 894 (1950).

power in one patent conditions its license on the licensee's acceptance of a package of patents.[204] In this case the underlying concerns of tying law as well as patent misuse are implicated. The 1988 Patent Misuse Reform Act discussed previously covers package licensing as well as tying, approving it unless the patentee has market power in the market for the desired patent.[205] However, the Copyright Act contains no such provision, and one post-1988 decision condemned "block-booking"—a form of package licensing—of television shows.[206] The court reasoned that by licensing shows in blocks the defendant licensor was foreclosing rival program producers from access to the licensee station's time slots. However, the court appears to have erred on the foreclosure issue; tying nearly always forecloses rivals from the particular buyer upon whom a tying arrangement is imposed. But the relevant foreclosure issue is whether the *market* is foreclosed. For example, if the market contained ten television stations, block-booking that entirely filled the programming slots of one station would nevertheless leave the other nine to receive the programming of rivals.[207]

5.5c5. *Patent Pools*

A patent pool occurs when a group of firms license their individually held patents to one another, or sometimes exchange licenses. The metaphor of the pool is taken from the oil industry, where multiple surface owners might have an interest in the same subterranean pool of oil. They could then profit and minimize conflict by drilling a single well and sharing the operating expenses and revenues.

In general, patent pools are treated under the rule of reason, and most are legal.[208] In *Zenith Radio*, however, the Supreme Court

---

[204] Hazeltine Research v. Zenith Radio, 388 F.2d at 33–35. The patents at issue covered devices for color televisions.

[205] The Act makes it lawful to "condition * * * the license of any rights to the patent * * * on the acquisition of a license to rights in another patent * * * unless * * * the patent owner has market power in the relevant market for the patent or patented product on which the license or sale is conditioned." 35 U.S.C.A. § 271(d). U.S. Dep't of Justice & Fed. Trade Comm'n, Antitrust Guidelines for the Licensing of Intellectual Property § 5.3 (1995), state that the agencies will evaluate package licensing under the same criteria as are applied to tying arrangements.

[206] MCA Television Limited v. Public Interest Corp., 171 F.3d 1265 (11th Cir. 1999).

[207] See § 10.6b2.

[208] For example, Standard Oil Co. v. United States, 283 U.S. 163, 51 S.Ct. 421 (1931). See Christina Bohannan & Herbert Hovenkamp, Creation Without Restraint: Promoting Liberty and Rivalry in Innovation, ch. 8 (2011); Erik N. Hovenkamp & Herbert Hovenkamp, Patent Pools and Related Technology Sharing, in Cambridge Antitrust Intellectual Property Handbook (Roger D. Blair and D. Daniel Sokol, eds. 2017).

approved a lower court finding that an *exclusive* patent pool was illegal *per se*.[209] The court interpreted the agreement at issue as one among competitors that they would not license their patents to others. Such an agreement could be an effective collusion facilitator, in that it could permit the firms to fix prices while deterring new entry.

A traditional economic defense of patent pools is that they are justified when the patents in the pool are complements. Because complements are used together, pooling can avoid "royalty" stacking problems that occur when two different sellers provide complementary goods. Separately, the two will typically charge a higher price than if their output was combined into a single seller.[210] By contrast, *competing* patents are used in the alternative rather than together, and pooling threatens to eliminate competition between them.

However, the patents contained in modern large pools, particularly in information technologies, often have many claims and are very difficult to interpret. This makes them harder to classify as complements or substitutes and many operate as both. A more robust explanation of patent pooling is that it enables the users of technology to avoid costly issues of validity and boundary interpretation. While individual boundaries are typically the best way to protect private property interests, in some cases the costs of identifying and defending individual boundaries makes them impractical. For example, a group of fishermen who share a common pond are likely to find it cheaper to share access, together with some rules that control catch size and support requirements, rather than have individual fences dividing up the body of water. This is true even though the fish are substitutes for one another, not complements. Patents, however, are not like fish in one important sense: patents are nonrivalrous, which means that one person's use does not diminish what is left over for others. This entails that output restrictions governing pooled patents are competitively more suspicious than output restrictions in fisheries, which are virtually a necessity.[211]

---

[209]   Zenith Radio Corp. v. Hazeltine Research, Inc., 395 U.S. 100, 113 n. 8, 89 S.Ct. 1562, 1571 n. 8 (1969).

[210]   See, e.g., Richard J. Gilbert, Antitrust for Patent Pools: A Century of Policy Evolution, 2004 Stan. Tech. L. Rev. 3. On royalty "stacking," see Herbert Hovenkamp, Antitrust and the Patent System: A Reexamination, 76 OSU L.Rev. 467 (2015); Erik N. Hovenkamp & Herbert Hovenkamp, "Tying Arrangements," Oxford Handbook of International Competition Policy (2015).

[211]   See Christina Bohannan & Herbert Hovenkamp, Creation Without Restraint: Promoting Liberty and Rivalry in Innovation 325–364 (2012).

One type of complementary relationship that virtually always justifies pooling is "blocking patents," which are patents that cannot be practiced without infringing one another. As a result, protected use of either patent requires licensing of both. As one court noted, if the claims made in patents are blocking, then "no third party would want just one license, and each party [licensor] is effectively precluded from licensing its own patent unless the other party agrees to licensing of its patent as well."[212]

5.5c6. FRAND: Patent Licensing and Standard-Essential Patents

In information technology markets such as computers or cellphones, standards are often used to guarantee interoperability as well as product quality.[213] Products developed under these standards are often patented, thus requiring participating producers to obtain patent licenses. Standard-setting in these markets is a "rolling" process, requiring continual updating and development of new standards for new technologies. Standard setting organizations (SSOs) usually require participants to disclose essential patents that they own, and agree to license them to all participants, including competitors, on fair, reasonable, and nondiscriminatory ("FRAND") terms.[214] Such patents are called "standard essential patents," or SEPs. FRAND declarations are made by patent holders, and represent their opinion that the patent in question is "essential," meaning that some portion of the standard cannot reasonably be practiced without infringing the patent. For the most part the SSO does not verify essentiality, although that may become an issue in subsequent patent infringement litigation. "Over-declaring" is common.[215] Nor does the SSO check patents for validity.

The Patent Act itself does not impose FRAND obligations. The obligations are voluntary, and patentees who are not involved in SSOs have no obligation other than market pressures to submit their patents to a standard or engage in FRAND licensing. In networked

---

[212] Boston Scientific Corp. v. Schneider, 983 F.Supp. 245, 271 (D. Mass.1997), dism'd by consent, 152 F.3d 947 (Fed.Cir. 1998) (alleged patent pool lawful when patents were found to be blocking).

[213] On standard setting, see § 5.4c.

[214] See, e.g., the IP policy of the Telecommunications Industry Association: "A license under any Essential Patent(s), the license rights which are held by the undersigned Patent Holder, will be made available to all applicants under terms and conditions that are reasonable and non-discriminatory."

[215] See Mark A. Lemley & Timothy Simcoe, How Essential are Standard-Essential Patents?, 104 Corn. L. Rev. 607, 527 (2019); Robin Stitzing, Pekka Saaskilahti, Jimmy Royer, and Marc Van Audenrode, Over-Declaration of Standard Essential Patents and Determinants of Essentiality (SSRN working paper, 11 Sep 2018), https://papers.ssrn.com/sol3/papers.cfm?abstract_id=2951617.

technologies, however, these market pressures can be significant. For example, if a patentee refuses to commit its patented technology to an industry standard, the SSO may adopt a different standard that is not believed to infringe those patents.[216] Under FRAND, royalties that cannot be established by agreement among the parties are typically determined by a court or arbitrator.[217]

The FRAND system facilitates competition by assuring new firms as well as existing ones that they will be able to operate on the networked technology. Royalties to the owners of these standard essential patents (SEPs) are generally measured by the value that the contributed patent makes to the standard.[218] Importantly, tribunals seek to measure these values "ex ante," or prior to the patent's adoption into a standard and at a time when there are a fuller range of competitive alternatives.[219] Once the standard is adopted and implementers have incorporated it into their own technologies, a standard essential patent is likely to be in a much stronger position, approaching monopoly in some cases.[220] Patents that are committed in this way are described as being "FRAND encumbered."[221]

When a firm makes a commitment to develop its products under a particular standard, it wants assurance that it will have a durable right to operate under that standard at reasonable royalty rates. This process naturally leads to considerable path dependence in standards, as it encourages firms to develop their technologies in ways that ensure interoperability.[222]

Violations of these FRAND obligations, including failure to disclose patented technology and refusal to license to all on FRAND

---

[216]   See D. Scott Bosworth, Russell W. Mangum III, & Eric C. Matolo, *FRAND Commitments and Royalties for Standard Essential Patents*, 19, in COMPLICATIONS AND QUANDARIES IN THE ICT SECTOR: STANDARD ESSENTIAL PATENTS AND COMPETITION ISSUES (2018).

[217]   See, e.g., Interdigital Tech. Corp. v. Pegatron Corp., 2016 WL 234433 (N.D. Cal. Jan. 20, 2016) (compelling arbitration). See Hovenkamp, et al., IP and Antitrust: An Analysis of Antitrust Principles Applied to Intellectual Property Law § 35.05 (3d ed. & Supp. 2019).

[218]   See, e.g., Microsoft Corp. v. Motorola, Inc., 795 F.3d 1024, 1041 (9th Cir. 2015). See Thomas F. Cotter, Erik Hovenkamp, & Norman Siebrasse, Demystifying Patent Holdup, 76 Wash. & Lee L. Rev. 1501 (2019).

[219]   E.g., Lucent Techs., Inc. v. Gateway, Inc., 580 F.3d 1301, 1325 (Fed. Cir. 2009) ("The hypothetical negotiation tries, as best as possible, to recreate the ex ante licensing negotiation scenario and to describe the resulting agreement.").

[220]   See Carl Shapiro, *Navigating the Patent Thicket: Cross Licenses, Patent Pools, and Standard Setting* 119, in 1 INNOVATION POLICY AND THE ECONOMY (Adam B. Jaffe, et al, eds., 2001).

[221]   E.g., FTC v. Qualcomm, Inc., *6, 2017 WL 2774406 (N.D. Cal. June 26, 2017).

[222]   Cotter, Hovenkamp, and Siebrasse, *supra* note 218.

terms, are breaches of the FRAND agreement. Contract partners or third party beneficiaries may sue to enforce them.[223] Only a subset violate the antitrust laws, however, and it can be important to distinguish FRAND violations that violate the antitrust laws from those that do not. Antitrust violations can produce treble damages in private litigation, or else they can be enforced by the Federal Trade Commission or the Antitrust Division of the Justice Department.

Here it is important to avoid the two extremes: first is thinking that a FRAND violation is more or less automatically an antitrust violation; and second is thinking that because an act is a FRAND violation it cannot also be an antitrust violation.[224] Breach of a contract does not require market power or injury to competition, while a rule of reason antitrust violation ordinarily does. However, when power and anticompetitive effects are established, it is no defense that the defendant's conduct also violated its FRAND commitments and thus was a breach of contract.

SSOs operated by multiple firms are joint ventures.[225] For bona fide joint ventures, the purpose of the antitrust laws is not to destroy the venture or undermine its principal purposes, but rather to evaluate how the challenged restraint operates within the venture and condemn unreasonably harmful restraints.[226] SSOs should be addressed accordingly. The goal of the standard setting venture is to facilitate competitive operation and entry, interoperability, as well as preserve appropriate competitive incentives for research and development. Antitrust analysis necessarily involves testing conduct against these goals, but only to the extent of looking for practices that are anticompetitive. This means it must identify practices that reduce market wide output unreasonably or that are unnecessarily exclusionary or harmful to consumers because of their impact on competition. Antitrust law has no statutory authorization to oversee the standard essential patent process aside from its power to police anticompetitive practices.

---

[223] See, e.g., Microsoft Corp. v. Motorola, Inc., 864 F.Supp.2d 1023 (W.D. Wa. 2012) (product developer was third party beneficiary entitled to enforce FRAND obligation); Realtek Semiconductor Corp. v. LSI Corp., 946 F.Supp.2d 998 (N.D. Ca. 2013).

[224] See Herbert Hovenkamp, FRAND and Antitrust, ___ Cornell L. Rev. ___ (2020) (forthcoming), available at https://papers.ssrn.com/sol3/papers.cfm?abstract_id=3420925.

[225] For treatment of SSOs as joint ventures, see 13 Phillip E. Areeda & Herbert Hovenkamp, Antitrust Law, Ch. 22B, C (4th ed. 2019).

[226] See 7 Phillip E. Areeda & Herbert Hovenkamp, Antitrust Law, Ch 15 (4th ed. 2017).

Illustrating the difference is *Rambus*, which involved patent "ambush."[227] Rambus failed to disclose patents that it was developing even as it was participating in developing standards that would infringe those very patents. Members who believed they were developing a public domain standard found out only later that they owed royalties to Rambus. While Rambus' conduct may have violated its contractual obligation,[228] the D.C. Circuit held that they did not violate § 2 of the Sherman Act because it was not shown that anyone was excluded from the market. The only harm was that users of the standard had to pay more than if the technology had been in the public domain as they had been led to believe. Thus the case was more akin to fraud rather than monopolization.

In the presence of technological path dependence, which is common, the *Rambus* decision can be quite harmful to innovation. By failing to disclose its patents, Rambus induced other participants to mold their technology around them. Later on, when that technology was developed and modification costly, the surprise did two things. First, it required manufacturers to pay royalties to Rambus that they did not anticipate. Second, the nondisclosure directed technological development down a path it otherwise might not have taken.

In many FRAND cases conventional antitrust doctrine may indicate liability quite aside from FRAND commitments. For example, Qualcomm was found to have significant market power and to have engaged in unlawful refusals to deal with competitors, tying, exclusive dealing, and loyalty discounts.[229] The court did not rely on FRAND commitments in reaching these conclusions. Rather, it relied on traditional antitrust criteria under the rule of reason.

In sum, the fact that a practice breaches a FRAND agreement neither establishes antitrust liability nor precludes it. On the latter point, many antitrust violations involve conduct that also violated contract or tort law or perhaps some other body of law. In those cases we do not say that the fact that certain conduct breaches a contract means that it cannot also violate the antitrust laws Rather, we analyze the conduct independently under each body of law. The one important "conflict" principle is that damages are not to be awarded

---

[227] Rambus, Inc. v. FTC, 522 F.3d 456 (D.C.Cir. 2008); for good discussion, see Thomas F. Cotter, Patent Holdup, Patent Remedies, and Antitrust Responses, 34 J. Corp. L.1151, 1179–80 (2009).

[228] In fact, the disclosure requirements at the time were very ambiguous. See *Rambus*, 522 F.3d at 461. Subsequently, many SSOs strengthened their disclosure requirements.

[229] FTC v. Qualcomm, Inc., 411 F.Supp.3d 658 (N.D.Cal. 2019), rev'd on other grounds, 969 F.3d 974 (9th Cir. 2020).

twice for the same harm. If the jury does award damages twice, then the judge must order remittitur of the duplication.[230]

While the FRAND violation itself does not establish an antitrust violation, it may provide facts that are essential to the antitrust analysis. Antitrust law takes markets as it finds them. For example, in the numerous antitrust decisions involving the NCAA,[231] a very large joint venture, the antitrust courts do not pretend that the joint venture does not exist. Rather, they assume that the venture itself performs a socially valuable function. Then they begin with its rules and the investments and commitments that its structure creates and considers how antitrust can be used to make the market function competitively on those assumptions. In this case, FRAND commitments can induce firms to direct their technology down a certain path. If extraction or modification is costly, reneging on these requirements can be an anticompetitive practice.

The standard setting process and the use of standard essential patents is well settled and assumed to be socially and economically beneficial. In that case the best use of antitrust law is to police the competitive process within that system. The FRAND system has its own rules and regulations and in the first instance enforcing them is not an antitrust function. But neither does the system create an antitrust immunity.

Further, this is one area where it is critical to keep an eye on longer run concerns for innovation. If a single firm reneges on its FRAND commitments with anticompetitive results and antitrust fails to intervene, other firms will follow. FRAND-enabled joint ventures will fall apart. Internationally, that could slow the rate of innovation and make the resulting products much more costly. Domestically, it could deprive United States innovators and manufacturers of a leadership role. A troublesome decision by a Ninth Circuit panel may be do just that.[232] The defendant had been able to evade most of its FRAND obligations by threatening to withhold chips from companies that refused to pay its significantly higher royalties. If that decision encourages other firms to do the same thing Congress may have to intervene to protect the FRAND

---

[230]   E.g., Fineman v. Armstrong World Indus., Inc., 980 F.2d 171, 218 (9th Cir. 1992) (where both antitrust claims and common law tort and contract claims were predicated on the same loss of future profits, plaintiff must be limited to a single recovery).

[231]   AMERICAN LAW REPORTS maintains a comprehensive list of the dozens of antitrust cases against the NCAA. See Application of Federal Antitrust Laws to Collegiate Sports, 87 A.L.R. Fed.2d 43 (2014, & updated weekly).

[232]   FTC v. Qualcomm, 969 F.3d 974 (9th Cir. 2020). For further discussion, see §7.5; and Hovenkamp, FRAND and Antitrust, *supra*.

system. Otherwise collaborative innovations requiring FRAND licensing could be in trouble.

5.5d.   Agreements Concerning Non-Patent Intellectual Property[233]

Economically speaking, the competitive concerns with copyrights, trademarks or other forms of intellectual property are about the same as those applying to patents, although more attenuated. For example, the *Broadcast Music* case discussed in § 5.2c really involved nothing more than package licensing of a product that was copyrighted rather than patented.[234] The important difference that made this particular package license problematic was that the arrangement was analyzed as an agreement *among competitors* to engage in blanket licensing. If a single actor unilaterally package licensed its copyrights—for example, if Lady Gaga licensed all her performances in a single package on a take-it-or-leave-it basis—competitive concerns are not readily apparent.[235] Nevertheless, certain practices such as the "block booking" of films have been condemned under just such circumstances. For example, in *Paramount Pictures* the Supreme Court condemned a film producer's policy of licensing its films only in blocks.[236]

§ 5.6   Characterization and Evaluation: The Per Se Rule and the Rule of Reason

5.6a.   The Supreme Court and the Per Se Rule

Consider the following statements, all from the Supreme Court:

The true test of legality is whether the restraint imposed is such as merely regulates and perhaps thereby promotes competition or whether it is such as may suppress or even destroy competition. To determine that question the court must ordinarily consider the facts peculiar to the business to which the restraint is applied; its condition before and after the restraint was imposed; the nature of the restraint and its effect, actual or probable.

---

[233]   See generally 12 Antitrust Law ¶ 2041e (4th ed. 2019) (GE rule and price-fixing of non-patent intellectual property), ¶ 2043c (pooling), 2044e (horizontal market divisions of non-patent intellectual property).

[234]   On package licensing of patents, see § 5.5c3.

[235]   For a suggestion to the contrary, see CBS v. American Society of Composers, Authors & Publishers, 562 F.2d 130, 140–141 & n. 29 (2d Cir. 1977), reversed and remanded sub nom. Broadcast Music, Inc. v. CBS, 441 U.S. 1, 99 S.Ct. 1551 (1979).

[236]   United States v. Paramount Pictures, 334 U.S. 131, 68 S.Ct. 915 (1948).

Justice Brandeis, in Board of Trade of City of Chicago v. United States, 246 U.S. 231, 238, 38 S.Ct. 242, 244 (1918).

> Under the Sherman Act a combination formed for the purpose and with the effect of raising, depressing, fixing, pegging, or stabilizing the price of a commodity * * * is illegal *per se.*

Justice Douglas, in United States v. Socony-Vacuum Oil Co., 310 U.S. 150, 223, 60 S.Ct. 811, 844 (1940).

> Whether or not we would decide this case the same way under the rule of reason used by the District Court is irrelevant.

Justice Marshall, in United States v. Topco Associates, Inc., 405 U.S. 596, 609, 92 S.Ct. 1126, 1134 (1972).

> [P]er se rules * * * are * * * directed to the protection of the public welfare; they are complementary to, and in no way inconsistent with, the rule of reason.

Chief Justice Berger, dissenting, in United States v. Topco Associates, 405 U.S. at 621, 92 S.Ct. at 1140.

> Contrary to its name, the Rule [of Reason] does not open the field of antitrust inquiry to any argument in favor of a challenged restraint that may fall within the realm of reason. Instead, it focuses directly on the challenged restraint's impact on competitive conditions. * * *

> There are * * * two complementary categories of antitrust analysis. In the first category are agreements whose nature and necessary effect are so plainly anticompetitive that no elaborate study of the industry is needed to establish their illegality—they are "illegal per se;" in the second category are agreements whose competitive effect can only be evaluated by analyzing the facts peculiar to the business, the history of the restraint, and the reasons why it was imposed. In either event, the purpose of the analysis is to form a judgment about the competitive significance of the restraint; it is not to decide whether a policy favoring competition is in the public interest, or in the interest of the members of an industry.

J. Stevens, in National Society of Professional Engineers v. United States, 435 U.S. 679, 688–692, 98 S.Ct. 1355, 1363–65 (1978).

> [The defendants] have joined together into an organization that sets its price for the blanket license it sells. But this is not a question simply of determining

whether two or more potential competitors have literally
"fixed" a "price." As generally used in the antitrust field,
"price fixing" is a shorthand way of describing certain
categories of business behavior to which the *per se* rule has
been held applicable. [However, when] two partners set the
price of their goods or services they are literally "price
fixing," but they are not *per se* in violation of the Sherman
Act. * * * Thus, it is necessary to characterize the
challenged conduct as falling within or without that
category of behavior to which we apply the label "*per se*
price fixing." That will often, but not always, be a simple
matter.

J. White, in Broadcast Music, Inc. v. CBS, Inc., 441 U.S. 1, 8–9, 99
S.Ct. 1551, 1556–57 (1979).

The costs of judging business practices under the rule
of reason * * * have been reduced by the recognition of *per
se* rules. Once experience with a particular kind of restraint
enables the Court to predict with confidence that the rule of
reason will condemn it, it has applied a conclusive
presumption that the restraint is unreasonable.

J. Stevens, in Arizona v. Maricopa Cty. Med. Society, 457 U.S. 332,
343–44, 102 S.Ct. 2466, 2473 (1982).

The rationale for *per se* rules *in part* is to avoid a
burdensome inquiry into actual market conditions in
situations where the likelihood of anticompetitive conduct
is so great as to render unjustified the costs of determining
whether the particular case at bar involves anticompetitive
conduct. (emphasis added)

J. Stevens, in Jefferson Parish Hospital District No. 2 v. Hyde, 466
U.S. 2, 16 n. 25, 104 S.Ct. 1551, 1560 n. 25 (1984), on remand, 764
F.2d 1139 (5th Cir. 1985).

In its opinion, the Court of Appeals assumed that the
antitrust laws permit, but do not require, the condemnation
of price fixing and boycotts without proof of market power.
The opinion further assumed that the *per se* rule
prohibiting such activity "is only a rule of 'administrative
convenience and efficiency," not a statutory command. * * *
This statement contains two errors. The *per se* rules are, of
course, the product of judicial interpretations of the
Sherman Act, but the rules nevertheless have the same
force and effect as any other statutory commands.
Moreover, while the *per se* rule against price fixing and

> boycotts is indeed justified in part by "administrative
> convenience," the Court of Appeals erred in describing the
> prohibition as justified only by such concerns. The *per se*
> rules also reflect a long-standing judgment that the
> prohibited practices by their nature have "a substantial
> potential for impact on competition." [citing *Jefferson
> Parish*]

J. Stevens, in FTC v. Superior Ct. Trial Lawyers Assn., 493 U.S. 411,
432, 110 S.Ct. 768, 780 (1990).

> There is always something of a sliding scale in appraising
> reasonableness, but the sliding scale formula deceptively
> suggests greater precision than we can hope for. . . .
> Nevertheless, the quality of proof required should vary with
> the circumstances." . . . Professor Areeda . . . emphasized
> the necessity, particularly great in the quasi-common law
> realm of antitrust, that courts explain the logic of their
> conclusions. "By exposing their reasoning, judges . . . are
> subjected to others' critical analyses, which in turn can lead
> to better understanding for the future."

J. Souter, in California Dental Assn. v. FTC, 526 U.S. 756, 780–781,
119 S.Ct. 1604 (1999), quoting an earlier edition of 7 Antitrust Law
¶ 1500. The "sliding scale" language was quoted once again in FTC v.
Actavis, 570 U.S. 136, 159, 133 S.Ct. 2223, 2237 (2013).

> depending upon the concerted activity in question, the Rule
> of Reason may not require a detailed analysis; it "can
> sometimes be applied in the twinkling of an eye."

J. Stevens, in American Needle, Inc. v. National Football League, 560
U.S. 183, 203, 130 S.Ct. 2201, 2216–2217 (2010), quoting NCAA v.
Board of Regents of Univ. of Okla., 468 U.S. 85, 110, 104 S.Ct. 2948
(1984), which was in turn quoting Phillip E. Areeda, The "Rule of
Reason" in Antitrust Analysis: General Issues 37–38 (Federal
Judicial Center, June 1981).

5.6b.   The Exaggerated Distinction Between Rule of Reason and Per Se Treatment

Courts and commentators often say that most practices
analyzed as antitrust violations are considered under a "rule of
reason," while the *per se* rule applies only to a limited number—
perhaps price fixing, horizontal territorial or customer division,
naked concerted refusals to deal, and arguably some tying
arrangements.

In fact, all legal analysis is *"per se"* to one degree or another.[237] The *per se* rule says that once we know a certain amount about a practice we can pass judgment on its legality without further inquiry. The difference between a *"per se"* and a "rule of reason" standard lies in how much we need to know before we can make that decision. A rational decision maker will collect information, beginning with the most relevant and easiest to gather, until he reaches a point at which the marginal cost of acquiring more exceeds its expected marginal return. In this case the "marginal return" is the increased accuracy of the final decision. If the cost of obtaining certain information is very high, and the chance is small that it will make the final decision more accurate, the rational decision maker will not seek the additional information. For this reason Justice Marshall was wrong in *Topco*, quoted in § 5.6a, when he said it was "irrelevant" whether a *per se* case would come out the same way under the rule of reason. Given some final, accurate decision, O, the *per se* rule rests on a judicial judgment that the court can approximate O with sufficient accuracy once it knows a few specific things. Further, learning more things is likely to be very expensive and unlikely to bring the court substantially closer to O. The *per se* rule manifestly does not rest on a judgment that the two antitrust rules are calculated *ex ante* to yield different decisions.

Even in a so-called rule of reason case, however, the parties will not produce *all* the marginally relevant information. They will produce sufficient information to satisfy some judicially created presumptions—for example, that a defendant with 90% of a well defined market has monopoly power, or that a merger between the two largest firms in a concentrated market or a very large pay-for-delay settlement in a patent infringement suit are anticompetitive. Every inquiry is cut off at some point; the label *"per se"* simply refers to a class of situations where we find it appropriate to cut the inquiry off at a relatively early stage. In order to be useful, of course, the label *per se* must also tell the court *how* the inquiry is to be truncated. Even under *per se* rules, some facts are relevant while others are not.

To this end, Justice Brandeis' statement of the rule of reason in *Chicago Board of Trade*, quoted in § 5.6a, has been one of the most damaging in the annals of antitrust. The statement has suggested to many courts that, if the analysis is under the rule of reason, then nearly everything is relevant. We need to know about the history of the business, its condition before the restraint was imposed, its condition after, peculiarities of the business that might make the restraint permissible here but not elsewhere, and so on. Taken

---

[237]　See Richard A. Posner, The Rule of Reason and the Economic Approach: Reflections on the *Sylvania* Decision, 45 U. Chi.L.Rev. 1, 14–15 (1977).

individually, each element of Justice Brandeis' summary of the rule of reason is accurate, and may apply in at least some circumstances. The problem with the statement is that it identifies the haystack but not the needle. It never tells us what facts are decisive for determining whether a practice merely "regulates" and thus "promotes" competition, or whether it may "suppress" or even "destroy" competition. Under the rule of reason, relevant facts are those that tend to establish whether a restraint increases or decreases output, or decreases or increases prices. Most other facts are irrelevant.[238]

If one examines two kinds of cases at opposite ends of the spectrum, the distinction between "rule of reason" and *"per se"* analysis is clear enough. Suppose that on the left side of our spectrum we place alleged monopolization involving the innovation policies of a single firm. On the right side we place naked price fixing. In the first case we insist on a well-developed inquiry into the defendant's market power and the competitive effects of its practices. In the second we require little more than proof of the price fixing agreement. We can quite easily conclude that the first practice requires rule of reason analysis while the second is illegal *per se*. The great majority of innovation, even by dominant firms, is competitive; indeed, provable anticompetitive innovation is extremely rare, and should be condemned only in the case of an unambiguously anticompetitive abuse by an unambiguously dominant firm. By contrast, naked price fixing rarely or never has anything to be said in its support.

But as soon as we try to fill in the space between these two practices the gray area seems rather large. Tying arrangements are said to be illegal *per se*, but the basic inquiries are more complicated and even require some proof of market power.[239] By contrast, vertical nonprice restraints are said to involve a rule of reason, nearly all cases are rather easily dismissed. A difficult *"per se"* tying arrangement case can involve an inquiry that is far more elaborate than an easy rule of reason case.

So what is the use of a *"per se"* label? As a practical matter, to label something illegal *per se* is simply a shorthand form for expressing one of two different concepts, or perhaps both together. The first concept is that we can determine the legality of a practice without inquiring into the market structure or the market power of those engaged in the practice. To the extent it still exists the *per se* rule against tying arrangements is clearly an exception to this rule,

---

[238]   See 11 Antitrust Law ¶ 1912b (4th ed. 2018); Herbert Hovenkamp, The Rule of Reason, 70 Fla. L. Rev. 81 (2018).

[239]   On RPM, see § 11.5; on tying, see § 10.3f.

but that simply reflects that the *per se* label for tie-ins was ill conceived from the beginning.[240] At least two-thirds of the time, a statement that a practice is illegal per se is simply shorthand for the conclusion that we can condemn this practice without defining a relevant market or measuring the defendant's market share.[241]

The second concept, far more difficult to manage, is that the label "illegal *per se*" entails that certain justifications or defenses will not be permitted.[242] But even under the *per se* rule some justifications can be considered. More importantly, the court must consider claimed justifications in determining whether the conduct falls inside or outside the *per se* rule.

We sometime hear the deceptively simple proposition that all the court needs to do is balance efficiency effects against anticompetitive effects and see which way the scale tips. But courts are not capable of measuring either efficiency or power over price with anything approaching scientific accuracy. Most such judicial measurements are simply hunches, based on several presumptions about the nature and effects of certain practices. For the most part a factual conclusion that a practice leads to lower market output and higher consumer prices is sufficient. This inquiry is inherent in the consumer welfare approach to antitrust.[243]

This reasoning process explains why the Court was forced to listen to the defendant's answering argument in *BMI*. Blanket licensing surely involved an agreement among competitors that affected price. However the non-exclusive nature of the agreement and the fact that there were thousands of participants made collusion impossible. Further, the defendants produced a plausible argument that the agreement resulted in substantially larger output and lower

---

[240]   See § 10.3f.

[241]   See, e.g., All Care Nursing Service v. High Tech Staffing Services, 135 F.3d 740 (11th Cir. 1998), cert. denied, 526 U.S. 1016, 119 S.Ct. 1250 (1999) (claim proceeded under per se theory, so relevant market was never alleged or proven; dismissed when court applied rule of reason).

[242]   See 7 Antitrust Law ¶ 1510 (4th ed. 2017) and 11 id. ¶ 1907 (4th ed. 2018). Compare General Leaseways v. National Truck Leasing Assn., 744 F.2d 588, 593 (7th Cir. 1984):

The per se rule would collapse if every claim of economies from restricting competition, however implausible, could be used to move a horizontal agreement not to compete from the per se to the Rule of Reason category. We are told, therefore, to apply the per se rule when "the practice facially appears to be one that would always or almost always tend to restrict competition and decrease output" [quoting *Broadcast Music*]. In other words, if the elimination of competition is apparent on a quick look, without undertaking the kind of searching inquiry that would make the case a Rule of Reason case in fact if not in name, the practice is illegal per se.

[243]   On this point, see Herbert Hovenkamp, Consumer Welfare in Competition and Intellectual Property Law, 9 Competition Policy Int'l J. 53 (2014).

prices. By contrast, the arrangement in *Engineers* was exclusive; it forbad the engineers from competing on price. Further, their argument that "excessive" price competition would force engineers to cut corners was impermissible, for it was an argument that the public had an interest in higher bid prices. That argument may or may not be sound, but it must be settled by legislation. The defendant will not be permitted to avoid condemnation by showing that low prices or high output are not in the best interest of consumers in the particular case.

5.6c.   Identifying Anticompetitive Conduct: A Tentative Road Map

Characterizing agreements among competitors as competitive or anticompetitive is not easy, and the following guide is not foolproof. Even this "road map" leaves some avenues uncharted. In evaluating a restraint the court should ask the following questions, most typically in this sequence:

1.   Does the agreement arguably threaten either to reduce output[244] or raise price in some nontrivial way?[245] If not, it should generally be declared legal. If yes, go to step two.

2.   Is the agreement naked or ancillary to some other joint venture or agreement that is itself plausibly efficiency creating or otherwise beneficial to consumers?[246] An agreement is naked if it is formed with the objectively intended purpose or likely effect of increasing price or decreasing output in the short run. As a result, a naked agreement is rational only on the premise that the participants have market power. By contrast, an ancillary agreement reduces cost or improves the product and can be profitable whether or not the firms have any market power.

---

[244] See the interesting analysis in Spinelli v. NFL, 903 F.3d 185 (2d Cir. 2018), holding that NFL control over photographer access to NFL games may have reduced the number of photographers but not the number of photographs because each photo could be reproduced an infinite number of times. Is that persuasive? What about quality or variety of the photographs? Would an agreement among publishers to reduce the number of titles be competitively harmless, simply because each title could be reproduced an infinite number of times?

[245] In the case of monopsony, or joint ventures among buyers, the query is whether the venture threatens to lower the buying price or reduce the quantity of the input. On monopsony, see § 1.2b.

[246] "Efficiency creating" refers to agreements that coordinate production or distribution in order to increase productive efficiency by improving quality or lowering costs; agreements that solve nontrivial free rider problems, including agreements to share intellectual property; market facilitators; and perhaps others. That is, the step 2 inquiry should give broad scope to the *domain* of efficiency-creating agreements.

If the agreement is naked, it is illegal,[247] although we may pause briefly to consider idiosyncratic or unfamiliar issues, as discussed below. If the arrangement is ancillary, continue on.

3.   Look at the market power held by the parties to the challenged restraint. How numerous are they? How concentrated is the market? Is there a substantial competitive market outside the venture? Are entry barriers high or low? Is the venture non-exclusive—that is, are participants to the venture free to offer the covered product or service outside the restraints imposed upon the venture? If this quick analysis suggests that the exercise of market power is not plausible, the challenged practice is legal. Proof of actual anticompetitive effects, properly defined, can be used as a substitute for formal market analysis. If the exercise of market power *is* plausible, go to step four.[248]

4.   Is there strong evidence that the challenged practice creates substantial efficiencies by reducing participants' costs or improving product or service quality? Once a prima facie case has been made the burden of proving efficiencies should be on the person whose conduct is at issue, and who should have better information about efficiencies than anyone. If not, the practice is illegal. If yes, go to step 5.

5.   Can the same efficiencies be achieved by reasonably available alternatives that have less potential to harm competition? If yes, the practice in its present form is illegal, although the injunctive remedy should be limited to condemning the current form or ordering the alternative. If no less restrictive alternative is available, go to step 6.

6.   Balancing. Hopefully, few cases require real balancing; but if a challenged restraint simultaneously produces opportunities for both anticompetitive practices and substantial efficiencies, a court must have a guide one way or the other. The best guide seems to be that if the threat to competition is real, and if the defendants cannot come up with a way of restructuring their venture so that this threat is substantially dissipated, the court's only conclusion must

---

[247]   As the Supreme Court has noted, as "a matter of law, the absence of proof of market power does not justify a naked restriction on price or output. * * *" The latter "requires some competitive justification even in the absence of detailed market analysis." FTC v. Indiana Federation of Dentists, 476 U.S. 447, 457, 106 S.Ct. 2009, 2017 (1986).

[248]   On the importance of market power in queries involving joint ventures, see Frank H. Easterbrook, The Limits of Antitrust, 63 Tex.L.Rev. 1, 19–23 (1984).

be to condemn the arrangement. At this point, intent and good faith may become relevant, particularly in cases where the defendants have technical expertise and their professional judgment must have a certain amount of deference if their market is to function properly. Nevertheless, any court faced with the prospect of balancing must go back to step 5 and look hard for workable less restrictive alternatives.

The road map solves many decisions that courts have found troublesome, although one should not exaggerate its ease of use. For example, evaluation of a case like United States v. Topco Associates, Inc.,[249] seems easy, although the Court got it wrong. The joint venture among Topco brand grocers, which included territorial division, flunks step 1 because in the absence of any information about the market the agreement arguably decreases output. It passes step 2, because the Topco stores were involved in considerable integration of their businesses, including joint production of Topco branded goods and joint advertising. Further, the joint venture solved "free rider" problems by ensuring that a Topco grocer's promotion efforts in its own territory accrued entirely to its own store. Step 3 should end the inquiry. The low market shares of the individual members—about 6% each in their respective territories—indicates that there was almost no chance that the defendants could profitably reduce output and charge monopoly prices.

The blanket licensing arrangement at issue in the *Broadcast Music* case is a little more difficult. Once again, the blanket licensing arrangement flunks step 1, since it clearly affected price or output. The arrangement passes the step 2 inquiry, but it then (at first glance) produces ambiguous results at the step 3 (market power) inquiry. The venture covers a large share of the relevant market and as a practical matter it is very difficult for an artist to market her work outside the venture. At the same time, however, the venture includes thousands of artists and it is non-exclusive: any artist is free to sell her work outside the venture. A careful examination of the venture in its market setting should convince a court that there is no reasonable way the blanket licensing agreement will lead to a market wide output reduction. When thousands of cartel members are given absolutely unrestrained freedom to make unlimited non-cartel sales, the cartel is virtually guaranteeing that its prices can never be higher than they would have been in a market in which the cartel did not exist. There was no reasonable prospect that the venture was a

---

[249]   United States v. Topco Associates, 405 U.S. 596, 607–608, 92 S.Ct. 1126 (1972).

socially harmful exercise of market power, notwithstanding its high market share.

If that analysis leaves some discomfort, the step 4 inquiry should settle the matter. The transactional efficiencies achieved by blanket licensing were truly extraordinary: many radio stations would have been unable to function if they had to purchase all their performance rights one at a time.[250] Further, this efficiency was present and manifest, not merely plausible. Even the plaintiff did not want to abolish blanket licensing; it merely wanted the defendants to subdivide the blanket licenses into categories.

Another difficult decision is *NCAA*, where the Supreme Court condemned an agreement among NCAA football colleges to restrict the number of times that each team's football games could be televised.[251] The Court of Appeals had held that the NCAA television restriction was illegal *per se* as an output-restricting agreement among competitors in the market for televised college football. The Court of Appeals rejected the NCAA's defense that the arrangement actually promoted competition in a different market—the market for live attendance at football games. That argument was well rejected. *All* output restrictions in one market tend to increase the demand in markets for substitute products. For example, it is no defense to price fixing in the beef industry that it will increase demand for pork and lamb.

The Supreme Court affirmed the lower court's judgment, but held that the conduct at issue must be evaluated under the rule of reason. The NCAA is a special "network" industry in which "horizontal restraints on competition are essential if the product [NCAA football games] is to be available at all." As the Court noted, NCAA football teams simply cannot produce their product without agreeing with each other about certain things, such as a playing schedule, the size and shape of the football field and the rules of the game, and on rules determining player eligibility. The Court restated this formulation in its *American Needle* decision, holding that the NFL was not a single entity but rather a combination of its teams reachable under the Sherman Act. However, for purposes of a challenge to the teams' agreement to give a single exclusive license to produce trademarked caps the rule of reason should apply.[252]

---

[250] See § 5.2c.

[251] National Collegiate Athletic Association v. Board of Regents (*NCAA*), 468 U.S. 85, 104 S.Ct. 2948 (1984).

[252] American Needle, Inc. v. NFL, 560 U.S. 183, 203, 130 S.Ct. 2201, 2216–2217 (2010). See also Major League Baseball Properties, Inc. v. Salvino, Inc., 542 F.3d 290 (2d Cir. 2008), which required the rule of reason to a similar practice in the baseball market.

However, the Court also suggested that a "detailed analysis" under the rule of reason might not be necessary and spoke of the possibility of a quick look application that could be applied "in the twinkling of an eye."

Further, some of these agreements clearly have an effect on price or "output." For example, the teams must agree with one another whether there should be ten games or twenty games in a football season. They might also have to agree about how gate receipts are to be divided among home and away teams. Other agreements, such as one concerning the size of the playing field, may have little or no effect on output. The Supreme Court effectively held that since the delivery of the product at issue *forced* the NCAA members to agree about certain things, and since some of these things necessarily affected output, all agreements among the teams should be subject to the rule of reason.[253]

The Court then went on to condemn the television restriction under the rule of reason. Faced with substantial evidence that the agreement made televised NCAA football less available, that some schools wanted to televise more football games than the rule permitted, and that no plausible procompetitive justifications for the rule had been offered, the rule seemed anticompetitive.

Using our road map, the NCAA agreement restricting televised games flunks step 1. While the NCAA joint venture generally is efficient, thus passing step 2, the agreement limiting television output seems to be naked: its only purpose was to reduce the output of televised games. The inquiry could properly have ended there, once the defendant failed to assert any procompetitive benefit from the output restriction.[254]

Step 3, the market power inquiry, was difficult and the resolution still indeterminate. The Court's quick definition of the market as college football games may have been too narrow. But in this case the uncertainties about the market can be set aside if we continue down the road map. At first glance, step 4 may not seem dispositive either. On the one hand, the venture overall seems to create substantial efficiencies. On the other, the court is not in a very good position to quantify these efficiencies and balance them against the costs of any reduction in television output. But more decisively,

---

[253]   *NCAA*, 468 U.S. at 100, 104 S.Ct. at 2959. But doesn't this go too far? Suppose another provision of the venture agreement fixed the price of sweatshirts bearing team logos. Is a full rule of reason inquiry necessary? For my criticism of the NCAA conclusion, see 11 Antitrust Law ¶ 1910d (4th ed. 2018).

[254]   See, e.g., Law v. NCAA, 134 F.3d 1010, 1020 (10th Cir.), cert. denied, 525 U.S. 822, 119 S.Ct. 65 (1998) (dispensing with power requirement in challenge to NCAA fix of maximum coaching salaries).

the plaintiff's challenge was not to the overall venture, but only to
the restriction on televised games; that restriction was not shown to
produce any acceptable consumer benefits. Notwithstanding all the
good things to be said about the NCAA venture overall, the
restriction on the number of games was simply not essential to the
economic success of the basic venture itself and, considered
separately, did not obviously produce any efficiencies. NCAA football
will not work without an agreement regulating the number of games
that the teams will play, but it probably does not require an
agreement fixing the price of hot dogs sold in the stadium or fixing
the number of games that can be televised. The correct remedy,
however, is not to condemn the entire venture but rather to condemn
that clause of the venture agreement restricting the number of
televised games.

5.6d.   The Truncated, or "Quick Look," Rule of Reason

The courts have always realized that the line between the *per se*
rule and the rule of reason is not as hard or as easy to locate as we
might wish. Beginning with the *NCAA* decision in 1984 and the
Indiana Dentists decision in 1986, the Supreme Court began to take
more seriously an intermediate form of inquiry that generally falls
under the rubric of "nearly naked" or "facially unreasonable"
restraints, the "quick look," or the "abbreviated" or "bobtailed" rule
of reason. Typically, we say that a restraint falls within this
classification if it is highly suspicious, almost to the point of
deserving *per se* condemnation. Nevertheless, some doubts remain,
perhaps resulting from the fact that our experience with the restraint
is so limited.[255] At the very least, we want to listen to the defendant's
justification for its restraint. If that justification seems both plausible
and sufficient to suggest that the restraint is profitable without
regard to any power that the defendants might have, then a full rule
of reason inquiry will be necessary. By contrast, if the justification
indicates that the restraint is naked we can apply the per se rule.
Viewed in this way the real issue concerns assignment of burdens of
proof. Under the rule of reason the plaintiff must show power and an
initial case of anticompetitive effect. The burden shifts to the
defendant mainly for defenses. By contrast, the "quick look" gives the
plaintiff a smaller set of burdens up front and places heavier burdens
on the defendant. In *Actavis* the Supreme Court suggested that the
principal difference is that under the quick look the defendant has

---

[255]   See 11 Antitrust Law ¶ 1911 (4th ed. 2018).

the burden to show a lack of anticompetitive effects, while under the rule of reason the burden to prove them is on the plaintiff.[256]

Whether by "quick look" or simply as part of the rule of reason's "sliding scale," a truncated inquiry is usually best reserved for circumstances where the restraint is sufficiently threatening to place it presumptively in the per se class,[257] but lack of judicial experience requires at least some consideration of proffered defenses or justifications. Further, the only justifications that are acceptable are those tending to show that the challenged restraint really does tend to increase output, and thus decrease price. The purpose is *not* to broaden the range of defenses for a restraint that is conceded to reduce output or increase price.

The Supreme Court has never been enthusiastic about the "quick look." The Court has used the term in only three decisions, and rejected its application in all three.[258] On the other hand, many decisions, including *Actavis, NCAA, Indiana Dentists,* and *American Needle,* acknowledged that the plaintiff's proof burdens could be shortened to one degree or another from the fullest possible rule of reason approach.[259] But these decisions are also consistent with the proposition that the Court lacked sufficient experience with the industries or practices in question to be fully comfortable with the per se rule. *NCAA, Indiana Dentists,* and *American Needle* all indicate some hesitation with networked markets, where interaction among competitors is fairly normal. The distinguishing feature of *Actavis* is the relevance of the patent system and the rise of an unprecedented practice (pay-for-delay settlements) that was entirely a creature of a complex regulatory provision.

Thinking of antitrust analysis as three silos labelled "rule of reason," "quick look," and "per se" does not capture what the courts are doing. As noted previously, all antitrust analysis proceeds on the premise that the fact finder collects information up to the point that its incremental value is no longer worth the costs of obtaining it. The price-fixing agreement in *Law* presented a much more obvious case for competitive harm than did the concerted refusal to deal arrangement in *Indiana Dentists.* Once the Tenth Circuit had listened to the NCAA's defense of price-fixing of coaches' salaries,

---

[256]   FTC v. Actavis, Inc., 570 U.S. 136, 159, 133 S.Ct. 2223, 2237 (2013).

[257]   Thus, for example, vertical nonprice restraints are never subjected to "quick look" analysis. See, e.g., Orson v. Miramax Film Corp., 79 F.3d 1358, 1367 (3d Cir. 1996), on remand, 983 F.Supp. 624 (D.Pa.1997).

[258]   Actavis, *supra*; California Dental Assoc. v. FTC, 526 U.S. 756, 777 (1999); Texaco, Inc. v. Dagher, 547 U.S. 1, 7 n. 3 (2006). See Herbert Hovenkamp, The Rule of Reason, 70 Fla. L. Rev. 81 (2018).

[259]   American Needle, Inc. v. NFL, 560 U.S. 183, 203 (2010).

they knew with sufficient assurance that they were looking at a naked restraint whose *only* possible impact was almost certain to be anticompetitive. That made the further, expensive inquiry into market power unnecessary.

In *California Dental* a five-member majority held that an agreement among dentists restricting price and quality advertising could not be assessed on a quick look, but required full rule of reason treatment. [260] The defendant's restraints were stated to be efforts to prevent deceptive advertising, but they were so aggressive that they virtually prohibited all price or quality advertising of any sort.[261] The Court rejected the abbreviated inquiry that the Ninth Circuit had approved, noting that the health care market was particularly vulnerable to unsubstantiated and difficult-to-verify claims.[262] Perhaps most significantly, the Court noted that the literature and economic theory had suggested the "plausibility of competing claims about the effects of the professional advertising restrictions. . . ."[263] This suggested at least some possibility that restrictions appearing to be overly broad on their face might end up being reasonable in the unusually complex market for dental services. At the very least, however, the allegations about price impact should have been enough to shift the burden of proof. While the Court did not state it, a complex market with poorly informed buyers also suggests vulnerability to collusion.

5.6e.   Reforming the Rule of Reason

The most beneficial reform in the rule of reason would be to lighten the plaintiff's initial burden and require more robust proof of offsetting defenses. While the ultimate burden of persuasion lies with the plaintiff, a manageable rule of reason inquiry requires the court to shift the burden of proof from one side to the other, depending on its view of the case. If evidence were always perfect and complete, assignment of the burden of proof would not matter. The evidence would be there, available to either side, and whoever had the burden

---

[260]   California Dental Ass'n v. FTC, 526 U.S. 756 (1999).

[261]   See Justice Breyer's dissent:

As implemented, the ethical rule reached beyond its nominal target, to prevent truthful and nondeceptive advertising. In particular, the Commission determined that the rule, in practice:

    (1)   "precluded advertising that characterized a dentist's fees as being low, reasonable, or affordable," [121 F.T.C. 190, 301 (1996)];

    (2)   "precluded advertising . . . of across the board discounts," ibid.; and

    (3)   "prohibit[ed] all quality claims," id., at 308.

California Dental, 526 U.S. at 783, 119 S.Ct. at 1618.

[262]   526 U.S. at 784–787, 119 S.Ct. at 1619–1621.

[263]   Id. at 778, 119 S.Ct. at 1616.

would bring it forward. Assignment of the burden becomes an issue when information is incomplete or is private and held by one party.

One important factor in deciding how proof burdens should be assigned is plausibility. The burden of proof should generally be given to the party with the claim that is hardest to believe. If the plaintiff's claim is implausible, make him prove it. If a defense seems far-fetched, make the defendant come forward with the evidence supporting it. If market structure makes anticompetitive results seem highly unlikely, then make the plaintiff prove the contrary; or alternatively, if structural evidence makes the practice look suspicious, force the defendant to show why it should be exonerated.

An equally important factor is the location and availability of evidence. The plaintiff has the initial burden of showing a restraint sufficient to arouse our suspicions, and there is no good reason to require more. As this stage the evidence is likely to come from the market's structure and participants generally, although some of it may be obtained from defendants in discovery. When this obligation is satisfied, the burden shifts to the defendant to provide a procompetitive or competitively neutral explanation. Here, the asymmetry in information is usually quite pronounced. The defendant is the author of its restraint and is in a better position than anyone else to understand and support its own expectations about effects. For this reason it makes sense that the original burden on the plaintiff be relatively modest: it should be required to show a competitively suspicious restraint. The fact that the restraint could be interpreted in two different ways, as the *California Dental* majority suggested, means that the competitively benign alternative must be considered, but it does not entail that the burden of doing so be placed on the plaintiff. The real detail about anticompetitive effects should come out in the defendant's case after the burden shifts, because then the information will be produced by the person who is in the best position to control it and has the best set of incentives.

The *California Dental* majority acted too quickly in giving the plaintiff the burden to show that the defendant's restraints on advertising were anticompetitive.[264] The defendant's professional association claimed a dominant share of California dentists as its members and provided significant membership advantages. However, its rules effectively forbad most price and quality claims as misleading, without individual inquiries into whether advertisements were misleading in fact. The CDA even prohibited

---

[264]   California Dental Assn. v. FTC, 526 U.S. 756, 784, 119 S.Ct. 1604 (1999).

dentists from advertising guarantees, condemning statements such as "we guarantee all dental work for 1 year."

A closely divided (5–4) Court approved these restraints. The majority noted the possibility that the rules were anticompetitive, but they might also be procompetitive or competitively harmless. To the extent they did little more than restrain misleading advertising they might actually increase consumer confidence in dentistry. But the Court jumped too quickly from the premise that restrictions on false and misleading advertising are a good thing, to the conclusion that these very broad restrictions, made and enforced by the dentists themselves, were an appropriate way to get the job done, particularly in light of the fact that both federal and state agencies were in place to police complaints about consumer abuses.

The Supreme Court found support for its position in evidence that most information in the dental care market is controlled by producers rather than consumers. But that is hardly an argument for giving producers control of advertising. The evidence revealed a market where customers are vulnerable. Suppliers can be trusted mainly to act in their own best interest.

The Court's requirement that the plaintiff prove everything is a throwback to the unstructured rule of reason of the *Chicago Board of Trade* case early in the twentieth century.[265] As a matter of pure logic the Court was certainly right when it said that competitor-created restraints on advertising could increase, decrease or have no impact at all on the output of dental services. As a matter of evidence and history, however, that position is myopic. As a matter of logic, a fox going into a hen house at night might be intending to kill chickens, to take a harmless nap, or to gather eggs and clean cages. But the farmer, knowing the history of foxes in hen houses, is not likely to wait until the fox's intentions are clear.

A long history of collusion shows that price-affecting restraints enforced by market dominating groups are highly suspicious unless they are reasonably ancillary to joint production. In this case, what should have aroused the Court's suspicion even more was the rather poor fit between the restraints themselves and proven fraudulent advertising. The rules and the way they were administered were not narrowly tailored to correct fraud; rather, they were designed to prevent dentists from advertising price and quality. Further, there was no showing that state and federal authorities were not up to the task of protecting consumers from false and misleading advertising.

---

[265]   Chicago Board of Trade v. United States, 246 U.S. 231, 38 S.Ct. 242 (1918).

Presumptions in rule of reason cases are designed to enable judges to draw on past experience to create shortcuts favoring the party with the most plausible claim. By contrast, the unstructured rule of reason tends to require the plaintiff to prove everything. A more appropriate opening presumption in *California Dental* would have been that given the market dominance enjoyed by the defendant sellers, and the acknowledged breadth of their advertising restrictions, the burden should have been on them to show that there was a significant danger of misleading advertising that was not effectively remedied by government enforcers, and that producer-controlled restraints were the least threatening way to solve the problem without injuring competition.

Chapter 6

EXCLUSIONARY PRACTICES AND THE DOMINANT FIRM: THE BASIC DOCTRINE OF MONOPOLIZATION AND ATTEMPT

Table of Sections

§ 6.1   The Monopolization Offense

Section 2 of the Sherman Act, 15 U.S.C.A. § 2, condemns "every person who shall monopolize * * *." Today "monopolization" refers to a number of activities that may be illegal when performed by a dominant firm.[1]

In one sense the law of monopolization is concerned with what Louis D. Brandeis once called "The Curse of Bigness."[2] Today even more than in Brandeis's time, Americans are dominated by giant firms. But big business and Americans always have had a love-hate relationship. Big corporations employ more Americans and pay them higher salaries than small businesses do. They do most of our research and development, introduce most of our new products, defend us, entertain and inform us, and pay much of our taxes.

Notwithstanding these bounties, Americans have always mistrusted big business. We have written and read about the "organization man" who has ceded his freedom and identity to his

---

[1]   On the measurement of market power, see Ch. 3.
[2]   Louis D. Brandeis, The Curse of Bigness (1934).

employer.[3] We believe that big business homogenizes us, over-standardizes us, and—worst of all—makes us pay high prices for shoddy products or poor service. Antitrust is properly concerned only with the last of these sins.

In United States v. Grinnell Corp.[4] the Supreme Court defined illegal monopolization to include two elements: "(1) the possession of monopoly power in the relevant market and (2) the willful acquisition or maintenance of that power as distinguished from growth or development as a consequence of a superior product, business acumen, or historic accident." Both of these elements must be established before the defendant is guilty of monopolization.

During the first half of the twentieth century the judicial definition of the monopolization offense experienced considerable flux. Courts generally agreed that the offense required a showing of the defendant's substantial market power. In the earliest cases, however, the defendant's market power was obvious, and courts spent little time discussing it.[5] Today the market power requirement is clearly established, although courts still have difficulty measuring market power and are not entirely clear about how much market power a defendant must have to be guilty of illegal monopolization.

Today the prevailing legal rule requires a showing that the defendant (a) has "monopoly power", which is substantial market power; and (b) has "exercised" that power.[6] What it means to "exercise" monopoly power is ambiguous. The sale of products at a monopoly price is certainly an "exercise" of monopoly power—however, courts have consistently held that even the monopolist may legally sell its product at its profit-maximizing price and reduce output to a level that will clear the market at that price.[7] Today, the

---

[3]   William H. Whyte, Jr., The Organization Man (1956).

[4]   384 U.S. 563, 570–71, 86 S.Ct. 1698, 1704 (1966).

[5]   For example, Standard Oil Co. of N.J. v. United States, 221 U.S. 1, 31 S.Ct. 502 (1911) (defendant controlled 90% of business of producing, shipping, refining and selling petroleum); United States v. American Tobacco Co., 221 U.S. 106, 31 S.Ct. 632 (1911) (86%); United States v. American Can Co., 230 Fed. 859 (D.Md.1916), appeal dismissed, 256 U.S. 706, 41 S.Ct. 624 (1921) (at least at one time, over 90% of can producing plants).

[6]   As the Supreme Court most recently reiterated:

It is settled law that this offense requires, in addition to the possession of monopoly power in the relevant market, 'the willful acquisition or maintenance of that power. . . . The mere possession of monopoly power, and the concomitant charging of monopoly prices, is not only not unlawful; it is an important element of the free-market system.

Verizon Communications Inc. v. Law Offices of Curtis V. Trinko, LLP, 540 U.S. 398, 407, 124 S.Ct. 872, 878–879 (2004).

[7]   See Berkey Photo, Inc. v. Eastman Kodak Co., 603 F.2d 263, 275 (2d Cir. 1979), cert. denied, 444 U.S. 1093, 100 S.Ct. 1061 (1980) (monopoly seller):

"exercise" of monopoly power requires an "exclusionary" practice—that is, a practice that deters potential rivals from entering the monopolist's market, or existing rivals from increasing their output in response to the monopolist's price increase.

Even here some qualification is in order. Not all exclusionary practices merit condemnation. Many of them make consumers better off: for example, research and development, or the production of a better product at a lower price. To say that illegal monopolization consists of monopoly power plus *any* exclusionary practice would cut far too broadly. A great deal of case law has been concerned with distinguishing the monopolist's "exclusionary" practices worthy of condemnation from those practices which, although exclusionary, should be tolerated or even encouraged.

One useful definition is that monopolistic conduct requires acts that:

(1) are reasonably capable of creating, enlarging or prolonging monopoly power by impairing the opportunities of rivals; and

(2) either (2a) do not benefit consumers at all, or (2b) are unnecessary for the particular consumer benefits claimed for them, or (2c) produce harms disproportionate to any resulting benefits.

In addition, the practice must be reasonably susceptible to a judicial remedy, which means that the court must be able to identify the conduct as anticompetitive and either fashion an appropriate deterrent or an equitable remedy likely to improve competition.[8]

§ 6.2   Monopoly Power and Illegal Monopolization

The monopoly power requirement in monopolization cases helps courts to characterize a firm's conduct and predict its consequences. Much of the "exclusionary" conduct at issue in litigated monopolization cases is ambiguous when considered alone. For example, in a competitive market a refusal to deal, a dramatic price

---

The mere possession of monopoly power does not *ipso facto* condemn a market participant. But, to avoid the proscriptions of § 2, the firm must refrain at all times from conduct directed at smothering competition. This doctrine has two branches. Unlawfully acquired power remains anathema even when kept dormant. And it is not less true that a firm with a legitimately achieved monopoly may not wield the resulting power to tighten its hold on the market. Accord Kartell v. Blue Shield, 749 F.2d 922 (1st Cir. 1984), cert. denied, 471 U.S. 1029, 105 S.Ct. 2040 (1985) (monopsony buyer).

8   See 3 Antitrust Law ¶ 651 (4th ed. 2015).

reduction, or even tortious business practices are absolutely consistent with competition.

If a firm already has significant market power, however, courts have found these practices to be more threatening to the competitive process, and more likely to result in reduced output and higher prices.[9] If the evidence suggests a high degree of monopoly power, then a certain set of practices will condemn the defendant of illegal monopolization. If the evidence suggests a smaller amount of market power, then courts have used the law of attempt to monopolize, which carries stricter and more explicit conduct requirements. In all events, the plaintiff must provide reasonably specific allegations of substantial market power in its complaint—a conclusion required by the Supreme Court's *Twombly* decision, which tightened up antitrust pleading requirements.[10]

Before a firm can be guilty of illegal monopolization it must be the dominant firm in its market. Courts usually rely on market share data to determine whether the plaintiff has enough market power to be guilty of illegal monopolization. They fairly consistently hold that a 90% share of a well defined market is enough to support the necessary inference of market power. Several courts have found a market share on the order of 75% to be sufficient,[11] but if the share is lower than 70% courts become much more reluctant to find monopoly power.[12] Some courts hold as a matter of law that a share of less than 50% is insufficient, even if the defendant clearly had the power to raise its price by reducing output.[13] While "direct" evidence of market power as an alternative to traditional market definition has acquired considerable traction among economists, the courts have mostly been resistant to the idea that market dominance can be

---

[9]   As Justice Scalia noted in his *Kodak* dissent:

Where a defendant maintains substantial market power, his activities are examined through a special lens: Behavior that might otherwise not be of concern to the antitrust laws—or that might even be viewed as procompetitive— can take on exclusionary connotations when practiced by a monopolist.

Eastman Kodak Co. v. Image Technical Services, Inc., 504 U.S. 451, 488, 112 S.Ct. 2072, 2093 (1992) (Scalia, J., dissenting).

[10]   Bell Atlantic Corp. v. Twombly, 550 U.S. 544, 127 S.Ct. 1955 (2007).

[11]   See United States v. Grinnell Corp., 384 U.S. 563, 571, 86 S.Ct. 1698, 1704 (1966) (87% sufficient); United States v. Paramount Pictures, Inc., 334 U.S. 131, 68 S.Ct. 915 (1948) (suggesting that 70% is sufficient).

[12]   See Moore v. Jas. H. Matthews & Co., 473 F.2d 328, 332 (9th Cir. 1972), appeal after remand, 550 F.2d 1207 (9th Cir. 1977), supplemented, 1980 WL 1793 (D.Or.1980), reversed on other grounds, 682 F.2d 830 (9th Cir. 1982) (market share of 65%–70% raised a fact question). See 3B Antitrust Law ¶ 807d (4th ed. 2015) (collecting all decisions).

[13]   See Valley Liquors v. Renfield Importers, 822 F.2d 656 (7th Cir.), cert. denied, 484 U.S. 977, 108 S.Ct. 488 (1987) (50% insufficient as a matter of law for monopolization).

established without proof of a relevant market. A few have suggested the possibility.[14] As direct methods of assessing power become more refined and widely accepted, this is very likely to change.

As Chapter 3 develops, market share percentages are imperfect surrogates for market power. Indeed, even when markets are defined with great care a significant amount of approximation is usually involved. *First*, our data are incomplete and often imperfect. *Second*, traditional market share measurements require the court to include differentiated or geographically dispersed substitute products as either completely inside or completely outside the market. Inclusion understates the defendant's market power while exclusion overstates it. Our traditional market definition criteria do not readily permit compromise positions.[15]

As a result, it would be unwise to attempt to establish a "sliding scale" relationship between the egregiousness of the conduct and the required amount of market power. Our measures are not sufficiently calibrated. At the same time, however, some kinds of conduct are plausibly anticompetitive on smaller market shares than other kinds. For example, predatory pricing is reasonable strategic behavior only for firms with extremely large market shares. Although it has been formally treated as part of the law of attempt, predatory pricing should be treated as part of the law of substantive monopolization.[16] Likewise, various vertical contracting arrangements by which a firm seeks to "foreclose" rivals from the market could effectively be anticompetitive only on large market shares.

By contrast, monopolization through abuse of government process might be reasonable anticompetitive conduct on a much lower share. For example, a firm with a 50% market share and numerous small rivals of 5% or 10% each might use improper litigation to restrain its rivals' expansion or increase their costs.[17] In sum, one must examine the logic of the alleged exclusionary practice in order to determine the minimum requisite market share to make the practice anticompetitive. Courts often fail to do this.

Equally important is the relationship between market power and entry barriers. If entry is easy, even a very large market share fails to establish the defendant's market power. As soon as it raises its price to monopoly levels new competitors will appear and the price

---

[14]   See Broadcom Corp. v. Qualcomm, Inc., 501 F.3d 297, 307 (3d Cir. 2007) (dicta accepting that dominance can be proved "through direct evidence of supracompetitive prices and restricted output").

[15]   On the problem of imperfect substitutes, see § 3.3a.

[16]   See § 8.4a.

[17]   See § 7.12.

increaser's market share will drop rapidly until it lowers its price once again.[18] Although courts in monopolization cases have not always taken ease of entry as seriously as they should, several have noted that entry is easy and then concluded that the defendant lacked substantial market power.[19]

§ 6.3   Conduct Requirements—Is Bad Conduct Necessary?

Over the years both Congress and antitrust scholars have proposed a variety of "no fault" monopoly approaches that would condemn a firm with persistent, substantial market power without evidence of impermissible exclusionary conduct. The idea is worth brief discussion because it helps illustrate the ambiguity of conduct requirements in monopolization cases.

The framers of the Sherman Act did not intend to condemn someone "who merely by superior skill and intelligence * * * got the whole business because nobody could do it as well as he could * * *."[20] Such "monopolization" and the monopoly profits that may result are essential to economic development. Firms innovate because they expect their successes to produce economic returns. Eventually the high profits will attract other producers into the market. Collectively these producers will increase output and prices will be driven to the competitive level. A rule that condemned all prices higher than, say, average cost could stop innovation dead. The continual creation of monopoly, and its eventual correction by competitive entry is part of a never-ending process that explains most of the technical achievements of modern industry in market economies.[21]

There are other reasons for not condemning mere monopoly. Many markets are large enough to support only one or two firms efficiently. In a natural monopoly market a single incumbent would have lower costs than two or more equally efficient incumbents. Some natural monopoly markets are recognized as such and price regulated by the State, but many are not.[22]

---

[18]   See, e.g., Tops Markets v. Quality Markets, 142 F.3d 90 (2d Cir. 1998); on entry barriers, see § 1.6.

[19]   Tops Markets, 142 F.3d at 90; United States v. Syufy Enterp., 903 F.2d 659, 664–669 (9th Cir. 1990) (no entry barriers to exhibiting of films); Ball Memorial Hosp. v. Mutual Hosp. Ins., 784 F.2d 1325, 1335–1336 (7th Cir.), rehearing denied, 788 F.2d 1223 (7th Cir. 1986) (insurance business requires cash and risk management, for which there are ample supplies and markets).

[20]   21 Cong.Rec. 3151–52 (1890).

[21]   See Christina Bohannan & Herbert Hovenkamp, Creation Without Restraint: Promoting Liberty and Rivalry in Innovation, ch. 1 (2011).

[22]   For a monopolization case in a market that was probably a natural monopoly, see Union Leader Corp. v. Newspapers of New England, Inc., 284 F.2d 582 (1st Cir.

Most advocates of no fault monopolization rules rely on the fact that exclusionary conduct is often difficult to discover and, when discovered, difficult to interpret. We expect persistent, long-term monopoly profits to invite entry. When entry has not occurred, perhaps we should infer the existence of exclusionary practices even though we do not have convincing evidence of them. Such a rule is not so much a "no fault" monopolization doctrine as a rule that fault can be inferred from the existence of persistent monopoly power and profits.

§ 6.4   Identifying Monopolizing Conduct

The law of monopolization requires a showing that the defendant has monopoly power and has engaged in impermissible "exclusionary" practices with the design or effect of protecting or enhancing its monopoly position. This section assumes that the power requirement has been established.

In antitrust litigation most practices are considered to be analyzed under a rule of reason. A *per se* rule is generally appropriate only after judges have had long experience with a certain practice, and have concluded that the practice produces many pernicious results and almost no beneficial ones. The rule of reason was originally formulated by the Supreme Court in a monopoly case as a means of distinguishing permissible from impermissible exclusionary practices.[23] The meaning and scope of the rule of reason in monopolization cases are nevertheless ambiguous.[24]

The § 2 conduct test is sometimes stated as conduct that is rational (that is, profit-maximizing) only on the premise that it will destroy competition. This is sometimes called the "no economic sense" test.[25] The Supreme Court found this definition satisfied in *Aspen*, where a dominant ski company refused to continue a joint venture with a rival.[26] The joint venture in marketing ski packages was mutually beneficial to both firms and increased total market output; however, it was more essential for the smaller plaintiff than the larger defendant. The defendant could thus profit from terminating

---

1960), cert. denied, 365 U.S. 833, 81 S.Ct. 747 (1961); see also, Herbert Hovenkamp, Vertical Integration by the Newspaper Monopolist, 69 Iowa L. Rev. 451 (1984).

[23]   Standard Oil Co. of N.J. v. United States, 221 U.S. 1, 31 S.Ct. 502 (1911).

[24]   Most recent Supreme Court analysis of the rule of reason appears not in monopolization cases but in cases involving agreements among competitors. These are discussed in Ch. 5.

[25]   See 3 Antitrust Law ¶ 651b3 (4th ed. 2015).

[26]   Aspen Skiing Co. v. Aspen Highlands Skiing Corp., 472 U.S. 585, 105 S.Ct. 2847 (1985).

the venture only on the premise that the plaintiff would suffer a sharp decline in sales at the defendant's expense.

An alternative that is sometimes given is the "sacrifice" test, that a monopolist is willing to sacrifice short-term profits in order to reap the benefits of monopoly down the road. Although the Supreme Court did not explicitly require sacrifice in *Aspen*, in approving the lower court's liability finding it observed that the defendant "was willing to sacrifice short-run benefits and consumer goodwill in exchange for a perceived long-run impact on its smaller rival.[27] The Government favored a combination of the sacrifice and "no economic sense" tests in the *Trinko* case, arguing in its amicus brief that a monopolist's refusal to deal is unlawful only if it "involves a sacrifice of profits or business advantage that makes economic sense only because it eliminates or lessens competition. . . ."[28]

But such tests must be used circumspectly. Many forms of totally legitimate investment involve the "sacrifice" of profits today for development of a resource that will injure rivals at some point in the future. This could be said of the construction of a large efficient plant, or also of a costly research project that ends up in a market-shifting innovation. Both require a large investment up front, but neither is something antitrust wants to condemn. On the other side, some unilateral conduct can be anticompetitive even if it involves little or no sacrifice. For example, a firm that induces others to invest in a certain way that creates significant path dependence and then changes its course can cause significant competitive harm even if there is no sacrifice. Even in *Aspen*, for example, the evidence suggested that the defendant obtained immediate benefits from terminating the joint venture at issue. The plaintiff lost market share as well as its ability to compete for multi-slope lift tickets almost immediately.[29] In sum, the "sacrifice" test produces unacceptably high false positives as well as false negatives.

It is also important to distinguish the private plaintiff's burden of proof in an action for damages or an injunction from the government's burden in an enforcement action. As Chapter 16

---

[27]   *Aspen*, 472 U.S. at 610–611. See also Advanced Health-Care Servs. v. Radford Community Hosp., 910 F.2d 139, 148 (4th Cir. 1990) (if defendant makes a "short-term sacrifice" in order to further "exclusive, anticompetitive objectives," it has monopolized).

[28]   Brief for the United States and the Federal Trade Commission as Amici Curiae Supporting Petitioner, 2003 WL 21269559, at *16–17, Verizon Communications, Inc. v. Law Offices of Curtis V. Trinko, 540 U.S. 398, 124 S.Ct. 872 (2004).

[29]   See *Aspen* 472 U.S. at 607–608. See also the lower court's opinion. "By refusing to cooperate with the plaintiff, defendant became the only business in Aspen that could offer a multi-day multi-mountain skiing experience. 738 F.2d 1509, 1521 (10th Cir. 1984).

develops, the private plaintiff seeking damages must show causation and quantifiable injury to itself. The private plaintiff seeking an injunction has a slightly smaller burden: it must show threatened injury to itself, but the amount need not be quantified provided that it is substantial. The government acting as enforcer, however, has the power to enjoin violations, and a violation can be inferred if the natural and likely consequences of an act are injury to competition. When conduct (1) by a firm with monopoly power is (2) clearly harmful to competitors; and (3) not supported by a reasonable business justification or more harmful than necessary given the justification that is offered, then the inference is strong that the challenged act is anticompetitive. This proof is sufficient to support the government's suit in equity, although not the private plaintiff's action.

Given that equitable relief is available, what kind should it be? Historically, breakup of the offending firm was the preferred remedy, but increasingly today the government and the courts have tended to favor remedies that limit the guilty monopolist's conduct. That trend reflects a long history of questionable and unsuccessful structural remedies, many of which undoubtedly did more harm than good.[30]

The case law of monopolization contains categorical statements that subjective intent is not an element of illegal monopolization, and categorical statements that it is. In *Alcoa* Judge Hand purported to "disregard any question of 'intent,'" concluding that "no monopolist monopolizes unconscious of what he is doing."[31] In *Grinnell*, however, the Supreme Court defined the offense of monopolization to include "the willful acquisition or maintenance of [monopoly] power * * *."[32]

Historically the intent requirement in monopolization cases has followed the formulation of the criminal law. In *attempt* cases, the law may require a specific intent to achieve the prohibited result. That requirement is elaborated in § 6.5. In the case of the completed offense, however, courts either dispense with an intent requirement, or else infer intent from evidence of monopoly power plus exclusionary practices.

Evidence of intent comes in two kinds, objective and subjective. Objective evidence of intent is evidence inferred from the defendant's

---

[30]   On antitrust remedies, see Peter C. Carstensen, Remedies for Monopolization From Standard Oil to Microsoft and Intel: The Changing Nature of Monopoly Law from Elimination of Market Power to Regulation of its Use, 85 S.Cal.L.Rev. 815 (2012).

[31]   United States v. Aluminum Co. of America, 148 F.2d 416, 431–32 (2d Cir. 1945). See also Ball Memorial Hospital v. Mutual Hospital Insurance, 784 F.2d 1325, 1338 (7th Cir. 1986) ("intent to harm rivals is not a useful standard in antitrust").

[32]   United States v. Grinnell Corp., 384 U.S. 563, 570–71, 86 S.Ct. 1698, 1704 (1966).

conduct. Subjective evidence of intent is evidence such as statements that indicate that the defendant consciously had a certain end in mind. A general requirement of subjective intent in monopolization cases vastly complicates discovery, and protects those companies who carefully and systematically destroy any paper trail of monopolistic purpose. The result is a great deal of arbitrariness.

Most courts have at least tacitly agreed with Justice Hand that, since no monopolist is unconscious of what it is doing, clear evidence of an impermissible exclusionary practice by a firm with monopoly power is the only proof of intent required. That is virtually the same thing as saying that the law of monopolization does not contain a separate intent requirement. Nevertheless, in *Aspen* the Supreme Court found intent to be relevant to both attempt and substantive monopolization. In monopolization, "evidence of intent is merely relevant to the question whether the challenged conduct is fairly characterized as 'exclusionary' or 'anticompetitive. * * * ' "33

On its face the *Aspen* statement is not very helpful, but it contains the germ of an important observation. Many kinds of conduct, such as the refusal to deal with a competitor in *Aspen*, is extremely difficult for courts to characterize. In such cases evidence of intent can aid courts in the characterization problem. However, evidence such as this should then be confined to those situations where (1) the defendant clearly has sufficient market power to justify the conclusion that it is capable of monopolization; and (2) the challenged conduct is sufficiently threatening that evidence of intent will lead the court in one direction or the other.

§ 6.5   The Offense of Attempt to Monopolize

The offense of attempt to monopolize is one of the most complex of federal antitrust violations. On the one hand, many acts alleged to be illegal attempts may also be illegal monopolization or violations of another antitrust law. In such cases a separate "attempt" offense is superfluous. On the other, expansive use of the attempt offense to reach conduct not condemned by the other antitrust laws may do more harm than good to the competitive process. If attempt analysis focuses too heavily on unfair conduct and too little on market power

---

33   Aspen Skiing Co. v. Aspen Highlands Skiing Corp., 472 U.S. 585, 105 S.Ct. 2847 (1985). Likewise, Spectrum Sports v. McQuillan, 506 U.S. 447, 113 S.Ct. 884 (1993), suggests that intent remains important in an attempt case. See § 6.5.

But see Conwood Co. v. United States Tobacco Co., 290 F.3d 768 (6th Cir. 2002), cert. denied, 537 U.S. 1148, 123 S.Ct. 876 (2003), where the court seemed overwhelmed by evidence of bad intent and ended up condemning conduct that was mainly procompetitive. See § 7.13.

the offense can operate to protect inefficient businesses from their more efficient rivals.[34]

Nonetheless, the statute is clear. Section 2 condemns every "person who shall monopolize or attempt to monopolize * * *."[35] At common law the attempt to commit a crime could be illegal even though the language of the relevant criminal statute condemned only the completed act. One of the great architects of the modern American common law, Justice Oliver Wendell Holmes, Jr.,[36] read the common law formulation of attempt into the Sherman Act in 1905. In Swift & Co. v. United States the defendants were accused of attempting "to obtain a monopoly of the supply and distribution of fresh meats throughout the United States * * *."[37] Their defense was that the indictment failed to allege specific acts that were themselves illegal. To this Justice Holmes responded:

> * * * Where acts are not sufficient in themselves to produce a result which the law seeks to prevent,—for instance, the monopoly—but require further acts in addition to the mere forces of nature to bring that result to pass, an intent to bring it to pass is necessary in order to produce a dangerous probability that it will happen. * * * But when that intent and the consequent dangerous probability exist, this statute, like many others and like the common law in some cases, directs itself against that dangerous probability as well as against the completed result.[38]

The three elements of the attempt offense today are taken directly from Holmes's formulation. The plaintiff must establish the defendant's: 1) specific intent to control prices or destroy competition in some part of commerce; 2) predatory or anticompetitive conduct directed to accomplishing the unlawful purpose; and 3) a dangerous probability of success.

6.5a.   Attempt Law's Specific Intent Requirement

Intent has often been antitrust's ghost in the machine. Courts use it to help them make sense of conduct that they do not fully understand. Problematically, however, the essence of competition is the intent to triumph over one's rivals. One of the most perplexing problems in antitrust policy is discerning between illegitimate and

---

[34]   See generally, Edward H. Cooper, Attempts and Monopolization: A Mildly Expansionary Answer to the Prophylactic Riddle of Section Two, 72 Mich.L.Rev. 375 (1974).

[35]   15 U.S.C.A. § 2.

[36]   See Oliver Wendell Holmes, Jr., The Common Law 65 (1881).

[37]   196 U.S. 375, 393, 25 S.Ct. 276, 278 (1905).

[38]   Id. at 396, 25 S.Ct. at 279.

legitimate intent—a problem that looms distressingly large if intent is the only thing we have to help us characterize ambiguous conduct.

The most commonly stated position is that specific intent is an established element of the attempt offense, approved by the Supreme Court, and cannot be considered irrelevant.[39]

The problem goes much deeper than mere identification of evidence of intent. Intent, once determined, must be evaluated. Most courts agree that mere intent to do better than or to vanquish one's rivals is insufficient to warrant condemnation. Intent of the following kinds, however, has been found sufficient: 1) intent to achieve monopoly power, or to acquire sufficient power to control price;[40] 2) intent to exclude competition;[41] or 3) intent to perform the specific act fulfilling the conduct requirement of the attempt offense.

None of these descriptions adequately distinguishes harmful from competitive intent. Intent to "exclude" is consistent with both efficient practices (research and development) and inefficient ones (predatory pricing). The last alternative—intent to engage in the specific act that satisfies the conduct requirement of the attempt offense—is inadvertently used by courts who hold that the requisite intent can be inferred from the conduct itself. This standard can become dangerously overdeterrent bootstrapping unless courts put strict limits on the kind of conduct that satisfies the requirement, and insist upon a meaningful showing of dangerous probability that the conduct is both anticompetitive (inefficient) and reasonably calculated to yield a monopoly. If these restrictions are followed, however, the intent requirement becomes superfluous.[42]

As a general matter subjective intent should either be irrelevant, or else should be used only to help a court characterize ambiguous conduct. Economists would prefer to analyze the structure of a market and determine from objective evidence whether (1) conduct is anticompetitive or efficient, (2) whether the danger of monopoly is real, and (3) whether the conduct at issue was reasonably

---

[39] See Times-Picayune Pub. Co. v. United States, 345 U.S. 594, 626, 73 S.Ct. 872, 890 (1953): "While the completed offense of monopolization under § 2 demands only a general intent to do the act, 'for no monopolist monopolizes unconscious of what he is doing,' a specific intent to destroy competition or build monopoly is essential to guilt for the mere attempt * * *."

[40] See Photovest Corp. v. Fotomat Corp., 606 F.2d 704, 711 (7th Cir. 1979), cert. denied, 445 U.S. 917, 100 S.Ct. 1278 (1980).

[41] See United States v. Empire Gas Corp., 537 F.2d 296, 302 (8th Cir. 1976), cert. denied, 429 U.S. 1122, 97 S.Ct. 1158 (1977).

[42] For example, General Indus. Corp. v. Hartz Mount. Corp., 810 F.2d 795, 802 (8th Cir. 1987) ("specific intent need not be proven by direct evidence but can be inferred from the defendant's anticompetitive practices or other proof of unlawful conduct.").

calculated to create a monopoly. Judges are often less sanguine about their ability to evaluate conduct exclusively on objective evidence, against the background of a particular market structure. They are particularly skeptical when the analysis requires a fair amount of economic sophistication. Predatory pricing is one example. Finally, judges are inclined to let ambiguous evidence go to the jury and to regard intent, conduct and dangerous probability as three factual elements that must be established separately.[43]

The trend in most courts is to use the intent requirement as a liability-restricting rather than liability-expanding device. Some courts use specific intent as an aid in characterizing ambiguous conduct. If the conduct is sufficiently close to the line that it could go either way, knowledge of specific intent or its absence can help the court decide whether to condemn it. In such cases of ambiguous conduct, specific intent generally becomes an additional requirement that the plaintiff must establish. However, if conduct considered alone clearly offers "the basis for a substantial claim of restraint of trade,"[44] most courts are far more willing to dispense with a separate showing of specific intent. They either ignore the intent requirement or else hold that the particular conduct alleged is sufficiently clear that evil intent can be inferred. In *Spectrum Sports*, the Supreme Court approved a formulation of the attempt offense that permits intent to be proven from objective evidence. "Unfair or predatory conduct may be sufficient to prove the necessary intent to monopolize."[45] However, the Court also held that intent could not be inferred from dangerous probability of success alone.[46]

6.5b.   "Dangerous Probability of Success"

Occasionally the circumstances surrounding an alleged attempt to monopolize indicate clearly the potential harm to competition. If there are only two firms in a relevant market and one dynamites the other's plant the danger to competition is clear. In most cases, however, the danger is difficult to evaluate. The purpose of the "dangerous probability" requirement is to avoid overdeterrence in situations when the defendant's conduct is difficult to assess or the

---

[43]   For example U.S. Philips Corp. v. Windmere Corp., 861 F.2d 695, 698–703 (Fed.Cir. 1988), cert. denied, 490 U.S. 1068, 109 S.Ct. 2070 (1989) (letting the jury decide whether defendant's internal memoranda statements such as "let's pound them [our competitors] into the sand" were simply sales talk or sufficient evidence of anticompetitive intent.).

[44]   See *Inglis*, 668 F.2d at 1028.

[45]   Spectrum Sports v. McQuillan, 506 U.S. 447, 459, 113 S.Ct. 884, 892 (1993).

[46]   Ibid. ("We hold that petitioners may not be liable for attempted monopolization * * * absent proof of a dangerous probability that they would monopolize a particular market and specific intent to monopolize.").

market in which the conduct occurred is not clearly conducive to monopoly.

The "dangerous probability" requirement was traditionally controversial. For example, the Ninth Circuit found the requirement unnecessary if the conduct that formed the basis of the attempt claim was also a per se violation of the antitrust laws.[47] But in *Spectrum Sports* the Supreme Court made clear that (1) "dangerous probability of success" is a required showing in any attempt case, (2) that dangerous probability of success cannot be inferred from intent alone but must be proven separately;[48] and (3) that the dangerous probability requirement in turn requires the plaintiff to define and prove a relevant market which is threatened with monopolization.[49]

Spectrum Sports also held that the dangerous probability requirement cannot be met merely by showing that conduct alleged to be an attempt violates a different antitrust law. For example, tying arrangements, mergers and certain refusals to deal have all been treated as illegal attempts.[50] In any event, in such cases the violation of § 2 is usually inconsequential: a plaintiff's remedy is usually not greater when the same activity violates two statutes instead of one.

In *Philadelphia Taxi*, the Third Circuit held that conduct by defendant Uber, an online transportation network company, did not constitute an unlawful attempt to monopolize.[51] That conduct

---

[47] Lessig v. Tidewater Oil Co., 327 F.2d 459, 474 (9th Cir. 1964), cert. denied, 377 U.S. 993, 84 S.Ct. 1920 (1964). The Supreme Court's *Spectrum Sports* decision expressly overruled *Lessig. Spectrum Sports*, 113 S.Ct. at 891–892.

[48] *Spectrum Sports* also overruled such decisions as Mt. Lebanon Motors, Inc. v. Chrysler Corp., 283 F.Supp. 453 (W.D.Pa.1968), affirmed on other grounds, 417 F.2d 622 (3d Cir. 1969), which approved a jury verdict of attempted monopolization. The court directed a verdict for the defendant on the plaintiff's monopolization claim because Chrysler faced substantial competition from other automobile manufacturers, but held that the attempt to monopolize could be inferred from the intent alone. The conduct complained of was that Chrysler ended its franchise agreement with the plaintiff and began selling its cars directly through a factory owned outlet. Query: what market was Chrysler monopolizing?

[49] *Spectrum Sports*, 113 S.Ct. at 892 (intent alone insufficient to establish dangerous probability of success; the claim also "requires inquiry into the relevant product and geographic market and the defendant's economic power in that market."). In fact, the Supreme Court had assessed the requirement earlier. See Walker Process Equip., Inc. v. Food Machinery & Chem. Corp., 382 U.S. 172, 177, 86 S.Ct. 347, 350 (1965): "To establish monopolization or attempt to monopolize * * * it would then be necessary to appraise the exclusionary power of the illegal * * * claim in terms of the relevant market for the product involved."

[50] See Kearney & Trecker Corp. v. Giddings & Lewis, Inc., 452 F.2d 579, 598 (7th Cir. 1971), cert. denied, 405 U.S. 1066, 92 S.Ct. 1500 (1972) (tying arrangement); Knutson v. Daily Review, Inc., 548 F.2d 795 (9th Cir. 1976), cert. denied, 433 U.S. 910, 97 S.Ct. 2977 (1977), on remand, 468 F.Supp. 226 (1979), affirmed, 664 F.2d 1120 (9th Cir. 1981) (acquisition of competitors).

[51] Philadelphia Taxi Ass'n, Inc. v. Uber Techs., Inc., 886 F.3d 332 (3d Cir. 2018).

included evasion of regulatory requirements that applied to taxicabs, failure to purchase taxicab medallions that taxicabs were required to bear, failure to pay drivers minimum wages, hiring away rivals, failure to obtain vehicle insurance, and offering consumers lower prices than traditional taxicabs charged. The court observed that, while Uber's prices were alleged to be lower, they were not alleged to be predatory. While some of the other activities may have violated regulatory requirements, they did not for that reason alone constitute antitrust violations, and their overall impact was to introduce more rather than less competition into the market. In any event the Philadelphia Parking Authority, which was in charge of enforcing most of these regulations, had not relinquished its role. The hiring away of drivers was not anticompetitive because the drivers were actually used by Uber. Finally, looking at overall availability of ride-for-hire services, they increased rather than decreased during the relevant time period.

Reliable evidence of specific intent can be difficult to find and inconclusive when it is found. Conduct can be equally ambiguous. Often the simplest way to assess the danger a defendant's conduct poses is to examine the market in which the alleged attempt occurred. If the defendant's conduct is ambiguous, arguably consistent with both monopolization and competition on the merits, examination of the market will help a court determine whether a dangerous probability of monopoly existed. If the answer is no, the court should go no further.

More importantly, since evaluation of conduct is imprecise, examination of the market's proclivity to monopolization will reduce the rate and costs of error. The possibility for error is two-fold. First, a legal rule that is too harsh on defendants will tend toward overinclusiveness or overdeterrence: that is, it may recognize all (or most) true instances of conduct likely to cause monopoly, but it will sometimes condemn competition on the merits as well. Secondly, a legal rule that is too harsh on plaintiffs will tend toward underinclusiveness or underdeterrence: it may recognize most instances when monopolization is unlikely, but in the process may overlook some instances when monopoly is a real threat.[52]

Both kinds of errors can impose economic costs on society. Overinclusive rules are inefficient when they brand efficiency as monopolistic. The result is that firms charge higher prices than necessary in order to avoid legal liability, and they refrain from doing things that benefit consumers but that may harm competitors.

---

[52]   See Paul L. Joskow & Alvin K. Klevorick, A Framework for Analyzing Predatory Pricing Policy, 89 Yale L.J. 213, 222–39 (1979).

Furthermore, to the extent that the more efficient firms refrain from exploiting their efficiencies to the full extent, the market becomes attractive to other, less efficient firms. The result will be higher costs and prices.

Underinclusive rules are also inefficient. A rule that fails to recognize incipient monopolization will permit the growth of some monopolies. Both the monopolist's reduced output and its anticompetitive efforts to maintain its monopoly position are socially costly. A perfect legal rule would avoid both overdeterrence and underdeterrence. Unfortunately, when conduct is ambiguous, the legal rule is necessarily an oversimplification of reality. For example, no comprehensible legal rule can weigh all the relevant variables in a predatory pricing case.[53] Recognizing that the rule will sometimes miss the mark, courts must nevertheless strive to minimize the costs of such errors.

Although the *Spectrum Sports* decision[54] required the plaintiff to define a relevant market in an attempt case, it said little about the kind of proof of market power or market share necessary to support the claim. Courts have expressed concern that the attempt offense can be used anticompetitively to condemn "unfair" business conduct when there is little likelihood of monopoly. This has generally led to the requirement that the plaintiff in an attempt case must show that the defendant has a certain minimum market share. The Fourth Circuit has articulated the market share requirements for attempt cases this way:

> (1) claims of less than 30% market shares should presumptively be rejected; (2) claims involving between 30% and 50% shares should usually be rejected, except when conduct is very likely to achieve monopoly of when conduct is invidious, but not so much so as to make the defendant per se liable; (3) claims involving greater than 50% share should be treated as attempts at monopolization when the other elements for attempted monopolization are also satisfied.[55]

---

[53]   See Ch. 8.

[54]   *Spectrum Sports*, 113 S.Ct. at 884.

[55]   M & M Medical Supplies and Service v. Pleasant Valley Hospital, 981 F.2d 160, 168 (4th Cir. 1992) (en banc).

Most other courts use numbers in the same range,[56] with a few indicating that a rising market share is a stronger indicator of sufficient power.[57]

But generalizing about market share requirements in this fashion is problematic. The plausibility of an attempt to monopolize depends on a host of factors, of which market share is only one. Further, the market power requirements in attempt cases vary with the conduct alleged to be an attempt. A firm that seeks to create a monopoly by dynamiting its competitor's plants does not need market power—only a saboteur and a match. The same thing generally applies to other kinds of conduct that have been held to be an attempt to monopolize, such as bad faith litigation or patent fraud. However, in Lorain Journal Co. v. United States[58] the defendant was accused of refusing to sell newspaper advertising to any purchaser who also purchased advertising on a nearby radio station. Lorain Journal's scheme could not have succeeded unless it held a dominant market share. If there were competing daily newspapers in the relevant area, anyone who wanted to advertise in both a newspaper and the radio station would have purchased its newspaper advertising from a newspaper that did not assess the restriction.

Thus it is impossible to generalize: some attempts to monopolize require the defendant to have significant market power while others do not. Further, the success of a particular attempt scheme often depends not on the defendant's market power, but on its relatively large market share. Predatory pricing is such an offense: the act of predatory pricing does not require a defendant to have the ability to sell its output at a price higher than marginal cost. On the contrary, the offense itself involves selling at a price often lower than short-run marginal cost. However, predatory pricing is prohibitively expensive and unlikely to yield a monopoly unless the predator has a fairly large market share to begin with.[59]

In all cases it is important to remember that the attempt offense is designed to reach conduct likely to create a monopoly. The attempt offense was not designed to condemn the exercise of present market power. Nor was it designed, however, to condemn conduct unlikely to give the defendant a monopoly. At the very least a plaintiff should be required to identify some market in which the defendant's activities,

---

[56]   See 3B Antitrust Law ¶ 807 (4th ed. 2015).

[57]   See 3B Antitrust Law ¶ 807e2 (4th ed. 2015) ("A rising market share is more likely to suggest a dangerous probability of success than a falling share."); Fiberglass Insulators v. Dupuy, 856 F.2d 652 (4th Cir. 1988) (correct to focus on resulting market share of 51% rather than initial market share of 5%).

[58]   342 U.S. 143, 72 S.Ct. 181 (1951).

[59]   See § 8.4.

if allowed to run their course, plausibly would have generated a monopoly.

One uncertainty is how *Spectrum Sports'* relevant market requirement will play out in a case where significant market power is established by "direct" proof not requiring a market definition. As noted earlier, such proof can be superior in markets where the data are available, and is more accurate in product differentiated markets.[60] At the same time, however, the plaintiff must be able to identify a grouping of sales over which the exercise of market power will be plausible. In most cases this problem should solve itself. That is, the evidence of high margins or low elasticity of demand will necessarily pertain to some identifiable set of sales, and these would at least presumptively constitute the market.

---

[60]   See § 3.9.

Chapter 7

EXCLUSIONARY PRACTICES IN MONOPOLIZATION AND ATTEMPT CASES

Table of Sections

§ 7.1 Introduction

The chapter discusses various practices that have been branded by courts or plaintiffs as monopolistic. Before these practices can be condemned under § 2 of the Sherman Act, the defendant's product must be found to have monopoly power or "dominance,[1] and the general considerations and definitions given in the previous chapter apply. The same conduct may also constitute an "attempt" to monopolize if the firm is currently not a monopolist in the market at issue, but threatens to become one. The "power" showing in attempt cases is less, but the conduct requirements are stricter.[2] By contrast, any practice that will support a charge of attempt will also support a charge of illegal monopolization, provided that the higher market power requirements of the latter offense are met.

Since the Sherman Act was passed, many practices have been condemned as illegal monopolization if the firm that carried them out had sufficient market power. These include:

espionage or sabotage

mergers

reduction of output

expansion of capacity or output

predatory, below cost, pricing

price discrimination

---

[1]   See Ch. 3.

[2]   See § 6.5.

price discounts, including quantity discounts, "loyalty" discounts (those requiring a buyer to take a specified minimum percentage of its needs from the seller), and "bundled" discounts (those requiring the buyer to purchase a "bundle" of two or more goods)

refusals to deal

vertical integration

tying arrangements

supply or price "squeezes"

predatory or "manipulative" research and development; altered complementary products

failure to predisclose research and development

attempts to "leverage" a monopoly in one area or market into an unfair advantage in a second area or market

raising rivals' costs

patent abuses, including improperly brought infringement suits, patent acquisitions and "accumulation," and refusal to license

abuse of government process through vexatious litigation or administrative claims

business torts

Predatory pricing, discounting practices, and related pricing issues are considered in Chapter 8. As § 6.1 notes, the mere buying and selling of goods at the monopoly price is not a qualifying exclusionary practice.

§ 7.2   Merger and Monopoly

A merger is rarely an "exclusionary" practice. The knowledge that a prospective entrant might be bought up would encourage it to enter a market. A merger or acquisition could "exclude" or discourage someone from entering a market only if the merger created a new firm that had lower costs and was harder to compete with than the two firms had been before the merger.

Nonetheless, a merger *can* create a firm with monopoly power, and this firm could then reduce output and raise prices. Further, it might be tempted to engage in exclusionary practices in order to entrench its position. Courts have fairly consistently held that the

Sherman Act condemns mergers to monopoly.[3] The most notable exception was the 1920 U.S. Steel case. United States Steel Company had been formed in 1901 by the merger of some 180 firms controlling around 90% of the market.[4] But by 1920 its market share had declined to 50%, largely because it pursued a strategy of setting high prices that encouraged entry.[5] A divided Supreme Court refused to condemn the conduct as monopolization, noting (a) that the firm was no longer a monopoly, given the new entry; (b) that the government had waited about a decade before bringing suit; (c) that the merger seemed to be a consequence of natural developments in the industry, such as economies of scale caused by new technology.

Several early monopolization cases, particularly the *American Can* decision, involved allegations that a dominant firm bought its rivals' plants and shut them down in order to keep market output low. The success of such a tactic would depend on the circumstances. For example, if entry is easy the practice might invite further new entrants, attracted by the opportunity to sell out at a high price.[6] But easy entry markets are not susceptible to monopolization in any event.

The § 2 prohibition reaches not only the acquisition of an actual rival, but also of a likely entrant or a nascent firm. Indeed, one of the most effective ways for a dominant firm to maintain its monopoly position[7] is to acquire incipient rivals as they appear on the horizon.[8] This is particularly true of intellectual property acquisitions—for example, a firm whose monopoly depends on patented technology might acquire an exclusive right in potentially competing patents developed by others, thus staving off a competitive uprising. Section 2 is presumptively violated by the monopolist's acquisition of an exclusive right in a patent or other intellectual property right at the

---

[3]   Northern Securities Co. v. United States, 193 U.S. 197, 24 S.Ct. 436 (1904); Standard Oil Co. of N.J. v. United States, 221 U.S. 1, 31 S.Ct. 502 (1911); United States v. First Nat'l Bank & Trust Co. of Lexington, 376 U.S. 665, 84 S.Ct. 1033 (1964). See also 3 Antitrust Law ¶ 701 (4th ed. 2015); and 4 id. ¶ 911–912 (4th ed. 2016); Barak Orbach & Grace Campbell Rebling, The Antitrust Curse of Bigness, 85 S.Cal.L.Rev. 605 (2012).

[4]   United States v. United States Steel Corp., 251 U.S. 417, 40 S.Ct. 293 (1920).

[5]   See Alfred D. Chandler, Scale and Scope: Dynamics of Industrial Capitalism 126–129 (1990).

[6]   United States v. American Can Co., 230 Fed. 859 (D.Md.1916), appeal dismissed, 256 U.S. 706, 41 S.Ct. 624 (1921).

[7]   On maintenance of monopoly power as a § 2 offense, see § 6.4b.

[8]   See 3 Antitrust Law ¶ 701d (4th ed. 2015).

heart of its monopoly power, although acquisitions of non-exclusive rights are generally lawful.[9]

One practice that requires further antitrust attention is when a large platform, such as Google, Amazon or Facebook, acquires a nascent rival. Most of these acquisitions do not fall within current merger law because the acquired firms are either too small or else they are complements rather than competitors of the acquiring firms.[10] The danger, however, is that by systematically buying up these small firms the acquiring entities preclude their emergence as viable competitors in the future. After all, the large platforms started out their own lives as tiny entities.[11] Nevertheless, it is not clear that § 2 is the appropriate vehicle, since it requires either a monopoly or a dangerous probability that one will be created. It is not much of a stretch, however, to regard a large platform's systematic acquisitions of smaller firms as an attempt to monopolize.

A variation of the *American Can* buy-and-shut-down strategy is the "killer acquisition," which occurs when a firm acquires a highly innovative young firm, typically in tech or pharmaceuticals, not to integrate its innovation, but rather to remove its productive capacity or research projects from the market.[12] Such acquisitions produce none of the efficiencies of mergers because the acquired firm is simply shut down. Further, to the extent such acquisitions shut down promising technologies they can operate as significant restraints on innovation. The social costs of such restraints can be much higher than for ordinary price restraints.[13]

Today § 7 of the Clayton Act condemns most horizontal mergers involving firms with sufficient market power to be found guilty of illegal monopolization.[14] As a result, the courts have come to rely less on the Sherman Act.

---

[9]   See 4 Antitrust Law ¶ 912d (4th ed. 2016); Herbert Hovenkamp, Antitrust and the Patent System: A Reexamination, 76 OSU L.J. 467 (2015).

[10]   For further development, see § 12.3c.

[11]   See Kevin Bryan and Erik Hovenkamp, Startup Acquisitions, Error Costs, and Antitrust Policy, 87 Univ. Chi. L. Rev. 331 (2020); Herbert Hovenkamp, Antitrust and Platform Monopoly, 130 Yale L.J. ___ (2021) (forthcoming), available at https://papers.ssrn.com/sol3/papers.cfm?abstract_id=3639142.

[12]   Id., and Colleen Cunningham, et al., Killer Acquisitions (2018), available at https://papers.ssrn.com/sol3/papers.cfm?abstract_id=3241707.

[13]   See Herbert Hovenkamp, Restraints on Innovation, 29 Cardozo L. Rev. 247 (2007).

[14]   See § 12.1.

§ 7.3   Output Expansion; Strategic Capacity Construction

In *Alcoa* Judge Hand held that Aluminum Company's continual expansion of capacity to meet anticipated market demand was "exclusionary" because it denied potential competitors a fair share of the market.[15] But expansion of capacity will exclude an *equally efficient* rival only if the monopolist increases output to the point that it must sell at marginal cost. That is, if a firm builds a plant so large that it can service all the output demanded at a competitive price, there will be no economic profits to attract equally efficient competitors into the market. If the monopolist produces less than that, however, the monopoly profits will attract any rival capable of producing at the same costs.

The foregoing may not apply, however, when economies of scale are significant. In that case, the established firm might take strategic measures designed to deprive potential rivals of the opportunity to enter at the efficient scale.[16] For example, it might build a very large plant, but operate it at only half capacity. The low output serves to keep prices high, but the excess capacity, observable by prospective rivals, serves to deter new entrants.

But even assuming that expansion of capacity can sometimes be anticompetitive, antitrust policy cannot condemn it unless it is able to separate efficient from anti-competitive expansions. In the *du Pont* (titanium dioxide) case, the Federal Trade Commission concluded that this was virtually impossible and criticized Judge Hand for jumping too quickly to the conclusion that Alcoa's output expansion was anticompetitive. Du Pont had developed a new method for producing titanium dioxide, a paint whitener, and then built a plant large enough to supply foreseeable demand for the entire market, thus depriving other firms of access. The Commission faulted *Alcoa* for saying "nothing about the scale economies inherent in Alcoa's expansion" or addressing whether "Alcoa's additional output conformed to demand estimates or resulted in excess capacity."[17] Since *du Pont*, output or capacity expansion has not been condemned under § 2 unless it resulted in predatory prices, which must be lower than the relevant measure of cost.

---

[15]   United States v. Aluminum Co. of America, 148 F.2d 416, 431 (2d Cir. 1945).

[16]   See § 8.3b, on strategic pricing behavior.

[17]   E.I. du Pont de Nemours & Co., 96 F.T.C. 653, 747 (1980).

§ 7.4   Price Discrimination; Leasing Practices

Price discrimination occurs when a seller obtains different rates of return from the same product from different groups of customers. Price discrimination is a complex subject and price discrimination comes in different kinds, or "degrees," that can have different economic effects. Most price discrimination is concerned with extraction, not exclusion. That is, its purpose and generally its effect is not to exclude anyone from the market, but rather to enable a seller to earn higher profits from relatively isolated or idiosyncratic customers. Nevertheless, some courts have considered price discrimination by the monopolist to be an exclusionary practice warranting condemnation. In United States v. United Shoe Machinery Co. (USM), Judge Wyzanski condemned the defendant for obtaining a high rate of return from leases of machines in which it had no competitors, and a much lower rate of return from leases of machines in which competition was greater.[18] In this case leasing may have facilitated price discrimination by preventing arbitrage. That is, if USM had simply sold its machines, those charged a relatively low price would have resold to those asked to pay a higher price. Leasing enabled USM to keep the machines from being transferred and also to monitor use, with lease rates tied to intensity of use.

The ability to engage in persistent price discrimination is evidence of at least minimal market power.[19] But is price discrimination itself an exclusionary practice? Suppose that a monopolist has costs of $1.00 per widget. It identifies two sets of customers who are willing to pay different prices, selling to one set at $1.00 per widget (a competitive but nevertheless profitable price), and to the other set at $1.50 per widget. Now a court forbids it to price discriminate. The firm will either sell to both sets of customers at $1.00, or else it will sell only to the high preference customers at a price of $1.50. Which price maximizes the seller's profits will vary from one situation to another.

Clearly, if the monopolist's non-discriminatory profit-maximizing price is $1.00, its earlier price discrimination was not "exclusionary." On the contrary, the sales at a price of $1.50 to the high preference purchasers would attract new competitors into at least that part of the market. However, if the monopolist's non-discriminatory profit-maximizing price is $1.50, then its price discrimination was exclusionary. If forbidden to price discriminate

---

[18]   110 F.Supp. 295, 340, 341 (D.Mass.1953), affirmed per curiam, 347 U.S. 521, 74 S.Ct. 699 (1954).

[19]   See § 3.9b.

the monopolist would charge $1.50 for all units, and those customers willing to pay only $1.00 would not be served.[20]

However, the price discrimination in the above example is exclusionary because it *increases* the monopolist's total output. Price discrimination in the real world sometimes results in larger output than non-discriminatory pricing, and sometimes it does not. When the price discrimination results in a larger output, then the practice also has the effect of excluding competitors. When it does not result in a larger output, it usually excludes no one. On the contrary, the higher profits that accrue from price discrimination will invite new entry.

Price discrimination may cause anticompetitive exclusion when the market has developed institutions that require sharing of technology or assets and price discrimination threatens to undermine these. This can occur in the context of standard setting that involves cross-licensing of patents. The targets of such discrimination may either be forced from the market or experience higher costs.[21]

§ 7.5   Unilateral Refusals to Deal I: General Doctrine

In United States v. Colgate & Co.[22] the Supreme Court reiterated the ancient common law doctrine that "[i]n the absence of any purpose to create or maintain a monopoly" a private trader may freely "exercise his own independent discretion as to parties with whom he will deal." The rule remains good law.

The *Colgate* doctrine of refusal to deal contains two explicit exceptions. First, the decision not to deal must be "independent." The per se legality rule does not apply to concerted refusals, which are discussed in Chapter 5. Second, the refusal must occur "[i]n the absence of any purpose to create or maintain a monopoly."[23] If a unilateral refusal to deal is ever illegal, it is when the refusal is undertaken by a monopolist, or by someone who threatens by the refusal to become one.

In *Aspen Skiing* the Supreme Court held that a larger skiing company (Ski Co.) violated the antitrust laws when it refused to continue its participation in a joint venture with a smaller company

---

[20]   See 3 Antitrust Law ¶ 721 (4th ed. 2015). Richard A. Posner, Antitrust Law 81–82, 205 (2d ed. 2001), is somewhat more willing to condemn price discrimination as exclusionary.

[21]   See § 7.5c.

[22]   250 U.S. 300, 307, 39 S.Ct. 465, 468 (1919).

[23]   250 U.S. at 307, 39 S.Ct. at 468.

(Highlands).[24] Assuming that the market was properly defined as downhill skiing in Aspen, Colorado, the two firms shared the market, but the defendant was roughly three times as big as the plaintiff and controlled three mountains to the plaintiff's one.

For some time, Ski Co. and Highlands had participated in various ventures to market "All Aspen" tickets that would permit skiers to ski all four mountains at their will. Actual use was monitored and the two firms split revenues in proportion. Of course, price or output affecting agreements among competitors are suspect under § 1 of the Sherman Act, particularly when they involve the only two firms in the market. In the 1970's the Colorado Attorney General's office had challenged the joint venture and obtained a consent decree permitting the venture to continue, provided that the firms set ticket prices unilaterally.[25]

In the late 1970s Ski Co. began to insist on larger divisions of the revenues. The arrangement fell apart when Ski Co. insisted on a formula giving Highlands only 12.5% of the revenue, even though historical usage suggested its percentage should be 14% or 15%. Ski Co. then offered its own three mountain ticket, and refused to cooperate with Highlands' efforts to give its own customers access to Ski Co.'s mountains. For example, Ski Co. refused to sell Highlands lift tickets to Ski Co.'s mountains even at full price, so that Highlands could include the tickets in its ski packages. This repeated refusal to continue participation in the joint venture was challenged by the plaintiff under § 2.

In affirming lower court findings of monopolization, the Supreme Court asserted two propositions: first, a monopolist does not have a general obligation to cooperate with rivals; but second, some refusals to deal may have "evidentiary significance" and may produce liability in certain occasions. In this instance, Ski Co. *had* participated in the joint venture for many years, and then refused to do so without offering "any efficiency justification whatever for its pattern of conduct."[26]

The Court concluded that mere failure to provide a sensible business explanation for the change was insufficient for condemnation. The plaintiff also had to show that the refusal to deal had a negative impact on consumers as well as on the plaintiff itself. In this case the evidence was clear that skiers preferred the combined

---

[24]   Aspen Skiing Co. v. Aspen Highlands Skiing Corp., 472 U.S. 585, 105 S.Ct. 2847 (1985).

[25]   Id. at 591 & n.9, 105 S.Ct. at 2851 & n.9.

[26]   Id. at 608, 105 S.Ct. at 2860.

four mountain ticket, and that Ski Co's refusal deprived them of that choice.[27]

7.5a.   Protecting the Incentive to Invest

While *Aspen* is sometimes conflated with the "essential facility" doctrine,[28] the two doctrines rest on inconsistent rationales. The *Aspen* rule creates an incentive for firms to invest by protecting previous joint investment decisions from anticompetitive repudiation by a dominant firm. In sharp contrast, the essential facility doctrine discourages competitive investment and is best left to regulatory policy rather than antitrust law.

The *Aspen* defendant's refusal to deal harmed both a rival and consumers. Customers were better off to be able to purchase the four-mountain package. To be sure, this could have been accomplished through a merger, but it would have been a merger to monopoly. The refusal to deal robbed consumers of a package that the market had provided in the past and apparently could have provided in the future had the defendant cooperated.

The Court's rules for recognizing an anticompetitive unilateral refusal to deal seem to be quite cautious. First, there must have been a pre-existing dealing relationship and the plaintiff's investment in reliance on this commitment. Second, the defendant's termination of this relationship must be without a good justification. Third, the refusal to continue in this relationship must be shown to harm consumers, as well as the plaintiff.

Reading *Aspen* to create a *new* obligation to deal where no arrangement had existed before would be a significant extension of its holding. In its 2004 *Trinko* decision the Supreme Court described *Aspen* as "at or near the outer boundary of § 2 liability."[29] On *Aspen's* facts, that seems clear. The harm to competition seemed minimal. While the skiing joint venture was profitable to the firms, the plaintiff did not make substantial investment or redeployment of its resources in reliance on the venture. Cancelling the venture largely restored the status quo ante. A joint venturer's abandonment of an established relationship can be much more harmful to competition when the venture induces and directs significant new investment,

---

[27]   Id. at 606, 105 S.Ct. at 2859.

[28]   See § 7.7.

[29]   Verizon Communications, Inc. v. Law Offices of Curtis V. Trinko, LLP, 540 U.S. 398, 409, 124 S.Ct. 872, 879 (2004).

redirecting investment in ways that are very costly to reverse.[30] As this happens the case for antitrust intervention is stronger.

In any event, *Trinko*'s characterization of *Aspen* as at the outer boundary of § 2 liability should not be read as some free floating conclusion about all refusal to deal cases. Monopolization cases are highly fact specific and Justice Scalia's characterization should be read as a description of *Aspen's* facts, nothing more.

The FRAND process provides a good example of how the *Aspen* rule should work. As part of the process of developing standards for new technology in networked industries, which require interconnection, firms agree to disclose their patents that they deem essential to a proposed standard and to license them to all participants on "fair, reasonable, and nondiscriminatory" (FRAND) terms.[31] These agreements can reasonably be expected to steer subsequent product development in the direction of these agreed-upon standards. Under the FRAND commitment, participants can develop the standards in the confidence that the technology they are adopting is available to them at a cost similar to the costs paid by other, similarly situated firms. That is, the process facilitates competitive development of complex networked technologies involving a large number of participants. If one firm that has developed a dominant position in an essential component then withdraws its commitment, that could impair competition significantly. This is essentially what happened in the *Qualcomm* case, where a firm that had made FRAND commitments on its patents, but later selectively licensed them only to noncompetitors or tied licenses to its own hardware and at prices significantly higher than the FRAND rate.[32] In that case the injury to competition must be reckoned as significantly greater than it was in *Aspen*. In a troublesome decision, a Ninth Circuit panel reversed.[33] The court ignored the higher prices that Qualcomm's behavior caused, holding that there was inadequate evidence of harm to competitors. That conclusion stood antitrust's consumer welfare principle on its head. More problematically, the FRAND system is socially valuable but fragile. Breach of contract actions had not been successful in restraining Qualcom's activities. If other firms follow Qualcomm's

---

[30] See Thomas Cotter, Erik Hovenkamp, and Norman Siebrasse, Demystifying Patent Holdup, 76 Washington & Lee L. Rev. 1501 (2019).

[31] For further analysis, focusing on joint venture aspects of FRAND, see § 5.5c6.

[32] FTC v. Qualcomm, 411 F.Supp.3d 658 (N.D. Cal. 2019); see Herbert Hovenkamp, FRAND and Antitrust, ___ Cornell L. Rev. ___ (2020), available at https://papers.ssrn.com/sol3/papers.cfm?abstract_id=3420925.

[33] FTC v. Qualcomm, 969 F.3d 974 (9th Cir. 2020).

lead the FRAND system could well fall apart unless subsequent decisions or Congress intervene.

Aspen is sensibly restricted to the unjustified repudiation of a commitment that substantially affected market investment. The violation consists in the defendant's participation in a venture reasonably intended to produce reliance and promote development, and then changing course in a manner that both undermines those intentions and leads to reduced output, higher prices, or impaired innovation. This conduct element distinguishes *Aspen* from the "essential facility" doctrine. The *Aspen* rule serves to encourage investment in technologies where ongoing cooperation is essential. By contrast, the essential facility rule treats firms as simply incapable of investing on their own. In its *Novell* decision the Tenth Circuit added as a requirement something that the *Aspen* Court had suggested but did not require: namely, that the refusal involve a "willingness to sacrifice short term profits" that would be irrational but for its anticompetitive effect.[34] The *Novell* court then noted the lack of evidence that Microsoft suffered any loss from its alleged withdrawal of technical information necessary to make Wordperfect work efficiently in a Windows environment. In cases involving joint investment, however, the sacrifice requirement seems unnecessary and counterproductive. One problem with sacrifice tests generally is that it is hard to distinguish "sacrifice" from investment. Most costly investments involve losses in the short run followed by gains later on. Further, the eventual gains are often strongly correlated with losses by competitors, particularly in concentrated markets.

Another problem is that sacrifice is irrelevant to the amount of competitive harm. It is rational for a firm to repudiate a commitment when it stands to earn more by doing so. Adding a requirement that repudiation must produce immediate losses, followed only later by profit only serves to immunize certain anticompetitive refusals.

Aspen applies only to unreasonable refusals to deal—without a "business justification," as the Supreme Court put it. For example, firms may coinvest in a technology that later proves to be unworkable, and antitrust policy should not require firms to stay with business decisions that are not working. In the *Qualcomm* case the defendant's repudiation was not driven by investments in technology that had proven worthless. To the contrary, it was precisely because the technology was so valuable that Qualcomm was motivated to repudiate its commitments to participate in the FRAND process.

---

[34]   Novell, Inc. v. Microsoft Corp., 731 F.3d 1064, 1075 (10th Cir. 2013).

In any event, the record in *Aspen* indicates that the defendant did not sacrifice anything. On the one hand, it lost participation in a profitable joint revenue-sharing venture with the plaintiff. However, it simultaneously gained from the fact that it obtained all of the revenue from the remaining sales. This tradeoff was actually positive: Ski Company made more sales and more money after it terminated the joint venture, even in the short run.[35]

The way to approach *Aspen*-style refusals to deal is not to require "sacrifice," which is difficult to apply and adds nothing to or understanding of the amount of competitive harm. Rather, the court should examine the nature and amount of investment that venturers reasonably made in reliance on the joint venture, and consider the effects of the defendant's unjustified repudiation. *Aspen's* real bite is when joint activity sets development on a particular path that is costly to change, and the defendant is then able to hijack a substantial portion of those gains to itself in a way that limits competition. If a firm can lawfully undermine investment in this way it will destroy the incentive of future firms to make such investments. For example, FRAND obligations create a system that is intended to promote shared but competitive development of technology. If a firm is able to renege on these obligations and thereby transfer to itself a dominant position, the result can be reduced output and higher prices in the short run, and reduced innovation in the longer run.

Refusal to deal cases that raise these issues often present problems in vertical integration. For example, as long as Microsoft did not make Microsoft Office, including its word processing program Microsoft Word, it would have every incentive to make Wordperfect interconnect with Windows as smoothly as possible. Windows and Wordperfect are complements and operating systems become more valuable as complements such as application programs work better. Once Microsoft became a downstream competitor, however, its incentives changed. It could profit by degrading Wordperfect for the benefit of its own Microsoft Word. The European Union competition authority made a similar observation in its *Microsoft* case involving servers, or specialized computers that process internet, email, and other communications traffic. Microsoft shared its protocols liberally with non-Microsoft server manufacturers as long as Microsoft itself was not in the server operating system market. Once it entered that market, however, it began to degrade its technological information to

---

[35] See the discussion of the record, Reply Brief for Petitioner, *Aspen*, No. 84-510, 1985 WL 669989 (March 20, 1985), showing that there was no sacrifice of either volume or profits.

non-Microsoft manufacturers for the benefits of its own server system.[36]

These facts suggest a rationale for a broader antitrust duty to deal law in networks where technological compatibility and interconnection are essential.[37] The problem is less severe in lower tech networks such as real estate boards, where access is controlled by a group of firms who can act only by agreement and the emergence of dominant firms is less common. The remedies problem can be difficult, although it can sometimes be addressed through a nondiscrimination rule. For example, in the EU case the tribunal required that Microsoft's provision of information to non-Microsoft servers had to be in all respects identical to that provided to Microsoft servers.

The presence of effective government regulation can also change the picture, as the Supreme Court's 2004 *Trinko* decision indicates.[38] The plaintiff was a customer of AT&T, which in this case was a competitive local exchange carrier, or CLEC. Under the 1996 Telecommunications Act the defendant Verizon, an incumbent local exchange carrier, or ILEC, was required to enter an interconnection agreement providing for sharing of its network elements with any CLEC who requested such interconnection.[39] The antitrust dispute arose when Verizon failed to provide such access in a timely fashion. The plaintiff complained that the failure was not an oversight but rather was "part of an anticompetitive scheme to discourage customers from becoming or remaining customers" of CLECs. The complaint requested damages as well as a mandatory injunction ordering Verizon to fill orders for new services from CLECs on the same terms and timing as it took care of its own customers.[40]

The Supreme Court noted the "tension" that exists whenever a court is asked to require a monopolist to share its lawfully acquired inputs:

> Firms may acquire monopoly power by establishing an infrastructure that renders them uniquely suited to serve

---

[36]   Case T-201/04, Microsoft Corp. v. Comm'n, 2007 E.C.R. II-3601, ¶ 4. See Herbert Hovenkamp, The Obama Administration and § 2 of the Sherman Act, 90 Boston Univ.L.Rev. 1611 (2010).

[37]   See 3B Antitrust Law ¶ 772h (4th ed. 2015).

[38]   Verizon Communications, Inc. v. Law Offices of Curtis V. Trinko, LLP, 540 U.S. 398, 124 S.Ct. 872 (2004).

[39]   Telecommunications Act of 1996, § 151(a), Pub. L. No. 104–104, 110 Stat. 56 (1996).

[40]   *Trinko*, 540 U.S. at 404, 124 S.Ct. at 877. Significantly, the 1996 Telecommunications Act also requires CLECs to provide such access on "just, reasonable, and nondiscriminatory' terms." 47 U.S.C. § 251(c)(3).

their customers. Compelling such firms to share the source of their advantage is in some tension with the underlying purpose of antitrust law, since it may lessen the incentive for the monopolist, the rival, or both to invest in those economically beneficial facilities.[41]

Further, the Court noted, forced sharing blends the roles of antitrust court and regulator by requiring antitrust courts to act as "central planners," determining price, output, and other terms of dealing.[42]

The Court also noted that forced sharing requires firms to cooperate rather than compete, and cooperation can "facilitate the supreme evil of antitrust: collusion."[43] As a result, antitrust has traditionally been very reluctant to impose sharing obligations even on proven monopolists.

In *Trinko*, contrary to *Aspen*, the complaint did not "allege that Verizon voluntarily engaged in a course of dealing with its rivals, or would ever have done so absent statutory compulsion."[44] Because there was no initial voluntary cooperation, "the defendant's prior conduct sheds no light upon the motivation of its refusal to deal— upon whether its regulatory lapses were prompted not by competitive zeal but by anticompetitive malice." Indeed, defendant Ski Company had even refused to sell to the plaintiff at its own retail price, "suggesting a calculation that its future monopoly retail price would be higher." In sharp contrast, the Telecommunications Act required Verizon to interconnect at very low rates of compensation, almost certainly lower than it could earn from making its own retail sales. The plaintiffs were effectively asking for an antitrust rule requiring a defendant to give up *more* profitable business in order to make lower price sales to a rival.

The Court also observed that *Aspen* involved a situation where the defendant refused to sell something that "it already sold at retail" in any event. That also explained the *Otter Tail* case, where the defendant simply refused to wholesale, or "wheel," power that it was already transmitting to others.[45] It would also distinguish the subsequent *Qualcomm* decision where the assets at issue were patents—discrete property interests that are readily subject to

---

41   Id. at 407–408, 124 S.Ct. at 879.

42   Ibid.

43   Ibid.

44   Ibid.

45   Id. at 410, 124 S.Ct. at 880, citing Otter Tail Power Co. v. United States, 410 U.S. 366, 93 S.Ct. 1022 (1973).

independent transfer and where an obligation to do so had already been created.[46] In *Trinko*, however,

> the services allegedly withheld are not otherwise marketed or available to the public. The sharing obligation imposed by the 1996 Act created 'something brand new'—'the wholesale market for leasing network elements.' The unbundled elements offered pursuant to § 251(c)(3) exist only deep within the bowels of Verizon; they are brought out on compulsion of the 1996 Act and offered not to consumers but to rivals, and at considerable expense and effort.[47]

Further, in *Trinko*, unlike either *Aspen* or *Otter Tail* the plaintiff was asking the defendant not merely to share out of its excess capacity, but also to design and build additional systems that it must then share with rivals.

The Court concluded that these facts would require it to stretch liability for a unilateral refusal to deal significantly beyond *Aspen*, and it declined to do so.

7.5b.   Scope of Duty to Deal

Ordering a firm to deal invariably involves the court in setting the terms of sale, including but not limited to price. In the process we will have turned the defendant into a virtual public utility. Antitrust, it should be recalled, is designed to be a *market alternative* to price regulation, not merely price regulation by another name.

One limitation that often works is to limit the dealing duty to inputs for which the defendant has already made a market commitment. Alternatively, the court must be assured that the market is unable to supply the input in question. The Ninth Circuit lost sight of this in its *Kodak* decision after remand from the Supreme Court.[48] It concluded that once a relevant market was defined for all Kodak parts,[49] Kodak had a duty to sell every part in that market whether or not the part could readily be produced or obtained from alternate sources.[50] By requiring Kodak to supply all these things the court reduced the likelihood that the plaintiffs would develop alternative sources of their own. As a result, the market for fixing Kodak copy machines became less rather than more competitive.

---

[46]   FTC v. Qualcomm, 411 F.Supp.3d 658 (N.D. Cal. 2019), rev'd on other grounds, 969 F.3d 974 (9th Cir. 2020).

[47]   540 U.S. at 410, 124 S.Ct. at 880.

[48]   Image Technical Services, Inc. v. Eastman Kodak Co., 125 F.3d 1195 (9th Cir.1997), cert. denied, 523 U.S. 1094, 118 S.Ct. 1560 (1998).

[49]   For the problems with this market definition, see § 3.3b.

[50]   See 3A Antitrust Law ¶ 765 (4th ed. 2015).

By contrast, the *Aspen* plaintiff was not asking the defendant to supply it everything it needed to do business. It wanted only continued participation in a joint marketing venture whose terms had previously been settled by agreement among the parties. A dealing order is less disruptive to the extent a court can identify prices or other terms of dealing that have already been established in market transactions. For example, a dealing order that requires a firm to honor FRAND commitments does no more than require the firm to adhere to contract provisions that it has already agreed to.

7.5c.   Refusals to Deal in Cooperative Networks

A common feature of networked markets is that the collective action of more than a single producer and buyer is necessary to make the market work.[51] For example, a network's output is often a set of complementary goods or services offered by multiple sellers, such as local and long distance communications or computer hardware, software, and communications. Networks frequently show economies of scale in consumption, which are sometimes called "network effects." This means that customers value the network more as it becomes larger and has a greater number and variety of participants. For example, a telephone is worthless as a communication device if it cannot be connected to anyone else's telephone. Telephones become more valuable as they can be linked into a single system and the number of users increases. An optimal system would permit everyone to talk to everyone else. The same thing is true today of computers. They communicate with the world via the internet, and depend on compatibility among both users and many types of suppliers. To the extent that the installed base of a particular type of computer becomes larger, software becomes more profitable to write and cheaper to purchase.

Cooperative investment of this kind also produces significant path dependence, which means that extraction from an existing cooperative framework can be very costly, although it is sometimes justified, particularly when the existing technology has become obsolete.[52] For example, no matter how much co-investment had given rise to the technology for analog video recording (VHS) tapes,

---

[51]   See Yochai Benkler, The Wealth of Networks: How Social Production Transforms markets and Freedom (2006).

[52]   On path dependence, see Stanley J. Liebowitz and Stephen E. Margolis, Path Dependence, Lock-in and History, 11 J. L., Econ., and Org. 205 (1995); Joseph Farrell and Garth Saloner, Installed Base and Compatibility: Innovation, Product Preannouncements, and Predation, 76 Am.Econ.Rev. 940 (1986). On the special problem of path dependence in technology networks, see Thomas Cotter, Erik Hovenkamp, and Norman Siebrasse, Demystifying Patent Holdup, 76 Wash. & Lee L. Rev. 1501 (2019).

once the digital video disc (DVD) made this technology obsolete, no one should be condemned for refusing to support it.[53]

While regulatory regimes such as the Telecommunications Act[54] create interconnection obligations, antitrust may be a superior device for doing so. First, antitrust is less likely to be affected by interest group pressures. Second, if the antitrust laws are properly applied they tend to be more selective, generally imposing interconnection only in the presence of a history that justifies it, clear dominance, and relatively clear necessity if competition is to be created or maintained. This may minimize the consequences of one forceful critique of traditional regulation by government agencies, which is that they impede innovation.[55] Properly applied, antitrust is able to be "surgical" in its approach to compelled dealing, ordering it only when competitive alternatives have been found to be deficient. By contrast, the interconnection obligations imposed by the 1996 Telecommunications Act are global, imposing very broad sharing obligations, in some cases even where competition could thrive without them.

To be sure, using antitrust to force interconnection imposes its own difficulties. The problems of determining interconnection prices and the scope of the obligation do not go away simply because the dispute occurs in a network. Resolutions such as requiring nondiscriminatory treatment, or calling for ongoing monitoring of interconnection obligations are hardly perfect, but they are not uncommon in markets subject to more explicit regulation, and almost certainly better in many situations than not requiring adequate interconnection at all. In any event, privately created institutions such as FRAND are often in place to provide assistance.[56] To the extent a FRAND agreement establishes mechanisms for resolving disputes and determining royalties, antitrust's most difficult problem has been solved.

---

[53]   For good historical perspective, see Peter S. Menell, Envisioning Copyright Law's Digital Future, 46 N.Y.L. Sch. L. Rev. 63 (2003).

[54]   Telecommunications Act of 1996, § 151(a), Pub. L. No. 104–104, 110 Stat. 56 (1996).

[55]   At a very general level, the more regulated an economy the less innovation its firms produce. See OECD, GOING FOR GROWTH 68 (2006).

[56]   See § 7.11d3.

§ 7.6 Unilateral Refusal to Deal II: Vertical Integration, Price Squeezes, Tying and Exclusive Dealing[57]

Refusals to deal are a common consequence of vertical integration. The integrated firm begins to deal only with its newly-developed (or newly-acquired) suppliers or outlets, and terminates its relationship with independent firms.[58] Antitrust has always had a problematic love-hate relationship with vertical integration, particularly if it involves dominant firms. The policy has ranged from harsh, virtual per se rules against a firm's acquisition or even its construction of its own stores, to the position often associated with the Chicago School that vertical integration should be virtually legal per se.[59]

7.6a. *Kodak* and Aftermarket Opportunism

The Supreme Court's 1992 *Kodak* decision suggested that if a photocopier manufacturer controlled 100% of a properly defined market for its own replacement parts, its refusal to deal with an independent firm that serviced such photocopiers could be monopolistic.[60] The Court briefly considered whether a firm can have substantial market power in a market for its own replacement parts. More problematically, it suggested that a firm could monopolize by refusing to deal with others in markets for its own replacement parts if the firm was engaged in a program of "willful acquisition" of a monopoly—the monopoly, once again, being defined in terms of its own brand of parts and the servicing of its own equipment.

Kodak was only the second largest seller of photocopiers, and its share of the general photocopier market (some 23%) was too small to support any § 2 claim. However, the theory of the complaint was that Kodak was taking advantage of "locked in" customers who had already purchased a Kodak photocopier by forcing them to purchase

---

[57]   Vertical integration by the monopolist is explored more fully in §§ 9.2–9.3.

[58]   If the monopolist's vertical integration is by merger, exclusive dealing contract, or tying arrangement, they may be analyzed under both the Clayton Act and the Sherman Act. These are considered at greater length in chs. 9 & 10.

[59]   On the problematic history of vertical integration as an antitrust problem, see Herbert Hovenkamp, The Law of Vertical Integration and the Business Firm: 1880–1960, 95 Iowa L.Rev. 863 (2010); William E. Kovacic, The intellectual DNA of Modern U.S. Competition Law for Dominant Firm Conduct: The Chicago/Harvard Double Helix, 2007 Colum. Bus. L. Rev. 1 (2007). On vertical integration and the Chicago School, see Herbert Hovenkamp, Robert Bork and Vertical Integration: Leverage, Foreclosure, and Efficiency, 79 Antitrust L.J. 983 (2014).

[60]   Eastman Kodak Co. v. Image Technical Services, 504 U.S. 451, 112 S.Ct. 2072 (1992).

their subsequent repair service from Kodak as well.[61] To be sure, someone who already owns a Chrysler that needs a new transmission may be stuck, for only a Chrysler transmission will fit into a Chrysler automobile. But customers purchasing goods in a competitive market will generally regard monopoly prices for services and replacement parts as a higher price for the original good, and normally they will buy elsewhere.

Nevertheless, (1) some customers may not be well informed and Chrysler might be able to charge a higher-than-market price as a result; or (2) Chrysler might change its pricing policy or its policy of dealing with third party suppliers after a significant number of customers are already locked-in to Chrysler automobiles.

A firm that controls a monopoly at one stage of a distribution process can seldom enlarge its monopoly profits by monopolizing one or more additional stages as well. As a result, claims that a firm "monopolizes" simply by controlling the distribution of its own product, replacement parts, or service should be viewed skeptically.

It is in fact possible for most firms to charge above cost prices for aftermarket replacement parts, notwithstanding a modest market share of the foremarket. For example, if one adds up all of the off-the-shelf prices for the parts needed to reconstruct an automobile, the price is far higher than if the automobile were purchased in one piece from a car dealer. Much of the excess is a function of the fact that distribution and inventorying of aftermarket parts is costly. Part of it is a result of attempts to engage in price discrimination.[62]

But part of the problem is precisely the one that the Supreme Court's *Kodak* decision confronted: even well-informed customers lack perfect information; they tend to overemphasize the immediate price of original equipment, and to discount the price of subsequent repair. As a result, even a seller with a 5% market share can probably charge high prices for aftermarket parts.

But not every market imperfection is an antitrust problem—and certainly not a § 2 problem, which requires a dominant firm. The real problem of *Kodak* is that if it is taken seriously there is no good means of stopping it short of being willing to call hundreds of nondominant manufacturers and other sellers "monopolists" simply because the products require brand specific aftermarket parts or service.

---

[61] The economic literature does contain several models of profit-maximization in markets where existing customers have switching costs—that is, they are locked in to their past seller's particular brand. See Herbert Hovenkamp, Antitrust and Information Technologies, 68 Fla. L. Rev. 419 (2016).

[62] See 10 Antitrust Law ¶ 1740 (4th ed. 2018).

7.6b.   Vertical Integration and Refusals to Deal: Price or Supply "Squeezes"

A common criticism of vertical integration is that it can raise entry barriers. Vertical integration by the monopolist allegedly creates a barrier to entry in the monopolist's market because any prospective entrant must come in at two levels instead of one. For example, if a monopolist aluminum manufacturer did all its own fabricating there would be no independent market for fabricators. Anyone who wanted to enter aluminum manufacturing might also have to enter aluminum fabricating.

In a simple situation vertical integration by the monopolist creates an entry barrier only if the integration lowers the monopolist's costs. In that case a new entrant at a single level would find it difficult to compete. However, in more complex situations a requirement of two level entry can magnify risk, particularly if entry is independently risky at both levels.

Vertical integration can also complicate entry if the two levels have differential economies of scale or if one level is regulated. For example, a firm seeking to enter at the market level with fewer scale economies would not be able to compete unless it also entered at the other level, where efficient production would require much higher output. If efficient production of bicycles requires an output of 10,000 per month, but efficient retailing requires a single-store output of only 100 per month, widespread vertical integration may force those wishing to retail bicycles to manufacture them as well. If bicycle production is subject to collusion or oligopoly but large retailers have been effective at forcing the manufacturers to compete with one another, manufacturer integration into retailing could make an oligopoly or cartel more effective. Relatedly, vertical integration can change the outcomes of bargaining between firms in ways that result in higher prices or that raise rivals' costs. These issues are discussed in our treatment of vertical mergers.[63]

The price or supply "squeeze" is a variation of the refusal to deal. Suppose that a vertically integrated monopolist at the manufacturing level owns some of its retail outlets and also sells its product to independent retailers. The independent retailers have a difficult time competing with the retailers owned by the monopolist, however. They allege that the monopolist always favors its own outlets in times of short supply, and sometimes refuses to sell to independents altogether. Further, the monopolist either charges the independents

---

[63]   See § 9.5; and Michael H. Riordan, Anticompetitive Vertical Integration by a Dominant Firm, 88 Am. Econ. Rev. 1232 (1998).

a higher price for the product than it charges its own dealers, or else the outlets owned by the monopolist resell the product at a price that the independents are unable to match. The first of these practices is sometimes referred to as a "supply squeeze," and the second as a "price squeeze". Economically they are more-or-less the same: the integrated monopolist allegedly manipulates the market price in order to injure the unintegrated rivals, who are squeezed both by short supply and by their own high costs relative to those of the monopoly-owned outlets.[64]

Alleged price and supply "squeezes" often result because vertically integrated firms have lower costs than do independent firms who must rely on the market. The monopolist who reduces its costs by vertical integration will sell to the consumer at a lower price, and independent dealers will be unable to compete.[65]

In *linkLine* the Supreme Court categorically rejected claims of a price squeeze directed by a vertically integrated monopolist against an unintegrated rival.[66] The Court held that if a monopolist has no duty to deal with a rival in the wholesale, or upstream, market, its price squeeze would not be unlawful unless prices in the retail, or downstream, market were predatory under the standards it had developed for predatory pricing cases, which require prices below cost. The defendant AT & T was a vertically integrated monopolist which wholesaled digital subscriber line (DSL) service to rival Internet service providers (ISPs) but also provided its own DSL-based Internet service to its own customers. The plaintiffs alleged that the defendant charged such a high price for its wholesale DSL service and such a low price on its retail service that the rivals could not make a reasonable profit on the spread between what they had

---

[64]   In *Alcoa* Judge Hand discussed the supply and price squeeze at some length. Alcoa allegedly used the squeeze against independent fabricators of its ingot. United States v. Aluminum Co. of America, 148 F.2d 416, 436–438 (2d Cir.1945).

[65]   One possible exception arises when the dominant firm takes advantage of a vertically related firm's specialized investment and effectively transfers the latter's revenues above variable costs to itself. In Bonjorno v. Kaiser Aluminum & Chemical Corp., 752 F.2d 802 (3d Cir.1984), cert. denied, 477 U.S. 908, 106 S.Ct. 3284 (1986), the court found liability where Kaiser was found to have used a price squeeze to drive fabricator Bonjorno's revenue down to a level just sufficient to cover its average variable costs, but insufficient to enable it to earn a profit. See Erik Hovenkamp & Herbert Hovenkamp, The Viability of Antitrust Price Squeeze Claims, 51 Ariz. L.Rev. 273 (2009). As a general matter a firm does not have an obligation to enable other firms to earn profits. But in the absence of vertical integration firms may be in a position to take anticompetitive advantage of the irreversible, or "sunk" investments of others. See the discussion of transaction cost economics in § 1.8; and see Benjamin Klein, Robert G. Crawford & Armen A. Alchian, Vertical Integration, Appropriable Rents, and the Competitive Contracting Process, 21 J.L. & Econ. 297 (1978); Oliver E. Williamson, The Mechanisms of Governance 120–145 (1996).

[66]   Pacific Bell Tel. Co. v. LinkLine Communic., Inc., 555 U.S. 438, 129 S.Ct. 1109 (2009).

to pay and what they received from their own customers. As the Court observed, however:

> AT & T could have squeezed its competitors' profits just as effectively by providing poor-quality interconnection service to the plaintiffs, as Verizon allegedly did in *Trinko*. But a firm with no duty to deal in the wholesale market has no obligation to deal under terms and conditions favorable to its competitors. If AT & T had simply stopped providing DSL transport service to the plaintiffs, it would not have run afoul of the Sherman Act. Under these circumstances, AT & T was not required to offer this service at the wholesale prices the plaintiffs would have preferred.[67]

As to the downstream prices, the principal assertion in the plaintiff's complaint was that they were "too low," but without reference to cost. But the Court had addressed this issue in *BrookeGroup* as well as in its *Cargill* decision, and concluded that "too low" is meaningless unless it is understood in relation to some objective standard, such as cost. As a result, the plaintiff's case amounted to nothing more than

> an amalgamation of a meritless claim at the retail level and a meritless claim at the wholesale level. If there is no duty to deal at the wholesale level and no predatory pricing at the retail level, then a firm is certainly not required to price *both* of these services in a manner that preserves its rivals' profit margins.[68]

7.6c.   Quasi-Tying and Exclusive Dealing—Technological Ties

Tying and exclusive dealing are most commonly addressed under § 3 of the Clayton Act or § 1 of the Sherman Act. The Clayton Act was designed to go after certain anticompetitive practices under a more aggressive standard than the Sherman Act encompassed. Indeed, only recently have the courts put real teeth into the market power requirements for exclusive dealing and tying. Today the minimum market share hovers in the range of 30%–40%, which is probably about right for most markets although it may be too harsh on plaintiffs in networked industries were interoperability is essential.[69]

---

[67]   *LinkLine*, 129 S.Ct. at 1119.

[68]   Id. at 1120. On *Brooke Group* and the law of predatory pricing, see §§ 8.3–8.5, 8.8.

[69]   On the market share requirements for unlawful tying and exclusive dealing, see §§ 10.3, 10.8e.

It makes sense to relax the technical requirements of the tests for tying and exclusive dealing tests when we are dealing with a monopolist rather than a firm with a 30% or 40% market share. In any event, the general test for monopolization would require that. A § 2 offense requires an exclusionary practice which harms rivals unnecessarily,[70] whether or not the technical tying requirements have been met. One difference between the § 2 tying or exclusive dealing offense and the traditional § 1 or Clayton § 3 offenses is the lack of any agreement requirement in the former. Monopolization is a unilateral practice.

The § 2 decisions on forced bundling generally do not discuss the "separate product" requirement in tying cases, because they do not follow the tying logic at all; rather they go straight to the question whether the practice is unreasonably exclusionary under the circumstances. This is simply another way of saying that a monopolist's unilateral "ties" can be unlawful under the general § 2 test whether or not they involve the "separate products" that tying law requires.

In its *Microsoft* decision the D.C. Circuit found that Microsoft violated § 2 of the Sherman Act by "commingling" the computer code for its Windows computer operating system and its Internet Explorer web browser.[71] This unilateral act effectively required all purchasers of Microsoft Windows to accept a pre-installed version of Internet Explorer as well. Since computer manufacturers did not wish to support two versions of the same program, the effect of commingling was virtually to eliminate Internet Explorer's principal rival, Netscape, from the original distribution portion of the browser market. This in turn made it much more difficult for Netscape to develop tools that would have made computers compatible with a large number of different operating systems. The court also found that Microsoft offered no procompetitive justification for commingling.

The courts have also condemned exclusive dealing under § 2 when the defendant was a dominant firm. For example, while the Supreme Court never used the term "exclusive dealing" in the *Lorain Journal* case, the practice condemned under § 2 was just that.[72] The defendant newspaper forbad its own advertising customers from buying advertising from a competitor. The Supreme Court never considered what percentage of the market was foreclosed by Lorain Journal's practices—an essential requirement in exclusive dealing

---

[70]   See § 6.4.

[71]   United States v. Microsoft Corp., 253 F.3d 34, 66 (D.C. Cir. 2001).

[72]   Lorain Journal Co. v. United States, 342 U.S. 143, 72 S.Ct. 181 (1951).

cases.[73] Once again, the question in the § 2 case is whether the practice injures rivals unnecessarily and without business justification, and the technical requirements for exclusive dealing by nondominant firms are not the only way of approaching this problem. In *Dentsply* the Third Circuit sustained a government's challenge to exclusive dealing by a market dominating seller of materials used for filling teeth and for manufacturing artificial teeth.[74] Dentsply's market share in these materials ranged from 67% to 80%. Dentsply sold its material through a network of dealers who, with a few exceptions, were required to sell Dentsply materials exclusively to their customers, who were mainly dental laboratories that filed dentists' orders for specific artificial teeth or teeth substitutes. The impact was to restrict unreasonably the development of competing sources of dental materials.[75]

Use of § 2 against exclusive dealing or tying might seem strange, given that § 1 reaches agreements under more aggressive standards than § 2 employs, and also that § 3 of the Clayton Act[76] reaches both exclusive dealing and tying of commodities when competition is threatened. Fundamentally, however, both tying and exclusive dealing are "exclusionary" practices of the kind that ordinarily fall within the purview of § 2. Further, as noted above, while § 2 is more restrictive in its market power requirement it is less categorical in its other requirements.

§ 7.7 Refusal to Deal III: The "Essential Facility" Doctrine

The so-called "essential facility" doctrine is one of the most troublesome, incoherent and unmanageable of bases for refusal-to-deal liability under Sherman § 2. One big task confronting the antitrust laws is finding the proper division between refusal to deal doctrine that is conducive to investment and innovation, and that

---

[73] On the foreclosure requirement in exclusive dealing, see § 10.9e. In *Lorain Journal*, by contrast, the only evidence of foreclosure was that "[n]umerous Lorain County merchants testified that, as a result of the publisher's policy, they either ceased or abandoned their plans to advertise over WEOL." 342 U.S. at 149, 72 S.Ct. at 184.

[74] United States v. Dentsply International, Inc., 399 F.3d 181 (3d Cir. 2005), cert. denied, 546 U.S. 1089, 126 S.Ct. 1023 (2006). See also McWane, Inc. v. FTC, 783 F.3d 814 (11th Cir. 2015), cert. denied, 136 S.Ct. 1452 (2016), which was applying § 5 of the FTC Act, but used Sherman Act § 2 standards with reference to a firm whose market share was above 90%.

[75] Id. at 190–191: "By ensuring that the key dealers offer Dentsply teeth either as the only or dominant choice, [Dentsply's exclusive dealing] has a significant effect in preserving Dentsply's monopoly. It helps keep sales of competing teeth below the critical level necessary for any rival to pose a real threat to Dentsply's market share. As such, [the exclusive dealing] is a solid pillar of harm to competition."

[76] 15 U.S.C. § 14.

which encourages passivity. The principal problem with the essential facility doctrine in its current form is that it clearly falls into the latter category.

The essential facility doctrine proclaims that the owner of a properly defined "essential facility" has a § 2 imposed duty to share it with others. But this definition leaves numerous questions unanswered, among them: 1) what is a qualifying "essential facility"? 2) does the duty to deal extend only to rivals, or also to vertically related firms or others? 3) when is the refusal to deal unjustified? and 4) How is a court to determine the scope and terms of any compelled dealing.

It is also critical not to confuse the essential facility doctrine with the more general antitrust doctrine of refusal to deal developed in § 7.5. *Aspen's*[77] refusal to deal doctrine is conduct based and involves a firm's reneging on a previous commitment in a competitively harmful way. By contrast, the essential facility doctrine is asset-based, holding that mere ownership of a bottleneck asset may obligate a firm to share the asset with others.

The essential facility doctrine is said to have originated in the Supreme Court's *Terminal Railroad* decision,[78] which required a group of firms controlling a railroad bridge and transfer and storage facilities at the Mississippi River to share these facilities with other railroad lines. But the case makes a poor ancestor for the essential facility doctrine, because it was a § 1 case, involving an agreement among multiple firms who controlled the facility.

Of course, once a properly defined "essential facility" is at issue, it really should not matter whether the facility is controlled by a single firm or a group of firms acting in concert. But if someone is dubious about the essential facility doctrine as a distinct principle of antitrust liability, then the difference between concerted and unilateral action becomes quite important. Concerted refusals to deal are condemned more easily than unilateral refusals, with less elaborate proofs of actual competitive effects.[79] For this reason, the focus on unilateral conduct makes it critical that "essential facility" be defined with rigor.

The first Supreme Court decision that looks like a modern essential facility case is *Otter Tail Power*, which used § 2 to condemn a public utility's refusal to "wheel" or distribute power for municipal

---

[77]   Aspen Skiing Co. v. Aspen Highlands Skiing Corp., 472 U.S. 585, 105 S.Ct. 2847 (1985). See § 7.5.

[78]   United States v. Terminal R.R. Assn., 224 U.S. 383, 32 S.Ct. 507 (1912). See 3A Antitrust Law ¶ 772b1 (4th ed. 2015).

[79]   See § 5.4a.

utility companies that wished to supply their own electricity by purchasing it elsewhere.[80] *Otter Tail's* apparent purpose was to force the municipalities to become its own customers. Otter Tail may have controlled a natural monopoly, depending on how one views the market for "wholesale" as opposed to retail electric power under then existing technology. Further, Otter Tail was a regulated utility.

The next Supreme Court case contributing substantially to the "essential facility" doctrine is the *Aspen* decision, discussed previously.[81] The Supreme Court did not decide that case on essential facility grounds, but a great deal of *Aspen's* language has been incorporated into more recent essential facility cases.

In *MCI*, the Seventh Circuit stated the essential facility doctrine in a way that has influenced numerous subsequent decisions. The doctrine has four elements:

> (1) control of the essential facility by a monopolist; (2) a competitor's inability practically or reasonably to duplicate the essential facility; (3) the denial of the use of the facility to a competitor; and (4) the feasibility of providing the facility.[82]

Finally, while the Supreme Court's *Trinko* decision, discussed in § 7.5, refused "either to recognize * * * or to repudiate" the essential facility doctrine, it placed severe limitations on future essential facility claims.[83] The court generally limited essential facility claims to situations where (a) the claimed facility is essential in the sense that rivals are unable to supply it for themselves, (b) where the facility being claimed is something that the defendant owns fully developed and is actually selling to others, (c) where the sale to rivals would be "rational" in the sense that it is at least as profitable to the defendant as alternative sales, and (d) where there is no regulatory agency actively supervising a compulsory sharing requirement.

7.7a.   What Is a Qualifying "Essential Facility"?

Most of the things found by courts to be essential facilities have fallen into one of three classifications: (1) natural monopolies or joint venture arrangements subject to significant economies of scale;[84] (2)

---

[80]   Otter Tail Power Co. v. United States, 410 U.S. 366, 93 S.Ct. 1022 (1973).

[81]   Aspen Skiing Co. v. Aspen Highlands Skiing Corp., 472 U.S. 585, 105 S.Ct. 2847 (1985).

[82]   MCI Communic. Corp. v. AT&T, 708 F.2d 1081, 1132–1133 (7th Cir.), cert. denied, 464 U.S. 891, 104 S.Ct. 234 (1983).

[83]   Verizon Communications, Inc. v. Law Offices of Curtis V. Trinko, LLP, 540 U.S. 398, 411, 124 S.Ct. 872, 881 (2004).

[84]   E.g., United States v. Terminal R.R. Assn., 224 U.S. 383, 32 S.Ct. 507 (1912); Associated Press v. United States, 326 U.S. 1, 65 S.Ct. 1416 (1945).

structures, plants or other valuable productive assets[85] that were created as part of a regulatory regime, whether or not they are properly natural monopolies;[86] or (3) structures that are owned by the government and whose creation or maintenance is subsidized.[87] What all these structures have in common is that those who have control over or access to them may have significant cost advantages over those who do not.

Since monopolization is a market power offense, the owner of a properly defined essential facility must possess sufficient market power; alternatively, the claimed facility must serve as a bottleneck that permits market power to be exercised. If competitive alternatives are available, the facility can hardly be characterized as "essential."[88]

7.7b.   The Extent of the Duty to Deal

The trend in judicial decisions is to limit the essential facility doctrine to refusals to deal with firms that compete with the defendant in some market.[89] This conclusion seems appropriate as a general matter, although there are some qualifications. First, although public utilities may have a duty to serve all paying customers, that duty is generally imposed by legislation, and it is not the province of an antitrust court to decide when the duty should be imposed in the absence of a statute requiring it.[90] Second, a refusal to deal with a firm that does not compete at any level with the defendant rarely has anticompetitive consequences. Of course, one must distinguish the situation where the vertically related firm is also an actual or potential rival of the defendant. For example, in

---

[85]   An "essential facility" need not be a tangible asset. See *Bellsouth*, id., holding that a customer list could be an essential facility. The plaintiff ultimately lost because the defendant was willing to give the substance of the list, but not the format in which it was contained.

[86]   For example, Otter Tail Power Co. v. United States, 410 U.S. 366, 93 S.Ct. 1022 (1973); Verizon Communications, Inc. v. Law Offices of Curtis V. Trinko, LLP, 540 U.S. 398, 411 (2004).

[87]   For example, Hecht v. Pro-Football, 570 F.2d 982 (D.C.Cir. 1977), cert. denied, 436 U.S. 956, 98 S.Ct. 3069 (1978) (public athletic stadium).

[88]   E.g., Pittsburg County Rural Water Dist. No. 7 v. City of McAlester, 358 F.3d 694 (10th Cir.), cert. denied, 543 U.S. 810, 125 S.Ct. 44 (2004) (municipality's refusal to sell water to rural water district not essential facility doctrine where plaintiff admitted there were other sources of water and defendant's water treatment plant was not the only one in the area); Castelli v. Meadville Medical Center, 702 F.Supp. 1201 (W.D.Pa.1988), affirmed, 872 F.2d 411 (3d Cir. 1989) (hospital not essential facility, since there were several others within the geographic market).

[89]   For example, Interface Group v. Massachusetts Port Authority, 816 F.2d 9 (1st Cir. 1987); Garshman v. Universal Resources Holding, 824 F.2d 223 (3d Cir. 1987).

[90]   The Supreme Court so held in Verizon Communications, Inc. v. Law Offices of Curtis V. Trinko, LLP, 540 U.S. 398 (2004).

Fishman the defendant controller of Chicago Stadium was also an intending purchaser of the Chicago Bulls, as was the plaintiff.[91] As a result, the defendant stood simultaneously in a vertical (lessor-lessee) and competitive relationship with the defendant, and the refusal should be regarded as directed against a competitor.

7.7c.   Reasonableness of Refusal to Deal

Sherman § 2 should be applied only to refusals to deal that threaten higher prices or reduced output in some relevant market, or that threaten to perpetuate monopoly power already owned. As a result, the plaintiff must show that the refusal to deal is exclusionary, or anticompetitive in the economic sense. With respect to private plaintiffs, the "antitrust injury" doctrine confirms this requirement, and there is no reason for thinking that doctrine does not apply in essential facility cases.[92]

Nevertheless, some courts have applied the essential facility doctrine even when it seemed quite clear that competition was largely unaffected by the defendant's refusal to deal. For example, in *Fishman v. Wirtz* the defendant refused to make the Chicago Stadium available to the plaintiff, who consequently lost the opportunity to purchase the Chicago Bulls professional basketball team.[93] But the Bulls were already playing at Chicago Stadium, and it was not clear that there would be more competition in any market as a result of the defendant's refusal to deal. The dispute at hand was about ownership of the Bulls, not about the insertion of competition via a second team into a monopolized market.[94]

To view the problem in another way, if the controller of an essential facility—say, a natural gas pipeline—is already leasing space to a dozen shippers of natural gas, competition may not be affected by the controller's refusal to lease the line to yet another shipper. That decision may harm the shipper, but it does not appear to make any market less competitive. Alternatively, if two firms vie to ship in a natural monopoly pipeline, and one wins by unfair means, the unfairness goes to the *identity* of the monopolist, not to the question whether the market will be monopolized or competitive. In the first of these cases the antitrust injury requirement is not met; in the second, it may or may not be met depending on the nature of the dispute. If the low price bidder for a natural gas contract was ousted

---

[91]   Fishman v. Estate of Wirtz, 807 F.2d 520 (7th Cir. 1986).

[92]   See § 16.3. See also Flip Side Productions, Inc. v. Jam Productions, Ltd., 843 F.2d 1024 (7th Cir.), cert. denied, 488 U.S. 909, 109 S.Ct. 261 (1988) (applying antitrust injury doctrine to essential facility claim).

[93]   Fishman v. Estate of Wirtz, 807 F.2d 520 (7th Cir. 1986).

[94]   See Judge Easterbrook's dissent, 807 F.2d 520 at 563–564.

by unfair means, then its replacement by a higher price bidder could be anticompetitive even though at any given time the essential facility could be occupied by only one firm.

7.7d. Essential Facility Doctrine Inconsistent with General Antitrust Goals; *Aspen* Contrasted

One problem with the logic of the "essential facility" doctrine is that, if the doctrine is restricted to refusals calculated to create or perpetuate monopoly power, then the more general antitrust rules respecting refusals to deal seem quite adequate for the job.[95] But if the limitation is not imposed, then the essential facility doctrine loses its mooring in § 2 of the Sherman Act. It begins to operate as a "fair access" statute that forces one set of private firms to accommodate another set even when competition is not improved. As a result, the doctrine is either superfluous or else inconsistent with basic antitrust principles.

Further, compelling a single firm to deal requires a court to set terms and conditions of the sale, thus turning it into a kind of regulatory agency. Suppose that the defendant owns a gas pipeline from origin point X to market point Y. The cost of gas at point X is $10.00 per unit, and the cost of pipeline shipment to point Y is $2.00 per unit. But X is a monopolist and charges a delivered price of $15.00 per unit, thus capturing $3.00 in excess profits per unit shipped. Now a gas producer at point X, wishing to ship to point Y itself, uses the essential facility doctrine to obtain a judicial injunction ordering the defendant to lease space on its pipeline. What price will the defendant charge?

Unless constrained by the court's order the defendant will charge its profit-maximizing price of $5.00 per unit shipped, reducing its own shipments accordingly. The result is that the amount of gas shipped through the pipeline will remain unchanged and the price will not budge. The pipeline owner simply obtains its monopoly overcharge through the lease of the pipeline rather than as a markup on the shipped gas.

In that case application of the essential facility doctrine has done nothing to improve consumer welfare. When forced to share, the monopolist owner of an essential facility will charge the plaintiff the same monopoly price that it would otherwise charge to customers. The only way that the court can avoid this result is by ordering

---

[95]   See §§ 7.6–7.7. See generally Phillip Areeda, Essential Facilities: an Epithet in Need of Limiting Principles, 58 Antitrust L.J. 841 (1989).

sharing *and* regulating the price. At that point the pipeline has become, for all practical purposes, a public utility.

A final consequence of forced sharing is that, once the plaintiff has been given the right to share the defendant's pipeline, it loses its incentive to build its own pipeline.[96] In this sense, the essential facility doctrine is manifestly hostile toward the general goal of the antitrust laws. It serves to undermine rather than encourage rivals to develop alternative inputs of their own. In the pipeline situation, real competition occurs when a second or third pipeline are built, and they are most likely to be built when rivals are forced to build them, rather than obtaining judicially mandated access to the defendant's pipeline.

This is one of the most important differences between the essential facility doctrine and the *Aspen* refusal to deal rule.[97] The essential facility doctrine tends to discourage firms from making their own investments to the extent they can piggyback on someone else's assets. By contrast, the *Apen* rule encourages firm to invest by protecting the integrity of joint investments from subsequent anticompetitive manipulation by a dominant firm.

§ 7.8   "Predatory" Product Design and Development; Failure to Predisclose; Altered Complementary Products

Many private plaintiffs have alleged that the defendant was a monopolist and that it "manipulated" the product or the market in such a way as to prevent the plaintiff from competing. These practices have included physical bundling or other strategic selection of technologies, "predatory" research and development, failure to predisclose certain technical or design innovations, and strategic use of brand name advertising.

7.8a.   Predatory Product or Process Innovation

One set of claims of monopolization by bundling was raised in several cases initially brought against IBM. In *California Computer Products*[98] the defendant manufactured central processing computer units and various "peripherals" such as memory devices, monitors, and controllers. The plaintiff manufactured only disk drives, a type

---

[96]   See *Trinko*, 124 S.Ct. at 879 ("Compelling such firms to share the source of their advantage is in some tension with the underlying purpose of antitrust law, since it may lessen the incentive for the monopolist, the rival, or both to invest in those economically beneficial facilities").

[97]   See § 7.5.

[98]   California Computer Products, Inc. v. IBM Corp., 613 F.2d 727 (9th Cir. 1979).

of memory device. The defendant introduced a new line of computers in which the memory and central processing units were assembled in the same box and sold as a single product. The defendant was generally able to show that the new units performed faster and were less expensive than their predecessors. However, the plaintiffs characterized the new line of computers as "technological manipulation" designed only to eliminate the independent market for separate memory units. The court refused to condemn such innovation.

Should the development of a new product that reduces or eliminates the market for some existing product manufactured by a competitor ever be illegal monopolization?[99] Two possibilities come to mind: 1) if it is undisputed that the new product is not superior to the old product, but is perhaps even inferior; 2) if there is clear evidence that the defendant's intent in developing the new product was to destroy the independent market for the competitor's product.

Both situations raise significant problems of administration. First, whether a new product is "superior" or "inferior" to an old product is entirely a matter of consumer preference, not of judicial decision.[100] If IBM's new computer system with the built-in memory was inferior to the old system in the eyes of consumers, they would switch to the newer one.

The question of bad intent is even clearer: every inventor "intends" his invention to injure the competing products of close competitors, for that is the only way his own invention is likely to find a market. Suppose that Henry Ford knew absolutely that production of the Model T would destroy the business of a carriage maker across the street. Should its development be illegal? Certainly not. Suppose that Henry Ford developed the Model T for no other reason than to ruin the business of the carriage maker, whom he disliked intensely? While we might wish to condemn such behavior, there is simply no way to distinguish between "legitimate" and "illegitimate" manifestations of intent. Intent is merged into the completed result, in this case a new product whose development

---

[99]   The Ninth Circuit thought not. See id. at 744:

IBM, assuming it was a monopolist, had the right to redesign its products to make them more attractive to buyers—whether by reason of lower manufacturing cost and price or improved performance. It was under no duty to help Cal Comp or other peripheral equipment manufacturers survive or expand. * * * The reasonableness of IBM's conduct in this regard did not present a jury issue.

[100]   See Automatic Radio Mfg. Co. v. Ford Motor Co., 272 F.Supp. 744 (D.Mass.1967), affirmed, 390 F.2d 113 (1st Cir. 1968), cert. denied, 391 U.S. 914, 88 S.Ct. 1807 (1968), where the innovation may have been an aesthetic improvement, but not a technical one.

injures or destroys certain competitors. No reasonable basis exists for concluding that the development of a new product or group of products is illegal monopolization. Such a rule would certainly do far more harm to the innovative processes in a market economy than it would promote competitive efficiency.[101] *Ex ante*, it would entitle firms injured by the technological development of another to a discovery trip through their records in search of anything that might be construed as bad intent. Better to start at the onset by making intent irrelevant.

Cases like this are dangerous for antitrust policy makers. In its *Allied Orthopedic* decision the Ninth Circuit rejected the plaintiff's claim that the defendant Tyco's introduction of new type of pulse oximeter system violated the antitrust laws and that lower court should have balanced "the benefits of Tyco's alleged product improvement against its anticompetitive effects." The court reasoned that:

> There is no room in this analysis for balancing the benefits or worth of a product improvement against its anticompetitive effects. If a monopolist's design change is an improvement, it is "necessarily tolerated by antitrust laws," unless the monopolist abuses or leverages its monopoly power in some other way when introducing the product.

Further,

> To weigh the benefits of an improved product design against the resulting injuries to competitors is not just unwise, it is unadministrable. There are no criteria that courts can use to calculate the "right" amount of innovation, which would maximize social gains and minimize competitive injury.[102]

By contrast, in *C.R. Bard* the Federal Circuit approved a jury's verdict finding anticompetitive product design.[103] Bard produced a patented gun that took tissue samples by injecting a small disposable needle beneath the surface of the skin. Formerly the needles had been sold by multiple firms, one of which was the plaintiff. However,

---

[101]   For a contrary view see Janusz A. Ordover & Robert D. Willig, An Economic Definition of Predation: Pricing and Product Innovation, 91 Yale L.J. 8 (1981). For a response, see J. Gregory Sidak, Debunking Predatory Innovation, 83 Col.L.Rev. 1121 (1983).

[102]   Allied Orthopedic Appliances Inc. v. Tyco Health Care Group LP, 592 F.3d 991, 1000 (9th Cir. 2010). See Herbert Hovenkamp, Antitrust and Information Technologies, 68 Fla. L. Rev. 419 (2016).

[103]   C.R. Bard, Inc. v. M3 Sys., Inc., 157 F.3d 1340, 1371 (Fed.Cir. 1998), cert. denied, 526 U.S. 1130, 119 S.Ct. 1804 (1999), on remand, 120 F.Supp.2d 1145 (N.D.Ill.2000).

Bard redesigned the gun so as to accept only its own needles. There was some evidence that the redesigned gun was not an improvement over the earlier version and that Bard's only purpose in redesigning it was to make rivals' needles incompatible. The plaintiff could probably have manufactured the redesigned needle but for the fact that the new needle was itself patented.[104] The court permitted a jury to find unlawful monopolization on these facts. It affirmed a jury instruction that "conduct that involves the introduction of superior products" is not exclusionary, but that if the "conduct is ambiguous, direct evidence of a specific intent to monopolize may lead you to conclude that the conduct was intended to be and was in fact exclusionary or restrictive."[105]

Design patents can raise similar issues when the product covered by the patent needs to interconnect with a different product. For example, in the *Ford Global* decision the court held that it was not unlawful under patent law for an automobile manufacturer to protect some of its aftermarket repair parts with design patents. As a result, competing makers of aftermarket parts could not make repair parts that duplicated the original equipment parts but would have to have different designs that did not infringe the patent.[106] While design patents may not be "functional," the court held that consumer preference for replacement parts that were identical to original equipment parts was not a "function." There were no antitrust issues and the decision exhibits one unfortunately typical myopia in patent litigation, which is to ignore the impact on competition.

7.8b.   Failure to Predisclose New Technology

In *Berkey Photo* a rival claimed that Kodak, a camera and film monopolist, violated § 2 by failing to predisclose information about a new product package. Kodak had developed a revolutionary new camera that pleased consumers and may have performed better than equivalently priced cameras. The camera also used a new type of film in a patented cartridge that was difficult for rivals to duplicate. Kodak then introduced the new camera and film cartridge simultaneously. Eventually competing manufacturers would very likely be able to copy both the camera and the film and bring them to market themselves. During the interval, however, the camera

---

[104]   See *C.R. Bard*, 157 F.3d at 1370.

[105]   Ibid.

[106]   Automotive Body Parts Assn. (ABPA) v. Ford Global Tech., LLC, 930 F.3d 1314 (Fed. Cir. 2019).

monopolist would enjoy not only the monopoly profits in its new camera, but would also be the only provider of the new film.[107]

Competing film manufacturers are undoubtedly injured by this failure to predisclose. They would have been better off if they also could have had film on the market the day the new camera was introduced. Is competition injured? Kodak could probably make all available monopoly profits by selling the camera at its profit-maximizing price. It would then have to charge a competitive price for the film anyway. In this case, however, Kodak very likely used its domination of both camera and film to price discriminate. The high use photographer who shoots 20 rolls of film per day may value the new camera much more highly than the person who shoots 3 rolls per year. By transferring part of the available monopoly profits from the camera to the film, Kodak may have been able to obtain a higher overall rate of return from the higher intensity users.[108]

While Kodak's failure to predisclose may have facilitated price discrimination, such discrimination is generally not socially harmful. Indeed, it probably permitted the monopolist to sell more cameras than it would have otherwise. That will generally benefit consumers, and in the long run it may even mean a larger market for the competing film manufacturers. In *Berkey* the Second Circuit refused to require a monopolist to predisclose new technology, and no court since has assessed that requirement.

7.8c. *Microsoft*: Unnecessarily Harmful Redesigns and Licensing Requirements

In order to understand the Government's case against Microsoft one must know a little about the economics of computer operating systems such as Windows. These systems are said to be subject to "positive network externalities," which means that they become more valuable to a particular user as the system has a larger number of other users. The classic example of positive network externalities is the telephone system. Even the highest tech telephone is virtually worthless if it cannot be connected to anyone else. As soon as the phone can be connected to at least one other subscriber it acquires value, and the value to each user increases as the number of other subscribers increases. As a result, a system with a large number of

---

[107] Berkey Photo, Inc. v. Eastman Kodak Co., 603 F.2d 263 (2d Cir. 1979), cert. denied, 444 U.S. 1093, 100 S.Ct. 1061 (1980).

[108] In this case the failure to predisclose operates in the same way as a variable proportion tying arrangement. See § 10.6e. Price discrimination is less likely in a case like *Automatic Radio* where one product was an automobile and the other product a car radio. Most purchasers of one car will buy only one car radio, Automatic Radio Mfg. Co. v. Ford Motor Co., 272 F.Supp. 744 (D.Mass.1967).

subscribers is more desirable to a new subscriber than a system with few subscribers, assuming that the two systems cannot be hooked together. This state of affairs can give dominant firms a significant advantage over rivals.[109]

The sources of network externalities for Windows or any computer operating system are manifold, but mainly they include (1) users' needs for compatibility and interchange with other users, and (2) software developers' need to develop for a large number of users. An operating system with a large installed base will always be more attractive to both users and software developers than an equally good operating system with a smaller installed base.

Microsoft's network advantage depended on its ability to keep Windows sufficiently incompatible with other computer operating systems that users cannot run software or perform other tasks on different systems interchangeably. Netscape and Sun Microsystem's Java computing language, which enabled software to be run on multiple operating systems, threatened this advantage. An illustration that may help you think of the problem is a country with two telephone systems that cannot be connected together. One system has older technology but has been around longer and has 100,000 subscribers. The newer system has superior technology but only 100 subscribers. Notwithstanding its inferior technology, the large installed base gives the older firm a very significant advantage over the new firm, because consumers place a high value on being interconnected with as many other people as possible. As a result, the larger system has less incentive to improve its technology or cut its price.

But suppose that someone develops a switch that enables the two systems to be connected together, so that a subscriber to one system can readily talk to people on the other system, and vice versa. The network advantages can now be aggregated across the two systems, and there is no unique advantage to being on one system or the other. Consumers will be able to choose a telephone on the basis of other factors, such as who has the better technology, price, or service.

Netscape, enhanced by Java, threatened to produce the "switch" that would connect multiple operating systems, thus destroying Microsoft's significant network advantage over rival systems. Bill Gates expressed the fear that these programs would "commoditize" the operating system market. In particular, Java's "write once, run

---

[109] See Richard A. Posner, Antitrust Law 245–258 (2d ed. 2001); Herbert Hovenkamp, The Antitrust Enterprise: Principle and Execution, ch. 12 (2005). On the case law, see 13 Antitrust Law ¶¶ 2220–2221 (4th ed. 2019).

anywhere" strategy threatened to make different operating systems completely compatible on both the user end and the software writing end.[110] The result would be the emergence of a traditional product differentiated market in which one could choose a Microsoft or non-Microsoft operating system based entirely on price, features, speed, support, and so on. Compatibility with other users would not be a factor.

The government's theory was that Microsoft did everything in its power to keep this switch from being deployed, and thus to preserve the incompatibility of different operating systems. Among the practices that the government challenged were: (a) Microsoft "commingled" Windows and Internet Explorer code, giving IE a decisive advantage over Netscape in people's choice of a web browser; (b) it prevented computer manufacturers from removing Microsoft icons, including Internet Explorer icons, from the desktop or start menu of the computers they sold, or from modifying the "boot," or startup sequence so as to favor non-Microsoft products; (c) it prevented computer manufacturers from altering the Windows desktop, or interface that shows the various icons for the programs that the system includes; (d) it induced software developers by various contractual devices to favor Internet Explorer over Netscape as a web browser choice; (e) it pressured Apple Computer to use Internet Explorer rather than another browser in its own office systems; (f) it placed pressure on Intel, a major chip manufacturer, to withdraw developmental support for chips that ran the Java multi-platform computing language. The D.C. Circuit condemned all these practices, although it exonerated a few others.[111]

§ 7.9   The Troublesome "Leverage" Theory; Nonmonopolistic Advantage in Second Market

Already in the 1940s the Supreme Court declared that a firm was forbidden to use monopoly power in one market to acquire a competitive advantage in a second market.[112] The meaning and scope

---

[110] See United States v. Microsoft, 84 F.Supp.2d 9, 29–30 (D.D.C. 1999) (findings of fact 74–77).

[111] United States v. Microsoft Corp., 253 F.3d 34, 66 (D.C. Cir. 2001). The parties then entered a consent decree, which was approved by the D.C. Circuit in Massachusetts v. Microsoft Corp., 373 F.3d 1199, 1209 (D.C. Cir. 2004). See Herbert Hovenkamp, The Antitrust Enterprise: Principle and Execution, Ch. 12 (2005).

[112] United States v. Griffith, 334 U.S. 100, 107–109, 68 S.Ct. 941, 945–947 (1948) (firm used dominant position in some theaters to obtain a competitive advantage in other locations); United States v. Paramount Pictures, 334 U.S. 131, 174, 68 S.Ct. 915, 937 (1948) (similar).

of these decisions have remained ambiguous ever since,[113] but in its broadest form the rule has been read to prevent a monopolist from obtaining a competitive advantage in a second market "even if there has not been an attempt to monopolize the second market."[114] The liability comes from the "abuse" of economic power already held in the first market; not from any threat that monopoly will be created in the second market.

This leverage theory has been applied most frequently to claims that a monopolist used restrictive agreements or vertical integration to obtain an unfair advantage over rivals in the secondary market. For example, in *Kerasotes* the defendant was charged with taking advantage of its monopoly position as a movie exhibitor in some cities to negotiate exclusive contracts that covered other cities where it had no monopoly.[115]

In its *Spectrum Sports* decision the Supreme Court appeared to reject the leverage theory altogether.

> § 2 [of the Sherman Act] makes the conduct of a single firm unlawful only when it actually monopolizes or dangerously threatens to do so. The concern that § 2 might be applied so as to further anticompetitive ends is plainly not met by inquiring only whether the defendant has engaged in "unfair" or "predatory" tactics.[116]

Although this statement was dicta, the *Spectrum Sports* decision seemed quite categorical in its insistence that the threat of monopoly in a properly defined relevant market is the Sherman Act's only true concern. As a result, several decisions accept only a narrow version of the leverage theory that involves using monopoly power in one market to create a second monopoly in a related market. In the process, however, they generally hold that all the elements of an attempt to monopolize offense must be met for the second market. This effectively robs the leverage theory of its distinctiveness.[117]

---

[113]   See 3 Antitrust Law ¶ 652 (4th ed. 2015).

[114]   Berkey Photo v. Eastman Kodak Co., 603 F.2d 263, 276 (2d Cir. 1979), cert. denied, 444 U.S. 1093, 100 S.Ct. 1061 (1980) (ultimately not finding liability on this theory); Kerasotes Mich. Theatres v. National Amusements, 854 F.2d 135, 138 (6th Cir. 1988), cert. dismissed, 490 U.S. 1087, 109 S.Ct. 2461 (1989) (reversing dismissal of leverage claim).

[115]   Kerasotes Mich. Theatres v. National Amusements, 854 F.2d 135 (6th Cir. 1988).

[116]   Spectrum Sports v. McQuillan, 506 U.S. 447, 459, 113 S.Ct. 884, 892 (1993), on remand, 23 F.3d 1531 (9th Cir. 1994).

[117]   See, e.g., Cost Management Services v. Washington Natural Gas, 99 F.3d 937, 952 (9th Cir. 1996) (accepting as "viable" a revised theory of leveraging as "an attempt to use monopoly power in one market to monopolize another market," but "under this

In its *Trinko* decision in 2004 the Supreme Court spoke more decisively than it had in *Spectrum Sports*:

> The Court of Appeals also thought that respondent's complaint might state a claim under a "monopoly leveraging" theory. * * * We disagree. To the extent the Court of Appeals dispensed with a requirement that there be a "dangerous probability of success" in monopolizing a second market, it erred.[118]

That statement very likely ended the long run of a controversial doctrine.

§ 7.10   Raising Rivals' Costs (RRC); Market Preemption

A monopolist may be able to create or secure its own position by raising its rivals' costs relative to its own.[119] As a monopolistic strategy, RRC has some attractions over alternatives such as predatory pricing.[120] The predator must forego immediate substantial losses from price cutting in the hope that it will be able to charge monopoly prices later, after rivals have been forced out of the market. By contrast, RRC produces profits to the strategizer immediately, and nothing so catastrophic as a firm's forced exit from the market need happen. This makes RRC theories more plausible in many circumstances than theories about absolute competitor exclusion. One of the major contributions of the imperfect and monopolistic competition revolution is the idea that both competition and harm exist in degrees. RRC then becomes an important alternative to absolute foreclosure, or exclusion.[121]

Another characteristic of RRC is that the cost-increasing strategies in question depend on assumptions about bargaining behavior that can be quite complex. Nevertheless, the ideas have

---

theory [the plaintiff] must establish each of the elements normally required to prove an attempted monopolization claim. . . .").

[118]   Verizon Communications, Inc. v. Law Offices of Curtis v. Trinko, LLP, 540 U.S. 398, 414, 124 S.Ct. 872, 883 n. 4 (2004), citing Spectrum Sports, 506 U.S. at 459, 113 S.Ct. 892.

[119]   See generally Steven C. Salop & David T. Scheffman, Raising Rivals' Costs, 73 Amer.Econ.Rev. 267 (1983); Thomas G. Krattenmaker & Steven C. Salop, Competition and Cooperation in the Market for Exclusionary Rights, 76 Am.Econ.Rev. 109 (1986); E. Thomas Sullivan, On Nonprice Competition: an Economic and Marketing Analysis, 45 U.Pitt.L.Rev. 771, 776–785 (1984).

[120]   On predatory pricing, see Ch. 8.

[121]   For further development see § 1.8.

gained very considerable traction and have been incorporated into the antitrust agencies' Vertical Merger Guidelines.[122]

Writers have offered a variety of theories explaining how a firm might raise its rivals' costs. Many of them involve concerted action by numerous firms, and are included in the general discussion of concerted refusals to deal.[123] Strategies that could involve only a single firm, and are thus reachable only under § 2, include the following:

> 1) A large firm might petition the government for regulations that have a more severe impact on smaller firms. For example, a regulation requiring airplanes to use three-person flight crews might cost much more for a small airline flying tiny planes than a large airline flying mainly large planes over long routes.[124] Such conduct is probably protected activity under the *Noerr-Pennington* doctrine, if it is directed at a government agency, although it may not be if it is directed at a private standard-setting association.[125]

> 2) A dominant firm engages in litigation against the smaller firm. Assume that litigation costs the same amount for both parties—perhaps $100,000 per year. The established incumbent who files the action has an output of 100,000 units per year, while the recent entrant who is the defendant has an output of 10,000 units per year. In this case the litigation costs the established firm $1.00 per unit, and the new entrant $10.00 per unit. If the new entrant has

---

122 U.S. Dept. of Justice and FTC, Vertical Merger Guidelines § 4.a (June 30, 2020), available at https://www.ftc.gov/system/files/documents/reports/us-department-justice-federal-trade-commission-vertical-merger-guidelines/vertical_merger_guidelines_6-30-20.pdf. For further discussion, see § 9.5.

123 For an extensive development of concerted activities that can raise rivals' costs, see Thomas G. Krattenmaker & Steven C. Salop, Anticompetitive Exclusion: Raising Rivals' Costs to Achieve Power over Price, 96 Yale L.J. 209 (1986) (evaluating many strategies); and Herbert Hovenkamp, Antitrust Policy, Restricted Distribution, and the Market for Exclusionary Rights, 71 Minn.L.Rev. 1293 (1987) (evaluating and expressing doubts about many proffered strategies).

124 On economies of scale in regulatory compliance, see George R. Neumann & Jon P. Nelson, Safety Regulation and Firm Size: Effects of the Coal Mine Health and Safety Act of 1969, 25 J.L. & Econ. 183 (1982); B. Peter Pashigian, The Effect of Environmental Regulation on Optimal Plant Size and Factor Shares, 27 J.L. & Econ. 1 (1984). Others are discussed in Herbert Hovenkamp, Antitrust Policy After Chicago, 84 Mich.L.Rev. 213, 277 (1985).

125 See generally ch. 18; and see Steven C. Salop, David T. Scheffman & Warren Schwartz, "A Bidding Analysis of Special Interest Legislation: Raising Rivals' Costs in a Rent Seeking Society," in Federal Trade Commission, Political Economy of Regulation: Private Interests in the Regulatory Process 103 (1984).

not yet begun to produce, the costs will be felt even more strongly.

3) A large capital intensive firm may bargain with a union in such a way as to cause marketwide wage increases, knowing that the impact of the increase will be felt much more heavily by smaller, labor-intensive firms.[126]

4) A dominant firm leading the race in research and development intentionally selects a technology for which scale economies are substantial, knowing that the fringe firms will have to follow along. Alternatively, a firm may create an array of patents on marginal or even nonexistent innovations, knowing that other firms will either have to invent around the patents or else litigate their validity.[127]

While all of these strategies may be anticompetitive under appropriate conditions, not every practice that raises a rival's costs is unlawful. Indeed, probably the most common practice that raises a rivals' costs is output expansions that force a rival to reduce its output, thus depriving it of scale economies, or that force a rival to engage in more aggressive promotion in order to compete. To state the latter point differently, aggressive production by a large firm may force rivals to spend resources in order to stay in the game. But such practices are the heart of competition, even though they make a rival's efforts more costly.[128]

Only a few judicial decisions have explicitly invoked the literature on RRC in condemning alleged monopolization.[129] One district court decision approved a jury verdict on the theory that Blue Cross used cost-cutting techniques with respect to its own customers to raise the costs of others.[130] However, in *Ball Memorial Hospital*, the Seventh Circuit found an alleged strategy of RRC to be

---

[126] See Oliver E. Williamson, Wage Rates as a Barrier to Entry: the Pennington Case in Perspective, 82 Q.J.Econ. 85 (1968).

[127] See Richard J. Gilbert & David M. G. Newbery, Preemptive Patenting and the Persistence of Monopoly, 72 Am.Econ. Rev. 514 (1982).

[128] See Richard A. Posner, Antitrust Law 196–197 (2d ed. 2001), concluding that raising rivals' costs is a useless formulation for identifying exclusionary practices.

[129] See National Org. for Women v. Scheidler, 968 F.2d 612 (7th Cir. 1992), reversed on nonantitrust grounds, 510 U.S. 249, 114 S.Ct. 798 (1994) (rejecting claim that anti-abortion picketers violated antitrust laws by raising costs of abortion clinics; Query: are anti-abortion picketers and abortion clinics "rivals" for Sherman Act purposes?); Premier Electrical Constr. Co. v. National Electrical Contractors Assoc., 814 F.2d 358, 368 (7th Cir. 1987) (finding that agreement to make businesses contribute money to collective bargaining process could operate to raise rivals' costs).

[130] Reazin v. Blue Cross & Blue Shield of Kan., 635 F.Supp. 1287 (D.Kan.1986), affirmed, 899 F.2d 951 (10th Cir.), cert. denied, 497 U.S. 1005, 110 S.Ct. 3241 (1990).

implausible.[131] The theory was that Blue Cross forced hospitals to accept extra low rates for its own subscribers, thus requiring them to charge the patients of other insurance companies (or those without insurance) extra high rates. But Blue Cross was found not to have market power, and the court was hard pressed to see how such a strategy could be pursued by a competitive firm.

One frequently litigated instance of RRC is market preemption. For example, in *Syufy Enterprises* the defendant was condemned under § 2 for purchasing exclusive licenses to exhibit motion pictures over a larger geographic area than the court thought justified, given that the area was significantly larger than the area from which the defendant actually drew viewing customers.[132] Other firms have also been accused of monopolization by "overbuying" or stealing essential inputs from competitors. For example, in *Potters Medical Center* the court denied summary judgment on the plaintiff hospital's claim that the defendant hospital stole local physicians by using bonuses to get them to send their patients exclusively to the defendant's hospital.[133]

Customer pre-emption occurs when a dominant firm purchases from its own customers or others the right that they not purchase from a competitor. Such cases have always been difficult to analyze. First, they must be classified. Some are no more than exclusive dealing or tying arrangements, and these may be quite efficient even when the upstream party is a monopolist.[134]

The more problematic exclusionary contracts are those where the contract (1) excludes a specific named competitor; or (2) where the contract is "naked"—that is, it is not attached to the sale of any other product or service at all. An example of the first is *Lorain Journal*, where the defendant refused to sell advertising to buyers who also purchased advertising from nearby radio station WEOL.[135] An example of the second is the allegation in *Alcoa* that the defendant once purchased from utilities a promise that they would not provide electricity to Alcoa's competitors or potential competitors.[136] Alcoa

---

[131]   Ball Memorial Hospital v. Mutual Hospital Insurance, Inc., 784 F.2d 1325 (7th Cir.), rehearing denied, 788 F.2d 1223 (7th Cir. 1986).

[132]   Syufy Enters. v. American Multicinema, 793 F.2d 990 (9th Cir. 1986), cert. denied, 479 U.S. 1031, 107 S.Ct. 876 (1987). See also McWane, Inc. v. FTC, 783 F.3d 814 (11th Cir. 2015), cert. denied, 136 S.Ct. 1452 (2016) (dominant firm used exclusive dealing to raise rival's cost by foreclosing access to distributors).

[133]   Potters Med. Center v. City Hosp. Assn., 800 F.2d 568 (6th Cir. 1986).

[134]   See generally ch. 10.

[135]   Lorain Journal Co. v. United States, 342 U.S. 143, 72 S.Ct. 181 (1951).

[136]   United States v. Aluminum Co. of Am., 44 F.Supp. 97, 121, 144 (S.D.N.Y.1941), reversed in part, 148 F.2d 416 (2d Cir. 1945).

purchased no electricity itself from these utilities; so the only apparent purpose of the contract was to exclude the rivals.

Another form of customer pre-emption is the contract penalty. The dominant firm may enter into a long-term lease with its customers, and charge a substantial penalty for early termination. If the penalty is sufficiently large and covers enough customers, a prospective rival may not be able to attain a scale sufficient to make entry profitable.[137] If the customers have perfect information and know that the impact of signing such an agreement is continuation of the monopoly, they may refuse to sign. But in the usual case the customers' information will be imperfect and the prospects of new entry uncertain.[138] Several cases have involved such clauses, although in most the judicial analysis has not been all that helpful.[139]

Modeling situations in which exclusionary contracts such as these might be anticompetitive is relatively easy. Problematically, however, the antitrust tribunal must run the process *backwards*. That is, it begins with the contract containing the allegedly anticompetitive provision, and must then determine whether the provision is anticompetitive or competitive. The great majority of contract penalty clauses are nothing more than devices to make contract participants perform, and that purpose is undoubtedly competitive.

Finally, a "most-favored-nation" clause in a contract guarantees a buyer or seller that its deal will be at least as good as the deal given any rival. They are sometimes referred to as "price protection" clauses. As a general proposition, seeking the best deal seems like harmless, procompetitive behavior. MFN clauses are harmless when they are undertaken unilaterally by firms without market power. They can create competition problems, however, when they are thought to facilitate collusion or, as is more relevant here, make the

---

[137]   See Philippe Aghion & Patrick Bolton, Contracts as a Barrier to Entry, 77 Am. Econ. Rev. 388 (1987); Joseph Brodley & Ching to Albert Ma, Contract Penalties, Monopolizing Strategies, and Antitrust Policy, 45 Stan. L. Rev. 1161 (1993).

[138]   Even if entry is likely, each customer knows that the prospective entrant needs only a portion of the customer base in order to enter. Suppose that the dominant firm offers a high lease price without the penalty clause, but a lower price with the penalty clause. Each customer will likely pay the lower price and take the penalty clause, hoping that enough other customers will pay the higher price to make the new entry profitable. See Steven C. Salop, Practices that (Credibly) Facilitate Oligopoly Coordination, in New Developments in the Analysis of Market Structure 265, 272–273, 278–284 (Joseph E. Stiglitz & G. Frank Mathewson eds. 1986).

[139]   Telex Corp. v. IBM, 510 F.2d 894 (10th Cir. 1975), cert. dismissed, 423 U.S. 802, 96 S.Ct. 8 (1975) (upholding lease cancellation penalties where rival lessors used them too).

offerings of firms competing with a dominant firm less attractive, particularly when the competitors are discounters.

For example, a new health or dental plan that wants to offer lower fees will have a difficult time finding dentists if the dentists are required by contract to lower their prices to the dominant plan as well.[140] Such requirements can make it more difficult for smaller firms or new entrants to compete.[141] Alternatively, an insurer might "purchase exclusion" by agreeing to pay higher rates to health care providers who agree to exclusive provision contracts. Such a case is really about using MFNs to purchase exclusive dealing.[142] In any event, a unilaterally imposed MFN clause must be addressed under the rule of reason. They have efficiency explanations, such as encouraging dealer investment in a supplier's product by promises to the effect that the supplier will not favor a different dealer.[143] Used in that way, they are no more harmful than vertical nonprice restraints, particularly if MFN status is conditioned on dealer performance—for example, "as long as you show healthy sales performance you will get as favorable a price as any dealer in your territory." By contrast, horizontal agreements to impose MFNs may be per se unlawful attempts to facilitate collusion.[144]

§ 7.11   Unreasonably Exclusionary Practices Involving Patents or Other Intellectual Property Rights

Dominant firms have also been condemned under the antitrust laws for abusing rights created under the patent laws. A patent itself implies a property right to prevent others from duplicating a certain product or process. But this power to exclude is not unlimited, and courts have often found patentees guilty of exclusionary practices, particularly if they have tied some unpatented article to the patented

---

[140]   E.g., United States v. Delta Dental of Rhode Island, 943 F.Supp. 172 (D.R.I. 1996).

[141]   United States v. Medical Mut. of Ohio, 1999–1 Trade Cas. (CCH) ¶ 72,465 (N.D. Ohio 1999) (MFN allegedly "stifled" the development of new or less costly health plans).

[142]   E.g., Aetna, Inc. v. Blue Cross Blue Shield of Michigan, 2012 WL 2184568 (E.D.Mich. 2012) (denying motion to dismiss).

[143]   Jonathan Baker & Judith A. Chevalier, The Competitive Consequences of Most-Favored-Nation Provisions, 27 Antitrust 20 (Spring, 2013); Steven C. Salop & Fiona Scott Morton, Developing an Administrable MFN Enforcement Policy, 27 Antitrust 15 (Spring, 2013); Aaron S. Edlin, Do Guaranteed-Low-Price Policies Guarantee High Prices, and Can Antitrust Rise to the Challenge?, 111 Harv. L. Rev. 528 (1997).

[144]   United States v. Apple, Inc., 952 F.Supp.2d 638 (S.D.N.Y. 2013), affirmed, 791 F.3d 290 (2015), cert. denied, 136 S.Ct. 1376 (2016) (ebook publishers agreed to require Amazon to charge higher prices at behest of Amazon's competitor, Apple).

one, accumulated patents in order to make entry into the monopolized market difficult, or in a few situations if they have refused to license the patent to others. In addition, enforcing a patent obtained by fraud or inequitable conduct may violate § 2 of the Sherman Act,[145] as can attempts to enforce a patent known by the holder to be invalid or unenforceable. Several of these practices are discussed in other chapters.[146]

The "monopoly" that is sometimes said to result from an enforceable patent is not the same thing as the "monopoly" or monopoly power which is a predicate for illegal monopolization. Indeed, it would be better not to speak of a patent "monopoly" at all; a patent is an exclusive right in intellectual property limited to its claims. A patented product may compete intensely with similar products which are either unpatented or covered by different patents.[147] As a result, a single patent seldom defines the scope of a relevant market for antitrust purposes. The Supreme Court made this position clear already in its *Walker Process* decision, where it required an antitrust plaintiff claiming patent abuses to allege and prove a relevant market.[148] It expanded this holding to all antitrust claims including tying in the *Illinois Tool Works* decision, which reversed a half century old presumption that a patent creates market power.[149]

7.11a. *Walker Process*: Improper Infringement Suits on Unenforceable Patents

In *Walker Process*[150] the patentee brought an infringement suit against a rival. The rival counterclaimed that (1) the patentee had obtained the patent by committing a fraud on the patent office; and (2) its enforcement action under such a patent was an attempt to monopolize. The Supreme Court agreed. Justice Clark's opinion for the Court presented the question as "whether the maintenance and

---

[145] Walker Process Equip., Inc. v. Food Machinery & Chem. Corp., 382 U.S. 172, 86 S.Ct. 347 (1965).

[146] Improprieties in patent licensing and the complex relationship between antitrust policy and patent "misuse" are taken up in § 5.5. Tying arrangements involving patented articles are discussed further in ch. 10.

[147] On the relation between patents and market power, see § 3.9d.

[148] *Walker Process*, 382 U.S. at 177, 86 S.Ct. at 350; see § 6.5b.

[149] Illinois Tool Works Inc. v. Independent Ink, Inc. (ITW), 547 U.S. 28, 126 S.Ct. 1281 (2006); and see § 3.9d. See also Spectrum Sports v. McQuillan, 506 U.S. 447, 455, 113 S.Ct. 884, 890 (1993) (dicta; patent cannot be presumed to define a relevant market).

[150] Walker Process Equip., Inc. v. Food Machinery & Chem. Corp., 382 U.S. 172, 86 S.Ct. 347 (1965).

enforcement of a patent obtained by fraud on the Patent Office[151] may be the basis of an action under § 2 of the Sherman Act. . . ."[152]

If a patentee obtains a patent fraudulently (usually by giving material, false information in a patent application), the patent itself can become unenforceable. In that case, under *Walker Process* the attempt to enforce a fraudulently obtained patent may violate either § 2 of the Sherman Act or § 5 of the FTC Act.[153] In *Walker Process* itself the patentee Food Machinery had filed a sworn statement in the PTO that it neither knew nor believed that its invention had already been used in the United States for more than one year prior to the filing of the patent application.[154] In fact, Food Machinery itself had been involved in such use, and the use invalidated the patent. By contrast, merely obtaining a patent by fraud, although unlawful under the Patent Act, is not an antitrust violation until the patentee actually tries to enforce the patent against someone else or use it in some other anticompetitive manner.[155]

Procedurally, the *Walker Process* antitrust claim most often appears as a counterclaim brought by the defendant in an infringement suit.[156] The patentee sues, charging infringement. The

---

[151]   Referring to the United States Patent and Trademark Office, or PTO.

[152]   *Walker Process*, 382 U.S. at 173. The doctrine is also generally held to apply to threats to sue or warning letters to customers. That is, they are protected as long as the infringement claim is reasonably founded. See, e.g., Innovation Ventures, LLC v. N.V.E., Inc., 694 F.3d 723 (6th Cir. 2012) (defendant's sending of letter stating that rival committed trademark infringement and false marking and suggesting that retailers sell its product exclusively did not violate the Sherman Act when there was no evidence that the letter caused injury and in any event could easily be rebutted). See 1 Antitrust Law ¶ 205f (5th ed. 2020).

[153]   On the latter, see Charles Pfizer & Co. v. FTC, 401 F.2d 574, 579 (6th Cir. 1968), cert. denied, 394 U.S. 920, 89 S.Ct. 1195 (1969) (false statements to patent office in order to procure monopoly of potent drug violated § 5 of FTC Act).

[154]   The Patent Act provides that "[a] person shall be entitled to a patent unless * * * [the] invention was patented or * * * in public use or on sale in this country, more than one year prior to the date of application for patent in the United States. * * *"35 U.S.C.A. § 102(b).

[155]   FMC Corp. v. Manitowoc Co., 835 F.2d 1411, 1418 & n. 16 (Fed.Cir. 1987) ("Mere procurement of a patent, whatever the conduct of the applicant in the procurement, cannot without more affect the welfare of the consumer and cannot in itself violate the antitrust laws."). Accord Cygnus Therapeutics Sys. v. ALZA Corp., 92 F.3d 1153 (Fed.Cir. 1996).

[156]   Currently the courts are divided on the question whether challenges that patent infringement litigation itself violates the antitrust laws must be brought as compulsory counterclaims, which means that they will be lost if they are not brought. Holding that they are not compulsory: Tank Insulation Int'l, Inc. v. Insultherm, Inc., 104 F.3d 83, 88 (5th Cir.1997); Hydranautics v. FilmTec Corp.,70 F.3d 533, 536–37 (9th Cir.1995). Holding that they are compulsory: Critical-Vac Filtration Corp. v. Minuteman Int'l, Inc., 233 F.3d 697, 702–04 (2d Cir.2000); see also Genentech, Inc. v. Regents of the Univ. of Cal., 143 F.3d 1446, 1455–56 (Fed.Cir.1998), vacated on other grounds, 527 U.S. 1031, 119 S.Ct. 2388 (1999). See 3 Antitrust Law ¶ 706e (4th ed. 2015).

defendant denies that the patent is valid because of the claimed fraud on the patent office, and then counterclaims that the infringement action violates the antitrust laws. The antitrust plaintiff is thus typically the defendant in the underlying infringement action, and the antitrust defendant the plaintiff in the underlying action.

7.11b. Enforcement of Patent Known to Be Invalid or Unenforceable; *Noerr* Issues

Courts have often found that an established firm's improper litigation or appeals to an administrative agency can be an illegal exclusionary practice. Although firms have a First Amendment right to petition the government for redress of their grievances, this right does not extend to baseless claims filed in an adjudicative setting against a rival or prospective entrant for the purpose of excluding the rival from a certain market.[157]

The question arises in *Walker Process* and similar contexts when a firm brings patent infringement suits against rivals even though (a) the firm procured its own patent fraudulently; or (b) it knows that its own patent is unenforceable, invalid or expired, or that the rival's product or process does not infringe its patent. Whether such a lawsuit is used to raise a rivals' costs[158] or simply as an entry deterrence device, it can be a § 2 violation if the plaintiff in the patent suit either has or threatens to acquire substantial market power. *Most Walker* Process claims are asserted by infringement defendants as counterclaims; however, consumers who believe they have paid more as a result of an unreasonably enforced patent may also sue.[159]

At the same time, however, courts are quite sensitive to the fact that patent holders, even if they are dominant firms, have constitutionally protected legal rights to enforce their claims in court.[160] For this reason they have been reluctant to accept too readily the argument that such suits are improperly brought. They have assessed such requirements as proof of "knowing and willful patent fraud," apparently meaning that the antitrust plaintiff must produce evidence that the antitrust defendant actually knew that the patent it was enforcing was invalid or not infringed.[161] Other courts

---

[157] See § 18.3.

[158] See § 7.10.

[159] See DDAVP Direct Purchaser Antitrust Litig., 585 F.3d 677 (2d Cir. 2009). See also Ritz Camera & Image, LLC v. SanDisk Corp., 772 F. Supp. 2d 1100 (N.D. Cal. 2011), aff'd, 700 F.3d 503 (Fed. Cir. 2012).

[160] The same thing applies to trade secrets. See AvidAir Helicopter Supply, Inc. v. Rolls-Royce Corp., 663 F.3d 966 (8th Cir. 2011) (if a firm had a valid and enforceable trade secret, a lawsuit to protect it could not be an antitrust violation).

[161] Argus Chem. Corp. v. Fibre Glass-Evercoat Co., 812 F.2d 1381, 1385 (Fed.Cir. 1987).

have held that such claims must be established by clear and convincing evidence.[162]

Whether or not fraud is involved, all of these cases implicate every person's constitutional right to seek redress in court. In general, a lawsuit brought to enforce intellectual property rights cannot constitute a § 2 violation unless it is a "sham"—brought in bad faith and not in order to obtain a particular judicial result, but rather to harass a rival. In its *Professional Real Estate (PREI)* decision, the Supreme Court held that a copyright owner's enforcement suit on a novel question of law could not be deemed a "sham" where there were no important factual issues in dispute, the infringement suit was intended by the copyright owner to bring the requested relief, and there was a plausible legal basis for the claim.[163] In a very brief footnote, the Court stated that it was not deciding the extent to which a litigant's "fraud or other misrepresentations" before a court might constitute sham.[164]

PREI is thus a fairly narrow decision, not dispositive of the great majority of claims based on bad faith patent infringement actions. The questions in these cases do not typically concern the technical interpretation of a term in the statute about which reasonable people could differ, as *PREI* did.[165] Rather, they concern allegations that the plaintiff in the infringement action (the antitrust defendant) had in its possession facts showing that the patent application process was corrupted, that the patent was invalid or that the defendant in the infringement action was not an infringer. *Professional Real Estate* requires the antitrust plaintiff to show that the infringement action was "objectively baseless." If it is not, then the suit cannot form the basis for an antitrust violation. If it is, then further discovery into the antitrust defendant's intent in bringing the suit is appropriate.[166] But *all* suits that fit into the *Walker Process* definition of attempts to enforce patents obtained by fraud, or the *Handgards* definition of attempts to enforce patents known to be invalid, are "objectively baseless" in this sense. That is, someone knowing all the facts would also know that the suit had no merit.

---

[162]   E.g., Loctite Corp. v. Ultraseal Ltd., 781 F.2d 861 (Fed.Cir. 1985); SmithKline Diagnostics, Inc. v. Helena Labs., 859 F.2d 878, 891 (Fed.Cir. 1988); FMC Corp. v. Manitowoc Co., 835 F.2d 1411, 1415 (Fed.Cir. 1987).

[163]   Professional Real Estate Investors v. Columbia Pictures Industries, 508 U.S. 49, 113 S.Ct. 1920 (1993).

[164]   *Professional Real Estate*, 508 U.S. at 61 n. 6, 113 S.Ct. at 1929 n. 6., citing *Walker Process*.

[165]   See § 15.3b.

[166]   *Professional Real Estate*, 508 U.S. at 60, 113 S.Ct. at 1928.

At least one court has held that the improper appropriation of a *valid* patent from someone else is not an antitrust violation, because the "theft" creates no monopoly. It merely transfers the monopoly from one person to another.[167] That analysis may be true as a general matter, but there might be cases where the amount of market power conferred by a patent depends on the identity of its holder. For example, suppose firm *X* has patented process *A*, which gives it a cost advantage over rivals and permits it to charge supracompetitive prices. Now firm *Y* develops patented process *B*, which is as efficient or perhaps even a little better than *B*. *Y* intends to use process *B* itself, or perhaps license it to others; but *X* obtains the patent through fraud, and then sits on the new technology. In this case the mere "transfer" of a patent from one firm to another could perpetuate *X*'s monopoly and deprive consumers of competition between firms using the alternative processes.

Several courts have extended the baseless litigation and improper use rules to other forms of intellectual property. For example, in *CVD* the court held that trade secret litigation pursued by a dominant firm in bad faith could constitute an antitrust violation.[168] In *Lasercomb* the court stated in dicta that copyright litigation brought in bad faith could constitute an antitrust violation as well.[169]

In its important *DDAVP* decision the Second Circuit held that consumers who claimed that they paid more for a drug because of a pioneer drug manufacturer's improper patent enforcement activities against a generic manufacturer could bring their own treble damages lawsuit.[170] In this case the defendant's had allegedly filed a petition with the FDA requesting additional testing of a generic equivalent drug even though they knew such testing was unnecessary. The court also held that the consumers did not have to wait to file their claim until after the merits of the patentee's challenge had been resolved.

---

[167] Brunswick Corp. v. Riegel Textile Corp., 752 F.2d 261 (7th Cir. 1984), cert. denied, 472 U.S. 1018, 105 S.Ct. 3480 (1985). The antitrust plaintiff had disclosed its invention in confidence to the defendant, which promised to keep it secret. Then, while the PTO searched for the plaintiff's misplaced patent application, the defendant filed its own patent application, which was granted.

[168] CVD v. Raytheon Co., 769 F.2d 842, 851 (1st Cir. 1985), cert. denied, 475 U.S. 1016, 106 S.Ct. 1198 (1986) (in this case the alleged facts were not trade secrets at all; the antitrust defendant "regularly published * * * detailed information related to the [technology] in periodic reports. * * *").

[169] See Professional Real Estate Investors v. Columbia Pictures Industries, 508 U.S. 49, 113 S.Ct. 1920 (1993).; Lasercomb America v. Reynolds, 911 F.2d 970, 977 (4th Cir. 1990); accord DSC Communications Corp. v. DGI Techs., Inc., 81 F.3d 597, 601 (5th Cir. 1996) (possible copyright misuse to prevent competitor from designing a competing switch).

[170] DDAVP Direct Purchaser Antitrust Litigation, 585 F.3d 677 (2d Cir. 2009), cert. denied, 561 U.S. 1038, 130 S.Ct. 3505 (2010).

In this case the FDA had rejected the sham petition, but the pendency of the petition may have delayed the introduction of the generic drug.[171]

Finally, note that an improperly brought infringement action satisfies the *conduct* portion of a monopolization or attempt to monopolize claim. It does not satisfy any structural requirements pertaining to relevant market definition, market share, or dangerous probability of success in creating a monopoly. Each of those elements must be established by separate proof.[172]

7.11c.   Accumulation; Nonuse

The continuing development and actual use of new patented devices should never be treated as an illegal exclusionary practice. The disincentive created to research and development would far outweigh any injury to the competitive process that might result. A more difficult question arises, however, when the monopolist acquires or becomes the exclusive licensee of related patents and refuses to use them or relicense them to others. Suppose that Firm A has developed patented process X and uses it to manufacture widgets. Under both the patent and antitrust laws A may use process X exclusively; it need not license the process to any competitor.[173] Now, however, an inventor develops process Y, which will manufacture widgets at about the same price as process X. The inventor does not want to manufacture widgets herself, but proposes instead to license the process to anyone who wants it. Firm A then pays the inventor a high price for the exclusive license to use process Y. However, firm A never employs process Y. It continues to manufacture widgets using process X, and continues to have a monopoly in the widget market.

In this case the chance of injury to competition is more substantial. Firm A has its monopoly profits in widgets to protect. Any new entrant into the widget market, using process Y, will face competition from A as well as from other possible licensees of process Y. As a result, firm A may be willing to pay more for the exclusive right to use (or in this case to prevent the use of) process Y than any potential competitor would. The systematic acquisition and non-use of patents licensed from others should therefore be an antitrust concern, in appropriate cases. Nevertheless, in the *Paper Bag* the

---

[171]   Id. at 694.

[172]   See 1 Antitrust Law ¶ 208 (4th ed. 2013).

[173]   In the *SCM* case, id., the district court held that creating antitrust liability "for a monopolist's unilateral refusal to license patents" would pose "a threat to the progress of science and the useful arts not warranted by a reasonable accommodation of the patent and antitrust laws." 463 F.Supp. at 1014.

Supreme Court held that a firm's acquisition of a patent from its inventor and refusal to license it to others was lawful, even though the record made clear that the infringement plaintiff, a dominant firm, acquired the unused patent for the purpose of keeping its technology off the market.[174]

Another problem, not yet fully addressed in the decisions, occurs when a non-practicing entity buys up all of the patents covering alternative technologies in an industry, thereby threatening to monopolize it. In *Intellectual Ventures* a court initially sustained such a complaint.[175] Note that a merger between three competing firms that exhausted all alternatives in that market would very likely be unlawful. Should a series of patent acquisitions accomplishing the same thing be treated any differently? Although the Patent Act makes the transfer of existing patents lawful, it does not approve anticompetitive transfers.[176]

While nonuse of a patent is not an antitrust violation, remedies for patent infringement may be limited by the Supreme Court's *eBay* decision.[177] Under *eBay* a patentee is not automatically entitled to an injunction but must meet the usual requirements for equitable relief. One of these is that a damages remedy would be inadequate. Since a nonpracticing entity can monetize a patent only by obtaining royalties, a damages remedy does seem to be adequate. The lower courts have tended to deny injunctions to patentees who are not practicing the patents in question. Further, the distinction between unused patents that are developed internally and those that are acquired from others seems important, particularly if the acquiring firm is dominant and acquired the patents in order to keep their technologies from competing with the acquirer's technology. In general, however, the courts have not adopted this distinction.[178] The best rule would be to permit dominant firms to acquire a *non*exclusive license to technology closely related to their dominant

---

[174]   See Continental Paper Bag Co. v. Eastern Paper Bag Co., 210 U.S. 405, 28 S.Ct. 748 (1908). On the *Paper Bag* litigation, see Christina Bohannan & Herbert Hovenkamp, Creation Without Restraint: Promoting Liberty and Rivalry in Innovation, ch. 7 (2011).

[175]   Intellectual Ventures I, LLC v. Capital One Financial Corp., 99 F.Supp.3d 610 (D.Md. 2015). Subsequently, many of the patents in question were found invalid. See Intellectual Ventures I, LLC v. Capital One Bank (USA), 792 F.3d 1363 (Fed. Cir. 2015), 850 F.3d 1332 (Fed. Cir. 2017). In another decision, however, it vacated the antitrust holding on grounds of collateral estoppel. Intellectual Ventures I, LLC v. Capital One Financial Corp., 937 F.3d 1359 (Fed. Cir. 2019). See Erik Hovenkamp & Herbert Hovenkamp, Buying Monopoly: Antitrust Limits on Damages for Externally Acquired Patents, 25 Tex. Intel. Prop. L.J. 39 (2017).

[176]   35 U.S.C. § 261.

[177]   eBay Inc. v. MercExchange, L.L.C., 547 U.S. 388 (2006).

[178]   See 3 Antitrust Law ¶¶ 705, 707 (4th ed. 2015).

technology. A nonexclusive license enables them to use the technology they are able to use, but does not give them the power to deny access to others.[179]

In *Trebro* the Federal Circuit held that a firm that acquired but did not use a patent could obtain an injunction shutting down a competitor who infringed the plaintiff's unused patent but not any patent that the plaintiff actually practiced.[180] The court created an exception to *eBay* for a firm that is actually competing with the infringement defendant, although not infringing any patent that the plaintiff was actually using. This rationale excessively subordinates competition policy to a poorly articulated value in patent law—effectively permitting a dominant firm to acquire patents on competing technologies and thus deny entry to competitors, even if it is not practicing these particular patents itself. The purpose of the Patent Act is to facilitate innovation, not to permit people to withdraw it from the market altogether. The *Trebro* decision highlights an ongoing concern about patent-antitrust policy: antitrust economics has developed empirical and technical tools for evaluating market performance that patent law, which is much more insular, has not come close to matching. Perhaps as a result, antitrust law does a far better job of accommodating patent policy than patent law does of accommodating competition policy.[181]

7.11d. Unilateral Refusal to License, Simple and Conditional

7.11d1. Absolute Refusal to License

A 1988 amendment to the Patent Act provides:

(d) No patent owner ... shall be ... deemed guilty of misuse or illegal extension of the patent right by reason of his having done one or more of the following: ... (4) refused to license or use any rights to the patent; or (5) conditioned the license of any rights to the patent or the sale of the patented product on the acquisition of a license to rights in another patent or purchase of a separate product, unless, in view of the circumstances, the patent owner has market

---

[179] Bohannan & Hovenkamp, Id.

[180] Trebro Mfg. Inc. v. Firefly Equipment, LLC, 748 F.3d 1159 (9th Cir. 2014). See Erik N. Hovenkamp & Thomas F. Cotter, Anticompetitive Patent Injunctions, 100 Minn. L. Rev. 871 (2015).

[181] See Herbert Hovenkamp, The Rule of Reason and the Scope of the Patent, 52 San Diego L. Rev. 515 (2015).

power in the relevant market for the patent or patented product on which the license or sale is conditioned.[182]

This provision makes clear that under the Patent Act a simple refusal to license a patent cannot be "misuse" of a patent.[183] It is also consistent with many decisions holding that the owner of a patent has no duty to license its patent to others.[184] Whether the quoted provision creates an *antitrust* immunity for refusals to license is dubious. When Congress wants to create an antitrust immunity, it uses explicit immunizing language, as it has done on many occasions.[185] By contrast, the statutory wording here, "misuse or illegal extension of the patent right," is classic misuse language. Most likely Congress was seeking to limit the reach of patent "misuse" claims, while saying nothing about antitrust violations.[186]

In its *Kodak* decision the Ninth Circuit held that a firm had a duty to sell its patented parts and share its copyrighted diagnostics software with rivals.[187] First, looking at the statute quoted above, the court concluded that it did no more than state pre-existing law.[188] That was true in the sense that no case had ever condemned a simple refusal to license, and the statute simply declared that such refusals are not misuse. Indeed, the court acknowledged that it could "find no reported case in which a court has imposed antitrust liability for a unilateral refusal to sell or license a patent or copyright."[189] But at that point there was a logical disconnect with the court's conclusion

---

[182]   35 U.S.C.A. § 271(d).

[183]   On patent "misuse," see § 5.5.

[184]   The decisions include Cygnus Therapeutics Sys. v. ALZA Corp., 92 F.3d 1153, 1160 (Fed.Cir.1996) (patentee "under no obligation to license;" antitrust claim dismissed); Genentech v. Eli Lilly & Co., 998 F.2d 931, 949 (Fed.Cir.1993), cert. denied, 510 U.S. 1140, 114 S.Ct. 1126 (1994) (same; patentee's "right to select its licensees, to grant exclusive or non-exclusive licenses or to sue for infringement and the pursuit of optimum royalty income, are not of themselves acts in restraint of trade"); Data General Corp. v. Grumman Systems Support Corp., 36 F.3d 1147 (1st Cir.1994); USM Corp. v. SPS Techs., 694 F.2d 505, 513 (7th Cir. 1982), cert. denied, 462 U.S. 1107, 103 S.Ct. 2455 (1983) (may license "only on such terms as [the patentee] sees fit"); United States v. Studiengesellschaft Kohle, m.b.H., 670 F.2d 1122, 1131 (D.C.Cir.1981) (finding no cases imposing a duty to license, and refusing to create one). The copyright cases are similar: e.g., Tricom v. Electronic Data Systems Corp., 902 F.Supp. 741, 743 (E.D.Mich.1995) (owner of copyrighted software may not be compelled to license). Other decisions are discussed in 3 Antitrust Law ¶ 709 (4th ed. 2015).

[185]   E.g., Charitable Donation Antitrust Immunity Act, 15 U.S.C. § 37(b) ("the antitrust laws . . . shall not apply to charitable gift annuities. . . ."); Confirmation of Antitrust Status of Graduate Medical Resident Matching Programs, 15 U.S.C. § 37b(b)(2) (it "shall not be unlawful under the antitrust laws to sponsor. . .").

[186]   On patent "misuse," § 5.5b.

[187]   Image Technical Services v. Eastman Kodak Co., 125 F.3d 1195 (9th Cir. 1997), cert. denied, 523 U.S. 1094, 118 S.Ct. 1560 (1998).

[188]   125 F.3d at 1215.

[189]   *Kodak*, 125 F.3d at 1216.

that the defendant did have such a duty. It reasoned that because the statute declared existing law it was not entitled to be taken seriously and thus left room for a decision manifestly inconsistent with its words.

Further, the duty that the *Kodak* decision declared was a very broad one. The court reasoned that a patent rightfully creates a power to exclude from one market, not more. In the case at hand, a refusal to license a part excluded rivals from parts but also disabled them from servicing Kodak photocopiers. As the court reasoned, the patent entitled Kodak to protect its parts monopoly but not its service monopoly. As a result, it was for the jury to decide whether Kodak's intended merely to protect the former, or to create or maintain monopoly power in the latter.

But this reasoning rests on a flawed understanding of a patent. A patent describes an invention, not a market. Many patents, particularly for intermediate goods, might be used in final products or processes that operate in a wide variety of markets. For example, a patented mixing process might be applied to paint, peanut butter, and prescription drugs. A patented microprocessor circuit might be used in personal computers, navigation systems, or bread machines. At this writing, no other circuit has followed this *Kodak* line of reasoning.[190]

In any event, nothing in the Patent Act exonerates a larger scheme of monopolization in which a refusal to license is a component. For example, it may apply to "product hopping," in which the owner of a patented pharmaceutical drug withdraws it from the market prior to expiration, thus forcing users to switch to a newer version of the drug with a longer remaining patent life.[191] This strategy can succeed because generic versions of the older drug often cannot enter under state law restrictions that require them to be identical with a drug that is currently on the market. Significantly, however, the injury to competition in this case is what occurs *after* the patent on the first drug has expired and generic entry would otherwise be possible. In sum, product-hopping creates a situation in which refusal to license a patent serves to prolong the firm's exclusivity beyond the expiration of that patent.

---

[190]   The Federal Circuit Court of Appeals disagreed in a similar case brought against Xerox. ISO Antitrust Litigation, 203 F.3d 1322, 1325–1326 (Fed. Cir. 2000), cert. denied, 531 U.S. 1143, 121 S.Ct. 1077 (2001). See 3 Antitrust Law ¶ 709 (4th ed. 2015).

[191]   New York v. Actavis, PLC, 787 F.3d 638 (2d Cir. 2015), cert. dismissed, 136 S.Ct. 581 (2015).

7.11d2.   Conditional Refusals to License

Conditional refusals to license rest on a different footing than simple refusals. A conditional refusal might be one of the following: (1) I will license you my patented photocopier only if you agree to purchase my paper and ink; (2) I will license you my patented photocopier only if you agree not to obtain photocopiers from anyone else; or (3) I will license you my patented photocopier only if you agree to give me a royalty free license for your paper collating attachment. The first of these is a tying arrangement, the second exclusive dealing, and the third a reciprocity agreement.

Significantly, § 3 of the Clayton Act applies to a "condition or understanding" that limits a firm's ability to deal with a competitor, and to goods "whether patented or unpatented."[192] Further, § 271(d) of the Patent Act as quoted above expressly permits simple refusals to license, but also indicates in § 271(d) that tying can still be unlawful if the patentee "has market power in the relevant market for the patent or patented product. . . ."[193]

These statutes indicate that basic antitrust principles govern the use of tying arrangements, exclusive dealing, or reciprocity in the licensing of patented processes or products. In each case, condemnation requires an agreement, market power or significant market foreclosure, and some assessment of anticompetitive effects.[194]

7.11d3.   Refusal to License FRAND-Encumbered Patents

Negotiations during standard setting often involve competing offers of technology to be adopted by a standard-setting organization (SSO), typically for a network such a cellular communications. Patentees may compete to have their technology adopted. A "standards essential patent" (SEP) is one that has been adopted as an "essential" component in the network. The price for this status is frequently a "FRAND" (or "RAND") obligation, which is a promise to license the patent to network participants at "fair, reasonable, and nondiscriminatory" royalties. Neither the royalty rate nor the scope of the obligation to license are typically specified up front.

The courts are leaning to the view that the owner of a "FRAND-encumbered" patent has a duty to license it to a network participant. That seems clear enough under contract law, although whether it

---

[192]   15 U.S.C.A. § 14.
[193]   35 U.S.C.A. § 271(d)(5).
[194]   See § 10.6 (tying) and § 10.8 (exclusive dealing).

also constitutes an antitrust violation is less clear.[195] In the first instance this is a question of the meaning of the FRAND agreement and not antitrust law, although antitrust becomes relevant when power and competitive injury requirements are met.[196]

The FRAND commitment means that the patentee has promised to license to anyone willing to pay a FRAND-determined royalty. Requesting an injunction would be inconsistent with that contractual commitment, and the equitable doctrine of "unclean hands" would bar the injunction with respect to that patent.[197] At least one district court has denied a patentee an injunction in violation of its FRAND commitment.[198] This issue of patentee misconduct was an oversight in a "Policy Statement on Remedies for Standards-Essential Patents," issued in 2019 by the Justice Department, the Patent Office and the National Institutes of Standards and Technology.[199]

7.11e.   Patent "Ambush" and Failure to Disclose, Particularly in Standard Setting

Many patent applications are rejected upon initial submission, but often applicants can revise their applications, removing or revising rejected claims and even adding new claims that were not in the original application. A patent "continuation" is an application for additional claims made on a patent that was previously applied for.[200] Such "late claims" may not be disclosed promptly. Second, they can be written on technology that may not have been available at the time

---

[195]   See Apple, Inc. v. Motorola, Inc., 757 F.3d 1286 (Fed. Cir. 2014) (three way split, with two judges out of three finding a licensing duty); Microsoft Corp. v. Motorola, Inc., 696 F.3d 872 (9th Cir. 2012) (granting injunction preventing patentee who had made such commitments from enforcing injunction claims in a German court). However, see the discussion of the Ninth Circuit's troublesome *Qualcomm* decision, *supra*, § 7.5a.

[196]   For further discussion, see Herbert Hovenkamp, FRAND and Antitrust, ___ Cornell L. Rev. ___ (2020), available at https://papers.ssrn.com/sol3/papers.cfm?abstract_id=3420925.

[197]   See, e.g., Gilead Sciences, Inc. v. Merck & Co., Inc., 888 F.3d 1231 (Fed. Cir. 2018); Precision Instrument Mfg. Co. v. Automotive Maint. Mach. Co., 324 U.S. 806, 65 S.Ct. 993 (1945); Keystone Driller Co. v. General Excavator Co., 290 U.S. 240, 54 S.Ct. 146 (1933).

[198]   HTC Corp. v. Telefonaktiebolaget LM Ericsson, 2019 WL 4734950 (E.D.Tex. May 22, 2019).

[199]   https://www.justice.gov/atr/page/file/1228016/download.   See   Herbert Hovenkamp, Justice Department's New Position on Patents, Standard Setting, and Injunctions, The Regulatory Review (Jan. 6, 2020), available at https://www.thereg review.org/2020/01/06/hovenkamp-justice-department-new-position-patents-standard-setting-injunctions/.

[200]   The Patent Act provides for continuations in 35 U.S.C.A. § 132. See Bohannan & Hovenkamp, Creation Without Restraint: Promoting Liberty and Rivalry in Innovation ch. 3 (2011); Mark A. Lemley & Kimberly A. Moore, Ending Abuse of Patent Continuations, 84 B.U. L. Rev. 63 (2004).

the original claim was filed but was developed during the period between the original claim and the continuation filing. Once a patent issues its enforcement date relates back to the date the original application was filed, so this creates a problem of retroactivity. Someone else can invent something that was not covered by the claims in the original patent, but is covered by the late added claims.

The possibility of such abuses reveals one of the more deficient aspects of the patent system's failure to provide adequate notice to inventors.[201] While patents may be a species of property, they are property with a woefully inadequate system for providing adequate public notice prior to someone else's investment decision.[202] If a patentee can manipulate the continuation process to cover technology developed by others prior to the date that late claims were added or notice of them properly given, the policy reduces rather than increases the incentive to innovate. An inventor might do a thorough patent search and not find any prior claim on his invention but later be made the subject of an infringement suit on the basis of a continuation application.

Nevertheless, there is probably little room for application of the antitrust laws, given that the Federal Circuit has expressly approved the use of continuation applications to write updated claims on a competitor's existing products or technology. The primary fix for this problem lies within the patent law themselves.

The *Rambus* case involved a research company that was in the business of patenting designs for computer memory technology. One significant feature of computer memory chips is that they must be compatible with a variety of computers. This requires that chip producers develop a common set of standards for performance and interoperability. The Electronic Industries Association, a trade association including memory chip manufacturers, developed the Joint Electron Devices Engineering Council (JEDEC) whose assignment was continuously to develop and maintain interoperability standards for such chips. Rambus was a member of JEDEC during the early 1990s, after it had filed an original patent application. During that period the members of JEDEC knew about Rambus' 1990s patent application; however Rambus did not disclose that it had additional continuation applications in process. According

---

[201] See James Bessen & Michael J. Meurer, Patent Failure: How Judges, Bureaucrats, and Lawyers Put Innovators at Risk 62–65 (2008), noting, inter alia, that the number of continuation applications had increased seven fold in the previous 20 years.

[202] See Herbert Hovenkamp, Notice and Patent Remedies, 88 Tex.L.Rev. Online ("See Also") 221 (2011); Bohannan & Hovenkamp, Creation Without Restraint: Promoting Liberty and Rivalry in Innovation, chs. 3–4 (2011).

to the FTC, Rambus also took advantage of its membership in JEDEC to formulate additional claims written on the very technology that JEDEC was in the process of developing, all of which would obtain the original 1990 priority date once a patent with these new claims issued.

These patents were subsequently found to be valid and infringed, but then the FTC brought an antitrust action alleging that Rambus had manipulated the patent issuance and standard setting process in order to obtain excessive royalties in its portion of the memory technology market. But the D.C. Circuit rejected the FTC's conclusion that "deceit merely enabling a monopolist to charge higher prices than it otherwise could have charged" constituted an act of monopolization.[203] Significantly, the FTC could not show that JEDEC was misled into adopting Rambus' technology to the exclusion of technology owned by someone else. Other decisions have not hesitated to find the requisite exclusion when a firm's failure to disclose led the SSO to adopts its technology to the exclusion of specific rivals.[204]

§ 7.12 Business Torts as Antitrust Violations

The term "business torts" refers to a variety of practices, including fraud & misrepresentation, inducement of breach of conduct, "stealing" of a rival's key employees, forcible interference with customers or the movement of products, passing off, false advertising or product disparagement.

Antitrust claims based on business torts require extreme caution, for two reasons. First, state law already provides ample remedies.[205] Second, the fit between tortious and anticompetitive conduct is poor. Most torts are not anticompetitive in the antitrust sense. Tort law almost never requires a structural analysis of the market or a showing that the defendant has market power, and it typically measures injury only by looking at the plaintiff's business losses, not by inquiring whether the market suffered lower output or

---

[203] Rambus, Inc. v. FTC, 522 F.3d 456 (D.C. Cir. 2008), cert. denied, 555 U.S. 1171 (2009).

[204] E.g., Actividentity Corp. v. Intercede Group, PLC, 2009 WL 8674284 (N.D. Cal. Sep. 11, 2009). For further development, see 3 Antitrust Law ¶ 712 (4th ed. 2015). See also Broadcom Corp. v. Qualcomm, Inc., 501 F.3d 297 (3d Cir. 2007), a nonantitrust case, in which the court applied equitable estoppels against a patentee who made promises to a standard setting organization concerning its patenting and royalty intentions and later reneged on these promises.

[205] See, e.g., Daniel B. Dobbs, The Law of Torts 1257–1318, 1343–1384 (2000).

higher prices. As a result, most business torts have only a *de minimis* effect or no effect at all on competition.[206]

In *Conwood* the Sixth Circuit approved an antitrust damages award of over $1 billion for conduct, most of which was tortious but probably not anticompetitive.[207] The defendant and plaintiff were two out of four manufacturers of moist snuff, a tobacco product sold in small tins on racks behind retail counters. The defendant had a dominant but declining market share. Historically, each of the four firms had provided retailers with its own rack for displaying its products, but in response to requests for more compact display the defendant had pioneered an integrated rack that held the products of all four firms. In some of the 300,000+ retail stores that sold moist snuff the defendant had deployed the integrated rack at the retailers request; this was true, for example, of Wal-Mart, the largest single retailer. In others the defendant had obtained permission from retailers to change racks. In yet others it had replaced the racks without permission and dumped the rivals' racks. The evidence also showed that when filling the racks the defendant tended to give itself more facings, or display space, then it gave to rivals, although the percentage of facings was not as high as its market share.[208] The Sixth Circuit approved the district court's decision not to require evidence showing what percentage of rack substitutions were made at the request of retailers, how many were made with permission and how many were tortious. But it also approved a damages methodology that looked at the plaintiffs' overall loss of market share.[209] The result was that the court awarded damages for the activity of designing a new display rack and installing it at a retailer's request or with its permission.

The plaintiff had to replace approximately 20,000 racks per month at a cost of $100,000. However, there were more than 300,000 stores. Far from showing a substantial injury, this indicated *de minimis* replacement costs of roughly 33 cents per store per month, and that one store in fifteen needed a new rack each month. Since the racks were $5 or $6 dollar items it seems clear that the plaintiff suffered no competitive injury from the conduct. The plaintiff continued to earn high profits throughout the complaint period.

---

[206]   See 3A Antitrust Law ¶¶ 780–782 (4th ed. 2015).

[207]   Conwood Co. v. United States Tobacco Co., 290 F.3d 768 (6th Cir. 2002), cert. denied, 537 U.S. 1148, 123 S.Ct. 876 (2003).

[208]   See *Conwood*, 290 F.3d at 775.

[209]   On the damages methodology in *Conwood*, see §§ 17.6b, 17.6c.

Fortunately, *Conwood* is an outlier case. Most courts have been quite circumspect about antitrust claims based on business torts. As a result, few antitrust violations have been found.[210]

§ 7.13 Conduct Requirements in Attempt Cases

Any act that is legal for a monopolist in the market in which it has monopoly power should be legal for a nonmonopolist: the conduct requirements for attempt should be substantially stricter than the requirements for illegal monopolization.[211] This means that activities that are only "marginally" illegal for monopolists are almost certainly legal for nonmonopolists. Price discrimination,[212] failure to predisclose new technology,[213] aggressive research and development,[214] expansion of capacity,[215] acquisition of or refusal to license patents,[216] and some dealer terminations and exclusive dealing contracts[217] may be legal when they are performed by a monopolist. They are then necessarily legal when they are performed by a nonmonopolist.[218]

---

[210] See, e.g., Taylor Pub. Co. v. Jostens, 216 F.3d 465 (5th Cir. 2000) (false statements about defendant's own prices); American Professional Testing Serv. v. Harcourt Brace Jovanovich, 108 F.3d 1147 (9th Cir. 1997) (disparagement of rival, the antitrust plaintiff).

[211] Transamerica Computer Co. v. IBM Corp., 698 F.2d 1377, 1382 (9th Cir.), cert. denied, 464 U.S. 955, 104 S.Ct. 370 (1983) (if conduct is not monopolization, it is not attempt either).

[212] See Pacific Eng'g & Prod. Co. v. Kerr-McGee Corp., 551 F.2d 790 (10th Cir.), cert. denied, 434 U.S. 879, 98 S.Ct. 234, rehearing denied, 434 U.S. 977, 98 S.Ct. 543 (1977).

[213] Berkey Photo, Inc. v. Eastman Kodak Co., 603 F.2d 263 (2d Cir. 1979), cert. denied, 444 U.S. 1093, 100 S.Ct. 1061 (1980).

[214] California Computer Products v. IBM Corp., 613 F.2d 727, 744 (9th Cir. 1979).

[215] E.I. du Pont de Nemours & Co., 96 F.T.C. 653 (1980).

[216] See SCM Corp. v. Xerox Corp., 645 F.2d 1195 (2d Cir. 1981), cert. denied, 455 U.S. 1016, 102 S.Ct. 1708 (1982).

[217] Paschall v. Kansas City Star Co., 727 F.2d 692 (8th Cir.) (*en banc*), cert. denied, 469 U.S. 872, 105 S.Ct. 222 (1984).

[218] See 3B Antitrust Law ¶ 806 (4th ed. 2015).

Chapter 8

PREDATORY AND OTHER EXCLUSIONARY PRICING

Table of Sections

---

§ 8.1 Introduction

In its traditional form, "predatory pricing" refers to a practice of driving rivals out of business by selling at a price below cost. The predator's intent is to charge monopoly prices after rivals have been

333

dispatched or disciplined. Predatory pricing is analyzed under the antitrust laws as illegal monopolization or attempt to monopolize under § 2 of the Sherman Act, or sometimes as a violation of Clayton Act § 2, generally called the Robinson-Patman Act.

Courts once believed that predatory pricing was easy for a well-financed firm to accomplish, and that it was a common means by which monopolies came into existence.[1] Later on many economists, legal writers and courts rejected that position, concluding that predatory pricing is in fact very expensive, risky, and not plausible in the vast majority of markets in which it has been alleged to occur.[2] A few legal scholars believed that anticompetitive predatory pricing in any market is irrational and virtually never happens.[3] Today the pendulum has partially shifted back. While predation strategies are often complex there is widespread consensus today that they exist and can sometimes be anticompetitive. The antitrust rules that courts currently apply to predation claims are largely a product of the earlier anti-enforcement period. As a result, there is also a growing consensus that current predation rules are underdeterrent.

The legal tests for predatory pricing have changed with judicial attitudes about how frequently it occurs. When courts believed predatory pricing was common, plaintiffs could sometimes establish it by showing that the defendant firm was large, the victim small, that prices in the predated area went down, and the defendant intended to harm its rivals.[4] Later, increased skepticism about the frequency of predatory pricing led courts to develop much stricter tests. Since 1975 when the Areeda-Turner test was introduced,[5] only

---

[1]   For example, in the early twentieth century it was widely believed that the Standard Oil monopoly was created this way. Whether that was true remains controversial. See John McGee, Predatory Price Cutting: The Standard Oil (N.J.) Case, 1 J. L. & Econ. 137 (1958) (debunking predatory pricing theory); Christopher R. Leslie, Revisiting the Revisionist History of Standard Oil, 85 S.Cal.L.Rev. 573 (2012) (debunking McGee); Daniel A. Crane, Were Standard Oil's Rebates and Drawbacks Cost Justified?, 85 S.Cal.L.Rev. 559 (2012) (finding the answer ambiguous); Elizabeth Granitz & Benjamin Klein, "Monopolization by 'Raising Rivals' Costs': The Standard Oil Case," 39 J.Law & Econ. 1 (1996) (arguing that Standard mainly acquired its dominant position by agreements with railroads and others imposing higher costs on rivals).

[2]   See 3A Antitrust Law, Ch. 7C (4th ed. 2015).

[3]   For example, Robert H. Bork, The Antitrust Paradox: A Policy at War With Itself 144–55 (1978; rev. ed. 1993); Frank Easterbrook, Predatory Strategies and Counterstrategies, 48 Univ.Chi.L.Rev. 263 (1981).

[4]   E.g., Utah Pie Co. v. Continental Baking Co., 386 U.S. 685, 87 S.Ct. 1326, rehearing denied, 387 U.S. 949, 87 S.Ct. 2071 (1967).

[5]   See § 8.2.

a few plaintiffs have prevailed in predatory pricing actions.[6] But no circuit has held that pricing at below cost is *per se* legal.

Few antitrust allegations are more sensitive or difficult for courts to assess than predatory pricing claims. Low prices are a principle if not the primary goal of antitrust policy. In a predatory pricing case, however, a court must consider a charge that a price is unlawful because it is too low. Further, the relationship between any firm's prices and its costs is ambiguous and difficult to compute. If the judge uses an overdeterrent rule the result will be inefficiently high prices.

Predatory pricing is not condemned because it results in current lower prices. It is condemned because, if successful, it will eventually result in reduced output and higher prices. A price is predatory if it is reasonably calculated to drive rivals from the market today or else discipline them so that the predator can enjoy profitable monopoly pricing in the post-predation period.

For such a scheme to succeed, several things must be true. First, the victims must be sufficiently weak or have sufficiently high costs that the predator can drive them from business or make them obey. Second, the market must be structured in such a way that the predator can predict a profitable period of above cost pricing. Third, the discounted present value of the future period of monopoly pricing must be greater than the present losses that the predator incurs during the predatory period. The following sections analyze these requirements and describe some of the difficulties that courts have encountered in evaluating predatory pricing claims.

§ 8.2 When Is a Price Predatory? The Areeda-Turner Test

Competition drives prices to marginal cost.[7] When a firm considers whether to produce one additional unit, it weighs the added revenues the additional sale will generate against the added costs of production and sale. Two things are generally true: 1) prices in competitive markets tend toward marginal costs; 2) dropping a price below short-run marginal cost is not reasonable profit-maximizing

---

[6]   But there have been some. See U.S. Philips Corp. v. Windmere Corp., 1992–1 Trade Cas. ¶ 69,778, 1991 WL 338258 (S.D.Fla.1991) (evidence of drastic price reductions by a firm threatened by new entrant and holding 90% of a market characterized by substantial barriers to entry was sufficient to show monopolization under the Sherman Act).

[7]   See W. Kip Viscusi, John M. Vernon, & Joseph E. Harrington, Jr., Economics of Regulation and Antitrust, ch. 4 (5th ed. 2019); and see § 1.1.

behavior, unless the resulting losses are more than offset by future gains.

Marginal cost pricing is consistent with competition; supramarginal cost pricing is consistent with monopoly.[8] But prices lower than marginal cost are consistent with neither. In an influential article published in 1975, Professors Areeda and Turner argued that a price lower than reasonably anticipated short-run marginal cost is predatory, while a price equal to or higher than reasonably anticipated short-run marginal cost is nonpredatory.[9]

Areeda and Turner argued further that use of short-run marginal cost as a benchmark for predation is impractical, because marginal cost is extraordinarily difficult to compute.[10] Marginal cost can be difficult to compute in litigation when the relevant question is whether over some past, extended period of time a seller's prices were lower than its marginal costs, unless the disparity between the two is large.

Therefore Areeda and Turner proposed a surrogate: average variable cost (AVC). A firm's total production costs can be divided into two kinds, fixed and variable. A fixed cost is one that does not change with variations in output over a given time period; a variable cost is one that does. For example, over a one-year period the capital cost of the plant itself is a fixed cost: it will have to be paid whether or not the firm produces, and the amount of the payment will not change as output varies. However, most labor costs, the costs of basic raw material or ingredients, and utility costs are generally variable. A bakery that increases its bread production by 100 loaves per day for three weeks likely will not enlarge its plant. However it will spend more money on flour, salt, and probably electricity and labor.

In litigation, AVC is theoretically easier to compute than marginal cost. One must identify which costs are variable, add them up, and divide by the number of units produced. Under the Areeda-Turner test, a price above AVC is presumed to be lawful. A price

---

[8]   See § 1.2.

[9]   Phillip Areeda & Donald Turner, Predatory Pricing and Related Practices Under Section 2 of the Sherman Act, 88 Harv.L.Rev. 697 (1975). The current formulation of the Areeda-Turner test is contained in 3A Antitrust Law Ch. 7C-3 (4th ed. 2015).

[10]   While marginal cost is difficult to compute, it may not always be difficult to determine that a price is below marginal cost. For example, suppose that a gasoline retailer pays a wholesale price of $1.00, including taxes, and sells the same gasoline at a price of 90 cents. In that case we do not need to know precisely what marginal cost is in order to know that the price is below it. See 3A Antitrust Law ¶ 740a (4th ed. 2015); and Rebel Oil Co. v. Atlantic Richfield Co. *(Rebel Oil II)*, 146 F.3d 1088, 1094 & n. 1 (9th Cir.), cert. denied, 525 U.S. 1017, 119 S.Ct. 541 (1998).

below AVC, if other prerequisites are met, is conclusively presumed to be illegal.[11]

§ 8.3 Predatory Pricing: Application and Criticism of the Areeda-Turner Test

Many courts initially adopted the Areeda-Turner test with little qualification.[12] Academics were more critical, and a lively scholarly debate ensued about the proper legal standards for predatory pricing.[13] Eventually this debate influenced courts as well, and some circuits that initially embraced the Areeda-Turner test had second thoughts. Today nearly all circuits adopt a version of the test. However, several deviate in some respects from Areeda and Turner's original formulation.

The Areeda-Turner test has been subjected to two broad classes of criticism: 1) Even assuming marginal cost is the proper benchmark for predation, AVC is often a poor surrogate; 2) short-run marginal cost is not an appropriate benchmark for identifying predation: although few prices below short-run marginal cost are nonpredatory, a price higher than short-run marginal cost can also be "anticompetitive."

8.3a. The Average Variable Cost (AVC) Surrogate

Figure 1 illustrates some of the problems of the AVC test. The figure shows the cost functions of a plant of roughly optimal size. Its competitive rate of output is Q_c, which is at the intersection of the demand curve and the firm's marginal cost curve.[14] At this rate of output and with a market price of P_c, the firm is earning enough to cover its average total costs (AC), and more than AVC.

At the competitive rate of output, marginal costs are higher than AVC. More importantly, the two are diverging: if the firm increases its output, marginal costs and AVC will be even further apart. Under the Areeda-Turner rule, however, the firm legally would be able to increase its output all the way to Q_p and drop its price to P_p. At levels of output higher than optimum capacity (where predation can be

---

[11] 3A Antitrust Law, ¶ 723. A price above average total cost (the sum of fixed and variable costs divided by the number of units of output) is *per se* legal under the Areeda-Turner test.

[12] See Herbert Hovenkamp, The Areeda-Turner Test for Exclusionary Pricing: A Critical Journal, 46 Rev. Indus. Org. 209 (2015).

[13] The debate is summarized in James Hurwitz & William Kovacic, Judicial Analysis of Predation: the Emerging Trends, 35 Vand.L.Rev. 63 (1982); Joseph Brodley & George Hay, Predatory Pricing: Competing Economic Theories and the Evolution of Legal Standards, 66 Cornell L.Rev. 738 (1981).

[14] The demand curve slopes downward because, although the firm may not have market power, it will make more sales if it lowers its price.

expected to occur),[15] marginal cost and AVC tend to be quite far apart, with marginal cost higher than AVC. The result is that the Areeda-Turner test can give the predator considerable room for maneuvering. In fact, under the Areeda-Turner rule a firm could compute its AVC and legally sell at a price one cent higher, all the while imposing significant losses on its victim. One answer, of course, is that when AVC and marginal cost diverge substantially, a price below marginal cost will generally be easier to recognize and the AVC surrogate may be unnecessary.[16]

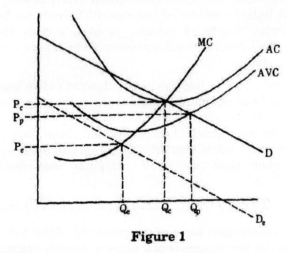

Figure 1

Precisely the opposite happens in a sick industry, plagued with excess capacity. As § 8.4b below shows, an industry with substantial excess capacity is not a plausible candidate for predatory pricing because the predator cannot reasonably look forward to a period of monopoly pricing. Shifted demand curve D_e in Figure 1 shows the consequences of excess capacity. Price will drop to P_e and output to Q_e, less than the optimal rate of output for the plant. Marginal cost and AVC also diverge, but this time AVC is higher. Under the Areeda-Turner test a firm pricing its output at marginal cost could nevertheless be guilty of predatory pricing.[17]

---

[15]   Since predatory pricing is a short-run phenomenon, the predator would ordinarily wish to do it without constructing an additional plant, even though during the predatory period output must be very high. As a result, we anticipate that predation will occur most often at inefficiently high levels of output.

[16]   See 3A Antitrust Law ¶ 740c (4th ed. 2015).

[17]   In the short-run a firm would ordinarily cease production if the price dropped to a level below its average variable costs—that is, it could then minimize losses by producing nothing at all. However, the firm must consider the cost of ceasing production and restarting it. If it intends to stay in business and wants to retain certain customers or contracts, short periods of producing at a price lower than AVC may be more profitable than ceasing production. In any case, prolonged periods of

In short, the Areeda-Turner test makes predatory pricing easy to "prove" in markets where it is almost certain not to occur, but more difficult to prove in markets that are conducive to predation.

8.3b. The Problem of Long-Run, Strategic Behavior; "Predatory" Prices Above Cost

Other criticisms of the Areeda-Turner test are more complex. Although there are numerous variations, the academic literature has suggested variations on the predatory pricing story that the Areeda-Turner test fails to consider. For example, multiple-benefit predation occurs when the predator that operates in numerous markets engages in well publicized price cutting in one as a threat, with the result that oligopoly prices are maintained elsewhere. A variation on this story is that one or more oligopolists respond to a price cutter (or other kind of innovator) with predation in order to send a message to other oligopolists that such competitive excursions will not be tolerated.

Critics have also argued that the Areeda-Turner test ignores the possibility of limit pricing, or strategic entry deterrence. Suppose, for example, that an industry operating at optimal efficiency can produce widgets at $1.00 each. Demand at that price is 1000 per year. The minimum efficient scale (MES) for a widget plant is 250 widgets per year. Such a market has room for three or four efficient firms. However, a firm could construct a single efficient plant producing 1000 widgets annually and satisfy the entire market.

A single dominant firm that built a plant capable of producing 1000 widgets per year could effectively deter future competitors. Having built a 1000-widget plant, the dominant firm could actually produce widgets at a rate of perhaps 700 per year and sell them at a monopoly price of $1.50. Any time a prospective entrant appeared, however, the dominant firm could increase its output to, say, 900 widgets per year and drop its price to slightly more than $1.00. Even though the current price is highly profitable and the prospective entrant has access to the same technology, it would see that *post*-entry prices will probably be unprofitable. In particular, if demand is not sufficient to enable the firm to achieve MES *after* entry occurs, the new entrant will face higher costs than the incumbent. The post-entry price might then be too low to enable the entrant to earn a

---

pricing below AVC are not likely to occur in an industry with excess capacity. See Paul Joskow & Alvin Klevorick, A Framework for Analyzing Predatory Pricing Policy, 89 Yale L.J. 213, 251 n. 77 (1979).

profit, even though that price is above the incumbent's marginal costs and average variable costs.[18]

In this way the excess capacity of the dominant firm can stand ready as a weapon in its hands: prospective entrants know that the incumbent can easily increase output and reduce price in response to any attempt at entry or output expansion. Such a strategy will work best in an industry where assets are specialized and a great deal of the investment required for entry is "sunk"—that is, the new entrant will not be able to recover these costs in the event of failure.[19] Further, the strategy is "sustainable," which means that the dominant firm can pursue it indefinitely because it is profitable even in the short run.

Most economists acknowledge that strategies such as limit pricing occur and can be anticompetitive. The fundamental problem is that no one has developed the tools for evaluating such claims and determining appropriate relief. In general, the fact that an anticompetitive pricing strategy is sustainable entails that it is "above cost" in the short run, and this makes evaluation far more difficult. Further, it typically forces the court to look at the one thing—subjective intent—that has proved consistently to be the undoing of a rational predatory pricing policy. The worst of all possible rules would be one that (1) permitted prices to be proved predatory even when they exceed average total cost; and (2) permitted plaintiffs to establish (1) on the basis of evidence drawn from intent.

In any event, the Supreme Court's *Brooke* decision[20] limited predation claims to those where prices are below average cost. To be sure, price-cost relationships were not at issue and the Court refused to decide the proper cost test for predatory pricing. Further, the case was brought under the Robinson-Patman Act rather than the Sherman Act. However, since the Robinson-Patman Act is more expansive than the Sherman Act,[21] any restriction that applies to Robinson-Patman Act predation must apply to Sherman Act predation as well.

---

[18]   The illustration is a simplification of Williamson, *supra*, 292–301. It is simply explained in George Hay, A Confused Lawyer's Guide to the Predatory Pricing Literature 155–202, in Strategy, Predation, and Antitrust Analysis (S. Salop, ed. 1981).

[19]   See § 1.6 on sunk costs as barriers to entry.

[20]   Brooke Group Ltd. v. Brown & Williamson Tobacco Corp., 509 U.S. 209, 210, 113 S.Ct. 2578, 2581 (1993).

[21]   See § 8.8.

§ 8.4   Structural Issues: When Is Predatory Pricing Plausible? Recoupment

Figure 2 illustrates some of the problems facing the putative predator.

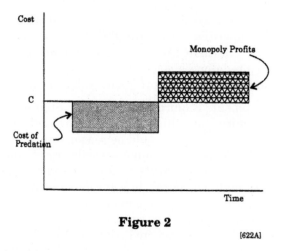

Figure 2

[622A]

The central line labeled C measures the predator's costs, which formally are its total costs. This line represents a finite time period sufficiently long to cover both the predation period and the period of post-predation monopoly pricing. The shaded rectangle on the left, which hangs below line C, represents the costs of predatory pricing, which consists of two elements: the duration of the pricing scheme and the extent of loss per unit sold. The first of these is measured by the horizontal length of the rectangle, and the second is measured by its height. The cross-hatched rectangle on the right, which sits atop line C, represents the monopoly returns from predatory pricing. The size of these returns depends on their duration, measured by the horizontal length of the cross-hatched rectangle, and also the amount of monopoly profit per unit sold, measured by the cross-hatched rectangle's height.

Predatory pricing is not a profitable strategy unless the present value of the cross-hatched rectangle on the right is larger than the shaded rectangle on the left. Indeed, the cross-hatched rectangle must be discounted in two quite distinct ways. *First,* money to be received in the future is worth less than money in my pocket today. Indeed, if the underlying interest rate is 10%, a dollar a year from now is worth only ninety cents, two years from now is worth eighty-one cents, and so on.[22] *Second,* the cross-hatched rectangle must be reduced if the probability that the predatory pricing scheme will succeed is anything less than one hundred percent, taking into account several possibilities: (1) the rivals will prove tenacious and stay in the market, so the monopoly period will never materialize; (2) the rivals will be driven from the market, but shortly after the monopoly price increase new entrants will appear, driving prices back to the competitive level; (3) the predator will be caught, convicted of a Sherman Act violation, enjoined and assessed damages. If a predator believes there is only a 50–50 chance of success, the size of anticipated profits must be cut in half.

The recoupment requirement as the Supreme Court has articulated it requires something close to dollars-and-cents proof that the predatory pricing strategy could be reasonably predicted to have a positive payoff. This seems unnecessarily strict, imposing high evidentiary burdens on plaintiffs in an area where speculation is likely to be very high. Of course, in some cases easy entry or robust competitors suggest that recoupment is not possible, and the case should be dismissed. But in close cases the recoupment calculation is heavily affected by the predicted size of the defendant's post-predation market share as well as market elasticities of demand and supply. These numbers are difficult enough to measure when one is looking at the current market, but measurement problems can become intractable when we need to predict them in a post-predation market that has not yet materialized. Such an estimate requires accurate predictions about the time new entry will take, the ability of surviving rivals to expand their output, or of customers to identify substitutes. In sum, the recoupment requirement was a reaction to a line of cases that found predation in markets where it could not plausibly have occurred—but it was an overreaction.[23]

8.4a.   The Predator's Market Position; Predatory Pricing in Oligopoly

As a matter of legal theory, courts have traditionally dealt with predatory pricing claims as attempts to monopolize. As a matter of economics, this seems wrong. Predatory pricing and other pricing

---

[22]   See Brooke Group Ltd. v. Brown & Williamson Tobacco Corp., 509 U.S. 209, 210 113 S.Ct. 2578, 2581 (1993): "The plaintiff must demonstrate that there is a likelihood that the predatory scheme alleged would cause a rise in prices above a competitive level that would be sufficient to compensate for the amounts expended on the predation, including the time value of the money invested in it."

[23]   See 3A Antitrust Law ¶¶ 725b, c, 726d5 (4th ed. 2015). See also Aaron S. Edlin, Predatory Pricing: Limiting *Brooke Group* to Monopolies and Sound Implementation of Price-Cost Comparisons, 127 Yale L.J. Forum 996 (2018); Christopher R. Leslie, Predatory Pricing and Recoupment, 113 Colum. L. Rev. 1695 (2013).

strategies are generally plausible only for firms that are *already* dominant in their markets. Indeed, predatory pricing may require a higher market share than other practices (such as baseless patent litigation) that are generally condemned as substantive monopolization. For many years courts largely ignored structural issues in predatory pricing cases and focused instead on price/cost relationships. More recently, however, some have discovered that the quickest road to a resolution may be to look at structure first. If structural analysis indicates that predatory pricing simply cannot be a profitable strategy in a particular market, then further inquiry need not be made into price/cost relationships. As the discussion in § 8.7 shows, many courts recognize this.[24] The Supreme Court's *Brooke* decision, discussed below, is a bold turn in this direction. There the court assumed that (1) prices were below average variable cost and (2) the defendant's anticompetitive intent was clear. However, it dismissed the complaint because an analysis of market structure convinced it that "recoupment" was not likely.

One objection to this focus on structure is that if the goal of antitrust law is deterrence, then the law should look at conduct rather than results. Refusing to find predatory pricing in competitive markets sounds a little like failing to find attempts generally. The common law offense of "attempt," after all, is directed toward *failures*. Someone who points a gun at someone and pulls the trigger may be convicted of an attempt even though the powder is wet or the firing pin defective. *He* thought the gun would work, and if we want to deter murders, that should be the thing that counts. So, the argument goes, if the goal of antitrust law is deterrence, then we want to deter people from attempting antitrust violations, even those where the likelihood of success is small. Indeed, the attempt itself can be socially costly. Failed predation has been described as a "gift" to consumers, because it produces low prices today and no subsequent monopoly prices later.[25] But it is hardly a gift to competitors, and it may impose costs on others, such as those from whom the competitor purchases its inputs. Indeed, it may even hurt

---

[24] For example, American Academic Suppliers v. Beckley-Cardy, 922 F.2d 1317, 1319 (7th Cir. 1991) ("Firms found guilty of attempting to monopolize are typically, and in predatory pricing cases must always be, monopolists.").

[25] See Judge Easterbrook's opinion in A.A. Poultry Farms v. Rose Acre Farms, 881 F.2d 1396, 1401 (7th Cir. 1989), cert. denied, 494 U.S. 1019, 110 S.Ct. 1326 (1990) ("Price less than cost today, followed by the competitive price tomorrow, bestows a gift on consumers. * * * Because antitrust laws are designed for the benefit of consumers, not competitors, a gift of this kind is not actionable.").

See also *Brooke* decision, *supra*: "Although unsuccessful predatory pricing may encourage some inefficient substitution toward the product being sold at less than its cost, unsuccessful predation is in general a boon to consumers. * * *" 509 U.S. at 224, 113 S.Ct. at 2588.

some consumers to the extent that the "false" signaling about price leads them to make investments or alter their activities in some other fashion.[26]

This approach to the attempt offense makes considerable sense when the conduct under examination is unambiguous. The pointing of a gun at someone's head is a fairly unambiguous act, and it generally remains unambiguous even after it turns out that the gun is defective or the powder wet. Not so with predatory pricing. By all odds, we do a very poor job of identifying the line between predatory and non-predatory prices. Conceptually, our scheme for measuring price/cost relationships is full of holes, as the previous discussion reveals. Questions about how costs should be classified, what cost level is predatory, and under what circumstances, all yield highly disputed and variant answers.[27] Further, even if we all agreed about the basic concepts, we haven't done well enough in *measuring* the appropriate costs to make the scheme workable with tolerable accuracy.

So the courts have taken a rational actor approach.[28] They presume that firms are profit maximizers, and that their managers have at least an intuitive knowledge of the kinds of strategies that will and will not work in their respective areas. Then we ask ourselves "Could a manager who knows these things about the market she works in believe that her firm could profitably drop price today, dispatch rivals, and charge monopoly prices later?" If our economic answer to that question is no, it helps us characterize the ambiguous conduct. No, a rational person would not have done this. So assuming this particular defendant's manager is rational, that must not be what happened.

In *Brooke Group* the plaintiffs were not complaining about an actual or threatened monopoly, but rather of a lockstep oligopoly several decades old. While the Court purported to apply a rational actor approach, it understated the risks of predation. It assumed that oligopolies are inherently unstable, notwithstanding ample evidence that they are in fact quite stable across a wide range of circumstances.[29] Further, the predatory scheme in *Brooke Group* was

---

[26]   For example, predatory pricing in product A may encourage a customer of product A, who uses A as an input into product B, to enter the market for B or expand her capacity there, since the market appears quite profitable. But once the A price is increased to the competitive level, that entry or expansion may turn out to be unprofitable.

[27]   See §§ 8.5–8.6, *infra*.

[28]   See 3A Antitrust Law ¶ 725a (4th ed. 2015).

[29]   See Herbert Hovenkamp and Fiona Scott-Morton, Framing the Chicago School of Antitrust Analysis, ___ Univ. Penn. L. Rev. ___ (2020) (forthcoming), available at https://papers.ssrn.com/sol3/papers.cfm?abstract_id=3481388.

not intended to destroy a rival, but only to convince it that staying within the highly profitable oligopoly framework was a better option than defecting. As we suggest later, the Supreme Court very likely exaggerated the risks and underestimated payoffs to predatory pricing in oligopoly.[30]

When a court evaluates a predatory pricing claim, it should consider several additional structural features of the relevant market.

8.4b.   Barriers to Entry

The rationale for predatory pricing is the sustaining of losses today that will give a firm monopoly profits in the future. The monopoly profits will never materialize, however, if new entrants appear soon after the successful predator attempts to raise its price. Predatory pricing will be profitable only if the market contains significant barriers to new entry.

There is one important difference between entry analysis in predatory pricing cases and, say, merger cases. In the latter, the only relevant question is whether entry is likely to reverse any price increase that the merger might otherwise cause.[31] In predatory pricing cases one must also consider whether predatory pricing occurred in the first place. In answering this question, historical evidence of entry can prove quite helpful.

In a merger case, evidence of recent entry is not necessarily good proof that entry barriers are low. Each new entrant adds to total market output and drops the market price, and entry is not attractive unless the prospective entrant predicts that the market will be profitable *after* its own output is added to that of others in the market. As a result, a market that was conducive to entry before firm A entered, may not be conducive after A is already there and producing. For this reason, the federal government's Merger Guidelines play down the significance of historical evidence of entry in merger analysis.[32]

By contrast, the claim in a predatory pricing case must be that the market was *already* unprofitable during the predation period— that is, output was already higher and prices lower than required for profitability. This claim is directly contradicted by the fact that one or more firms entered *during* the predatory period. Such entry entails that the entering firm believed prices were sufficiently high that it

---

[30]   See § 8.8.
[31]   On entry barriers and merger policy, see § 12.6.
[32]   See id.

could make a profit. Any price low enough to impose losses on established rivals is necessarily low enough to make entry by an equally efficient firm unprofitable.[33]

§ 8.5   Judicial Adaption of the Areeda-Turner Test: Price/Cost Relationships and Intent

Courts initially embraced the Areeda-Turner test for predatory pricing with enthusiasm.[34] Eventually, however, they created various exceptions and qualifications to the test. No court has completely rejected every aspect of the test, however, and the basic Areeda-Turner AVC paradigm continues to influence every circuit that has considered a predatory pricing case since 1975.

8.5a.   Price/Cost Relationships

The Areeda-Turner test *sounds* simple: a price lower than AVC is illegal, and the court can refer to a "laundry list" describing which costs should be considered fixed and which variable. An accountant using this formulation would find it rather easy to testify about the relationship between a defendant's prices and its costs.

As some courts discovered, however, computing variable costs is not always as easy as first appeared.[35] Second, the presumption that the average variable cost surrogate should be used only when AVC is relatively close to marginal cost was unworkable. Third, the proposed "laundry list" of fixed and variable costs did not account for the wide variety of industries in which predatory pricing might occur— concrete and college textbooks, bakery bread, industrial chemicals, and so on. Fourth, the test seemed unable to take strategic long-term behavior into account. Finally, at high output levels the test was a paradise for defendants, and virtually none lost a case.[36]

---

[33]   See, e.g., Affinity LLC v. GfK Mediamark Res. & Intelligence, LLC, 547 Fed. Appx. 54 (2d Cir. 2013) (rejecting predatory pricing claim where market was competitively structured and had low entry barriers); Stearns Airport Equip. Co. v. FMC Corp., 170 F.3d 518 (5th Cir. 1999) (large number of foreign firms coming into market indicated entry barriers to low to support predatory pricing claim).

[34]   See § 8.2.

[35]   For some of the difficulties, see United States v. AMR Corp., 335 F.3d 1109 (10th Cir. 2003); William Inglis & Sons Baking Co. v. ITT Continental Baking Co., 461 F.Supp. 410, 418 (N.D.Cal.1978), affirmed in part, reversed in part, 668 F.2d 1014 (9th Cir. 1981), cert. denied, 459 U.S. 825, 103 S.Ct. 57 (1982).

[36]   This, of course, is consistent with Areeda's and Turner's premise that bona fide predatory pricing occurs only rarely. See Joseph Brodley & George Hay, Predatory Pricing: Competing Economic Theories and the Evolution of Legal Standards, 66 Cornell L.Rev. 738, 768–89 (1981).

8.5b.   Intent

Many courts have been uncomfortable with Areeda's and Turner's refusal to consider the defendant's intent. They have responded by "softening" the rule. The Ninth Circuit, for example, has held that a price below AVC creates a rebuttable presumption of predation.[37] A price above AVC but below average total cost creates a rebuttable presumption of nonpredation.[38] Prior to *Brooke* that court also held that a price above average total cost is not conclusively legal, as it would be under the Areeda-Turner formulation, but created a strong presumption of legality.[39] Other circuits have also expressed their willingness to soften the hard presumptions of the Areeda-Turner test.[40]

The relevance and meaning of the defendant's intent continues to be a fiercely debated issue. Invariably, when courts admit evidence of intent, they find it difficult to distinguish between predatory and competitive acts. As a result, the Supreme Court's *Brooke* decision[41] goes very far in the direction of making intent evidence irrelevant— or at least, making it a limiting rather than expanding factor. That is, absence of anticompetitive intent may still disprove predation, but its presence will not establish it unless structural factors are also present. Although *Brooke* was brought under the Robinson-Patman Act,[42] everything the Supreme Court said about intent applies with equal force to Sherman Act predation claims, since the latter statute requires even stronger proof. In *Brooke*, the evidence of the defendant's anticompetitive intent was "more voluminous and detailed than in any other reported case."[43] Nevertheless, the Court dismissed the complaint because its structural analysis convinced it that predatory pricing was not a profitable strategy.

---

[37]   William Inglis & Sons Baking Co. v. ITT Continental Baking Co., Inc., 668 F.2d 1014, 1036 (9th Cir. 1981), cert. denied, 459 U.S. 825, 103 S.Ct. 57 (1982).

[38]   Id. at 1035–36.

[39]   Transamerica Computer Co. v. IBM Corp., 698 F.2d 1377, 1388 (9th Cir.), cert. denied, 464 U.S. 955, 104 S.Ct. 370 (1983).

[40]   For example, D.E. Rogers Assoc., Inc. v. Gardner-Denver Co., 718 F.2d 1431, 1437 (6th Cir. 1983), cert. denied, 467 U.S. 1242, 104 S.Ct. 3513 (1984). See 3A Antitrust Law ¶ 728c (4th ed. 2015).

[41]   Brooke Group Ltd. v. Brown & Williamson Tobacco Corp., 509 U.S. 209, 113 S.Ct. 2578 (1993).

[42]   The decision is discussed at some length in § 8.8.

[43]   *Brooke*, 509 U.S. at 248, 113 S.Ct. at 2601.

§ 8.6   Judicial Adaption of Areeda-Turner: Identifying Relevant Costs; Multi-Product Firms; Customer-Specific Pricing

Suppose that an established firm selling 100 products is accused of predatory pricing in one of them. How should the relevant costs be calculated? When a firm decides whether the addition of a new product is profitable, it compares *incremental* costs and gains, rather than total averages. For example, suppose the addition of a new product is being considered by a ninety-nine item grocery store. The store, which is very small, generally has only one employee on duty at a time, and the single employee can quite easily handle the new item in addition to the previous ninety-nine. In that case, incremental labor costs are zero, even though labor is a variable cost as a general matter. The same thing could be said of utilities, another variable cost item. It probably costs no more to heat and light the store with the one hundred items than with the ninety-nine, so utilities contribute little or nothing to *incremental* variable costs. At the margin, the cost of selling an additional item may be no more than the wholesale price of the item itself. If that is the case, then the wholesale price should be the only relevant variable cost for purposes of analyzing alleged predation in that item.[44]

An alternative rule requiring that costs be averaged operates as a deterrent to firms to do efficient things, such as add products where the cost of adding them is less than the additional revenue they produce. That is to say, the alternative rule prevents firms from achieving available economies of *scope*, which are economies that result from a firm's ability to do two things at once. It should not be the policy of the antitrust laws to prevent firms from adding products when the incremental cost of their doing so is less than the revenue they produce.[45] For example, in *International Travel*[46] a major airlines was accused of predatory pricing in its cut rate, or

---

[44]   The Supreme Court's opinion in Brooke Group Ltd. v. Brown & Williamson Tobacco Corp., 509 U.S. 209, 113 S.Ct. 2578 (1993), does not discuss this issue, although it was almost certainly relevant to cost determination. B & W was accused of predatory pricing in "generic" cigarettes. But generic cigarettes were probably nothing more than ordinary cigarettes, manufactured in the same production facilities, perhaps with lower quality tobaccos, wrappers, and so on. If there were excess capacity to begin with, then relevant variable costs should include only the *incremental* costs of making the generics.

[45]   Compare William Inglis & Sons Baking Co. v. Continental Baking Co., 942 F.2d 1332, 1336 & n. 6 (9th Cir. 1991), vacated in part 981 F.2d 1023 (1992), on remand, 1993 WL 424235 (N.D.Cal. 1993), affirmed in part, reversed in part, 82 F.3d 424 (9th Cir. 1996) (predatory pricing should be limited to costs "uniquely incurred" in making an additional sale).

[46]   International Travel Arrangers v. NWA (Northwest Airlines), 991 F.2d 1389 (8th Cir.), cert. denied, 510 U.S. 932, 114 S.Ct. 345 (1993).

"supersaver" fares. However, the airline's overall fare structure was profitable and the alternative to supersaver fares would have been empty seats, which produced no revenue at all. If an airline can fill an additional seat on an already scheduled flight for $100, the antitrust laws should not prevent it from doing so, provided that the *incremental* cost of servicing that passenger is less than $100. The court correctly held that price-cost relationships should be determined from the airline's overall fare structure, not simply by looking at its lowest fares.

Closely related to the above problem is the allocation of variable costs when a firm is alleged to engage in predatory pricing in one of its many products, but the products are more or less interchangeable parts of the seller's inventory and most of their cost demands are non-unique. Consider once again the grocer who sells ninety-nine items but is accused by a rival of predatorily pricing only one, milk. Allocation of variable costs in such situations can impose enormous measurement problems. For example, one would have to figure out how much of the employees' time was spent stocking and selling milk as opposed to other items, how much of the utility bill went to taking care of the space occupied by the milk in the refrigerated case, and so on.

This problem of separating out relevant costs and revenues becomes especially important in industries with substantial fixed costs, where pricing is based on competitive bids that may vary from one sale to the next. Suppose, for example, that the prevailing price of custom made machine parts has been $12.00, but the market has been somewhat soft. An opportunity for a large sale comes along, and the winner takes it with a bid of $9.00. A rival charges that this particular bid, although not the defendants other sales at the $12.00 price, is predatory. Once again, the relevant costs for determining predation are the *incremental* costs that the firm must incur in filling the order. For example, perhaps the firm already has workers who are underutilized, floor space in its shop that is heated and lit but is currently not being used, delivery trucks that are running with half loads, and so on. The incremental cost of producing the additional order should not include a pro rata share of the labor, utilities or gasoline for the trucks—these costs are already being incurred to support output at the current level. A predatory pricing rule that counts them tends to deter firms from using their productive assets efficiently.

The economic source of cost allocation problems such as these is rather easily identified. Variable costs are lumpy. One cannot generally buy a truck to deliver only one sack of peanuts per week, or hire a laborer to work only ten minutes per week. Even constituent parts come in large sizes. For example, if flour comes in fifty pound sacks, which will make 200 loaves of bread, the baker who makes 150 loaves may end up throwing one fourth of the sack away. In that case, it may be profitable for the baker to seek out a buyer for fifty additional loaves of bread, *even* if the buyer does not pay a price equal to the wholesale cost of the flour. For this reason, competition "on the margin" often occurs at prices that seem, at first glance, to be too low.

§ 8.7   Judicial Adaption of Areeda-Turner: Structural Issues and Recoupment

The initial impact of the Areeda-Turner test on judicial decisions was to turn the attention of litigants to issues of price/cost relationships. Courts often paid scant attention to structural issues. This was both ironic and unfortunate, because often analysis of structural issues would take the court to a much easier and more certain decision than analysis of the complexities of the AVC test. For example, in the *Inglis* case the court barely acknowledged the fact that the bakery market contained several competitors, and the defendant was only the second largest. In addition, entry was easy and the industry had a large amount of excess capacity. Computation of the defendant's market share including the excess capacity of competitors indicates that the defendant had approximately 8% of the market.[47]

The Supreme Court has noted the importance of structural issues. In dicta in a merger decision it stated:

> In order to succeed in a sustained campaign of predatory pricing, a predator must be able to absorb the market shares of its rivals once prices have been cut. If it cannot do so, its attempt at predation will presumably fail, because there will remain in the market sufficient demand for the competitors' goods at a higher price, and the competitors will not be drawn out of business. In this case, [the defendant's] 20.4% market share after the merger suggests it would lack sufficient market power to engage in predatory pricing * * *. Courts should not find allegations

---

[47]   William Inglis & Sons Baking Co. v. ITT Continental Baking Co., 461 F.Supp. 410 (N.D.Cal.1978), affirmed in part, reversed in part, 668 F.2d 1014 (9th Cir. 1981), cert. denied, 459 U.S. 825, 103 S.Ct. 57 (1982). Even the plaintiff's plant was sold to a competitor who remained in business after the plaintiff went bankrupt. For an analysis of the market in the *Inglis* case, see Herbert Hovenkamp & Avarelle Silver-Westrick, Predatory Pricing and the Ninth Circuit, 1983 Arizona State L.J. 443, 464–67.

of predatory pricing credible when the alleged predator is incapable of successfully pursuing a predatory scheme.[48]

In its 1993 *Brooke* decision the Supreme Court dismissed a predation claim under the Robinson-Patman Act after its structural analysis indicated that "recoupment"—or post-predation recovery of the expense of predatory pricing—was unlikely.[49]

In *A.A. Poultry* the Seventh Circuit held that if structural evidence indicated a healthy competitive market, with repeated entry and a likely market share under ten percent, then the complaint should be dismissed without inquiry into the relationship between the defendant's prices and costs.[50] A later Seventh Circuit decision then held that predatory pricing claims should be regarded as implausible unless the defendant "already has monopoly power" at the time of the alleged predatory campaign.[51]

Finally, the length of any claimed period of predatory pricing is relevant. Plaintiffs are quite naturally inclined to allege long periods of predation, because their damages are usually based on lost profits during the predatory period, up to the maximum permitted by the antitrust statute of limitation, which is four years. But the longer the period of alleged predation, the less plausible the basic claim, simply because predatory pricing is such an extraordinarily expensive strategy. Markets have so many uncertainties that it is generally difficult for firms to plan such things more than a few months in advance. Further, the longer the period of predation, the longer the required period of monopoly sales to make the predation profitable.[52] In the *Matsushita* case, the Supreme Court expressed disbelief that an alleged predatory pricing scheme could have lasted two decades.[53] Indeed, when considered *ex ante*, it seems quite inconceivable that a firm would embark on a strategy of loss selling for as much as two years, if it anticipates that this duration will be needed to dispatch the victim. In *Brooke* the Supreme Court noted the implausibility of

---

[48]   Cargill v. Monfort of Colo., 479 U.S. 104, 119, 107 S.Ct. 484, 494 (1986). See also Matsushita Electric Indus. Co. v. Zenith Radio Corp., 475 U.S. 574, 585 n. 8, 106 S.Ct. 1348, 1355 n. 8 (1986) (defining predation as activity undertaken by a firm with "a dominant share of the relevant market").

[49]   Brooke Group Ltd. v. Brown & Williamson Tobacco Corp., 509 U.S. 209, 113 S.Ct. 2578 (1993). See § 8.8.

[50]   A.A. Poultry Farms v. Rose Acre Farms, 881 F.2d 1396 (7th Cir. 1989), cert. denied, 494 U.S. 1019, 110 S.Ct. 1326 (1990).

[51]   American Academic Suppliers v. Beckley-Cardy, 922 F.2d 1317, 1319 (7th Cir. 1991).

[52]   See Kenneth Elzinga & David Mills, Testing for Predation: Is Recoupment Feasible?, 34 Antitrust Bull. 869 (1989).

[53]   Matsushita Electric Indus. Co. v. Zenith Radio Corp., 475 U.S. 574, 591, 106 S.Ct. 1348, 1358 (1986).

claims of lengthy predation, but it did not indicate that the eighteen month predation period alleged in that case was too long.[54] In the Spirit Airlines case, by contrast, the 6th Circuit found a predation claim by a tiny airline against a much larger rival to be highly plausible. Gate access requirements made entry barriers very high and the recoupment period in this case was very short.[55]

§ 8.8   Predatory Pricing and the Robinson-Patman Act

Predatory pricing can also violate § 2 of the Clayton Act, which was amended in 1936 by the Robinson-Patman Act. The Act forbids sales of the same product at two different prices under certain conditions. Robinson-Patman lawsuits brought by competitors alleging price predation are known as "primary-line" cases.[56] These applications are largely governed by the original language created in 1914 when the Clayton Act was passed, rather than the 1936 Robinson-Patman Act amendments.

The framers of the Clayton Act adhered to a peculiar "recoupment" theory of predatory pricing. They realized that extended periods of loss selling made predation costly. They concluded that a predator "must of necessity recoup its losses in the particular communities or sections where [its] commodities are sold below cost or without a fair profit by raising the price of this same class of commodities above their fair market value in other sections or communities * * *."[57]

In the view of the Robinson-Patman Act's framers, most predators were large firms that operated in several geographic markets. Their victims were small firms that operated in only one. Under this recoupment theory a predator could "subsidize" its below-cost sales in one market by raising its price in a different market. Predation would thereby be cost-free.

The most obvious criticism of this theory is that a reasonable profit-maximizing firm would *already* be charging its profit-

---

[54]   *Brooke Group*, 509 U.S. at 231, 113 S.Ct. at 2592.

[55]   Spirit Airlines, Inc. v. Northwest Airlines, Inc., 431 F.3d 917, 929–930, 950–951 (6th Cir. 2005) (defendant recouped its predation investment "within months of Spirit's exit from the market").

[56]   15 U.S.C.A. § 13(a): "It shall be unlawful for any person * * * to discriminate in price between different purchasers of commodities of like grade and quality * * * where the effect of such discrimination may be substantially to lessen competition or tend to create a monopoly * * *."

[57]   Senate Report No. 698, 63d Cong., 2d Sess. 3 (1914). This "recoupment" theory of predatory pricing is at least a generation older than the Clayton Act. See Henry Stimson, Trusts, 1 Harv.L.Rev. 132, 134 (1887).

maximizing price in each market in which it operated. In that case a price increase in any market would produce less, not more revenue.

The Robinson-Patman Act may, however, require A to make a hard choice. It can cut price in one market only by making matching cuts in other markets. This could make predation much more expensive. Further, predatory pricing is difficult to identify: it requires a sophisticated knowledge of cost figures that are generally in the exclusive control of the predator and may not become available until after an action has been filed. Price differences, however, are easily detectable: if A sells its output at 80 cents in market #3 and at $1.00 in markets #1 and #2, competitors will know almost immediately.[58] The problem is that this still does not tell us whether the lower price is predatory.

Utah Pie Co. v. Continental Baking Co., one of the most criticized antitrust decisions of the Supreme Court, was such a case.[59] The defendants were three, independently-acting sellers of frozen pies, each of whom had less than 20% of the relevant market.[60] The plaintiff's market share was about 50%. The evidence showed a period of intense competition in which prices went down, although the plaintiff continued to show a profit throughout the complaint period.[61] The defendants actively competed for customers, not only with the plaintiff, but also with each other.[62] The defendants' violation was to sell pies in the Salt Lake City market at a lower price than they sold them in other cities. The Court never explained what would have happened if the three defendants had driven the plaintiff out of business: they still would have been in competition with each other. Further, the court did not discuss the relationship between the defendants' prices and their costs, except to observe that some prices were "below cost."[63] In *Utah Pie* the Supreme Court almost certainly used the Robinson-Patman Act to condemn hard competition rather

---

[58] See 14 Antitrust Law ¶¶ 2332, 2341 (4th ed. 2019); Herbert Hovenkamp, Judicial Reconstruction of the Robinson-Patman Act: Predatory Differential Pricing, 17 U.C. Davis L.Rev. 309 (1983).

[59] Utah Pie Co. v. Continental Baking Co., 386 U.S. 685, 87 S.Ct. 1326 (1967).

[60] The relevant market was frozen dessert pies in Salt Lake City, Utah.

[61] At the beginning of the complaint period the market share of plaintiff Utah Pie was 66.5%. The market shares of the defendants were: Carnation, 10.3%; Continental, 1.3%; Pet, 16.4%. By the end of the complaint period the plaintiff's share had dropped to 45.3%, but it was still making a profit. Pet's share had risen to 29.4%. *Utah Pie*, 386 U.S. at 692, n. 7, 87 S.Ct. at 1330.

[62] Id. at 695, 87 S.Ct. at 1332.

[63] Id. at 703 n. 14, 87 S.Ct. at 1336 n.14.

than predation. The result was to protect the plaintiff's monopoly position and force consumers to pay a higher price.[64]

One way to avoid the anticompetitive trap of *Utah Pie* is to interpret the Robinson-Patman Act to condemn differential pricing when it is predatory but tolerate or even encourage it when it is competitive. But how does a court tell the difference? By determining if the sales in the low-price market were made below cost and with the reasonable expectation that they would dispatch or discipline competitors in that market so that the predator could charge monopoly profits in the future.

In its important *Brooke* decision,[65] the Supreme Court responded to these developments in several ways: (1) it essentially (although not expressly) overruled *Utah Pie*; (2) it held that the fundamental inquiry in primary-line Robinson-Patman cases was the same as in Sherman Act predatory pricing cases—namely, whether the plaintiff is charging below cost prices today in order to earn monopoly profits tomorrow; (3) however, it found one important difference between Sherman Act and Robinson-Patman Act predatory pricing—the former applies only to predatory pricing that facilitates single-firm monopoly, but the latter applies to predatory pricing that might facilitate oligopoly as well; (4) it emphasized the importance of structural issues; (5) it made pricing below cost dispositive, although it declined to identify the relevant measure of cost; and (6) it held that below cost prices (in this case, below AVC) plus the clearest possible manifestations of anticompetitive intent were not sufficient to trigger liability; the plaintiff must also show that post-predation monopoly profits made the predation profitable, or else that the predator could reasonably anticipate such profitability at the time it embarked on the predatory pricing scheme.

The *Brooke* case arose in the highly concentrated cigarette industry, where six firms dominated the market. Philip Morris, the largest, commanded a 40% share, and R.J. Reynolds had about 28%. The defendant, Brown & Williamson (B & W) was the third largest firm, with a market share of about 12%. The plaintiff Liggett & Myers (Liggett), formerly the Brooke Group, was small and struggling with a market share of 2.3% at the beginning of the period. The industry was a "textbook" oligopoly, with prices moving in lockstep through

---

[64]   See Ward Bowman, Restraint of Trade by the Supreme Court: the *Utah Pie* Case, 77 Yale L.J. 70 (1967); Kenneth Elzinga & Thomas Hogarty, *Utah Pie* and the Consequences of Robinson-Patman, 21 J.L. & Econ. 427 (1978).

[65]   Brooke Group Ltd. v. Brown & Williamson Tobacco Corp., 509 U.S. 209, 113 S.Ct. 2578 (1993).

twice yearly price increases.[66] However, overall demand for cigarettes was declining as a result of controversies about health, and the firms were developing substantial excess capacity.

In 1980 Liggett introduced a generic, unadvertised cigarette sold in a simple black and white box which it sold for some 30% less than the general price. The insertion of price competition into this tightly oligopolistic industry was unprecedented and succeeded immediately. Other oligopolists felt obliged to respond in kind. First, R.J. Reynolds repackaged one of its brands as a generic and cut the price as well. Then the defendant B & W entered with a generic packaged in an identical box to Liggett's box and began to undercut Liggett's price. During an 18 month price war which ensued, B & W allegedly cut its prices substantially lower than average variable cost. The record was filled with memorandum evidence to the effect that B & W's purpose was to discipline Liggett and force it to get its price up to an oligopoly level. Eventually B & W succeeded, since Liggett could not sustain the below cost pricing. The price of generic cigarettes rose and stabilized at oligopolistic levels, somewhat below the price of premium cigarettes but at a much smaller discount than previously.

Liggett sued under the Robinson-Patman Act, because B & W's price cuts were effectuated through promotional discounts that were given to different distributors in varying degrees; as a result there was price "discrimination," or two different prices, under that statute. Although it received a substantial damage award in the district court, the judge set the judgment aside and the Fourth Circuit affirmed, holding essentially that B & W's 12% market share made predation implausible.

The Supreme Court affirmed, although on different grounds. It began with the premise that the Robinson-Patman Act must be interpreted in a manner consistent with other antitrust statutes. As a result, the fundamental inquiry in Sherman Act and Robinson-Patman predatory pricing cases was the same: does the evidence indicate that the defendant engaged in predatory pricing with the reasonable expectation that present below-cost prices would be more than offset by future monopoly (or oligopoly) prices?[67] The one important difference was that the Sherman Act, which reaches "monopolizing" conduct, focuses on single firm conduct calculated to achieve monopoly profits. By contrast, the "substantially lessen

---

[66]   See id. at 2599 (Stevens, J., dissenting); see Frederic M. Scherer & David Ross, Industrial Market Structure and Economic Performance 250 (3d ed. 1990), upon which the Court relied.

[67]   *Brooke,* 509 U.S. at 222–223, 113 S.Ct. at 2587–2588.

competition" language of Robinson-Patman permits other kinds of anticompetitive results, such as predation that might facilitate or preserve oligopolistic price coordination.[68]

Under either statute, however, the plaintiff must show that prices were below cost:

> As a general rule, the exclusionary effect of prices above a relevant measure of cost either reflects the lower cost structure of the alleged predator, and so represents competition on the merits, or is beyond the practical ability of a judicial tribunal to control without courting intolerable risks of chilling legitimate price-cutting.[69]

The Court did not specify the appropriate measure of cost, but the parties had assumed that it was average variable cost.[70]

In addition to showing below cost prices, however, the plaintiff must also demonstrate "that the competitor had a reasonable prospect, or, under § 2 of the Sherman Act, a dangerous probability, of recouping its investment in below-cost prices."[71] As the Court noted:

> Recoupment is the ultimate object of an unlawful predatory pricing scheme; it is the means by which a predator profits from predation. Without it, predatory pricing produces lower aggregate prices in the market, and consumer welfare is enhanced. Although unsuccessful predatory pricing may encourage some inefficient substitution toward the product being sold at less than its cost, unsuccessful predation is in general a boon to consumers. * * *[72]

In order to determine whether such recoupment is possible, the plaintiff must show not only that the intended target of predatory pricing would give in and either exit the market or raise prices; it must also show that "there is a likelihood that the predatory scheme alleged would cause a rise in prices above a competitive level that would be sufficient to compensate for the amounts expended on the predation, including the time value of the money invested in it."[73] This showing "requires an estimate of the cost of the alleged

---

[68]   Ibid.

[69]   Id. at 223, 113 S.Ct. at 2588.

[70]   Id. at 223 n. 1, 113 S.Ct. at 2588 n. 1.

[71]   Brooke Group Ltd. v. Brown & Williamson Tobacco Corp., 509 U.S. 209, 224, 113 S.Ct. 2578, 2588 (1993).

[72]   Ibid.

[73]   Ibid.

predation and a close analysis of both the scheme alleged by the plaintiff and the structure and conditions of the relevant market."[74]

The Court then accepted in principle that predation in order to facilitate oligopoly could violate the Robinson-Patman Act. However, where the beneficiaries of predation are a group of firms rather than a single firm, the predators must "agree on how to allocate present losses and future gains among the firms involved, and each firm must resist powerful incentives to cheat on whatever agreement is reached."[75]

Brooke considerably increases the plaintiff's burden in a predatory pricing case, whether under the Sherman Act or the Robinson-Patman Act. If the plaintiff cannot show a substantial likelihood that the defendant would have enjoyed post-predation monopoly profits, then summary judgment is appropriate, notwithstanding prices lower than average variable cost and clear evidence of predatory intent. In this sense, *Brooke* is a "structural" case and carries predatory pricing analysis out of the area of price-cost relationships into the area of post-predation recoupment.

At the same time, the *Brooke* decision, just as the cases challenging tacit collusion directly,[76] underscores the absolute ineffectiveness of the antitrust laws in dealing with oligopoly. The judicial tendency is to "fly speck"—to look for deviations from perfect lock step pricing or other regimentation as indicating that the plaintiff's oligopoly theory is too weak. But no oligopoly is perfect. Indeed, it is doubtful that an oligopoly exists that would satisfy the *Brooke* Court's standard for proving predatory pricing in an oligopolistic market. The defendant need only show that a non-trivial number of secret discounts occur, and that nonprice competition exists. But only in textbooks do oligopolists succeed in charging everyone precisely the same supracompetitive price. In the real world, oligopoly serves as a device by which firms divide up customers, obtaining high prices from the small, poorly informed or previously committed. Others will negotiate more advantageous treatment. This does not mean that the oligopoly is performing badly. It simply means that oligopoly markets confront change and diversity, just as other markets. Notwithstanding that, the cigarette oligopoly at issue had been extremely durable.

---

[74]   Ibid., citing Kenneth Elzinga & David Mills, Testing for Predation: Is Recoupment Feasible?, 34 Antitrust Bull. 869 (1989).

[75]   Id. at 227, 113 S.Ct. at 2590, citing Matsushita Electric Indus. Co. v. Zenith Radio Corp., 475 U.S. 574, 588–590, 106 S.Ct. 1348, 1356, 1358 (1986).

[76]   See § 5.6.

Brooke Group's largely factual conclusion that recoupment is less likely in oligopoly setting than in monopoly settings seems quite wrong and should be revisited. Oligopolies put firms to the choice whether it is more profitable to cooperate or to defect, which is hardly the same thing as threatening them with destruction if they do not successfully resist. In oligopoly, predation is a tool of discipline, not of destruction. *Brook Group* reflects a disbelief in oligopoly theory that was a hallmark of Chicago School economics in the 1960s and 1970s but that has been thoroughly repudiated today.[77]

§ 8.9   More Complex Exclusionary Pricing Strategies, Particularly Discounts

This section briefly examines pricing practices that do not clearly fit within the traditional "predatory pricing" definition. In some cases the practices have been analogized to predatory pricing, but in others they are treated more like tying or exclusive dealing.

8.9a.   Quantity and Loyalty Discounts

Suppose the defendant offers buyers a discount that increases continuously as the firm's aggregate purchases increase over a one year period. Alternatively, suppose that the discount increases as the buyer's share of purchases from the defendant increases. For example, a buyer might get a 5% discount if it purchases 25% of its needs from the defendant, a 7% discount if it purchases 50% of its needs from the defendant, and so on.

Of course, these discounts could be predatory pricing if the discounted price satisfied the tests for prices below cost and recoupment that the courts generally employ.[78] But let us suppose that even the price receiving the largest discount is fully profitable—that is, above the defendant's average total cost. Can the price nevertheless be anticompetitive and unlawful? Most courts have approved simple, above cost quantity discounts—that is, where the discount is attached to the gross number of units that someone purchases.[79] To be sure, a quantity discount might induce a customer to purchase more from a single seller. For example, a buyer who needs 100 automobiles for its fleet might be induced to purchase all 100 from a single manufacturer rather than 50 each from two different manufacturers if the first manufacturer offers a quantity discount. But it is not easy to see anything anticompetitive in this

---

[77]   See Herbert Hovenkamp and Fiona M. Scott Morton, Framing the Chicago School of Antitrust Analysis, ___ Penn. L. Rev. ___ (2020) (forthcoming), available at https://papers.ssrn.com/sol3/papers.cfm?abstract_id=3481388.

[78]   See § 8.5.

[79]   E.g., Barry Wright Corp. v. ITT Grinnell Corp., 724 F.2d 227 (1st Cir. 1983).

strategy. Rival sellers can make the same offer. About the only thing we can say about quantity discounts is that they encourage buyers to aggregate particular purchases rather than spread them around.

The market share or "loyalty" discount has been somewhat more controversial, and a good case can be made for condemnation in some cases even if no price ever falls below cost. Such discount strategies typically tag the discount to the purchaser's taking a certain percentage of its needs from the seller. For example, the buyer might get a 5% discount for purchasing at least 80% of its needs from the seller, and a 10% discount for purchasing at least 90% of its needs from that seller. Often these discount schemes have multiple tiers, and often they aggregate purchases over an extensive time period, such as one year. In that case they may take the form of a rebate that will be given to a buyer at the end of the year if it has purchased at least the specified percentage from the seller.

If the discount is attached to a purchaser's taking 100% of its needs from a seller then we are looking at a kind of quasi exclusive dealing. Indeed, the exclusive dealing provision contained in § 3 of the Clayton Act explicitly applies to a seller who offers a "discount from, or rebate upon" its price in exchange for the buyer's promise not to deal with a competitor.[80] As developed in Chapter 10, exclusive dealing is tested under the rule of reason. Most of it is lawful and is an everyday occurrence (for example, most car dealers sell only a single manufacturer's brand of new cars and most fast food franchises sell only the products supplied or authorized by their franchisors). However, a few are unlawful if they are unreasonably exclusionary, which does not require a showing of prices below cost.

When the specified market share for the discount is less than 100%, then the name "exclusive dealing" does not fit as well. Of course, there is still an agreement between the seller and buyer, so the cases routinely involve challenges under both § 1 and § 2 of the Sherman Act.

In the *Concord Boat* case the Eighth Circuit refused to condemn Brunswick's policy of giving boat builders a discount if they purchased a specified minimum percentage of their motors from Brunswick.[81] The discounts were not alleged or shown to bring motor prices below cost and the court observed that a customer could switch "at any time" to a different supplier who offered an equally good deal. Indeed, in this case the prices were stated to be so far above cost that the plaintiffs, who were purchasers, were asking for overcharges as

---

[80]   15 U.S.C.A. § 14.

[81]   See, e.g., Concord Boat Corp. v. Brunswick Corp., 207 F.3d 1039 (8th Cir.), cert. denied 531 U.S. 979, 121 S.Ct. 428 (2000).

damages. In that case, however, it is hard to see how the price can be "exclusionary." By contrast in *ZF Meritor* the Third Circuit held that a more generalized "rule of reason" approach more akin to exclusive dealing should be applied to such discounting practices rather than a price/cost test. It then largely affirmed a jury's verdict for the plaintiff, notwithstanding that none of the defendant's prices were shown to be below its costs.[82] A dissenter objected that if the prices were in fact above the defendant's costs an equally efficient rival would have been able to match them.[83]

One rationale for condemning loyalty discounts that are nominally above cost arises if a significant portion of the purchases from the dominant firm are "nondiscretionary," in the sense that customer demand for this manufacturer is so strong and invariant that the intermediary has no choice but to stick with the dominant firm's product for that set of purchases. For example, suppose that boaters are divided into two types. Sixty percent have extremely strong preferences for Bruswick motors and will not substitute; the remaining forty percent are more price sensitive and will shop for the best deal. Now Brunswick offers a market share discount that tops out at 90% of purchases. In that case the boat builder who takes less than 90% of its needs from Brunswick loses the discount not only on the last few motors but also on the 60% of motors that it must purchase from Brunswick anyway. These cases resemble bundled discounts[84] more than loyalty discounts. They might occur when there is a very large installed base of the dominant firm's technology and customers have no choice but to purchase complimentary goods that are consistent with this technology.[85]

In *Allied Orthopedic,* the Ninth Circuit rejected discounting practices challenged under both §§ 1 and 2 of the Sherman Act.[86] The product in question was pulse oximetry devices that collect information about a hospital patient's heart and blood oxygen and transmit this information to a screen. Tyco sold these devices to hospitals principally through hospital group purchasing organizations (GPOs), whose contracts typically provided for discounts conditioned on a hospital's purchase of minimum market shares. Hospitals were free to purchase elsewhere, although they

---

[82]   ZF Meritor, LLC v. Eaton Corp., 696 F.3d 254, 267 (3d Cir. 2012).

[83]   Id. at 311–312.

[84]   See § 8.9b.

[85]   See, e.g., Masimo Corp. v. Tyco Health Care Group, 350 Fed. Appx. 95 (9th Cir. 2009) (hospitals forced to purchase minimum amount of Tyco sensors which were used with very large installed base of Tyco monitors).

[86]   Allied Orthopedic Appliances Inc. v. Tyco Health Care Group LP, 592 F.3d 991 (9th Cir. 2010).

could lose Tyco's discount if they purchased more than a specified percentage elsewhere. Even Tyco's fully discounted prices were not alleged to be below cost; to the contrary, the plaintiffs were purchasers seeking damages for overcharges on the theory that the prices contained an element of monopoly markup. Tyco had at least two rivals, Masimo and GE.

The Ninth Circuit found it "significant that the market-share discount and sole-source" "agreements did not contractually obligate Tyco's customers to purchase anything from Tyco."[87] At least one of the rivals was selling generic sensors at a lower price than Tyco's price and the plaintiff's expert "never explained why price-sensitive hospitals would adhere to Tyco's market-share agreements when they could purchase less expensive generic sensors instead." In sum, "any customer subject to one of Tyco's market-share discount agreements could choose at anytime to forego the discount offered by Tyco and purchase from a generic competitor."[88]

The single-product discounting decisions are undoubtedly influenced by the fact that in the last two decades the Supreme Court has considered three types of pricing strategies involving single products—simple predation in *Brooke Group*, predatory purchasing in *Weyerhaeuser*, and price squeezes in *linkLine*.[89] In all three it has made "cost" the benchmark. While cost-based tests make administration easier, they almost certainly overlook many instances of anticompetitive behavior. Notwithstanding its technical softness, the Third Circuit's more open ended approach outlined in *ZF Meritor* seems best calculated to address the full range of issues.

8.9b.   Package Pricing and Bundled Discounts

8.9b1.   *The Varieties of Bundled Discounts*

Discounts are often attached to a buyer's purchase of two different things together, and packaging of this sort can arise in a wide variety of circumstances. A bundled discount may be a way that a seller competes, by offering to throw an extra good into a deal rather than cutting the price. Alternatively, it may be a way of spreading revenue. For example, a seller may offer a primary good at an

---

[87]   Id. at 996.

[88]   Id. at 997. See Daniel A. Crane, Bargaining Over Loyalty, 92 Tex. L.Rev. 253 (2013).

[89]   For simple predation see § 8.3, Brooke Group Ltd. v. Brown & Williamson Tobacco Corp., 509 U.S. 209, 210, 113 S.Ct. 2578, 2581 (1993); for predatory purchasing see § 8.10, Weyerhaeuser Co. v. Ross-Simmons Hardwood Lumber Co., Inc., 549 U.S. 312, 127 S.Ct. 1069 (2007); for price squeezing see § 7.6b; and Pacific Bell Tel. Co. v. LinkLine Commc'ns, Inc., 555 U.S. 438, 451–452, 129 S.Ct. 1109, 1120 (2009).

extremely low price, perhaps even zero, conditioned on the buyer's agreement to purchase aftermarket goods or supplies from that seller.[90] Finally, a seller may offer a lower price to those buyers who purchase the seller's full line of products or some subset of two or more products.

As an example of the first situation, suppose that Ford's costs for a particular model are $25,000 and the market price is $27,000. During a period in which competition is intensifying Ford responds by including a car stereo system at no additional charge, even though the system costs $500. The result seriously injures a manufacturer of aftermarket car stereos, who can no longer profitably sell such stereos to purchasers of Ford automobiles. It claims predatory pricing. Has Ford sold at "below cost"?

If we look only at the price of the stereo system, Ford has clearly sold it at a price (zero) lower than any measure of cost. But if we look at the price of the car-plus-stereo, it is fully profitable. On these facts, Ford should not be convicted of predatory pricing. First, oligopolists typically compete not by cutting price but by adding quality or product variety, and we do not want to undermine this avenue of competition. Second, a contrary rule would invite antitrust plaintiffs to break products down into their constituent parts, claiming that while the package as a whole was sold at a price above cost, this or that component was not. Third, the strategy of including the stereo is fully sustainable in the sense that even after the stereo is included, the cost of the car (now $25,500) is still considerably less than the price. The courts are divided on the issue.

Bundled discounts might be thought to threaten competition when the dominant firm makes several goods while rivals make only one good or perhaps some subset of the dominant firm's offering. For example, in *LePage's* the defendant made a variety of office products and gave wholesale purchasers a discount that was aggregated over the variety of products they bought.[91] In that case the rival producing a single product may be able to match the defendant's effective price only by offering a discount on its single product that is equal to the discount given on the entire package offered by the defendant. To illustrate, suppose that 3M supplied a large retailer with Scotch tape, Post-it notes, and staples. The retailer ordinarily uses $100,000 of each of these products per year, and 3M offers an aggregated discount

---

[90]   E.g., Kentmaster Mfg. Co. v. Jarvis Products Corp., 146 F.3d 691 (9th Cir. 1998), amended, 164 F.3d 1243 (9th Cir. 1999) (defendant sold commercial meat cutters at price of zero but buyers had to purchase its replaceable cutting blades for the life of the equipment; no violation).

[91]   LePage's v. 3M, 324 F.3d 141 (3d Cir. 2003) (en banc), cert. denied, 542 U.S. 953, 124 S.Ct. 2932 (2004).

of 10% provided that the buyer takes $300,000 in any combination of all three products. An equally efficient tape manufacturer could match the tape discount. But by purchasing its tape from LePage's the retailer would also be losing discount on the Post-it notes and the staples. Indeed, in an extreme case LePage's could steal the sale only by offering a 30% discount on its tape, sufficient to match 3M's discounted tape price as well as the lost discount on the Post-its and the staples. In sum, the smaller the subset of goods that the competitor offers, the larger the proportionate discount it will have to offer in order to match the dominant firm's bundled price. By contrast, if the plaintiff and the defendant both sell the full range of goods then ordinary predatory pricing rules should apply.[92]

8.9b2. The "Attribution" Test for Bundled Discounts

In *LePage's* the Third Circuit sustained a verdict for the plaintiff without any requirement of below cost pricing. Other decisions have disagreed.[93] The *LePage's* court believed that bundled discount resembled tying more than predatory pricing. The defendant is simply bundling the goods together by using a discount rather than an absolute bundling requirement. To be sure, the bundled discount cases do not have the look and feel of predatory pricing. Neither the defendant's individual prices nor its bundled price is below cost. As a result the prices are fully "sustainable," in the sense that they are profitable and the seller can keep selling in this fashion indefinitely.

In light of this some decisions subsequent to *LePage's* have adopted an "attribution test" in order to determine whether a bundled discount really has exclusionary power, just as an absolute tying contract would have. After all, discounts are presumptively a good thing and we do not want to condemn them without good reason for thinking that they exclude rivals unreasonably. Under the attribution test one simply attributes the entire discount on all products in the package to the product for which exclusion is claimed. If the resulting price is less than the defendant's cost, then the package discount is exclusionary as against a rival who makes only the excluded product.[94]

To illustrate, suppose the defendant's costs of two products are A=$6 and B=$4. Its standalone prices for the two goods are A=$9 and

---

    [92]   See Aerotec Int'l., Inc. v. Honeywell Int'l, Inc., 4 F.Supp.3d 1123 (D.Ariz. 2014) (discussing this point).

    [93]   E.g., F.T.C. v. Church & Dwight Co., Inc., 665 F.3d 1312 (D.C. Cir. 2011) (dicta indicating that *LePage's* decision condemning bundled discounting without any showing of prices below a relevant measure of cost is not the law of the Second Circuit and has been widely criticized).

    [94]   See Cascade Health Solutions v. PeaceHealth, 515 F.3d 883 (9th Cir. 2008) (applying attribution test).

B=$6, or a total of $15. However, the defendant offers a price of $12 to any purchaser of one A and one B together. Note first that the $12 price is well above the defendant's costs of the two goods, which is $10. But suppose a rival who makes only B and has the same $4 costs, wants to compete? It can offer a price as low as $4, but in that case the customer will have to pay the standalone price of $9 for A, bringing the total to $13. The only way the rival can compete with the defendant's bundle is by offering B at a price of $3 or less, which is less than the rival's costs. In sum, this pricing scheme can exclude even an equally efficient rival who operates in only a subset of the grouping of sales covered by a bundled discount.

The attribution test is economically identical to asking whether the *incremental* price of the bundle when product B is added is sufficient to cover B's incremental cost.[95] The reason the bundle in the previous illustration is exclusionary is because the defendant charged $3 more for the AB package than for A alone, even though B cost it $4. This "incremental cost" test is actually more accurate than the "attribution" test that the courts use because the attribution test creates false positives when there are economies of joint production or provision.

While the Ninth Circuit applied the attribution test in its *Cascade* decision,[96] it later suggested somewhat ambiguously in *Doe* that the Supreme Court's *linkLine* decision rejecting a price squeeze claim had effectively ruled out all Sherman Act challenges to pricing where the price was above cost.[97] Of course, not only *linkLine* but also *Brooke Group* and *Weyerhaeuser* assumed predatory pricing in a single product. As a result, anything stated in *linkLine* about the appropriate test for *bundled* discounts was dicta. There is no reason for thinking that the Court's references to below cost pricing in *linkLine* had been given with bundled pricing in mind. Nevertheless, it remains the case that a bundled price that flunks the attribution test is typically above cost and fully sustainable. Further, in most circumstances it is a rational and procompetitive act. Supreme Court jurisprudence has been extremely cautious about antitrust challenges to low prices.

It is important to bear in mind that the test for bundled pricing is fundamentally a "bundling" test, not a predatory pricing test. That

---

[95]   On this point, see Erik Hovenkamp & Herbert Hovenkamp, Exclusionary Bundled Discounts and the Antitrust Modernization Commission, 53 Antitrust Bull. 517 (2008).

[96]   See Cascade Health Solutions v. PeaceHealth, 515 F.3d 883 (9th Cir. 2008).

[97]   Doe v. Abbott Labs., 571 F.3d 930, 935 (9th Cir. 2009), discussing Pacific Bell Tel. Co. v. linkLine Commc'ns, Inc., 555 U.S. 438, 451–452, 129 S.Ct. 1109, 1120 (2009). On price squeezes and the *linkLine* decision, see § 7.6b.

is, the gravamen of the complaint is that the defendant is "tying" two things together, but is doing so by a conditional discount rather than by a contract or technological design. The law of tying does not require prices below cost. Rather it requires some condition imposed by the seller that serves to deny competitors access to the market for the second product. For example, if a printer monopolist should tie ink cartridges, market access could be denied to rival cartridge manufacturers even if the monopolist is charging more than cost for both the printers and the ink. By the same token, a bundled discount on the combination of printer plus cartridges can make it impossible for a rival making only cartridges to compete, not because of a contractual obligation, but because of its inability to match the price even though the overall price is above cost. So the attribution test measures only the fact of tying; it does not measure for the other elements of illegality that might serve to justify a tie.

§ 8.10 Predatory Buying and Most-Favored-Nation Clauses in Purchase Agreements

In *Weyerhaeuser* the Supreme Court considered the standard to be applied to alleged predatory purchasing of hardwood sawlogs that were to be processed into finished hardwood. The Ninth Circuit had upheld a district court judgment that the defendant violated § 2 of the Sherman Act by engaging in predatory overbuying—that is, paying a higher price for sawlogs in order to deny access to rival sawmills.[98] The record suggests that while Weyerhaeuser had a dominant position in the market for acquiring and sawing alder logs in the Pacific Northwest, it sold the finished hardwood in a much more competitive market in which it lacked significant power. The lower court had rejected a cost-based test and approved a jury instruction that a violation could be found if the "Defendant purchased more logs than it needed or paid a higher price for logs than necessary. . . ." The instructions apparently provided no additional guidance on how the jury was to identify a price that was "higher . . . than necessary," or how to determine whether the defendant "purchased more logs than it needed."

In its unanimous reversal the Supreme Court held that predatory purchasing must be subject to the same "below cost" and "recoupment" standards as are applied in cases involving predatory selling.[99] The Court also emphasized that during the period

---

[98]   Weyerhaeuser Co. v. Ross-Simmons Hardwood Lumber Co., Inc., 549 U.S. 312, 127 S.Ct. 1069 (2007). For a critique of the economic analysis see Rebecca Haw, Adversarial Economics in Antitrust Litigation: Losing Academic Consensus in the Battle of the Experts, 106 Nw.U.L.Rev. 1261 (2012).

[99]   Id. at 1074. On these requirements in predatory pricing, see §§ 8.2–8.7.

preceding and covered by the litigation Weyerhaeuser had made significant investments in its sawmills for cutting the red alder logs in question, increasing production in every facility that it owned in the area.[100] Weyerhaeuser also used the most modern technology, designed mainly to increase the amount of recoverable hardwood from a red alder log. By contrast, plaintiff Ross-Simmons "appears to have engaged in little efficiency-enhancing investment." The Court noted that the requirement that prices be below-cost was necessary because a rule condemning above-cost pricing as predatory would either end up punishing firms because of their lower cost structure or else require analysis that is beyond the practical ability of the courts to manage.[101] Further, such a rule could chill "legitimate" price cutting. As for recoupment, the Court noted that a putative predator would not likely launch into a program of below-cost sales without a reasonable prospect that it could recoup its investment.[102]

The Court also observed that predatory buying, with its threat of monopsony on the purchasing side of a market, is "analytically similar" to predatory selling:

> A predatory bidder ultimately aims to exercise the monopsony power gained from bidding up input prices. To that end, once the predatory bidder has caused competing buyers to exit the market for purchasing inputs, it will seek to "restrict its input purchases below the competitive level," thus "reduc[ing] the unit price for the remaining input[s] it purchases." The reduction in input prices will lead to "a significant cost saving that more than offsets the profit[s] that would have been earned on the output." Ibid. If all goes as planned, the predatory bidder will reap monopsonistic profits that will offset any losses suffered in bidding up input prices.[103]

Further, the Court observed, the two practices were not merely formally similar. They were also similar in ways that bore on risk and likelihood of success, and the antitrust policy's concerns with overdeterrence. Both predatory selling and predatory purchasing are high risk-low payoff strategies. Further, both price cutting by the seller and aggressive bidding by the buyer are the "very essence of competition,"[104] making it particularly hard to distinguish improper

---

[100]   *Weyerhaeuser,* 127 S.Ct. at 1072.

[101]   Id. at 1074.

[102]   Id. at 1075, citing Brooke Group and Matsushita Electric Industrial Co. v. Zenith Radio Corp., 475 U.S. 574, 106 S.Ct. 1348 (1986).

[103]   *Weyerhaeuser,* 127 S.Ct. at 1075–1076, citing Herbert Hovenkamp, The Law of Exclusionary Pricing, 2 Competition Policy Intl., No. 1, pp. 21, 35 (Spring 2006).

[104]   *Weyerhaeuser,* 127 S.Ct. at 1077.

from legitimate behavior. As to the latter, there are "myriad" legitimate rationales for increasing a purchase price:

> A firm might bid up inputs as a result of miscalculation of its input needs or as a response to increased consumer demand for its outputs. A more efficient firm might bid up input prices to acquire more inputs as a part of a procompetitive strategy to gain market share in the output market. A firm that has adopted an input-intensive production process might bid up inputs to acquire the inputs necessary for its process. Or a firm might bid up input prices to acquire excess inputs as a hedge against the risk of future rises in input costs or future input shortages. There is nothing illicit about these bidding decisions. Indeed, this sort of high bidding is essential to competition and innovation on the buy side of the market.[105]

Because the plaintiffs had conceded that they could not show either recoupment or buying prices so high as to drive the defendant's reselling prices below its costs, the Court rejected the predatory buying theory.[106]

A few courts have considered "most-favored-nation" (MFN) clauses, which in this situation amount to a dominant buyer's insistence that it obtain a price at least as low, or lower than, the price given to any rival. For example, Blue Cross as well as other insurers sometimes ask physicians or pharmacists to promise that they will charge BC patients no more than any other patient paid for the same good or service. As the Seventh Circuit noted in finding no antitrust violation, even a monopsonist is entitled to pay as little as it can.[107] By contrast, in a case brought by the government the court found that similar conduct could violate § 1 of the Sherman Act.[108]

Should antitrust be more concerned when the monopsonist insists on paying *less* than any rival pays? Perhaps. If the seller, such as a hospital, has large fixed and joint costs, it may be in a position to shift these from one group of patients to another. For example, if

---

[105]   Ibid.

[106]   For further analysis, see 3A Antitrust Law ¶ 747 (4th ed. 2015).

[107]   See Blue Cross & Blue Shield United v. Marshfield Clinic, 65 F.3d 1406, 1415 (7th Cir.1995), cert. denied, 516 U.S. 1184, 116 S.Ct. 1288 (1996) (upholding such a contract).

[108]   United States v. Blue Cross Blue Shield of Michigan, 89 F.Supp.2d 665 (E.D.Mi. 2011). Cf. Shane Group, Inc. v. Blue Cross Blue Shield of Michigan, 825 F.3d 299 (6th Cir. 2016) (disapproving settlement in class action case challenging most-favored-nation clauses). And see Health Alliance Plan of Mich. v. Blue Cross Blue Shield of Michigan, 2017 WL 1209099 (E.D. Mi. March 31, 2017) (partially denying motion to dismiss on exclusionary MFN claim).

the hospital's average fixed costs for a hospital stay are $100 per night but a dominant insurer insists on paying $90, the hospital might respond by making some set of more vulnerable patients pay $120. This may be a way of raising the costs of nondominant insurers.[109]

---

[109]   Cf. Elizabeth Granitz & Benjamin Klein, "Monopolization by 'Raising Rivals' Costs': The Standard Oil Case," 39 J.Law & Econ. 1 (1996) (noting that Standard Oil required railroads to give it rebates that brought its transport rates below those of rival oil shippers). On the MFN problem in online markets, see Jonathan B. Baker & Fiona Scott Morton, Antitrust Enforcement Against Platform MFNs, 127 Yale L.J. 20176 (2018).

Chapter 9

VERTICAL INTEGRATION AND VERTICAL MERGERS

Table of Sections

§ 9.1   Introduction

A firm is vertically integrated whenever it performs for itself some function that could otherwise be purchased on the market. A lawyer who washes her own office windows and a pizza parlor that makes its own deliveries are both vertically integrated firms. The examples should illustrate that all firms are vertically integrated to some degree. A rule that prohibited firms from providing for themselves anything that could be procured on the market would impose catastrophic costs on society.

A firm can integrate vertically in three different ways. First, and most commonly, it can enter a new market on its own. The pizza parlor that purchases its own delivery car and the lawyer who washes her own windows in order to cut operating costs have integrated vertically by new entry.

Second, a firm can integrate vertically by acquiring another firm that is already operating in the secondary market. A lawyer wishing to wash her own windows would be unlikely to acquire a window washing firm. However, a gasoline refiner might acquire its own distributors or retail stations; a manufacturer might acquire its own retail outlets; or an electric utility might acquire its own working wind farm.

Third, a firm might enter into a long-term "relational" contract with another firm under which the two firms coordinate certain aspects of their behavior. Although such long-term contracts are market exchanges, they can eliminate many of the uncertainties and risks that accompany frequent uses of the market.

Under a variety of theories, all three forms of vertical integration have been condemned. Vertical integration by new entry generally raises antitrust issues only when the integrating firm is a monopolist. It is analyzed under § 2 of the Sherman Act.[1] Vertical acquisitions are analyzed as mergers, most often under § 7 of the Clayton Act. Vertical integration by long-term contract is often condemned under § 1 of the Sherman Act if it is found to involve resale price maintenance or some other agreement in restraint of trade.[2] Vertical integration by contract can also be condemned as illegal tying or exclusive dealing under § 3 of the Clayton Act or § 1 of the Sherman Act.[3]

Some markets are more conducive to vertical integration by merger rather than by new entry. Vertical integration by new entry increases the capacity of the level into which the integration occurs. If a city has three movie theaters and a major film producer integrates vertically into the theater market by building a new theater, the city will have four. As a general matter, the firm that wants to integrate by new entry must determine whether the new store or plant will be profitable at *post*-entry prices. If minimum efficient output by the new enterprise greatly increases total market output, post-entry prices could be much lower than current prices. By contrast, if the firm integrates into the area by acquiring an existing plant or store, capacity in the area will remain the same and prices may not change.

A firm can integrate vertically in two different directions. If a firm integrates into a market from which it would otherwise obtain some needed raw material or service (such as the utility that purchases a wind farm or the lawyer who washes her own windows), the integration is said to be "backward," or "upstream." If a firm integrates in the direction of the end-use consumer (such as the oil refiner that acquires its own retail stations), the integration is said to be "forward," or "downstream."

---

1   15 U.S.C.A. § 2.

2   See Ch. 11.

3   See Ch. 10.

Both the economic theory and the antitrust law of vertical integration have gone through dramatic cycles. Much of economics and antitrust law prior to 1970 reflected a deep suspicion of vertical integration, and the result was aggressive antitrust rules, including per se illegality for some forms of vertical integration by contract, such as tying and resale price maintenance.[4] That all changed in the 1970s when Chicago School writers such as Robert Bork argued the absolutely contrary position[5]—namely that vertical integration and vertical contracting are virtually never competitively harmful and should be governed by benign antitrust rules approaching per se legality.

Today most people who think seriously about these issues believe that Bork was about as far off on the right as 1960s vintage antitrust policy was on the left.[6] Bork very largely ignored the importance of intellectual property rights, networks, and information technologies—all areas where the opportunities for harm from vertical practices can be significantly greater than Bork imagined. Further, Bork's simple illustrations of vertical integration that involve monopolists did not account for the more varied situations in which vertical integration occurs and where more strategic behavior is possible. When a large firm faces a number of rivals, vertical integration often results in higher rather than lower prices as well as consumer harm.[7]

These newer models are not as hostile toward vertical integration as was the literature from the 1960s and earlier. They generally acknowledge that vertical integration is very often beneficial, primarily because it reduces costs. Their real bite occurs in more concentrated markets where firms interact in more complex ways. At this writing (2021) we are in a period of intellectual foment. A few vertical integration rules, such as the per se rule against tying, are excessively aggressive. Others, however, such as very benign attitudes toward vertical mergers, are quite underdeterrent.

---

[4]   See Herbert Hovenkamp, The Opening of American Law: Neoclassical Legal Thought, 1870–1970, ch. 12 (2015).

[5]   Robert Bork, The Antitrust Paradox: A Policy at War With Itself 225–245 (1978; rev. ed. 1993).

[6]   For more intermediate positions, see Oliver E. Williamson, Markets and Hierarchies: Analysis and Antitrust Implications (1975); George J. Stigler, The Organization of Industry (1983 ed.).

[7]   See, e.g., Michael H. Riordan, Anticompetitive Vertical Integration by a Dominant Firm, 88 Am. Econ. Rev. 1232 (1998); Thomas G. Krattenmaker & Steven C. Salop, Anticompetitive Exclusion: Raising Rivals Costs to Achieve Power Over Price, 96 Yale L.J. 209 (1986); Patrick Rey & Jean Tirole, A Primer on Foreclosure, in 3 Handbook of Industrial Organization 2145 (Mark Armstrong & Robert Porter, eds., 2007).

§ 9.2   The Economics of Vertical Integration

9.2a.   The Implications of Coase's Work; Transaction Cost Economics

Many of our economic insights into vertical integration are a result of the important work of Ronald Coase. In "The Nature of the Firm," published in 1937, Coase laid the foundation for the modern neoclassical rationale for vertical integration.[8] Coase argued that use of markets is expensive, and a firm can avoid these costs by doing certain things for itself. With respect to any decision that the firm must make, it will generally compare the costs of using the market against the cost of internal production. The aggregation of such decisions determine the degree to which a firm is integrated vertically.

Transaction cost economics (TCE) is a form of economic analysis that is heavily indebted to Coase. In a traditional market everyone deals with everyone else. Firms produce and offer their product to anyone who wants to buy it. But in the TCE world, which resembles modern reality much more fully, large firms such as Microsoft, General Motors, and McDonalds, develop specialized products or services. Other, typically smaller firms develop specialized complementary products or services that interact with these products. For example, GM does not just need "engine blocks." Rather, it needs engine blocks that are specifically designed for an automobile it is manufacturing. It can do one of two things: first it can give some other firm specifications, perhaps including some intellectual property licenses, and rely on the other firm to develop a suitable product and price it competitively. If the transaction costs of reaching this agreement are suitably low, GM will likely enter a long-term bargaining relationship with this firm. If the transaction costs are too high, GM will decide to produce the engine blocks itself. By the same token, Microsoft Windows depends on a complex interaction of a number of firms with specialized commitments to a specific computer operating system, to the computers that run it, and to the software and communications technologies that it accesses.

Transaction Cost Economics takes a kind of microscopic look at these relationship and tries to sort out the answers to such questions as when do firms rely on trading partners rather than internal

---

[8]   Ronald H. Coase, The Nature of the Firm, 4 Economica (n.s.) 386 (1937). For more recent Coasian perspectives on the firm and vertical integration, see the other essays collected in Ronald H. Coase, The Firm, the Market, and the Law (1988); The Nature of the Firm: Origins, Evolution, and Development (Oliver E. Williamson & Sidney Winter, eds. 1991); Herbert Hovenkamp, Coase, Institutionalism, and the Origins of Law and Economics, 86 Ind. L.J. 499 (2011).

production? What explains long-term and highly specialized contracts? Why are some contractual arrangements exclusive? The result is a position on questions about vertical mergers, tying, exclusive dealing, resale price maintenance and similar practices that is very considerably more tolerant than the old "hostility tradition" that dominated antitrust analysis in the 1970s and earlier. At the same time, however, it does see somewhat more room for strategic anticompetitive behavior than the old Chicago School saw.

9.2b.   Cost Savings, Technological and Transactional

Most vertical integration results from a firm's desire to reduce its costs. The lawyer washes her own windows because she "cannot afford" to have them done by an outside firm. More often than not, the same motivation impels the manufacturer to build or acquire its own retail stores, or the grocery chain to operate its own dairies or farms. Often little formal economic analysis goes into these decisions. A firm simply becomes dissatisfied with the way someone else is providing a service and believes it can do better itself.

Some cost savings from vertical integration result from technological economies. The classic example is the steel mill combined with a rolling mill. The steel mill produces steel in the form of ingots. The rolling mill presses very hot steel ingots into various shapes used in fabricating bridges, buildings, or other steel structures. If the steel mill sold the ingots on the open market they would have to be transported and reheated—two processes which are very expensive in proportion to the value of the steel. By contrast, the steel mill that operates its own rolling mill can produce ingots as they are needed and roll them in the same plant while they are still hot. Although steel mills and rolling mills are both large machines producing distinct products, most steel mills own and operate their own rolling mills.

Such economies in technology generally cannot be achieved by vertical merger, because they require new construction of fully integrated plants. However, this does not mean that vertical mergers contain little potential for producing efficiencies. Technological efficiencies are only a small proportion of the economies that can be achieved by vertical integration. Firms can also achieve "transactional" efficiencies by avoiding the costs of using the marketplace.[9] In fact, there is no *technological* reason why the steel mill and the rolling mill could not be separate firms located in the same building and having a contractual relationship with each other.

---

[9]   The classic statement of this theory is Coase, Nature of the Firm, *supra*.

Such a relationship would be impractical for other reasons, however: two firms would be forced to deal with each other exclusively even though they likely would have inconsistent goals (each wants to maximize its own profits, and the two may have different profit-maximizing rates of output). The costs of writing a contract that would satisfy both firms and cover every contingency might be very high.[10]

Use of the market can be expensive. Negotiating costs money. Dealing with other persons involves risk, and the less information one firm has about the other, the greater the risk.[11] The two parties to a bargain almost always have different incentives. Suppose a manufacturer of aircraft agrees to buy its aircraft radios from another firm. Once the contract price has been established, the aircraft manufacturer wants the best radio it can get for the price, for that will increase the satisfaction of its aircraft customers at no additional costs to itself. The radio producer, by contrast, wants to produce as inexpensively as possible a radio that satisfies the specifications in the purchase agreement. The firms might try to outline in detail all the specifications of the radio. Such a contract may be negotiated several years before the radios are delivered. The aircraft itself is a developing and changing product, subject to new technology and unforeseen economic constraints. If the contract were drafted to anticipate every possible change, the contract negotiations would be prohibitively expensive. Sooner or later the radio manufacturer will have some discretion—perhaps in whether to use a more expensive component that clearly meets the specifications in the contract, or a cheaper component that is marginal. The radio manufacturer is likely to use the cheaper component if he predicts that it will meet the standard. If he miscalculates, or if the standard is ambiguous, there may be a dispute and perhaps costly litigation.

These problems multiply as the final cost of a product becomes more uncertain, as is frequently the case when projects require ongoing research and development. If the aircraft manufacturer is not purchasing a radio "off the shelf" but is having a new type of radio designed, neither the aircraft producer nor the radio producer knows its final cost. If the aircraft manufacturer insists on a "firm" bid—i.e., if the radio manufacturer is asked to bear the risk of the uncertain final cost—the radio manufacturer will calculate the risk into its bid price. That risk premium may be very large. In sum, the cost of

---

[10]   Oliver Williamson, Markets and Hierarchies: Analysis and Antitrust Implications 83–84 (1975).

[11]   On the relation between information and vertical integration, one of the classic studies is K. Arrow, Vertical Integration and Communication, 4 Collected Papers of Kenneth J. Arrow 185 ([1975] 1984).

specifying everything in advance is often prohibitively high, because people do not have perfect foresight. But any shortfall makes the contractual arrangement incomplete, and may permit each of the parties to engage in strategic behavior that benefits itself at the expense of the other.[12]

One alternative is for the parties to enter a "cost-plus" contract, under which the radio manufacturer develops the radio and adds a specified mark-up to its costs. In that case, however, the radio manufacturer loses its incentive to reduce costs. In fact, the higher its costs, the higher the percentage mark-up will be.

The second alternative is for the radio manufacturer to submit an estimated bid that can be adjusted in the future for "overruns," or unanticipated cost increases. The United States Government, particularly the Department of Defense often purchases equipment under such contracts. Similar problems occur here, however. First, all the information about costs originates with the seller, and the buyer often cannot be sure that the seller is spending the money efficiently. Second, the transaction costs of accounting for and justifying cost overruns with respect to each component in a complex product can be high, perhaps more than the cost of the components themselves.

The best alternative may be for the aircraft manufacturer to produce its own aircraft radios.[13] To be sure, this is not always feasible. If minimum efficient scale (MES) of a radio plant is 1000 units per year, but the aircraft manufacturer produces only 40 aircraft per year, its production costs per radio might far exceed the uncertainty and transaction costs described above. Whether a particular instance of vertical integration will reduce a firm's costs is an empirical question that depends on the structure of the markets and the technology involved in the manufacturing process.[14] Since

---

[12]   The literature on this subject is large and good. In addition to other works of Oliver Williamson cited throughout this chapter, see Oliver E. Williamson, Transaction-Cost Economics: the Governance of Contractual Relations, 22 J.L.Econ. 233 (1979); Ian MacNeil, Contracts: Adjustment of Long-Term Economic Relations Under Classical, Neoclassical, and Relational Contract Law, 72 Nw.U.L.Rev. 854 (1978); Dennis Carlton, Vertical Integration in Competitive Markets Under Uncertainty, 27 J.Indus. Econ. 189 (1979). On the rise of "neoclassical" and later "relational" contracting, see Herbert Hovenkamp, The Opening of American Law: Neoclassical Legal Thought, 1870–1970 (2015) at 124–129.

[13]   For a real world application, see Benjamin Klein, Vertical Integration as Organizational Ownership: the Fisher Body-General Motors Relationship Revisited 213, in The Nature of the Firm (Williamson & Winter eds. 1991), and Ronald H. Coase, The Acquisition of Fisher Body by General Motors, 43 J.L. & Econ. 15 (2000).

[14]   See Benjamin Klein, Vertical Integration as Organization Ownership, 4 J.L. Econ. & Org. 199 (1988).

technology changes through time, incentives for vertical integration change as well.

Asset specificity often creates a motive for vertical integration. As a general proposition, the more specialized productive assets must be, the less satisfactory or competitive an independent market for them will be. For example, so long as the radio can be produced generically for a large number of aircraft, we can expect to see a large and perhaps robustly competitive market for it. But as soon as the radio becomes unique to one or a small number of specialized purchasers, then use of the market becomes more costly. First, the seller must invest in specialized productive facilities that will be used to satisfy only one or a small group of customers. Second, the buyer will probably have to rely on a small group of sellers.[15]

When a firm supplies a certain product or service for itself, the "price" it pays equals the cost of producing the product or service. As a result, *if* a firm can produce the product or service as cheaply as existing independent producers can, then any imperfection in the market for that product or service will make it more expensive to buy than to produce. All markets contain some imperfections. For example, a firm almost always has better information about itself than about other firms. Lack of information about an outside supplier or outlet increases a firm's risks, and therefore its costs. Firms transacting business in the market are inclined to overstate both their capacity and their financial stability. Often the true information is easy to disguise. On the other side, the firm negotiating a contract may often be asked to produce information that it would prefer to keep confidential. Vertical integration enables a firm substantially to solve both these problems of information "impactedness" and confidentiality.

§ 9.3   Plausible Anticompetitive Consequences of Vertical Integration

In a simple case involving an upstream monopolist and a downstream firm who uses the monopolist's product as its only input, a firm cannot increase its market power by vertical integration unless the integration also reduces costs. For example, a monopoly manufacturer of bicycles generally cannot increase its monopoly profits by becoming a distributor or retailer of bicycles as well. The profit-maximizing price of bicycles is determined on the demand side

---

[15]   The theory is summarized in Paul Joskow, Asset Specificity and the Structure of Vertical Relationships: Empirical Evidence 117 in *The Nature of the Firm* (Williamson & Winter eds. 1991); Oliver Williamson, The Vertical Integration of Production: Market Failure Considerations 24, in Oliver Williamson, Antitrust Economics: Mergers, Contracting, and Strategic Behavior (1987).

by the amount that final consumers of bicycles are willing to pay. If the total cost of manufacturing a bicycle and distributing it to a cyclist is $70.00, but the profit-maximizing price is $90.00, the $20.00 in monopoly profits could be claimed by any single monopolist in the distribution chain, provided that the other links in the chain are competitive. If the monopoly manufacturer is already obtaining $20.00 in monopoly profits from sales to distributors, it will not be able to make more monopoly profits by acquiring its own distributor.

9.3a.   Strategic Control of Inputs

Vertical integration in imperfectly competitive markets may permit firms to raise prices by manipulating inputs. This literature generally criticizes the Chicago School analysis of vertical integration by the monopolist for considering only the two extremes of monopoly and perfect competition, and for disregarding the fact that inputs can often be substituted for one another.[16] In cases of oligopoly with differentiated products and inputs that can be used in variable proportions, the story is more complex.

For example, suppose an upstream bauxite monopolist charges a high price for bauxite that is converted into alumina, and then combined with tin to make various aluminum alloys. Importantly, the proportions of bauxite and tin can vary considerably, and many buyers do not care what the precise compound is. We assume tin is sold competitively. Downstream smelters will respond to the bauxite monopoly by using relatively less bauxite and relatively more tin to the degree that customers find the substitution acceptable. This substitution means that the demand for bauxite, and thus its price, tends to go down. By integrating vertically into smelting, the bauxite monopolist can restore the proportions to their previous level, and thus raise the demand for bauxite once again.

The economic effect of vertical integration in this case is twofold: (1) the mixture of inputs may be restored to the optimal, or competitive, level, thus increasing productive efficiency; but (2) the relative size of the monopolized market is enlarged. Which of these effects outweighs the other is an empirical question.

9.3b.   Price Discrimination

Price discrimination occurs when a firm can profitably obtain different rates of return on different groupings of sales. The economic consequences of price discrimination vary from situation to situation.

---

[16]   See Frederic M. Scherer & David Ross, Industrial Market Structure and Economic Performance 522 (3d ed. 1990); Roger Blair & David Kaserman, Law and Economics of Vertical Integration and Control 48–50 (1983).

Suppose that a monopoly manufacturer of Polish sausages discovers that it has two different groups of customers with different demands for sausages. One group purchases the sausages in grocery stores for home consumption. The profit-maximizing price for that group of customers is 25 cents per sausage. The other group of customers buys the sausages from concessionaires at public events such as baseball games. The profit-maximizing price for them is $1.00 per sausage.

If the firm must charge the same price to all buyers, its profit-maximizing price will depend on the circumstances. At one extreme it might charge 25 cents to all customers and make sales in both concessions and grocery stores. However, it might also charge $1.00 per sausage, in which case it will make higher profits from concession sales but lose most grocery store sales. Alternatively, it might find a profit-maximizing price somewhere between 25 cents and $1.00. Where that price lies depends on the marginal cost of the sausages and the relative size and demand elasticities of the two groups of customers.

The firm might make substantially more money by price discriminating—by selling sausages for 25 cents each in grocery stores and for $1.00 each through concessionaires. Any attempt to price discriminate raises two problems, however. First is the Robinson-Patman Act, which might prevent the firm from selling the same product to two classes of buyers at two different prices. The second problem is arbitrage. If grocers were sold sausages for 25 cents each (less their mark-up), but concessionaires were charged $1.00 each (less their mark-up), the concessionaires would have a simple solution. They would go to grocery stores and fill their shopping carts with 25 cent Polish sausages. The sausage maker would end up making all his sales to grocery stores at the lower price.

The solution for the Polish sausage maker is to enter the concessions business itself, either by new entry or else by acquiring an existing concessionaire. Then the manufacturer will be able to retail its sausages directly to baseball fans at $1.00 each, while continuing to make 25 cent sales to grocery stores.

There is no good reason for condemning price discrimination *simpliciter* under the antitrust laws. On the one hand, price discrimination often results in higher output than a monopolist's nondiscriminatory pricing. For example, if the Polish sausage maker were forced to sell all sausages at the same price, it might decide to charge $1.00 and make only the concession sales. In that case many grocers and their customers would be impoverished. On the other hand, any imperfect price discrimination scheme produces a certain amount of inefficiency, both from less-than-competitive output and from the costs of operating the price discrimination scheme itself.

9.3c.   Foreclosure, Raising Rivals' Costs, and Entry Barriers

One of the most durable theories of harm from vertical integration is that it can "foreclose" rivals from a market or raise their costs and lead directly to consumer harm. Today, such explanations are taken much more seriously than they were in the late twentieth century, but they are also easy to exaggerate.

If a manufacturer of shoes acquires a chain of shoe stores it may sell its manufactured shoes only through its own stores, and the stores may stop buying shoes from other manufacturers. Before complete exclusivity would occur on both sides, however, the manufacturer's output and the shoe stores' demand must be roughly the same. If the manufacturer is large, it likely will continue to make some sales to other shoe stores as well. Ordinarily, however, if vertical integration produces lower costs, we would expect the integrated firm to take advantage of these economies by self-dealing up to its fullest available capacity. In that case, vertical integration would injure unintegrated rivals but it would very likely benefit consumers.

Most cases are more complex. For example, suppose that a market dominant hospital should acquire the largest local anesthesiology group or else enter into an exclusive contract for its services. Depending on the anesthesiology group's market share, rival hospitals might be denied adequate anesthesiological services, or competing anesthesiological groups might be denied access to this hospital. While they might not be absolutely excluded from the market, the integration may deny them access to the most favorable trading partners, forcing them to bear higher costs or offer inferior service.

The problem in information technologies can be more severe than in more traditional manufacturing industries. For example, an independent owner of programming, such as digital films, would very likely maximize its profits by licensing as broadly as possible. Digital media can be duplicated indefinitely, so there are no shortages that need to be allocated. Suppose, however, that the media company enters either an exclusive contract or a merger with an internet or satellite program transmitter. Now incentives change. The transmitter may be able to charge more by offering certain program exclusively, and will thus have an incentive to black out or deny programming access to customers who get their programming from a rival transmitter.

§ 9.4   Vertical Mergers and Antitrust Law

Historically, vertical mergers did not fare well under the antitrust laws. Most of the law of vertical mergers was written at a time when protection of small businesses rather than encouragement of efficiency was the underlying antitrust policy.[17]

Early vertical merger decisions drew from the common law of trade restraints, which placed heavy reliance on the defendant's intent. For example, in the 1911 *American Tobacco Co.* case the Supreme Court found that "the conclusion of wrongful purpose and illegal combination is overwhelmingly established" by the defendants' "gradual absorption of control over all the elements essential to the successful manufacture of tobacco products, and placing such control in the hands of seemingly independent corporations serving as perpetual barriers to the entry of others into the tobacco trade."[18]

This emphasis on evil intent prevailed for forty years. In United States v. Yellow Cab Co., the Supreme Court held that a manufacturer of taxicabs (Checker) violated § 1 of the Sherman Act[19] by acquiring cab operating companies in several large American cities, if it intended by the acquisition to suppress competition in the taxi operating market.[20] The Court found that as a result of the acquisition the operating companies might be forced to purchase their taxicabs exclusively from Checker, and other manufacturers of cabs would be excluded from competing for their business. The alleged result was that the cab companies "must pay more for cabs than they would otherwise pay, their other expenditures are

---

[17]   For example, Brown Shoe Co. v. United States, 370 U.S. 294, 82 S.Ct. 1502 (1962), which condemned a vertical merger because it permitted the post-merger defendant to undersell its unintegrated rivals. On this history, see Herbert Hovenkamp, The Opening of American Law: Neoclassical Legal Thought, 1870–1970, Ch. 12 (2015).

[18]   United States v. American Tobacco Co., 221 U.S. 106, 182–83, 31 S.Ct. 632, 649 (1911). The *American Tobacco* trust included horizontal and conglomerate, as well as vertical acquisitions.

[19]   Prior to its 1950 amendments, § 7 of the Clayton Act, which covers most mergers today, did not apply to vertical acquisitions.

[20]   332 U.S. 218, 67 S.Ct. 1560 (1947). The Court later affirmed a lower court finding that there was no such intent. United States v. Yellow Cab Co., 338 U.S. 338, 70 S.Ct. 177 (1949). See also United States v. Paramount Pictures, 334 U.S. 131, 174, 68 S.Ct. 915, 937 (1948), holding that a vertical merger "runs afoul of the Sherman Act if it was a calculated scheme to gain control over an appreciable segment of the market and to restrain or suppress competition, rather than an expansion to meet legitimate business needs * * *."

increased unnecessarily, and the public is charged high rates for the transportation services rendered."

The Court's analysis is perplexing. No vice president has yet figured out how a vertically integrated firm can become rich by selling to itself at an inflated price. More likely, the cab companies (which already had monopolies in the individual cities) were buying taxicabs in a competitive market but charging regulated monopoly prices to taxicab riders. By acquiring the cab companies, Checker was able to transfer these monopoly returns to itself. Alternatively, if the taxicab fares were price-regulated, then Checker could charge supracompetitive prices to its own operating companies, and the increased costs could be shown to the regulatory agency as justification for a fare increase.[21]

In any case, the Court's alternative argument against the merger became more prominent in the case law—namely, that Checker's acquisition of the operating companies excluded other cab manufacturers "from that part of the market represented by the cab companies under [its] control * * *." Anticompetitive "foreclosure" occurs only if one of the integrating firms has a significant market presence. Suppose that eight firms manufacture identical typewriters and fifty firms retail them. If a manufacturer acquires one retailer, the manufacturer likely will begin selling its typewriters through this retailer. This will force some realignment of buyers and sellers—firms that formerly dealt with one of the merging firms may have to find each other and enter new contracts. No one will be foreclosed, however. Product differentiation may change this result to the extent that some transaction relationships become more favorable than others. The 2020 Vertical Merger Guidelines discussed below discuss some of the possibilities.[22]

After 1950 the Supreme Court condemned vertical mergers under the foreclosure theory, even when both merging levels were competitive.[23] In 1950 § 7 of the Clayton Act was amended, in part to clarify that the statute applied to vertical as well as horizontal mergers.[24] More importantly, the legislative history of amended § 7

---

[21]   On vertical integration as a rate regulation avoidance device, see § 9.3d *supra*.

[22]   See § 9.5.

[23]   In 1948, however, the Supreme Court refused to condemn a vertical merger under the foreclosure theory when the vertical acquisition left several alternative buyers and sellers in the market, when one of the merging firms accounted for only 3% of the market for rolled steel, and that firm's previous suppliers could easily switch both their production and their business elsewhere. United States v. Columbia Steel Co., 334 U.S. 495, 507–510, 68 S.Ct. 1107, 1114–1115 (1948).

[24]   Before its 1950 amendments § 7 applied only to mergers that might lessen competition "between" the acquiring and acquired firms. A vertical merger involves firms that were not competitors before the merger. The legislative history of the 1950

reveals that Congress wanted stronger merger standards that would condemn acquisitions in their "incipiency," before they had a chance to work their full evil.

The Supreme Court's first big vertical merger case after § 7 was amended was United States v. E. I. du Pont de Nemours & Co.[25] The action had been filed in 1949 under original § 7, and the amendments did not apply to acquisitions that occurred before 1950. Nevertheless, the Court applied the policy of the Amendments. It found a violation in du Pont's 1917–19 acquisitions of a 23% stock interest in General Motors Co. Du Pont was a manufacturer of finishes and fabrics for automobiles. General Motors, a manufacturer of automobiles, purchased such finishes and fabrics for its manufactured cars. The primary issue, as the Court saw it, was

> whether du Pont's commanding position as General Motors' supplier of automotive finishes and fabrics was achieved on competitive merit alone, or because its acquisition of the General Motors' stock, and the consequent close intercompany relationship led to the insulation of most of the General Motors' market from free competition.[26]

As formulated, this question raised the specter of judicial inquiry into whether a firm's own dealings with upstream parents or downstream subsidiaries were on the competitive merits or simply a consequence of the ownership interest.

The Court went much further in the first vertical merger decision under amended § 7. In Brown Shoe Co. v. United States,[27] it condemned a shoe manufacturer's acquisition of a shoe retailer when the manufacturer's market share was about 5% and the retailer's national market share was about 1%. In justifying condemnation on such small market shares the Court cited a " 'definite trend' among shoe manufacturers to acquire retail outlets," followed by a " 'definite trend' for the parent-manufacturers to supply an ever increasing percentage of the retail outlets' needs, thereby foreclosing other manufacturers from effectively competing for retail accounts." The "necessary corollary" of these trends, concluded the Court, was "the foreclosure of independent manufacturers from markets otherwise open to them." The result was that other shoe manufacturers and retailers were forced to integrate vertically as well.

Celler-Kefauver Amendments to § 7 is discussed in 4 Antitrust Law ¶¶ 902–903, 1002 (4th ed. 2016); and in Brown Shoe Co. v. United States, 370 U.S. 294, 315–23, 82 S.Ct. 1502, 1518–23 (1962).

[25]   353 U.S. 586, 77 S.Ct. 872 (1957).

[26]   Id. at 588–589, 77 S.Ct. at 875.

[27]   370 U.S. 294, 82 S.Ct. 1502 (1962).

What did the Court mean by foreclosure "forcing" vertical integration in a market as atomized as the shoe industry? Clearly it could not mean that independent shoe retailers were unable to find independent manufacturers willing to sell them shoes. In 1963 less than 10% of American shoes were distributed through manufacturer-owned-or-operated stores.[28] The real cause of the "foreclosure" was the efficiency of the vertically integrated firms. By vertically integrating, firms were able to reduce their costs. Competition among vertically integrated firms drove prices below the costs of the unintegrated firms. They were forced to integrate not because outlets or sources of supply were unavailable, but because only vertical integration would enable them to compete with integrated firms.

A related argument against vertical mergers is that they enhance the merging firm's market power by making entry into the industry more costly or more difficult. If incumbents are vertically integrated a prospective entrant may have to enter at two levels instead of one. The Supreme Court relied on this "barrier to entry" argument in Ford Motor Co. v. United States,[29] when it condemned Ford's acquisition of Autolite, a spark plug manufacturer.

The barriers to entry argument must also confront the fact that efficiency itself is a barrier to entry. If vertical integration is efficient—for example, if two processes that formerly cost $30 can be performed for $28.00 by a vertically integrated firm—then vertical integration is a "barrier to entry" in the sense that unintegrated rivals will have higher costs. However, vertical integration in a competitive market which produces no cost savings will not produce a barrier to entry either. If the vertically integrated firm still faces $30.00 in costs, as do its pairs of unintegrated rivals, then entry at each separate level will be as profitable as before.

The arguments have more force, however, when one of the integrating firms has a dominant market position. If the world's only aluminum producer acquires an aluminum fabricator and refuses to sell to independent fabricators, the result will be complete foreclosure for existing fabricators and a substantial entry barrier for potential fabricators—neither will be able to obtain aluminum.

Alternatively, suppose that the aluminum monopolist fears competitive entry. Aluminum requires bauxite for its production, however, and the world contains only two known bauxite fields— Field A and Field B. The aluminum monopolist already owns Field A. By acquiring Field B and refusing to sell bauxite to any competitor,

---

[28]   See John Peterman, The *Brown Shoe* Case, 18 J.L. & Econ. 81, 117 (1975).

[29]   405 U.S. 562, 92 S.Ct. 1142 (1972). For the same theory, see the United States v. American Tobacco Co., 221 U.S. 106, 182–83, 31 S.Ct. 632, 649 (1911).

the aluminum monopolist could delay competitive entry into aluminum production indefinitely. Alternatively, alternative bauxite fields may exist but their product is inferior and requires higher processing costs. In that case the dominant firm will be imposing higher operating costs on rivals, which could either deter them from entering or else permit it to charge higher prices after they are in the market.

The Supreme Court has not decided a vertical merger case since *Ford Motor* in 1972. During that time circuit courts become increasingly critical of the foreclosure and entry barrier theories. For example, in Fruehauf Corp. v. FTC[30] the Second Circuit refused to enforce an FTC ruling condemning a vertical merger under § 7 and ordering divestiture. Fruehauf, the largest manufacturer of truck trailers in the United States, with about 25% of that market, acquired Kelsey-Hayes, which controlled about 15% of the market for heavy duty truck and trailer wheels. The FTC alleged that the acquisition foreclosed about 6% of the market for heavy duty wheels. However, the court was

> unwilling to assume that any vertical foreclosure lessens competition. Absent very high market concentration or some other factor threatening a tangible anticompetitive effect, a vertical merger may simply realign sales patterns, for insofar as the merger forecloses some of the market from the merging firms' competitors, it may simply free up that much of the market * * * for new transactions * * *.

The Court then went on to require some showing of an anticompetitive effect, in addition to the mere fact of foreclosure. The FTC had alleged one anticompetitive effect: that in times of shortage Fruehauf would deny wheels to its competitors in the trailer market. The Court found no evidence that this would happen. It tentatively agreed with the FTC's finding that barriers to entry into the wheel market were high, based on evidence that entry required a minimum investment of $10–$20 million, and that minimum efficient scale for a new plant would be about 9% of the market. However, the Court found no evidence that these barriers would require any new entrant to come into the market at both levels, or would make entry at a single level more difficult.

More recently, the attention in vertical merger cases has shifted away from simple foreclosure, or denial of access, and toward raising rivals' costs.[31] For example, a vertical merger might tie up so much

---

30   603 F.2d 345 (2d Cir. 1979). Quotation at 352 n. 9.

31   On RRC as a monopolistic device, see Michael H. Riordan & Steven Salop, Evaluating Vertical Mergers: A Post-Chicago Approach, 63 Antitrust L.J. 513 (1995).

of a market that a rival is denied sufficient output to attain scale economies. When that happens the rival's costs will rise and the integrator can raise its price as well.

To illustrate, suppose that the relevant universe contains ten identical cable systems, six of which are owned by Firm X, while the others are independent. Further, there are two programmers who compete to supply programming to the ten systems. A program costs $10, which must be recovered in licensing fees. If a programmer licenses to all ten systems, programming fees must be at least $1 per system; if each programmer licenses only half the systems, the fee must be at least $2 per system. Firm X now acquires (or is acquired by) one of the two programmers and the post-merger firm uses only its own programming in its cable systems. As a result, the rival programmer can no longer license to more than four stations, thus requiring it to charge license fees of at least $2.50. The dominant firm can then raise its own fees proportionately.

This was basically the theory of the consent decree that the FTC obtained in the *Time-Warner* case in 1996.[32] The allegation was that a major cable television operator's (TW) acquisition of a major provider of cable television programming (Turner) threatened to prevent rivals in the programming market "from achieving sufficient distribution to realize economies of scale." This would give TW the opportunity to raise its own programming prices, which were passed on to consumers in the form of higher cable rates. Somewhat similarly, the NBC Universal/Comcast joint venture, which was approved by a consent decree,[33] was concerned with Comcast's position as a provider of internet broadband services that was dominant in many areas, and NBC's substantial output of programming that could compete with other forms of internet programming. In part, the firms had to consent that they would not prioritize NBC programming over non-NBC programming.

Information technologies, particularly digital content, can present greater problems of foreclosure or raising rivals' costs than other markets.[34] Video programming is a nonrivalrous good. For example, once *The Irishman* has been produced as a film and digitized, its owner can make an infinite number of copies at almost zero cost. There is no scarce output that must be allocated, and the costs of serving one customer do not rise because someone else is

---

[32] Time-Warner, 5 Trade Reg. Rep. ¶ 24,104 (consent decree, FTC, 1996).

[33] United States v. Comcast Corp., U.S. Dep't of Justice, http://www.justice.gov/atr/case/us-and-plaintiff-states-v-comcast-corp-et-al (Feb. 20, 2011); United States v. Comcast Corp., 2011 WL 5402137 (D.D.C. Sept. 1, 2011).

[34] For fuller discussion, see Herbert Hovenkamp, Antitrust and Information Technologies, 68 Fla. L. Rev. 419 (2016).

being served as well. As a result, a nonintegrated producer of digital programming almost always has an incentive to sell to all customers willing to pay. To be sure, it may profit by price discriminating, but it generally cannot profit by simply withholding programming from a particular class of buyers.

If an independent programmer integrates vertically with an internet access supplier, however, incentives change. The vertically integrated firm may deny programing to customers who are served by a different access supplier in order to induce them to switch. It may also be in a position to bargain for higher access rates, holding out the threat of switching as an inducement. The result might be both higher access prices and reduced access to programming.

In the *AT&T/Time-Warner* vertical merger case the court approved an access supplier's acquisition of a very large holder of digital content, Time Warner, by AT&T, which owned some cable companies as well as DirectTV.[35] In one troublesome conclusion, the district court accepted the defendant's argument that the post-merger firm would not seek to maximize profits overall, but would continue to maximize the profits of Time-Warner standing alone, which it would do by licensing to everyone.[36] Precisely the point of such an acquisition, however, is that the vertical merger would enable the integrated firm to enlarge overall profits by suppressing offerings in the downstream market. For example, it might selectively deny Time-Warner programming to the customers of rival systems in order to get customers to switch to one of its own. The plaintiff's expert relied on a bargaining model, under which the post-merger firm is a profit-maximizer and would be able to use its platform as a lever to either force the customers of rival systems to pay more or else to switch to an AT&T system. Standalone profits for Time-Warner might go down, at least in the short run, but the overall profits of the post-merger firm would rise. In any event the theory that the firm would not maximize total profits is inconsistent with the economic theory of the firm, as well as with the Supreme Court's decision in *Copperweld*, which is that a firm must be viewed as a single entity for antitrust purposes, no matter what its internal structure.[37]

Vertical acquisitions such as *AT&T/Time-Warner* can cause substantial harm by either excluding rivals or raising their costs. One possible fix is to condition the merger on rules that guarantee rival

---

[35]   United States v. AT&T, 916 F.3d 1029 (D.C. Cir. 2019), affirming 310 F.Supp.3d 161 (D.D.C. 2018).

[36]   See 310 F.Supp.3d at 222–223.

[37]   Copperweld Corp. v. Independence Tube Corp., 467 U.S. 752 (1984). See § 4.6.

firms nondiscriminatory access to programming.[38] While such an order may not work in industries where the product is tangible and subject to output constraints, it may produce positive results when the product is nonrivalrous and capable of infinite reproduction, such as digital programming. In such cases the vertical merger gives the acquiring firm everything it needs to improve its own offering, thus realizing the benefits of vertical integration; however, the nonexclusion requirement also helps ensure that the merging firm will not be in a position to restrict distribution anticompetitively.

§ 9.5   The Vertical Merger Guidelines

For many years antitrust enforcers, academics, and even judges have complained that the enforcement agencies need new guidelines for vertical mergers. Guidelines that included vertical mergers were last revised in 1984 at the height of Chicago School hostility toward harsh antitrust treatment of vertical restraints.[39] Finally in 2020, the Agencies issued new vertical merger Guidelines.[40] As of this writing, no judicial decisions have interpreted them.

The Vertical Guidelines borrow heavily from the 2010 Horizontal Merger Guidelines concerning general questions of market definition, entry barriers, partial acquisitions, treatment of efficiencies, and the failing company defense.[41] However, the Vertical Guidelines de-emphasize traditional terminology describing vertical mergers as linking an upstream "market" and a downstream "market." Instead, they use the term "relevant market" to speak of the market that is of competitive concern, and the term "related product" to refer to some product, service, or grouping of sales that is either upstream or downstream from this market, or in some cases a complement.[42] So, for example, if a truck trailer manufacturer should acquire a maker of truck wheels and the market of concern was trailer manufacturing, the Agencies would identify that as the relevant market and wheels as the "related product."[43]

The Guidelines indicate that they will measure markets and market shares in the same way as the Horizontal Merger Guidelines,

---

[38]   E.g. Gregory S. Crawford, et al., The Welfare Effects of Vertical Integration in Multichannel Television Markets, 86 Econometrica 891 (May 2018).

[39]   See 4A Antitrust Law ¶¶ 1005c, 1006h (4th ed. 2014).

[40]   U.S. Dept. of Justice and FTC, Vertical Merger Guidelines (June 30, 2020), available at https://www.ftc.gov/system/files/documents/reports/us-department-justice-federal-trade-commission-vertical-merger-guidelines/vertical_merger_guidelines_6-30-20.pdf.

[41]   See Ch. 12, and DOJ and FTC, Horizontal Merger Guidelines (Aug. 19, 2010), available at https://www.justice.gov/atr/horizontal-merger-guidelines-08192010.

[42]   Id., § 3.

[43]   Cf. Fruehauf Corp. v. FTC, 603 F.2d 345 (2d Cir. 1979).

but that they do not rely on the market share thresholds for presumptive illegality in the horizontal guidelines.[44] Indeed, nothing in the Vertical Guidelines expressly links a presumption of illegality to any particular market share. Nevertheless, at least some of the anticompetitive strategies the Guidelines discuss require significant shares. For example, one of the given illustrations is of an orange juice manufacturer who uses a vertical merger with an orange grower to charge higher orange prices to competing orange juice manufacturers or perhaps even stop supplying them.[45] Oranges are a commodity, however, and such a strategy could never work unless the acquired orange grower accounted for a significant share of orange production in the relevant region.

The Agencies do appear to be admonished by the Second Circuit's *Fruehauf* decision, now 40 years old, which was the last big, fully litigated vertical merger case prior to *AT&T/Time Warner*.[46] The message in the *Fruehauf* court's rejection of the FTC's theory was that foreclosure numbers standing alone do not mean very much. There must be some theory about how foreclosure leads to lower output and higher prices. The Vertical Guidelines provide several examples and illustrations.

The Guidelines divide the universe of adverse competitive effects into Unilateral Effects[47] and Coordinated Effects.[48] The discussion of unilateral effects is largely based on bargaining theory similar to that used in the treatment of unilateral effects from horizontal mergers in the 2010 Horizontal Merger Guidelines.[49] Basically, a price increase is more profitable if the losses that accrue to one merging participant are recaptured by or diverted to the merged firm as a whole. These principles have been a relatively uncontroversial part of industrial organization economics for decades. The Vertical Guidelines recognize both foreclosure and raising rivals' costs as concerns, as well as access to competitively sensitive information.[50]

---

[44]   Id., § 3.

[45]   Id., § 4, Example 2.

[46]   United States v. AT&T, Inc., 916 F.3d 1029 (D.C.Cir. 2019).

[47]   Id., § 4.

[48]   Id., § 5.

[49]   See this volume, § 12.3d.

[50]   Vertical Merger Guidelines, *supra*, § 4. For analysis, see Herbert Hovenkamp, Competitive Harm Under the Vertical Merger Guidelines, ___ Rev. Indus. Org. ___ (2021) (forthcoming); and William P. Rogerson, Modelling and Predicting the Competitive Effects of Vertical Mergers: The Bargaining Leverage Over Rivals (BLR) Effect, available at https://www.ftc.gov/system/files/attachments/798-draft-vertical-merger-guidelines/rogerson_verticalguidelines1_2.pdf.

The Guidelines note:

A vertical merger may diminish competition by allowing the merged firm to profitably use its control of the related product to weaken or remove the competitive constraint from one or more of its actual or potential rivals in the relevant market. For example, a merger may increase the vertically integrated firm's incentive or ability to raise its rivals' costs by increasing the price or lowering the quality of the related product. The merged firm could also refuse to supply rivals with the related products altogether ("foreclosure").

As for economic methodology, the Vertical Guidelines observe:

Where sufficient relevant data are available, the Agencies may construct economic models designed to quantify the net effect on competition. The Agencies may employ merger simulation models to assist in this quantitative evaluation. These models often include independent price responses by non-merging firms and may incorporate feedback from the different effects on incentives. The Agencies do not treat merger simulation evidence as conclusive in itself, and they place more weight on whether merger simulations using reasonable models consistently predict substantial price increases than on the precise prediction of any single simulation.[51]

These methodologies generally compare the firms' predicted bargaining position before and after the merger on the assumption that the firms seek maximization of profits or value. They then query whether equilibrium (i.e., stable) prices in the post-merger market will be higher than those prior to the merger. In making that determination the Guidelines indicate that the Agency will consider:

(1) *Ability*: By altering the terms by which it provides a related product to one or more of its rivals, the merged firm would likely be able to cause those rivals (a) to lose significant sales in the relevant market (for example, if they are forced out of the market; if they are deterred from innovation, entry, or expansion, or cannot finance those activities; or if they have incentives to pass on higher costs through higher prices) or (b) to otherwise compete less aggressively for customers' business.

(2) *Incentive*: The merged firm, as a result of the merger, would likely find it profitable to foreclose rivals, or offer

---

[51]   § 4.

inferior terms for the related product, because it benefits significantly in the relevant market when rivals lose sales or alter their behavior in response to the foreclosure or to the inferior terms.[52]

This approach, which reflects important developments in empirical economics, does entail that there will be increasing reliance on economic experts to devise, interpret, and dispute the relevant economic models.

In a brief section the Vertical Guidelines also state a concern for mergers that will provide a firm with access or control of sensitive business information that could be used anticompetitively. The Guidelines do not provide a great deal of elaboration on this point.[53]

The Vertical Guidelines also discuss an offset for elimination of double marginalization.[54] Double marginalization in this context occurs when two vertically related independent firms each have market power and each maximizes its profits independently because they are unable to coordinate their output. As a result, output is even lower and price even higher than it is when there is only one monopolist. Double marginalization does not invariably occur, however. In many cases two firms that are involved in ongoing business should be able to eliminate double marginalization by contract. The Coase Theorem, for example, states that parties in that position will bargain to the joint maximizing result, and double marginalization is not joint maximizing. To the extent that is true, elimination of double marginalization cannot be counted as a "merger specific" efficiency.[55] Rather, the defendants must show that it cannot be eliminated by contract or other means.

The theory of double marginalization applies to both vertically related firms and to producers of complements, such as independent patent owners who license to a common manufacturer. However, the vertical situation is much more amenable to contractual elimination because vertically related firms deal with each other routinely and are in a position to reach joint-maximizing bargains that will eliminate double marginalization. By contrast, the producers of complementary products do not ordinarily deal with each other.

---

[52]   § 4a.

[53]   § 4b.

[54]   Id., § 6. On reducing double marginalization as mitigating competitive concerns in some cases, see 4A Antitrust Law ¶ 1022.

[55]   See Jonathan B. Baker, Nancy L. Rose, Steven C. Salop, and Fiona Scott Morton, Five Principles for Vertical Merger Enforcement Policy, 33 Antitrust 12 (Summer 2019); Steven C. Salop, Invigorating Vertical Merger Enforcement, 127 Yale L.J. 1962 (2018). On the tension between double marginalization and the Coase Theorem, see Herbert Hovenkamp, Competitive Harm, *supra.*

Finally, the Guidelines note a concern that certain vertical mergers may enable "coordinated interaction," or collusion.[56] This could occur, for example, if the merger eliminated a maverick buyer who formerly played rival sellers off against one another. In other cases the merger may give one of the partners access to information that could be used to facilitate collusion or discipline cartel cheaters.

These Guidelines are relatively short. They incorporate by reference many of the relevant points from the 2010 Guidelines for horizontal mergers. In any event, they may not provide as much detail as merging firms or federal courts might hope for, but they are an important step toward specifying the increasingly economic approaches that the agencies take toward merger analysis, one in which direct empirical estimates play a larger role, with a comparatively reduced role for more traditional approaches depending on market definition and market share.

While the new Vertical Guidelines leave the overall burden of proof with the challenger, they have clearly weakened the presumption that vertical mergers are invariably benign, particularly in highly concentrated markets or where the products in question are differentiated. Second, the Vertical Guidelines emphasize approaches that are more economically sophisticated and empirical. Consistent with that, concerns about foreclosure and raising rivals' costs are once again taken more seriously.[57]

---

[56]   Id., § 5.

[57]   See Baker, et al., Five Principles, *supra.*

Chapter 10

TIE-INS, RECIPROCITY, EXCLUSIVE DEALING AND MOST-FAVORED-NATION AGREEMENTS

Table of Sections

§ 10.1   Introduction: The Judicial Test for Tie-Ins

A tie-in, or tying arrangement, is a sale or lease of one product or service on the condition that the buyer take a second product or service as well. Tie-ins may be illegal under § 1 of the Sherman Act or § 3 of the Clayton Act.[1] Tie-ins have also been challenged under more aggressive standards under § 5 of the FTC Act,[2] and unilaterally imposed bundling by dominant firms can violate Sherman Act § 2. Tying arrangements involving patent licenses or patented products may sometimes invoke the patent "misuse" doctrine, discussed in Chapter 5.

This test from the Second Circuit captures the law quite well:[3] 1) There must be separate tying and tied products; 2) there must be "evidence of actual coercion by the seller that in fact forced the buyer to accept the tied product"; 3) the seller must possess "sufficient economic power in the tying product market to coerce purchaser acceptance of the tied product * * *"; 4) there must be "anticompetitive effects in the tied market * * *"; and, 5) there must

---

[1]   15 U.S.C.A. § 14:

It shall be unlawful . . . to lease or make a sale or contract for sale of goods, wares, merchandise, machinery, supplies, or other commodities, whether patented or unpatented . . . or fix a price charged therefor, or discount from, or rebate upon, such price, on the condition, agreement, or understanding that the lessee or purchaser thereof shall not use or deal in the goods, wares, merchandise, machinery, supplies, or other commodities of a competitor or competitors of the lessor or seller, where the effect of such lease, sale, or contract for sale or such condition, agreement, or understanding may be to substantially lessen competition or tend to create a monopoly in any line of commerce.

[2]   See § 10.3e.

[3]   Yentsch v. Texaco, Inc., 630 F.2d 46, 56–57 (2d Cir. 1980).

be "involvement of a 'not insubstantial' amount of interstate commerce in the tied product market * * *."

The Supreme Court has never articulated a complete test of its own. The circuit courts have assembled their tests from various statements contained in different Supreme Court opinions. The circuits are close to unanimous in requiring elements 1, 3 and 5 of the test set forth above. Further, if the "coercion" requirement in element 2 means only that the seller must insist that the buyer take the tied product as well as the tying product, courts agree that the plaintiff must show number 2.

The fourth element, "anticompetitive effects," is the most ambiguous, with some courts permitting broad-based inquiries into the effect of the arrangement on competition. Others use the term as a synonym for coercion and still others as a synonym for antitrust injury. If a tying arrangement is really a *per se* violation of the antitrust laws, as the Supreme Court has often stated, then a separate analysis of anticompetitive effects is peculiar. The whole point of *per se* analysis is to avoid expensive individualized inquiries concerning competitive effects of particular arrangements. As a result, the use of an "anticompetitive effects" requirement probably reflects considerable doubt about the wisdom of the *per se* rule.

The fifth element of the test for *per se* illegality—a "not insubstantial" amount of commerce in the tied product market[4]—is pure formalism. To the extent that tying law is concerned with limits on competition facilitated by foreclosure or increased collusion, the correct number should be some *percentage* of a relevant market foreclosed by the arrangement. The "quantitative substantiality" rule that tying law uses states a minimum dollar amount which generally does not vary with the size of the market.

Both courts and commentators have suggested several reasons why sellers impose tie-ins: 1) someone with a monopoly in the tying product can use a tie-in to create a second monopoly in the tied product and reap two sets of monopoly profits instead of one; 2) a monopolist can use a tie-in to raise barriers to entry and thereby protect its monopoly status, or ties by a sufficiently dominant firm can cause inefficient market foreclosure; 3) tie-ins by a group of firms can facilitate oligopoly or collusion; 4) a tie-in can enable a price-regulated seller to avoid or conceal avoidance of price regulation; 5)

---

[4]   See Northern Pacific Rwy. v. United States, 356 U.S. 1, 6, 78 S.Ct. 514, 518 (1958) (tie-ins "are unreasonable in and of themselves whenever a party has sufficient economic power with respect to the tying product to appreciably restraint free competition in the market for the tied product and a 'not insubstantial' amount of interstate commerce is affected"); *Jefferson Parish, supra,* at 8 (quoting *Northern Pacific*).

tie-ins can facilitate or conceal predatory pricing; 6) tie-ins can permit monopoly sellers to engage in or conceal price discrimination without violating the Robinson-Patman Act; alternatively tie-ins can facilitate nondiscriminatory metering; 7) tie-ins may increase productive or transactional efficiency by improving the quality of a product, lowering its costs, or by facilitating its distribution.

§ 10.2 Tying Arrangements and Consumer Welfare

Nearly every product or service can be divided into components or parts. A coat can be sold without its buttons, a desk without its drawers and a jar of pickles can probably be sold without its lid. The market would come to a standstill, however, if the antitrust laws gave every customer a legal right to atomize his purchases as much as he chose.

Why then a law of tying arrangements? Quite simply, some forced package sales have been perceived by both Congress and the courts as causing competitive harm to the seller's customers or competitors. The law of tie-ins is concerned with identifying those forced combined sales that can credibly injure competition.

An antitrust policy maker might take a number of approaches to this problem. One would be to adopt a rule that maximized consumer welfare in the very short run. Such a rule might permit any consumer to subdivide any purchase to any extent. A store selling a coat would be required to snip off a single button for any customer who wanted to buy it. Such a rule would impose enormous costs on sellers, and consumers would end up paying higher prices for products.

Nevertheless, a legal policy designed to maximize the welfare of consumers will not necessarily make every single consumer better off in every situation.[5] Consider Captain Ahab, for example, who would greatly prefer to buy a single right shoe rather than a pair. Unfortunately for Ahab, most shoe stores sell shoes only in pairs, because the cost of stocking, returns, and record-keeping would soar if stores sold individual right shoes and were stuck with the remaining left shoes. These costs would be passed on to consumers, all of whom would pay a higher price for shoes. Although shoe sellers' (nearly) universal policy of selling shoes only in pairs makes most consumers better off, it injures a small number of consumers who would prefer a single shoe.[6]

---

[5]   See Erik Hovenkamp & Herbert Hovenkamp, Tying Arrangements and Antitrust Harm, 52 Ariz. L. Rev. 925 (2010).

[6]   The Supreme Court ignored this in Fortner Enter., Inc. v. United States Steel Corp., 394 U.S. 495, 503–504, 89 S.Ct. 1252, 1258–1260 (1969) (*Fortner I*), when it held

A law of tying arrangements concerned with efficiency and competition must try to identify those forced combined sales that generate consumer gains that outweigh consumer losses. However, it is usually impossible to measure how all consumers are affected by a forced combined sale. Therefore tests must be devised for determining when particular tying arrangements injure consumers as a group.

§ 10.3   Market Power and Per Se Unlawful Ties; Sherman v. Clayton Act Tests

In Times-Picayune Pub. Co. v. United States[7] Justice Clark tried to establish some differences between the law of tie-ins as considered under § 1 of the Sherman Act and § 3 of the Clayton Act. Justice Clark believed that the Clayton Act must have broader coverage than the Sherman Act. Otherwise § 3 of the Clayton Act would be superfluous. The Sherman Act applied only to agreements actually "in restraint of trade," while the Clayton Act reached every agreement the effect of which "may be substantially to lessen competition."

Justice Clark concluded that a plaintiff can have the benefit of a *per se* rule under § 1 of the Sherman Act by showing *both* that the seller had sufficient market power in the tying product to restrain competition in the tied product *and* that the tie-in restrained a substantial volume of competition in the market for the tied product. If the plaintiff could show only one of these, however, the tie-in might still be a violation of § 3 of the Clayton Act under the rule of reason.[8]

Justice Clark's distinction made little sense in either law or economics, and it raised two unfortunate possibilities: 1) that some tie-ins could be found illegal even though the seller had no market power in the tying product market; 2) that if a seller had market power, its tie may be illegal *per se*: that is, evidence about the actual pro-competitive or efficiency effects of a particular arrangement would be irrelevant. Fortunately, subsequent case law has softened both of these rules. [9]

---

that the tying arrangement could be condemned if it affected any "appreciable number of buyers."

[7]   345 U.S. 594, 73 S.Ct. 872 (1953). The alleged tie-in was that the defendant sold identical advertisements in its morning newspaper and evening newspaper as a package, and refused to sell advertising in either newspaper separately.

[8]   Times-Picayune Pub. Co. v. United States, 345 U.S. 594, 608–09, 73 S.Ct. 872, 880 (1953).

[9]   Moore v. James H. Matthews & Co., 550 F.2d 1207, 1214 (9th Cir. 1977) ("The practical difference between the two standards has eroded steadily since Justice

10.3a. The Rationale and Development of Tying's Market Power Requirement[10]

Suppose that a market contains 100 sellers of identical wheat, and one seller requires a buyer to purchase a chicken for $2.00 as a condition of taking the wheat. Some purchasers who want a chicken anyway might purchase the "package" from the farmer, if both the wheat and the chicken were competitively priced. Anyone who did not want a chicken, however, would treat the requirement as an increase in the price of wheat and buy wheat from a competitor who did not impose a chicken tie. Anticompetitive tie-ins are implausible in competitive markets.

Today most courts have adopted a single test under both the Clayton and Sherman acts that requires both market power and a significant amount of commerce in the tied product market. No recent decision has condemned a tie when there was an express finding that the defendant lacked market power in the tying product. Nevertheless, an occasional court acknowledges the possibility of a Clayton Act rule-of-reason violation without a power showing. In *Town Sound* the Third Circuit concluded that "even if [the defendant's] position is the sounder as a matter of economics, and even if [the defendant] accurately predicts the direction in which the Supreme Court is heading, still-binding precedent forecloses our adopting" a rule requiring the plaintiff to prove market power in the tying product.[11]

The Supreme Court has never provided a useful rule for determining *how much* market power the seller must possess before the tying arrangement is illegal. Historically the Court did not take market power in tying cases very seriously. Many of the earliest cases involved patent "misuse" claims, where the Court found that the antitrust defendant improperly tied unpatented goods to the patented product or the patent license.[12] These decisions spoke generally of a patent "monopoly," or the attempt to leverage the

---

Clark's attempt to draw a fine line" between the two). See 9 Antitrust Law ¶ 1719b (4th ed. 2018).

[10]   See 10 Antitrust Law ¶¶ 1731–1740 (4th ed. 2018).

[11]   Town Sound and Custom Tops v. Chrysler Motors Corp., 959 F.2d 468, 485 (3d Cir.), cert. denied, 506 U.S. 868, 113 S.Ct. 196 (1992). The statement was dicta, and the court went on to approve the arrangement.

[12]   For example, Motion Picture Patents Co. v. Universal Film Mfg. Co., 243 U.S. 502, 37 S.Ct. 416 (1917); Carbice Corp. v. American Patents Development Corp., 283 U.S. 27, 51 S.Ct. 334 (1931). See Christina Bohannan & Herbert Hovenkamp, Creation Without Restraint: Promoting Rivalry in Innovation, Ch. 6 (2011). On the historical development of the patent tying case law, which long antedated the Sherman Act, see Herbert Hovenkamp, Antitrust and the Design of Production, 103 Corn. L. Rev. 1155, 1173–1193 (2018).

power of the patent beyond its lawful scope.[13] However, they almost never considered whether the defendant actually had market power in any market. Likewise, *International Salt* and *Paramount*, where the Supreme Court began to articulate the modern law of tie-ins, never required significant market power in the tying product.[14]

In *Times-Picayune* the Supreme Court appeared to require the seller's "dominance" in the tying product market.[15] By contrast, in the *Northern Pacific Rwy.* case a few years later, the Court assessed a much weaker requirement that the defendant control a "substantial" amount of the tying product and failed even to define a relevant market.[16] The Court interpreted *Times-Picayune* to require no more "than sufficient economic power to impose an appreciable restraint on free competition in the tied product. * * *"[17] In Fortner Enterprises, Inc. v. United States Steel Corp. (*Fortner I*) the Court not only found it unnecessary to define a relevant market for the tying product, but held that market power in the tying product could be inferred from the fact that the seller had "unique economic advantages over his competitors."[18]

But in the second *Fortner* case the Court greatly qualified this position and held that market power could not be inferred from the fact that the seller merely sold the tying product (credit) cheaper in order to obtain sales of a relatively high priced tied product (prefabricated houses).[19] Under *Fortner II*, simple "uniqueness" of the tying product was not sufficient to meet the market power requirement unless there were a separate showing that the uniqueness at issue really created market power. The defendant's financing terms were said to be "unique" because it offered lower interest rates and was willing to take higher risks than competitors, but it made these loans only to purchasers of its rather overpriced houses. As the Court pointed out, this was not market power, but only "a willingness to provide cheap financing in order to sell expensive houses." If "the evidence merely shows that credit terms are unique because the seller is willing to accept a lesser profit—or to incur

---

[13]   See Herbert Hovenkamp, The Rule of Reason and the Scope of the Patent, 52 San Diego L. Rev. 515 (2015).

[14]   International Salt Co. v. United States, 332 U.S. 392, 68 S.Ct. 12 (1947); United States v. Paramount Pictures, 334 U.S. 131, 68 S.Ct. 915 (1948).

[15]   *Times-Picayune*, 345 U.S. at 611, 73 S.Ct. at 882.

[16]   Northern Pacific Rwy. v. United States, 356 U.S. 1, 6–8, 78 S.Ct. 514, 518–519 (1958).

[17]   Id. at 11, 78 S.Ct. at 521.

[18]   394 U.S. 495, 505, 89 S.Ct. 1252, 1259 (1969).

[19]   United States Steel Corp. v. Fortner Enterprises (Fortner II), 429 U.S. 610, 621–622, 97 S.Ct. 861, 868–869 (1977).

greater risks—than its competitors, that kind of uniqueness will not give rise to any inference of economic power."[20]

The use of vague and diluted market power requirements was halted, at least for Sherman Act cases, in Jefferson Parish Hosp. Dist. No. 2 v. Hyde. The plaintiff anesthesiologist alleged that the hospital illegally tied the use of its operating rooms to a particular firm of anesthesiologists. The Court found that a market share of 30% in the tying product market was insufficient, because 70% of the market continued to be available to patients who wanted to use a different anesthesiologist than the one employed by the defendant. Finally, the Court appeared to require definition of a relevant market and computation of market share, at least if the tying product is not patented.[21]

10.3b. Tying Arrangements in Imperfectly Competitive Markets; Locked-In Customers[22]

Could tie-ins be used in moderately competitive markets to exploit certain consumers? The Supreme Court thought so in the *Kodak* case.[23] Kodak sold photocopy machines in a product differentiated market, where its market share was about 23%. Under the challenged policy, only those who purchased their repair service from Kodak could purchase Kodak's replacement parts, and Kodak controlled the production of many of these parts. The tying challenge came from independent firms that serviced Kodak photocopiers and wanted to purchase repair parts from Kodak. The policy was alleged to be a tying arrangement in which the replacement parts were the tying product and the service was the tied product.[24]

The holding in *Kodak* was relatively narrow: lack of market power in a primary market need not entail, as a matter of law, lack of market power in aftermarkets. But the Court's opinion engaged in far-ranging speculation about how a manufacturer of a branded durable good could use tying arrangements to exploit "locked-in" customers—those who had already purchased a Kodak photocopier

---

[20] Id. at 622, 97 S.Ct. at 869.

[21] The Court's dicta clung to the presumption that a patented tying product conferred market power. Id. at 16. Presumably, no relevant market need be defined in such a case. See § 10.3c.

[22] See also § 3.3.

[23] Eastman Kodak Co. v. Image Technical Services, Inc., 504 U.S. 451, 112 S.Ct. 2072 (1992).

[24] After remand the tying claim dropped out for lack of any "agreement," but the Ninth Circuit affirmed liability under § 2 of the Sherman Act. See Image Technical Services, Inc. v. Eastman Kodak Co., 125 F.3d 1195 (9th Cir. 1997), cert. denied, 523 U.S. 1094, 118 S.Ct. 1560 (1998); and §§ 3.3a; 7.6, 7.11d1.

and could now be victimized by restrictive practices affecting aftermarkets for service and replacement parts.

Given that the market for photocopiers was competitive, could Kodak have the requisite market power in the market for replacement parts? A well informed consumer would treat high service prices as a price increase in the basic product, and purchase its photocopier from a rival.[25] However, the Court reasoned, in certain moderately competitive markets for durable goods, a seller could use a tie-in to take advantage of "locked in" customers who had already purchased the defendant's durable good and now needed replacement parts and service that would fit. The lock-in would make at least some customers willing to pay a higher price for Kodak's parts, given the costs of abandoning their existing machines and purchasing others. The Court reasoned that if the gains from high services prices were great enough to offset any lost sales to better informed customers who would forego the package, then the tie would be both profitable and injurious to consumer welfare, notwithstanding a competitive primary market for photocopiers.

The Court observed that consumers of durable goods needing frequent maintenance are not in an equally good position to engage in "lifecycle" pricing—that is, pricing that takes both the price of the original good and the cost of subsequent maintenance into account. For those whose purchase decision is driven mainly by the cost of the initial durable good (the photocopier itself), subsequent exploitation through high service prices might be possible. Although some customers were sensitive to subsequent repair costs and presumably calculated them into the total cost of owning a photocopier, other customers operated on a much shorter horizon. The Court then noted that if the costs of service are presumed to be small in relation to the total purchase price, and information about service costs is difficult and expensive to obtain, then one could not presume that consumers would gather the information. This might make anticompetitive practices in the aftermarket profitable, notwithstanding competition in the primary market.[26]

The *Kodak* Court probably exaggerated the costs of obtaining information about aftermarket repairs. Information about repair costs is common to large classes of consumers; it does not have to be gathered individually for each. If a firm persistently charged more than other firms for aftermarket services, there is no obvious reason

---

[25]   See Queen City Pizza, Inc. v. Domino's Pizza, Inc., 124 F.3d 430 (3d Cir. 1997), cert. denied, 523 U.S. 1059, 118 S.Ct. 1385 (1998).

[26]   *Kodak*, 504 U.S. at 473, 112 S.Ct. at 2085.

why this information would not leak out to most consumers who are at least moderately attentive.

Kodak also considered whether the manufacturer of durable, branded goods could be found to have market power in unique replacement parts.[27] Kodak's 23% market share in the photocopier market[28] was even less than the defendant had in the *Jefferson Parish* case, where the Supreme Court had refused to condemn a tie-in on a market share of around 30%.[29] However, the "aftermarket" for replacement parts included many items that would fit only on Kodak photocopiers, and a significant minority were manufactured by either Kodak or its licensees exclusively. Without addressing the uniqueness question at any length,[30] the Court suggested that there might be a relevant market for *Kodak-brand* parts and service.[31] In that case, of course, Kodak's market share might be 100%.

Lower courts have resisted the broader implications of *Kodak*. They generally limit the case to situations where (1) the alleged tied product is purchased *after* customers are "locked-in" by virtue of a previous purchase; and (2) where the defendant changed its aftermarket pricing policy after a significant number of customers had made their purchase, or a significant number of customers can actually show that they were misinformed about aftermarket prices.[32] Nearly all courts also agree that in tying claims brought by franchisees, market power must be established by looking at the franchisor's market position in the general market in which it sells. To be sure, after a franchisee has signed a contract requiring it to take all of its requirements of, say, pizza dough from the franchisor the franchisee is locked in and cannot buy cheaper dough elsewhere. But since the requirement is enforceable only if spelled out in the franchise contract, the franchisee already knew about the requirement at the time it decided to enter into the franchise arrangement.[33]

---

[27]   The problem is analyzed in more detail in § 3.3.

[28]   See Image Technical Service, Inc. v. Eastman Kodak Co., 903 F.2d 612, 616, n. 3 (9th Cir. 1990).

[29]   Jefferson Parish Hosp. Dist. No. 2 v. Hyde, 466 U.S. 2, 104 S.Ct. 1551 (1984); see § 10.3a.

[30]   On "uniqueness" as conferring market power, see § 10.3d.

[31]   *Kodak*, 504 U.S. at 484, 112 S.Ct. at 2091 & n. 31. The issue is explored more fully in § 3.3a.

[32]   See generally 10 Antitrust Law ¶ 1740 (4th ed. 2018).

[33]   Maris Distributing Co. v. Anheuser-Busch, 302 F.3d 1207 (11th Cir. 2002), cert. denied, 537 U.S. 1190, 123 S.Ct. 1260 (2003); Queen City Pizza, Inc. v. Domino's Pizza, Inc., 124 F.3d 430 (3d Cir. 1997), cert. denied, 523 U.S. 1059, 118 S.Ct. 1385 (1998). See 2A Antitrust Law ¶ 519 (4th ed. 2014).

Twenty years of litigation under Kodak has expended millions of dollars in legal fees and not produced a single defensible decision finding market power on the basis of lock-in. Academic commentary has been overwhelmingly negative as well.[34]

10.3c. Intellectual Property and the Presumption of Market Power

Historically, courts presumed a seller's market power in the tying product when it was patented[35] or copyrighted.[36] A few lower courts recognized the same presumption when the tying product was trademarked.[37] In its 2006 *Illinois Tool Works* decision the Supreme Court overruled the presumption.[38]

This hardly means that the possession of intellectual property is totally irrelevant to the market power question. Patents can serve to reduce the supply competition facing a firm by making its product harder to duplicate. If elasticity of demand is already low as well, the result of the patent may be to define a relevant market in which the patent holder's share is substantial. But the patent itself is only one piece of evidence in this inquiry into market power.

A 1988 amendment to the Patent Act protects patentees from "misuse" challenges if they tie patented products "unless, in view of the circumstances, the patent owner has market power in the relevant market for the patent or patented product on which the license or sale is conditioned."[39] This appears to be Congressional acknowledgement that market power is not inherent in a patent grant, but must be separately proven.[40] The Supreme Court relied heavily on this statute and its history in overruling the market power

---

[34] For a summary of the criticism and an argument that *Kodak* should be overruled, see Herbert Hovenkamp, Post-Chicago Antitrust: A Review and Critique, 2001 Col.Bus.L.Rev. 257.

[35] See International Salt Co. v. United States, 332 U.S. 392, 68 S.Ct. 12 (1947), and see Jefferson Parish, 466 U.S. 2, 16, 104 S.Ct. 1551, 1560 (1984) (dictum).

[36] United States v. Loew's, Inc., 371 U.S. 38, 48, 83 S.Ct. 97, 103 (1962); United States v. Paramount Pictures, Inc., 334 U.S. 131, 158, 68 S.Ct. 915, 929 (1948); Digidyne Corp. v. Data General Corp., 734 F.2d 1336, 1341–42 (9th Cir. 1984).

[37] Photovest Corp. v. Fotomat Corp., 606 F.2d 704 (7th Cir. 1979), cert. denied, 445 U.S. 917, 100 S.Ct. 1278 (1980); Siegel v. Chicken Delight, Inc., 448 F.2d 43 (9th Cir. 1971), cert. denied, 405 U.S. 955, 92 S.Ct. 1172 (1972).

[38] Illinois Tool Works Inc. v. Independent Ink, Inc., 547 U.S. 28, 126 S.Ct. 1281 (2006).

[39] 35 U.S.C.A. § 271(d)(5).

[40] See 10 Antitrust Law ¶ 1737c (4th ed. 2018).

presumption for patents.[41] The lower courts have extended this holding to copyrights and trademarks.

10.3d. The Rationale for Per Se Illegal Tie-Ins

The judicial test described in § 10.1 accounts poorly for the economic functions of tying arrangements in sellers' distribution schemes. The test is not well designed to enable a court to determine whether a particular tie-in is socially harmful. Whether it is used as a collusion facilitator, for price discrimination, metering, or rate regulation avoidance are all but irrelevant to the formal judicial analysis. At the same time, the test has mired countless courts in analysis of issues that are not central to the economic functions of tie-ins and their potential to harm competition.

As previously observed, a forced package sale by a seller without market power must be efficiency creating or else the seller could not successfully sell its product this way. "Efficiency-creating" means that the gains that accrue to customers who benefit from the combination are greater than the losses that accrue to those who are injured, and that the gains can be realized only if the combination is forced on everyone.

For example, a shoe store does not need market power to force all its customers to buy shoes in pairs. If it sold shoes singly it would face higher costs that would be passed on to customers. These costs would outweigh the benefit to the relatively small number of people who would be better off if they could buy a single shoe. Likewise, stores with no market power force customers to buy coats with their buttons, automobiles with their spare tires and dressed geese with their gizzards—even though there are people who would prefer all these "tying" products without their respective "tied" products. Often courts have addressed this consumer welfare problem by deciding that the two items were in fact a single legal "product."[42]

If a seller is in a competitive market, its forced combination sale is probably efficient. It does not follow, however, that if the seller has market power its forced combination sale is inefficient. One must therefore dispute Justice Clark's suggestion in *Times-Picayune*[43] that if a seller has market power, its tie-in involving a significant amount of interstate commerce is *per se* illegal—that is, illegal without regard to possible procompetitive effects. Even a monopoly seller of shoes

---

[41]   Illinois Tool Works Inc. v. Independent Ink, Inc., 547 U.S. 28, 126 S.Ct. 1281 (2006). See also Sheridan v. Marathon Petroleum Co., LLC, 530 F.3d 590 (7th Cir. 2008) (similar; trademark).

[42]   See § 10.5.

[43]   Times-Picayune Pub. Co. v. United States, 345 U.S. 594, 73 S.Ct. 872 (1953).

would sell them in pairs. It would be efficient for the monopolist to do so, and both the monopolist and its customers are better off when the monopolist has lower costs.

Are tie-ins even arguably within the category of practices, such as price fixing, that are almost always harmful? The Supreme Court concluded that they were in Northern Pacific Rwy. Co. v. United States.[44] Justice Black wrote:

> Indeed, "tying agreements serve hardly any purpose beyond the suppression of competition * * *." They deny competitors free access to the market for the tied product, not because the party imposing the tying requirements has a better product or a lower price but because of his power or leverage in another market. At the same time buyers are forced to forego their free choice between competing products. For these reasons * * * [t]hey are unreasonable in and of themselves whenever a party has sufficient economic power with respect to the tying product to appreciably restrain free competition in the market for the tied product and a "not insubstantial" amount of interstate commerce is affected.

The result of *Northern Pacific* has been that often when the defendant has market power in the tying product the court has condemned its tie-in, even when the forced combined sale was probably in the best interest of consumers.[45] In the *Jefferson Parish* case, four concurring Justices were ready to jettison the *per se* rule for tying arrangements, but as of this writing it remains the law.[46] Although the 1992 *Kodak* decision is hardly explicit on the issue, the majority described the law of tying arrangements as if a *per se* rule were being applied.[47]

---

[44]   356 U.S. 1, 6, 78 S.Ct. 514, 518 (1958). The Court was quoting Standard Oil Co. of Calif. v. United States, 337 U.S. 293, 305–306, 69 S.Ct. 1051, 1058 (1949).

[45]   See Hyde v. Jefferson Parish Hosp. Dist. No. 2, 686 F.2d 286, 294 (5th Cir. 1982), reversed, 466 U.S. 2, 104 S.Ct. 1551 (1984). In reversing, however, the Supreme Court concluded that "It is far too late in the history of our antitrust jurisprudence to question the proposition that certain tying arrangements pose an unacceptable risk of stifling competition and therefore are unreasonable 'per se.' " 466 U.S. at 8, 104 S.Ct. at 1556.

[46]   Jefferson Parish, 466 U.S. at 32, 104 S.Ct. at 1569.

[47]   See Eastman Kodak Co. v. Image Technical Services, Inc., 504 U.S. at 461, 112 S.Ct. at 2079 (1992):

A tying arrangement is "an agreement by a party to sell one product but only on the condition that the buyer also purchases a different (or tied) product, or at least agrees that he will not purchase that product from any other supplier." [citation omitted] Such an arrangement violates § 1 of the Sherman Act if the seller has "appreciable economic power" in the tying product market and if the arrangement affects a substantial volume of commerce in the tied market.

§ 10.4   When Are Products Tied Together?

Clearly, if a seller freely permits the buyer to take or decline a second product there is no tie. The buyer must somehow be forced, or coerced, into accepting the tied product. This coercion could result from (1) an absolute refusal to sell the tying product without the tied product; (2) a discount, rebate or other financial incentive given to buyers who also take the tied product; (3) technological design that makes it impossible to sell the tying product without the tied product.

10.4a.   Coercion by Contract, Condition, or Understanding

The term "coercion" seems clear enough. Coercion is at the heart of most exclusionary practices. As the Second Circuit stated most simply, "* * * there can be no illegal tie unless unlawful coercion by the seller influences the buyer's choice."[48] Nonetheless, the coercion doctrine has become beguiling in tie-in analysis. The term "coercion" has been used by courts in tie-in cases to mean several things: 1) whether purchasers were actually forced to take the tied product as a condition of taking the tying product, or had the option of taking the tying product alone; 2) whether the defendant-seller had market power in the market for the tying product; 3) whether a particular purchaser would have taken the tied product anyway, and therefore was not injured by being "forced" to take it; 4) whether the tie-in foreclosed other options that the customer would have exercised but for the tying arrangement.

The first meaning of "coercion" is the correct one when we are considering whether two products are tied together. If a customer for item A is free to take or refuse item B as he pleases, there is no tie-in. At the other extreme, if all purchasers of item A must also take item B there is coercion, or "conditioning," in this sense. In the middle are several possibilities. One, which arises often in class actions, concerns transactions that are individually negotiated by class members, some of whom received more pressure from the seller than others to take the tied product, depending on the economic position of each purchaser-class member. In such cases the fact of coercion

---

Likewise, in his dissenting opinion Justice Scalia treated the issue as one of per se illegality. 504 U.S. at 486, 112 S.Ct. at 2092.

[48]   American Mfrs. Mut. Ins. Co. v. American Broadcasting Paramount Theatres, Inc., 446 F.2d 1131, 1137 (2d Cir. 1971), cert. denied, 404 U.S. 1063, 92 S.Ct. 737 (1972) (dismissing complaint; no pressure by defendant to take tied product). See 10 Antitrust Law ¶ 1753 (4th ed. 2018).

must be established on an individual basis, and most courts have refused class action certification.[49]

Some courts infer coercion, or conditioning, from an explicit contractual provision requiring purchase of the tied product.[50] Other courts have refused to infer coercion if there is no such explicit contractual provision.[51] No basis exists in reason or economics, however, for the Sixth Circuit's broad rule that coercion, or conditioning is not "an element of an illegal tying arrangement" if the contract explicitly provides for the purchase of both tying and tied products. By that reasoning a contract to purchase "one thousand bolts and one thousand nuts" eliminates any need for the plaintiff to prove coercion, in spite of the fact that the plaintiff may have wanted to buy the nuts and bolts in the same transaction. The evidence in the Sixth Circuit case suggested as much.[52]

The Supreme Court probably put the issue to rest in Jefferson Parish Hosp. Dist. No. 2 v. Hyde, although its analysis is ambiguous.[53] The Court said that tying arrangements warrant condemnation when the seller has sufficient market power "to force a purchaser to do something that he would not do in a competitive market." Furthermore, condemnation would be warranted only if the tie restrains "competition on the merits by forcing purchases that would not otherwise be made." The Court then upheld the hospital-anesthesiologist tie, because there were several other hospitals in the market. As a result, a patient who wanted a different anesthesiologist than the one provided by the defendant could easily seek out an alternative. This analysis appears to preclude a tying claim when the plaintiff cannot show that at least some purchasers took the tied product only because they were forced to.

A final emergent area of controversy is tying by "default" rules. Is it tying if the Android operating system for smartphones comes with Google Search pre-installed, even though the customer has the

---

[49]   Federal Rule of Civil Procedure 23(b)(3), which governs most class actions in antitrust cases, is generally interpreted to require that the "fact" of injury be established by common proof for all class members; otherwise certification is inappropriate. See 7A Charles Wright, Arthur Miller, & Mary Kay Kane, Federal Practice and Procedure § 1778 (3d ed. 2015).

[50]   Bogosian v. Gulf Oil Corp., 561 F.2d 434 (3d Cir. 1977), cert. denied, 434 U.S. 1086, 98 S.Ct. 1280 (1978) (if various station lessees can show similar lease provision that they must sell only defendant's gasoline, then coercion has been established.).

[51]   See Cia, Petrolera Caribe, Inc. v. Avis Rental Car Corp., 735 F.2d 636, 638 (1st Cir. 1984).

[52]   Bell v. Cherokee Aviation Corp., 660 F.2d 1123, 1131 (6th Cir. 1981). See the well-reasoned dissent at pp. 1134–36, noting that nearly all customers preferred to purchase fuel and maintenance services from the company that stored their aircraft.

[53]   466 U.S. 2, 12, 104 S.Ct. 1551, 1558–59 (1984).

right to install a different search engine? At this writing, the European Commission seems to say yes, while the American courts are more reluctant.[54]

10.4b. Proof of a Relevant Tying "Agreement;" Uncommunicated Conditions

Section 1 of the Sherman Act reaches tying arrangements only when there is a "contract," "combination," or "conspiracy."[55] Clayton Act § 3 requires a sale "on the condition, agreement, or understanding" that a tied product is required.[56] Suppose a seller simply refuses to sell to products separately, but will sell them together. Does the buy-sell agreement itself satisfy the requirement of a tying "agreement?" Most courts say yes.[57] The act of coercion is not the agreement that results in an actual sale, but the refusal to sell one product without another.[58] The inference of a tie becomes even stronger if a buyer requested the tying good alone but was turned down, and later entered a contract covering both goods.[59]

A tie generally cannot be inferred from a completely uncommunicated condition if the seller sells to some buyers by contracts that include provision of the second product and by other contracts that do not so provide. The presumption of tying becomes stronger as the percentage of buyers who would prefer not to have the second product grows, and as the instance of contracts not covering the second product declines.[60] Likewise, courts often conclude that tying can be presumed when the defendant uses a form contract covering both products, particularly when it refuses to sell otherwise than by this form.[61] Significantly, however, not even 100% bundling establishes tying conclusively. It may establish no more than that all customers want the two products together. For example, a shoe wholesaler may use a form contract that specifies "___ pairs of shoes," with the blank to be filled in for each purchase. As § 10.5 develops, universal bundling even in competitive markets generally

---

[54]   See Herbert Hovenkamp, Antitrust and Platform Monopoly, 130 Yale L.J. ___ (2021) (forthcoming); Daniel A. Hanley, A Topology of Multisided Digital Platforms, 19 Conn. Pub. Int. L.J. 271 (2020).

[55]   15 U.S.C.A. § 1.

[56]   15 U.S.C.A. § 14.

[57]   E.g., Systemcare v. Wang Laboratories Corp., 117 F.3d 1137 (10th Cir. 1997) (en banc) (overruling older Tenth Circuit decisions to the contrary).

[58]   See 10 Antitrust Law ¶ 1754 (4th ed. 2018).

[59]   See id. at ¶ 1756c.

[60]   See id., ¶ 1756.

[61]   See, e.g., IBM Corp. v. United States, 298 U.S. 131, 134, 56 S.Ct. 701 (1936) (apparent form contract requiring lessees of IBM's computers to use its tabulating cards).

indicates that the two goods are in fact a single product. Of course, a high bundling percentage has evidentiary significance because it shows that the seller is not making any sales except as a package. But the plaintiff would still have to show that at least some customers would have preferred the tying without the tied product.

10.4c.   Package Discounts

Another sort of conditioning occurs when the tie-in appears not as an absolute requirement, but as a discount or other favorable term to a customer who takes two products together.[62] If the discount is sufficiently steep in relation to the markup on the second product, then a rival who makes only the second product will not be able to compete effectively.[63] Of course, if other rivals make the same full bundle then they should be able to match the discounter's pricing scheme and there will be no bundling.

Section 3 of the Clayton Act condemns tying not only when the defendant absolutely requires the purchaser to take the tied product, but also when it offers a "discount from, or rebate upon" the purchase price in exchange for tying.[64] That provision condemns ties only where the effect of the tie may be substantially to lessen competition. If other rivals can readily match the discount, then competition is not lessened.

10.4d.   Coercion by Package Design; Technological Ties

Forced package sales can also result from technological innovations that make joint production plus refusal to sell separately cheaper than separate production. The alleged tying arrangement in the *Times-Picayune* case is an early example.[65] The defendant was accused of refusing to sell classified advertising separately in its morning and evening newspapers. However, the record established that the newspaper set type once for the classified section of its morning and evening editions, thus saving considerable money.

Some technological ties may be used for no other purpose than to ensure that the purchasers buy aftermarket parts only from the plaintiff. For example, one decision noted a practice followed by the defendant printer manufacturer as well as many others of using an electronic microchip on an ink cartridge to ensure that only

---

[62]   See, e.g., Collins Inkjet Corp. v. Eastman Kodak Co., 781 F.3d 264 (6th Cir. 2015) (finding sufficient evidence to support preliminary injunction in case where defendant offered a lower price to buyers who took tying and tied product together).

[63]   The test is developed in § 8.9b2.

[64]   15 U.S.C.A. § 14.

[65]   Times-Picayune Pub. Co. v. United States, 345 U.S. 594, 73 S.Ct. 872 (1953).

cartridges produced by the manufacturer could be used in the printer.[66] Even this microchip might be thought of as a quality control mechanism to the extent that use of rivals' ink cartridges produces inferior results. But that is a proposition that would have to be established. One problem with the microchip is that it excludes *all* competitors' cartridges, not just those that might be inferior. Keep in mind, however, that this issue relates only to the fact of bundling. A plaintiff would still have to show market power and anticompetitive effects.

In a true technological tie the "tying" results from product design rather than from a contract. As a result the tying requirement seems to be unilateral rather than contractual, and § 2 of the Sherman Act is the preferred vehicle for challenging it. As a result, they are not subject to per se analysis but must be addressed under the rule of reason. In Microsoft the D.C. Circuit Court condemned Microsoft's "commingling" of Windows and Internet Explorer computer code into a single program as unlawful monopolization.[67] However, it remanded an orthodox § 1 tying claim of the same products, and the government subsequently dropped the claim. In the *Apple iPod/iTunes* litigation Apple was accused of continuously managing its software in such a way as to create incompatibilities between iTunes, a large music database, and non-Apple electronic devices. As a result, the complaint alleged, it was much more difficult for consumers to switch from Apple devices to non-Apple devices because they were threatened with loss of a substantial portion of their music libraries.[68] Apple ultimately prevailed on a jury verdict concluding that the redesigns were genuine product improvements.

Another tech tie strategy, recently approved by the Federal Circuit Court of Appeals in a nonantitrust case, is to use design patents to limit rivals' ability to sell substitutes. In *Ford Global* that court approved the use of design patents on replaceable crash parts for automobiles.[69] Traditionally the market for such parts has contained several competitors in addition to the original manufacturer, and customers and insurers often prefer the competitors because their parts are cheaper. By approving a design patent the court effectively ensured that parts made by rivals would

---

[66]   Static Control Components, Inc. v. Lexmark Intern., Inc., 487 F.Supp.2d 861, 871 (E.D. Ky. 2007) (describing "lock-out" microchip technology on printer cartridges).

[67]   United States v. Microsoft Corp., 253 F.3d 34, 65–67 (D.C. Cir.), cert. denied, 534 U.S. 952, 122 S.Ct. 350 (2001).

[68]   Apple iPod iTunes Antitrust Litigation, 2014 WL 4809288 (N.D. Cal. Sep. 26, 2014) (denying Apple's motion for summary judgment). See John M. Newman, Anticompetitive Product Design in the New Economy, 39 Fla.St.U.L.Rev. 681 (2012).

[69]   Automotive Body Parts Assn. (ABPA) v. Ford Global Tech., LLC, 930 F.3d 1314 (Fed. Cir. 2019).

have to have a slightly different look from original equipment parts so that they would not commit design patent infringement.

§ 10.5   The Requirement of Separate Tying and Tied Products

10.5a.   Introduction; Basic Competitive Market Test

A tying arrangement does not exist unless the defendant bundles "separate" tying and tied products, and generally refuses to sell the tying product without the tied product.[70] But determining when two products are "separate" has proven to be a vexing issue.

Most forced package sales are the product of simple efficiency. For example, consumer retailing would come to a standstill if every purchaser were legally entitled to buy automobiles without tires or dressed geese without their gizzards. The competitive market is generally efficient in this manner: if it is less costly to bundle things together under competitive conditions or consumer satisfaction improves, competition leads to forced bundling. For that reason shoes and gloves are sold almost exclusively in pairs, automobiles are universally sold with their tires, and personal computers are mainly sold with hard drives preinstalled. Importantly, there is no *technological* reason that these items cannot be packaged and sold separately; their combination is entirely a result of consumer preference or cost savings in the distribution or selling process.

Thus the basic test for tying: *the alleged tying and tied items are separate products if the tying item is commonly sold separately from the tied item in a well functioning market.*[71] Note that the relevant question is whether the tying product is commonly sold without the tied product under ordinary competitive conditions, not vice-versa. For example, one observing the automobile market generally sees that (1) automobiles are almost never sold without tires; but (2) tires are frequently sold without automobiles. The second statement is true because tires wear out more quickly than automobiles, and thus there is a significant aftermarket for replacement as well as some specialty tires. But under the basic test someone claiming that an automobile manufacturer or dealer unlawfully tied tires to cars would have to show that under ordinary competitive conditions cars

---

[70]   Or alternatively, charges a higher price when the tied product is not included. On package discounts, see § 10.4c.

[71]   See 10 Antitrust Law ¶¶ 1744–1745 (4th ed. 2018).

are commonly sold without their tires. Failing this, there would be a single product and no tying arrangement.[72]

Thus *Jefferson Parish* concluded that whether "one or two products are involved" depends "on the character of the demand for the two items. . . ."[73] And in *Kodak* the Supreme Court concluded that "for [photocopier] service and parts to be considered two distinct products, there must be sufficient consumer demand so that it is efficient for a firm to provide service separately from parts."[74]

10.5b. "New" Products

In *Jerrold Electronics* the defendant had developed an early form of cable system using a large antenna, booster receivers, and cable connections going to numerous homes.[75] The items were physically separate, but the defendant would sell them only in complete installations. The court concluded that when this system was first introduced, knowledge about its assembly and operation was very limited, thus justifying Jerrold in insisting on package provision. For example, if the package contained items A, B, and C and pictures were fuzzy, the consumer might get lost in finger pointing, where the maker of A blamed the maker of B for the problem, and so on. The court concluded that during this early period the defendant could insist that it sell all the components, and not merely stipulate quality and specifications so that others could supply them as well.[76] However, once this introductory period was passed, this rationale no longer applied and the court found separate products.[77]

While the new product rationale makes sense, it invites two critical questions of fact: *first*, when is an amalgamation of formerly separate products really a "new" product, and when is it just plain tying? *second*, how long should a market dominating defendant be entitled to rely on the "new product" rationale for finding a single product?

---

[72]   The contemporaneity of demand is therefore relevant. For example, since electric motors and replacement parts are required by customers at different times (the parts only after the motor breaks), courts find separate products for the two. Parts & Elec. Motors, Inc. v. Sterling, Inc., 826 F.2d 712, 720 (7th Cir. 1987).

[73]   Jefferson Parish Hosp. Dist. No. 2 v. Hyde, 466 U.S. 2, 19 104 S.Ct. 1551, 1562 (1984).

[74]   Eastman Kodak Co. v. Image Technical Services, Inc., 504 U.S. 451, 462, 112 S.Ct. 2072, 2079 (1992).

[75]   United States v. Jerrold Electronics Corp., 187 F.Supp. 545 (E.D. Pa. 1960), affirmed per curiam, 365 U.S. 567, 81 S.Ct. 755 (1961).

[76]   Id. at 559.

[77]   Id. at 560. See 10 Antitrust Law ¶ 1746 (4th ed. 2018).

On the first question, there has to be some reason for thinking that (a) the combination works better than separate provision; and (b) the consumer of the package cannot achieve the same result by combining the goods for him-or herself. That is to say, the combination works better when it is assembled by the seller than by the buyer.[78] In *Microsoft* the D.C. Circuit rather tentatively concluded under this test that Microsoft and Internet Explorer were separate products, but that the degree of innovation represented by an integrated Windows/Internet Explorer package called for rule of reason analysis.[79] Under that analysis the separate products test is much less important.[80]

10.5c. Efficiency—"Economies of Joint Provision"

One obvious defense to a tying arrangement is that joint provision is cheaper than separate provision. The efficiencies generated by forced combined sales can be broadly grouped into two kinds, transactional, and productive or technological. The sale of shoes only in pairs is a good example of a transactional efficiency. Presumably shoes cannot be manufactured more cheaply in pairs than by the piece. However, they probably can be distributed and sold far more cheaply in pairs. If a store had to offer a solitary left shoe to the occasional customer who wanted one it would be stuck with the right shoe, and a very long wait until another customer came along who wanted only a right shoe of the same size and style. The shoe store would probably return it or order a new mate for it. If the additional costs generated by these extra maneuvers are greater than half the cost of a pair of shoes, it would be more efficient to force the one-legged purchaser to take a pair, even if he throws the left shoe away.

In *Times-Picayune* the Supreme Court permitted a newspaper to require advertisers to buy space in both its morning and evening newspapers simultaneously. Advertising in the two was found to be a single product, which Justice Clark identified as "readership."[81] While that conclusion was not particularly enlightening, Justice Clark also noted that when the sale of morning and evening advertising was combined into a single transaction, most of the costs of running an advertisement—soliciting, billing and setting type— were performed only once instead of twice. The newspaper could

---

[78]   See id., ¶ 1746.

[79]   United States v. Microsoft Corp., 253 F.3d 34, 89 (D.C.Cir.), cert. denied, 534 U.S. 952, 122 S.Ct. 350 (2001).

[80]   See § 10.7c.

[81]   Times-Picayune Pub. Co. v. United States, 345 U.S. 594, 613, 73 S.Ct. 872, 883 (1953).

lower the cost of advertising by running identical advertising sections in its morning and evening newspapers.[82] In his dissenting opinion in *Fortner* fifteen years later, Justice White made a similar observation: "if the tied and tying products are functionally related, they may reduce costs through economies of joint production and distribution."[83] And in her *Jefferson Parish* concurrence, Justice O'Connor concluded that "When the economic advantages of joint packaging are substantial the package is not appropriately viewed as two products, and that should be the end of the tying inquiry."[84] Judge Posner has also concluded that two items should be considered a single product if there were "rather obvious economies of joint provision."[85]

Nevertheless, the five-Justice *Jefferson Parish* majority appeared to reject the idea that the efficiency of joint provision could justify finding a single product. It concluded that whether separate products exist depends "not on the functional relation between" the two items, but rather "on the character of the demand" for them.[86]

The requirement of "rather obvious economies" seems to be a sensible single-product test, although one would want to interpret the phrase to mean "rather obvious and significant economies." That is to say, a provable and significant efficiency serves to undermine the plaintiff's prima facie case rather than merely warranting consideration as a defense to a presumptively unlawful arrangement. The law of monopolization under § 2 of the Sherman Act takes a similar approach, permitting even an absolute monopolist to create technological innovations that bundle formerly separate products, provided that there is a good business justification for the bundling.[87]

---

[82]   Id.

[83]   Fortner Enter., Inc. v. United States Steel Corp., (Fortner I), 394 U.S. 495, 514 n. 9, 89 S.Ct. 1252, 1264 n. 9 (1969), (J. White, dissenting).

[84]   Jefferson Parish Hosp. Dist. No. 2 v. Hyde, 466 U.S. 2, 40–41, 104 S.Ct. 1551, 1573 (1984) (O'Connor, J., concurring). However, Justice O'Connor went on to conclude that "since anesthesia [the alleged tied product] is a service useful to consumers only when purchased in conjunction with hospital services [the tying product], the arrangement is not properly characterized as a tie between distinct products." But under this rule all package sales of complementary products (products that must be consumed together) would be viewed as sales of single products. Justice O'Connor's proposal would effectively wipe out three-fourths of the law of tying arrangements, for most involve complementary products: for example, IBM v. United States, 298 U.S. 131, 56 S.Ct. 701 (1936) (computers and computer cards); International Salt Co. v. United States, 332 U.S. 392, 68 S.Ct. 12 (1947) (salt injecting machines and salt).

[85]   Jack Walters & Sons Corp. v. Morton Bldg., Inc., 737 F.2d 698, 703 (7th Cir. 1984). The court concluded that a manufacturer's prefabricated building kits and its trademark were not separate products.

[86]   *Jefferson Parish*, 466 U.S. at 19.

[87]   See §§ 7.5–7.6.

An conspicuous and significant cost savings is clearly such a justification.

§ 10.6   Competitive Effects

As noted previously, the per se rule for tying does not explain how ties affect competition. As a result, courts have often condemned tie-ins without understanding the economic function of the arrangement in the defendant's distribution scheme. If tying doctrine is to be rationalized, however, economic effects must be explored. This Section looks at the major theories that have been presented to explain why firms use tying arrangements.

10.6a.   The Leverage Theory: Using Tie-Ins to Turn One Monopoly into Two; Tipping

The leverage theory is the oldest theory under which tie-ins have been condemned. Under the theory, a seller who has a monopoly in one product, which is often patented, uses a tie-in to create a "limited" monopoly in a second product that is essential to the use of the tying product. Suppose that a seller has a patent monopoly in a freezer that preserves ice cream in transit better than any competing technology. The freezer requires solid carbon dioxide ("dry ice"), a common substance, as a refrigerant. The seller requires all purchasers of its freezer to buy its dry ice as well. In condemning this arrangement Justice Brandeis wrote in 1931 that it permitted

> the patent-owner to "derive its profit, not from the invention on which the law gives it a monopoly, but from the unpatented supplies with which it is used" [and which are] "wholly without the scope of the patent monopoly" * * *. If a monopoly could be so expanded, the owner of a patent for a product might conceivably monopolize the commerce in a large part of the unpatented materials used in its manufacture. The owner of a patent for a machine might thereby secure a partial monopoly on the unpatented supplies consumed in its operation.[88]

Such "leveraging" is not a plausible way to increase monopoly profits. Suppose that seller A has a monopoly in a patented glass jar. Each jar requires one lid, but the lids are not patented and are manufactured by many competitors. A produces jars for $1.00, but she sells them at $1.50, which is her profit-maximizing price. The competitive price of lids is 30 cents.

---

[88]   Carbice Corp. of Amer. v. American Patents Development Corp., 283 U.S. 27, 31–32, 51 S.Ct. 334, 335–36 (1931).

A decides to manufacture lids herself and sell a jar and a lid as a package. What is A's profit-maximizing price for the package? The answer, quite clearly, is $1.80. A's computation of her profit-maximizing price for jars as $1.50 was *predicated* on the fact that lids were sold for 30 cents. Since every jar must have a lid, buyers place a certain value on the package. Someone who buys a jar and a lid for $1.80 is generally indifferent whether the price is $1.00 for the jar and 80 cents for the lid, or $1.50 for the jar and 30 cents for a lid. As long as the proportion of jars to lids is constant the purchaser will attribute a price change in either to the price of the entire package. The jar monopolist cannot make any more monopoly profits by monopolizing the lid market as well.

The theory that a monopoly seller can use a tie-in to enlarge current monopoly profits has been condemned repeatedly by commentators for a half century.[89] In a few judicial opinions judges have also noted the implausibility of the leverage theory.[90]

10.6b. Entry Barriers, Foreclosure, and Collusion

10.6b1. Entry Barriers and Tying Arrangements

Tying arrangements may raise entry barriers in the market for either the tying or the tied product. For example, suppose a newspaper company publishes both a morning newspaper and an evening newspaper. A second firm attempts to enter the market with an evening newspaper. The incumbent firm responds by requiring all purchasers of advertising in its morning paper to buy an identical advertisement in the evening paper. The unit pricing scheme will foreclose the new entrant from advertisers who want to advertise in the morning, because they will be required to place their evening advertising in the incumbent's evening newspaper instead of the competitor's.[91]

The theory that tying arrangements raise barriers to entry can be susceptible to the same criticism that can be raised against all "entry barrier" arguments: namely, the fact that something is an entry barrier says nothing about whether it is socially harmful or

---

[89] For example, see Ward Bowman, Tying Arrangements and the Leverage Problem, 67 Yale L.J. 19 (1957); Richard Markovits, Tie-ins, Leverage, and the American Antitrust Laws, 80 Yale L.J. 195 (1970).

[90] For example, Hirsh v. Martindale-Hubbell, Inc., 674 F.2d 1343, 1349 n. 19 (9th Cir.), cert. denied, 459 U.S. 973, 103 S.Ct. 305 (1982).

[91] See Times-Picayune Pub. Co. v. United States, 345 U.S. 594, 73 S.Ct. 872 (1953).

beneficial.[92] Efficiency itself is a remarkably strong barrier to entry. Suppose the daily newspaper can show that by forcing all advertisers to buy space in both morning and evening newspapers it can print identical advertising sections in the two newspapers and thereby set type once instead of twice. The largest cost of running an advertisement is the cost of setting the type. The cost saving can be realized, however, only if *all* purchasers of advertising advertise in both the morning and evening editions. Unit pricing may permit the incumbent to sell an advertisement in both newspapers together for $7.00, while the potential entrant must charge $5.00 for the evening advertising alone. The "barrier to entry" results from the lower cost of the unit pricing scheme.[93]

The more difficult question is whether tying can create entry barriers for reasons other than efficiency. That is most clearly possible when products are differentiated or covered by intellectual property rights. For example, a firm that is dominant in the tying market can use tying to favor its own technology in a product differentiated tied market. That was essentially the story of Microsoft and the Internet Explorer browser tie, which excluded Netscape even though Netscape at the time was a superior product.[94] But this largely pushes the issue from entry barriers, which are concerned mainly with prospective rivals, to foreclosure.

10.6b2. Foreclosure; Market Share

Jefferson Parish shifted the emphasis in tying cases away from leverage and toward foreclosure, or the degree to which a tie-in denies market access to rivals.[95] This shift in emphasis also turns the appropriate market "power" inquiry into one concerning market *share*. That is, when the challenged anticompetitive effect is foreclosure we want to know something about the *coverage* of the restraint, not necessarily about the short-run ability of the seller to set prices above the competitive level.

The foreclosure and entry barrier concerns are closely related, although foreclosure applies to existing firms as well as prospective entrants. The real foreclosure threat is that the tie might facilitate single firm dominance or oligopoly by denying market access to more

---

[92]   See Harold Demsetz, Barriers to Entry, 72 Amer.Econ.Rev. 47 (1982); Richard Schmalensee, Economies of Scale and Barriers to Entry, 89 J.Pol.Econ. 1228 (1981). And see § 1.6.

[93]   See Record at 1127–29, which noted the cost savings from single setting of type. *Times-Picayune, supra.*

[94]   See § 10.4d.

[95]   Jefferson Parish Hosp. Dist. No. 2 v. Hyde, 466 U.S. 2, 41–42, 104 S.Ct. 1551, 1573 (1984).

aggressive competitors or potential entrants. A tie that forecloses a large percentage of the market is not anticompetitive if entry into both the tying and tied product markets is easy. When entry is difficult, however, the concerns are real.

10.6c.   Tie-Ins as Price Discrimination and Metering Devices; Franchise Agreements

Sellers often use tying arrangements to facilitate price discrimination.[96] Although courts sometimes acknowledge this fact,[97] the presence of price discrimination has had little impact on judicial analysis or determination of legality.

Although price discrimination can be very profitable, it is often difficult for sellers to accomplish for three reasons. First, certain forms of it are illegal under the Robinson-Patman Act,[98] which can prevent the sale of the same product at two different prices. Second, in order to engage in at least some types of price discrimination, a seller must identify and segregate different groups of customers for whom the elasticity of demand differs. That is, the seller must be able to distinguish in some relatively low-cost way buyers who place a high value on the seller's product from buyers who place a much lower value on it but are still willing to pay a price that is profitable to the seller. Finally, the seller must be able to prevent arbitrage, which occurs when favored purchasers (those charged a lower price) resell the product to disfavored purchasers (those charged a higher price).

A seller can solve all three problems by using a variable proportion tying arrangement, in which different customers use different amounts of the tied product.[99] For example, a monopoly seller of computer printers might believe that a buyer planning to make 1000 printed pages per week values the machine more highly than a buyer intending to print only 100 pages per week. The seller may sell the printer subject to a condition that all purchasers buy their ink cartridges from the seller as well.[100] The seller prices the printer at the competitive level or perhaps even lower. However, the seller charges a high price for ink cartridges, because those who print

---

[96]   See Ward Bowman, Tying Arrangements and the Leverage Problem, 67 Yale L.J. 19 (1957); Richard Markovits, Tie-ins and Reciprocity: A Functional, Legal and Policy Analysis, 58 Tex.L.Rev. 1363, 1407–10 (1980).

[97]   See United States Steel Corp. v. Fortner Enter., 429 U.S. 610, 616 n. 7, 97 S.Ct. 861, 866 n. 7 (1977) (Fortner II); Fortner Enter., Inc. v. United States Steel Corp., 394 U.S. 495, 513, 89 S.Ct. 1252, 1264 (1969) (Fortner I) (White, J., dissenting).

[98]   15 U.S.C.A. § 13.

[99]   See 9 Antitrust Law ¶ 1711 (4th ed. 2018).

[100]   See Henry v. A.B. Dick Co., 224 U.S. 1, 32 S.Ct. 364 (1912).

more copies use more cartridges. If the rate of return on the machine itself is 5% and the rate of return on the cartridges is 40%, the seller's net rate of return will be much higher from the 1000 page per week user than from the 100 page user.[101]

Should tie-ins designed to achieve price discrimination be illegal? A monopolist may legally charge its nondiscriminatory profit-maximizing price. Many commentators argue that price discrimination is preferable because it results in higher output than nondiscriminatory monopoly pricing.[102] This argument applies unfailingly only to perfect price discrimination, however—that is, price discrimination in which every buyer pays its reservation price (i.e., the highest price it is willing to pay) for the product. Imperfect price discrimination does not necessarily result in increased output, and sometimes the output may be even less than it is under nondiscriminatory monopoly pricing. The effect of imperfect price discrimination on output presents a fairly complex question.[103]

Price discrimination by tie-in is common in franchise agreements.[104] By price discriminating the franchisor takes advantage of the fact that some franchise locations are far more profitable than others, but that almost any location profitable enough to keep the franchisee in business will also be profitable to the franchisor. The result of the variable proportion tie is that the very small franchise, which would not exist at all if the franchisor charged each franchisee its nondiscriminatory profit-maximizing price, can be profitable to both franchisee and franchisor. Consumers will also be better off. Those injured by such a scheme are the very successful franchisees who, because of the price discrimination, are forced to pay more than the franchisor's nondiscriminatory profit-maximizing price.

---

[101] Suppose the printer is priced at $1,000 and lasts one fifty-week year. Profits on the printer are $50.00, or $1.00 per week. Ink is priced at 1 cent per sheet, of which 40% is profit. The profits from the 1,000 sheet-per-week user will be $4.00 on ink and $1.00 on the printer, per week. The profits from the 10,000 page-per-week user will be $40.00 on ink and $1.00 on the printer per week. The net rate of return on sales in the first case is about 17%, and in the second about 34%.

[102] See, e.g., 3 Antitrust Law ¶ 721 (4th ed. 2015); Robert Bork, The Antitrust Paradox: A Policy at War With Itself 394–98 (1978; rev. ed., 1993).

[103] See Richard A. Posner, Antitrust Law 202–206 (2d ed. 2001), who for the time being would not condemn tying arrangements merely because they enable price discrimination; but he also notes that the welfare effects of price discrimination ties are uncertain.

[104] For example, Queen City Pizza v. Domino's Pizza, 124 F.3d 430 (3d Cir.), cert. denied, 523 U.S. 1059, 118 S.Ct. 1385 (1998); Kypta v. McDonald's Corp., 671 F.2d 1282 (11th Cir.), cert. denied, 459 U.S. 857, 103 S.Ct. 127 (1982) (tying the franchise license to a variable-rate rental of the franchise location); Krehl v. Baskin-Robbins Ice Cream Co., 664 F.2d 1348 (9th Cir. 1982) (in which the tied product was ice cream).

Not all variable proportion ties are used for price discrimination. The tie may simply be a metering device, designed to measure costs that vary with intensity of use. To use the mimeograph machine and paper as an example, if wear and tear on a lessor's machine varies directly with the number of copies, the lessor may tie paper to the machine in order to meter the costs that the lessee's use imposes on the lessor. There is no price discrimination if the price of the paper is calculated precisely to cover the wear and tear caused by each use.

§ 10.7 Tie-Ins and Efficiency: Toward a General Rule of Reason

10.7a. Efficiencies and Tying Law's Idiosyncratic Per Se Rule

The so-called per se rule applied to tying arrangements is idiosyncratic in two respects. One, it is unique in requiring proof of market power in the tying product.[105] Second, even when market power is established courts ordinarily permit the defendant to offer various defenses.

10.7b. Nonforeclosing Ties; Full-Line Forcing and Unwanted Tied Products; Lack of Consumer Injury

The dominant theory of ties today is that they harm competition by excluding, or "foreclosing," rivals, mainly in the tied product market, or else by raising their costs. By contrast, under the leverage theory discussed in § 10.6 the harm is thought to be "extraction" rather than foreclosure. The theory is that the tie permits the seller to charge more by tying two things together, and that this can happen even if no rivals are foreclosed. The "restraint of trade" standard of § 1 of the Sherman Act contemplates price increasing conduct as well as foreclosing conduct.

One particular type of nonforeclosing tie that arises in the context of franchise or other authorized dealer contracts is so-called "full-line forcing." Full-line forcing occurs when a manufacturer insists that its dealer carry a full line of the manufacturer's product, rather than the models that the dealer finds most profitable. Most courts have found full-line forcing legal since the 1970's, sometimes by concluding that the manufacturer's "line" is a single product.[106]

---

[105]   See § 10.3.

[106]   For example, Southern Card & Novelty v. Lawson Mardon Label, 138 F.3d 869 (11th Cir. 1998).

An economic objection to full-line forcing is hard to find. Full line requirements help manufacturers achieve economies of scale or scope in distribution. Manufacturers use independent dealers as a substitute for self-distribution, and they can sell their products only if the dealers offer and promote them. If a manufacturer makes models A, B and C, and its authorized dealer refuses to sell C, then the manufacturer must find a second dealer to sell C, retail C itself, or drop C from that particular region. The better alternative is to dismiss the dealer and find one willing to sell the manufacturer's full line. Significantly, full-line forcing is an output-*increasing* activity; the manufacturer's only rationale for imposing it is to get all of its product variations before customers.

Further, in the absence of exclusive dealing no rival is foreclosed.[107] That is to say, unless the manufacturer also imposes exclusive dealing, this dealer is free to sell the products of other firms.[108] The requirement is onerous only to the dealer itself, which must bear the costs of carrying a product that it does prefers not to have. Further, no theory has emerged explaining how a manufacturer can charge higher prices by requiring dealers to sell its full line.

Indeed, full-line forcing is one member of a set of "no competitive injury" ties that occur when the customer is forced to take a product that it does not want *at all*. No rival can be foreclosed by such a tie because the customer would not purchase from someone else even if no tying had been imposed. As the Supreme Court observed in *Jefferson Parish*, tying cannot be per se unlawful "when a purchaser is 'forced' to buy a product he would not have otherwise bought even from another seller in the tied product market. . . ." In that event, "there can be no adverse impact on competition because no portion of the market which would otherwise have been available to other sellers has been foreclosed."[109]

The Ninth Circuit's *Brantley* decision, decided under the rule of reason, is a good illustration of the unwanted tied product.[110] The plaintiffs were complaining that the defendant's bundling practices forced them to take cable channels that they did not want. They would have preferred more *a la carte* pricing in which they would pay

---

[107]   See 9 Antitrust Law ¶ 1724c (4th ed. 2018); and 10 Id. at ¶ 1747e2 (4th ed. 2018).

[108]   Exclusive dealing is covered in § 10.8.

[109]   Jefferson Parish Hosp. Dist. No. 2 v. Hyde, 466 U.S. 2, 16, 104 S.Ct. 1551 (1984).

[110]   Brantley v. NBC Universal, Inc., 675 F.3d 1192, 1201 (9th Cir. 2012). For further discussion see Herbert Hovenkamp, Antitrust and the Patent System: A Reexamination, 76 OSU L.J. 467 (2015).

only for the channels they actually watched. The Ninth Circuit rejected the claim, concluding that it did not "allege the types of injuries to competition that are typically alleged to flow from tying arrangements. . . . [T]here is effectively 'zero foreclosure' of competitors," and compelling the purchase of unwanted products is not itself an injury to competition."

Finally, consumers are not injured by arrangements such as full line forcing, for the tying requirement does not apply to them. While the dealer is required to carry a full line, the dealer's customer can pick and choose among the items as he or she pleases.[111]

10.7c.   Conclusion: Moving Tying Law Toward a Rule of Reason

The antitrust world would be a much better place if its per se rule were jettisoned and tying practices subjected to rule of reason treatment. Tying is not even arguably in the category of highly suspicious restraints for which the per se rule is reserved.

Tying analysis under the rule of reason would look quite different than it does now. Market power in either the tying or tied product would still be required. The "separate products" requirement would become less significant and perhaps fade completely out of existence. As noted before, the principal purpose of the requirement was to screen out obviously competitive arrangements under what purported to be a per se rule. But when the court can go straight to competitive consequences it really does not matter whether the products are separate. Rather, if market power and foreclosure effects were proven, what *would* matter is whether the arrangement was justified as saving costs, producing superior products, or otherwise pleasing customers. "Separate products" might be a convenient shorthand for describing ties that flunk these tests, but it need not be.

In *Illinois Tool Works* the per se rule for tying arrangements was not at issue, but only the question whether a patent presumptively conferred market power on a tying product.[112] But in its opinion the Court spoke repeatedly about the excessive hostility toward ties

---

[111]   See, e.g., Roy B. Taylor Sales v. Hollymatic Corp., 28 F.3d 1379 (5th Cir. 1994), cert. denied, 513 U.S. 1103, 115 S.Ct. 779 (1995), which found no violation when the defendant required a dealer to carry the defendant's rather high priced hamburger patty paper as a condition of carrying its hamburger patty making machine. Customers, however, were free to buy the machine from the dealer and either make their own paper or buy it somewhere else. As a result, rival makers of patty paper were not foreclosed.

[112]   Illinois Tool Works, Inc. v. Independent Ink, Inc., 547 U.S. 28, 126 S.Ct. 1281 (2006).

exhibited in a past era and also about tying's efficiency potential. It even suggested that the per se rule had been designed exclusively for patent ties.[113] In sum, the Court did everything except explicitly overrule the general per se tying rule. That chip should be the next one to fall.

§ 10.8   Exclusive Dealing

An exclusive dealing arrangement is a contract under which a buyer promises to buy its requirements[114] of one or more products exclusively from a particular seller. Exclusive dealing arrangements have been condemned under § 1 of the Sherman Act and § 3 of the Clayton Act, as well as § 5 of the FTC Act.[115] As Chapter 7 notes, one important relatively recent development in the law of exclusive dealing is application of § 2 of the Sherman Act when the firm imposing it is a "monopolist."

10.8a.   Anticompetitive Foreclosure and Its Variations

10.8a1.   The Foreclosure Theory of Exclusive Dealing

Exclusive dealing arrangements have been disapproved under the same "foreclosure" theories that courts have applied in vertical merger and tying cases.[116] For example, if independent gasoline retailers agree to buy all their gasoline needs from one refiner and no one else, the stations are "foreclosed" from other gasoline refiners for the duration of their contracts. In Standard Oil Co. of California v. United States (*Standard Stations*)[117] the Supreme Court found such contracts illegal when they collectively foreclosed 6.8% of the gasoline market to the defendant's refiner competitors. Since exclusive dealing arrangements were common in the market, the total percentage of independent stations "foreclosed" from the market by *all* refiners who used such contracts was considerably higher.[118]

Did such contracts make the market less competitive? All the arguments concerning the foreclosure theory presented in Chapter 9 on vertical integration apply equally to exclusive dealing. The

---

[113]   Id. at 42.

[114]   In antitrust analysis, common law requirements contracts are generally treated as exclusive dealing. For example, Taggart v. Rutledge, 657 F.Supp. 1420, 1443–1445 (D.Mont. 1987), affirmed mem., 852 F.2d 1290 (9th Cir. 1988).

[115]   15 U.S.C.A. § 45. See FTC v. Brown Shoe Co., 384 U.S. 316, 86 S.Ct. 1501 (1966); and § 10.3e in this volume.

[116]   See § 9.3c.

[117]   337 U.S. 293, 69 S.Ct. 1051 (1949).

[118]   Id. at 295. Only 1.6% of the retail stations had "split pumps"—that is, sold gasoline from two or more different refiners.

competitive threat, if any, is generally less in exclusive dealing than in more durable and extensive forms of vertical integration, such as vertical mergers. Unlike mergers, exclusive dealing contracts usually do not govern every aspect of an independent firm's business. Further, exclusive dealing contracts are of limited duration. Every so often, depending on contract terms that could range from a few months to many years, the supplier must bid anew against competing suppliers.[119]

Exclusive dealing might foreclose competition inefficiently if the upstream firm has a dominant market position and entry into the downstream market is restricted. As long as new downstream facilities can readily be constructed, effective foreclosure is unlikely. But suppose that geographic location is critical to business survival, and two or three sites for resale locations are substantially better than alternatives. In that case, a dominant upstream firm could "foreclose" competition—thus making entry more difficult—by entering into exclusive dealing contracts with all of the preferred downstream locations.

For antitrust, the end game of all practices, including exclusionary contracting, is harm to consumers, usually measured by reduced output and higher prices in the downstream market. This is the all important difference between tort law and antitrust. Harm to a competitor might be a method of unfair competition. But exclusive contracting violates the antitrust laws when it causes harm to those who buy. The Ninth Circuit got this precisely wrong in its *Qualcomm* decision. The District Court had painstakingly reviewed the record to show how the defendant's exclusive dealing and exclusionary discounting practices resulted in higher prices, but the Ninth Circuit rejected this evidence, holding that what was relevant was harm to competitors.[120]

10.8a2. Raising Rivals' Costs

Many of the foreclosure theories of exclusive dealing become more robust if one views them, not as excluding rivals from a market altogether, but as raising rivals' costs by relegating them to inferior products or distribution channels.[121] For example, Standard Oil very

---

[119]   The exclusive dealing contracts in the *Standard Stations* case were of varying terms. Many, however, were from year-to-year, requiring a 30 day notice by either party for termination. Id. at 296, 69 S.Ct. at 1053. In such cases competitive bidding for the contracts could be substantial, even though a station carried the gasoline of only one supplier at any given time. See United States v. El Paso Natural Gas Co., 376 U.S. 651, 84 S.Ct. 1044 (1964).

[120]   FTC v. Qualcomm, 411 F.Supp.3d 658 (N.D. Cal. 2019), rev'd, 969 F.3d 974, 999–1000 (9th Cir. 2020).

[121]   See 11 Antitrust Law ¶ 1804 (4th ed. 2018).

likely enlarged its monopoly by agreeing with railroads that they would give it preferential scheduling and lower prices than any competing shipper of petroleum products.[122] American Can for a time bought up the full output of can machine makers, thereby forcing rival can makers to resort to inferior technology.[123] Or Toys 'R' Us, the country's largest toy purchaser, forced suppliers to promise that competing discounters would receive only differentiated versions of toys or large bundles that customers would have to take all at once.[124] Likewise, in *McWane* the court agreed with the Federal Trade Commission that a dominant supplier of pipe fittings and related supplies used exclusive dealing anticompetitively to make it more difficult for a smaller firm that did not offer a full line of such fittings to compete.[125] Under the exclusive dealing arrangement dealers could not substitute away from McWane unless they carried all of their trade to the only rival, but the rival was not able to supply them. In so doing the dominant firm, with more than 90% of the market would be able to maintain its position for a longer time by hindering its rival's growth.

10.8a3. Defining Markets to Measure Vertical Foreclosure[126]

Before anticompetitive foreclosure can occur a firm with a relatively large percentage of the upstream market must foreclose a significant percentage of access to the downstream market. To illustrate, suppose that firm X makes 80% of the world's solar-powered wrist watches and enters into exclusive dealing agreements with 100% of the jewelry stores in an area. If jewelry stores were the only places that such watches could be sold, it would be very difficult for competing watch makers to find suitable outlets. But if such watches are efficiently sold through department stores, discount stores, or over the internet, then the restraint might not be all that significant.[127] As a result, it is always important to look at the entire range of distribution channels through which efficient distribution

---

[122]   Elizabeth Granitz & Benjamin Klein, Monopolization by "Raising Rivals' Costs:" the Standard Oil Case, 39 J. L. & Econ. 1 (1996).

[123]   United States v. American Can Co., 230 F. 859, 875 (D. Md. 1916), appeal dismissed, 256 U.S. 706, 41 S.Ct. 624 (1921) ("[F]or a year or two after defendant's formation it was practically impossible for any competitor to obtain the most modern, up-to-date, automatic machinery."). See 11 Antitrust Law ¶ 1801a (4th ed. 2018).

[124]   Toys 'R' Us, 5 Trade Reg. Rptr. ¶ 24516 (F.T.C. 1998), affirmed, 221 F.3d 928 (7th Cir. 2000). Since the agreement was imposed on toy manufacturers it was a form of output contract rather than an exclusive dealing contract.

[125]   McWane, Inc. v. FTC, 783 F.3d 814 (11th Cir. 2015).

[126]   See 2A Antitrust Law ¶ 570 (4th ed. 2014).

[127]   See 11 Antitrust Law ¶ 1802d (4th ed. 2018).

can occur; exclusive dealing that shuts off only one distribution channel might permit ample competition through others.[128]

10.8b.   Exclusive Dealing as a Cartel Facilitator

Exclusive dealing may facilitate collusion by denying buyers an opportunity to force sellers to bid against each other. This reduces the opportunities for cartel cheating. For example, if gasoline refiners are colluding, gasoline distributors might be able to force the refiners to bid against each other and reach agreements with individually negotiated secret terms. But if the cartel members agreed to use exclusive dealing contracts with their distributors, thus making them "branded" resellers, then this bidding could be reduced. Of course, exclusive dealing should be condemned under this theory only if (1) the upstream market shows signs of being conducive to collusion; and (2) the exclusive dealing is sufficiently widespread to create the inference that it is being used as a cartel facilitator. Unfortunately, the fact that exclusive dealing is efficient in a market also tends to make it widespread. Firms must either adopt efficient practices or else lose market share to those who do. If upstream markets are highly concentrated and conducive to collusion, but the exclusive dealing itself seems to be efficient, then the policy maker might wish to approve exclusive dealing only for short periods. If exclusive dealing contracts must be re-bid frequently, most of the benefits of exclusive dealing will be retained, but the competitive threat will be greatly diminished.

10.8c.   The Difference Between Exclusive Dealing and Tying

As noted in § 10.7c, if tying arrangements were subjected to a rule of reason there would be far less need to determine whether a particular agreement was exclusive dealing or tying. The two practices would be analyzed in roughly the same way, as they should be. Today, the principal reason for litigation efforts to distinguish exclusive dealing from tying is the fact that tying opens up the possibility of a per se rule.

In fact, exclusive dealing can have a greater anticompetitive impact than tying, depending on the circumstances. For example, suppose that Minolta agreed to supply copy machines to a photocopy store and tied paper and other supplies. The copy store would not be able to use non-Minolta paper in these machines. Unless Minolta also imposed exclusive dealing, however, the store would be free to use Xerox or Toshiba machines, and could use the paper of others in those

---

[128]   See id. at ¶ 1821d4 (4th ed. 2018).

machines. To the extent the copy store could vary proportions, it might respond to high priced Minolta paper by using the Minolta machines less and the non-Minolta machines more. By contrast, if Minolta imposed exclusive dealing on either machines or paper, then the store would have to take all its requirements of that product from Minolta. In sum, tying arrangements apply to tying *products*, while exclusive dealing applies to *stores* or even *firms*. The foreclosure caused by tying is less to the extent that a firm can use or sell multiple brands of the tying product.[129]

While tie-ins and exclusive dealing typically perform similar economic functions, courts have distinguished the two, applying a more lenient test to exclusive dealing. The chief difference between exclusive dealing and tying is that in exclusive dealing the court recognizes no distinct "tying" product. A good example is Justice O'Connor's concurring opinion in the *Jefferson Parish* case.[130] Once Justice O'Connor decided that hospital services and anesthesiology were the same "product" and could not constitute a tying arrangement, she dealt with the arrangement as an exclusive dealing contract. In fact, however, a "tying" product exists even in exclusive dealing contracts—namely, the right of the retailer to sell the supplier's merchandise and perhaps to display a sign showing itself to be an "authorized dealer." That right is worth more to the high volume seller than to the low volume seller. As a result, exclusive dealing is probably used to facilitate price discrimination just as tie-ins.[131] That was almost certainly true in *Standard Stations*. Standard had a great deal invested in public recognition of its name. By entering exclusive dealing contracts with stations, permitting them to display the Standard brand, and charging a supracompetitive price for its gasoline, Standard was in effect selling its name as well as its gasoline to the retailer; however, it was selling its name at a price that varied with the amount the retailer sold.[132] Of course, once the court has decided that no tying arrangement exists, because the alleged tying and tied products are actually one, then the plaintiff may have nothing left but an exclusive dealing claim. This often happens in vertical litigation involving franchise arrangements.

---

[129]   See 11 Antitrust Law ¶ 1800b (4th ed. 2018).

[130]   Jefferson Parish Hosp. Dist. No. 2 v. Hyde, 466 U.S. 2, 44, 104 S.Ct. 1551, 1575–1576 (1984).

[131]   See § 10.6e.

[132]   See Krehl v. Baskin-Robbins Ice Cream Co., 664 F.2d 1348 (9th Cir. 1982), in which the plaintiff-franchisees were permitted to display the defendant's trademark but also required to sell the defendant's ice cream exclusively. The plaintiffs and the court characterized this as a tying arrangement; however the difference between *Baskin-Robbins* and *Standard Stations* is difficult to discern.

10.8d.   Efficiency Explanations and Defenses for Exclusive Dealing

The exclusive dealing arrangement stands between the vertical merger and the individual sale as a device for facilitating distribution of a manufacturer's product to the ultimate consumer. Markets are uncertain, some much more uncertain than others.[133] Long-term, flexible contracts can minimize the costs and risks to both parties of dealing with these uncertainties. For example, no retail gasoline dealer knows in advance precisely what its sales will be over some future period. Nor may he have anything approaching reliable information about the status of suppliers. Some markets are so uncertain that no reasonable investor will build an outlet unless she has advance assurance of a steady source of supply.[134] If summer travel is brisk, the gasoline retailer needs to know that it can obtain enough gasoline, and relying on the spot market for short-notice purchases can be risky and expensive.

The refiner, by contrast, wants a steady outlet for its product. Customers become accustomed to buying a particular brand at a particular location. A customer's ability to know in advance that a particular station carries a brand he prefers makes the customer better off. The exclusive dealing arrangement gives both refiners and ultimate consumers the advantages of outright refiner ownership of retail stations, but permits the refiner to avoid the high capital costs of investing in stations. The exclusive dealing contract may also provide incentives at the retailer level. If the refiner owns its own stations, the station operator is merely an employee. The independent dealer is a businessman who usually maximizes his profits by selling as much as possible of the refiner's gasoline.

Additionally, vertical integration by contract gives both parties to the agreement an economic interest in productive facilities. For example, the value of a gasoline refinery results from future sales of refined gasoline. By arranging in advance for a steady stream of such sales, the refiner essentially shares the risk of the investment with the gasoline retailers.[135] In general, the more specialized the plant,

---

[133]   For an important discussion of the use of vertical integration to avoid market uncertainties, see Oliver Williamson, Markets and Hierarchies 82–131 (1975). On the history of United States antitrust policy toward vertical integration by contract, see Herbert Hovenkamp, The Law of Vertical Integration and the Business Firm: 1880–1960, 95 Iowa L. Rev. 863 (2010).

[134]   See Great Lakes Carbon Corp., 82 F.T.C. 1529, 1656 (1973) ("a prudent refiner will not install [an expensive] facility unless he has in hand, at the time that investment decision is made, a contract for the disposition of the [product] to be produced."). See 11 Antitrust Law ¶ 1811 (4th ed. 2018).

[135]   See 11 Antitrust Law ¶ 1814 (4th ed. 2018).

the greater this risk will be. If the refiner builds without this assurance, retailers can later take advantage of the refiner's sunk costs and bargain for any price sufficient to cover the variable costs of refining gasoline.[136] As a result, the refiner unsure about future demand is likely to build a smaller refinery than it would if the demand were certain, or else not build at all. This situation is exacerbated if information in the market is poor. For example, if I am planning to build a refinery but I do not know what competing refiners are planning to build, I may fear there will be excess refining capacity. By guaranteeing my market through long-term requirements contracts, I can spread this risk and reduce my uncertainty.[137]

For all the reasons outlined above, exclusive dealing is a classic example of what is sometimes called "relational" contracting—that is, of contracting that permits parties to make fairly long term arrangements that reduce their risk and to account for the fact that they do not know everything about the future.[138] Vertical integration by ownership involves much heavier investment in markets where others are already specialists and capacity may be adequate. Simple contracts that specify quantity are too inflexible to consider the market's uncertain future meanderings.

10.8e.   The Legal Standard for Exclusive Dealing Contracts

The district court's opinion in *Standard Stations* had created a virtual *per se* rule against requirements contracts if the percentage of the market foreclosed by the agreement exceeded about 7%. In affirming the district court, the Supreme Court appeared to approve this *per se* approach to exclusive dealing contracts.

Twelve years later the Court retreated from that position in Tampa Elect. Co. v. Nashville Coal Co.[139] The most significant part of the *Tampa* decision was its definition of the relevant market,

---

[136]   For one likely instance of this see Great Atlantic & Pacif. Tea Co. v. F.T.C., 440 U.S. 69, 73, 99 S.Ct. 925, 929 (1979), where A & P was able to obtain a very low bid from Borden milk company, allegedly in violation of the Robinson-Patman Act, because Borden had just built an enormous plant in the area in reliance on A & P's continued business, and feared underutilization if it did not retain A & P's account.

[137]   See Wesley Liebeler, Antitrust Law and the New Federal Trade Commission, 12 Sw.U.L.Rev. 166, 186–196 (1981); Howard Marvel, Exclusive Dealing, 25 J.L. & Econ. 1 (1982).

[138]   On antitrust policy and relational contracting, see Herbert Hovenkamp, Harvard, Chicago and Transaction Cost Economics in Antitrust Analysis, 55 Antitrust Bull. 613 (2010).

[139]   365 U.S. 320, 81 S.Ct. 623 (1961), on remand, 214 F.Supp. 647 (M.D. Tenn.1963).

which reduced effective foreclosure to lower than 1%.[140] As a result, the Court's discussion of the legal standard to be applied can be considered dicta. In an ambiguous but potentially powerful statement, the Court concluded that:

> To determine substantiality [of foreclosure] in a given case, it is necessary to weigh the probable effect of the contract on the relevant area of effective competition, taking into account the relative strength of the parties, the proportionate volume of commerce involved in relation to the total volume of commerce * * * and the probable immediate and future effects which pre-emption of that share of the market might have on effective competition therein.[141]

As in any case where proof of foreclosure share is decisive, a relevant market must be defined.[142] But care must be taken that the *correct* relevant market is used, particularly when the upstream party operates in one geographic market and the downstream party in another. For example, suppose a national company refining and wholesaling gasoline in regional markets enters into exclusive dealing contracts with gasoline stations, as in *Standard Stations*. The first question is, What is the threatened danger to competition? In the typical case, as *Standard Stations* was, the stations promised to sell nothing but Standard's own gasoline. If the perceived threat is foreclosure of suppliers—that is, exclusive dealing makes it impossible for refiners other than Standard to sell gasoline to these stations—then the relevant market is the regional one in which the refiners operate.[143] Likewise, if the threatened harm is collusion at the refiner level, one must look to the refining market. By contrast, if the threatened harm is retailer collusion, then the retail market must be identified.

The courts today follow *Tampa*'s suggested rule of reason approach.[144] In addition, foreclosure on the order of 30% to 40% is generally necessary if the action is under § 1 of the Sherman Act

---

[140]   See § 3.6.

[141]   365 U.S. at 329, 81 S.Ct. at 629.

[142]   For example, Morgan, Strand, Wheeler & Biggs v. Radiology, Ltd., 924 F.2d 1484, 1489–1490 (9th Cir. 1991) (exclusive dealing claim dismissed where the plaintiffs failed to define relevant product and geographic markets). On market definition, see Ch. 3.

[143]   For example, Ryko Mfg. Co. v. Eden Serv., 823 F.2d 1215, 1233 (8th Cir. 1987), cert. denied, 484 U.S. 1026, 108 S.Ct. 751 (1988) (looking at degree of foreclosure in supply market).

[144]   See McWane, Inc. v. FTC, 783 F.3d 814, 833–836 (11th Cir. 2015) (exclusive dealing requires rule of reason analysis); Roland Mach. Co. v. Dresser Indus., 749 F.2d 380, 393 (7th Cir. 1984) (same).

against a nondominant firm.[145] The concurring Justices in *Jefferson Parish* opined that 30% was insufficient where they could find no additional anticompetitive effects.[146] When the action is under § 2 of the Sherman Act against a dominant firm, lower percentages will suffice.

Most courts look at actual impact on competition and not merely on the foreclosed market share.[147] That can cut in both directions. The *Jefferson Parish* conclusion that 30% was insufficient obtained in a market in which no evidence appeared that the exclusion was being used for anticompetitive purposes. Efficiency explanations dominated. Indeed, it is difficult to understand what motive a hospital would have for making the anesthesia market less competitive. By contrast, *Microsoft*, where the defendant was intending to exclude rival browser Netscape,[148] should call for less categorical foreclosure requirements. Condemnation would be appropriate on lower foreclosure shares.

Tampa's rule of reason also requires courts to examine numerous other factors, including (1) the duration of the contracts; (2) the likelihood of collusion in the industry, and the degree to which other firms in the market also employ exclusive dealing; (3) the height of entry barriers; (4) the nature of the distribution system and distribution alternatives remaining available after exclusive dealing is taken into account; and (5) other obvious anti-or pro-competitive effects. Among the latter, the most often cited are prevention of free riding and encouragement of the dealer to promote the supplier's product more heavily.

As noted previously, long contracts should generally be regarded as more problematic than short ones, because substantial

---

[145]   For example, Sewell Plastics, Inc. v. Coca-Cola Co., 720 F.Supp. 1196, 1212–1214 (W.D.N.C.1989), affirmed mem., 912 F.2d 463 (4th Cir. 1990) (40% insufficient).

[146]   *Jefferson Parish*, 466 U.S. at 45, 97 S.Ct. at 1575 (O'Connor, J., concurring): "Exclusive dealing is an unreasonable restraint on trade only when a significant fraction of buyers or sellers are frozen out of a market by the exclusive deal." The concurrers then found 30% coverage inadequate because they could find no anticompetitive effects.

[147]   For example, Advanced Health-Care Servs. v. Radford Community Hosp., 910 F.2d 139, 151 (4th Cir.1990); Collins v. Associated Pathologists, Ltd., 844 F.2d 473, 478–479 (7th Cir.), cert. denied, 488 U.S. 852, 109 S.Ct. 137 (1988).

See also Roland Mach. Co. v. Dresser Indus., 749 F.2d 380, 393–395 (7th Cir.1984), concluding that in order to prove unreasonable exclusive dealing a plaintiff first must prove that it is likely to keep at least one significant competitor of the defendant from doing business in a relevant market. If there is no exclusion of a significant competitor, the agreement cannot possibly harm competition. Second, he must prove that the probable (not certain) effect of the exclusion will be to raise prices above (and therefore reduce output below) the competitive level, or otherwise injure competition.

[148]   United States v. Microsoft Corp., 253 F.3d 34, 66 (D.C. Cir. 2001). See § 7.8c.

competition generally emerges when the contracts must be renegotiated. Indeed, a market saturated with exclusive dealing contracts could be fiercely competitive, if the contracts were short term and the parties bid vigorously for the contracts themselves. This is frequently the case for service contracts, where exclusive dealing greatly reduces transaction cost fees. For example, a factory probably does not want to negotiate each day to have its trash hauled away. Rather, it will take competitive bids from trash hauling firms, and the winner will get an exclusive contract with a stated duration, perhaps one year. When the contract expires a new round of bidding will begin. Such a market is likely to operate competitively even though every factory and commercial trash hauler in the area uses a contract that is exclusive over its lifetime.

Likewise, exclusive dealing that "forecloses" a large percentage of one mode of distribution will have little anticompetitive effect if another mode is available. Closely related is the question of entry barriers. Exclusive dealing should be condemned only when it facilitates monopoly pricing, and this is not likely to occur if entry is easy. Of course, meaningful entry must either occur at both levels covered by the exclusive dealing arrangement, or else there must be sufficient free capacity at one level to give a new entrant at the other level a ready source of supply. For example, exclusive dealing between oil refiners and service stations will facilitate monopoly pricing only if prospective competitors cannot easily and quickly enter. If the exclusive dealing is so widespread that anyone wishing to be a refiner must also open a chain of service stations, then one must consider whether there are substantial barriers to two-level entry. The difficulty of entry should generally be evaluated under standards similar to those developed in the 2010 Horizontal Merger Guidelines.

§ 10.9 Vertical Most-Favored-Nation (MFN) and "Anti-Steering" Clauses

A most-favored-nation (MFN) clause requires a purchaser or seller to grant to the defendant prices or terms that are at least as favorable as the price or terms offered to rivals. Sometimes the contracts even name specific rivals.[149] While MFN clauses differ from exclusive dealing, they can have similar effects to the extent that

---

[149] See, e.g., Dennis W. Carlton, The Anticompetitive Effects of Vertical Most-Favored-Nation Restraints and the Error of *Amex*, 2019 Colum. Bus. L. Rev. 93 (2019); Denis W. Carlton & Ralph A. Winter, Vertical Most-Favored-Nation Restraints and Credit Card No-Surcharge Rules, 61 J.L. & Econ. 215 (2018); Jonathan B. Baker & Fiona Scott Morton, Antitrust Enforcement Against Platform MFNs, 127 Yale L.J. 2176 (2018); Stephen C. Salop & Fiona Scott Morton, Developing an Administrable MFN Enforcement Policy, 27 Antitrust 15 (Spring 2013).

they penalize firms for dealing with rivals. In a few cases the MFN is offered in exchange for explicit exclusive dealing—I'll give you a discount if you promise to deal with me exclusively.[150] In general, however, because they provide for preferential treatment rather than outright exclusion, MFNs are thought to impose a smaller threat of harm than exclusive dealing. Further, they have procompetitive effects. For example, they may guarantee firms that they are not getting a poorer bargain than rivals are getting.

The structural analysis of MFN clauses proceeds by looking at the defendant's position in the upstream market and foreclosure or raising rivals' costs in the downstream market. For example if a health insurance company has 80% of the market for insurance and its MFN clauses cover 70% of insured patents, these patients may then be effectively out of competitive play for rival insurers. Otherwise, they can serve them only at higher costs.[151]

The Court will also have to look at the nature of the MFN clauses, however. At one extreme, MFN clauses that require no more than matching of prices given to someone else may cause no exclusionary harm. To be sure, there could be other types of harms. For example, price-matching clauses can facilitate collusion to the extent that they tend to equalize prices across the market. They may also limit the opportunities for firms to engage in price discrimination, much of which is efficient.

At the other extreme, an MFN could make dealing with a rival so costly that the market dries up, creating an effect akin to exclusive dealing. For example, suppose A sells to B under an arrangement requiring A's price to anyone else to be at least 20% higher than the price given to B. In that case no other firms might be willing to pay A's price. This can impose higher costs on rivals. For example, in the late nineteenth and early twentieth century Standard Oil obtained "preferential rebates" from railroads in exchange for large volume commitments.[152] This effectively raised the costs of competing oil shippers.[153]

---

[150] ProMedica Health Sys., Inc. v. FTC, 749 F.3d 559, 571 (6th Cir. 2014) (defendant offered one provider an organization a 2.5% rate discount if the provider would exclude a rival hospital from its network).

[151] E.g., United States v. Delta Dental of R.I., 943 F. Supp. 172, 176–80 (D.R.I. 1996) (insurer had MFN agreement with 90 percent of practicing dentists, and its plans covered 35–45 percent of persons with dental insurance in the state).

[152] See David Millon, The Sherman Act and the Balance of Power, 61 S.Cal.L.Rev. 1219 (1988).

[153] See Elizabeth Granitz & Benjamin Klein, Monopolization By "Raising Rivals' Costs": The Standard Oil Case, 39 J.L. & Econ. 1, 2 (1996); Daniel A. Crane, Were Standard Oil's Rebates and Drawbacks Cost Justified?, 85 S. Cal. L. Rev. 559 (2012).

Anti-steering clauses, which limit customer ability to shop for lower prices, are more pernicious than simple MFNs. They can interfere with customers' ability to make maximizing choices. The Supreme Court failed to see this in its *AmEx* decision, which approved American Express's policy of forbidding merchants from offering a discount to customers in exchange for their use of a different credit card that carried a lower fee.[154] Credit cards are "two-sided" markets, in which transactions on one side (with customers) are offset by transactions on the other side (with merchants). Another example is the Uber platform, a two sided-market in which drivers and passengers make exchanges for rides. A higher fare will produce more drivers but fewer rides, or vice-versa. The operator of the platform maximizes its returns by seeking the correct balance between the two.

For some purposes, particularly those involving the computation of revenue, competitive effects on two sided markets can be assessed only by looking at both sides, because harms on one side can be offset by benefits on the other side.[155] For example, the fact that credit cards are free to cardholders hardly suggests predatory pricing, because one must consider the revenue that card issuers obtain from merchants as well. The same thing is true of over-the-air television, which is free to viewers but produces revenue from advertisers.

What the Supreme Court failed to see in *AmEx* is that exclusionary practices can be quite another matter and often do not involve offsetting burdens and benefits. Facing the high fees charged by American Express for using its card, merchants were motivated to offer card carrying customers a lower price in exchange for use of a less costly card.

For example, if the merchant credit card fee on a large purchase were $30 on an American Express card but $20 on a Visa card, the merchant might offer the customer a $5 discount on the price in exchange for her use of the Visa card. The anti-steering rule prevented this transaction from occurring. In the process the rule made *both* the customer and the merchant worse off: it denied the customer the discount that the customer would have received for using a cheaper card and the merchant the lower costs that would

---

[154]   Ohio v. American Express Co., 138 S.Ct. 2274 (2018).

[155]   On the economics and other distinctive features of two-sided platforms, see § 1.4b. For more elaborate economic discussion, see Jean-Charles Rochet & Jean Tirole, Platform Competition in Two-Sided Markets, 1 J. Eur. Econ. Ass'n 990 (2003); Michael Katz & Jonathan Sallet, Multisided Platforms and Antitrust Enforcement, 127 Yale L.J. 2142 (2018).

have resulted from this substitution.[156] The price would be lower with steering, and both product volume and aggregate credit card usage would increase. The only beneficiary from the restriction was American Express, the owner of the platform, which was able to shield its high fees from a lower price competitor.

In sum, the Court failed to perform the kind of transaction-specific Coasean analysis that is required for vertical contractual practices.[157] If it had, it would have seen that the *AmEx* facts showed a direct link between the challenged conduct and higher consumer prices. Indeed, each instance of steering prevented by *AmEx's* rule resulted in (1) a higher price for that purchaser; (2) loss of revenue to the merchant; and (3) injury to the competing, lower cost card that would have obtained the transaction.

The district court found that a merchant's overall prices were higher as a result of the no-steering rule, and the record appeared to support that conclusion. But that issue is really a red herring. The plaintiff was not seeking to enjoin the defendant's entire business, but only the anti-steering rule. In that case the court should examine the effects of the challenged rule, and in this case it was clear that each and every time the anti-steering rule prevented a customer from using a cheaper card the effective price was higher.

One lesson of *Amex* is that one must not be misled by overgeneralized rhetoric, and the economics of two-sided markets has produced a great deal of it. There is no substitute for doing a close transaction-based analysis in order to see who is being harmed and who is benefitted from a particular practice.

---

[156] See Erik Hovenkamp, Platform Antitrust, 44 J.Corp. L. 713 (2019); Herbert Hovenkamp, Platforms and the Rule of Reason: the American Express Case, 2019 Col. Bus. L. Rev. 35 (2019).

[157] On this point, see Herbert Hovenkamp, The Looming Crisis in Antitrust Economics, ___ Boston Univ. L. Rev. ___ (2020) (forthcoming) (SSRN working paper, Feb. 2020), available at https://papers.ssrn.com/sol3/papers.cfm?abstract_id=3508832.

Chapter 11

INTRABRAND RESTRAINTS
ON DISTRIBUTION

Table of Sections

---

§ 11.1   Introduction

This chapter deals with two broad categories of vertical management by contract. One is vertical price fixing, or resale price maintenance (RPM), which is manufacturer or supplier regulation of the price at which a product is resold by independent dealers.[1] The second category is most generally classified as vertical nonprice restraints. Among the most common of these is vertical territorial division, which is supplier regulation of the location or sales territories of its distributors or retailers. Another important vertical nonprice restraint is the customer restriction, which limits the classes of buyers with whom a distributor or other reseller may deal. But vertical nonprice restraints come in numerous other varieties, including restrictions preventing a dealer from selling a particular model, limitations on mail-order sales, limitations on the kinds of contracts that dealers can write with customers, or limitations on the number of dealers that a supplier will permit in a given city or other area.

The restraints described in this chapter are denominated "intrabrand," because they regulate a dealer's sales of a single brand without creating limitations on its sales of brands made by other suppliers. By contrast, "interbrand" distribution restraints limit the way downstream firms can use brands made by someone other than the firm imposing the restraint. The principal interbrand distribution restraints are tying arrangements and exclusive dealing, which are the subject of the previous chapter. Intrabrand distribution restraints are governed by § 1 of the Sherman Act. Interbrand distribution restraints are covered by § 3 of the Clayton Act as well.[2] Frequently a supplier uses both kinds of restraints simultaneously. For example, a supplier might provide in its dealer contracts that a dealer may sell only in a designated territory and deal only in the

---

[1]   In this chapter the words "upstream firm," "manufacturer," or "supplier" are used more-or-less interchangeability to refer to the upstream party to a vertical agreement. The words "downstream firm," "distributor," "dealer," "reseller," or "retailer" generally refer to the downstream party. The downstream party is an intermediary between the manufacturer and the end use consumer.

[2]   Clayton Act § 3, 15 U.S.C.A. § 15, makes it unlawful to lease or sell goods, etc., "on the condition, agreement or understanding that the lessee or purchaser thereof shall not use or deal in the goods * * * of a competitor * * * of the lessor or seller. * * *" This language does not reach restraints imposed entirely on the supplier's own brand.

supplier's brand. This would be a combination of a vertical territorial restraint (intrabrand) and exclusive dealing (interbrand). In the balance of this chapter the term "vertical restraint" refers to an intrabrand restraint.

Until fairly recently the two sets of practices were governed by two different legal standards. Today, however, all are governed by the rule of reason, although application may vary depending on the type of restraint.

§ 11.2 Perceived Competitive Threats of Minimum RPM and Vertical Territorial Restraints

11.2a. Introduction

Courts have suggested different reasons why RPM should be illegal. One is that it permits a manufacturer to take advantage of its retailers and deny them the freedom to set a price most advantageous to themselves.[3] Another is that RPM is really a manifestation of price fixing among the retailers, who have involved the manufacturer in the agreement so that it can help police the cartel.[4] A variation of the second is that a powerful individual dealer in its territory may insist that minimum prices be imposed on its retailer rivals.

The first argument seems quite specious as a general proposition. The retailer's mark-up is the price a manufacturer pays to have its product distributed, and a manufacturer should be able to have its product distributed in the most efficient manner—that is, the one that maximizes its profits. Naturally, the manufacturer wants to keep distribution costs as low as possible. Any firm is best off if other firms in the distribution chain behave as competitively as possible.[5] Any profits from a retailer's mark-up accrue to the retailer, not to the manufacturer.

11.2b. Vertical Restraints as Collusion Facilitators; Powerful Individual Dealers

The second argument noted above is that RPM is really carried out at the instigation of the retailers, who are engaged in price fixing. There are good reasons why retailers would want to involve their

---

3   Simpson v. Union Oil Co., 377 U.S. 13, 20–21, 84 S.Ct. 1051, 1056–57, rehearing denied, 377 U.S. 949, 84 S.Ct. 1349 (1964); United States v. A. Schrader's Son, Inc., 252 U.S. 85, 99, 40 S.Ct. 251, 253 (1920).

4   Dr. Miles Medical Co. v. John D. Park & Sons Co., 220 U.S. 373, 407–08, 31 S.Ct. 376, 384–85 (1911), overruled, Leegin Creative Leather Products, Inc. v. PSKS, Inc., 551 U.S. 877, 127 S.Ct. 2705 (2007).

5   See § 9.2b, c.

suppliers in a cartel. The suppliers may be in a better position to monitor the pricing activities of the retailers, since the manufacturers normally deal with each retailer, but the retailers do not normally deal with each other. In addition, if the manufacturers manage to take advantage of the *Colgate*[6] exception, they will be able to enforce RPM legally.

Such retailer cartels are alleged to come in two kinds. If the manufacturers in the market have little market power and product differentiation is minor, then the retailers of any single manufacturer could not raise the price of the manufacturer's product to monopoly levels. Customers would switch to a different brand. For example, if Sylvania makes 5% of the nation's televisions and consumers do not differentiate Sylvania TVs significantly from other brands, then, a cartel of Sylvania retailers could not charge a monopoly price for Sylvania televisions. Customers would switch to Sony, Toshiba, LG or some other brand. In this situation only an "interbrand" cartel will work—that is, a cartel encompassing enough brands of televisions that the price fixers collectively have significant market power. Likewise, the RPM agreements facilitating the cartel would have to come from all these manufacturers.

By contrast, if Sylvania were a television monopolist, itself capable of charging a monopoly price, then the cartel of Sylvania retailers could likewise charge a monopoly price. The RPM agreements facilitating the cartel need come only from this monopoly manufacturer.[7] If the product is differentiated substantially, then a cartel of that brand's dealer might be able to charge a higher price, depending on the extent of competition with other brands.

RPM and vertical territorial restrictions can be evidence of retailer collusion only if 1) the manufacturer imposing the restriction is either a monopolist in the retailer's area or significant product differentiation gives that brand sufficient market power; or 2) the restriction is used by a high percentage of the manufacturers in the market. Either of these phenomena would support the inference that the retailers subject to the restriction collectively have enough market power to engage in price fixing.

A wealth of history shows that dealers have attempted to use RPM imposed by suppliers to facilitate horizontal dealer collusion. Indeed, the *Dr. Miles* decision first condemning RPM was the

---

[6]   See United States v. Colgate & Co., 250 U.S. 300, 39 S.Ct. 465 (1919), discussed in § 11.4b.

[7]   See 8 Antitrust Law ¶ 1604 (4th ed. 2017). Further, if multibrand dealers had market power locally, they might be able to cartelize a product in which the supplier lacked market power.

byproduct of one of the biggest dealer cartels in American history—
an agreement by members of national associations of wholesale and
retail druggists to fix the price of proprietary medical drugs.[8] In many
of the early RPM decisions, there was strong evidence of horizontal
as well as vertical collusion.[9] One of the most widely publicized
incidents of dealer forced RPM occurred in the 1930's and involved
the same industry as *Dr. Miles*. When the manufacturer of Pepsodent
toothpaste stopped using RPM, druggists responded *en masse* by
relegating Pepsodent to second class distribution or not distributing
it at all, and the druggists' trade association campaigned for what
amounted to a boycott. The manufacturer gave in and restored
RPM.[10]

11.2b1. Dealer Power; Policy Implications

Most of the Chicago School analysis urging *per se* legality of
RPM presumed that the power of either individual dealers or dealer
cartels was rare. Retail stores generally do not require highly
specialized building or other productive assets, and stores selling one
set of products can often change or add others readily. In sum entry
is easy, and suppliers can quickly find new distribution outlets. Most
importantly, manufacturers can always integrate into distribution
themselves if resellers persist in charging monopoly prices.

But there is ample experience belying these assumptions. Large
multi-brand chain stores almost certainly produce sufficient
economies of scale and scope in retailing to give them substantial cost
advantages over single-brand stores or small, individual stores. To
that extent, entry into the market cannot be presumed to be easy—
and not even vertical integration by manufacturers is likely to occur
unless the manufacturer's output is broad enough to support brand-
specific retailing.

A well designed rule of reason inquiry would look into things
that were largely unnecessary under the old rule of per se illegality.
Chief among these are the market power of those imposing the
restraint. Further, dealers must often deal in multiple brands.

---

[8]   See Herbert Hovenkamp, Enterprise and American Law, 1836–1937 at 342–
345 (1991).

[9]   See, e.g., Continental Wall Paper Co. v. Voight & Sons Co., 148 Fed. 939 (6th
Cir. 1906), affirmed, 212 U.S. 227, 29 S.Ct. 280 (1909) (refusing to enforce RPM
contract between colluding members of manufacturing association and price-cutting
reseller); Loder v. Jayne, 142 Fed. 1010 (C.C. Pa.), affirmed, 149 Fed. 21 (3d Cir. 1906)
(finding conspiracy among drug manufacturers to fix prices and impose RPM on
retailers).

[10]   Thomas Overstreet, Jr., & Alan Fisher, Resale Price Maintenance and
Distributional Efficiency: Some Lessons from the Past, 3 Contemp. Policy Issues 3, 45–
50 (1985). Similar incidents are recounted in Laura Phillips Sawyer, American Fair
Trade: Proprietary Capitalism and the "New Competition," 1890–1940 (2018).

Manufacturers are typically more able to control resellers who deal exclusively in their own brand, because they have a great deal of leverage over the reseller. Indeed, the manufacturer could deprive the reseller of all its inventory. But when the product must be sold by large multibrand stores, then the tables are often turned. Such resellers can acquire a great deal of leverage over suppliers.

Second, the product must be one that can be sold at a supracompetitive price. The important question is not the product's nationwide market share, assuming it is distributed in a national market, but its share in the municipality or other geographic area where retail customers shop and can seek out alternatives. At the same time, we are not looking for the power to engage in monopolistic exclusionary practices, but merely the power to raise price profitably. A share in the range of 40–50 percent should be sufficient, given that the market is typically subject to both product differentiation and spatial differentiation among sellers—that is, the retailer taking advantage of the restraints is likely to be in a favored position vis-a-vis other retailers. In general, issues of retail distribution and retailer power are highly fact specific, warning us against overgeneralization.

11.2b2. Manufacturer Collusion and Vertical Restraints

Writers have also argued that vertical restrictions may facilitate collusion at the manufacturer rather than the retailer level. As § 4.1 noted, vertical integration can enable a cartel to police its members more carefully. Sales made to wholesalers or distributors are generally large, secret, and individually negotiated. The cartel member has an incentive to cheat by shading price, providing extra services, engaging in reciprocity,[11] or accepting secret rebates. Since the chances of detection increase with the number of such cheating sales, it is important that each sale be large. Retail prices, by contrast, are generally public, relatively standardized at particular locations, and individual transactions are small. Effective price concessions can be communicated only by public advertising, which competitors will see. By imposing RPM or territorial restrictions on retailers, a manufacturers' cartel may be able to monitor prices and number of sales at the retail level.

The manufacturers' cartel will work, however, only if its members collectively control enough of the market to wield monopoly power. Furthermore, price or output verification by vertical restrictions will work only if all cartel members use it. As a result the restrictions are evidence of a manufacturers' cartel only if most

---

[11]   On reciprocity, see § 10.8.

manufacturers in the market are using them. Presumptively, at least, if fewer than half of the manufacturers in a properly defined market are using a restraint, it is not likely to be a facilitator of manufacturer collusion.

11.2c.   Price Discrimination

Vertical restrictions, particularly vertical territorial or product assignments, may be designed to facilitate price discrimination by the manufacturer. Price discrimination occurs when the seller makes higher profits from one set of customers than from another. The two most significant practical barriers to price discrimination are the difficulty of identifying and segregating groups of customers willing to pay different prices, and the difficulty of preventing arbitrage. Arbitrage occurs when favored purchasers (those who pay the lower price) resell the product to disfavored purchasers and frustrate the price discrimination scheme.

Vertically imposed territorial or customer restrictions can enable a manufacturer to solve both these problems. For example, suppose that the manufacturer produces a disinfectant used by both hospitals and restaurants. The hospitals have fewer available substitutes for the disinfectant, and they are willing to pay a higher price than the restaurants. The manufacturer could discriminate in price between the two groups of customers by using two different distributors, giving one the exclusive right to sell to hospitals, and the other the exclusive right to sell to restaurants. Alternatively, the manufacturer could engage in "dual distribution," by selling to the hospitals itself but using an independent distributor for the restaurants. These restrictions help the manufacturer segregate the customers and prevent arbitrage, because each class of customers deals with a different seller and has little reason to know that a different group of customers is buying the same product from someone else. Both vertical customer restraints and vertical territorial restraints have been used by manufacturers to facilitate price discrimination in this way. For example, in the *Clairol* case the manufacturer produced a hair coloring agent, which it sold in two different bottles, one for solons and one for retail customers. Although the two bottles contained the same ingredients, Clairol sold the salon version for 46 cents less per bottle. Its restraint system, which survived challenge, forbad distributors of the salon version from making that version available to general retailers.[12]

Should vertical restraints be condemned simply because they facilitate price discrimination? The efficiency effects of such

---

[12]   Clairol v. Boston Discount Center of Berkley, 608 F.2d 1114 (6th Cir. 1979).

restraints is almost impossible to measure. Price discrimination schemes often increase output and rarely exclude rivals.[13] At the same time, however, price discrimination does not invariably increase output, and it can be costly to administer. As a basic premise, the best answer seems to be that the existence of third degree price discrimination alone should not warrant condemnation of a restraint.

§ 11.3   Vertical Restraints and Efficiency

11.3a.   The Free-Rider Problem

Some manufacturers use intrabrand restraints not to facilitate price fixing, which reduces output, but to enlarge output by encouraging retailers to market the manufacturer's product more aggressively and efficiently.

Often the manufacturer is attempting to avoid one of the many variations of the "free rider" problem. Suppose that Chrysler Motor Co. has two auto dealerships in Wichita. Dealer A is stocked with a full inventory of cars (which the dealer carries at its own expense), has a large and expensive showroom, many sales agents who spend a great deal of time displaying cars and giving test drives to prospective purchasers, and an excellent service department that makes many pre-sale and post-sale adjustments to new cars. Dealer B, located across town, rents one room in a warehouse, has no inventory, gives no test rides, has no service department, and does all its negotiating over the telephone.[14]

The point-of-sale services given by Dealer A are costly, and Dealer A must charge about $500 more than it pays for a new car just to cover its distribution costs. By contrast, Dealer B does quite well with a mark-up of $100. What do you do as a new car buyer? Perhaps you will go to Dealer A's large showroom, look at the cars, test drive one or more, collect a good deal of information, and leave, telling the salesperson that you will "think about it." Then you go to Dealer B and place an order for the car you want.

The information you obtained from Dealer A was essential to your decision making. For example, you probably would not have purchased a Chrysler had you not been permitted to test drive one. You avoided paying for the information you gathered, however, by purchasing from a different dealer who did not supply the information and was able to sell the car at a lower price. You and

---

[13]   See 3A Antitrust Law ¶ 720 (4th ed. 2015).

[14]   For a roughly similar story, see United States v. General Motors Corp., 384 U.S. 127, 86 S.Ct. 1321 (1966).

Dealer B in this case took a "free ride" on the point-of-sale information offered by Dealer A.

Unfortunately, Dealer A does not make money giving test drives; the dealer must sell cars. It will not stay in business long if everyone takes advantage of its information system but purchases their cars from Dealer B. Further, if Dealer A goes out of business Chrysler's Wichita sales will decline substantially, because most customers insist on being able to obtain this vital information *somewhere* before they purchase a particular brand of automobile. In order to compete effectively with other automakers, Chrysler must have a mechanism for providing potential customers with test drives and other vital information.

Suppose, however, that Chrysler requires its Wichita dealers to charge the same resale price for various models of automobiles—say, $24,000 for a particular model. Now you as customer have no incentive remaining to make your purchase from the cut-rate dealer, which must charge the same price anyway. You will go to the dealer who does the best job of providing the kind of information and customer service that is important to you when you buy a car. The cut-rate dealer will have to clean up its act or lose business. In fact, with the final output price given, the two dealers will compete with each other, not in price, but in the amount of services they can deliver. Competition between them will drive the level of services up to the point at which their marginal costs equal the maintained price.[15]

Similar analysis applies to vertical territorial restraints. Instead of establishing a resale price, Chrysler might simply terminate Dealer B (the cut-rate dealer) and give Dealer A the exclusive right to retail new Chryslers in Wichita. Now Chrysler can be assured that its customers will obtain the point-of-sale information and services that they want. Dealer A will have a contract with Chrysler, which tells the dealer how much service to provide. The dealer no longer has the disincentive of a cut-rate dealer stealing its customers. Further, Dealer A is not a monopolist: it still competes with other automobile retailers in Wichita, and cannot take a free ride on their services. For example, a customer will not test drive a Ford in order to determine whether she wants to purchase a Chrysler.

---

[15]   See Lester Telser, Why Should Manufacturers Want Fair Trade? 3 J.L. & Econ. 86 (1960).

11.3b.   Variations on the Free-Rider Problem and Alternative Explanations

11.3b1. *Purchase of Preferred Distribution Services; Shelf Space; Quality Certification*

Many commodities sold subject to RPM or nonprice restraints seem not to require significant consumer educational services at the point of sale. Among these are toothpaste, candy, blue jeans, men's underwear, pet supplies, and beer. Competitive explanations for vertical restraints in products that appear to require no point-of-sale services have been manifold. The following discussion summarizes those that appear most plausible and that seem to apply to a broad range of situations.

Products sold subject to RPM, but where point-of-sale services seem insubstantial, often share one characteristic: multi-brand or multi-product retailers have an advantage over single-product retailers. For example, few stores deal exclusively in Levi's brand blue jeans. Jeans are distributed most efficiently if they can be placed in a large number of stores in a single city. In that case demand in each location will be insufficient to sustain the entire store. As a result Levi's are most generally sold in clothing stores which offer other brands of blue jeans as well as other types of clothing, or even in department stores that sell a wide array of products.

When Levi Strauss sells its blue jeans through, say, Macy's Department Stores, Levi is effectively purchasing distribution services from Macy's. Importantly, these services are not fungible. Macy's has preferred shelf space in the center of the store, and less satisfactory space hidden in the corners. Further, if Macy's has a very positive image in the eyes of consumers, its handling of a product serves as a kind of certification that the product is good.[16] It hires people to assemble displays, and has considerable discretion about how much expense and effort will go into one particular item's promotion rather than another's. The high margins guaranteed by RPM can serve as an inducement to Macy's to give Levi's favorable treatment.

11.3b2. *Facilitating Resale Density*

Firms also use RPM to obtain high density of distribution. For some relatively inexpensive but space-consuming products, it is more important to manufacturers to have them available on every corner, so to speak, than to have them available at the lowest possible price.

---

[16]   See Howard P. Marvel & Stephen McCafferty, Resale Price Maintenance and Quality Certification, 15 Rand. J.Econ. 346 (1984).

RPM may guarantee relatively high cost outlets a sufficient margin to carry a product.[17] Suppose that newspapers could be sold by discounters or large grocery stores at $2.00, but that small convenience stores would not carry them at a price lower than $3.00. Newspapers have two groups of buyers. Group A is willing to pay $3.00 for a newspaper, but they will also walk or drive the extra block or two, or put up with the longer line, in order to buy their newspaper for $2.00. Group B will buy their newspaper from whichever store is closest or most convenient, giving little thought to the higher price. In this situation, without RPM the discounters will sell the newspaper for $2.00 and the convenience stores will sell it for $3.00. The convenience stores will lose all of group A, and this may make carrying newspapers unprofitable. With RPM, both must charge $3.00. Then both groups of customers will shop the convenience stores as much as the discounters. The effect of the RPM may be to make it profitable for both groups of stores to sell the newspaper, thus increasing density of distribution.

11.3b3. Protection of Dealer Margins; Enforcement of Distribution Contracts

Vertical restraints can also be mechanisms for enforcing distribution contracts by making termination costly to dealers. Contracts between manufacturers and dealers can apply to the full range of products and dealer services that manufacturers wish their dealers to provide. A supplier "enforces" a contract with a dealer by terminating the dealer or taking some less drastic disciplinary measure, such as reducing the supply of a profitable item. But these enforcement threats are credible only if the dealership in the manufacturer's products is profitable. One conceptual difficulty with the traditional free-rider model is that dealers compete in the giving of nonprice services until their costs rise to the price. Dealers make only a competitive rate of return. A dealer who is earning no more than a competitive return on product A may not be injured very much if its manufacturer terminates the dealer.

Resale price maintenance and vertical nonprice restraints may thus serve to ensure that dealers earn positive profits by protecting them from significant intrabrand competition. The effect of the profits is that termination of a dealership is costly to the dealer, thus giving it a powerful incentive to honor the terms of whatever contractual understanding it has with the supplier. The value of this

---

[17]   Pauline Ippolito & Thomas R. Overstreet, Resale Price Maintenance: an Economic Assessment of the FTC's Case Against the Corning Glass Works, 39 J.L. & Econ. 285 (1996) (finding seller density as most likely explanation for resale price maintenance of simple glass items).

conception of distribution restraints is that it applies across the full range of products and services that we see governed by price and nonprice restrictions.[18]

§ 11.4 The Agreement Requirement in Vertical Restraints Cases

11.4a. Agreements—Horizontal and Vertical, Price and Nonprice

Both RPM and vertical nonprice restraints are challenged under § 1 of the Sherman Act as contracts, combinations or conspiracies in restraint of trade. Just as with the law of horizontal price fixing, illegal vertical restraints cannot be condemned without evidence of a qualifying agreement among two or more firms to impose the restraint. The agreement need not be with the plaintiff—for example, it could be an agreement with a supplier and the disciplined dealer's competitor.[19] The agreement could also be one among suppliers to impose RPM or vertical nonprice restraints on dealers below. But a purely unilateral decision to impose such restraints is not reachable under § 1.

The conceptual differences between a horizontal agreement and a vertical agreement are significant. For example, competitors meeting together to discuss market prices may provoke considerable suspicion. But a supplier and a dealer are necessarily parties to a buyer-seller agreement, and they presumably discuss prices all the time.[20] As a result, in vertical restraints cases the evidentiary focus tends to be the *content* of agreements, while horizontal cases tend to focus on the *fact* of agreement. As § 11.5d notes, when courts determine whether vertical agreements concern "price," they are much stricter than when they make that determination respecting horizontal agreements. A horizontal agreement that merely "affects price" can be illegal per se. By contrast, a vertical agreement does not count as a "price agreement" unless it establishes a rather specific price or price level.

---

[18]   See Benjamin Klein & Kevin M. Murphy, Vertical Restraints as Contract Enforcement Mechanisms, 31 J.L. & Econ. 265 (1988). Compare Business Electronics Corp. v. Sharp Electronics Corp., 485 U.S. 717, 728, 108 S.Ct. 1515, 1521 (1988) (suggesting that vertical non-price restraints ensure that dealers earn enough profits to pay for necessary services).

[19]   However, a purely horizontal agreement among suppliers to terminate a dealer for failing to adhere to a vertical restriction is best dealt with as a concerted refusal to deal. See § 5.4.

[20]   See 11 Antitrust Law ¶ 1902d (4th ed. 2018).

The basic agreement requirement for price and nonprice restraints is the same.[21] Nevertheless, historically the per se rule forced the agreement requirement to loom much larger in RPM cases. Under the *Dr. Miles* rule, proving a qualifying price "agreement" was often tantamount to establishing the violation. Today, however, most vertical agreements of both price and nonprice varieties are presumptively legal, with exceptions only for those that represent unreasonable exercises of unilateral or collusive market power. Indeed, vertical restraints imposing territorial boundaries, store locations, customer restrictions and the like, are often specified in writing in distribution agreements that are signed by both supplier and dealer. In such cases existence of an agreement is not disputed.

11.4b. The *Colgate* Doctrine

The Supreme Court first stated the agreement requirement for vertical restraints in United States v. Colgate & Co.[22] The *Colgate* decision was the unforeseen result of a badly drafted indictment, which neglected to "charge Colgate * * * with selling its products to dealers under agreements which obligated the latter not to resell except at prices fixed by the company." Rather, the indictment alleged 1) that Colgate entered into sales contracts with retailers; 2) that it separately announced an intention not to make such contracts with retailers who sold for less than Colgate's posted retail prices; 3) that it subsequently refused to deal with price cutters, as it announced. In an era inclined to equate the "agreement" requirement in antitrust with common law contract doctrine, the Court quite easily separated the sales contract on the one hand from Colgate's apparently "unilateral" refusal to deal on the other. The Sherman Act was not designed to "restrict the long recognized right of a trader or manufacturer [to] announce in advance the circumstances under which he will refuse to sell."[23]

One of the difficulties with *Colgate* is its excessive formalism that sends people looking for qualifying legal "agreements." *Colgate* stands for the controversial proposition that when a manufacturer simply announces its intention not to deal with price cutters and dealers respond by not cutting price, there is no violation because

---

[21]   See Parkway Gallery Furniture v. Kittinger/Pennsylvania House Group, 878 F.2d 801, 805 (4th Cir. 1989) (agreement requirement is same for price and nonprice restraints, and for rule of reason and per se violations).

[22]   250 U.S. 300, 39 S.Ct. 465 (1919).

[23]   On the relation between *Colgate* and the Supreme Court doctrine of liberty of contract, see Edward P. Krugman, Soap, Cream of Wheat and Bakeries; the Intellectual Origins of the *Colgate* Doctrine, 65 St. John's L. Rev. 827 (1991).

there was no "agreement" between the manufacturer and the price cutting retailer.[24]

In order to claim the *Colgate* exception the manufacturer can do no more than announce its intent not to deal with price cutters, and later refuse to deal with a violator. As the Supreme Court held in *Parke, Davis*, if the manufacturer warns, threatens, or intimidates its retailers in any way, it is likely to fall out of the exception and into the then existing *per se* prohibition.[25]

Its formalism notwithstanding, the *Colgate* doctrine retains vitality. In *Monsanto* the Supreme Court expressly refused to overrule *Colgate*, holding that it continues to be "of considerable importance that independent action by the manufacturer * * * be distinguished from price-fixing agreements."[26] In fact, the Court went so far as to say that an agreement could not be inferred from the fact that a supplier terminated one dealer in response to a second dealer's complaints about the first dealer's price cutting.

One serious analytic problem with the *Colgate* doctrine as originally developed, is that it seems inimical to the basic rationale for RPM and other vertical restrictions. Such restrictions are a form of vertical integration which enable a manufacturer to achieve optimal distribution of its product. The restrictions should be approved when their potential for creating efficiency is apparent, and condemned only when there is some potential for economic harm.

Colgate, however, is predicated on the natural right of retailers to be free from manufacturers. In order to claim the exception a manufacturer must *avoid* becoming too involved with its retailers. Vertical integration often necessitates a great deal of cooperation and communication between a manufacturer and the retailers who make up its distribution system. One of the chief advantages that a manufacturer obtains from outright ownership of its own retail outlets is the right to operate the stores, displaying and pricing the merchandise as it sees fit. Often the manufacturer is a specialist, while the retailer is a generalist. However, *Colgate* tends to approve RPM only when the level of vertical integration between manufacturer and retailer is very small. The result is that RPM is

---

[24]   See United States v. A. Schrader's Son, Inc., 264 Fed. 175, 183 (N.D. Ohio 1919), reversed, 252 U.S. 85, 40 S.Ct. 251 (1920): "Personally, and with all due respect, * * * I can see no real difference * * * between the Dr. Miles Medical Co. case [refusing to enforce an RPM agreement] and the Colgate Co. case. * * * The tacit acquiescence of the wholesalers and retailers in the prices thus fixed is the equivalent for all practical purposes of an express agreement * * *."

[25]   United States v. Parke, Davis & Co., 362 U.S. 29, 80 S.Ct. 503 (1960).

[26]   Monsanto Co. v. Spray-Rite Serv. Corp., 465 U.S. 752, 763, 104 S.Ct. 1464, 1470 (1984).

most available in those situations where it is least valuable—where there is no organized "distribution system" at all.

11.4c.   Dealer Terminations

One effect of the old *per se* rule against RPM and the *Colgate* exception was a rule once adopted by several circuit courts that a supplier could not lawfully terminate a distributor "in response to" a competing distributor's complaints that the terminated distributor had been cutting prices. Different courts characterized this conduct in different ways.

In *Monsanto*, the Supreme Court held that a court could not infer the existence of an RPM agreement "merely from the existence of complaints, or even from the fact that termination came about 'in response to' complaints." Rather, the evidence must show "a conscious commitment to a common scheme designed to achieve an unlawful objective."[27] In this case the evidence was sufficient to support the jury's finding of a "common scheme" to set resale prices. As the court noted, however, most cases involving allegations that a supplier terminated one dealer in response to another dealer's complaints arose in the context of distribution systems that contained nonprice restrictions. As a result the termination may not have been the result of illegal RPM at all, but was really motivated by a dealer's violation of territorial restraints. Any rule that prevented a "manufacturer from acting solely because the information upon which it acts originated as a price complaint would create an irrational dislocation in the market."

The Supreme Court's conclusion about the relevance of price complaints is hard to dispute. A supplier generally imposes RPM or nonprice restraints in order to combat free riding problems, to force dealers to comply with their distribution contracts or to make an adequate investment in distributing the supplier's product.[28] Furthermore, free riding injures *both* the supplier and dealers who compete with the free rider. As a result, no inference of an agreement can be drawn from the fact that a dealer or retailer complained. The complaining dealer is reporting a violation by a competing dealer that injures the complainant; the supplier is responding by disciplining a violation that injures the supplier. The supplier is acting in its *individual* best interest and no agreement can be inferred.[29]

---

[27]   Monsanto Co. v. Spray-Rite Svce. Corp., 465 U.S. 752, 768 (1984).

[28]   See § 11.3.

[29]   See for example, Helicopter Support Sys. v. Hughes Helicopter, 818 F.2d 1530 (11th Cir. 1987) (mere fact that dealer complains, which suggests that it would benefit from competing dealer's termination, insufficient to establish agreement).

So in determining agreement, one must look at the supplier's *independent* best interest—that is, what would the supplier's best interest be on the assumption that some generic dealer, totally lacking in market power, had made the complaint? For example, Apple Computer Company met this test when it convinced the court that its ban on low price mail order sales was necessary because it believed that optimal customer education required a face-to-face transaction.[30] The fact finder should also consider the validity of the reasons advanced for terminating the plaintiff.[31]

11.4d. The Agreement Requirement and Antitrust Policy Respecting Vertical Restraints; Restraints Initiated by Powerful Dealers

Suppose a powerful local dealer forces its suppliers to impose RPM on competitors in order to support its own higher resale prices.[32] We could properly infer an "agreement" between the powerful dealer and the various suppliers, for the latter are not acting according to their independent best interest. Independently, they would rather expand their output by selling to the powerful dealer's lower price competitors. They accede to the RPM only to avoid losing the powerful dealer's business. In this case an agreement requirement also helps one distinguish between competitive and anticompetitive uses of vertical restraints.[33]

§ 11.5 Resale Price Maintenance in the Courts

11.5a. From Dr. Miles to Leegin

In Dr. Miles Medical Co. v. John D. Park & Sons Co.[34] the Supreme Court held that a contract between a manufacturer and dealer, requiring the dealer to resell the manufacturer's product at a

---

[30]   O.S.C. v. Apple Computer, 792 F.2d 1464, 1467–1468 (9th Cir. 1986).

[31]   For example, McCabe's Furniture v. La-Z-Boy Chair Co., 798 F.2d 323, 329 (8th Cir. 1986), cert. denied, 486 U.S. 1005, 108 S.Ct. 1728 (1988) (considering supplier's claim that dealer termination was necessary to assure quality of dealer services).

[32]   For example, Garment District v. Belk Stores Servs., 799 F.2d 905 (4th Cir. 1986), cert. denied, 486 U.S. 1005, 108 S.Ct. 1728 (1988).

[33]   See Watson Carpet & Floor Covering, Inc. v. Mohawk Indus., Inc., 648 F.3d 452 (6th Cir. 2011) (sustaining complaint that carpet manufacturer conspired with certain carpet dealers to exclude the plaintiff, a competing carpet dealer). See also 8 Antitrust Law ¶ 1604 (4th ed. 2017).

[34]   220 U.S. 373, 400, 31 S.Ct. 376, 381 (1911). One year earlier the Dr. Miles Co. had signed a consent decree agreeing not to participate with drug retailers in the horizontal price fixing of drugs. Park was an "aggressive cutter"—a pharmacy that did not participate in the cartel, but instead cut prices. RPM was clearly being used to facilitate horizontal collusion. See Jayne v. Loder, 149 Fed. 21, 25 (3d Cir. 1906); and see Herbert Hovenkamp, Enterprise and American Law: 1836–1937 at ch. 25 (1991).

specified price was unenforceable because it was contrary to the policy of the Sherman Act. The Court could not determine why a manufacturer would want to impose such a requirement upon its dealers. It admitted that "the advantage of established retail prices primarily concerns the dealers," who would receive "enlarged profits" as a result. The injury that the Court perceived was that only "favored" dealers would be able to realize these profits. Presumably there were disfavored dealers who could not obtain a fair share of the market unless they cut the resale price.

On this rationale was born the rule that "vertical price-fixing" or resale price maintenance (RPM) is illegal *per se*. The Court found no theory under which the manufacturer would be benefitted by RPM. Since under the Court's theory the end result was higher retail prices, the only thing that accrued to the manufacturer was reduced output, and therefore lower profits. The Court rejected with almost no comment the principal defense given: that the success of Dr. Miles' Medicine depended on the density of its distribution, and the typical pharmacy would be loathe to sell something commonly traded at a discounted price.[35]

The *Dr. Miles* decision followed the traditional common law rule that agreements in restraint of trade, although not affirmatively illegal, were unenforceable among the parties. Indeed, the court made only two brief references to the Sherman Act, and then only to observe that its meaning and that of the common law were probably the same.

After nearly a century of debate among academics and lawyers, a divided (5–4) Supreme Court overruled *Dr. Miles* in its 2007 *Leegin* decision.[36] The defendant Leegin was a manufacturer of leather garments which it sold through specialty retailers under the "Brighton" brand. The plaintiff PSKS was a discount retailer that operated "Kay's Kloset" and refused to abide by resale prices that Leegin specified as a condition of supply. As the Supreme Court noted, in the century since *Dr. Miles* the Court had "rejected the rationales on which" it was based, including its reliance on common law restraints on alienation and "formalistic" doctrine rather than "demonstrable economic effect," as well as *Dr. Miles* failure to

---

[35] The Court did note: "If there be an advantage to the manufacturer in the maintenance of fixed retail prices, the question remains whether it is one which he is entitled to secure by agreements restricting the freedom of trade on the part of the dealers who own what they sell." 220 U.S. at 407–408, 31 S.Ct. at 384. It then answered in the negative. On the "density of distribution" rationale for RPM, see § 11.3b2.

[36] Leegin Creative Leather Products, Inc. v. PSKS, Inc., 551 U.S. 877, 127 S.Ct. 2705 (2007).

distinguish horizontal from vertical price fixing.[37] The Court then turned to the legal economic literature, where the consensus seemed quite strong that RPM was procompetitive much of the time.[38] It observed that the effects of RPM were frequently analogized to the effects of vertical nonprice restraints, which had been subject to rule of reason treatment for some thirty years.[39] Respecting the commonly stated free rider explanation for RPM:

> Absent vertical price restraints, the retail services that enhance interbrand competition might be underprovided. This is because discounting retailers can free ride on retailers who furnish services and then capture some of the increased demand those services generate. Consumers might learn, for example, about the benefits of a manufacturer's product from a retailer that invests in fine showrooms, offers product demonstrations, or hires and trains knowledgeable employees.[40] Or consumers might decide to buy the product because they see it in a retail establishment that has a reputation for selling high-quality merchandise. If the consumer can then buy the product from a retailer that discounts because it has not spent capital providing services or developing a quality reputation, the high-service retailer will lose sales to the discounter, forcing it to cut back its services to a level lower than consumers would otherwise prefer. Minimum resale price maintenance alleviates the problem because it prevents the discounter from undercutting the service provider. With price competition decreased, the manufacturer's retailers compete among themselves over services.[41]

Further, RPM can "increase interbrand competition by encouraging retailer services that would not be provided even absent free riding," which it would do by guaranteeing the retailer's margin on certain products for which retailer risk and cost were high.[42]

---

[37]   Id. at 884–885.

[38]   Id. at 888–890, citing Herbert Hovenkamp, The Antitrust Enterprise: Principle and Execution 184–191 (2006); Robert H. Bork, The Antitrust Paradox 288–291 (1978); ABA Section of Antitrust Law, Antitrust Law and Economics of Product Distribution 76 (2006); Frederic M. Scherer & David Ross, Industrial Market Structure and Economic Performance 558 (3d ed. 1990); and two amicus briefs.

[39]   See Continental T. V. v. GTE Sylvania, 433 U.S. 36, 97 S.Ct. 2549 (1977).

[40]   Citing Richard A. Posner, Antitrust Law 172–173 (2d ed. 2001).

[41]   *Leegin*, 551 U.S. at 891, citing Howard P. Marvel & Stephen McCafferty, Resale Price Maintenance and Quality Certification, 15 Rand J. Econ. 346, 347–349 (1984).

[42]   Id. at 892.

On the other side RPM could be used to facilitate dealer collusion, or to impose higher consumer prices at the behest of a powerful dealer who demands that the manufacturer stop serving or discipline its price cutting competitors.[43]

For the Court these offsetting possibilities made the rule of reason the only appropriate vehicle for assessing RPM and justified jettisoning the century-old *Dr. Miles* precedent. The four dissenters led by Justice Breyer did not deny the first portion of that proposition, although they did disagree about the balance of potentially beneficial and harmful effects. Justice Breyer acknowledged that, were the Court writing on a clean slate, more lenient treatment than a harsh per se rule might be appropriate. But the slate was hardly clean, and a century worth of limiting and defining doctrine had grown up around the per se rule. As a result of this doctrine implementation of RPM rules had proven "practical over the course of the last century, particularly when compared with the many complexities of litigating a case under the 'rule of reason' regime."[44] He concluded that the new rule would:

> likely raise the price of goods at retail and that it will create considerable legal turbulence as lower courts seek to develop workable principles. I do not believe that the majority has shown new or changed conditions sufficient to warrant overruling a decision of such long standing. All ordinary *stare decisis* considerations indicate the contrary.[45]

The *Leegin* decision binds neither Congress nor state legislatures and courts. Congress has tampered with RPM on more than one occasion. A few states have reinstated or preserved the per se rule for sales within their borders, by either legislation or judicial decision.[46] Whether such statutes survive preemption or Constitutional challenge very likely depends on the extent to which the state statute purports to reach extraterritorial conduct or conduct

---

[43]   *Leegin*, 551 U.S. at 893–894, citing 8 Antitrust Law ¶ 1604.

[44]   Id. at 924 (Breyer, J., dissenting).

[45]   Id. at 929.

[46]   See, e.g., O'Brien v. Leegin Creative Leather Prods., Inc., 294 Kan. 318, 277 P.3d 1062 (2012) (retaining per se rule); Alan Durush v. Revision LP, 2013 WL 1749539 (C.D. Cal. 2013) (suggesting but not deciding that California still follows per se rule); People v. Tempur-Pedic Int'l, Inc., 95 A.D.3d 539, 944 N.Y.S.2d 518 (App. Div. 2012) (under New York law RPM agreements are not affirmatively challengeable but they are not enforceable either). See also Md. Code Ann., Com. Law §§ 11–201 et seq. (2009); and see Michael A. Lindsay, From the Prairie to the Ocean: More Developments in State RPM Law, 11 Antitrust Source 1 (August 2012).

that has no economic effect within the state, as well as the extent to which it might discriminate against interstate commerce.

11.5b.   The Meaning of "Resale"—Consignment Exception

Under *Dr. Miles*, the per se rule against resale price maintenance applied only when the supplier sold a good to the dealer and then attempted to regulate the price at which the good was resold. If nothing was resold, then the rule did not apply. For example, suppose the franchisor of a hair cutting salon instructs individual franchisees that a certain type of haircut must cost $12.00. The RPM rule does not apply, for nothing is being resold.[47] Under the rule of reason this distinction between resales of products, and services that are merely licensed, would seem to lose most of its importance. For example, if a sufficiently powerful haircut franchisee should exist, it might be able to force the franchisor to raise the haircut prices charged by other franchisees. This situation would be economically identical to that of the powerful dealer who forces RPM upon rival dealers. We might think it unlikely that any individual haircut store could ever acquire such power, but that is a different matter.

In United States v. General Electric Co.,[48] the Court held that the *Dr. Miles* rule does not apply to a consignment agreement in which the retailer is the manufacturer's agent rather than a purchaser and reseller, and title to the merchandise remains with the manufacturer. Once again, nothing was being "sold" to the dealer; thus there was no "resale" to the customer.

Theoretically, everything that can be achieved by a sale and resale can also be achieved by a properly drawn consignment contract. For that reason, firms sometimes attempt to evade *Dr. Miles* by simply relabelling their agreements "consignments" rather than contracts for sale. Historically, courts were rather wooden about applying this consignment, or "agency" exception to the RPM rule, emphasizing such metaphysical questions as when "title" to goods passes from one person to another.[49]

But since the mid-1960s the courts have tried to find viable economic distinctions between resale and consignment agreements, justifying a *Dr. Miles* exception for the latter. In Simpson v. Union

---

[47]   See 8 Antitrust Law ¶ 1622 (4th ed. 2017); and Great Clips v. Levine, 1991–2 Trade Cas. ¶ 69671, 1991 WL 322975 (D. Minn. 1991) (not unlawful RPM for haircut franchisor to restrict franchisee's pricing of haircuts).

[48]   272 U.S. 476, 47 S.Ct. 192 (1926).

[49]   For example, see *General Electric*, 272 U.S. at 484–485.

Oil Co.,[50] the Supreme Court applied *Dr. Miles* to a "consignment agreement" between a large refiner and its retail gasoline stations. All risks of loss were on the station operators, who leased their stations from the refiner. The operators also faced some risk of lower market prices, since their commissions rose or fell with changes in retail prices. The refiner refused to renew the plaintiff's lease because the plaintiff sold gasoline at less than the refiner's stipulated resale price.

In condemning the arrangement, Justice Douglas expressly approved a bona fide consignment arrangement under which an owner took a single article to a dealer who would sell the article as the owner's agent. However, when such arrangements are used "to cover a vast gasoline distribution system, fixing prices through many retail outlets," then "the antitrust laws prevent calling the 'consignment' an agency * * *." Union Oil's consignment device was nothing more than a "clever manipulation of words."

The *Simpson* rule did not draw the traditional line between bona fide consignment arrangements and resale agreements. Justice Douglas rested the distinction on whether the producer had a distribution "system" or was simply negotiating a single sale of a single article. For this reason Justice Stewart wrote in dissent that *Simpson* really overruled *General Electric*.[51] *Simpson* effectively held that there was no consignment exception for large manufacturers with established distribution networks.

Consignment agreements persist in certain situations as an alternative to sale and resale. Two things make consignment attractive to certain retailers. First, consignment can enable a retailer to obtain inventory without tying up capital or credit. Second, under consignment agreements a supplier typically assumes more of the risks of loss, nonsale or price decline than under a resale agreement. For example, sometimes highly perishable products such as bread are distributed to small grocers on consignment. Under the agreement the wholesaler baker comes to the store each morning, dropping off fresh loaves and picking up loaves left unsold from the previous day. The grocer pays only for the loaves that were sold. The baker—who likely has a specialized outlet for "day old" bread—can sell the outdated bread more efficiently than the grocer. By this mechanism most of the risk of nonsale is retained by the manufacturer.

Consignment can also permit certain suppliers to reach a market more efficiently, particularly if market demand for the

---

[50]   377 U.S. 13, 84 S.Ct. 1051 (1964).

[51]   Id. at 21–22, 84 S.Ct. at 1057.

product is highly uncertain. An unknown artist, for example, may give her painting or sculpture to a retail gallery on consignment. The artist and gallery will agree on a retail price, from which the gallery will take its percentage if the work is sold. If it is not sold within a certain time, the artist and gallery may renegotiate the price or the artist may withdraw the work. By this mechanism the gallery avoids investing its capital in a high risk enterprise. The artist, by contrast, is likely to have more confidence (perhaps unwarranted) in her ability to sell to the public than the gallery does. If the gallery were forced to pay for the painting before resale it would probably demand a much larger discount from the artist's expected resale price than the artist would wish to accept.

In *Illinois Corporate Travel* the court had little difficulty in concluding that a travel agent is not a buyer-reseller of tickets for the airlines.[52] The agents carried no inventory of seats, but simply accessed a computer to sell seats out of the airlines' own inventory. There was no risk of non-sale. Equally important to the court was the fact that the market was created and defined totally by the airlines, not the travel agents, and that the market seemed to require consistency in the communication of prices. Finally, the travel agents had very little involvement in the delivery of the service being sold. They printed the tickets, but they had almost nothing to do with providing air transport service itself.[53] Customers did not merely purchase a "ticket," which is intrinsically worthless; they purchased a ride on an airplane, which the travel agent did not sell. *Illinois Corporate Travel* reflects the trend to limit *Simpson*'s holding that consignment should not be found when the good is distributed through a large distribution system. The array of travel agents used by the national airlines certainly qualifies as a large "system," but the consignment label clearly applies nevertheless.

In a consignment agreement such as this, supplier regulation of the price becomes imperative. Once the dealer's profits are fixed, the dealer's interest is to sell as much as possible, without regard to cost, and she bears virtually none of the costs of the actual plane trip. The only entity capable of efficient pricing is the airline.

The consignment exception has less importance under *Leegin*'s rule of reason for resale price maintenance. For example, the consignment exception has never been particularly important in the law of vertical nonprice restraints, which has been governed by a rule

---

[52]   Illinois Corporate Travel, Inc. v. American Airlines, 806 F.2d 722, 725 (7th Cir. 1986), after remand, 889 F.2d 751, 752–753 (7th Cir. 1989), cert. denied, 495 U.S. 919, 110 S.Ct. 1948 (1990).

[53]   Id. at 725.

of reason for most of antitrust history. Further, the anticompetitive threat posed by RPM—such as when it is asserted at the behest of a powerful dealer—has little to do with whether the underlying transaction is a consignment or a sale. As a result, the rule of reason should be able to take us straight to the issue of competitive vs. anticompetitive behavior, without being sidetracked by an issue that is of little economic consequence. So far, however, that has not been the case. The real focus of the consignment question has not been on the competitive analysis of RPM, but rather on whether there is an agreement between two independent actors. That is to say, once the court has decided that the reseller is a consignee rather than a reseller they treat him as an agent, or as an actor who is technically "inside the firm." That makes the conduct unilateral rather than conspiratorial and takes it out of § 1 of the Sherman Act altogether.

11.5c.   Maximum RPM

Although the old *per se* rule against minimum RPM had many supporters, few people have had good things to say about the Supreme Court's *Albrecht* decision that *maximum* resale price maintenance is also illegal *per se*.[54] Nevertheless, the *Albrecht* rule lasted thirty years until overruled by the Supreme Court in *State Oil*.[55]

Few Supreme Court decisions had proven more anticompetitive than *Albrecht*. A manufacturer generally establishes maximum resale prices in order to prevent retailers from charging a monopoly price, either because the latter had formed a cartel or because individually they had monopoly power in their respective geographic markets. In *Albrecht,* the dealers (newspaper delivery agents) were monopolists: each had an exclusive territory. Even a small monopolist such as a newspaper carrier has the power to reduce output and raise price. One set of victims of this monopolization was newspaper customers, who must either pay a higher price or cancel their subscriptions. Another victim, however, was the newspaper, which obtained no additional revenues from the higher price but made fewer sales because of the subscription cancellations.

Maximum RPM enables manufacturers to control chronic price fixing by dealers. The feared collusion could be either tacit or express. For example, if a product is fungible and dealers are concentrated and in close proximity, they may be tempted to follow one another's price without competing too aggressively. The result will be oligopoly

---

[54]   Albrecht v. The Herald Co., 390 U.S. 145, 88 S.Ct. 869 (1968). See Roger Blair & Gordon L. Lang, Albrecht After ARCO: Maximum Resale Price Fixing Moves Toward the Rule of Reason, 44 Vand. L. Rev. 1007 (1991).

[55]   State Oil Co. v. Khan, 522 U.S. 3, 118 S.Ct. 275 (1997).

behavior which serves the dealers well, but reduces the supplier's sales. Maximum RPM can force a dealer to set price closer to the competitive level. As a result, maximum RPM can also serve to eliminate or at least reduce double marginalization, or situations where vertically related firms set monopoly markups separately.

As a general rule, any action by a supplier to reduce the market power of its dealers makes both the supplier and consumers better off. Output will be higher, prices lower and the supplier will obtain larger profits. This is what the defendant was attempting to do in *Albrecht*.[56] Any antitrust policy that places a high value on either efficiency or consumer welfare should approve bona fide maximum RPM agreements. That is, whether one believes the goal of the antitrust laws is either efficiency or stopping monopoly wealth transfers away from consumers,[57] the *per se* rule against maximum RPM is perverse.

The *Khan* case accepted these criticisms and ended the regime of *Albrecht*. Plaintiff Khan had a lease with defendant State Oil that made it unprofitable for Khan to add more than a 3.25 cents per gallon markup to gasoline, a clear violation of the *Albrecht* rule.[58]

The Court pointed out that since its *Sylvania* decision in 1977 the Court had been far more sensitive to the question of actual competitive effects of vertical arrangements.[59] When *Albrecht* was decided both price and nonprice restraints were considered to be unlawful per se, and this fact had disinclined the court to parse out the particular economic effects of maximum resale price maintenance.[60]

The Supreme Court made clear that it was not holding that maximum RPM was per se lawful. Rather, like most antitrust practices involving an agreement between two firms, it is to be subjected to the rule of reason.[61] It then remanded to the courts below to reconsider the decision under the rule of reason, although it did not provide any guidance as to the content of such a rule.[62]

---

[56]   See § 9.2.

[57]   On these alternative goals, see § 2.1.

[58]   See 8 Antitrust Law ¶¶ 1635–1638 (4th ed. 2017).

[59]   *Khan*, 522 U.S. at 13–15, 118 S.Ct. at 280–281, referring to Continental T. V. v. GTE Sylvania, 433 U.S. 36, 97 S.Ct. 2549 (1977); see § 11.6.

[60]   522 U.S. at 14–15, 118 S.Ct. at 281.

[61]   522 U.S. at 22, 118 S.Ct. at 285.

[62]   On remand, Judge Posner dismissed the complaint. 143 F.3d 362 (7th Cir. 1998).

11.5d. The Difference Between Price and Non-Price Agreements

The plaintiff in a vertical restraints case must prove a qualifying "agreement" between two or more firms. At a time when price agreements were subject to a per se rule while nonprice agreements received the rule of reason and were very generally approved, much rested on the plaintiff's ability to prove that the agreement in question pertained to price.

Under *Leegin*, however, the distinction between price and nonprice restraints has much less importance, given that both types of restraints are now governed by a rule of reason. But that does not mean that the distinction is irrelevant either. Even under the rule of reason price restraints may be treated more harshly than nonprice restraints. For example, if resale price maintenance is being used to facilitate a dealers' cartel it is no answer that the cartel did not set a specific price but only engaged in conduct that generally served to push prices up. We routinely condemn cartels that do exactly that.[63] The rule of reason is not concerned with price as such, but rather with conduct that tends to reduce market output below competitive levels in order to push up the price. For example, if a powerful dealer should insist that other dealers be forced to keep prices up it should not be a defense that the pressure was not particularly specific as to the price level.

§ 11.6 Vertical Nonprice Restraints Under the Rule of Reason

Vertical nonprice restrictions vary with the nature of the product and its distribution system. A manufacturer might specify the locations of its retail outlets and not deal with anyone who resells the product somewhere else. The manufacturer might restrict the number of retailers with whom it will deal in a particular city, sometimes by giving a particular retailer a contractually-guaranteed exclusive right to sell there. Occasionally a manufacturer makes this decision after it has established multiple dealerships in a city, and then it must terminate one or more existing dealerships. Many lawsuits alleging illegal territorial restrictions are brought by such terminated dealers. Territorial restraints are sometimes placed on traveling distributors rather than retailers, with each distributor assigned to a primary or exclusive territory.[64] Sometimes

---

[63]   See §§ 4.4–4.5.

[64]   In some cases a distributor is permitted to make sales in another distributor's territory, but is required to compensate the latter dealer. See Ohio-Sealy Mattress Mfg. Co. v. Sealy, 585 F.2d 821, 829 (7th Cir. 1978), cert. denied, 440 U.S. 930, 99 S.Ct.

manufacturers assign particular customers to a distributor by size or type, and forbid other distributors from making sales to those customers.

Finally, in addition to territorial and customer restrictions are literally hundreds of kinds of restrictions on the way a product is sold. For example, a supplier may require resellers to wear particular uniforms, to display the seller's trademarks in a particular way, to wash vehicles regularly, or to be open evenings or seven days a week. The restrictions in this category are rarely challenged under the antitrust laws, because they seem to have little impact on competition. Such restrictions are an integral part of the franchising system, which accounts for a sizeable percentage of the distribution of goods and services in the United States. As a consequence of these restrictions, all restaurants controlled by a particular franchisor across the country—say, all McDonalds' outlets—may have a certain similarity to one another, in spite of the fact that nearly all are independently owned.

Supreme Court analysis of vertical territorial restrictions took a very different path from its analysis of RPM. In White Motor Co. v. United States, the Supreme Court refused to condemn a truck manufacturer's vertical territorial restrictions under a *per se* rule.[65] Neither did the Court approve rule of reason analysis, however. Rather, it held that the district court had acted too quickly in fashioning a *per se* rule condemning the practice and should have waited until after a trial.

Then, in United States v. Arnold, Schwinn & Co. the Supreme Court declared illegal *per se* all territorial restrictions imposed by a manufacturer on either a distributor or a retailer.[66] No further economic analysis was necessary to convince the Court that territorial restraints in sales transactions were "so obviously destructive of competition that their mere existence is enough" to warrant condemnation. However, the Court distinguished sales from consignment agreements in which the manufacturer "completely retains ownership and risk of loss."[67]

The *Schwinn* era came to an abrupt end in 1977, only a decade after it began, when *Schwinn* was expressly overruled by Continental

---

1267 (1979). This indicates that the assigned dealer has made an investment in its own territory which will be misappropriated unless compensation is paid.

[65]   372 U.S. 253, 83 S.Ct. 696 (1963). The restrictions gave exclusive territories to independent distributors and also reserved certain named customers to the manufacturer.

[66]   388 U.S. 365, 87 S.Ct. 1856 (1967).

[67]   See § 11.5b.

T.V., Inc. v. GTE Sylvania Inc.[68] Sylvania, a struggling television manufacturer with 1% to 2% of the national market sought to improve its market performance by selling exclusively through a small group of carefully selected retailers. Its purpose was to minimize the amount of competition among Sylvania dealers located in the same city, and to enable them to compete better with other brands. Sylvania both limited the number of dealers that could operate in any particular area, and required each dealer to sell its products only from locations specified in its franchise contract. From 1962, when this strategy was implemented, to 1965, Sylvania's share of the television market increased to 5%.

Plaintiff Continental T.V. was a San Francisco retailer who became unhappy when Sylvania licensed an additional dealer in San Francisco. Continental began selling more televisions manufactured by other television makers and opened an unauthorized store in Sacramento. Sylvania responded first by reducing Continental's wholesale credit, and eventually by terminating its franchise.

The Court could have distinguished *Sylvania* from *Schwinn*. For example, Sylvania's market share was much lower than Schwinn's. Such distinctions might justify different outcomes under a rule of reason. However, they could not permit Sylvania to escape from the *per se* rationale developed in the *Schwinn* case. The Supreme Court overruled *Schwinn* and adopted a rule of reason for all nonprice vertical restrictions. The Court then suggested that vertical territorial restraints lessened or eliminated *intrabrand* competition—that is, competition among different distributors or retailers of the same manufacturer. For example, under Sylvania's location clause, there would be fewer Sylvania dealers in Sacramento than if Continental had been permitted to move there. However, Sylvania's increase in market share indicated that vertical restraints could improve *interbrand* competition—competition among different brands of the same product.

11.6a. Balancing "Intrabrand" and "Interbrand" Competition

Sylvania's rule of reason for nonprice restraints is deceptively easy to formulate. Vertical territorial restraints may lessen competition among the dealers of the manufacturer imposing the restraints. However, they may increase competition among the brands of different manufacturers. The rule of reason requires a court to weigh these two effects against each other and determine whether the net result is competitive or anticompetitive. More commonly,

---

[68]   Id.

courts say that "a vertical restraint may be reasonable if it is likely to promote interbrand competition without overly restricting intrabrand competition."[69]

However, *Sylvania's* analysis left unresolved questions and logical riddles. First, what does it mean to say that intrabrand competition is "lessened"? Further, how does a court *balance* an increase in interbrand competition against a decrease in intrabrand competition? Indeed, is it even rational to speak of two different kinds of "competition," intrabrand and interbrand, that somehow pull against each other?

This much seems inescapable: Sylvania was a struggling television manufacturer with a market share of less than 5%. Absent collusion with other brands, it could not profitably obtain a higher price for televisions by reducing the number it sold. To be sure, if the manufacturer miscalculated about the effect of the restriction, the result might be that it would simply sell fewer units—that is apparently what happened in the *Schwinn* case. However, rival manufacturers would immediately make up the difference. Neither Sylvania nor its retailers had the power to lessen competition in any meaningful sense of that word. Today several circuits hold that intrabrand competition cannot be "lessened" at all unless the manufacturer imposing the restraints has market power.[70]

Even when the manufacturer is a monopolist, however, someone must explain how it can increase its profits by dividing territories. More importantly, will these increased profits come from reduced output or increased output? The most plausible explanations for vertical territorial restrictions, even when the manufacturer is a monopolist, is that they ensure dealer compliance with distribution contracts.[71] In that case, the restrictions are designed to increase output—not a very good argument that intrabrand competition has been "lessened."

The second problem with *Sylvania's* rule of reason concerns the court's capacity to measure something as intangible as the balance between interbrand and intrabrand competition. For the comparison to be sensible, one would have to balance intrabrand competition against overall productive efficiency. On the one hand, the restraints could be said to reduce intrabrand competition insofar as product

---

[69] Continental T.V., Inc. v. G.T.E. Sylvania Inc., 694 F.2d 1132, 1137 (9th Cir. 1982).

[70] JBL Enter., Inc. v. Jhirmack Enter., Inc., 698 F.2d 1011, 1017 (9th Cir. 1983), cert. denied, 464 U.S. 829, 104 S.Ct. 106 (1983) (market share of 4.2% or less too small); Valley Liquors, Inc. v. Renfield Importers, Ltd., 678 F.2d 742, 743 (7th Cir. 1982) ("balance tips in defendant's favor" if defendant lacks "significant market power").

[71] See § 11.3b4.

differentiation and the smaller number of Sylvania dealers permitted each to raise price above its marginal cost. On the other hand, the restraints improved the quality of Sylvania's distribution scheme and thus made Sylvania perform better vis-a-vis its manufacturer competitors.

But even assuming this was the Supreme Court's meaning, this balancing test does not provide anything that is very useful to a court. Antitrust tribunals measure both competition and productive efficiency by extremely crude approximations—often little more than hunches guided by a few historically developed presumptions.

11.6b. Sylvania's Impact in the Lower Courts

The rule of reason has come close to creating complete nonliability for vertical nonprice restraints. If one counts litigated cases, there are no more than a half dozen plaintiff victories.[72] Of course, others might have settled at an earlier stage.

Nearly all courts weigh the market power of the firm employing the restraints. Even though the *Sylvania* formulation suggests that vertical restraints reduce "intrabrand" competition—thus suggesting a single brand market—the courts generally formulate market definition in traditional terms. Most courts presume that before a restraint can have an adverse impact on competition, it must be shown to affect a substantial share of a properly defined relevant antitrust market. The market analysis is less elaborate than in monopolization or merger cases, and there is only vague agreement on market share thresholds or the meaning of market power once it is found. Several decisions found market power lacking without making an explicit determination of market share.[73] In several circuits the defendant's lack of significant market power appears decisive.[74] In any event, the cases are subject to the Supreme Court's insistence in its *AmEx* decision that a relevant market be defined in

---

[72]   See Douglas H. Ginsburg, Vertical Restraints: de Facto Legality Under the Rule of Reason, 60 Antitrust L.J. 67 (1991), who counts three plaintiff victories at the circuit level and one remand for trial. The three decisions were Graphic Prods. Distrib, Inc. v. ITEK Corp., 717 F.2d 1560 (11th Cir. 1983); Multiflex, Inc. v. Samuel Moore & Co., 709 F.2d 980 (5th Cir. 1983); and Eiberger v. Sony Corp. of Amer., 622 F.2d 1068 (2d Cir. 1980).

[73]   See Murrow Furniture Galleries v. Thomasville Furniture Industries, 889 F.2d 524, 528–529 (4th Cir. 1989); Ryko Mfg. Co. v. Eden Servs., 823 F.2d 1215, 1231 (8th Cir. 1987), cert. denied, 484 U.S. 1026, 108 S.Ct. 751 (1988); Bi-Rite Oil Co. v. Indiana Farm Bureau Co-op, Ass'n., 908 F.2d 200, 204 (7th Cir. 1990).

[74]   *Bi-Rite, supra* 908 F.2d at 204 (7th Cir.); Valley Liquors, Inc. v. Renfield Importers Ltd., 678 F.2d 742, 745 (7th Cir. 1982). Other decisions are discussed in 8 Antitrust Law ¶ 1645 (4th ed. 2017).

a vertical restraints case, even if power can be assessed as well or better by some alternative means.[75]

If the defendant is found to have sufficient market power, its restraints are not necessarily illegal. At that point the courts generally consider the manufacturer's explanation for the restriction being challenged; if a legitimate business explanation is offered, that fact counts heavily in favor of legality. The proffered defenses are typically that the restraints make dealers more efficient, encourage the optimal range of dealer services, or eliminate free riding. The array of permissible defenses is as varied as the products to which restraints are applied. For example, suppliers may use location clauses to facilitate the inspection of inventory for quality or freshness.[76] They may regulate product safety or integrity by limiting distribution to specified dealers. Restraints may be used to assure dealer efficiency by giving the dealer an unambiguous territory known to customers.[77] Courts have often cited a supplier's need to control dealer free riding as justifying restraints.[78]

Sylvania's language notwithstanding, nothing in these lower court decisions comes close to "balancing" interbrand and intrabrand competition. That formulation has simply proved unworkable. Rather the courts appear to adopt a formulation that, at risk of over generalization, looks like this one: *First*, they make sure there is a qualifying vertical nonprice agreement.[79] Then, assuming they find no horizontal agreement, they estimate the defendant's market power in the products or services made subject to the restraint. If that amount falls under roughly 25% or so, they ordinarily dismiss the complaint. As the amount increases beyond 25%, the court insists that the supplier produce a credible and provable justification for the restraint. If such a justification is found, then nothing but a strong, specific showing of anticompetitive effects in the interbrand market will condemn the restraint.[80]

---

[75]   Ohio v. American Express Co., 138 S.Ct. 2274, 2285 n. 7 (2018). See § 3.9e.

[76]   Adolph Coors Co. v. A & S Wholesalers, 561 F.2d 807, 811 (10th Cir. 1977).

[77]   Newberry v. Washington Post Co., 438 F.Supp. 470, 475 (D.D.C. 1977) (restraints by dominant newspaper necessary to ensure prompt, undisrupted delivery).

[78]   O.S.C. Corp. v. Apple Computer, 792 F.2d 1464, 1468 (9th Cir. 1986); Muenster Butane v. Stewart Co., 651 F.2d 292, 297 (5th Cir. 1981).

[79]   On the "agreement" requirement, see § 11.4; on the difference between price and non-price agreements, see § 11.5d.

[80]   See, for example, *O.S.C.*, 792 F.2d at 1467–68: "Apple [the defendant] met its burden by proffering 'an entirely plausible and justifiable explanation." In this case:

> that the mail order prohibition was imposed to ensure Apple's products were sold only by face-to-face transactions. * * * Apple's market strategy requires sales support such as assessing the needs of prospective purchasers, assembling the particular package to meet those needs, hands-on instruction, education and

11.6c. Boycott Claims

Many plaintiffs have tried to avoid *Sylvania*'s liability defeating rule of reason by characterizing the supplier's refusal to deal or dealer termination as a boycott.[81] Under appropriate circumstances boycotts, or concerted refusals to deal, can be illegal *per se*. However, the *per se* classification must be limited to horizontal agreements by competitors.[82] To apply the "boycott" label to a purely vertical agreement between one dealer and a supplier to terminate a second dealer, deprives *Sylvania*'s rule of reason of much of its meaning. In any event, the Supreme Court put the issue to rest in its *NYNEX* decision, holding that an agreement between a single utility and a single supplier of services to the utility could not be unlawful per se.[83] Even if there was no legitimate business reason for the agreement (in this case, to facilitate fraudulent overcharging of regulated rates), the per se rule was apt only if two or more *competing* firms agreed with each other to exclude someone else.[84] In sum, collective *horizontal* action is essential to any claim of a per se unlawful boycott.

11.6d. Exclusive Dealerships, Sole Outlets, and Refusals to Deal

A firm may designate a single dealer as its distributor in a certain area, and refuse to sell its product to others intending to resell it there. A supplier may even terminate one or more existing dealers in order to create an exclusive dealership.[85] If this act is unilateral, § 1 is not implicated at all,[86] but even an agreement giving a dealer an exclusive right is judged under the rule of reason and is usually legal.[87] Even *Schwinn*,[88] which applied the *per se* rule to nonprice

---

training, and follow-up servicing. Mail order sales inherently cannot supply that necessary support.

[81]   See Dart Indus. v. Plunkett Co., 704 F.2d 496, 499 (10th Cir. 1983); Carlson Machine Tools v. American Tool, 678 F.2d 1253, 1258 (5th Cir. 1982).

[82]   See § 5.4.

[83]   NYNEX Corp. v. Discon, 525 U.S. 128, 119 S.Ct. 493 (1998); see § 5.4d.

[84]   See *NYNEX*, 525 U.S. at 135, 119 S.Ct. at 498, discussing *Business Electronics*.

[85]   For example, Crane & Shovel Sales Corp. v. Bucyrus-Erie Co., 854 F.2d 802 (6th Cir. 1988); Rutman Wine Co. v. E. & J. Gallo Winery, 829 F.2d 729 (9th Cir. 1987).

[86]   See § 11.4.

[87]   Golden Gate Acceptance Corp. v. General Motors Corp., 597 F.2d 676, 678 (9th Cir. 1979); Ark Dental Supply Co. v. Cavitron Corp., 461 F.2d 1093, 1094 (3d Cir. 1972).

[88]   United States v. Arnold, Schwinn & Co., 388 U.S. 365, 376, 87 S.Ct. 1856, 1864 (1967). See § 11.6.

restraints, recognized that exclusive dealerships rarely raise competitive concerns.[89]

Nevertheless, there may be cases where threats to competition are plausible, but only in the presence of market power or a cartel. The agreement for an exclusive dealership or sole outlet in a given area cannot be anticompetitive if there is robust interbrand competition.[90]

One anticompetitive possibility is the dealer who has upstream market power (vis-à-vis the manufacturer) in its resale area. It may insist on an exclusive dealership in order to eliminate competing dealers in the same brand. This would of course go against the supplier's interest because it would lead to reduced output in that area.[91] Such facts cannot be presumed.

11.6e.   Dual Distribution

Sometimes a manufacturer reserves particular territories or customers to itself. A "dual distribution" system is one in which the supplier distributes part of its product through independent resellers and part through its own employees. In some cases the independent dealers and the supplier's company dealers may compete at the resale level; in other cases they may not. In any event, the supplier may wish to control competition between the two by placing territorial or customer restrictions on the various dealers.

Courts were once quite hostile toward vertical restraints imposed in the context of dual distribution. They viewed them as inherently suspect and essentially as horizontal rather than vertical agreements. In *Sylvania* the Supreme Court suggested in an ambiguous footnote, probably not referring to dual distribution, that some arrangements may present "occasional problems in differentiating vertical restrictions from horizontal restrictions." The latter would clearly be "illegal *per se.*"[92] This language has suggested

---

[89]   "[A] manufacturer * * * may select * * * certain dealers to whom, alone, he will sell his goods. If the restraint stops at that point—if nothing more is involved than vertical 'confinement' of the manufacturer's own sales of the merchandise to selected dealers, and if competitive products are readily available to others, the restriction, on these facts alone, would not violate the Sherman Act." Ibid.

[90]   See Packard Motor Car Co. v. Webster Motor Car Co., 243 F.2d 418, 420 (D.C. Cir.), cert. denied, 355 U.S. 822, 78 S.Ct. 29 (1957) ("virtual per se legality" where there is "effective competition * * * at both the seller and buyer levels. * * *"); See Paddock Pub. v. Chicago Tribune Co., 103 F.3d 42, 47 (7th Cir. 1996) (wire service's provision to only one newspaper in an area not unlawful when there were numerous competing services).

[91]   For further analysis, see 8 Antitrust Law ¶ 1654 (4th ed. 2017).

[92]   Continental T. V. v. GTE Sylvania, 433 U.S. 36, 58 n. 28, 97 S.Ct. 2549, 2561 (1977).

to some courts that they must determine whether restrictions in a dual distribution system are "really" horizontal or vertical.[93] Here, *Leegin* is of little effect: the issue is not whether the restraint pertains to price but rather whether it is really a horizontal restraint disguised as a vertical restraint.

However, the same analysis generally applies to dual distribution systems as to all other vertical restraints. A manufacturer who has no market power cannot use dual distribution to create it. Furthermore, even a monopoly manufacturer generally cannot increase its market power by insulating its wholly-owned retail outlets, even if the effect is to injure competing, independent retailers. If the manufacturer has market power, any monopoly profits earned at the retailer level could also be earned at the manufacturer level.[94]

Dual distribution networks are even more susceptible to free rider problems than wholly independent networks are. Manufacturer-owned outlets have no incentive to take a free ride, for their profit-and-loss statement is the same as that of their parent. Knowing this, the independent dealers have a strong incentive to free ride: the manufacturer-owned outlet is forced to provide the point-of-sale services and is unlikely to respond to the free rider by cutting services and price itself.

Further, at least one thing suggests that the manufacturer engaged in dual distribution is *not* participating in a retailer cartel: the fact that the manufacturer can and is selling part of its output through its own stores. Any retail cartel would transfer monopoly profits away from the manufacturer and toward the independent retailers. The manufacturer's best response to retailer price fixing is to enter retailing itself and keep the monopoly profits. The manufacturer engaged in dual distribution has already entered. Indeed, the existence of a dual distribution scheme is often evidence that the manufacturer is trying to combat chronic retailer collusion or poor performance by forcing independent retailers to match its prices and dealer services.

---

[93] For example, Photovest Corp. v. Fotomat Corp., 606 F.2d 704 (7th Cir. 1979), cert. denied, 445 U.S. 917, 100 S.Ct. 1278 (1980); Coleman Motor Co. v. Chrysler Motors Corp., 525 F.2d 1338 (3d Cir. 1975). Both decisions spoke of a "conspiracy" between the supplier and its wholly owned distributor subsidiary. Such claims of intra-enterprise conspiracy are now forbidden by the Supreme Court's decision in Copperweld Corp. v. Independence Tube Corp., 467 U.S. 752, 104 S.Ct. 2731 (1984). For fuller treatment of the case law, see 8 Antitrust Law ¶ 1605 (4th ed. 2017).

[94] On the "leverage" theory—that a monopolist one can use vertical arrangements to turn one monopoly into two—see § 7.9; in the context of tying arrangements, see § 10.6a.

As a general rule the existence of dual distribution should not be an aggravating factor in courts' analysis of vertical restrictions. The trend in decisions is toward this view.[95]

95   See Illinois Corporate Travel v. American Airlines, 889 F.2d 751, 753 (7th Cir. 1989), cert. denied, 495 U.S. 919, 110 S.Ct. 1948 (1990) ("dual distribution * * * does not subject to the per se ban a practice that would be lawful if the manufacturer were not selling directly to consumers."). See also Jacobs v. Tempur-Pedic Intern., Inc., 626 F.3d 1327 (11th Cir. 2010) (dual distribution did not transform a resale price maintenance scheme into horizontal conspiracy).

Chapter 12

MERGERS OF COMPETITORS

Table of Sections

---

§ 12.1   Introduction: Federal Merger Policy and the Horizontal Merger Guidelines

A merger occurs when two firms that had been separate come under common ownership or control.[1] The word "merger" has a broader meaning in federal antitrust law than in state corporation law.[2] In many cases a "merger" for antitrust purposes is merely the purchase by one firm of some or all of the assets of another firm. A merger of corporations also occurs when one corporation buys some or all of another corporation's shares. The antitrust laws also use the word "merger" to describe a consolidation: two original corporations cease to exist and a new corporation is formed that owns the assets of the two former corporations.[3]

---

[1]   "Control" is relevant because leases or contractual arrangements amounting to less than fee simple ownership can be challenged as mergers. See 5 Antitrust Law ¶ 1202 (4th ed. 2016). See also McTamney v. Stolt Tankers & Terminals, 678 F.Supp. 118 (E.D.Pa. 1987) (contract to purchase productive assets plus effective control was an "acquisition" for Clayton § 7 purposes).

[2]   See J.D. Cox & T.L. Hazen, Corporations, ch. 22 (3d ed. 2019). However, see California v. American Stores Co., 872 F.2d 837, 845 (9th Cir.), affirmed on other grounds, 495 U.S. 271, 110 S.Ct. 1853 (1990) (state corporate law should be used to determine when an acquisition had occurred).

[3]   For example, United States v. Rockford Memorial Corp., 717 F.Supp. 1251 (N.D. Ill. 1989), affirmed, 898 F.2d 1278 (7th Cir.), cert. denied, 498 U.S. 920, 111 S.Ct. 295 (1990).

A "horizontal" merger occurs when one firm acquires another firm that manufactures the same product or a close substitute, *and* both firms operate in the same geographic market. In short, the firms were actual competitors before the merger occurred. If the two firms were not actual competitors before the merger, then the merger will be treated either as "vertical" or "conglomerate" depending on the relationship between the firms.

Today the great majority of merger cases are brought by the Antitrust Division of the Department of Justice (Division) and the Federal Trade Commission (FTC).[4] A few are brought by private plaintiffs, but their success rate has not been high.[5] In 2010 the Division and the FTC jointly issued revised Guidelines outlining their enforcement policies respecting horizontal mergers. These Guidelines serve as a useful starting point for assessing the competitive effects of mergers.[6] This chapter integrates the discussion of case law, Guidelines and fundamental economic theory in a way that indicates the importance and appropriate domain of each.[7] The Merger Guidelines are only Guidelines and they are not binding on courts. Nonetheless, over the years the courts have paid close attention to the Guidelines, generally giving the government the benefit of the doubt.

The goal stated by the Horizontal Merger Guidelines is to prevent the enhancement of market power that might result from mergers. The 2010 Guidelines state that "[a] merger enhances market power if it is likely to encourage one or more firms to raise price, reduce output, diminish innovation, or otherwise harm customers as a result of diminished competitive constraints or incentives."[8] Clearly the focus on enhancement of market power is not limited to price. The Guidelines also worry that a merger might curtail innovation, such as in cases where the acquired firm is engaged in innovation activities that are likely to capture revenues from the acquiring firm and a merger might serve to diminish those

---

[4]   Collectively, the Division and the FTC are frequently referred to below as the "Agencies."

[5]   See § 14.3a.

[6]   U.S. Dept. of Justice and Federal Trade Commission, Horizontal Merger Guidelines (Aug. 2010), available at https://www.ftc.gov/sites/default/files/attachments/merger-review/100819hmg.pdf.

[7]   Those parts of the Guidelines dealing with market definition are analyzed mainly in Ch. 3. Vertical mergers are analyzed under the 2020 Vertical Merger Guidelines.

[8]   2010 Horizontal Merger Guidelines, § 1.

efforts.[9] For the most part these are "long run" effects, perhaps not showing up until years after a merger occurred (or was prevented from occurring). These concerns are taken up in §§ 12.3d & e.

Finally, identifying effective remedies for anticompetitive mergers is a complex problem that the Antitrust Division has addressed comprehensively in a Manual that was substantially revised in 2020.[10]

12.1a.   The Relevance of Market Structure to Merger Analysis

In the 1960's and earlier, industrial organization theory was governed by the "Structure-Conduct-Performance" (S-C-P) paradigm, which suggested that as industries became more concentrated the firms within them would naturally find collusive or oligopolistic conduct more profitable. The result would be poor industry performance.[11] The importance of the S-C-P paradigm was that market structure *entailed* poor performance, because the structure itself made oligopoly conduct inevitable; that is, given a highly concentrated structure, the profit-maximizing strategy for a firm was to behave oligopolistically.

In the 1970's the S-C-P paradigm came under increasing attack from those who argued that (1) high concentration was necessary for firms in many markets to attain economies of scale and scope; and (2) markets could continue to perform competitively even at high concentration levels.[12] Nevertheless, concentration remains functionally relevant.[13] While the old S-C-P paradigm assumed that

---

[9]   Id., § 6.4. The issue is pursued in Christina Bohannan & Herbert Hovenkamp, Creation Without Restraint: Promoting Liberty and Rivalry in Innovation, Ch. 7 (2012).

[10]   U.S. Dept. of Justice, Merger Remedies Manual (Sep. 2020), available at https://www.justice.gov/atr/page/file/1312416/download. The FTC did not join in the promulgation of these Guidelines. However, it has published its own guide, entitled "Negotiating Merger Remedies: Statement of the Bureau of Competition of the Federal Trade Commission", available at https://www.ftc.gov/tips-advice/competition-guidance/merger-remedies.

[11]   Important works include Edward S. Mason, Price and Production Policies of Large-Scale Enterprise, 29 Am. Econ. Rev. 61 (1939); H. Michael Mann, Seller Concentration, Barriers to Entry, and Rates of Return in Thirty Industries, 1950–1960, 48 Rev. Econ. & Stat. 296 (Aug. 1966). The S-C-P paradigm is discussed more fully in § 1.7. On the history and theory, see Herbert Hovenkamp, The Opening of American Law: Neoclassical Legal Thought, 1870–1970, ch. 11 (2015).

[12]   For example, Harold Demsetz, Industry Structure, Market Rivalry, and Public Policy, 16 J. L. & Econ. 1 (1973); Yale Brozen, Concentration, Mergers, and Public Policy (1983). Other literature is summarized in Richard A. Posner, The Chicago School of Antitrust Analysis, 127 Univ. Pa. L. Rev. 925 (1979).

[13]   See Jonathan B. Baker, Market Concentration in the Antitrust Analysis of Horizontal Mergers, in Antitrust Law & Economics (Keith Hylton, ed., 2009).

high concentration *entailed* poor performance, the new approach tends to view high concentration as merely a *prerequisite* for or perhaps an important ingredient in poor performance. This entails that evaluation of non-structural evidence is essential to predicting the behavior of the post-merger market. The 2010 Horizontal Merger Guidelines demonstrate this influence by the way in which they take various factors other than market share into account in predicting the consequences of a merger.[14] In addition, we have become much more sensitive to the impact of economies of scale and scope in production and distribution.[15]

Today there is increasing evidence that we have exaggerated the efficiency effects of mergers and underestimated their anticompetitive effects. Too many harmful mergers that result in reduced output or higher prices have been approved. These conclusions are substantially the result of more effective empirical testing of the behavior of post-merger firms.[16] As a result, a strong case can be made that mergers should be scrutinized more closely, and that the Merger Guidelines should be revised accordingly. Further, significant efficiencies should not be presumed. Rather, they must be proven and shown to be merger specific—that is, unlikely to be attainable by means other than the merger.

12.1b. The Basic Concerns of Merger Policy: Reduced Market Output or Innovation, Higher Prices, and Offsetting Efficiencies

Because the horizontal merger involves two firms in the same market, it produces two consequences that do not flow from vertical or conglomerate mergers: 1) after the merger the market contains one firm less than before; 2) the post-merger firm ordinarily has a larger market share than either of the partners had before the merger.[17] Today one principal concern of merger policy is that horizontal

---

[14]   However, see United States v. Oracle Corp., 331 F.Supp.2d 1098, 1122–1123 (N.D.Cal. 2004), which criticized the 1992 Horizontal Merger Guidelines in force at that time for being excessively structural.

[15]   For a survey of the S-C-P literature from relatively sympathetic writers, see James W. Meehan & Richard J. Larner, The Structural School, its Critics, and its Progeny: An Assessment 179, in Economics and Antitrust Policy (Richard J. Larner & James W. Meehan eds. 1989).

[16]   See John Kwoka, Mergers, Merger Control, and Remedies: A Retrospective Analysis of U.S. Policy (2014).

[17]   However, the post-merger firm's share could be either larger or smaller than the sum of the pre-merger shares of the two merging firms. If the merger makes the firm more efficient it would increase its output, giving it a larger share. If the merger facilitates the exercise of market power the firm would reduce output and to an extent rivals would pick up the slack, giving the post-merger firm a smaller share. See 4 Antitrust Law ¶ 932a (4th ed. 2016).

mergers may facilitate market wide express or tacit collusion or oligopoly behavior.[18] The 2010 Guidelines use the term "coordinated interaction" to refer to these behaviors.[19] A second concern is that a merger may facilitate a "unilateral" price increase by the post-merger firm, while other firms in the market may increase their price slightly or not at all.[20] Mergers may additionally create opportunities for price leadership or in some cases eliminate aggressive firms or firms that refuse to cooperate in a cartel.

If mergers produced no beneficial consequences, but only anticompetitive ones, we could justifiably condemn all of them under a *per se* rule. Most mergers are legal, however because they can increase the efficiency of firms by enabling them to attain efficient levels of manufacturing, research & development, or distribution more rapidly than the firms could accomplish by internal growth. Mergers of nondominant firms may make markets more competitive by creating more substantial rivals for the dominant firm. Further, mergers may permit firms to acquire productive assets without the social cost that internal growth plus the bankruptcy of some firms might entail. Finally, mergers tend to assign productive assets away from less efficient managers and toward more efficient ones, where the assets will be more valuable. Alternatively, they may permit the firm to achieve economies in management by eliminating duplication. At least some of these efficiencies are ordinarily passed on to consumers.

Economies of scale can be broadly grouped into two kinds: economies of plant size, and various multi-plant economies. Generally a horizontal merger does not increase plant size,[21] but rather increases the number of plants that are controlled by a single management. This suggests that a merger will not often decrease the costs of operating a single plant, but it may yield substantial multi-plant economies. For example, it may be cheaper per unit to purchase 1,000,000 units of some raw material at a time rather than 200,000. Further, the costs per unit of research and development decrease as the number of units a firm produces increase.

The kinds of efficiencies that can be achieved by horizontal merger vary immensely from one industry to another. They are largely a function of highly individualized technology and

---

[18] On collusion and Cournot oligopoly, see § 4.2.

[19] 2010 Horizontal Merger Guidelines, § 7.1, available at https://www.ftc.gov/sites/default/files/attachments/merger-review/100819hmg.pdf.

[20] 2010 Guidelines, § 6.

[21] Although there are exceptions. If one farmer purchases an adjacent farm, she may combine and operate them as a single plant. Likewise, if one airline purchases another, the fleets of planes will very likely be operated together as one.

distribution systems. Some industries, such as retail grocers, banks, and trucking companies, may be able to reduce costs significantly and improve consumer welfare by horizontal mergers. Others, such as delicatessens and small French restaurants, may work more efficiently as single-store operations.

The most difficult problem in determining an appropriate merger policy is that the field of mergers cannot be divided into mergers that encourage collusion or increase market power on the one hand, and mergers that create efficiency on the other. Many mergers do both at once. To be sure, there are cases at the extremes where we can confidently predict that the efficiency produced by a particular merger far outweighs the predictable danger of noncompetitive behavior, or vice-versa. But many legally questionable mergers produce ambiguous results.

Given that collusion is illegal under the Sherman Act anyway, why do we bother committing resources to evaluating mergers as transactions that *might* result in higher prices? Why not simply wait until prices actually rise? The most important answer is that the Sherman Act has turned out to be a woefully inadequate instrument for going after oligopoly or other collusion-like behavior.[22] Further, of the collusion reachable under § 1, only a small percentage is detected. Even worse, if the feared consequence of a merger is a unilateral price increase there is not much antitrust can do. Under United States antitrust law a firm acting unilaterally may set any price it wishes. Since we cannot go after oligopoly directly under § 1, we do the next best thing. We try to prevent (taking efficiencies and other factors into account) the creation of market structures that tend to facilitate Cournot or collusion-like outcomes.[23] This "prophylactic" purpose is central to merger policy today.[24]

---

[22]   See §§ 4.4–4.5.

[23]   See FTC v. Elders Grain, 868 F.2d 901, 905 (7th Cir. 1989), which approved a preliminary injunction against a merger, noting:

The penalties for price-fixing are now substantial, but they are brought into play only where sellers actually agree on price or output or other dimensions of competition; and if conditions are ripe, sellers may not have to communicate or otherwise collude overtly in order to coordinate their price and output decisions; at least they may not have to collude in a readily detectable manner.

[24]   See Herbert Hovenkamp, Prophylactic Merger Policy, 70 Hasting L.J. 45 (2018). The same reasoning applies to anticompetitive patent acquisitions: once a firm acquires an outside patent its enforcement via infringement action is usually constitutionally protected. That is why an acquisition that is predictably anticompetitive should be enjoined. Cf. Intellectual Ventures, LLC v. Capital One Fin. Corp., 280 F.Supp.3d 691 (D.Md. 2017), aff'd on other grds, 937 F.3d 1359 (Fed. Cir. 2019) (erroneously concluding that patent acquisition was lawful because subsequent assertion of the patent would be protected).

§ 12.2　Efficiency and Merger Policy

Horizontal mergers can create substantial efficiencies even as they facilitate collusion or enlarge market power. Courts and other policy makers have entertained three different positions concerning efficiency and the legality of mergers:

　　1)　mergers should be evaluated for their effect on market power or likelihood of collusion, and efficiency considerations should be largely irrelevant;

　　2)　mergers that create substantial efficiencies should be legal, or there should be at least a limited "efficiency defense" in certain merger cases;

　　3)　mergers should be condemned *because* they create efficiencies, in order to protect competitors of the post-merger firm.

For reasons developed in § 12.4d, the burden of proving efficiencies should rest with the merging firms.

12.2a.　The Dubious Legacy of the Warren Era

The merger policy of the Warren Court in the 1960's adopted the third proposal from this list: it condemned mergers *because* they created certain efficiencies. For example, in Brown Shoe Co. v. United States the Supreme Court held that a horizontal merger between competing retailers of shoes was illegal because the large, post-merger firm could undersell its competitors. The Court concluded that Congress desired "to promote competition through the protection of viable, small, locally owned businesses," and the creation of a large company with lower costs would frustrate this goal. "Congress appreciated that occasional higher costs and prices might result from the maintenance of fragmented industries and markets," the Supreme Court acknowledged, but it "resolved these competing considerations in favor of decentralization."[25]

Brown Shoe's critics have attacked the opinion for protecting competitors at the expense of consumers.[26] But that critique must come to terms with the relatively clear legislative history of the 1950 Celler-Kefauver Amendments to § 7. The *Brown Shoe* opinion read it correctly. In 1950 protection of the "viability" of small businesses who

---

[25]　370 U.S. 294, 344, 82 S.Ct. 1502, 1534 (1962). On the history, see Herbert Hovenkamp, The Opening of American Law: Neoclassical legal Thought, 1870–1970, Ch. 11 (2015).

[26]　For example, Robert H. Bork, The Antitrust Paradox: A Policy at War With Itself 198–216 (1978; rev. ed. 1993).

were being "gobbled up" by larger companies was much more on Congress's mind than low consumer prices or high product quality.[27]

Brown Shoe and successor cases such as *Von's Grocery*[28] can be criticized, however, not for the goals they chose but for their efficacy in achieving them. *Von's* involved a merger between the third largest and the sixth largest grocery chains in greater Los Angeles. The market was unconcentrated, however, and the combined share of these two chains was 7.5% of sales. Both chains were family owned and operated. The largest firm in the market, which was not a party to the merger, had a market share of only 8%. The market exhibited a "trend" toward concentration with many individual stores being purchased by chains, suggesting that the larger chains were able to undersell the smaller chains and the individual mom-and-pop grocers.

If a medium-sized chain is prevented from acquiring existing stores, it likely will respond by building new stores of its own, particularly if expansion will strengthen its position vis-a-vis larger chains. The result will be that very small chains or single store companies will find themselves unable to compete with larger firms, and unable to sell their stores to competitors. Not only will they lose the power to compete, but they might also lose most of the value of their most substantial capital asset—their stores.[29] It is therefore far from clear that the rule of *Brown Shoe* and *Von's Grocery* gave small businesses the kind of protection that Congress had in mind.

12.2b. Assessing the Efficiency Effects of Horizontal Mergers

12.2b1. The Welfare "Tradeoff" Model

Today the idea that mergers should be condemned because they create efficiency has clearly been abandoned. While the Supreme Court itself has never recognized an "efficiencies defense" to a prima facie unlawful merger, both the Merger Guidelines and several lower courts have done so.[30] Importantly, the query into efficiencies comes into play *only* after the merger has been found presumptively anticompetitive by structural and behavioral analysis.[31] If a merger

---

[27] See Derek Bok, Section 7 of the Clayton Act and the Merging of Law and Economics, 74 Harv.L.Rev. 226, 234 (1960); Herbert Hovenkamp, The Antitrust Enterprise: Principle and Execution, Ch. 9 (2004).

[28] United States v. Von's Grocery Co., 384 U.S. 270, 86 S.Ct. 1478 (1966).

[29] See Richard A. Posner, Antitrust Law 129 (2d ed. 2001).

[30] See, e.g., Saint Alphonsus Medical Center-Nampa, Inc. v. St. Luke's Health Sys., Ltd., 778 F.3d 775, 783 (9th Cir. 2015); FTC v. H.J. Heinz Co., 246 F.3d 720–722 (D.C.Cir. 2001).

[31] See §§ 12.3–12.6.

poses no competitive threat to begin with, then analysis of possible efficiencies is unnecessary.

The argument for an "efficiency defense" in merger cases is suggested by Figure 1, which illustrates a merger that gives the post-merger firm measurably more market power than it had before the merger.[32] As a result, the firm reduces output from Q_1 to Q_2 on the graph, and increases price from P_1 to P_2. Triangle A_1 represents the monopoly "deadweight loss" that results from reduced output.[33]

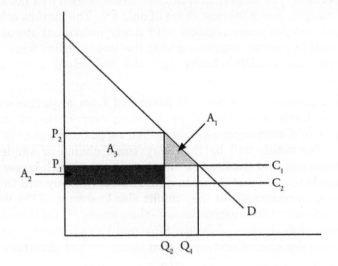

Figure 1

At the same time, the merger produces measurable economies, which show up as a reduction in the firm's costs from C_1 to C_2. Rectangle A_2 represents efficiency gains that will result from these economies. If A_2 is larger than A_1 the merger produces a *net* efficiency gain, even though it permits the firm to raise its price from the pre-merger level. Further, Figure 1 suggests that A_2 can be larger than A_1. The efficiency gains illustrated by A_2 are spread over the entire output of the post-merger firm. The deadweight losses in A_1 are spread over only the reduction in output. If the post-merger firm reduced its output by 10%, each of the 90% of units still being

---

[32]   The source is Oliver E. Williamson, Economies as an Antitrust Defense: the Welfare Trade-Offs, 58 Amer.Econ.Rev. 18 (1968); see also, Oliver E. Williamson, Economies as an Antitrust Defense Revisited, 125 U.Pa.L.Rev. 699 (1977); Herbert Hovenkamp, Appraising Merger Efficiencies, 24 GMU L.Rev. 703 (2017). 4A Antitrust Law ¶¶ 970–976 (4th ed. 2016).

[33]   See the discussion of the social cost of monopoly in § 1.3b.

produced would contribute to the efficiency gains; the deadweight loss, however, would accrue over only the 10% reduction.[34]

By his own admission, Williamson's analysis was highly simplified and it is vulnerable to some criticisms. First, the model assumes a merger to monopoly. But most collusion facilitating mergers involve firms whose aggregate share is significantly less than 100%. For example, suppose a 20% firm should acquire a 10% firm, greatly increasing the threat of collusion-like behavior. In that case, the increased coordination that results from the merger enables *both* the merging and the non-merging firms to increase their prices. However, the efficiency gains are spread across *only* the output of the two merging firms, which account for only 30% of the market's output.[35]

Second, the analysis assumes that the efficiencies are strictly "merger specific," which means that only the merger that reduces competition can produce them. Often efficiencies can be attained in less harmful ways, including licensing as an alternative to acquisition, partial spinoffs to other sellers, or other restructuring that minimizes harmful consequences while permitting the firms to achieve most efficiency gains.

Third, the efficiencies that Williamson's model illustrates usually must come from some effect *other* than scale economies, because in the tradeoff situation illustrated in Figure 1 output is actually lower than it had been before, going from Q_1 down to Q_2. To be sure, some mergers can enable firms to take advantage of scale economies even as they reduce output. An example might be two firms that each have an inefficient 5000 unit plant. After a merger the firm might produce 8000 units efficiently out of a single larger plant. Note that the merger itself does not achieve this result, however. It simply leaves the firm with two inefficiently small plants. This is not to suggest that there are no efficiencies that can be attained at reduced output; however, the universe of efficiencies that occur at lower rather than higher output may be small, particularly when one adds in the requirement that they must be merger specific.

Fourth, some care must be taken to ensure that the cost savings are not merely "pecuniary." For example, a merger that creates a monopoly on the selling side might also create significant power on the buying side, enabling the firm to suppress the prices that it pays. But in that case any gains to the merging firm could be more than

---

34   Williamson, *Economies, supra,* 58 Amer.Econ.Rev. at 22–23.
35   For further development, see 4A Antitrust Law ¶ 970e (4th ed. 2016).

offset by the losses that accrue to its suppliers, and the case for overall efficiency evaporates.

Fifth, one of the most severe limitations of the Williamson model was its assumption of a market that was perfectly competitive prior to the merger but monopolized afterward. This would be a rarity in merger law. More likely the market prior to a challengeable merger or joint venture was already noncompetitive, but to a lesser degree. For example, a marginally challengeable merger today might change the market from one having four firms to one having three firms. Both might be noncompetitive. One of the reasons that Williamson's picture shows a small deadweight loss is because when one starts with a perfectly competitive market the sales are taken from "marginal" consumers who place a low value on the product. As a result, loss of these sales entails a fairly low deadweight loss. At higher price levels the amount of surplus per consumer is much greater, making an output reduction of the same magnitude more costly. Further, at these higher levels any efficiency gains must be spread over a lower output.

Figure 2 illustrates this situation. It shows exactly the same market as the first figure, and with a merger or other practice that produces the same per unit cost reduction. In this case, however, the market was already noncompetitive to begin with, reflecting *P1* prices that are higher than cost *C1*. This difference has two effects. First, consumer losses are larger because output is being taken from consumers whose willingness to pay is higher in relation to the product's cost. Second, because output is already lower to begin with, the efficiency gains resulting from a further output reduction are spread over a smaller number of units.   An important corollary is that as price-cost margins prior to a merger are higher, greater efficiency gains will be needed to offset the merger's anticompetitive price effects.

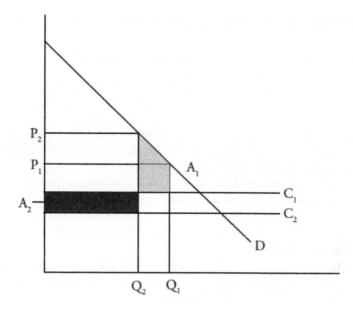

Figure 2

Finally, note that the "tradeoff" model applies to a limited range of situations—namely, where the efficiency gain is sufficiently large to offset the deadweight loss, but not so large that it actually results in a lower price than before the merger or joint venture occurred. If the gains were that large there would be no tradeoff; both consumers and producers would be better off. It is difficult to say what percentage of mergers, joint ventures or other practices lead to both increased market power and a higher price, but have offsetting production gains that exceed consumer losses.

To say this differently, the Williamson tradeoff model assumes a general welfare test for antitrust harm, where consumer losses and producer gains are netted out. If the model is consumer welfare, then the merger illustrated in the two above figures would be unlawful even if the efficiency gains (A_2) were greater than the deadweight loss (A_1).[36] Any deadweight loss at all would condemn the merger. As this proposition suggests, one reason that the consumer welfare principle entirely dominates antitrust analysis is administrability. Any time measurement makes a difference—that is, where a practice both facilitates an actual output reduction resulting from market power but also produces efficiencies—the fact finder would have to quantify these effects and net them out. That would require a cardinal

---

[36]   On the difference between total welfare and consumer welfare in antitrust law, see § 2.3c.

measurement of deadweight loss and offsetting gains in production efficiency.

12.2b2. Must Efficiencies Be "Passed On"?

The welfare tradeoff model of merger efficiencies treats all efficiency gains the same way, no matter who gets the benefit. Suppose that two firms selling widgets at a competitive price of $1.00 merge. As a result of the merger the post-merger firm has enough market power to reduce output and increase the price of widgets to $1.05. In addition, the firm's marginal costs drop from $1.00 per widget to 90 cents per widget. In this case the merger results in an *actual* output reduction and an *actual* price increase for consumers. Although the overall effect of the merger is efficient, the benefits of the increased efficiency accrue mainly to the post-merger firm in the form of higher profits.[37]

At the same time, a rule requiring *all* efficiency gains to be passed on to consumers is unacceptable as well. A more acceptable rule that takes both economic and political concerns into account is that the defendants must show that efficiencies created by the merger are sufficiently large to keep post-merger prices at or below pre-merger levels.[38] For example, if a merger threatens monopoly or oligopoly raising the price from the pre-merger level of $1.00 to $1.10, efficiencies must be sufficient to drive the post-merger price back to the $1.00 range or lower. The 2010 Horizontal Merger Guidelines do not quite declare flatly that they will challenge any merger whose efficiency effects are insufficient to reverse a price increase completely. Rather they state the efficiencies must be "of a character and magnitude such that the merger is not likely to be anticompetitive in any relevant market." The enforcement Agency will then "consider whether cognizable efficiencies likely would be sufficient to reverse the merger's potential to harm customers in the relevant market, e.g., by preventing price increases in that market." The Guidelines also add in a footnote that the Agency will generally focus on the immediate price impact of a merger. They will not necessarily ignore, but they will give less weight to efficiencies that are likely to result only over the longer run.[39] Interpreting the 2010

---

[37] FTC v. University Health, 938 F.2d 1206, 1222–23 (11th Cir. 1991) (defendant "must demonstrate that the intended acquisition would result in significant economies and that these economies ultimately would benefit competition and, hence, consumers").

[38] See 4A Antitrust Law ¶ 971d (4th ed. 2016).

[39] 2010 Horizontal Merger Guidelines, § 10 & n. 15. The footnote observes that if the efficiencies relate mainly to fixed costs they will be unlikely to show up in the very short term, but may appear in the longer run. In particular, the Guidelines add in the that efficiencies in the conducting of research and development will not likely affect short term prices.

Guidelines the Sixth Circuit was more categorical. In rejecting an efficiencies defense offered by merging hospitals it observed that the defendant "did not even attempt to argue . . . that this merger would benefit consumers (as opposed to only the merging parties themselves) in any way."[40]

12.2b3. Efficiencies Must Be "Merger-Specific" and "Extraordinary"

The welfare tradeoff model has force only because we assume that the efficiencies in question could not be obtained by means other than merger. But many efficiency gains can be attained by other means, although perhaps less readily. For example, a merger may result in the termination of an inefficient CEO and his replacement by a more aggressive one, but stockholders or an attentive Board of Directors could do the same thing.[41] A merger might facilitate a firm's simplification of its distribution system or specialization of its plants, but these things would very likely happen without the merger as well. They might simply take longer.

Nearly anything that can be accomplished by a firm can also be accomplished by contract. In fact, the modern economic conception of a firm regards it as a bundle, or "nexus," of contracts. One corollary is that contractual alternatives to mergers are often available, and in many cases will be less threatening to competition. For example, plausible alternatives to merger are joint ventures or licensing agreements, particularly where the efficiency gains are in such activities as research and development. Joint participation in R & D can be highly efficient and, if properly limited, need not raise significant concerns about coordination of prices or output. The same thing is frequently true of intellectual property licensing, which can enable firms to share a technology while continuing to compete with each other in other ways. For example, in the *St. Luke's* hospital merger case the Ninth Circuit accepted the district court's conclusion that the hospital in question could have acquired access to a shared electronic database by licensing or other means as an alternative to merger.[42]

Finally, one must keep in mind that the concentration standards for assessing mergers[43] are premised on the proposition that all mergers produce some efficiency gains. As a result, they take into

---

[40]   ProMedica Health Sys., Inc. v. FTC, 749 F.3d 559, 571 (6th Cir. 2014).

[41]   See FTC v. Owens-Illinois, Inc., 681 F.Supp. 27, 53 (D.D.C.), vacated as moot, 850 F.2d 694 (D.C.Cir. 1988) (accepting this defense).

[42]   Saint Alphonsus Medical Center-Nampa, Inc. v. St. Luke's Health Sys., Ltd., 778 F.3d 775, 791 (9th Cir. 2015); see 4A Antitrust Law ¶ 973c (4th ed. 2016).

[43]   See § 12.4b.

account the "ordinary" efficiency gains that can be expected to result from a merger.[44] The kinds of efficiencies that qualify for the defense must be "extraordinary," going beyond these expected savings.

§ 12.3   Estimating Anticompetitive Consequences I: Mergers Facilitating Unilateral Price Increases

12.3a.   Introduction

The anticompetitive consequences of mergers can be grouped under two general headings. Under the first comes mergers that permit the post-merger firm to make a significant price increase, while other firms in the market either keep their price the same or take a much smaller increase. The second classification, which is discussed in § 12.4, includes mergers that facilitate collusion or other forms of coordinated interaction, thus permitting all firms in the market to increase their price.

12.3b.   Merger to Monopoly

The "classic" example of a merger facilitating a unilateral price increase is the merger to monopoly.[45] Such mergers deserve the highest level of antitrust scrutiny, and generally should be condemned even if barriers to entry are low. The need for rivals to be permitted to exist and grow is simply too important in such a market.

Suppose that the antitrust rule were that mergers to monopoly were legal in a market with low entry barriers. As each new entrant came into the market, it could expect an offer to be bought up by the dominant firm. Further, each of those offers would be profitable, for the value of being able to participate in a monopoly would be greater than the value of being a competitive rival against a dominant firm.

12.3c.   Unilateral Effects in Product Differentiated Markets[46]

A market is product differentiated when different sellers offer distinctive variations. While their products compete with one another to greater or lesser degrees, customers distinguish among them and may be willing to pay more for one variation. Our basic models of cartels and oligopoly assume undifferentiated products, but in the

---

[44]   See, e.g., FTC v. Staples, 970 F.Supp. 1066, 1090 (D.D.C. 1997) (rejecting savings in employee health insurance costs as a qualifying efficiency); and see 4A Antitrust Law ¶ 974a (4th ed. 2016).

[45]   See 4 Antitrust Law ¶ 911 (4th ed. 2016).

[46]   The related theory of unilateral effects resulting from capacity constraints or differential costs is not developed here; see 4 Antitrust Law ¶ 915 (4th ed. 2016).

real world this is the exception rather than the rule. Product differentiation is relevant to the extent that (1) the product produced by one merging firm differs from that produced by another, meaning that the pre-merger competition between them is less than it would be if they produced identical output; and (2) the output of the merging firms differs from that of other firms in the market.

Courts historically tended to ignore product heterogeneity as a factor in merger law, largely because so little was known about the relationship between the degree and nature of product differentiation, and the nature and likelihood of noncompetitive results. Product differentiation has appeared much more prominently in formal economic and policy analysis of mergers.

Under the right circumstances, product differentiation can give firms a bit of protected space within which supracompetitive price increases can be profitable. This problem is well known in the economics literature and is illustrated by a model that economist Harold Hotelling used already in 1929.[47] The degree to which a merger in a product differentiated market might facilitate a *unilateral* price increase by the post-merger firm depends on (1) the relative "closeness" in product space of the merging firms to one another; and (2) the relative distance between the post-merger firm's product offering and the offerings of others in the market; and (3) the relative inability of other firms to redesign their products to make them close to the output of the merging firms. This requires the Agencies to consider a variety of factors about the relationship between the two merging firms, between the post-merger firm and other competitors, and between the firms and the customers of each. For example, there must be a significant number of customers who regard the products of the two merging firms as particularly close substitutes.[48] Further, it must be apparent that other firms in the market will not reposition themselves to take advantage of the price increase.

---

[47]   Harold Hotelling, Stability in Competition, 39 Econ. J. 41 (1929).

[48]   2010 Horizontal Merger Guidelines, § 6.1. See also F.T.C. v. Whole Foods Market, Inc., 548 F.3d 1028 (D.C. Cir. 2008) (siding with FTC and concluding that there could be a much narrower market of premium natural and organic foods supermarkets in which the merger created a dominant firm, even though it would have been inconsequential in a broader market that included all supermarkets; see the opinion on remand, in which the district court concluded that the dispute turns almost entirely on market definition. F.T.C. v. Whole Foods Market, Inc., 592 F.Supp.2d 107 (D.D.C. 2009)). The case finally settled on March 6, 2009, by an agreement which required some divestment of individual stores to one or more FTC-approved buyers, as well as of the "Wild Oats" brand.

The closer the products made by the two merging firms, the more likely that the merger will produce a substantial price increase.[49] However, they need not be the "closest" rivals before the merger can have sufficiently anticompetitive consequences. In *Whole Foods* the FTC and later the D.C. Circuit distinguished between "marginal" customers, who would shop the lowest price, and "core" customers who would be loyal to high end natural food stores even after a price increase.[50] Whether the latter group was significant enough to make a price increase profitable presented an empirical question. Further, something must prevent other firms in the market from repositioning their output to make it more like that of the merging firms, thus enabling them to take advantage of the price increase. In making this assessment the agencies may use a methodology called "critical loss analysis," which begins with a price increase of a given magnitude, and then consider how many sales must be lost before this particular price increase would become unprofitable.[51] Then it considers whether the actual level of sales lost in response to a given price increase exceeds the critical level.[52] If the actual level is greater than the critical level, then the price increase is unprofitable and the market must be drawn more broadly. In some cases a large price increase might be profitable while a smaller one would not be; in others a small increase might be profitable while a larger one would not be. In most cases the merger in question has not occurred, so the merger must be "simulated," with the relevant losses estimated from demand elasticities.

As the figure below illustrates, suppose that a market has six firms, A through F, making a differentiated product. The firms' products are differentiated, but by different amounts, as indicated by the distances between them. A's marginal cost is $1.00, its current price is $2.00, and at that price it sells 100 units. Its residual price elasticity of demand is 2, which means that a 10% price increase, to $2.20, will yield a 20% demand reduction, to 80 units. Note that this price increase is unprofitable. Pre-increase profits were $100. But post-increase profits are $1.20 per unit, times 80 units, or $96.

---

[49]   2010 Horizontal Merger Guidelines, § 6.1, available at https://www.ftc.gov/sites/default/files/attachments/merger-review/100819hmg.pdf.

[50]   FTC v. Whole Foods Markets, Inc., 548 F.3d 1028 (D.C. Cir. 2008).

[51]   See 4 Antitrust Law ¶ 914a (4th ed. 2016); Carl Shapiro, The 2010 Horizontal Merger Guidelines: From Hedgehog to Fox in Forty Years, 77 Antitrust L.J. 49 (2010).

[52]   See City of New York v. Group Health, Inc., 2008 WL 4974578 (S.D.N.Y. Nov. 21, 2008) (critical loss analysis relevant to determination of amount of price increase that would likely occur subsequent to a merger).

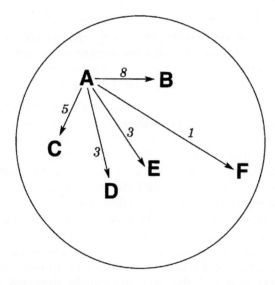

But when firm A raises its price, where do the customers go? Let us assume that of the 20 units that are lost, 8 (40%) go to B, the closest rival, 5 (25%) go to C, the second closest rival, and 3, 3 and 1 units respectively go to rivals D, E & F. This percentage rate at which customers substitute from A to B, or from A to C, is called a "diversion ratio." Assume also that all rivals have the same costs.

In this case an A-C merger would make the price increase profitable. While the price increase to $2.20 reduces A's own profits by $4.00, it increases C's profits by $5.00 (that is, C sells 5 more at a profit of $1.00 each). As a result of the merger, sales by C that were previously lost are "recaptured" by A. A merger with B would be even more profitable, since 8 sales, and $8.00 in increased profit, go to B. But the important point is that a merger with *either* B or C would make A's 10% price increase profitable, even though C is only the second closest rival. Thus either merger would be challengeable if we regarded a merger facilitating a 10% price increase as unlawful. A merger with firms D, E, or F would not be challenged.

Measuring diversion ratios empirically can be a fairly manageable problem, particularly in markets where there are electronic records of transactions. For example, if a sporting goods chain sells several brands of running shoes and the price of Adidas rises by 10%, scanner data might reveal the number of customers who switched away from Adidas, and the relative numbers that switched to Nike, Saucony, Asics, and so on.

One important technical tool that has been developed to facilitate this analysis is "upward pricing pressure," or UPP. UPP is an econometric tool that involves weighing the upward pressure resulting from the above described effects against any reductions in marginal cost that might result from merger efficiencies. Under the Guidelines approach if the predicted effect on prices is positive, or "upward," then the merger should be challenged.

Before consumer data tells us reliably that a merger among two makers of similar products is anticompetitive, we also need to collect information about other factors. These include mainly manufacturers' ability to re-configure their products in response to higher profits in one segment. Making higher quality baby food may require little more than selecting different ingredients, and perhaps some advertising announcing the quality change. On the other hand, for Ford to enter the market niche occupied by BMW and Mercedes may require years of planning and design. We also need to know something about the ability of retailers to re-design their sales efforts. The multi-brand retailer has its own profit incentives to push those products that sell the best and can be expected to disfavor product variations selling at monopoly prices.

12.3d. Mergers That Threaten Innovation

The 2010 Horizontal Merger Guidelines contain a Section that did not appear in previous Guidelines concerning mergers that threaten competition by limiting "innovation and product variety."[53] The concern is mainly with unilateral effects that result from reductions in innovation competition. The Guidelines state:

> The Agencies may consider whether a merger is likely to diminish innovation competition by encouraging the merged firm to curtail its innovative efforts below the level that would prevail in the absence of the merger. That curtailment of innovation could take the form of reduced incentive to continue with an existing product-development effort or reduced incentive to initiate development of new products.
>
> The first of these effects is most likely to occur if at least one of the merging firms is engaging in efforts to introduce new products that would capture substantial revenues from the other merging firm. The second, longer-run effect is most likely to occur if at least one of the merging firms has capabilities that are likely to lead it to

---

[53]   2010 Horizontal Merger Guidelines, § 6.4. The 2010 Guidelines also contain a statement in its opening section that "A merger enhances market power if it is likely to encourage one or more firms to raise price, reduce output, diminish innovation, or otherwise harm customers as a result of diminished competitive constraints or incentives."

develop new products in the future that would capture substantial revenues from the other merging firm.

The Agencies evaluate the extent to which successful innovation by one merging firm is likely to take sales from the other, and the extent to which post-merger incentives for future innovation will be lower than those that would prevail in the absence of the merger.[54]

This concern is hardly fanciful and some version of it has been known in antitrust since the beginning of the twentieth century. In the *Paper Bag* patent litigation, which reached the Supreme Court in 1908, the dominant firm had acquired a patent in a technology that competed with technology it was already using. It did not use the patent at all, preferring to stick with its existing technology, but also refused to license it to others and filed a successful infringement action against a rival firm that developed technology that infringed the acquired patent.[55]

Closely related is the problem of "killer" acquisitions, which occur when a firm acquires another firm only to close it down. For example, a pharmaceutical company may acquire a smaller company that has ongoing research projects but perhaps no actual production in the same area. Then the acquirer shuts the firm down and cancels its projects, thus removing it as a competitive threat. The appropriate antitrust response should be harsh. Such a merger creates no efficiencies because the acquirer is not using the assets of the acquired firm. Indeed, the transaction resembles a cartel with an output reduction more than a merger.[56] The above-quoted passage from the Merger Guidelines applies because the post-merger firm is curtailing its innovation efforts as a result of the merger.

An appropriate remedy in some of these cases is to permit dominant firms to acquire *non*exclusive licenses in patents that lie at the heart of their power, but not exclusive licenses.[57] Prohibiting such acquisitions altogether often precludes firms from keeping their own technology up to date. In order to accomplish this, however, they do not need the patent's power to exclude; they need only access to patented technology developed by others. As a result, permitting the

---

[54]   Id.

[55]   Continental Paper Bag Co. v. Eastern Paper Bag Co., 210 U.S. 405, 429, 28 S.Ct. 748 (1908). For more on the litigation, see Christina Bohannan and Herbert Hovenkamp, Creation Without Restraint: Promoting Rivalry in Innovation, ch. 7 (2011).

[56]   See Colleen Cunningham, Florian Ederer, & Song Ma, Killer Acquisitions, available at https://papers.ssrn.com/sol3/papers.cfm?abstract_id=3241707 (giving several examples, mostly from the pharmaceutical industry).

[57]   See 3 Antitrust Law ¶ 707g (4th ed. 2015).

acquisition of nonexclusive licenses strikes about the right balance between denying a dominant firm access to essential technology and permitting it to exclude others from its market.

Patents are unquestionably "assets" reachable by § 7.[58] At the time a patent is acquired neither the government nor anyone else may know whether the acquiring firm intends to practice it. But the exclusive or nonexclusive nature of the assignment is knowable and exclusive assignments in areas subject to dominance should be regarded with suspicion. Further, exclusivity is rarely essential to protect any legitimate interest of the acquiring firm. Its legitimate interest is to be able to practice the best technology itself, but not to prevent others from using technology that it did not develop itself.

Of course, a nonexclusive license may be worth less to the acquirer than an exclusive license, and this may injure the inventor/assignor of the patent. Indeed, an exclusive right to the patent in the hands of the dominant firm who does not intend to use it could be worth more than a nonexclusive right held by that firm or others. But patents do not create entitlements to market monopolies any more than ownership of a production plant entitles one to a monopoly in its product market, or to sell it subject to an anticompetitive noncompetition agreement. That is, the general rule that assets can be freely transferred to the highest bidder clearly applies to patents, but it is just as clearly subject to the constraint that anticompetitive transactions can be enjoined when they fall within the prohibitions of the antitrust laws.

12.3e. Platform Acquisitions and Potential Competition

One merger problem on the horizon at this writing is large platform acquisitions of nascent firms. Google, Apple, Facebook, Amazon, and Microsoft have acquired hundreds of small startups.[59] The most likely explanation of such acquisitions is that the new rival threatens to become an aggressive competitor, even though it has not done so yet. In that case the effect of the merger is to prevent this new technology from developing in competition with that of the dominant firm. This explanation also accounts for the fact that many of the high tech startups that have been acquired are not competitors of the acquiring firm at the time of the acquisition. In some cases they

---

[58]   See 5 Antitrust Law ¶ 1202f (4th ed. 2016). See also Pharmaceutical Research and Mfrs. of Am. v. FTC, 790 F.3d 198 (D.C.Cir. 2015) (FTC had authority to require reporting of transfers of exclusive patent rights under the Hart-Scott-Rodino Act, given the possibility that some such acquisitions might be anticompetitive).

[59]   See Herbert Hovenkamp, Prophylactic Merger Policy, 70 Hastings L.J. 45, 70–73 (2018).

sell complements or an unrelated product. Of course, the general policy of the intellectual property laws is to encourage the dissemination of new technology, but in this case a *non*exclusive license will serve that purpose quite adequately. It will permit the dominant firm to have access to the technology at issue, while not denying it to others who might enter into competition with the dominant firm.[60]

For example, suppose that Facebook would like to acquire the text messaging app WhatsApp (an acquisition that actually occurred in 2014). If Facebook were limited to a nonexclusive license to all of WhatsApp's technology, it could still obtain everything needed to add WhatsApp's features to its program.[61] To be sure, WhatsApp would be worth much less if it could sell only a nonexclusive license to Facebook. That is because the deal has both an integration value and an exclusion value. A nonexclusive license would give Facebook WhatApp's full integration value, less perhaps the value of some key employees: Facebook would be able to offer all of WhatsApp's features. What Facebook would not get, however, is the value of excluding other firm's from WhatsApp's technology. IP acquisitions are unique in the sense that it is possible to segregate the integration value and the exclusion value by means of a nonexclusive license. This would enable the firms to obtain the socially beneficial aspects of the acquisition, but not the socially harmful aspects. In any event, while the acquisition price for a nonexclusive license would be less, it would leave WhatsApp intact and free to grant other nonexclusive licenses to other firms.

Finally, one must be wary of a conclusion in the Supreme Court's *AmEx* decision that the only thing that can compete with a two-sided platform is another two-sided platform.[62] This conclusion is factually incorrect and more problematically was stated as a conclusion of law. Taken literally it can make a merger between a two-sided platform and a more traditional firm is virtually per se legal because it cannot be considered a merger of competitors. One court has already decided that a merger of a two-side airline reservation platform (Sabre) and a more traditional airline service could not be a merger of

---

[60]   See, e.g., United States v. Baroid Corp., 59 Fed. Reg. 2610 (1994) (consent decree conditioning acquisition by large firm of competing technology on the granting of licenses to others). See Erik Hovenkamp, Startup Acquisitions, Error Costs, and Antitrust Policy, 87 Univ. Chi. L. Rev. 331 (2020).

[61]   At least some data indicated that Facebook viewed WhatsApp as a rising competitor and potential rival to Facebook's entire platform. See "Facebook Feared WhatsApp Threat Ahead of 2014 Purchase, Documents Shows", *Wall St. Journal*, Nov. 25, 2019; https://www.buzzfeednews.com/article/charliewarzel/why-facebook-bought-whatsapp.

[62]   Ohio v. American Express Co., 138 S.Ct. 2274, 2287 (2018).

competitors.[63] This conclusion, if not corrected, has the potential to do a great deal of mischief, but currently lower courts appear to be treating it as the law.

§ 12.4   Estimating Anticompetitive Consequences II: Mergers Facilitating Coordinated Interaction

The prevailing concern of merger law is to deter oligopolistic pricing or express collusion. Since many mergers have a significant but unmeasurable potential to create efficiencies,[64] an ideal antitrust policy would condemn mergers when the risk of oligopoly pricing or collusion is substantial and approve them when such risks are minimal.

Most economists agree that there is a relationship between the size, size distribution and number of firms in a market and the likelihood of collusion. More recently, many have come to believe that structure is not everything, although few regard it as irrelevant. In any event, they do disagree about the relevant numbers. Furthermore, markets differ from each other. One market containing six firms might be much more susceptible to collusion than another. Nevertheless, both the Merger Guidelines and the courts have tried to develop unitary structural rules for prima facie illegality that apply in all industries with a given level of concentration. Then they use several non-market share factors as mitigating or aggravating circumstances on a case-by-case basis. This approach was approved by the Supreme Court in United States v. Philadelphia Nat. Bank.[65] The non-market share factors include:

1)   Presence and Height of Entry Barriers

2)   Sophistication of Buyers, Suppliers or Others in a Position to Discipline Market Participants

3)   Sales Methods, Shipping Costs, Availability of Facilitating Practices

4)   Degree of Product Differentiation

---

[63]   United States v. Sabre Corp., 452 F.Supp.3d 97 (D.Del. 2020), vacated on other grounds, 2020 WL 4915824 (3d Cir. July 20, 2020). The parties subsequently abandoned their merger plans for other reasons.

[64]   See § 12.2.

[65]   374 U.S. 321, 355–66, 83 S.Ct. 1715, 1737–43 (1963). The Court compared market share percentages in merger cases in a wide variety of industries and concluded that the percentages in the case before it (combined market share more than 30%) "raise an inference that the effect of the contemplated merger of appellees may be substantially to lessen competition * * *." Id. at 365, 83 S.Ct. at 1742.

12.4a.   Measuring Market Concentration: The CR4 and the Herfindahl

Under practically every theory about how mergers can facilitate anticompetitive behavior, market concentration is relevant. If the feared consequence is collusion, it can readily be shown that price fixing is more likely to be successful as the number of price fixers declines. Collusion is particularly more likely to succeed if the colluders can eliminate firms that have been unwilling to participate in the cartel. As the number of cartel members is reduced, the ease with which an agreement can be reached increases; further, cheating becomes a smaller problem and it can often be detected more easily. The ability to eliminate a fringe firm not participating in the cartel can often spell the difference between success and failure, particularly if there are only one or a small number of such firms.[66]

If the feared result is Cournot oligopoly,[67] the inverse relationship between the number of firms and anticompetitive consequences is equally robust. In the orthodox Cournot oligopoly, output goes down and prices go up as the number of firms decreases. More complicated variants generally yield similar results. For example, the more easily one firm can observe the behavior of others, the more easily an oligopoly can be maintained. A small number of rivals is generally easier to observe than a large number, and "cheating" thus easier to detect.[68]

So concentration clearly matters. Nevertheless, the robustness of that conclusion belies much complexity about *how* it matters. The questions are manifold: (1) at what level does the number of firms in the market begin to make a measurable difference in performance? (2) what is the relevance of *variations* in firm size, whether in the market generally or among the merging partners? (3) what index, or measurement device, best captures the market concentration concerns of merger policy? (4) to what extent should differences among markets be taken into account? Although economists agree fairly broadly about the general relevance of concentration, they continue to dispute these questions. One's position on them affects both the weight given to a particular level of concentration and the choice of a rule, or "index," for measuring concentration.

12.4a1.   The Four-Firm Concentration Ratio (CR4)

In the 1960's and 1970's courts and the enforcement agencies most often looked at the "four-firm concentration ratio" (CR4) to

---

[66]   For analysis of these factors, see § 4.1.

[67]   See § 4.2.

[68]   See 4 Antitrust Law ¶ 930 (4th ed. 2016).

determine the degree of danger present in a particular market. The CR4 is computed by summing the market shares of the four largest firms in the market. Thus a market in which the four largest firms have market shares of 30%, 20%, 15%, and 10% has a CR4 of 75%.[69] Such a market was considered highly concentrated, and any merger in that market would be given close scrutiny. If the CR4 was much smaller, such as 25%, then a merger involving firms of somewhat larger market shares might still be legal. Under the original Merger Guidelines issued by the Division in 1968,[70] a merger of two firms of 4% market share each was presumptively illegal in a highly concentrated market (CR4 greater than 75%). If the market was less concentrated, mergers involving firms of 5% each were presumptively illegal. These Guidelines were substantially more tolerant of mergers than Supreme Court case law, which had condemned mergers in unconcentrated markets of firms whose combined post-merger market share was less than 8%.[71]

12.4a2. The Herfindahl-Hirschman Index (HHI)

The enforcement agencies now use the Herfindahl-Hirschman Index (HHI) instead of the CR4 to measure market concentration.[72] The HHI as used in the Horizontal Merger Guidelines is the sum of the squares of every firm in the relevant market. For example, if a market has 3 firms each with a market share of 25%, 1 firm of 15% and 1 firm of 10%, the HHI would be $25^2 + 25^2 + 25^2 + 15^2 + 10^2 = 2200$. Such a market (which has a CR4 of 90%) is considered moderately concentrated under the 2010 Horizontal Merger Guidelines, which set the threshold for "high" concentration at 2500.

Many economists believe that the HHI describes market structure and dangers of anticompetitive activity more accurately than the CR4 does. For example, the CR4 fails to account for distribution of market shares among the four largest firms. A market in which the four largest firms each have a 20% share has a CR4 of 80%. A market in which the largest firm has 77% and firms 2, 3 and

---

[69] Some economists prefer the 8-firm concentration ratio (CR8), which is the sum of the market shares of the eight largest firms. Courts, however, have used the CR4 almost exclusively.

[70] U.S. Dep't of Justice Merger Guidelines, reprinted in 4 Trade Reg.Rep. (CCH) ¶ 13,101 (1968).

[71] E.g., United States v. Von's Grocery Co., 384 U.S. 270, 86 S.Ct. 1478 (1966) (condemning merger where combined market share of merging firms was 7.5% and CR4 was 24.4%); United States v. Pabst Brewing Co., 384 U.S. 546, 86 S.Ct. 1665 (1966), on remand, 296 F.Supp. 994 (E.D.Wis. 1969) (condemning merger where firms' combined market share was 4.5% and CR4 less than 30%).

[72] For the history and early use of the Index, see Albert O. Hirschman, The Paternity of an Index, 54 Amer.Econ.Rev. 761 (1964); George J. Stigler, A Theory of Oligopoly, 72 J.Pol.Econ. 44 (1964).

4 each have 1% also has a CR4 of 80%. This is so because the price charged by a classical cartel is indifferent to the distribution of firm sizes. The cartel of four 20% firms will fix the same price as the cartel of one 77% firm and three 1% firms.

But in a non-cooperative oligopoly[73] the price rises as the disparity in firm size rises, and the HHI reflects this. Our experience also bears this out to some degree. A market with four equal size, equally efficient firms may behave quite competitively. An industry with one giant and several pygmies, however, will likely be conducive to "price leadership," a form of oligopolistic pricing in which the largest firm sets a supracompetitive price and the smaller firms, fearful of retaliation, follow with their own supracompetitive price. The HHI acknowledges that markets with the same CR4 may exhibit widely different degrees of competition. The HHI of the market containing four 20% firms will be around 1700 or 1800, depending on the size of the remaining firms. In the case of the market containing one 77% firm and three 1% firms, the HHI will be around 6000.

The question of variations in firm size is important, but it does not yield answers that are consistent, as the two concentration indices suggest. If the feared threat is price fixing and the industry is subject to scale economies, variations in firm size can make cartel bargains more difficult to reach and enforce. There will be more disagreements about the profit-maximizing price, because firms with different costs compute different profit-maximizing prices. There may also be less agreement about how the output reduction should be allocated.[74] For example, the HHI seems to be superior to the CR4 in predicting that a market in which one firm has a 77% market share and three others have 1% each will perform less competitively than a market with four 20% firms. But the HHI also predicts that a market in which the top four firms have 25%, 20%, 20%, and 15% will perform less competitively than the market with four 20% firms. The HHI in the former will be upwards of 1650, while that of the latter will be somewhere above 1600. *Any* amount of variation in firm size increases the HHI; that is, for any given number of firms, HHI is minimized when all firms are exactly the same size.[75] This prediction is not consistent with the notion that express collusion (or

---

[73]   On non-cooperative, Cournot-style oligopoly, see § 4.2.

[74]   The problems are discussed in § 4.1.

[75]   This is simply generalized. Suppose a market has n firms with market shares of A each. The HHI will be NA^2. Suppose now that one firm is larger by B, which entails that another firm or group of firms will be smaller by B, since the total must be 100%. Assume that the first firm's market share goes to $(A + B)$ and that the second firm's is now $(A - B)$. When both of these firms were size A, their joint contribution to the HHI was $2A^2$. But now their contribution is $(A + B)^2 + (A - B)^2$, which equals $A^2 + 2AB + B^2 + A^2 - 2AB + B^2$, which is the same as $2A^2 + 2B^2$. So the HHI has increased by $2B^2$.

cooperative oligopoly behavior) is most likely to succeed when all the firms are approximately the same size.

Is the HHI correct to assume that disparities in firm size yield higher rather than lower market prices in oligopoly markets? That question, it turns out, is extremely complicated and the answer varies among markets. For example, dominant firms in markets can facilitate price "leadership," which can be quite different from Cournot oligopoly. In the latter, each firm sets its own profit-maximizing output on the assumption that other firms will not change their behavior. Under price leadership, however, the dominant firm commonly sets the price under the assumption that the followers will match its price, because they fear retaliation. Price leadership models typically yield prices and output that approximate the cooperative, or *cartel*, level rather than the lower Cournot oligopoly level. Likewise, if oligopolies are thought of as repeated games, pricing and output approaching the cartel level may emerge.[76]

All of this underscores that our choice of an index is not only a question of mathematics, but also of the behavioral assumptions we make. One index may in fact be better for some measurement situations, while the other index is better for others.[77] In most industries, predicting the type of behavior that is most likely to occur would involve a great deal of guesswork. Presumably, firms acting in the abstract would prefer cooperative behavior, since it is more profitable.[78] However, their fallback position would be Cournot; so Cournot would express our minimum concern, and the relevant question would be, how successful would the firms be in keeping their prices *above* the Cournot level.

In addition, although the *theoretical* underpinning of CR4 and Cournot are fairly clear, the available empirical evidence is mixed: empirically it has not been shown that the CR4 consistently works better in one type of industry, while the HHI consistently works better in another type.

Another problem with the HHI is that an error in measuring the market share of a large firm will distort the measurement

---

[76]   See § 4.2.

[77]   See Marie-Paule Donsimoni, Paul Geroski & Alexis Jacquemin, Concentration Indices and Market Power: Two Views, 32 J. Indus. Econ. 419, 428 (1984): "[T]here is no such thing as an 'optimal' index of concentration, both because different industries behave differently as well as because no obvious widely accepted normative judgments exist to guarantee its optimality."

[78]   That is, perfectly cooperative behavior (for example a cartel where the profit-maximizing price is set accurately and no one cheats) yields the single-firm monopoly price. By contrast, Cournot behavior with two or more firms yields a price somewhat less than the single-firm monopoly price, which decreases as the number of firms increases. See § 4.2a.

substantially. This is a function of the fact that market share numbers in the HHI are squared, which exaggerates the impact of an error.[79] For example, assume that a market contains four firms with market shares of 35%, 15%, 10% and 10%. The CR4 is 70% and the HHI will be around 1700, depending on the size of the other firms in the market. Suppose, however, that the size of the largest firm is erroneously measured as 40%. In that case the four-firm concentration ratio goes to 75%—not a dramatic difference. The HHI, however, jumps to about 2100, and that difference is quite substantial. In fact, a 5 point error in the measurement of the largest firm has about the same impact on the HHI as a 5% error in the measurement of all three of the other firms in the CR4. For this reason, precise and careful market definition and share computation is essential to a court relying on the HHI, especially with respect to the largest firms in a fairly concentrated market.

Apropos of the last point, no matter which concentration index one chooses, the conclusions the index produces must be discounted when there is doubt about the quality of the underlying data, or when the market is too "thin" to produce very reliable information. For example, very small markets characterized by large, rather idiosyncratic sales do not provide very reliable numbers—indeed, the numbers may vary widely from one year to the next as firms bid, produce at capacity, and re-enter the market with further bids.[80] When differentiated products are placed into the same market, it will usually be defined too broadly, thus understating the degree of power.[81]

12.4b.   Market Share Thresholds Under the Horizontal Merger Guidelines

The 2010 Guidelines for horizontal mergers rely heavily on industrial organization theory to establish some prima facie indicators of when the Division or the FTC will challenge a particular merger. In brief, the Guidelines regard any market in which the *post-merger* HHI is below 1500 as "unconcentrated." Such a market has the equivalent of seven or eight roughly equal sized firms. "Mergers

---

[79]   For example, 20 is one third larger than 15. However, if the two numbers are squared, 400 is almost twice as large as 225.

[80]   Noting this is United States v. Baker Hughes Inc., 908 F.2d 981 (D.C.Cir. 1990).

[81]   On product differentiation and market definition or market power assessment, see § 3.4b.

resulting in unconcentrated markets are unlikely to have adverse competitive effects and ordinarily require no further analysis."[82]

If the post-merger HHI falls between 1500 and 2500, the market will be deemed "moderately" concentrated. Nevertheless the agencies will be unlikely to challenge a merger that produces an HHI increase of less than 100 points. If the increase is greater than 100 points, however, the likelihood of challenge increases and such mergers warrant further scrutiny.[83]

Markets where the post-merger HHI exceeds 2500 are regarded as highly concentrated. Even here, however, mergers producing an HHI increase of less than 100 points will not ordinarily be challenged. If the HHI increase falls between 100 and 200 points, then the merger will be regarded as having significant anticompetitive potential and will warrant close scrutiny. If the HHI increase exceeds 200 the merger "will be presumed to be likely to enhance market power," although this presumption can be rebutted by "persuasive evidence."[84]

In a market with a post-merger HHI above 2500 a dominant firm likely would be prohibited from acquiring any but the smallest of competitors. For example, if a firm with a 30% market share acquired a firm with a 4% share, the increase in HHI would be 240. The Agencies would probably challenge the merger, and the courts have agreed that mergers in or above that range in a properly defined relevant market are prima facie unlawful.[85]

The 2010 Guidelines deviate from stricter standards in the 1992 Guidelines and earlier, which had identified any market with a post-merger HHI above 1800 as highly concentrated and were more aggressive about challenging fairly small acquisition. However, the enforcement data indicate that particularly during the first decade of the 21st century the Guidelines were not followed very closely. For example, except in the petroleum industry, the FTC rarely challenged a merger when the *post*-merger HHI fell below 2000, unless they involved the largest firms in the market. The agencies challenged very few mergers where the post-merger HHI fell below

---

[82]   2010 Horizontal Merger Guidelines, § 5.3, available at https://www.ftc.gov/sites/default/files/attachments/merger-review/100819hmg.pdf.   For   further elaboration, see 4 Antitrust Law ¶ 932 (4th ed. 2016).

[83]   2010 Horizontal Merger Guidelines, § 5.3. See § 12.7.

[84]   2010 Horizontal Merger Guidelines, § 5.3.

[85]   FTC v. Penn State Hershey Med. Ctr., 838 F.3d 327 (3d Cir. 2016) (postmerger HHI of 5984 and HHI increase of 2582 sufficient for illegality). In addition, the court concluded, the post-merger hospital would control 76% of the market. See also Saint Alphonsus Medical Center-Nampa, Inc. v. St. Luke's Health Sys., Ltd., 778 F.3d 775, 786 (9th Cir. 2015) (HHI increase of 1607 and post-merger HHI of 6219).

2400, unless the merger increased the HHI by 300 points or more.[86] The 2010 revisions were an attempt to make the Guidelines a better predictor of actual agency practice.

12.4c.   The Weight to Be Given to Market Definition and Market Share Measures

Both concentration measures and estimates of market share are generalized attempts to predict the likelihood of anticompetitive behavior in a market. Often, however, information gleaned from the specific market at issue suggests that the concentration measures overstate or understate the competitive significance of a particular merger. This is particularly likely to occur when market conditions are in a state of flux, or when the concentration numbers either overstate or understate the degree of difference between products that are inside the market and those that are outside.

Further, market concentration/market share figures do not adequately account for the *degree* of difference between products inside or outside the market. If products defined as just outside the market are separated widely in product or geographical space from those defined as just inside, then those in the relevant market will have more power to raise price than if the separation is not so wide.

The 2010 Guidelines also place a heavier emphasis on direct evidence of competitive effects in defining markets: "[e]vidence of competitive effects can inform market definition, just as market definition can be informative regarding competitive effects."[87] The example offered concerns evidence that fewer firms offering a product causes price to rise significantly for that product—such evidence can *itself* establish a relevant product market.[88] The 2010 Guidelines also state that, in a merger situation involving "alternative and reasonably plausible candidate markets," direct evidence of

---

[86]   See FTC, Merger Challenges Data, Fiscal Years 1999–2003, available at https://www.ftc.gov/. One decision cited this data and then refused to condemn a merger that was on the margin of illegality according to the Guidelines, but whose numbers were significantly lower than previous mergers that the government had challenged. FTC v. Arch Coal, Inc., 329 F.Supp.2d 109, 129 (D.D.C.), case dismissed, 2004 WL 2066879 (D.C.Cir. 2004). In public hearings prior to the adoption of the 2010 Guidelines it became quite clear that Agency practice had deviated significantly from the standards that the 1992 Guidelines had articulated. See Carl Shapiro, The 2010 Horizontal Merger Guidelines: From Hedgehog to Fox in Forty Years, 77 Antitrust L.J. 49 (2010).

[87]   Id.

[88]   Compare the 2010 Guidelines with the 1992 Guidelines, § 1.1 ("In considering the likely reaction of buyers to a price increase, the Agency *will take into account* all relevant evidence, including . . . evidence that buyers have shifted or have considered shifting purchases between products in response to . . . competitive variables.") (emphasis added).

competitive effects is particularly valuable if the market shares resulting from the alternative markets yields disparate inferences regarding such effects.[89]

The 2010 Guidelines stress that market definition is an "inevitable simplification" in the sense that it imperfectly accounts for the fact that substitutes exist on a more-distant-to-closer spectrum. The 2010 Guidelines take the position that market shares of alternative products in markets that are defined *narrowly* are more likely to accurately measure their competitive significance. As a result, under the 2010 Guidelines, the Agencies proceed from the following understanding:

> Although excluding more distant substitutes from the market inevitably understates their competitive significance to some degree, doing so often provides a more accurate indicator of the competitive effects of the merger than would the alternative of including them and overstating their competitive significance as proportional to their shares in an expanded market.[90]

12.4d. How Should Concentration Count? The *Philadelphia Bank* Presumption

As the previous discussion suggests, predicting the competitive consequences of a merger is hardly an exact science. Several other factors must be taken into account, and each is susceptible to only "soft" measurement.

So does one simply throw them all into a pot and see what kind of stew comes out? In the *Philadelphia Bank* case, the Supreme Court concluded no.[91] Although numerous factors are relevant to predicting the consequences of a merger, market concentration must be considered more important than others. The Court acknowledged that a prediction of anticompetitive consequences

> is sound only if it is based upon a firm understanding of the structure of the relevant market; yet the relevant economic data are both complex and elusive. * * * [U]nless businessmen can assess the legal consequences of a merger with some confidence, sound business planning is retarded. * * * So also, we must be alert to the danger of subverting congressional intent by permitting a too-broad economic investigation.

---

[89]   2010 Guidelines, § 4.

[90]   Id.

[91]   United States v. Philadelphia Natl. Bank, 374 U.S. 321, 83 S.Ct. 1715 (1963).

[W]e think that a merger which produces a firm **[1]** controlling an undue percentage share of the relevant market, and **[2]** results in a significant increase in the concentration of firms in that market, is so inherently likely to lessen competition substantially that it must be enjoined **[3]** in the absence of evidence clearly showing that the merger is not likely to have such anticompetitive effects. * * *[92]

The bracketed numbers illustrate the burden shifting framework that courts apply. The plaintiff must show a combination of excessive post-merger concentration along with a significant increase in concentration. At that time the burden shifts to the defendant to rebut this prima facie case. The principal difference with today's practice is that the first relevant number in *Philadelphia Bank* was the market share of the post-merger firm, while today we usually look at the market's overall post-merger concentration.[93]

The rationales for placing the burden of proving efficiencies on the merging firms are clear. Defenses are all about engineering costs, economies of scale, distribution, management, transaction costs, IP portfolios, or make-vs-buy alternatives. For all of these the defendant is in a better position to have information about them and how they will be affected by the merger. Indeed, the motives for any merger are either increases in efficiency or increased market power or a combination. Presumably a rationally acting acquiring firm has relied on these to makes it decision. The merging firms are also in the better position in most cases to show that the claimed efficiencies are verifiable and merger specific. Once again, a rationally acting firm has presumably studied the alternatives to merger.

The *Philadelphia Bank* presumption may have been partly based on the Court's conclusion that Congress was concerned about concentration for its own sake, not because of its effect on prices. This invites us to consider whether the burden shifting framework is still correct even in a regime where we are inclined to think that competitive prices ought to be the exclusive goal of merger policy, and that high concentration is bad only when it yields higher prices. On the other hand, the quoted *Philadelphia Bank* statement makes clear

---

[92]   Id. at 362–363, 83 S.Ct. at 1741.

[93]   See Herbert Hovenkamp & Carl Shapiro, Horizontal Mergers, Market Structure, and Burdens of Proof, 127 Yale L.J. 1996, 1997–1998 (2018); Steven C. Salop, The Evolution and Vitality of Merger Presumptions: A Decision-Theoretic Approach, 80 Antitrust L.J. 269 (2015). On the evolution of structuralist approaches to antitrust policy, see Herbert Hovenkamp, The Opening of American Law: Neoclassical Legal Thought, 1870–1970, Ch. 12 (2015).

that the presumption was also based on the need for clear guidance for business managers in an area where guidance is elusive. Direct measure of competitive effects is technical and difficult, but firms typically have good instincts about who their competitors are and what are the market shares of the principal parties. This latter point serves to account for the durability of the burden-shifting approach.

While the D.C. Circuit's *Baker Hughes* decision suggested that the prima facie evidence rule is eroding,[94] other recent decisions have applied the *Philadelphia Bank* rule in fairly orthodox fashion.[95] In any event, the D.C. Circuit's subsequent *Heinz* decision, which relied heavily on structural evidence, largely repudiates the *Baker Hughes* denigration of structural evidence.[96] In its *ProMedica* decision the Sixth Circuit decisively adhered to the presumption and in the process endorsed the approach taken by the 2010 Merger Guidelines.[97] Speaking of the Guidelines' concentration thresholds, the court observed that the post-merger HHI of 4361 in that case, accompanying a 1078 point increase from the merger, "blew through those barriers in spectacular fashion.[98] Further, the court found that price in this market was directly and positively correlated with market share. As a result,

> These two aspects of this case—the strong correlation between market share and price, and the degree to which this merger would further concentrate markets that are already highly concentrated—converge in a manner that fully supports the Commission's application of a presumption of illegality.[99]

How about other factors? For example, should entry barriers be considered any differently in a regime where low consumer prices is merger law's goal, not merely the preservation of unconcentrated

---

[94]   United States v. Baker Hughes Inc., 908 F.2d 981, 991–992 (D.C.Cir. 1990).

[95]   E.g., United States v. Oracle Corp., 331 F.Supp.2d 1098, 1108 (N.D.Cal. 2004) (applying *Philadelphia Bank* and concluding that government had not made out a prima facie case of illegality based on market concentration); R.C. Bigelow, Inc. v. Unilever NV, 867 F.2d 102, 110 (2d Cir. 1989), cert. denied, 493 U.S. 815, 110 S.Ct. 64 (1989) (structure still starting point for analysis).

[96]   FTC v. H.J. Heinz Co., 246 F.3d 708 (D.C.Cir. 2001). See Jonathan B. Baker, Mavericks, Mergers, and Exclusion: Proving Coordinated Competitive Effects Under the Antitrust Laws, 77 N.Y.U.L. Rev. 135, 150 (2002).

[97]   ProMedica Health Sys., Inc. v. FTC, 749 F.3d 559, 568 (6th Cir. 2014). See also United States v. Bazaarvoice, Inc., 2014 WL 203966 (N.D.Cal. 2014) (following *Philadelphia Bank* presumption); In re Ardagh Group, 2014 WL 1493616 (FTC 2014) (same, post-merger HHI in 3500 range).

[98]   Ibid.

[99]   Id. at 570. See also Saint Alphonsus Med. Center v. St. Luke's Health Sys., Ltd., 2014 WL 407446 (D. Id. 2014), aff'd 778 F.3d 775 (9th Cir. 2015) (similar; high HHI numbers warranted condemning hospital merger).

markets? In this particular case, the basic balance should not change all that much. Low entry barriers serve to reduce our concern about mergers under *either* the *Philadelphia Bank* theory that concentration itself was Congress' concern, or the more economic theory that merger policy is concerned about noncompetitive pricing. Easy entry entails that markets will not be concentrated unless the incumbents are not earning profits.[100] To this extent, there is little basis for deviating from the *Philadelphia Bank* presumptions simply because we no longer think concentration *per se* is an important goal of merger enforcement. To be sure, entry barriers are relevant, but low entry barriers cannot be presumed and it is up to the defendant to provide evidence that they are in fact low.

Nevertheless, successive editions of the Merger Guidelines have gradually moved away from exclusive reliance on the *Philadelphia Bank* structural presumption.[101] Clearly, the target of merger policy today is reduced output and higher prices, not high concentration for its own sake. If structural evidence is still the most reliable and easily used basic indicator of likelihood of collusion, then *Philadelphia Bank*'s presumption continues to make sense. To this end, however, the "structural" rule that merger policy invites may not be anything as elaborate as the HHI or even the CR4. Perhaps the best indicator of likelihood of collusion in a market is the number of effective players, with effectiveness measured in terms of individual firms' realistic ability to upset collusion or oligopoly by cutting price. As that number exceeds eight or ten in the case of express collusion, or five to seven in the case of oligopoly, the likelihood of collusion diminishes rapidly.

Finally, one important class of mergers are among purchasers of labor that increase labor concentration, thus enabling the firms to reduce wages.[102] The evidence indicates that labor market concentration is as great or greater than product concentration, and that wages are at least as sensitive to concentration levels. For example, when two hospitals in a community merge, staff wages are likely to go down, because the hospitals face reduced competition for

---

[100]   Provided, that is, that entry barriers are measured under the Bainian formulation: an entry barrier is some condition in the market that permits the incumbent firms to earn monopoly profits while entry is deterred. On the difference between Bainian and Stiglerian entry barriers generally, see § 1.6. On entry barriers in merger cases, see § 12.6.

[101]   On this point, see Carl Shapiro, The 2010 Horizontal Merger Guidelines: From Hedgehog to Fox in Forty Years, 77 Antitrust L.J. 49 (2010) (discussing the 2010 Guidelines); Charles A. James, Overview of the 1992 Horizontal Merger Guidelines, 61 Antitrust L.J. 447 (1993) (discussing the 1992 Guidelines).

[102]   See 4A Antitrust Law ¶ 983 (4th ed. 2019)

certain workers.[103] Another result of these mergers is that they may limit labor competition even if the two firms do not compete in any product market. For example, a large platform seller such as eBay probably does not compete with a software producer such as Intuit, but both may hire computer engineers and thus compete intensely for particular workers.[104]

§ 12.5   The Significance of Product Differentiation

12.5a.   General Effects

Product heterogeneity has always provoked complexity in the analysis of markets. Most importantly, the perfect competition model does not work very well, and the deviations are difficult to account for systematically. Firms in product differentiated markets face individual demand curves that slope downward, although perhaps only slightly. At any given output level there will be different customers willing to pay different prices for the output of different sellers. Likewise, substantial product differentiation often entails that different firms have different costs, that they attain scale economies at different levels of output, and sometimes that they rely on different sets of inputs in their production processes. Product differentiation undermines every exercise in market definition to some degree. For example, if we decide that electric coffee pots and French presses are in the same market we treat them as perfect competitors, which is incorrect. On the other hand, if we put them into separate markets were end up treating them as if they do not compete at all, which is equally incorrect. Any market definition that includes significantly differentiated products tends to understate market power.

One effect of product differentiation is to enable post-merger firms to exact unilateral price increases when their merger involves two firms that are relatively proximate to each other in product space. But in most other situations the general effect of product differentiation is more benign. As § 4.1 noted, price fixing and cooperative oligopoly behavior can be frustrated if firms are unable to agree on the profit-maximizing cartel price. Product differentiation

---

[103]   See United States v. Anthem, Inc., 855 F.3d 345, 356, 371 (D.C. Cir.), cert. denied, 137 S.Ct. 2250 (2017) (condemning a merger on ordinary concentration grounds; then Judge Kavanaugh dissented and also noted the alternative ground that the merger might create monopsony power in provider markets).

[104]   For fuller discussion, see Ioana Marinescu & Herbert Hovenkamp, Anticompetitive Mergers in Labor Markets, 94 Ind. L.J. 1031 (2019); Suresh Naidu, Eric A. Posner & Glen Weyl, Antitrust Remedies for Labor Market Power, 132 Harv. L. Rev. 536 (2018). See California v. eBay, Inc., 2014 WL 4273888 (N.D. Cal. 2014) (approving settlement condemning agreement between eBay and Intuit not to hire one another's computer engineers).

frustrates collusion in this fashion for two different reasons. First, it may give firms different marginal costs, and firms whose costs differ maximize their profits at different prices. Second, product differentiation may entail that firms face different demand curves and this may give them different profit-maximizing prices.

12.5b.   More Extreme Product Differentiation: When Is a Merger Horizontal?

A merger is strictly "horizontal" only if 1) the two firms involved produce the same product (i.e., consumers cannot distinguish between the products of the two firms, or are completely insensitive to the differences); and 2) the firms sell the product in the same geographic market.

The real world contains few perfectly horizontal mergers. Identical gasoline stations across the street from each other are not exactly in the same market: one will be more attractive to west-bound traffic, the other to east-bound traffic. Nevertheless, a merger between them would almost certainly be treated as "horizontal" for antitrust purposes. Although customers may have preferences, the preferences are not strong enough to prevent substantial numbers of them from making a left turn rather than paying a monopoly price.

Discerning a line between horizontal and non-horizontal mergers that is meaningful for policy purposes is difficult, however. Courts characterize a merger as "horizontal" only after they have decided that the merger partners are in the same product and geographic markets. If they are not, courts characterize the competition between them as merely "potential" and the merger as "conglomerate." At that point, the mode of analysis changes significantly.[105]

Courts have characterized the following mergers as "horizontal": a merger 1) of a metal can manufacturer and a glass bottle manufacturer; 2) of a company that strip-mined coal and a company that deep-mined coal; 3) of a company that manufactured dry table wines and a company that manufactured sweet, fruity wines; 4) of a firm that manufactured heavy steel products and a firm that manufactured light steel products; 5) of a grocery chain whose stores were located in northeast Los Angeles and a grocery chain whose stores were located in southwest Los Angeles.[106]

---

[105] Potential competition mergers are discussed in Federal Antitrust Policy, Ch. 13.

[106] United States v. Continental Can Co., 378 U.S. 441, 84 S.Ct. 1738 (1964); United States v. General Dynamics Corp., 415 U.S. 486, 94 S.Ct. 1186 (1974); Coca-Cola Bottling Co., 93 F.T.C. 110 (1979); United States v. Columbia Steel Co., 334 U.S.

It is difficult to generalize about the degree of competition that existed between these pairs of merger partners. In some cases, such as *Continental Can*, cross elasticity of demand between the cans and bottles was high for some customers. The court found that beer bottlers were very sensitive to price and would have responded to a small price increase in cans by switching to bottles, or vice-versa.[107] By contrast, there were other customers who strongly preferred bottles to cans, and for whom the price of bottles would have to go very high before they would consider cans to be satisfactory substitutes.

Courts sometimes look at elasticity of supply when determining the extent to which two companies operate in the same relevant market. For example, United States v. Aluminum Co. of America (Rome Cable) involved the acquisition of a company that made copper and aluminum conductor by a much larger firm that made only aluminum conductor. The district court had found that aluminum and copper conductor should be placed in the same market because "there is complete manufacturing interchangeability between copper and aluminum, and manufacturers constantly review their product lines and 'switch readily from one * * * metal to another in accordance with market conditions.'"[108] The Supreme Court reversed, looking largely at demand conditions to hold that aluminum and copper conductor were separate products. The Supreme Court was probably wrong; if input costs were about the same and the firms could quickly substitute from aluminum to copper, or vice-versa, the competition between them was substantial.

The courts have tended to divide all non-vertical mergers into two kinds: "horizontal" and "conglomerate." Once the court has characterized a merger as "horizontal," the fact that the firms make products that are technically dissimilar, or sell them in somewhat different areas, is largely irrelevant. In *Von's Grocery*, for example, the court defined the relevant market as greater Los Angeles and simply added up the market shares of the two grocery chains who were parties to the merger. Once the merger had been classified as horizontal, it was no longer important that virtually all of Von's

---

495, 68 S.Ct. 1107 (1948); United States v. Von's Grocery Co., 384 U.S. 270, 86 S.Ct. 1478 (1966).

[107] 378 U.S. at 451–52, 84 S.Ct. at 1744.

[108] 377 U.S. 271, 285, 84 S.Ct. 1283, 1291–92 (1964) (J. Stewart, dissenting). See also Owens-Illinois, 5 Trade Reg.Rep. ¶ 23162 (F.T.C. 1992), which found that the market for glass containers contained several end users who would find substitution difficult—e.g., wine bottles, baby food bottles, etc. But on the supply side, glass bottle manufacturing equipment could be reconfigured in a few hours to permit the supplier to switch from one bottle to another. See § 3.5 for a more complete discussion of elasticity of supply.

stores were in the southwest part of the city and all the Shopping Bag stores in the northeast. Surely such a merger did not eliminate as much competition as a merger between two grocery chains all of whose stores were across the street from each other. In fact, Los Angeles was 70 or 80 miles wide, but the lower court found that the average shopper would drive only 10 minutes to buy groceries. The only pairs of Von's and Shopping Bag stores that actually competed with each other were a few pairs toward the middle of the city.[109] The Supreme Court's established framework left it only two alternatives, however: it could have looked at elasticity of supply and considered the likelihood that each chain would have built stores in the other chain's area in response to the second chain's price increase. In that case, it would have treated the merger as "conglomerate" and evaluated it under the potential competition doctrine. The alternative was to ignore the fact that the two chains had stores in different sections of town and treat the merger as purely horizontal. The Court chose the latter alternative.

§ 12.6 Barriers to Entry in Merger Cases

12.6a. The Appropriate Definition of Entry Barriers for Merger Policy

A barrier to entry is something that permits incumbents to price monopolistically for an unacceptable period of time before effective entry restores price and output to the competitive level. If barriers to entry are completely absent, any instance of monopoly pricing will be quickly driven down by new entry. Theoretically, even a merger to monopoly would not result in higher prices in such a market.[110]

The Supreme Court has sometimes cited high entry barriers as a rationale for condemning a particular merger,[111] but has seldom cited low entry barriers as a reason for approving one. The decision in *Von's Grocery*,[112] for example, has been criticized for ignoring the fact that entry barriers in the retail grocery business were extremely

---

[109] *Von's Grocery, supra* 384 U.S. at 295–96, 86 S.Ct. at 1492–93. (J. Stewart, dissenting). Justice Stewart concluded that the Von's and Shopping Bag stores actually in competition with each other accounted for "slightly less than 1% of the total grocery store sales in the area."

[110] On entry barriers generally, see § 1.6.

[111] For example, United States v. Phillipsburg Nat. Bank & Trust Co., 399 U.S. 350, 368–69, 90 S.Ct. 2035, 2045–46 (1970), citing state banking regulations that restrict entry as warranting condemnation of a horizontal merger. See also, FTC v. Procter & Gamble Co., 386 U.S. 568, 579, 87 S.Ct. 1224, 1230 (1967), discussed in § 13.4 below. See also ProMedica Health Sys., Inc. v. FTC, 749 F.3d 559, 556 (6th Cir. 2014) (citing barriers to entry for particular hospital services).

[112] United States v. Von's Grocery Co., 384 U.S. 270, 86 S.Ct. 1478 (1966).

low. As a result monopolistic pricing in that market was unlikely.[113] However, this criticism itself overlooks the fact that monopoly pricing was not the perceived evil of the merger in *Von's Grocery*. The perceived evil was the greater efficiency of the post-merger firm, which would force smaller grocers to go out of business or merge themselves. Superior efficiency is the world's greatest entry barrier, except perhaps for governmental entry restrictions.

In thinking of barriers to entry, it is usually best to focus on output rather than prices as the relevant variable. Setting price is easy to do and prices are easily changed. By contrast, before output is determined one must have a plant, and the size of one's existing plant determines the range over which output can be varied. Under monopoly or collusive pricing, the firms in the market must reduce market-wide output to less than the competitive output. In measuring entry barriers, one must then consider whether sufficient new production can come into the market within a reasonably short time to restore output to the competitive level. Once the competitive level of output is restored, prices will naturally fall to the competitive level as well.

Entry is seldom instantaneous, and it may take considerable time. Incumbent firms will be able to sustain any monopoly pricing scheme until entry occurs of sufficient magnitude to raise output to the competitive level. For the antitrust policy maker, the time question requires a policy choice about how long a period of monopoly pricing is tolerable. We may decide, for example, that monopoly pricing that can last only three months is not worth the commitment of substantial antitrust enforcement resources except in the case of easily formed and quickly abandoned price fixing schemes. If effective entry will occur within three months of a monopoly price increase, the social costs of any monopoly in that market will be smaller than the cost of identifying and enjoining it. In point of fact, however, the courts interpreting the antitrust laws have paid very little attention to this question of time, and there is no general judicial rule on the subject. By contrast, the 1992 Horizontal Merger Guidelines had suggested that entry barriers would be considered low for merger purposes when entry will occur "within two years from initial planning to significant market impact." The 2010 Guidelines do not commit themselves to a specific time, but they do require that entry "be rapid enough that customers are not significantly harmed by the merger, despite any anticompetitive harm that occurs prior to the entry."[114] The 2010 Guidelines place a heavier emphasis on the

---

[113]   See Richard A. Posner, Antitrust Law 127 (2d ed. 2001).

[114]   2010 Horizontal Merger Guidelines, § 9.1, available at https://www.ftc.gov/sites/default/files/attachments/merger-review/100819hmg.pdf.

history of entry ("recent examples of entry, whether successful or unsuccessful") than do previous Guidelines.[115]

For the antitrust policy maker, the problem of entry barriers revolves around three different issues: *first*, what is a suitable definition of barriers to entry? *second*, what kinds of market characteristics or practices qualify as entry barriers? *third*, what kinds of evidence in addition to the bare presence of these characteristics suggest that entry barriers are high enough to warrant antitrust intervention?

The definition of entry barriers given at the beginning of this section somewhat resembles the definition given by economist Joe S. Bain in the 1960's.[116] Bain tended to regard qualifying barriers to entry as market factors that deterred entry even as the firms already in the market were charging prices above the competitive level. This approach to entry barriers has some important advantages for antitrust policy purposes. Under it, one can measure the "height" of an entry barrier by the amount of monopoly pricing that will be permitted before entry occurs. For example, if firms in one market can raise prices 50% above cost without encouraging new entry, while firms in another market will encourage new entry as soon as they raise prices 20% above cost, we can say that entry barriers in the first market are higher than entry barriers in the second. We could generally say the same thing about duration. Entry barriers that permit two years' worth of monopoly pricing can be said to be more severe than entry barriers that permit only six months of monopoly pricing.

Nevertheless, some features of the Bainian definition of entry barriers seem unacceptable to some economists. First, the definition is circular: it tells us what the *result* of entry barriers is without telling us anything about their substance. Second, the Bainian definition seems to lump socially desirable practices into the category of entry barriers. For example, Bain would define scale economies as an entry barrier. If economies of scale are substantial, a dominant firm may be able to set a price well above its costs without causing new entry, for the residual market will not be large enough for a new firm to bring its costs down to the same level.

Largely for this reason, George Stigler redefined the entry barrier as "a cost of producing (at some or every rate of output) which must be borne by a firm which seeks to enter an industry but is not

---

[115]   Id., § 9.

[116]   Joe S. Bain, Barriers to New Competition: Their Character and Consequences in Manufacturing Industries (1962).

borne by firms already in the industry."[117] The Federal Trade Commission has occasionally adopted a Stiglerian definition of entry barriers. For example, its *Echlin* decision defined entry barriers as "additional long-run costs that must be incurred by an entrant relative to the long-run costs faced by incumbent firms."[118] However, in its subsequent *Flowers* decision, it reverted to a more Bainian definition.[119]

The Bainian definition is generally more consistent with antitrust policy, and most antitrust tribunals continue to use it. High entry barriers are not themselves an antitrust violation. If we had a rule of "no fault" monopolization, under which dominant firms could be penalized simply for having their dominant market positions, then a rule such as Stigler's makes sense. We should not use antitrust policy to punish a firm simply for attaining substantial scale economies. Although they can make entry difficult, scale economies are good for consumers.

12.6b.   What Constitutes an Entry Barrier?

In the final analysis, any merger policy that places a high value on economic efficiency and consumer welfare must designate as "barriers to entry" only those things that permit incumbent firms to engage in monopoly pricing while keeping outsiders from entering the market.

12.6b1.   Economies of Scale

As the previous discussion notes, economies of scale are an important entry barrier under the Bainian definition that antitrust most generally employs. Scale economies entail that the firm contemplating entry must always consider, not merely the cost of producing, but also the cost of acquiring enough sales to make its own entry into the market profitable. Most "limit pricing" strategies— under which incumbent firms set price in such a way as to make

---

[117]   George J. Stigler, The Organization of Industry 67 (1968). See also C. von Weizsacker, A Welfare Analysis of Barriers to Entry, 11 Bell J. Econ. 399, 400 (1980) (an entry barrier is a "cost of producing which must be borne by a firm which seeks to enter an industry but is not borne by firms already in the industry and which implies a distortion in the allocation of resources from the social point of view."); Harold Demsetz, Barriers to Entry, 72 Amer.Econ.Rev. 47 (1982) (barrier to entry is something that presents socially preferred entry from occurring).

[118]   Echlin Mfg., Co., 105 F.T.C. 410, 485 (1985). Other times the FTC has found Stiglerian barriers, although it may not have required them. For example, Owens-Illinois, 5 Trade Reg. Rep. ¶ 23162 (FTC, 1992) (environmental restrictions that applied to new furnaces but exempted existing furnaces a barrier to entry).

[119]   Flowers, 5 Trade Reg. Rep. ¶ 22523 at p. 22,217 & n. 10 (Oliver dissent) (FTC, 1989).

entry unattractive—depend on the existence of scale economies.[120] If a firm can make one unit per year at the same per unit cost that other firms face in making hundreds of units per year, then pricing strategies of this kind can generally not deter entry. Incumbents could exclude others only by selling their own output at cost or less. Cost prices are, of course, competitive; and below cost prices would be an unpromising entry deterrence strategy.

If economies of scale are substantial, the prospective entrant is forced to consider what the market price will be *after* its own entry is taken into account. For example, assume that minimum efficient operation in a market requires an output of 30 units. When this efficient cost level has been attained, the market would clear at an output of 100 units, assuming the price were competitive. Suppose the market currently contains three firms that are producing 30 units each, and price is about 15% above the competitive level. Will entry occur? Very likely not, even though prices are high. The new firm would have to reach an output level of 30 units in order to produce as efficiently as the incumbents. But any output level in excess of 10 units would mean that output would be too high to be sold at a profitable price. To be sure, if the prospective entrant forced its way in at the efficient level the other firms would lose money. But firms do not enter markets simply to impose losses on rivals. They enter in order to earn profits for themselves, and in this case the prospect of such profits is quite bleak.

12.6b2. Risk and Size of Investment; Sunk Costs

One important element in the calculus of the prospective entrant is the amount of risk. Courts historically tended to measure entry barriers by the absolute amount of money that it takes to enter an industry. But there is little reason for thinking that high investment, standing alone, deters entry. American and world capital markets are very efficient. If the investment is promising, it may be as easy to raise $100,000,000 as $100,000. Indeed, there may be some relevant scale economies in the raising of capital that make it relatively easier to raise the larger amount. High initial investment, standing alone, should not generally be treated as a qualifying entry barrier.

The relevant question for the prospective entrant is not how much it must invest, but rather how much it will lose if the enterprise fails. For this reason, irreversible or "sunk" costs count heavily in its calculus. For example, consider two firms contemplating entry into two markets where the absolute costs of entry are $1,000,000. The

---

[120] For a good summary of the economics literature, see Richard J. Gilbert, Mobility Barriers and the Value of Incumbency 475, in Handbook of Industrial Organization (Richard Schmalensee & Robert Willig, eds. 1989).

first market is general delivery services, which requires the firm to have a general purpose warehouse, some loading equipment such as fork lifts, and some general purpose delivery trucks. If the new business fails, virtually all of these assets can readily be redeployed in other markets, for all of them can be committed to a variety of uses. In such a market the risk of entry is not all that high, even though the firm might have to attain a high volume in order to get its costs down.

By contrast, a second firm must use most of its entry money to build a specialized chemical plant that can be used only for this particular market. If this business fails, the plant will have a salvage value of only 10 cents on the dollar. Given the same initial costs of entry, and scale economies of the same magnitude, entry is much less likely to occur into the second market than the first.

Some courts have recognized the value of asset specificity, or sunk costs, as entry barriers. For example, in *Illinois Cereal Mills* the court noted that corn mills are highly specialized plants that have little salvage value after they are abandoned. This supported the Federal Trade Commission's conclusion that entry barriers into the market were high.[121] The 2010 Horizontal Merger Guidelines define sunk costs as "entry or exit costs that cannot be recovered outside the relevant market."[122] That is to say, the specialized chemical plant in the above illustration may be capable of being sold, but it will have significant value only to another firm that intends to use it for the same purpose—that is, someone operating within the market.

12.6b3. *Advertising, Promotion, and Customer Loyalty*

Brand specific advertising in markets for branded products may constitute an entry barrier in both the Bainian and Stiglerian senses; nonetheless, there is a great deal of dispute about the height or meaningfulness of entry barriers produced by advertising. Simply put, if the effect of advertising dissipates very soon after the advertising occurs, then advertising is not much of a barrier to entry. The incumbent firm will have to keep on advertising in order to retain its lead, and prospective entrants can match the effect of the incumbent firm's advertising by spending an equivalent amount themselves. Of course, there are economies of scale in advertising— the large firm can spread its costs over more output—but that is a

---

[121]   FTC v. Illinois Cereal Mills, Inc., 691 F.Supp. 1131, 1138, 1144 (N.D.Ill. 1988), affirmed sub nom., FTC v. Elders Grain, 868 F.2d 901 (7th Cir. 1989) (degree of asset specialization suggested high entry barriers).

[122]   2010 Guidelines, § 5.1, available at https://www.ftc.gov/sites/default/files/attachments/merger-review/100819hmg.pdf.

barrier that comes from the scale economies rather than the advertising itself.

By contrast, if advertising has a cumulative effect that builds up over time, then the well established firm may have a distinct advantage over new entrants. Advertising costs are generally "sunk"—that is, once spent, the money cannot be recovered when the firm fails. Thus, if advertising has a cumulative, or capital, value, it may constitute a substantial entry barrier. Of course, the height of the entry barrier caused by advertising is also open to dispute, and once again depends on that portion of advertising expenditures that have a kind of built up or cumulative value.

Virtually the same analysis applies to things like customer loyalty, or goodwill. To the extent the effects accumulate, they can raise entry barriers. The only question of any real importance is how high such barriers are. In the great majority of cases, they are probably insignificant. But there are important exceptions. In markets where the product is complex, with many intricacies unfamiliar to the customer, and particularly where the product costs little relative to the customer's overall budget, goodwill and reputation count for a great deal. The customer must trust the seller because the relative cost of doing a complete product valuation oneself are rather high. By contrast, if the customer is in as good a position to evaluate the product or service as the producer is, then goodwill counts for much less.

12.6b4. Government Entry Restrictions, Including Intellectual Property

Government regulation, licensing and other entry restrictions collectively create among the greatest and most effective entry barriers. For example, if an environmental statute exempts existing plants from expensive compliance, new firms will face a cost that existing firms do not face. Such regulations are entry barriers only in the short run. Eventually, the old plants must be replaced and the new ones will need to comply. But in this case the short run could be a period of several years or even decades.

The role of government regulation in creating entry barriers is often used as part of an argument for the inefficiency of regulation. Regulation, after all, creates and encourages monopoly. But there is no necessary connection between the efficiency of regulation and its role in creating entry barriers. Regulation that is quite efficient in that it is a suitably tailored correction for a real market failure might nevertheless entail restrictions on entry, or requirements that increase the cost, risk or minimum efficient scale of new entry. By contrast, very poorly constructed regulatory policies might permit free entry.

The fact that an entry barrier originates from the government may have an effect on our antitrust analysis. Indeed, in some cases regulated industries are simply exempted from the application of the antitrust laws altogether.[123] Often, however, government regulation is evaluated in exactly the same way that other entry barriers are— that is, as creating a set of circumstances that make certain kinds of antitrust violations possible. For example, in its *Hospital Corporation* decision, the Seventh Circuit noted that a regulatory requirement that hospitals obtain a "certificate of need" could operate as a substantial entry barrier.[124] In this case, collusion that resulted from a merger would lead to an output reduction and excess capacity. But in proving need, a firm desiring to enter the market needed to show that the existing hospitals were currently operating at capacity. Thus the collusion itself could create the entry barrier.

Intellectual property rights often constitute a significant entry barrier.[125] Effective IP rights not only focus customer demand on the owner's product, but they also make it more difficult for rivals to produce in the owner's market niche. Of course, IP rights are both government created and valuable. As a result antitrust policy should not run roughshod over them. At the same time, however, the entry barrier question is neutral in that it asks only whether a price increase is possible, not whether it comes from a legitimate source. For example, two firms may each have strong patent portfolios that serve to discourage entry. But antitrust enforcers can still challenge a merger between the two if it facilitates the exercise of market power, and it does so without questioning the validity of any patent.

One final caveat: one must not reason too quickly from the observation that a firm owns IP rights to the conclusion that entry barriers into its market are high. Many IP rights are weak, narrow in scope, or easily avoided. In that case the IP portfolio may be little more than a nuisance.

12.6c.   Entry Barrier Analysis Under the 2010 Horizontal Merger Guidelines

The 1992 Merger Guidelines evaluated entry barriers by considering whether the merging firms could profitably maintain a

---

[123]   See ch. 16.

[124]   Hospital Corp. of Am. v. FTC, 807 F.2d 1381, 1387 (7th Cir. 1986), cert. denied, 481 U.S. 1038, 107 S.Ct. 1975 (1987).

[125]   See 2B Phillip E. Areeda & Herbert Hovenkamp, Antitrust Law ¶ 421h (4th ed. 2014).

price increase above premerger levels.[126] The 2010 Guidelines largely state the same concern, although they express it a little differently. They want to know whether the "prospect of entry into the relevant market will alleviate concerns about adverse competitive effects." If the output reduction necessary to support such a price increase would be undermined by new entry, then entry barriers are said to be low. The Guidelines have thus adopted a Bainian rather than a Stiglerian definition of entry barriers.[127] Under the 2010 Guidelines "Entry by a single firm that will replicate at least the scale and strength of one of the merging firms is sufficient." Entry by firms operating at a smaller scale may be sufficient "if such firms are not at a significant competitive disadvantage."[128]

In measuring likelihood of entry, the Guidelines note that entry can be counted as "likely" only if the prospective entrant anticipates that it will be profitable. This implies that the Agencies will rely on objective criteria in determining whether entry will effectively discipline monopoly pricing. "Entry is likely if it would be profitable accounting for the assets, capabilities, and capital needed and the risks involved, including the need for the entrant to incur costs that would not be recovered if the entrant later exits."[129]

Finally, entry will be deemed "sufficient" only if it would be on a large enough scale to "deter or counteract the competitive effects of concern."[130] This language was apparently intended to correct the problem that showed up in the *Waste Management* case.[131] Although entry occurred frequently, it was always at a very small scale that appeared to have little impact on the larger firms in the market.

The entry provisions contained in the 2010 Guidelines seem well calculated to add some rigor to entry barrier analysis in concentrated markets. They also suggest that ease of entry will not be presumed, but in most cases must be established. No matter how the burden of proof is formally assigned, a sizeable part of the burden of coming forward with the relevant evidence will lie with the merging firm or firms.

---

[126]   1992 Guidelines, § 3.0.

[127]   On the two definitions, see § 12.6a.

[128]   2010 Horizontal Merger Guidelines, § 9.3.

[129]   Id., § 9.2.

[130]   Id., § 9.3.

[131]   United States v. Waste Management, Inc., 743 F.2d 976, 976 (2d Cir. 1984). See § 12.6c.

§ 12.7   Observed Anticompetitive Behavior; Post-Acquisition Review

Suppose that a merger's competitive consequences are somewhat ambiguous on the standard market structure analysis, or even suggest that the merger is legal. Nonetheless, the firms in the market (either after the merger or both before and after) engage in a variety of practices that show that the market is not performing very competitively. For example, suppose that the firms follow a routine practice of publishing list prices once a month, all of which are nearly identical, and then refuse to negotiate discounts from those list prices, at least to certain classes of customers.[132] Or suppose that the firms have persistently followed a practice of price leadership under which a given firm announces the price increase and the others follow; or if the others fail to follow the leader quietly rescinds the increase. Should the merger be condemned on the basis of such evidence alone?

One good sign that a market is not performing competitively is the systematic willingness of sellers to engage in costly nonprice competition, coupled with a general unwillingness to reduce the price. Such behavior is costly, since the firm risks losing a sale; so it must have an explanation. In a competitive market, a seller should be indifferent as between offering a price cut of $1.00 or the inclusion of a service that costs $1.00, assuming there are no collateral costs. Under tacit or express collusion, however, the inclusion of the extra service may be a way of cheating on the cartel price without being detected.

Observed noncompetitive consequences are particularly important to the evaluation of mergers in markets that may be defined as too large, which often happens when products are differentiated. As noted in § 3.4, the Merger Guidelines may sometimes lead policy makers to commit the *"Cellophane"* fallacy by focusing too closely on high cross elasticity of demand at current market prices, and not taking into account that if a market is already subject to collusion, cross elasticity of demand will be high. The 1992 Guidelines had suggested that if there is evidence that collusion or collusion-like behavior is already occurring, the Agency will attempt to determine what the price would have been absent the collusion, and compute from that point.[133] But there seems to be a better

---

[132]   For example, Chicago Bridge & Iron Co. N.V. v. F.T.C., 534 F.3d 410 (5th Cir. 2008) (relying on post-acquisition evidence of anticompetitive behavior).

[133]   1992 Horizontal Merger Guidelines, § 1.11. See also United States v. Oracle Corp., 331 F.Supp.2d 1098, 1121–1122 (N.D.Cal. 2004) (discussing *Cellophane* fallacy in merger analysis).

solution: if there is evidence of such behavior, the merger should be condemned without further difficult inquiries into what the competitive price might have been and what would be the cross-elasticity of demand at that price. The 2010 Guidelines state that the Agencies will "presume that market conditions are conducive to coordinated interaction" if the firms have a history of express collusion.[134]

Observed behavior is particularly relevant to the analysis of mergers after they have occurred. Unlike earlier Guidelines, the 2010 Horizontal Merger Guidelines pay considerable attention to the review and analysis of already consummated mergers, making clear that the Government will challenge them in appropriate cases.[135] "Substantial weight" will be given to evidence of post-merger price increases. However, the Guidelines also note that the absence of such increases is not decisive, for the parties may be aware of the possibility of post-merger review and are moderating their behavior accordingly.[136]

§ 12.8   The "Failing Company" Defense and Related Factors Affecting Firm Viability

The failing company defense exonerates a merger that would otherwise be illegal under § 7. The legislative history of the 1950 Celler-Kefauver Amendments to § 7 makes clear that Congress intended some kind of exemption for acquisitions of "failing" companies.[137] However, the legislative history gives little guidance on the important questions of how "failing company" should be defined and what the scope of the defense ought to be.

The history of the failing company defense indicates that it was probably designed to protect the creditors, owners or stockholders, and employees of small businesses. In that case, the defense is more concerned with distributive justice than with efficiency. So regarded, the defense does a poor job of achieving its objective.[138] To be sure, the failing company defense can be beneficial to a small, "failing company" acquired by a larger firm and saved from bankruptcy. However, application of the defense can seriously injure a small

---

[134]   2010 Horizontal Merger Guidelines, § 7.2.

[135]   Id., § 2.1.1. See, e.g., Chicago Bridge & Iron Co. N.V. v. F.T.C., 534 F.3d 410 (5th Cir. 2008) (condemning a consummated merger).

[136]   Id. at § 2.1.1.

[137]   S.Rep. No. 1775, 81st Cong., 2d Sess. 7 (1950). See Paul M. Laurenza, Section 7 of the Clayton Act and the Failing Company: An Updated Perspective, 65 Va.L.Rev. 947 (1979); and see 4A Antitrust Law ¶¶ 951–954 (4th ed. 2016).

[138]   See Oliver Zhong, The Failing Company Defense after the Commentary: Let it Go, 41 Univ. Mich. J. L. Reform 745 (2008).

business that competes with a failing company acquired by a more efficient firm.

Notwithstanding Congress' historical concerns, a strong argument can be made that a narrowly applied failing company defense is economically efficient. The defense could serve to keep facilities in production that would otherwise be shut down. Of course, one of the goals of the bankruptcy laws is to permit firms to re-emerge as successful competitors. However, only a minority of failing firms are reorganized successfully in bankruptcy to re-emerge as productive entities.[139] At the same time, the relevant question is not what happens to the bankrupt *firm*, but what happens to its productive assets. Even if the firm ceases production, its assets might stay on the market after being resold to new investors or creditors. Productive assets are likely to be dismantled or taken out of production altogether only when the market contains excess capacity and the assets are highly specialized.

The failing company defense is well established in antitrust case law, although a qualifying "failing company" has been found only a few times.[140] Citizen Publishing Co. v. United States assessed the requirement that before the failing company defense can be used, the defendant must show 1) that the acquired firm is almost certain to go bankrupt and cannot be reorganized successfully; and 2) that no less anticompetitive acquisition (i.e., by a smaller competitor or a noncompetitor) is available as an alternative.[141] The statement on acquisitions of failing firms in the 2010 Horizontal Merger Guidelines is briefer than the one contained in the 1992 Guidelines. The 2010 Guidelines state:

> . . . a merger is not likely to enhance market power if imminent failure . . . of one of the merging firms would cause the assets of that firm to exit the relevant market.

---

[139] See Michael Bradley & Michael Rosenzweig, The Untenable Case for Chapter 11, 101 Yale L.J. 1043, 1075 (1992); Robert K. Rasmussen, The Efficiency of Chapter 11, 8 Bankr. Dev's J. 319 (1991).

[140] See California v. Sutter Health System, 84 F. Supp. 2d 1057 (N.D.Cal.), aff'd mem., 217 F.3d 846 (9th Cir. 2000), amended, 130 F.Supp.2d 1109 (N.D.Cal. 2001) (denying preliminary injunction where it seemed likely that defendant merging parties would meet requirements of failing company defense).

[141] 394 U.S. 131, 138, 89 S.Ct. 927, 931 (1969). The Newspaper Preservation Act, 15 U.S.C.A. §§ 1801–1804, permits "joint operating agreements" between two newspapers in the same city, and contains a weaker version of the "failing company" requirement. In order to enter into a JOA, the parties must show that at least one of the two newspapers "is in probable danger of financial failure * * *." See Michigan Citizens for an Independent Press v. Thornburgh, 868 F.2d 1285 (D.C.Cir.), affirmed by an equally divided Court, 493 U.S. 38, 110 S.Ct. 398 (1989), noting that the Act created a much broader defense than the antitrust failing company doctrine, and vested broad discretion in the Attorney General to approve newspaper joint ventures under the Act. See 4A Antitrust Law ¶ 955 (4th ed. 2016).

This is an extreme instance of the more general circumstance in which the competitive significance of one of the merging firms is declining: the projected market share and significance of the exiting firm is zero. If the relevant assets would otherwise exit the market, customers are not worse off after the merger than they would have been had the merger been enjoined.[142]

In addition to the failing company defense, the 2010 Guidelines also acknowledge a "failing division" defense, which might arise when a multidivisional firm decides to abandon a division which has a persistently negative cash flow and "the owner of the failing division has made unsuccessful good-faith efforts to elicit reasonable alternative offers."

Finally, a few decisions have concluded that, while an acquired firm was not a qualifying "failing company," its financial weakness indicated that pure market share or other structural characteristics tended to exaggerate the consequences of the merger.[143]

§ 12.9 Partial Acquisitions and Acquisitions "Solely for Investment"; Horizontal Shareholding

Section 7 of the Clayton Act condemns the acquisition of the "whole or any part" of the stock or assets of another firm if the requisite anticompetitive effects result. However, the section does "not apply to persons purchasing * * * stock solely for investment * * *."

The antitrust laws are concerned with the effects of certain practices on competition, not with the ownership of corporations. Legal "control" of a corporation should therefore not necessarily be the threshold for considering partial acquisitions under the Clayton

---

[142] 2010 Guidelines, § 11, available at https://www.ftc.gov/sites/default/files/attachments/merger-review/100819hmg.pdf.

[143] E.g., FTC v. Arch Coal, Inc., 329 F.Supp.2d 109, 157 (D.D.C. 2004):

Although not a failing firm in the technical sense, Triton is plainly a relatively weak competitor * * * with no convincing prospects for improvement. The evidence establishes that it faces high costs, has low reserves, has at best uncertain prospects for loans or new reserves, is in a weakened financial condition, and has no realistic prospects for other buyers. * * * Although defendants cannot avail themselves of a failing firm defense to defeat the FTC's antitrust challenge, Triton's weak competitive status remains relevant to an examination of whether substantial anticompetitive effects are likely from the transactions. The Court concludes that based on the evidence before it, plaintiffs' claims of Triton's past and future competitive significance * * * has been far overstated.

See also 4A Antitrust Law ¶¶ 962–963 (4th ed. 2016).

Act, and the Supreme Court has said as much.[144] As a general rule a person has legal control of a corporation if he owns and votes 50% or more of its shares. Realistically, however, ownership of far less than 50% will enable someone to have effective control of a corporation. In the case of a large corporation, ownership of 15% to 20% of the shares by one person could make him an enormous shareholder with tremendous influence in the buying, selling, entry and exit decisions of the corporation—particularly if all other shareholders were substantially smaller. The Supreme Court has not wasted much time deciding whether one company owned enough shares to have legal "control" of another company. More often than not, it has assumed control when the percentage of shares held was substantial. In United States v. E.I. du Pont de Nemours & Co.,[145] for example, it assumed that du Pont had substantial influence on General Motors' buying decisions even though du Pont owned only 23% of GM's shares.

Competition can be threatened, however, even if the acquiring firm's interest is so small that it has no influence at all over the acquired firm's decisions, a possibility that the 2010 Horizontal Merger Guidelines recognize.[146] Suppose that firms A and B are competitors and A acquires 15% of the shares of B. Clearly the competitive game has acquired a new twist. Under the rules of competition, A would like nothing better than to force B out of the market through A's greater efficiency. As a result of the partial acquisition, however, A suddenly has a strong financial interest in B's welfare. The risks of tacit or explicit collusion may increase dramatically.

There is one additional reason for carefully scrutinizing stock acquisitions of less than a controlling interest. Granted that there is no "control," there is also no opportunity for the creation of efficiency. Mergers, you will recall, receive rather complex rule of reason treatment because they pose serious dangers of noncompetitive behavior on the one side, but have the potential to create substantial economies on the other. If A acquires 5% of the shares of its competitor B, A may not have enough equity to "control" B. Neither, however, will the firms have common management or other bases for

---

[144] Denver & Rio Grande West. R.R. v. United States, 387 U.S. 485, 501, 87 S.Ct. 1754, 1763 (1967) ("control" does not determine Clayton Act issue). See also United States v. Dairy Farmers of America, Inc., 426 F.3d 850 (6th Cir. 2005) (partial stock acquisition could give firms incentive to eliminate competition between them).

[145] 353 U.S. 586, 77 S.Ct. 872 (1957). See also United States v. General Dynamics Corp., 415 U.S. 486, 94 S.Ct. 1186 (1974), where the acquiring firm owned 34% of the acquired firm's shares, but the parties agreed that there was "effective control."

[146] See 2010 Horizontal Merger Guidelines, § 13, available at https://www.ftc.gov/sites/default/files/attachments/merger-review/100819hmg.pdf.

obtaining the kinds of economies that make mergers socially valuable. In this case, the potential for social harm may be somewhat attenuated because the ownership interest is small—but the potential for social good has been reduced to nearly zero. That suggests a presumptive rule of condemnation.

The 2010 Horizontal Merger Guidelines generally acknowledge these issues, recognizing three situations in which partial acquisitions are of concern:

> "First, a partial acquisition can lessen competition by giving the acquiring firm the ability to *influence* the . . . conduct of the target firm." Second, it may also do so by lessening the acquiring firm's incentive to compete by giving the acquirer a stake in the target's financial performance. Finally, a partial acquisition can potentially harm competition by giving the acquirer access to the target firm's sensitive information—which can, in turn, facilitate coordinated interaction.[147]

One interesting issue that the courts have not addressed at this writing is application of the antitrust laws to so-called "horizontal shareholding" by mutual fund or other large investment firms. For example, a small number of fund managers might collectively own controlling interests in the airline industry. These may make it possible for them to coordinate airline pricing. In that case should their share purchases constitute acquisitions "solely for investment"? In most cases such firms do vote their shares, suggesting that the answer is no. That would almost certainly be the answer if it could be shown that large scale parallel shareholding by funds facilitated collusion in the product market.[148]

---

[147] Id. ("The risk of coordinated effects is greater if the transaction also facilitates the flow of competitively sensitive information from the acquiring firm to the target firm.").

[148] For further exploration, see Fiona Scott Morton & Herbert Hovenkamp, Horizontal Shareholding and Antitrust Policy, 127 Yale L.J. 2026 (2018); Einer Elhauge, Horizontal Shareholding, 129 Harv. L. Rev. 1267 (2016).

Chapter 13

PUBLIC ENFORCEMENT OF THE FEDERAL ANTITRUST LAWS

Table of Sections

§ 13.1 Public Enforcement Generally; the Antitrust Division

The public enforcement of the federal antitrust laws is largely in the hands of the Antitrust Division of the Department of Justice ("Division") and the Federal Trade Commission ("FTC"). Technically, only the Division has authority to engage in public enforcement of the Sherman Act. However, the FTC may bring actions challenging unfair methods of competition under § 5 of the Federal Trade Commission Act, which has been interpreted to include everything in the Sherman Act, plus a few practices that are not covered by the Sherman Act.[1] The Division and the FTC have concurrent authority to enforce the Clayton Act. Since the jurisdiction of the two agencies overlaps, they have developed clearance procedures for notifying each other before conducting investigations or filing actions. If both are found to be pursuing the same inquiry, the two agencies decide which will handle it, based generally on considerations of expertise, staff availability, and so on. If the matter involves likely criminal activity it will generally be referred to the Division, since the FTC does not have criminal jurisdiction.

Most of the time the two agencies co-exist amiably, but there are exceptions. For example, in 2019 the Antitrust Division intervened

---

[1] 15 U.S.C.A. § 45(a); FTC v. Cement Institute, 333 U.S. 683, 694, 68 S.Ct. 793, 800 (1948). On public enforcement generally, see Daniel A. Crane, The Institutional Structure of Antitrust Enforcement (2011). On the history of government antitrust enforcement in the twentieth century, see Herbert Hovenkamp, The Opening of American Law: Neoclassical Legal Thought, 1870–1970, Ch. 11 (2015).

in ongoing litigation brought by the FTC against Qualcomm,[2] and also took a position on standard essential patents that was more in line with views in old economy industries, as opposed to FTC positions that are more in line with digital and information technologies which have many more standard essential patents.[3]

Both the Division and the FTC occasionally issue written Guidelines, outlining their enforcement position on various matters. The most prominent of these, the 2010 Horizontal Merger Guidelines issued jointly by the Division and the FTC, are discussed in detail elsewhere.[4] In 2020 the Agencies joined in issuing Guidelines for vertical mergers.[5] In addition, the Division has issued numerous other enforcement guidelines, some of them in conjunction with the FTC.[6] The Division also issues Business Review Letters, evaluating business conduct contemplated by private parties.[7] Such a letter may state the Division's intention to challenge or not to challenge the conduct as of the date of the letter; but the Division is not bound to state its intent and sometimes refuses to do so. The Division also participates as amicus curiae in private antitrust actions, sometimes in behalf of defendants.[8] This practice has sometimes been criticized as falling outside the Division's jurisdictional authority to "prevent and restrain" antitrust violations.[9]

The Division's main antitrust enforcement activity is the launching of investigations and, if necessary, the subsequent pursuit

---

[2]   See FTC v. Qualcomm, Inc., 935 F.3d 752 (9th Cir. 2019) (granting DOJ request to stay relief requested by FTC and approved by district court). See Herbert Hovenkamp, FRAND and Antitrust, ___ Cornell L. Rev. ___ (2020) (forthcoming), currently available at https://papers.ssrn.com/sol3/papers.cfm?abstract_id=3420925.

[3]   See Department of Justice, USPTO, and National Institute of Standards and Technology, Policy Statement on Remedies for Standards-Essential Patents (Dec. 2019), available at https://www.justice.gov/atr/page/file/1228016. See Herbert Hovenkamp, The Justice Department's New Position on Patents, Standard Setting, and Injunctions, Regulatory Review (Jan 2020).

[4]   See Chs. 3 and 12.

[5]   U.S. Dept. of Justice and FTC, Vertical Merger Guidelines (June 30, 2020), available at https://www.ftc.gov/system/files/documents/reports/us-department-justice-federal-trade-commission-vertical-merger-guidelines/vertical_merger_guidelines_6-30-20.pdf. See § 9.5.

[6]   These Guidelines are available on the enforcement agency websites. See http://www.justice.gov/atr/ (U.S. Dep't of Justice, Antitrust Division); http://ftc.gov/ (Federal Trade Commission). They are also printed as appendices to the *Antitrust Law* treatise (current Supp.), as well as in volume 4 of Trade Regulation Reporter (CCH). Criminal antitrust actions are subject to the criminal sentencing Guidelines, but under the Supreme Court's decision in United States v. Booker, 543 U.S. 220, 125 S.Ct. 738 (2005), they are to be regarded as advisory rather than mandatory.

[7]   28 C.F.R. § 50.6 (2006).

[8]   For a listing of such briefs, see http://www.justice.gov/atr/antitrust-case-filings-alpha (last visited August 8, 2015).

[9]   See § 4 of the Sherman Act, 15 U.S.C.A. § 4.

of criminal or civil litigation. Investigations are initiated as a result of private complaints, inquiries conducted at the instigation of the Division itself, or as a result of private reporting, such as premerger notification.[10]

The Division and the FTC both maintain elaborate websites that provide detailed information on these activities. Readers are strongly advised to consult the websites before pursuing any action concerning the two government enforcement agencies, for their procedures and rules are subject to change and the websites are updated continuously.[11]

13.1a. Criminal Enforcement

The Division generally files criminal actions only for clear, intentional violations of the law. Nearly all of these are for explicit price fixing, bid rigging, or market division. In United States v. United States Gypsum, the Supreme Court held that the Division must prove criminal intent in order to obtain a criminal conviction.[12] This generally requires a showing either that the conduct had an anticompetitive effect and that the defendants knew of these probable effects, or else that the conduct was intended to produce anticompetitive effects, whether or not they actually occurred. A growing body of law has attempted to parse the meaning of these requirements. It seems clear that an effect on competition need not have occurred, provided that the defendants actually, subjectively intended that it occur.[13] In *Cinemette*, the court held that motion picture "split" agreements, a form of horizontal product division in which exhibitors agree not to bid competitively for the same film, could be the subject of a criminal indictment even though the practice was illegal per se in some circuits but not in others.[14] The court rejected the argument that because of the "uncertain legal status" of such agreements, no criminal intent could be inferred. Thus it seems that if the defendants do have an intent to injure competition they can be charged with a crime, even if the practice is not clearly illegal *per se.* By contrast, if the alleged violation is clearly illegal *per se,*

---

[10]   See § 14.3.

[11]   See www.ftc.gov, and http://www.justice.gov/atr/division-manual.

[12]   438 U.S. 422, 98 S.Ct. 2864 (1978).

[13]   United States v. Gravely, 840 F.2d 1156, 1161 (4th Cir. 1988).

[14]   United States v. Cinemette Corp. of Am., 687 F.Supp. 976 (W.D.Pa.1988). See Viking Theatre Corp. v. Paramount Film Distributing Corp., 320 F.2d 285 (3d Cir. 1963), affirmed per curiam by an equally divided court, 378 U.S. 123, 84 S.Ct. 1657 (1964) (refusing to apply per se rule); Admiral Theatre Corp. v. Douglas Theatre Co., 585 F.2d 877 (8th Cir. 1978) (same); United States v. Capitol Serv., 756 F.2d 502 (7th Cir.), cert. denied, 474 U.S. 945, 106 S.Ct. 311 (1985) (split agreements illegal per se). See 12 Antitrust Law ¶ 2013c (4th ed. 2019).

several courts have held that intent to enter into the conspiracy is all that is required; no showing must be made of a distinct intent to injure competition as such.[15]

For criminal violations of the Sherman Act, corporate defendants may currently be fined up to $100,000,000, or individuals up to $1,000,000. These particular numbers are stated in the Sherman Act itself and are periodically adjusted.[16] Further, individuals may receive prison sentences in addition to or instead of a fine.[17] Additionally, however, the Criminal Fines Improvements Act of 1984[18] provides that for violations generally committed since 1984, a fine may be measured by double the gain to the violators or the loss to the victim, or by the antitrust damages provisions, whichever is greater. Although fines measured in this manner may be greater than those explicitly authorized by the Sherman Act, they may be less than the provable treble damages in a private antitrust civil action.

The Division also maintains a corporate leniency, or amnesty, program which can save both a corporation and its officers from criminal prosecution if they come forward and make full disclosure of price fixing or other antitrust violations before the Division itself is aware of such activities.[19] In the *Empagran* case the Supreme Court deferred to the Government's argument that giving foreign plaintiffs expansive rights to sue foreign defendants under United States law would undermine this policy by increasing defendants' treble damage exposure, thus reducing the incentive to come forward with evidence of collusion.[20]

---

[15]   United States v. Brown, 936 F.2d 1042 (9th Cir. 1991).

[16]   15 U.S.C.A. §§ 1–3.

[17]   15 U.S.C.A. §§ 1, 2.

[18]   See 18 U.S.C.A. §§ 3621–3624; Criminal Fines Improvements Act of 1987 (re-enacted), 101 Stat. 1279, 1289. See U.S. SENTENCING GUIDELINES MANUAL (U.S.S.G.) § 2R1.1.(2012).

[19]   The program is outlined at http://www.justice.gov/atr/leniency-program (last visited August 12, 2015); for analysis see 4 Trade Reg. Rep. (CCH) ¶ 13,113 (2011) (corporations), ¶ 13,114 (2011) (individuals) (Aug. 10, 1993). See United States v. Stolt-Nielsen, S.A., 442 F.3d 177 (3d Cir. 2006) (while execution of a leniency agreement with the government might be raised by the defendant as a defense in a subsequent prosecution it could not be used to prevent the government from obtaining an indictment in the first place). See Joseph E. Harrington, Jr. & Myong-Hun Chang, When Can We Expect a Corporate Leniency Program to Result in Fewer Cartels?, 58 J.L. & ECON. 417, 443 (2015) (finding limited effectiveness).

[20]   F. Hoffmann-La Roche, Ltd. v. Empagran, 542 U.S. 155, 124 S.Ct. 2359 (2004), on remand, 388 F.3d 337 (D.C. Cir. 2004). The decision is discussed in § 21.2a, b.

13.1b.   Civil Enforcement

For civil investigations, the Division often issues Civil Investigative Demands (CIDs), which are subpoenas that can be issued to any person believed to have information pertaining to the investigation, and requiring documents, oral testimony, or answers to interrogatories.[21] Information obtained as a result of a CID may sometimes be shared with the FTC for its own investigation, or may occasionally be disclosed to Congress. Otherwise, it must be kept confidential and is expressly exempt from inquiries made under the Freedom of Information Act.[22]

Most civil antitrust investigations leading to challenges result in consent decrees, which are binding out-of-court settlements approved by the court. Consent decrees permit defendants to avoid the consequences of § 5(a) of the Clayton Act, which provides that a judgment in an antitrust case against a defendant becomes prima facie evidence of guilt in a subsequent private action based on the same violation.[23]

Consent decrees can later be enforced by the Division, just as any court judgment can, although they cannot form the basis for an antitrust action by a private plaintiff. Consent decrees are generally interpreted as contracts, and not by reference to the underlying law.[24] The success of such decrees has been somewhat controversial, although the overall record appears to indicate that they work better in practice than they do in theory.[25] In recent years the Division has consented to the modification or termination of many older consent decrees that are now considered to have gone too far, or where the defendants' position has changed materially—for example, if the

---

[21]   See Antitrust Civil Process Act, 15 U.S.C.A. §§ 1311–1314.

[22]   15 U.S.C.A. § 1314(g).

[23]   15 U.S.C.A. § 16(a).

[24]   But the consent decree often incorporates antitrust terms of art, and these are ordinarily interpreted according to antitrust principles. See, e.g., United States v. Microsoft Corp., 980 F.Supp. 537 (D.D.C.1997), reversed, 147 F.3d 935 (D.C.Cir. 1998) (relying heavily on antitrust law to interpret 1995 consent decree that would have forbidden Microsoft from bundling Windows 95 and Internet Explorer if the two were "separate products" for tying purposes). See 10 Antitrust Law ¶ 1746 (4th ed. 2018).

[25]   See Richard Epstein, Antitrust Consent Decrees in Theory and Practice: Why Less is More (2007) (quite critical); cf. Daniel A. Crane, Bargaining in the Shadow of Rate-Setting Courts, 76 Antitrust L.J. 207, 208 (2009) (examining antitrust consent decrees, particularly those with compulsory IP licensing provisions; noting high degree of success in getting parties to agree on rates without judicial intervention); Daniel A. Crane, Intellectual Liability, 88 Texas L. Rev. 253, 294 (2009) (similar). See also Harry First, The Case for Antitrust Civil Penalties, 76 Antitrust L.J. 127 (2009) (defending civil penalties as antitrust sanctions).

market has become much more competitive or the defendant is no longer the dominant player.[26]

Remedies for civil violations of the antitrust laws can include injunctions, as well as dissolution or divestiture for illegal mergers or occasionally monopolization. Just as any private plaintiff, the United States Government is also entitled to recover treble damages for injuries it suffers as a result of an antitrust violation—as, for example, in the case of federal government purchases subject to price fixing.[27]

§ 13.2   The Federal Trade Commission

The Federal Trade Commission is a regulatory agency established during the Wilson Administration in 1914.[28] The Commission consists of five Commissioners appointed by the President subject to Senate confirmation for seven-year terms. The FTC has authority to enforce the substance of all of the antitrust laws. This includes direct authority with respect to the Clayton Act and the Robinson-Patman Act. With respect to the Sherman Act, the FTC has no direct enforcement authority, but its authority to challenge "unfair methods of competition" under § 5 of the FTC Act[29] has been interpreted to include all practices condemned under the Sherman Act.

Further, in *Sperry & Hutchinson*, the Supreme Court held that the FTC has authority "to define and proscribe an unfair competitive practice, even though the practice does not infringe either the letter or the spirit of the antitrust laws."[30] As the Supreme Court later explained in *Indiana Dentists*, the "standard of 'unfairness' under the FTC Act is, by necessity, an elusive one, encompassing not only practices that violate the Sherman Act and the other antitrust laws

---

[26]   For example, *IBM*, 163 F.3d at 737; United States v. Western Elec. Co., 900 F.2d 283 (D.C.Cir. 1990) (partial removal of line-of-business restriction in 1983 consent decree, given changing market circumstances). See Steven C. Salop, Modifying Merger Consent Decrees to Improve Merger Enforcement Policy, Antitrust 15 (Fall, 2016).

[27]   15 U.S.C.A. § 15(a).

[28]   For a brief history, including some interesting oral histories, see https://www.ftc.gov/about-ftc/our-history. See also Martin Sklar, The Corporate Reconstruction of American Capitalism, 1890–1916 at 328–332 (1988); Timothy J. Muris and Bilal K. Sayyed, The Long Shadow of Standard Oil: Policy, Petroleum, and Politics at the Federal Trade Commission, 85 S.Cal.L.Rev. 843 (2012).

[29]   15 U.S.C.A. § 45.

[30]   FTC v. Sperry & Hutchinson Co., 405 U.S. 233, 239, 92 S.Ct. 898, 903 (1972).

but also practices that the Commission determines are against public policy for other reasons. * * *"[31]

As the *Indiana Dentists* statement suggests, the precise scope of the FTC's authority to "expand" the meaning of the Sherman Act is unclear and controversial. Further, it has come under increased scrutiny in recent years. Earlier cases had indicated that the FTC was entitled to condemn tying arrangements in the absence of market power[32] or exclusive dealing without a showing of likely injury to competition.[33] Subsequently, however, courts looked at expansive efforts by the FTC more critically. For example, in *Boise Cascade* the court upset FTC condemnation of a delivered pricing system used in common by several sellers, but where there was no evidence of an agreement among them.[34] The court concluded that the FTC had an obligation to show either an agreement or else evidence that noncollusive use of the system had a measurable anticompetitive effect. The Commission's decision in the *Dupont (Ethyl)* case met a similar fate.[35] The Commission challenged various "facilitating practices" alleged to yield collusion-like results in the absence of a Sherman § 1 price-fixing agreement. In overturning the Commission's decision condemning the practices, the court concluded that

> "before business conduct in an oligopolistic industry may be labeled 'unfair' within the meaning of § 5 a minimum standard demands that, absent a tacit agreement, at least some indicia of oppressiveness must exist such as (1) evidence of anticompetitive intent or purpose on the part of the producer charged, or (2) the absence of an independent legitimate business reason for its conduct."[36]

There are two views about the wisdom of the FTC's use of § 5 to go beyond the substance of the antitrust laws generally. One view looks to the substance of those laws, with their central concern for competition. If the case law under the antitrust laws defines our concerns for competition correctly, then it seems wrong for the FTC

---

[31]   FTC v. Indiana Fed'n of Dentists, 476 U.S. 447, 454, 106 S.Ct. 2009, 2016 (1986).

[32]   Atlantic Refining Co. v. FTC, 381 U.S. 357, 369–371, 85 S.Ct. 1498, 1506–1507 (1965).

[33]   FTC v. Brown Shoe Co., 384 U.S. 316, 321, 86 S.Ct. 1501, 1504 (1966).

[34]   Boise Cascade Corp. v. FTC, 637 F.2d 573, 579–582 (9th Cir. 1980). On reaching oligopoly behavior without proof of a qualifying agreement, see § 4.6.

[35]   E.I. du Pont De Nemours & Co. v. FTC, 729 F.2d 128, 139–142 (2d Cir. 1984).

[36]   729 F.2d at 139–140.

to go further. In effect, it would turn antitrust into the regulation of "unfair" rather than anticompetitive trade practices.[37]

But there is an alternative view, perfectly consistent with the proposition that the FTC's antitrust concern should be limited to identifying practices that are economically anticompetitive. The FTC is a regulatory agency, which is more specialized than courts and not as bound by strict rules of procedure and evidence. Further, its general remedy, at least in most cases, is a "cease and desist" order. Findings of violations of the FTC Act that are not also antitrust violations will not support subsequent private actions for treble damages. As a result, application of the FTC Act to practices that do not violate the other antitrust laws are appropriate when (1) the practice seems anticompetitive but is not technically covered by the antitrust laws; and (2) the social cost of an error seems to be relatively small.[38]

A good example is the use of the FTC Act to go after facilitating practices in oligopoly industries in the absence of an express agreement. Today there is widespread consensus that such practices can produce anticompetitive results, and that the Sherman Act's "agreement" requirement limits courts' ability to deal with the range of concerns that we associate with firms' coordination of price or output. Further, if the FTC's remedy is limited to prospective injunction against certain facilitating practices, such as advance price announcements or use of a common delivered pricing or basing point pricing scheme, then the social cost of an error is likely to be rather small. That is to say, advance posting of prices may produce certain economies even in a tightly oligopolistic industry prone to price leadership, but the threat to competition seems significantly larger. Another example is an unaccepted solicitation or offer to conspire to fix prices, which would not satisfy the Sherman § 1 "agreement" requirement but could nevertheless be anticompetitive. For example, an unaccepted solicitation can inform other firms of the offeror's willingness to engage in tacit, rather than express, collusion.[39]

In 2015 the FTC offered some very spare Guidelines for interpretation of § 5 beyond traditional antitrust. The Guidelines offer no examples but rather states three general principles:

---

[37]   See *Atlantic Refining*, 381 U.S. at 357; and *Brown Shoe*, 384 U.S. 316.

[38]   On this point, see Herbert Hovenkamp, The Federal Trade Commission and the Sherman Act, 62 Fla.L.Rev. 871 (2010).

[39]   On proof of agreement, see § 4.4. On unaccepted solicitations, see 6 Antitrust Law ¶ 1419e (4th ed. 2017).

- the Commission will be guided by the public policy underlying the antitrust laws, namely, the promotion of consumer welfare;

- the act or practice will be evaluated under a framework similar to the rule of reason, that is, an act or practice challenged by the Commission must cause, or be likely to cause, harm to competition or the competitive process, taking into account any associated cognizable efficiencies and business justifications; and

- the Commission is less likely to challenge an act or practice as an unfair method of competition on a standalone basis if enforcement of the Sherman or Clayton Act is sufficient to address the competitive harm arising from the act or practice.[40]

The ordinary remedy in an FTC action is a cease and desist order—although this may amount to forced dissolution or divestiture in the case of a merger. The FTC has authority to assess civil penalties, but only for violations of previously given cease and desist orders, or explicit violations of FTC rules and practices.[41] The courts are divided on the question whether the FTC's authority to obtain equitable relief includes the power to order "disgorgement," "restitution" or other equitable remedies that require the repayment of wrongfully acquired monies.[42] In general, the courts have interpreted such powers broadly. For example, in *American Stores* the Supreme Court held that the Clayton Act's authorization to plaintiffs to obtain equitable relief included the power to compel divestiture, or the forced breakup of a merging firm.[43] Further, a 2020 Supreme Court decision involving the Securities Act interpreted "equitable relief' to include disgorgement of actual improper gains, although not a penalty beyond that. The case for a similar interpretation seems about as strong for the FTC Act.[44]

Although the Commission receives many private complaints and acts upon them as it deems appropriate, only the FTC itself can

---

[40]   FTC, Statement of Enforcement Principles Regarding "Unfair Methods of Competition" under Section 5 of the FTC Act, available at https://www.ftc.gov/system/files/documents/public_statements/735201/150813section5enforcement.pdf.

[41]   See 15 U.S.C.A. § 45(*l*) & (m).

[42]   FTC v. Credit Bureau Center, LLC, 937 F.3d 764 (7th Cir. 2019) (denying the power); FTC v. Commerce Planet, Inc., 815 F.3d 593, 598–99 (9th Cir. 2016); FTC v. Ross, 743 F.3d 886, 890–92 (4th Cir. 2014) (recognizing it); FTC v. Bronson Partners, LLC, 654 F.3d 359, 365–66 (2d Cir. 2011)(recognizing it); FTC v. Direct Mktg. Concepts, Inc., 624 F.3d 1, 15 (1st Cir. 2010) (recognizing it).

[43]   California v. American Stores Co., 495 U.S. 271 (1990).

[44]   See Liu v. SEC, 140 S.Ct. 1936 (2020) (interpreting 15 U.S.C. § 78u(d)(5) ("any equitable relief that may be appropriate or necessary for the benefit of investors").

initiate its proceedings. The FTC has its own procedures for collecting and presenting evidence, generally governed by Section 5(b) of the FTC Act[45] and the Federal Administrative Procedure Act.[46] The initial adjudicative proceeding is given to an Administrative Law Judge (ALJ), who makes a preliminary decision. During this process the FTC provides its own complaint counsel, which generally has the burden of proof, just as the plaintiff in civil litigation. After the ALJ has issued a preliminary decision, it is either approved or disapproved by the Commission itself. If the Commission's decision is adverse to the respondent, it may seek review by the federal courts of appeals.[47] The court is generally obliged to accept the FTC's fact findings if they are supported by substantial evidence in the record as a whole. While courts generally give great weight to the Commission's interpretation of the *law*, they are not bound by it.

---

[45]   15 U.S.C.A. § 45(b).

[46]   5 U.S.C.A. § 554.

[47]   Preliminary injunctions are generally appealed to a federal district court.

Chapter 14

PRIVATE ENFORCEMENT

Table of Sections

§ 14.1 Introduction: § 4 of the Clayton Act

This chapter is concerned mainly with enforcement of the federal antitrust laws by private persons. Section 4 of the Clayton Act provides that "Any person injured in his business or property by reason of anything forbidden in the antitrust laws may sue * * * and shall recover three-fold the damages * * * sustained and * * * a reasonable attorney's fee."[1]

The simplicity of § 4's language belies the complexity of the many questions it has raised. The statute's coverage extending to "any person" is expansive. In a market economy a simple price fixing agreement has effects that injure everyone. Witness the impact of the OPEC embargoes in the 1970s, which resulted in higher prices not only of petroleum, but of everything that requires energy for its manufacture—industrial products, agricultural products, even other natural resources.[2] By its language, § 4 appears to give a cause of action to every person who is injured by a cartel or overcharging monopolist. The courts have concluded that the statute cannot be as broad as it purports to be, however, and they have devised ways to limit its scope.

Although private antitrust actions were filed soon after the passage of the Sherman Act, the number of such cases was not large until the 1950s. The number of private filings increased rapidly through the 1960s and exploded in the 1970s. While the number of private filings leveled off in the 1980s, it increased again in the 1990s. The private antitrust action continues to be the principal mechanism by which the antitrust laws are enforced. As many as 95% of antitrust cases are brought by private plaintiffs.

§ 14.2 Permissible Plaintiffs—Who Should Enforce the Antitrust Laws?

The Clayton Act's provision of mandatory treble damages plus attorney's fees to prevailing plaintiffs has put extraordinary pressure on courts to develop intelligible limits on antitrust enforcement rights. These statutory provisions encourage litigation by people for whom the amount of recovery discounted by the probability of success would otherwise be marginal. For example, a common law breach of contract action providing single damages and no attorneys fees might not be worth the risk; but if the action could be turned into an antitrust violation, the outcome may look much more appealing.

---

[1]   15 U.S.C.A. § 15.

[2]   See International Ass'n of Machinists v. OPEC, 649 F.2d 1354 (9th Cir. 1981), cert. denied, 454 U.S. 1163, 102 S.Ct. 1036 (1982) (act of state doctrine precluded antitrust lawsuit by labor union against OPEC).

Plaintiffs are continually tempted to turn every claimed business tort or contract breach into an antitrust violation as well.

Unfortunately, the courts have never been able to create an intelligible theory of private antitrust standing capable of being applied across the full range of potential cases. The law remains haphazard and inconsistent. On the one hand, the economics of enforcement suggests that its goal should be to maximize social wealth by deterring inefficient practices and permitting efficient ones. On the other, the courts have generally analyzed antitrust standing requirements in terms of compensation to victims. The result is significant inconsistency in rationales and rules.

§ 14.3 Antitrust's Special Requirement of Competitive Injury

Many practices illegal under the antitrust laws produce compensating efficiencies. Courts condemn them either because the anticompetitive effects are clear, while the efficiencies are ambiguous and incapable of measurement, or else because the anticompetitive effects appear to outweigh the efficiencies. Mergers and joint ventures in particular may simultaneously create efficiencies and increase the market power of the participating firms. Vertical integration, whether by contract or merger, has an even greater capacity to produce efficiencies, and an even smaller potential to be anticompetitive.

Increased market power creates a social cost while increased efficiency creates a social gain. But both can impose private losses. To characterize a certain practice as "efficient" is not to conclude that the practice benefits everyone, but only that aggregate benefits are greater than aggregate injuries. An antitrust policy dominated by efficiency concerns will attempt to distinguish purely private losses from those that coincide in some way with losses to society as a whole.

14.3a. "Antitrust Injury"; Private Merger Challenges

14.3a1. Mergers Alleged to Facilitate Exclusionary Practices

In Brunswick Corp. v. Pueblo Bowl-O-Mat, Inc.,[3] the plaintiff owned several bowling alleys and the defendant was a major national manufacturer of bowling equipment and operator of alleys. It sold bowling equipment to independent alleys on credit, and sometimes acquired alleys that were in financial trouble. Over a ten-year period

---

3   429 U.S. 477, 97 S.Ct. 690 (1977). On § 7 and mergers, see Ch. 12.

the defendant had taken over several defaulting alleys that competed with the plaintiff. Most of these acquired alleys would probably have gone out of business had they not been acquired by Brunswick. The plaintiff challenged the acquisition of two of the alleys under § 7 of the Clayton Act, claiming that its market share would have increased had the competing alleys been permitted to go out of business.

The *Brunswick* plaintiff's theory of action reaches the heart of the debate about whom the antitrust laws should protect: competition and consumers, or competitors. Horizontal mergers can facilitate monopolistic or collusive pricing by increasing concentration in the market. Consumers will pay higher prices, but the post-merger firm's output reduction and price increase will benefit other firms already in the market. They can charge higher prices under the "umbrella" created by the larger, post-merger firm.

But mergers can also increase the efficiency of the merging partners. Increased efficiency benefits consumers but invariably injures competitors. The plaintiff in *Brunswick* formerly had a languishing, spiritless rival. After the merger it faced a rejuvenated and aggressive competitor and prices would likely have gone down. Whether or not the merger was technically illegal, the plaintiff's injury was caused by increased competition from the post-merger firm, not by the market's increased proclivity toward monopoly pricing.

In denying recovery, the Supreme Court observed that many antitrust violations could cause "losses which are of no concern to the antitrust laws." In order to recover, a plaintiff must show not only that an antitrust law has been violated and the plaintiff injured. It must also show "*antitrust* injury, which is to say injury of the type the antitrust laws were intended to prevent and that flows from that which makes defendants' acts unlawful." Such an injury should "reflect the anticompetitive effect * * * of the violation * * *."[4] Today "antitrust injury" has been established as a requirement for private actions under virtually all of the antitrust laws. It has become an essential element of private plaintiff standing.

The antitrust injury doctrine applies only to private antitrust actions. The *Brunswick* opinion contrasted the "prophylactic" nature of Clayton § 7 with the "remedial" nature of § 4, the provision authorizing private damages actions. Section 7 was designed to reach mergers while the danger to competition was in its "incipiency," and somewhat uncertain.[5] By contrast, § 4 requires a private plaintiff to show actual injury. Since the merger contains two different

---

[4]   Id. at 489, 97 S.Ct. at 697.

[5]   See Ch. 12.

potentials for injury—one from the post-merger firm's increased market power and the other from its increased efficiency—it becomes important for the plaintiff to identify how it was injured.

14.3a2. Consumer Plaintiffs

The preferred plaintiff in a merger case is the consumer, who is benefitted by the merger's increased efficiency but injured by its post-merger price increase. Nevertheless, consumer challenges are relatively infrequent. As a general matter, if a merger is followed by a significant price increase and is challenged within four years of its occurrence (the statute of limitation period)[6] there is no reason why a consumer cannot challenge it. Naturally, the plaintiff will still have to prove that the merger was unlawful and that the merger caused the price increase.[7]

14.3b. "Antitrust Injury" Beyond § 7; Per Se Violations

Brunswick's contrast of § 7's prophylactic reach with the remedial nature of § 4 suggested that the antitrust injury doctrine applied only to mergers, not to other antitrust violations.[8] In J. Truett Payne Co. v. Chrysler Motor Corp.,[9] however, the Supreme Court applied the doctrine to a private action alleging illegal price discrimination under the Robinson-Patman Act. The Court held that a plaintiff winning a price discrimination suit was not entitled to "automatic" damages based on the difference between the higher price it paid and the lower price paid by others. Rather, the plaintiff must show that the price discrimination affected retail prices and thus caused it actual injury. Although the Court declared this conclusion to be "governed by" *Brunswick*, the decision seems to require proof of injury-in-fact rather than antitrust injury. The Court really said that notwithstanding the Robinson-Patman Act's prophylactic "may * * * substantially * * * lessen competition"

---

[6]   See 2 Antitrust Law ¶ 320 (5th ed. 2021).

[7]   See Midwestern Machinery v. Northwest Airlines, 167 F.3d 439 (8th Cir. 1999) (permitting consumer to challenge acquisition on grounds of increased price; rejecting district court's view that once the acquired firm' stock was dissolved and it ceased to exist as an independent entity, the merger qua merger could no longer be challenged). Steves and Son, Inc. v. Jeld-Wen, Inc., 345 F.Supp.3d 614 (E.D.Va. 2018), app. docketed, Apr. 16, 2019 (unlawful merger produced overcharge damages). See also Ritz Camera & Image, LLC v. SanDisk Corp., 700 F.3d 503, 507 (Fed. Cir. 2012) (consumers had antitrust standing to challenge overcharges resulting from defendant's enforcement of improperly obtained patent).

[8]   See Engine Specialties, Inc. v. Bombardier Ltd., 605 F.2d 1 (1st Cir. 1979), on rehearing, 615 F.2d 575 (1st Cir.), cert. denied, 446 U.S. 983, 100 S.Ct. 2964 (1980) (emphasizing prophylactic nature of § 7).

[9]   451 U.S. 557, 101 S.Ct. 1923 (1981). See 14 Antitrust Law ¶ 2371 (4th ed. 2019).

language, the plaintiff seeking damages must show actual, present injury.

The Robinson-Patman Act contains the same prophylactic language as Clayton § 7. But what about the Sherman Act? In *USA Petroleum* the Supreme Court extended the antitrust injury doctrine to a claim of maximum resale price maintenance, which at the time was unlawful *per se*.[10] The plaintiff, a gasoline retailer, claimed that a gasoline refiner was imposing maximum resale prices on dealers in competition with the plaintiff. The Supreme Court assumed that these prices were not predatory. It then held that the rationale for permitting dealers to complain about maximum RPM imposed upon *themselves* was that such price setting restrained their ability to compete as they saw fit. But a *competitor* of such a dealer would be complaining about its need to compete with above cost prices, and that is not antitrust injury.

14.3c.   Causation, Injury-in-Fact, Antitrust Injury Distinguished

The previous discussion should make clear that "injury" and "antitrust injury" are not the same thing. A private antitrust plaintiff must establish three quite independent requirements: (1) that it suffered an injury; (2) that its injury was caused by an antitrust violation; and (3) that the injury qualifies as "antitrust injury." Unfortunately, courts have not always kept the three requirements distinct. For example, in its *Matsushita* decision the Supreme Court observed that rivals could not recover from a cartel to increase prices, since competitors would be benefitted, not injured, by such a conspiracy. For that proposition it cited *Brunswick*.[11] But the *Brunswick* plaintiff was injured in fact; it was simply not a victim of antitrust injury. By contrast, the rival in the *Matsushita* illustration was not injured at all.

General standing doctrine requires a private plaintiff to prove injury-in-fact. Indeed, those with no cognizable injury at all may lack standing under Article III of the Constitution. In that case the independent standing requirements of the Clayton Act become superfluous. Nonetheless, Congress has the power to grant the right to sue even to those with negligible injuries.

---

[10]   Atlantic Richfield Co. v. USA Petroleum Co., 495 U.S. 328, 110 S.Ct. 1884 (1990). The per se rule against maximum RPM was subsequently overruled. See § 11.5c.

[11]   Matsushita Elec. Indus. Co. v. Zenith Radio Corp., 475 U.S. 574, 586, 106 S.Ct. 1348, 1355 (1986). See also *supra J. Truett Payne*, 451 U.S. 557.

A plaintiff must also show that the injuries were caused by the antitrust violation. Courts have articulated the causation requirement in different ways. In *Zenith* the Supreme Court required only that the violation be a "material cause" of the plaintiff's injury.[12] Under this requirement, if a plaintiff's business misfortunes resulted from many causes, it need show only that the defendant's antitrust violation was one of them. Cases following *Zenith* generally do not require the plaintiff to rank the causes and show that the antitrust violation somehow predominated among them.[13] Other courts have assessed a stronger requirement that the violation be shown to be a "substantial factor" in the plaintiff's loss.[14]

Is one articulation of the test better than the other? In most cases the difference is probably more semantic than real. Further, the plaintiff seeking damages will eventually have to separate out those damages caused by the antitrust violation from those caused by other factors.[15] This will require not only a ranking of causes, but also some assignment of weights to each one. Finally, if it seems quite clear that the antitrust violation was at best an insubstantial factor in the plaintiff's loss, or that there were many other plausible alternative explanations for the plaintiff's losses, then causation will fail under either test.[16]

Even severe injury-in-fact and causation do not entail antitrust injury. For example, an efficiency creating joint venture or merger

---

[12]   Zenith Radio Corp. v. Hazeltine Research, Inc., 395 U.S. 100, 114 n. 9, 89 S.Ct. 1562, 1571 n. 9, on remand, 418 F.2d 21 (7th Cir. 1969), cert. denied, 397 U.S. 979, 90 S.Ct. 1105 (1970).

[13]   For example, Amerinet v. Xerox Corp., 972 F.2d 1483, 1494 (8th Cir. 1992), cert. denied, 506 U.S. 1080, 113 S.Ct. 1048 (1993) ("in order to provide sufficient evidence of causation [the plaintiff] need only establish that [the defendant] violated the antitrust laws, that [the defendant's] alleged violations had a tendency to injure [the plaintiff's] business, and that [the plaintiff] suffered a decline in its business 'not shown to be attributable to other causes.' ").

[14]   For example, Loeb Indus. v. Sumitomo Corp., 306 F.3d 469 (7th Cir. 2002), cert. denied, 539 U.S. 903, 123 S.Ct. 2248 (2003) (conspiracy to manipulate market in copper future not shown to be cause of changes in price of scrap copper when any other factors affected that price); Watkins & Son Pet Supplies v. Iams Co., 254 F.3d 607 (6th Cir. 2001) (antitrust violation must be shown to be a "necessary predicate" of the harm).

[15]   See 2A Antitrust Law ¶ 338 (5th ed. 2021).

[16]   For example, J.B.D.L. Corp. v. Wyeth-Ayerst Labs., Inc., 485 F.3d 880 (6th Cir. 2007) (plaintiff could not show that defendant's rebate programs were a significant contributor to its own losses); Catlin v. Washington Energy Co., 791 F.2d 1343 (9th Cir. 1986) (plaintiff already showing most of its losses before alleged violation occurred).

may drive less efficient rivals out of the market altogether. But such firms are injured by more competition in the market, not less.[17]

Finally, the scope of injury that is required depends on the scope of relief that the plaintiff is requesting. The more you ask for, the more you must prove. If the plaintiff is seeking to dissolve a joint venture or break up a firm it must establish broad injury affecting a substantial part of the defendant's business. By contrast, if it is seeking merely an injunction against a particular anticompetitive rule, it needs to show the competitive harm caused by that rule. For example, in the *NCAA* case the plaintiff was challenging a specific rule that limited NCAA football teams to four nationally televised games annually.[18] It was not seeking to dissolve the NCAA as a joint venture. Accordingly, the Court approved an injunction after concluding that the rule itself was anticompetitive. The same thing should have applied in the *AmEx* case, where the plaintiff was seeking to enjoin the defendant's rule prohibiting merchants from steering customers to a cheaper credit card.[19] The plaintiff was not requesting that AmEx's entire business be shut down. However, both the majority and the dissent discussed whether retail prices overall were higher as a result of the rule. That issue was a red herring. It certainly would have been sufficient to support the injunction, but it was not necessary. The plaintiff's real proof requirement, which was readily met, was to show that those customers who would have wished to use a cheaper card but were denied the opportunity were injured because the rule denied access to a competitor.[20]

14.3d. Injunctive Relief

In its *Cargill* decision the Supreme Court held that the "antitrust injury" doctrine applies equally to suits seeking an injunction (or presumably divestiture) and suits seeking damages.[21] The "threatened" injury requirement of § 16 does not require a plaintiff to quantify its injury, but it must show some threatened injury. Further, the threatened injury must result from the impact of the challenged practice on competition. Just as a competitor may not obtain damages for the injuries that result from an efficiency-creating joint venture, so too it may not enjoin such a venture on the theory that it will be injured by the resulting efficiencies. The

---

[17]   E.g., Philadelphia Taxi Ass'n, Inc. v. Uber Techs., Inc., 886 F.3d 332 (3d Cir. 2018), cert. denied, 139 S.Ct. 211 (2018) (plaintiff, traditional taxicabs, were not injured by the increased competition brought about by Uber, a ride-hailing app).

[18]   NCAA v. Board of Regents of Univ. of Okla., 468 U.S. 85, 104 S.Ct. 2948 (1984). See § 5.6.

[19]   Ohio v. American Express Co., 138 S.Ct. 2274 (2018).

[20]   See § 10.9.

[21]   Cargill v. Monfort of Colo., 479 U.S. 104, 107 S.Ct. 484 (1986). See § 16.3a.

difference in proof of injury has to do not with the nature of the injury, but rather with § 4's separate requirements that the injury be quantifiable sufficiently to permit damages measurement.[22]

§ 14.4   Statutory and Judicial Rules Limiting Antitrust Standing

Clayton § 4 requires a plaintiff to be a "person," which includes natural persons, corporations, and unincorporated associations recognized by federal, state or foreign law. Municipalities, states and foreign governments are all permissible plaintiffs.[23]

14.4a.   "Business or Property"

Section 4 requires the antitrust plaintiff to show injury to its "business or property." In Reiter v. Sonotone Corp.,[24] the Supreme Court granted a damages action to a retail consumer who allegedly paid a higher price for a product because of a price fixing conspiracy. The consumer was injured in her "property" but not in her business. Today the term "property" in § 4 is nearly co-extensive with the common law concept: property is anything in which a person claims a legally recognized ownership interest.

The concept of "business or property" has sometimes been construed narrowly by lower courts. For example, in Reibert v. Atlantic Richfield Co.[25] the Tenth Circuit held that an employee discharged in the wake of a personnel consolidation brought about by a merger had no cause of action under Clayton § 7, the merger provision, because employment was not "business or property" within the meaning of § 4. A job is clearly a legally recognized property interest, however, and other courts have granted standing when the target of the antitrust violation was the labor market itself.[26] One set of examples in the large number of decisions addressing employer "no poach" agreements or other agreements limiting employee mobility.

---

[22]   Another important difference is that § 4 requires proof of injury that has already occurred. By contrast, one may obtain an injunction against injury that is merely threatened in the future, provided that it is antitrust injury. See Zenith Radio Corp. v. Hazeltine Research, Inc., 395 U.S. at 140, 89 S.Ct. at 1585.

[23]   However, foreign governments are generally restricted to recovery of actual rather than treble damages. 15 U.S.C.A. § 15(b). On foreign suits, see Pfizer v. Government of India, 434 U.S. 308, 318–320, 98 S.Ct. 584, 590–591 (1978). Although the United States as purchaser is not a "person" under the statute, a special provision permits it to seek treble damages. 15 U.S.C.A. § 15(a).

[24]   442 U.S. 330, 99 S.Ct. 2326, on remand, 602 F.2d 179 (8th Cir. 1979). See 2 Antitrust Law ¶ 345 (5th ed. 2021).

[25]   471 F.2d 727 (10th Cir.), cert. denied, 411 U.S. 938, 93 S.Ct. 1900 (1973).

[26]   See 2A Antitrust Law ¶ 352 (5th ed. 2021).

These violations occur in the labor market itself, and injured employees have standing.[27]

14.4b. Market Relationships; "Direct Injury" and "Target Area" Tests[28]

Courts have identified certain favored and disfavored classes of antitrust plaintiffs under Clayton § 4. Favored plaintiffs include customers and competitors of the violator. Disfavored plaintiffs include nonpurchasers, most potential competitors, employees of the violator, and stockholders, creditors, landlords, and employees of victims. Standing is sometimes denied to people in the favored categories and sometimes granted to those in the disfavored categories, but in each case there must be a good reason for deviating from a presumption that favors customers and competitors and disfavors most others.

14.4b1. "Direct Injury"

The "direct injury" test originated in Loeb v. Eastman Kodak Co.[29] The court denied standing to a stockholder in a corporation allegedly victimized by an antitrust violation. The holding was based on two rationales. First, the stockholder's injury was only an "indirect" consequence of the antitrust violation; the direct consequence was the injury to the corporation itself. Second, the court concluded that § 7 of the Sherman Act (Clayton § 4's predecessor) was not intended by Congress to "multiply suits" by conferring standing on thousands of stockholders "when their wrongs could have been equally well and far more economically redressed by a single suit in the name of the corporation."

Measure of the "directness" of an injury, as courts knew from their experience in tort law, would yield complicated metaphysical problems and no clear predictive rule. At the extremes it is perhaps easy to characterize an injury as "direct" or "indirect"—but in the middle are hundreds of cases in which the plaintiff's injury is clear but the chain of events between the act and the injury contains several, sometimes improbable links. The *Loeb* court's alternative observation was more sensible: that the corporation is a more efficient enforcer than its individual stockholders and should have the same information and incentives to sue.

---

[27]   E.g., Butler v. Jimmy John's Franchise, LLC, 331 F.Supp.3d 786 (S.D.Ill. 2018) (employees had standing to challenge intra-franchise agreements that restaurants would not steal one another's employees).

[28]   See 2 Antitrust Law ¶ 335 (5th ed. 2021).

[29]   183 Fed. 704, 709 (3d Cir. 1910).

The "efficient enforcer" doctrine can be pushed too far, however, when a less-than-optimal plaintiff with an actual competitive injury is rejected in favor of a theoretically superior plaintiff who has not sued.[30] The reasons for bringing or failing to bring an action are manifold and not always observable by outsiders. The more justifiable use of an "efficient enforcer" limitation is when an alternative plaintiff has actually sued for substantially the same injuries.

14.4b2. *"Target Area"*

The "target area" test was designed to eliminate some of the uncertainties of the direct injury test. As the Ninth Circuit formulated the test in Conference of Studio Unions v. Loew's Inc.,[31] the plaintiff must "show that he is within that area of the economy which is endangered by a breakdown of competitive conditions in a particular industry." The court then held that a labor union and its members were not the target of an alleged conspiracy between major motion picture producers and a second union to drive smaller motion picture companies out of business.

The target area test has proved just as problematic as the direct injury test. If standing under the target area test is limited to the defendant's *intended* victims, then the range of potential plaintiffs is often very small. However, if standing is expanded to include all persons whose injury is "foreseeable," then the target area test will often be unduly broad: when a firm is driven from business, it is certainly foreseeable that its employees and their union, its creditors, stockholders, suppliers and landlord will all be injured. All of these participate to some degree in that part of the economy that is threatened by the violation.

14.4b3. *Supreme Court Attempts at a More Useful Alternative*

Both the direct injury and target area tests for standing give a strong preference to consumers who suffer overcharge injuries or competitors injured by exclusionary practices. Occasionally courts even suggest that standing should be limited to these two classes of plaintiffs. But in Blue Shield of Virginia v. McCready,[32] the Supreme Court granted standing to a health insurance purchaser who alleged

---

[30] E.g., Gelboim v. Bank of Am. Corp., 823 F.3d 759 (2d Cir. 2016), cert. denied, 137 S.Ct. 814 (2017).

[31] 193 F.2d 51, 54–55 (9th Cir. 1951), cert. denied, 342 U.S. 919, 72 S.Ct. 367 (1952).

[32] 457 U.S. 465, 102 S.Ct. 2540 (1982).

that her insurance provider conspired with psychiatrists to exclude psychologists from her health policy's coverage.

The intended victims of the alleged conspiracy were clearly the psychologists. However, the defendant easily could foresee that any exclusion of psychologists from policy coverage would also injure purchasers of psychologists' services. Thus although Ms. McCready was not the "target" of the antitrust conspiracy, her injury was plainly foreseeable.

Without explicitly adopting either the "direct injury" or "target area" test, the Supreme Court granted standing by noting that plaintiff McCready was "within that area of the economy" that had been endangered by the "breakdown of competitive conditions" resulting from the alleged violation. Further, she was a victim of antitrust injury.[33] That is, her injury was a natural result of diminished competition in the market for medical services.

The Court then appeared to add one restriction to a broad rule granting standing to all plaintiffs who could allege antitrust injury, and whose injury-in-fact was both foreseeable and not *de minimis*: the injury must be "inextricably intertwined with the injury the conspirators sought to inflict on psychologists * * *."[34] The Court's "inextricably intertwined" language is empty rhetoric, however, and not well designed to achieve consistency in standing cases. A stockholder's injuries seem "inextricably intertwined" with the demise of the corporation in which he owns shares. Further, the Court paid little attention to the fact that another group of potential plaintiffs, the psychologists, were the direct target of the alleged conspiracy. Certainly they knew that the defendant had excluded them from its insurance coverage, and they had a strong incentive to sue.[35]

The Court qualified *McCready* in Associated General Contractors of California, Inc. v. California State Council of Carpenters,[36] which denied standing to a labor union alleging that the defendant association of contractors coerced various of its contractor members into dealing only with nonunion firms. The intended victims of the boycott were thus contractors who stood to lose building contracts unless they agreed to the association's demands.

---

[33]   Id. at 479, 102 S.Ct. at 2548.

[34]   Id. at 484, 102 S.Ct. at 2551.

[35]   In fact, the psychologists had sued. See Virginia Academy of Clinical Psychologists v. Blue Shield of Va., 624 F.2d 476 (4th Cir.), on remand, 501 F.Supp. 1232 (E.D.Va.1980), cert. denied, 450 U.S. 916, 101 S.Ct. 1360 (1981).

[36]   459 U.S. 519, 103 S.Ct. 897 (1983).

In holding that the union had not been "injured in its business or property," the Court treated the complaint as alleging an injury in the market for building projects, not in the labor market itself.[37] The outcome is easily rationalized if one considers first that employees ordinarily lack standing to sue for injuries that accrue to their employers, and secondly that in this case the plaintiff was not even the employees, but rather the union that represented them.

Nevertheless, the Court went on to note numerous difficulties in the plaintiff's complaint. First, the allegations were vague, and failed to identify precisely who was injured and how they were injured. Second, recognizing an antitrust damages action such as this one would present several problems of tracing and apportioning damages. Third, given that the real target of the alleged boycott was a group of contractors, the labor union was only a second-best plaintiff. Finally, there did not seem to be antitrust injury. Indeed, it was "not clear whether the Union's interest would be served or disserved by enhanced competition" in the contracting market.[38]

After two important Supreme Court decisions the law of standing in private antitrust actions is far from clear. None of the generalized, conceptual tests adequately predicts whether a particular plaintiff will be granted standing. Further, although they leave the older "direct injury" and "target area" tests somewhat in doubt, neither was overruled.

Nevertheless, one can draw a few generalizations that do in fact provide guidance. First, antitrust injury is a *sine qua non* for standing, as are both causation and injury-in-fact. Standing is never granted if one of these is found lacking, and the more tenuous the evidence the more likely the case will be dismissed on standing grounds. Second, consumers and competitors of the violator are presumptively granted standing. A weaker presumption of standing or perhaps no presumption either way attaches to boycott victims other than the immediately intended targets. This accounts for *McCready*. Other classes of victims, such as landlords, employees, stockholders, and creditors of victims, are presumptively denied standing. But the presumptions are rebuttable, and in close cases the court will determine whether there is another highly motivated

---

[37]   The Court noted that there was:

no allegation that any collective bargaining agreement was terminated as a result of the coercion, no allegation that the aggregate share of the contracting market controlled by union firms has declined, and no allegation that the Union's revenues in the form of dues or initiation fees have decreased.

459 U.S. at 542, 103 S.Ct. at 911.

[38]   Ibid. Indeed, more strenuous competition in the contractor market probably would have benefitted low cost contractors, which would likely be nonunionized.

group of potential plaintiffs in a position to enforce the antitrust laws more efficiently.

In addition, the court should also consider whether the particular plaintiff is in a unique position to discover an antitrust violation earlier than other potential plaintiffs would. In that case, granting standing could minimize the duration, and thus the social cost, of antitrust violations.[39]

§ 14.5 Special Problems of Antitrust Standing

14.5a. "Duplicative Recovery"

Courts also generally require that the injured business or property belong to the plaintiff and not to someone else. Occasionally, however, ownership of a particular property interest is ambiguous. In Hawaii v. Standard Oil Co. of California,[40] for example, the Supreme Court held that a state could not assert a damages claim for economic injuries to its citizens, or for injury to its general economy, if it was not itself a purchaser or competitor of the defendant. At that time, § 4 did not authorize a state's use of the common law doctrine of *parens patriae*, under which a governmental entity could bring an action asserting injuries to citizens within its protection. Since the citizens themselves had causes of action, the Court reasoned, any damages action brought by the State asserting the same injuries, or some more general injury to the state's economy, would yield duplicative recoveries. Section 4 was subsequently amended to permit *parens patriae* actions by states' attorneys general on behalf of natural persons residing in the state.[41]

14.5b. Derivative Injuries

The concept of "derivative" injury is slippery. The mere fact that an antitrust violation injures different groups of market participants does not entail that one group's injuries are merely derivative of the other. For example, predatory pricing directed initially at competitors will, if successful, yield higher prices for consumers. In this case we would not say that the competitors' injury is merely derivative of the consumers' injury. Both are participants in the immediate market. Further, their injuries are measured differently:

---

[39] On the preferred position of consumers in antitrust's remedial structure, see Daniel A. Crane, The Institutional Structure of Antitrust Enforcement (2011); Herbert Hovenkamp, The Antitrust Enterprise: Principle and Execution, chs. 2–4 (2005); Herbert Hovenkamp, Antitrust's Protected Classes, 88 Mich.L.Rev. 1 (1989).

[40] 405 U.S. 251, 92 S.Ct. 885 (1972).

[41] 15 U.S.C.A. § 15c.

consumers by the monopoly overcharge and competitors by loss of business opportunity.

Ideally, we would reserve the term "derivative" injury for those who claim the selfsame injury as someone else, and usually by their participation in some market other than the market that is the focus of the antitrust violation. A good example is the corporate shareholder, who will lose her investment when her stock becomes worthless as a result of another firm's antitrust violation. In this case, the loss of value in the shares is nothing other than the loss of business assets or potential profits that the corporation itself has experienced. We acknowledge this by saying that the shareholders' loss is entirely derivative of the loss suffered by the corporation itself, and generally deny standing to the shareholder. Roughly similar considerations apply to the landlords of antitrust victims, to their creditors, tax collectors, and customers with long-term contracts. In brief, when a firm is forced out of business in some market, its exit causes dislocations in numerous related markets where it does business. A court uses the term "derivative" to express its intuition that a particular damage claim is insufficiently distinguished from the claim of another to warrant a separate grant of standing.

The Supreme Court's *McCready* decision is helpful.[42] The Court permitted a health insurance consumer to sue her insurer for participating in an agreement with psychiatrists to exclude the services of clinical psychologists from medical policy coverage. In this case the psychologists were the competitors of the psychiatrists. Further, the psychologists had already maintained their own action.[43] Indeed the district court had considered the psychologists' and McCready's claim together, and had granted the psychologists standing while denying standing to McCready. The Supreme Court reversed the latter decision.[44] The psychologists had suffered one kind of injury—loss of profits in their profession—and McCready had suffered quite another, namely, reduced coverage on her health insurance policy.

---

[42]   Blue Shield of Va. v. McCready, 457 U.S. 465, 102 S.Ct. 2540 (1982). See § 16.4b3.

[43]   See Virginia Acad. of Clinical Psychologists v. Blue Shield of Va., 624 F.2d 476 (4th Cir.), on remand, 501 F.Supp. 1232 (E.D.Va.1980), cert. denied, 450 U.S. 916, 101 S.Ct. 1360 (1981).

[44]   *McCready*, 457 U.S. at 470 n. 4, 102 S.Ct. at 2543 n. 4.

§ 14.6 The Indirect Purchaser Rule

14.6a. Hanover Shoe, Illinois Brick, and Apple v. Pepper

In Hanover Shoe, Inc. v. United Shoe Machinery Corp.[45] the Supreme Court held that a direct purchaser from a monopolist could claim the entire monopoly overcharge as damages, even though the purchaser passed most of the overcharge on to its customers. The Court acknowledged that much of a monopoly overcharge is passed down the distribution chain and absorbed by the consumer. However, lawsuits by indirect purchaser consumers would be impractical. There might be thousands of such purchasers, each with only a "tiny stake in a lawsuit."

A decade later in Illinois Brick Co. v. Illinois[46] the Supreme Court followed *Hanover Shoe* in deciding that, since the direct purchaser has an action for the entire monopoly overcharge, the indirect purchaser should have none. It did not matter that the indirect purchaser could show that part of the overcharge had been passed on and that it had been injured as a result.

A monopoly overcharge at the top of a distribution chain generally results in higher prices at every level below. For example, if production of aluminum is monopolized or cartelized, fabricators of aluminum cookware will pay higher prices for aluminum. In most cases they will absorb part of these increased costs themselves and pass part along to cookware wholesalers. The wholesalers will charge higher prices to the retail stores, and the stores will do it once again to retail consumers. Every person at every stage in the chain likely will be poorer as a result of the monopoly price at the top.

One can calculate the percentage of any overcharge that a firm at one distributional level will pass on to those at the next level.

---

[45]   392 U.S. 481, 88 S.Ct. 2224 (1968).

[46]   431 U.S. 720, 97 S.Ct. 2061 (1977); see 2 Antitrust Law ¶ 346 (5th ed. 2021); and see Lucas Automotive Engineering v. Bridgestone/Firestone, 140 F.3d 1228 (9th Cir. 1998) (applying indirect purchaser rule so as to preclude indirect purchaser's challenge to a merger). A logical corollary of *Hanover* and *Illinois Brick* is that in states that accept indirect purchase lawsuits the direct purchaser's damages should be reduced by the amount that is passed on. However, the California Supreme Court has rejected that proposition. See Clayworth v. Pfizer, Inc., 49 Cal.4th 758, 111 Cal.Rptr.3d 666, 233 P.3d 1066 (2010) (the fact that pharmacies were able to pass on all or most of overcharge did not limit their recovery, at least in a situation where the statute of limitation on indirect purchaser recovery had run).

However, the computation requires knowledge of the prevailing elasticities of supply and demand.[47]

In Apple v. Pepper the Supreme Court adhered to the *Illinois Brick* rule but de-emphasized the question of passing on.[48] The plaintiffs were a class of iPhone users who purchased apps on Apple's App Store. They alleged that the App Store was a bottleneck for purchasing apps, and that Apple's 30% commission was a significant overcharge. Rejecting the defendant's argument that the plaintiffs were direct purchasers from the app sellers themselves, the Supreme Court found it "dispositive" that the customers paid their money directly to Apple, who then took out its commission and reimbursed the sellers.[49] It did not matter that the app makers set the retail price.

The Court also cited the language of § 4 of the Clayton Act, which "broadly affords injured parties a right to sue. . . ," but it then interpreted that language as granting such a right when "there is no intermediary between the purchaser and the antitrust violator." The dissenters rejected that reasoning and instead preferred a doctrine of proximate cause, analogous to tort law, in which damages claims would not be permitted to "go beyond the first step."[50] Both interpretations, it is worth noting, are inconsistent with the statute's grant of a damages action to "any person" who is injured.

Neither the majority nor the dissent confronted the voluminous economic literature tending to show that most intermediaries including the direct purchaser end up passing on most or in some cases all of any overcharge. Only the end user is not able to pass anything on, and as a result it often bears the largest and sometimes the only brunt of any overcharge.[51] In that case, the dissent would give the damages action to the wrong person, but the majority's rule would too in the more typical case where the first purchaser in line is a dealer or other intermediary rather than an end user.

Moreover, the complexities that the dissent cited would need to be confronted only if the app makers were suing for an *overcharge*. For intermediaries in any distribution chain, including the app producers in this case, the harm comes from lost sales volume, not

---

[47]   For the relevant formulas, see William M. Landes & Richard A. Posner, Should Indirect Purchasers Have Standing to Sue Under the Antitrust Laws? An Economic Analysis of the Rule of *Illinois Brick*, 46 U.Chi.L.Rev. 602 (1979).

[48]   Apple, Inc. v. Pepper, 139 S.Ct. 1514 (2019).

[49]   Id. at 1521.

[50]   Id. at 1526.

[51]   See Herbert Hovenkamp, Apple v. Pepper: Rationalizing Antitrust's Indirect Purchaser Rule, 120 Columbia L. Rev. Forum 14 (2020).

from the overcharge.[52] The fact that sales are digitized and marginal costs are very low suggests that estimating harm from lost sales volume need not be any more difficult to prove than lost profits generally, although one should not make light of the difficulties. The European Union takes a much more economically sophisticated approach, permitting damages to be proven by whatever methodology works best under the circumstances.[53]

Interestingly, neither the majority nor the dissent seemed particularly interested in the passing on issue that has so often dominated the indirect purchaser jurisprudence. For the majority this was mainly a problem in identifying who paid the money to whom. For the dissent the issue was proximate cause. Whether this signals a new course in indirect purchaser jurisprudence is at this writing difficult to say. One thing that is troublesome, however, is the Court's indifference to the questions of who is actually harmed by an antitrust violation, and how.[54]

14.6b.   Exceptions to the Illinois Brick Rule

The exceptions discussed in this Section should be read in light of the Supreme Court's decision in Apple v. Pepper, which suggests diminished importance for at least some of them. How that plays out in the lower courts remains to be seen.

14.6b1.   Pre-Existing Contracts

Suppose that a direct purchaser executes a 10-year contract to sell 1000 widgets per year at a price 10% higher than its costs. A year later, the firm's supplier enters into a cartel and raises the price of an input to monopoly levels. In that case the direct purchaser can pass on the entire monopoly overcharge for purchases under that contract.

Courts have generally recognized an exception to *Illinois Brick* for *fixed-quantity, fixed-mark-up* contracts that existed *before* the cartel price took effect. Indirect purchasers buying under such contracts can show that the entire monopoly overcharge was passed on to them; hence they should have the action for damages. It follows

---

[52]   Ibid.

[53]   See id., discussing European Union, Guidelines for National Courts on How to Estimate the Share of Overcharge which was Passed on to the Indirect Purchaser, 2019 O.J. (C 267) 4, 24, available at https://ec.europa.eu/competition/antitrust/actions damages/quantification_en.html.

[54]   See Herbert Hovenkamp, The Looming Crisis in Antitrust Economics, ___ Boston Univ. L. Rev. ___ (2020), available at https://papers.ssrn.com/sol3/papers.cfm? abstract_id=3508832.

that the direct purchaser should not have a damages action for purchases and resales made under such contracts.[55]

Most courts have held that this exception to the *Illinois Brick* rule applies only when the pre-existing contract is fixed *both* as to mark-up and quantity. If an indirect purchaser has a simple "cost-plus" contract, such as a requirements contract, it will respond to the cartel price increase by reducing the amount it purchases. In that case the direct purchaser will lose profits; thus the injury will be shared by the direct purchaser and the indirect purchaser.

In *UtiliCorp*, the Supreme Court adhered to this formulation in a case where the utility's customers were not obliged in advance to purchase a particular quantity.[56] The *UtiliCorp* plaintiffs were customers of a price regulated natural gas utility that had allegedly purchased gas at illegal monopoly prices. In a related case, the Seventh Circuit had held that the indirect purchasing consumers would have the damages action because (a) a price regulated utility is entitled under its cost-plus regulatory regime to pass on the full amount of any monopoly overcharge; and (b) at the regulated price, the price elasticity of demand for a good such as natural gas is extremely low—that is, customers would not likely reduce their purchases by significant amounts in response to the monopoly or cartel overcharge.[57]

In rejecting the Seventh Circuit's analysis, the Court concluded that the question of the utility's ability to pass on the overcharge was much more complex than the basic regulatory scheme suggested. State regulators did not uniformly permit utilities to raise their rates in response to gas price increases. Rather, the outcome varied from one situation to the next. Further, there was often considerable lag between the price increase and the rate increase, and the utility had to absorb the difference during the interval. The fact that these injuries did accrue to the utility entailed that it be permitted its own damage action. In that case, however, if "we were to add indirect purchasers to the action, we would have to devise an apportionment

---

[55]　In re Beef Industry Antitrust Litigation, 600 F.2d 1148 (5th Cir. 1979), cert. denied, 449 U.S. 905, 101 S.Ct. 280 (1980), on remand, 542 F.Supp. 1122 (N.D.Tex.1982), affirmed, 710 F.2d 216 (5th Cir. 1983), cert. denied, 465 U.S. 1052, 104 S.Ct. 1326 (1984).

[56]　Kansas & Missouri v. UtiliCorp United, 497 U.S. 199, 218, 110 S.Ct. 2807, 2818 (1990). The contracts at issue in *UtiliCorp* were not cost-plus, but the markup was set by regulatory agencies that presumably applied the same markup formulas to all purchases.

[57]　Illinois ex rel. Hartigan v. Panhandle E. Pipe Line Co., 852 F.2d 891, 697–899 (7th Cir. 1988) (en banc).

formula. This is the very complexity that *Hanover Shoe* and *Illinois Brick* sought to avoid."[58]

14.6b2. Injunction Suits

The measurement difficulties that prompted the indirect purchaser rule apply only to calculation of the *amount* of a particular purchaser's damages. Equity suits create no risk of duplicative recovery: it costs a defendant no more to comply with 10 identical injunctions than to comply with one. Lower courts generally have held that an indirect purchaser may seek an injunction against a cartel.[59] In *Apple*, the dissenters doubted this proposition, suggesting that only the first purchaser in line should have an action, even for an injunction.[60]

14.6b3. Cases Involving Vertical Agreements or Control

A third exception to *Illinois Brick*, which is really no exception at all, involves a middleman who is really part of the antitrust conspiracy. Suppose a cartel member sells to A, who resells to B, but A is also part of the price fixing conspiracy. B is not really an indirect purchaser, but a direct one. He should have a damages action.[61] One result of this rule is that indirect purchasers are encouraged to name their direct sellers as co-defendants in order to avoid dismissal at an early stage of the litigation. In fact, some courts have held that plaintiffs seeking to establish that direct purchasers were members of the conspiracy must name them as parties.[62] This rule seems sensible, at least where naming them is practicable. If they are not named they will not be bound by any legal conclusion that they are parties, will not have an opportunity to contest the allegation, and

---

[58] *UtiliCorp.*, 497 U.S. at 210, 110 S.Ct. at 2814. Finally, the court noted that many utilities are by law required to pass antitrust damage recoveries on to their customers in the form of rebates. Id. at 212, 110 S.Ct. at 2815.

[59] In re Warfarin Sodium Antitrust Litigation, 214 F.3d 395 (3d Cir. 2000), on remand, 212 F.R.D. 231 (D.Del.2002) (accepting indirect purchaser injunction claim); Campos v. Ticketmaster, 140 F.3d 1166 (8th Cir. 1998), cert. denied, 525 U.S. 1102, 119 S.Ct. 865 (1999) (indirect purchasers damage claim rejected, but could continue suit for injunction).

[60] Apple Inc. v. Pepper, 139 S.Ct. 1514, 1527 n. 1 (2019).

[61] See Arizona v. Shamrock Foods Co., 729 F.2d 1208 (9th Cir. 1984), cert. denied, 469 U.S. 1197, 105 S.Ct. 980 (1985) (parens patriae suit in behalf of dairy consumers alleging conspiracy involving both grocery stores and dairy producers). But see ATM Fee Antitrust Litig., 686 F.3d 741 (9th Cir. 2012), cert. denied, 571 U.S. 944, 134 S.Ct. 257 (2013) (rejecting claim that banks and ATM owners were engaged in a conspiracy to charge high fees to ATM users; the consumer plaintiff did not pay the fees directly to the ATM owners but rather to their banks, who transferred the fees to the ATM owners).

[62] See *Campos*, 140 F.3d at 1171 n. 4.

could even become plaintiffs themselves in a subsequent suit against the same defendants.

14.6c. Policy Implications of the Indirect Purchaser Rule; State Indirect Purchaser Statutes

Is the indirect purchaser rule a good one? Commentators have argued both sides with vehemence. Roughly half of the states have responded to *Illinois Brick* by amending their own antitrust statutes to allow damages actions by indirect purchasers.[63] In California v. ARC America Corp., the Supreme Court held that these statutes were not preempted by federal antitrust law.[64]

The most serious criticism of the indirect purchaser rule is that it appears inconsistent with § 4's mandate that damages should be designed to compensate plaintiffs. In the great majority of situations the indirect purchaser rule gives the entire damage action to the person who suffered the smaller injury—or, in some cases, no injury at all.

The concerns about tracing the overcharge through successive purchasers that led to *Illinois Brick* also seem largely misplaced. The argument was that computing that portion of the overcharge absorbed by the intermediary and that part passed on to consumers was largely intractable.[65] In fact, however, computing the indirect purchaser's overcharge need not, and ordinarily does not, involve any computation of pass on. In the typical case overcharge damages are measured by either the "yardstick" method or the "before-and-after" method. Neither requires computation of the pass on.

To illustrate, suppose manufacturers of liquor fix its price in Texas, from a competitive level of $10.00 to a cartel level of $14.00. Suppose that a bottle of liquor is sold to a retailer at the $14.00 price, and then the same bottle is sold to consumers for $16.00. Assume also that in a competitive market the retailer would have paid $10.00 and resold the liquor for $13.00. In sum, the retailer paid a $4.00

---

[63]   See 14 Antitrust Law ¶ 2412d (4th ed. 2019), which catalogs state deviations from the federal *Illinois Brick* rule.

[64]   490 U.S. 93, 109 S.Ct. 1661 (1989). See also Clayworth v. Pfizer, Inc., 49 Cal.4th 758, 111 Cal.Rptr.3d 666, 233 P.3d 1066 (2010) (permitting direct purchasers to recover notwithstanding that they had passed the overcharges on to indirect purchasers; court also observed that the statute of limitation on indirect purchaser recovery had run).

[65]   E.g., William M. Landes & Richard A. Posner, Should Indirect Purchasers Have Standing to Sue Under the Antitrust Laws? An Economic Analysis of the Rule of *Illinois Brick*, 46 U.Chi.L.Rev. 602 (1979).

overcharge for the liquor bottle and passed $3.00 of that overcharge on to customers.

In estimating consumer overcharge damages under the yardstick method the economist could identify some "yardstick" market similar to the affected market but without the price fixing. Suppose that market is Oklahoma, and that the same bottle of liquor in Oklahoma costs $13.00 at retail. In that case the consumer overcharge would be computed by comparing the $13.00 Oklahoma retail price with the $16.00 Texas retail price during the cartel period. The "pass on" would not ordinarily be computed at all, for all we are comparing is what the Oklahoma "yardstick" retail customer paid with what the customer in the price-fixed market paid.

The same thing is true of the before-and-after method. Under that methodology the expert would examine prices before the cartel came into existence and after it fell apart. She would find that in those two time period the retail customer paid $13.00 (after necessary adjustments are made), while during the cartel period that customer paid $16.00. Once again, no calculation of an "overcharge" would be necessary.

If we really wanted to compute the retailers "overcharge" injury we could do so by comparing markups. For example, during the cartel period the Texas retailers' markup was $2.00, while the Oklahoma retailers markup was $3.00. Of course, the markup does not capture the full amount of the retailers' injury, because it is injured not only by the reduced profits on each bottle sold, but also by the reduction in the number of bottles sold. But attempting to compute an overcharge never captures the losses resulting from lost volume. This is simply another way of observing that "overcharge" is not even theoretically the correct way of measuring the injury that accrues to a reseller who passes on some, but not all, of a cartel overcharge.[66]

To summarize, (a) the intermediary's injury is not measured by an "overcharge" at all, but by lost profits; (b) the indirect purchaser's damage can ordinarily be measured without reference to the amount "passed on" by the intermediary. As a result, the correct way to measure purchaser damages in a monopoly or price fixing case is lost profits to those who purchase and resell the product in question, and net overcharge to the final purchaser.

The Supreme Court's decision in Apple v. Pepper was an opportunity lost. *Illinois Brick* rested on grounds that were tenuous when it was decided and even more tenuous today. The Court's suggestion in *Illinois Brick* that an indirect purchaser rule would

---

[66]　See 2A Antitrust Law ¶¶ 395–396 (5th ed. 2021).

improve deterrence has never been established and is very likely incorrect. Today it is much clearer than it was forty years ago that the antitrust laws, particularly against price fixing, are underdeterrent. Further, today we have a better understanding of how downstream purchasers from a cartel or monopoly overcharge are injured, as well as an appreciation that different situations call for different resolutions. *Illinois Brick* was an unjustified bit of exceptionalism to the more general rules for business injury damages that has seriously hampered effective private enforcement against cartels. A better solution would be to permit experts to develop models accounting for injury in each particular case and subject these to the usual federal rules for considering expert testimony.[67]

14.6d. The Umbrella Plaintiff

Remotely related to the indirect purchaser is the buyer injured by "umbrella pricing" made possible by someone else's antitrust violation. Suppose that X, Y & Z fix the price of widgets at $1.50. The competitive price is $1.00. X, Y & Z control 85% of the market and Q, who is not part of the conspiracy, sells the remaining 15%.

The cartel will create a price "umbrella" under which Q will be able to raise her price to some level just under $1.50 and sell all she can produce. Suppose that P buys widgets from Q at $1.45. Clearly P has been injured by the cartel. P has no cause of action against Q, for Q has done nothing illegal. Instead P sues X, Y & Z, claiming that their cartel caused P's overcharge injuries.

In Mid-West Paper Products Co. v. Continental Group, Inc.[68] the Third Circuit rejected such a theory as speculative. It then analogized the umbrella claim to the indirect purchaser rule and concluded that computation of damages would present problems analogous to those in computing pass-on in indirect purchaser actions. In the *Beef Industry*[69] antitrust litigation, however, the Fifth Circuit permitted "inverted umbrella" sellers to recover from a buyer's cartel which depressed the wholesale price of beef.

Mid-West Paper's comparison of umbrella actions with indirect purchaser actions was not particularly apt. Computation of overcharge injuries from umbrella pricing need be no more difficult than computation of overcharge injuries in direct purchaser actions. Assuming that X, Y, Z and Q all operate in the same market and

---

[67]   See § 16.8c; and Herbert Hovenkamp, Apple v. Pepper: Rationalizing Antitrust's Indirect Purchaser Rule, 120 Col. L. Rev. Forum 14 (2020).

[68]   596 F.2d 573, 583–87 (3d Cir. 1979).

[69]   See United States Gypsum Co. v. Indiana Gas Co., Inc., 350 F.3d 623 (7th Cir. 2003) (refusing to dismiss umbrella claim).

produce fungible products, they would have the same competitive price. A direct purchaser from X, Y or Z would have to show the difference between the competitive price and the price she actually paid. A purchaser from noncartel member Q would have to show precisely the same thing. The fact that Q may have charged a lower price than the cartel will not complicate computation: P will merely recover the difference between the competitive price (which is the same for Q as it is for X, Y, and Z) and the price Q actually charged.

Chapter 15

ANTITRUST AND THE PROCESS
OF DEMOCRATIC GOVERNMENT

Table of Sections

§ 15.1   Regulation, Rent-Seeking and Antitrust Immunity

15.1a.   The Noerr Doctrine

Every natural person and business corporation in the United States has a right to "petition" the government for what it wants. This right is guaranteed even to those who want something extremely anticompetitive, such as a statutory monopoly, absolute freedom from price competition, or the forced removal of one's rivals from the market. This right applies at every level of government, state, federal and local, and to all three branches. The petitioning right includes the right to go before a regulatory agency in the executive branch; the right to lobby Congress, a state legislature or city council; and the right to bring or defend a case in court. The right's basic source is the First Amendment, although courts have found it in the legislative intent and policy of the Sherman Act as well.

Eastern Railroad Presidents Conference v. Noerr Motor Freight[1] involved an antitrust claim by truckers that railroads had organized a campaign intended to encourage shippers to use railroads rather than trucks for their shipping. First, the railroads allegedly petitioned state government officials for legislation that disadvantaged the truckers.[2] Second, the campaign presented the trucking companies in a false light, thus upsetting some of their customers. Many of the criticisms of trucking were publicly made by third parties, who appeared to be independent but were actually engaged by the railroads and financed by them.[3] The Court held two things: first, the direct petition to the government for legislation was immune from antitrust liability since Congress never intended the antitrust laws to interfere with the ordinary political process.[4] Second, the railroad statements presenting the truckers in a false light were also immune because they were in fact part of the general plan to make a case to the government for the legislation that the antitrust defendants desired.

Under *Noerr*, a firm that makes misleading or even untruthful claims to the government in order to get the government to injure the petitioner's competitors has antitrust immunity both (1) for any injury caused by the government response itself; and (2) for any consequences that flow from the fact that the public heard the misleading claims and responded by transferring their business away from the competitors. One basis for this doctrine is that in a government petitioning process all sides are entitled to have their say. If the railroads were portraying the trucking industry falsely, the truckers were in a position to correct the record—provided, of course, that they had the opportunity and resources to do so.

15.1b. Petitions to Governments Acting as Market Participants

Three years after *Noerr*, the Supreme Court held in United Mine Workers v. Pennington[5] that the defendant's efforts to influence a government agency to purchase its coal rather than the coal of competitors was immune. Once again, the conduct was a petition to

---

[1]   365 U.S. 127, 81 S.Ct. 523 (1961).

[2]   Id. at 129–130, 81 S.Ct. at 525. For example, the railroads lobbied against a bill that would have permitted trucks to carry heavier loads, and then persuaded a governor to veto it; they also lobbied for laws that increased taxes on heavily loaded trucks.

[3]   365 U.S. at 129, 81 S.Ct. at 525.

[4]   Id. at 135–137, 81 S.Ct. at 528–528.

[5]   381 U.S. 657, 85 S.Ct. 1585 (1965).

the government, although in this case the government was acting as a potential buyer, rather than a maker of laws.

Not all government purchase decisions are policy driven. If A tells the state "buy my office paper because it is made from recycled pulp," and the government responds, the government has made a policy decision reflecting its environmental concerns; *Noerr* immunity should follow. If A says "buy my office paper because I am the lowest bidder," and the price turns out to be the result of a rigged bid, no policy decision is implicated and *Noerr* should provide no shield in a subsequent antitrust suit.

In *Superior Court Trial Lawyers*[6] the Supreme Court limited *Pennington* and condemned a concerted boycott of legal services where the purchaser and immediate target of the boycott was the government itself. A group of trial lawyers representing indigent criminal defendants and paid by the District of Columbia collectively agreed to withhold their services until the District agreed to raise the rate of payment. When the District raised the rates, the boycott came to an end.

A number of observations about *Trial Lawyers* are relevant. First, a boycott of the same type directed at private customers would have been *per se* illegal.[7] Second, in this case the government was the customer. The principle that the government can be a victim of an antitrust violation and, in appropriate cases an antitrust plaintiff, is explicitly recognized by statute[8] and by case law that stretches back a century.[9] It would be quite irrational to decide that the government is a victim of an antitrust violation when it buys price-fixed goods, but that *Noerr* protects a group of private sellers agreeing with each other that they will withhold their services until a government purchase pays more. In sum, *Trial Lawyers* can be read for the narrow proposition that *Noerr* does not apply when the government is acting as a participant in a *private* market and the antitrust violation results from a privately initiated restraint that interferes with the ordinary process of competitive bargaining.

---

6   Ibid. See also Continental Ore Co. v. Union Carbide, 370 U.S. 690, 82 S.Ct. 1404 (1962), which refused to apply *Noerr* where the antitrust defendant had been appointed by the Canadian government as its agent for the regulation of vanadium sales in Canada, and then used this power to attempt to exclude competing vanadium sellers from the Canadian market. The Supreme Court characterized this as purely commercial activity, to which *Noerr* apparently did not apply.

7   See § 5.4.

8   15 U.S.C.A. § 15a (United States as plaintiff); 15 U.S.C.A. §§ 15c–15h (states as plaintiffs).

9   See Chattanooga Foundry & Pipe Works v. Atlanta, 203 U.S. 390, 27 S.Ct. 65 (1906) (permitting municipality to bring damage action for price fixing).

As the Federal Trade Commission observed:

> Permitting a price-fixing boycott directed at the government as buyer does not foster the *Noerr* goal of free exchange of information between people and the government. At the same time, prohibiting such conduct does not interfere with anyone's ability to choose to sell his services to the government or to make his views on the appropriate price known to the government.[10]

So the appeal to the government buyer or seller must be calculated to invoke a *policy* decision of the government. Further, as the Supreme Court noted, the antitrust injury caused by the trial lawyers' boycott resulted from the boycott itself, a private act, and not from the government's response. This suggests the following outcomes:

1. *Sellers engage in secret price-fixing against a government purchaser*: no immunity; no "petition" to the government is being made, and the injury is caused entirely by the private conduct.

2. *Seller engages in predatory pricing against competitors, where government is the customer*. Once again, there is no petition to the government, which probably does not even know that the price is predatory; the injury is caused by the predation, not by government action. To be sure, the injury is caused by the government's decision to accept the lowest bid, but this cannot be interpreted as a decision to condone predatory pricing.

3. *Sellers publicly boycott government purchaser until they receive higher prices*. *Noerr* provides no exemption, for the sellers are not treating the government as a government; they are using marketplace (not political) coercion. Further, the restraint itself results from purely private action. The government response in agreeing to pay higher prices does not create the restraint, but puts the restraint at an end. This is essentially the *Trial Lawyers'* case, which found no immunity.

4. *A group of sellers of steel electric conduit band together to convince the government that steel conduit is a better choice than plastic conduit in government buildings*. *Noerr* provides immunity, even if some of the information provided to the government is false. In this case, the

---

[10]   Superior Court Trial Lawyers, 107 F.T.C. 510, 562, 598 (1986), vacated, 856 F.2d 226 (D.C.Cir. 1988), reversed, 493 U.S. 411, 110 S.Ct. 768 (1990).

conspirators are seeking a policy decision. The government may or may not solicit evidence from both sides of the question, but if it fails to do so that is a failure of government process. The restraint is created, if at all, only when the government decides to listen to the private petitioners.

5. *A firm that deals with the government tells a government official "our employees will not vote for you, or we will give financial support to your opponent in the upcoming election, unless you buy more from us."* The results of such a proposal or threat might certainly be anticompetitive and corrupt, and may even be criminal. Nevertheless, the restraint occurs in the *political* rather than the private market. It is therefore not an antitrust violation.

§ 15.2   Petitions for Adjudicative Action

The right to petition the government also includes the right of business firms, acting unilaterally or in concert, to file a lawsuit or to bring a complaint before an agency acting in a quasi-judicial capacity.[11] Although the basic petitioning immunity is the same for judicial action as for legislative or executive action, the details are different. Since adjudicative claims do not involve governments as either purchasers or as the direct victims of antitrust violations, the petitioning immunity is subject to fewer exceptions. Furthermore, the adjudicative process has stricter "rules of conduct" that define the boundaries of acceptable behavior. For example, it is one thing to provide false information in the rough and tumble of a legislative campaign where communication lines are generally open. It is quite another to provide false information in a judicial setting, where an opponent may not have either the access or the resources to counter the challenge, and truthfulness is required by the rules of judicial procedure.

In Walker Process Equipment v. Food Machinery & Chemical Corp., the Supreme Court held that the wrongful filing of a civil suit could constitute an antitrust violation.[12] Walker, the antitrust plaintiff, had alleged that Food Machinery, the antitrust defendant, fraudulently obtained a patent by lying in its patent application

---

[11]   See 1 Antitrust Law ¶ 205 (5th ed. 2020). On joint filings by competing firms, see Primetime 24 Joint Venture v. NBC, 219 F.3d 92 (2d Cir. 2000) ("Where common legal or fact issues exist, the sharing of costs or other coordinated activity avoids wasteful duplication of effort and has no discernible effect on lawful competition.").

[12]   382 U.S. 172, 86 S.Ct. 347 (1965).

about prior sales that would have made the patent invalid.[13] Food Machinery then filed a patent infringement suit against Walker, but the suit was ultimately dismissed. Walker counterclaimed that the infringement suit itself violated § 2 of the Sherman Act. The Court held that if Food Machinery had knowingly obtained its patent by fraud and then filed an infringement suit, this suit would be stripped of its "exemption from the antitrust laws."[14] *Walker Process* failed to explore most of the fundamental issues raised by *Noerr*—indeed, it never cited *Noerr*. But implicitly at least, the Court held that certain kinds of lawsuits did not qualify for petitioning immunity, in this case because the plaintiff (later the antitrust defendant) knew that it had no basis in fact for its legal claim.

The Supreme Court tied *Noerr* and judicial petitions together in California Motor Transport Co. v. Trucking Unlimited,[15] where the plaintiffs alleged that the defendants had agreed with each other to deny the plaintiffs trucking licenses by instituting a series of lawsuits or objections before an administrative agency (the Interstate Commerce Commission) "with or without probable cause, and regardless of the merits of the cases."[16] In fact, most of the suits were not baseless; the firms had won 21 out of 40.[17]

First, the Supreme Court noted that the *Noerr* petitioning immunity applied in principle to petitions to all branches of government, and to requests for adjudicative as well as legislative action. Second, however, Justice Douglas' opinion found an exception to *Noerr* for petitions to the government that are merely a "sham," defined as "forms of illegal and reprehensible practice which may corrupt the administrative or judicial processes."[18] The Court also identified a pattern of "baseless, repetitive claims," made without regard to their merits, as constituting a sham. The Court noted the plaintiffs' allegation that the defendants had used procedural devices, not to win, but to delay and tie up the process, and thus "bar

---

[13]   Id. at 174, 86 S.Ct. at 349. The patent act prevents a firm from patenting something that has been sold in the U.S. for more than a year prior to the patent application. 35 U.S.C.A. § 102(b). For further discussion see § 7.11a of this book.

[14]   *Walker Process*, 382 U.S. at 175–177, 86 S.Ct. at 349–350.

[15]   404 U.S. 508, 92 S.Ct. 609 (1972).

[16]   Id. at 512, 92 S.Ct. at 612. See also Primetime 24 Joint Venture v. NBC, 219 F.3d 92 (2d Cir. 2000) (denying immunity when plaintiff alleged that national networks filed numerous complaints against satellite carrier "without regard to whether the challenges had merit").

[17]   *Trucking Unlimited*, 1967 Trade Cas. ¶ 72928 at 84744 (N.D.Cal. 1967); see Einer Elhauge, Making Sense of Antitrust Petitioning Immunity, 80 Calif. L.Rev. 1177, 1184 (1992).

[18]   404 U.S. at 513, 92 S.Ct. at 613.

their competitors from meaningful access to adjudicatory tribunals and to usurp that decisionmaking process."[19]

§ 15.3   The "Sham" Exception in Legislative and Adjudicative Contexts

The emergent meaning of "sham" is a petition to the government that is nothing more than a subterfuge designed to harass a rival. That is, the rival's injury is intended to result not from the governmental action, for no such action is really anticipated, but rather from the petitioning process itself. Thus, for example, a firm that engages a rival in costly litigation that it has no chance of winning, simply to exhaust the rival's resources, is engaging in a sham. The injury results not from an adverse judicial decision but rather from the litigation process itself.

Suppose a private party does wish government relief but uses improper or perhaps even illegal means to obtain it. Several cases have considered applying the term "sham" to such conduct— particularly to allegations of bribery of a government official, or allegations that the governmental decision maker somehow "conspired" with a private party to exclude the plaintiff from a market.

But the Supreme Court's *Columbia* decision defined "sham" strictly to apply only to those situations where the antitrust defendant's petition to the government is nothing more than a pretext, intended not to obtain government action but to harass a rival through the petitioning process itself.[20] The private antitrust defendant, a well established firm that sold outdoor billboards was faced with competition by the antitrust plaintiff, a newcomer. The defendant allegedly relied on his close relations with the city council and succeeded in obtaining an ordinance that prohibited the newcomer's billboards from being built, but grandparented in its own existing signs.

In finding that there was no sham, the Court ruled out virtually any possibility of claiming a "conspiracy" between a government official and a private party, where the alleged conspiracy was nothing other than a conspiracy to pass a certain statute, take a certain enforcement action, or otherwise engage in activities officially performed by the state. The only exception that the Court recognized

---

[19]   Id. at 512, 92 S.Ct. at 612.

[20]   City of Columbia & Columbia Outdoor Advertising v. Omni Outdoor Advertising, 499 U.S. 365, 381, 111 S.Ct. 1344, 1354 (1991) (although the defendant sought to exclude its rival from the market, it did so "not through the very process of lobbying, or of causing the city council to consider zoning measures, but rather through the ultimate product of that lobbying and consideration, viz., the zoning ordinances").

to *Noerr* petitioning immunity was a market participant exception, where the government itself participated in the market being restrained. But the Court said little about the nature or scope of such an exception. Further, it seems that such an exception would not be counted as a "sham," but merely as a situation where *Noerr* immunity would not apply. In this case, no matter how corrupt or unfair the process may have been, the antitrust defendant really did intend to obtain, and actually obtained, legislation favoring itself at the expense of the antitrust plaintiff.

In *Octane Fitness*, a nonantitrust case, the Supreme Court reiterated that the "sham" litigation exception to *Noerr-Pennington* is "narrow."[21] However, the threatened penalty of attorneys fees for litigation misconduct is far smaller than the threat of liability in antitrust cases based on the "sham" exception. As a result, heightened standards such as proof by clear and convincing evidence need not apply when the court is enforcing a provision that simply awards attorneys fees for improper litigation activities. The issue in *Octane Fitness* was whether such a provision in the Patent Act should be governed by *Noerr* standards.[22] Under the Court's unanimous decision ordinary litigation misrepresentation can continue to be penalized with attorneys fees under other rules, such as Federal Rule of Civil Procedure 11, without running afoul of Noerr's heightened requirements.[23]

One criticism of the now established definition of the "sham" exception is that many instances of governmental petitioning include *both* legitimate and the illegitimate processes. That is to say, the antitrust defendants in *Noerr* and perhaps *Columbia*, intended to use the *process* of petitioning to discourage or exclude rivals, just as much as the sought after governmental decision. In such cases of dual effect, is there a sham?

The qualified answer seems to be no, although the boundaries are not as clear as first appears. If the petitioner reasonably desires governmental action, and if there is an objectively reasonable chance that he will obtain it, then the conduct is not a "sham," notwithstanding that the rival will be injured more by the process than by the government decision itself.[24] *Noerr* itself spoke of the

---

[21]   Octane Fitness, LLC v. ICON Health & Fitness, Inc., 572 U.S. 545 at 556, 134 S.Ct. 1749 at 1757 (2014).

[22]   35 U.S.C. § 285.

[23]   Cf. Borough of Duryea, Pa. v. Guarnieri, 564 U.S. 379 at 390, 131 S.Ct. 2488 at 2496 (2011) (comparing "sham" exception to petitioning immunity to FRCP 11).

[24]   See Static Control Components, Inc. v. Lexmark Intern., Inc., 697 F.3d 387 (6th Cir. 2012), aff'd, 572 U.S. 118, 134 S.Ct. 1377 (2014) (objectively reasonable lawsuit could not be sham even if it was motivated by intent to harm a rival).

"incidental effect" of petitions to the government that were in fact intended to obtain governmental relief.[25]

15.3a.   Use of Abusive Methods; False Information

The *Columbia* decision reiterates that it is not antitrust's purpose to police the political process and correct its shortcomings:

> Any lobbyist or applicant, in addition to getting himself heard, seeks by procedural and other means to get his opponent ignored. Policing the legitimate boundaries of such defensive strategies, when they are conducted in the context of a genuine attempt to influence governmental action, is not the role of the Sherman Act.[26]

But are there any limits to the abuse of political process that the Sherman Act might correct? Suppose a petitioner uses falsified information in making a request to a legislative body or agency for something that will harm a rival. Worse yet, suppose a court litigant relies on false information in order to obtain a decision injuring a rival. Does *Noerr* protect either or both?

At the onset, one must distinguish between false information used to affect the outcome, and false information intended to raise a rival's costs. False information used for the second purpose can be a "sham" because the underlying motive of the person using it is simply to harass the rival. For example, if a firm falsifies its cost figures simply because it knows the rival must spend thousands of dollars uncovering the "mistakes," the sham exception would apply.

The hard case is the firm that uses false information in order to obtain the requested result. If the false information is being used *merely* to increase the rivals' burdens in defending against the claims, or to delay a decision on the rival's request, then the orthodox "sham" exception applies.[27] But if the false information really forms the basis of a government decision that would otherwise have been different, and if the victim can later establish these facts, then there will usually be a remedy under the laws of perjury, abuse of process, libel or slander, and the like. As a general matter, regulation of the

---

   25   Eastern Railroad Presidents Conference v. Noerr Motor Freight, 365 U.S. 127, 142, 81 S.Ct. 523, 532 (1961).

   26   *Columbia*, 499 U.S. at 381, 111 S.Ct. at 1355. Accord, Allied Tube & Conduit Corp. v. Indian Head, 486 U.S. 492, 508 & n. 10, 108 S.Ct. 1931, 1941 & n. 10 (1988). See also Baltimore Scrap Corp. v. David J. Joseph Co., 237 F.3d 394 (4th Cir. 2001), cert. denied, 533 U.S. 916, 121 S.Ct. 2521 (2001) which held that a lawsuit was protected by *Noerr* even though it was secretly financed by a competitor.

   27   See Litton Sys. v. AT & T, 487 F.Supp. 942, 956–58 (S.D.N.Y. 1980) (allegation that filing of false information delayed decision on plaintiff's request could define a "sham").

judicial process ought to be left to the laws and rules designed to control those processes, not to the antitrust laws.

15.3b. Baselessness in the Adjudicative Setting; Successful Claims

One problem with applying the term "sham" to judicial claims is that not every cause of action is a sure winner. Further, different minds may have different opinions about when it is worthwhile to proceed. The mere fact that a person loses is certainly not sufficient evidence that the claim was brought in bad faith.

In *Premier Electrical*, Judge Easterbrook attempted an economic test for "sham" petitioning:

> If the expected value of a judgment is $10,000 (say, a 10% chance of recovering $100,000) the case is not "groundless"; yet if it costs $30,000 to litigate, no rational plaintiff will do so unless he anticipates some other source of benefit. If the other benefit is the costs litigation will impose on a rival, allowing an elevation of the market price, it may be treated as a sham.[28]

There are several things to note about this test. First, "sham" is to be evaluated by a purely objective test; the question is not the state of mind of the person who brought the suit, but rather whether the suit's expected value exceeds its anticipated costs. Second, Judge Easterbrook makes clear that even litigation that is not absolutely "groundless" could be a sham. Indeed, even litigation that the plaintiff ultimately wins could be a sham if, *ex ante*, its expected value is less than its costs.

Third, but ignored by Judge Easterbrook's test, the benefits of litigation may come from other sources than the judgment itself, and one must consider what these are. *Premier Electrical* suggests that litigation could be used to raise a rivals' costs. But there could be quite legitimate reasons for bringing a lawsuit even when anticipated costs exceed immediate benefits. To call these lawsuits a "sham" would be inappropriate. For example, a commercial lender may spend $1000 noisily collecting a $300 debt. It does so, not because it is attempting to monopolize the money lending business, but because it wants to send the right message to its small debtors.[29] If it began to write off delinquent $300 debts because of the high cost of

---

[28]   Premier Electrical Constr. Co. v. National Elec. Contractors Ass'n, 814 F.2d 358, 372 (7th Cir. 1987).

[29]   Raising rivals' costs would certainly not be the reason. First, the debtor is not the creditor's competitor. Second, raising the debtor's costs is contrary to the creditor's interests.

collection, numerous small debtors would default. If the $1000 spent against debtor A also convinces debtor B, C and D that they had better pay up, then the litigation is profitable notwithstanding that it cost more than the anticipated recovery in the case involving A.

Fourth, implementing Judge Easterbrook's test in an antitrust lawsuit would be extraordinarily difficult. Suppose that a firm has a 2% chance of winning a patent infringement suit worth $10,000,000 if it does win, and litigation costs $500,000. In this case, the expected value of the recovery ($200,000) is much less than expected costs. But once again, the patent infringement suit may be designed to send a message to other rivals that the firm in question intends to enforce its patents, even if its claims are rather marginal.[30]

In deciding whether this lawsuit is a sham, the fact finder would have to determine (a) the percentage chance that the claimant would win; (b) the amount of the recovery; (c) the cost of bringing suit; (d) the value of the message sent to other rivals. No court has attempted these computations.

Should the presumption of a well brought claim be conclusive when the suit is successful? In *California Motor Transport*, the Supreme Court appeared to say no. That decision found that the plaintiffs properly alleged that a pattern of repetitive claims, half of which the antitrust defendant won, were in fact a "sham."[31] But there is an alternative explanation. There were apparently many shams among the twenty or so lawsuits that the *California Motor* antitrust defendants lost.[32] The gist of the claim was that the antitrust defendant had brought the suits without regard to merit, and won some by happenstance while it lost others. In *Burlington*, the Fifth Circuit concluded that the "determinative inquiry is not whether the suit was won or lost, but whether it was significantly motivated by a genuine desire for judicial relief."[33] However, then the court went on to note that it was "highly unlikely" that a meritorious suit would not be motivated by a genuine desire for relief.

In *Professional Real Estate*, the Supreme Court made the presumption that a successful suit is not a sham virtually conclusive.

---

[30]   See Erik N. Hovenkamp, Predatory Patent Litigation: How Patent Assertion Entities Use Reputation to Monetize Bad Patents (Northwestern Economics working paper, August 5, 2013), available at http://papers.ssrn.com/sol3/papers.cfm?abstract_id=2308115.

[31]   California Motor Transport Co. v. Trucking Unlimited, 404 U.S. 508, 513, 92 S.Ct. 609, 613 (1972).

[32]   See the district court's opinion, 1967 Trade Cas. (CCH) ¶ 72,928 at 84,744 (N.D.Cal. 1967).

[33]   *Burlington Northern*, 822 F.2d at 527–528, cert. denied, 484 U.S. 1007, 108 S.Ct. 701 (1988).

The Court held that "litigation cannot be deprived of [*Noerr*] immunity as a sham unless the litigation is objectively baseless."[34] The antitrust plaintiff Professional Real Estate (PRE) operated hotels and rented videodiscs containing motion pictures to patrons. The antitrust defendant, Columbia Pictures, sued PRE for violating Columbia's exclusive right to "perform" its copyrighted motion pictures, under the relatively novel claim that watching of a rented videodisc in a hotel room is a "performance." Columbia's copyright infringement case was hardly airtight. However, in other lawsuits filed by Columbia the Third Circuit had held that the watching of video cassettes in private screening rooms constituted a "performance."[35] PRE counterclaimed, alleging that the suit itself was a "sham." The Ninth Circuit first agreed with PRE on the underlying merits, holding that the viewing of videos in a hotel room is not a "performance."[36] However, it later agreed with the district court that since Columbia was "expecting a favorable judgment" in its copyright suit, that suit could not be a "sham." It dismissed PRE's antitrust counterclaim, approving the district court's refusal to permit PRE to engage in further discovery into questions concerning Columbia's motive in bringing the lawsuit in the first place.

In agreeing with the Ninth Circuit, the Supreme Court concluded that an "objectively reasonable effort to litigate cannot be sham regardless of subjective intent."[37] The Court then gave this test:

> First, the lawsuit must be objectively baseless in the sense that no reasonable litigant could realistically expect success on the merits. If an objective litigant could conclude that the suit is reasonably calculated to elicit a favorable outcome, the suit is immunized under *Noerr*, and an antitrust claim premised on the sham exception must fail.[38]

---

[34]   Professional Real Estate Investors v. Columbia Pictures Industries, 508 U.S. 49, 113 S.Ct. 1920 (1993).

[35]   See Columbia Pictures Industries v. Redd Horne, 749 F.2d 154 (3d Cir. 1984); Columbia Pictures Industries v. Aveco, 612 F.Supp. 315 (M.D.Pa. 1985), affirmed, 800 F.2d 59 (3d Cir. 1986).

[36]   Columbia Pictures Industries, Inc. v. Professional Real Estate Investors, Inc., 866 F.2d 278 (9th Cir. 1989).

[37]   Ibid.

[38]   The Court noted in a footnote:

A winning lawsuit is by definition a reasonable effort at petitioning for redress and therefore not a sham. On the other hand, when the antitrust defendant has lost the underlying litigation, a court must "resist the understandable temptation to engage in post hoc reasoning by concluding" that an ultimately unsuccessful "action must have been unreasonable or without foundation."

PRE, 508 U.S. at 60 n. 5, 113 S.Ct. at 1928 n. 5 (quoting Christiansburg Garment Co. v. EEOC, 434 U.S. 412, 421–422, 98 S.Ct. 694, 700–701 (1978)). See Avaya Inc., RP v. Telecom Labs, Inc., 838 F.3d 354, 404 (3d Cir. 2016) (fact that some of the claims made

Only if challenged litigation is objectively meritless may a court examine the litigant's subjective motivation. Under this second part of our definition of sham, the court should focus on whether the baseless lawsuit conceals "an attempt to interfere directly with the business relationships of a competitor," * * *[39]

The court then suggested that the common law tort of "malicious prosecution" captured most of the concerns that were relevant to identifying a "sham." "[T]he plaintiff [must] prove that the defendant lacked probable cause to institute an unsuccessful civil lawsuit and that the defendant pressed the action for an improper, malicious purpose."[40] In this context, probable cause requires no more than a "reasonabl[e] belie[f] that there is a chance that [a] claim may be held valid upon adjudication."[41] Further, since "the absence of probable cause is an essential element of the tort, the existence of probable cause is an absolute defense."[42]

15.3c. Single or Repetitive Claims

California Motor Transport defined sham in terms of "* * * a pattern of baseless, repetitive claims * * * which leads the factfinder to conclude that the administrative and judicial processes have been abused."[43] The Court was only describing the kinds of evidence that tends to show sham—a single baseless claim might be an oversight, but multiple claims cannot be so easily excused. At the time the first claim is rebuffed, the claimant should have been given reasons why it was improper. A firm which brings the same baseless claim a second time is more likely bringing the suit to harass.

A few courts have held quite categorically that a single baseless lawsuit cannot be a "sham."[44] But one lawsuit can be very expensive and can tie up the parties' resources for many years. As a result, to conclude categorically that a single lawsuit is never a "sham" would give firms carte blanche to use complicated, drawn out litigation strategically without fear of antitrust consequences. If the lawsuit was manifestly unreasonable, that fact should emerge either before

---

in the course of large antitrust case involving a four-month trial were frivolous did not serve to make the case itself a sham).

  [39] 508 U.S. at 50, 113 S.Ct. at 1922, quoting *Noerr*, at 144.

  [40] Id. at 61, 113 S.Ct. at 1929.

  [41] Ibid., citing Restatement (Second) of Torts § 675, Comment e, pp. 454–455 (1977).

  [42] 508 U.S. at 62–63, 113 S.Ct. at 1929.

  [43] California Motor Transport Co. v. Trucking Unlimited, 404 U.S. 508, 513, 92 S.Ct. 609, 613 (1972).

  [44] E.g., Loctite Corp. v. Fel-Pro, 1978–2 Trade Cas. ¶ 62204, 1978 WL 1385 (N.D.Ill. 1978).

the lawsuit is filed or while it is in progress. Further, sometimes "sham" takes the form of repetitive filings or demands made within a single lawsuit. The majority of circuits passing on the issue now hold that a single lawsuit can, under appropriate circumstances, be an antitrust violation. Other courts have recognized that a single lawsuit can be a sham, but only if it involves "serious misconduct."[45] In *Professional Real Estate*,[46] the Supreme Court made only a few passing references to "repetitiveness," but the clear implication was that repetition is not decisive either way. Rather, the fact that claims were brought repetitively is a piece of objective evidence to be used to determine bad faith.

The other side of the coin is that plurality of lawsuits does not necessarily prove sham. This is clearly true where the suits are brought in different jurisdictions. For example, state laws differ, so a loss on an issue in one state court does not dictate a loss on the same issue in the courts of a different state. Even where there is conflict among the federal circuit courts, a firm might be entitled to seek the ruling of a second federal court, if principles of collateral estoppel do not foreclose it.

Ultimately the meaning of repetitive claims presents a fact question, just as the question of substantive reasonableness itself.[47] The fact that challenged claims are repetitive can be of great importance, especially if the first dismissal gave the claimant objectively sound reasons for thinking that the subsequent claim is without merit.

15.3d.   Threat to Sue; Ex Parte Statements

Suppose a firm who believes its patent or copyright has been infringed by a rival writes a letter: "either stop selling this (product or process), or else I will sue." Clearly, the writing of such letters by dominant firms could chill competition. Is the letter itself protected under *Noerr*?

The answer must be yes, even though a threat to sue involves no petition to the government at all. Our entire dispute resolution process is designed to encourage people to resolve their differences if possible before litigating; and to settle out of court once litigation has

---

[45]   Razorback Ready Mix Concrete Co. v. Weaver, 761 F.2d 484, 487 (8th Cir. 1985). The court found no serious misconduct, and did not specify what it might be.

[46]   Professional Real Estate Investors v. Columbia Pictures Industries, 508 U.S. 49, 113 S.Ct. 1920 (1993).

[47]   See, e.g., USS-POSCO Indus. v. Contra Costa Cty. Bldg. & Constr. Trades Council, 31 F.3d 800, 811 (9th Cir. 1994) (repetitive nature of claims, even if some are upheld, is relevant to whether defendant had a "policy of starting legal proceedings without regard to the merits and for the purpose of injuring a market rival").

been filed. A rule that held that litigation is protected but that the pre-litigation "demand letter" is not would encourage firms to litigate first.[48]

Of course the threat of *baseless* litigation should not be given any more protection than the baseless litigation itself.[49] Likewise, a threat to sue by someone who has no intention of suing should be denied protection, for the simple reason that such a threat does *not* constitute a petition to the government, no matter how broadly defined.[50] For the same reasons, statements made by one party to litigation to an opponent's customers, to the media, or other private persons should not be protected. Suppose, for example, that a plaintiff in litigation sends a copy of the complaint to the defendant's customers. The sending of a document to a private person is not a petition to the government. Of course, if the plaintiff's purpose is to warn customers that they themselves will be legally liable for purchasing the defendant's product, then the letter would fall into the category of threats to sue, and should enjoy *Noerr* immunity if the lawsuit itself arguably has merit.

Finally, note that while the litigation and settlement process is protected by *Noerr*, the *content* of the settlement is not. A good illustration is "pay for delay" settlements, where the Supreme Court held in *Actavis* that a settlement of a patent dispute could be an antitrust violation.[51] As a result, the fact that a pay-for-delay settlement is a settlement does not immunize it from antitrust challenge by third parties. Occasionally a court is tripped by this. For example, a few have suggested, mainly in dicta, that if the settlement is overseen by a judge its substance might enjoy *Noerr* immunity.[52] Not only is that substantively incorrect, it also represents a fundamental misunderstanding of the jurisdiction of courts, which can bind only parties. A litigation settlement limits subsequent

---

[48]   See Rock River Communications, Inc. v. Universal Music Group, Inc., 745 F.3d 343, 352 (9th Cir. 2013) (if firm had a reasonable belief in its entitlement to relief at the time it sent out cease-and-desist notes about copyright infringement the activity was protected by *Noerr*).

[49]   CVD v. Raytheon Co., 769 F.2d 842, 850 (1st Cir. 1985), cert. denied, 475 U.S. 1016, 106 S.Ct. 1198 (1986) (applying same standard to threat to sue and lawsuit itself).

[50]   But see Cardtoons v. Major League Baseball Players' Ass'n, 182 F.3d 1132 (10th Cir. 1999), reversed on other grds. on rehearing, 208 F.3d 885 (10th Cir. 2000) which concluded that threats to sue made with probable cause were protected under *Noerr* even though the threats were never carried out.

[51]   FTC v. Actavis, Inc., 570 U.S. 136 at 143, 133 S.Ct. 2223 at 2228 (2013). See § 5.5c3.

[52]   Androgel Antitrust Litig., 2014 WL 1600331, at *6, 2014-1 Trade Cas. ¶ 78,744 (N.D. Ga. Apr. 21, 2014) (*Noerr* immunity may be justified if the parties "work with" the judge "to develop a judgment and order" that the judge signs).

actions by the parties, but it does not operate against others who were not parties to the litigation. For example, if competitors A and B settle a dispute with an anticompetitive market division agreement third parties such as consumers would still be able to challenge that agreement as an antitrust violation.[53] To hold otherwise would empower the court to bind people who were not parties to the litigation.

15.3e. Petitions for Invalid Legislation and Administrative Rules

The right to petition exists even if what the petitioner seeks subsequently turns out to be unconstitutional or unlawful. For example, suppose a taxicab firm requests a new municipal ordinance giving it a monopoly on travel from downtown to the airport. The ordinance is passed but is later held invalid under the "state action" doctrine because it was inadequately authorized by state law.[54] *Ex ante*, reasonable people could differ about the legality of the ordinance, and in this case the members of the city council apparently thought it was valid. The right to petition would lose much of its meaning if we attached a kind of strict liability to petitioners for ordinances subsequently found invalid.[55]

But to make the case a little stronger, suppose that the petitioner knew at the time the petition was made that the requested ordinance or administrative rule was unconstitutional or invalid. Once again, if the legislative body or agency accepts the petition, *and the injury is caused by the resulting rule*, then it would seem that *Noerr* should apply. In this case, the *cause* of the injury is the government's passage of the rule, which injures the plaintiff during the time it is in force.[56]

As noted above, however, petitioning activity is a "sham" when it is intended, not to obtain the explicitly requested response, but when the process itself is intended to impose burdens on rivals. The

---

[53] See 1 Antitrust Law ¶ 205g (5th ed. 2020).

[54] See Ch. 17.

[55] See In re Airport Car Rental Antitrust Litig., 521 F.Supp. 568, 583–585 (N.D.Cal. 1981), affirmed, 693 F.2d 84 (9th Cir. 1982), cert. denied, 462 U.S. 1133, 103 S.Ct. 3114 (1983) (*Noerr* immunity could exist even if requested action was invalid under "state action" doctrine); Greenwood Utilities Commn. v. Mississippi Power Co., 751 F.2d 1484, 1500 (5th Cir. 1985):

> * * * in the administrative context, an ultimate determination that agency action sought was unauthorized by statute should not remove protection for petitioning conduct directed to the agency to obtain that action. * * * [A] contrary result would * * * chill petitioning activity. * * *

[56] See *Airport Car Rental*, 521 F.Supp. at 574: "If plaintiff suffered injury, it resulted from the acts of public officials declining to lease space to plaintiff * * * and not the joint action of the defendants. * * *"

fact that the sought-for ordinance or rule is unconstitutional could certainly be evidence of sham. If any reasonable person acquainted with the law should know that the requested act is unlawful, the probability is increased that the request itself is not intended to elicit the government act, but only to harass the rival.

§ 15.4 Corruption of Private Decision Making Bodies

In Allied Tube & Conduit Corp. v. Indian Head,[57] the Supreme Court considered whether *Noerr* immunity extended to "petitions" made to a private standard-setting organization that had a great deal of influence on legislation. Indian Head, a maker of plastic conduit, alleged that Allied and other firms who manufactured steel conduit corrupted the processes of the National Fire Protection Association (NFPA) by packing a meeting with its own agents. NFPA was not a governmental entity, but rather a standard-setting association made up of private business firms. The defendants were able to obtain a decision from the standard-setting association disapproving plastic conduit for building construction. NFPA had no authority to pass legislation, of course, but its recommendations were closely followed by numerous state and local governments, which incorporated them into building codes.

In the *Allied Tube* case itself, the plaintiffs had claimed injury as a result of the stigma attached to plastic conduct as a result of the anti-plastic rule. With respect to such injuries, there was no relevant petition to the government. The Supreme Court began with the proposition that *Noerr* immunity might apply to petitions to private bodies, but only if the petition were nothing more than a kind of indirect attempt to obtain a subsequent governmental action. That is to say, *Noerr* does not exempt petitions to private bodies if the body itself then makes rules that are enforced through voluntary compliance or some other means:

> * * * where * * * an economically interested party exercises decision-making authority in formulating a product standard for a private association that comprises market participants, that party enjoys no *Noerr* immunity from any antitrust liability flowing from the effect the standard has *of its own force in the marketplace*.[58]

---

[57]   486 U.S. 492, 108 S.Ct. 1931 (1988). The Allied Tube petition is best viewed as a collusive restraint on innovation. See Christina Bohannan & Herbert Hovenkamp, Creation Without Restraint: Promoting Rivalry in Innovation, Ch. 5 (2011).

[58]   Id. at 510, 108 S.Ct. at 1942 (emphasis added).

For example, suppose that the great majority of retailers have a policy of selling electric appliances only if they meet standards promulgated by a trade association's private testing laboratory. A member of the association corruptly obtains a decision from the laboratory board disapproving the plaintiff's product, and numerous stores then decide not to sell that product. *Noerr* plays no role in such a case: no governmental action was sought, and none was obtained.

A much more problematic case arises if (1) the antitrust defendant corrupted the private standard-setting body; (2) the body responded with the anticompetitive rule; (3) local governments enact the anticompetitive rule into law simply on the basis of the standard-setting body's recommendation; and (4) the plaintiff's only injury results from the effect of the enacted laws themselves. Most of the concerns that *Noerr* evokes seem to apply. The failure is one of political process, not of market process. That is, in this case local governments are insufficiently attentive to the biases and distortions that might make recommendations from private trade associations unreliable.

But the problem cannot be disposed of quite this easily. In many areas private rule making takes place in highly technical areas where expertise is necessary and the cost of making fact determinations is extremely high. Furthermore, government officials are generalists and, especially at the local level, do not command the resources necessary to make their own inquiries into the reasonableness of professional recommendations. Following the private decision without a detailed inquiry into the merits is not necessarily a result of inattentiveness; it may be inherent in governmental process in technical areas of policy making.

The question then becomes whether those private market participants engaged in standard setting or rule making have a kind of "fiduciary duty" to the public—and, if so, whether the duty is to be enforced by the antitrust laws. As the degree of government abdication grows stronger, so does the case for denying *Noerr* immunity. Suppose, for example, that the state simply passes a statute stating "the standard for electric installations in this state is that promulgated by the National Fire Protection Association." In that case, corruption of NFPA that results in the exclusion of plastic conduit should not enjoy *Noerr* immunity even if the injury results entirely from subsequent government "enactment" of the NFPA standard. The government's "pre-commitment" has effectively made its act nothing more than ministerial. Of course, in most situations the government's prior commitment will be much more ambiguous, involving perhaps a historical pattern of following the private association's recommendations with little debate, but with no statutory commitment to do so.

Chapter 16

ANTITRUST AND FEDERAL REGULATORY POLICY

Table of Sections

§ 16.1 The Role of Antitrust in the Regulated Market

An industry is said to be "regulated" when the conduct of its sellers is subject to government control over the price a firm charges, the amount it can produce, the identity of the firms that can participate, or the quality of the product. All firms are "regulated" to some degree, but only few regulations create issues under the antitrust laws. As an abstract proposition, antitrust's task is: (1) to stand aside as a government pursues its regulatory goals, whatever those goals may be; (2) to make markets perform more competitively, given the regulatory regime that happens to control them; and (3) to scrutinize private conduct that is not effectively reviewed or controlled by the regulatory regime. The less room there is for competition and private discretion, the less the role for antitrust.

16.1a. Express or Implied Repeal

The case for limiting the role of antitrust in the regulated industries is strongest when the federal regulatory statute *expressly* exempts firms from antitrust liability. For example, the Shipping Act of 1984 contains a set of antitrust-like provisions that apply to common carriers regulated by the Federal Maritime Commission, and expressly prohibits private antitrust actions based on activities within the jurisdiction of that agency.[1] Likewise, federal statutes regulating railroads and trucking permit firms to engage in joint rate making without running afoul of the antitrust policy against collusion.[2] By contrast, in other cases, the federal regulatory statute may contemplate concurrent federal or even state antitrust authority. For example, in *Oneok* the Supreme Court concluded that provisions of the Natural Gas Act had been "meticulously" drafted in order to protect the authority of individual states to engage in regulation of natural gas transactions within their territory. Further, this included application of state antitrust law to gas sellers within the jurisdiction of the federal agency (FERC), at least state antitrust law did not conflict with the federal regulatory regime.[3]

Most regulatory statutes say nothing at all about the impact of the regulatory regime on antitrust jurisdiction. In these cases, any limitation on or exemption from antitrust must be considered as implied rather than express. Once again, the domain of such exemptions is narrow. As the Supreme Court has said, "Repeals of the antitrust laws by implication from a regulatory statute are strongly disfavored, and have only been found in cases of plain repugnancy between the antitrust and regulatory provisions."[4]

16.1b. The Relation Between Federal Regulation and Antitrust Jurisdiction: Two Views

The traditional approach to antitrust in the regulated industries viewed regulation as a closed box, and a particular market as either

---

[1]   46 U.S.C.A. § 1706. See Vehicle Carrier Servs. Antitrust Litig., 846 F.3d 71 (3d Cir. 2017), cert. denied sub nom. Alban v. Nippon Yusen Kabushiki Kaisha, 138 S.Ct. 114 (2017) (Shipping Act barred federal antitrust claims and, by reasonable inference, state antitrust claims).

[2]   Motor Carrier Act of 1980, 49 U.S.C.A. § 10706(b) ("A rail carrier * * * that is a party to an agreement of at least two rail carriers * * * that relates to rates * * * shall apply to the Commission for approval of that agreement. * * * If the Commission approves * * * the Sherman Act, the Clayton Act, the Federal Trade Commission Act * * * do not apply * * * with respect to making or carrying out the agreement"); Staggers Rail Act of 1980, 49 U.S.C.A. § 10706(a) (same).

[3]   See Oneok, Inc. v. Learjet, Inc., 575, U.S. 373, 135 S.Ct. 1591 (2015).

[4]   United States v. Philadelphia National Bank, 374 U.S. 321, 350–351, 83 S.Ct. 1715, 1735 (1963); 1A Antitrust Law ¶ 243 (5th ed. 2020).

inside or outside of the box. A market was either "regulated" or "unregulated." If the former, antitrust was generally unwelcome or at least seriously confined. Within this paradigm, the antitrust tribunal was generally called upon to determine the "pervasiveness" of the regulatory regime. All activities within a pervasively regulated regime were presumptively exempt from antitrust scrutiny.[5] This approach is built on a rather optimistic model of agency decision making. In an ideal regulatory regime, an agency considering a regulated firm's request would determine all relevant social and economic implications, including the impact on competition. Such a model would be efficient, because the entire record could be developed comprehensively, showing all effects of regulation in a single elaborate proceeding.

But the deregulation movement has changed our perceptions of both the nature and the domain of regulation. First, real world decision making is never as comprehensive or elegant as the previous paragraph suggests. Invariably, agencies do *not* pass on every relevant issue. No matter how "thick" the underlying regime, the agency does not collect all relevant information and consider all relevant factors. Indeed, often it may not consider certain antitrust-related issues at all.

In this regard, the lustre that regulation wore during the Progressive Era and New Deal has been tarnished considerably.[6] Today we are more likely to think of regulation as expensive, unwieldy, and highly imperfect insofar as its stated goal is to mimic market behavior. As a result, when market forces are working properly, we want them to have free rein, even *within* the regulated market.

Second, today we are more inclined to think of *all* markets as "regulated" to some degree. Antitrust itself is a form of "regulation"— that is, of sovereign intervention into the marketplace to force a solution different from the one that unrestrained private bargaining would produce. Viewed in this way, even property, tort and contract rules established under the common law are a form of regulation.

Within this perspective, the whole question of antitrust involvement becomes much more particularized, in two different senses. First, the pervasiveness of the general regulatory regime is

---

5   See Hughes Tool Co. v. Trans World Airlines, Inc., 409 U.S. 363, 93 S.Ct. 647 (1973) (finding pervasive scheme); Otter Tail Power Co. v. United States, 410 U.S. 366, 93 S.Ct. 1022 (1973) (no pervasive regulatory scheme for wholesale electric power; so no immunity); *Philadelphia Natl. Bank*, 374 U.S. at 352, 83 S.Ct. at 1735 (same).

6   For a historical glimpse, See Thomas K. McCraw, Prophets of Regulation (1984).

relatively unimportant.[7] Second, we generally do not divide the territory into "regulated" and "unregulated" firms. Rather, we consider whether the specific activity in question is or should be "regulated by the agency" or "regulated by the antitrust laws." What we really want to know is whether the conduct being challenged was instigated by a public regulatory agency, or perhaps approved after a fairly full review of the merits; or whether the challenged restraint resulted from the essentially unsupervised conduct of a private firm. If the latter, then it should be regarded as "market" conduct and the antitrust laws should presumptively apply.[8] In such cases, the court will generally deny the immunity unless application of the antitrust laws would create a "clear repugnancy" between the regulatory statute at issue and federal antitrust policy.[9]

In sum, whether the regulatory regime is "pervasive" is not nearly as important as is the answer to questions such as (1) whether the conduct being challenged was within the jurisdiction of the agency; (2) whether it was actually presented to the agency for review; (3) whether the agency appropriately reviewed potential anticompetitive consequences; (4) whether application of the antitrust laws in this particular instance would create inconsistent mandates or would frustrate the operation of the regulatory process; and (5) whether the agency has special expertise not generally available to antitrust tribunals to evaluate a particular claim.[10]

For example, in *Gordon* the Supreme Court held that antitrust scrutiny over alleged fixing of brokerage commissions would collide with the New York Stock Exchange's authority to set the rules governing how brokerage rates should be set.[11] In *Credit Suisse* the Supreme Court spoke much more categorically about implied immunity doctrine.[12] The plaintiffs, stock purchasers, alleged an

---

[7]   See 1A Antitrust Law ¶ 243e (5th ed. 2020).

[8]   National Gerimedical Hosp. v. Blue Cross, 452 U.S. 378, 101 S.Ct. 2415 (1981) (immunity denied where no regulatory agency was empowered to supervise the challenged conduct).

[9]   Id. at 389, 101 S.Ct. at 2422.

[10]   For interesting historical perspective, see Howard Shelanski, Justice Breyer, Professor Kahn, and Antitrust Enforcement in Regulated Industries, 100 Cal. L. Rev. 487 (2012). See also Herbert Hovenkamp, Regulation and the Marginalist Revolution, 71 Fl. L. Rev. 455 (2019) (on contestable market theory as applied in regulation); and Symposium on the history of regulation, introduced by Laura Phillips Sawyer and Herbert Hovenkamp, New Perspectives on Regulatory History, 93 Bus. Hist Rev. 659 (2019).

[11]   Gordon v. New York Stock Exchange, 422 U.S. 659, 95 S.Ct. 2598 (1975). Accord Stock Exchanges Options Trading Antitrust Litigation, 317 F.3d 134 (2d Cir. 2003); Friedman v. Salomon/Smith Barney, 313 F.3d 796 (2d Cir. 2002), cert. denied, 540 U.S. 822, 124 S.Ct. 152 (2003).

[12]   Credit Suisse Securities (USA), LLC v. Billing, 551 U.S. 264, 127 S.Ct. 2383 (2007).

enormous conspiracy among the writers of IPOs (initial public
offerings, or first issuances of stock) to manipulate the market
through restrictions on how new stock offerings were sold, with the
result that these stock prices were greatly inflated. IPOs are typically
issued through "syndicates," or joint ventures, of investment banking
firms, largely in order to reduce risk. The syndicates themselves had
been common in the industry and legally approved for half a
century.[13]

Looking back over its previous implied immunity decisions in
the securities industry, the Court found that the "centrality" of the
challenged conduct to the regulatory agency's supervisory role was
crucial to a finding of immunity. The Court found these factors
important:

> (1) the existence of regulatory authority under the
> securities law to supervise the activities in question; (2)
> evidence that the responsible regulatory entities exercise
> that authority; and (3) a resulting risk that the securities
> and antitrust laws, if both applicable, would produce
> conflicting guidance, requirements, duties, privileges, or
> standards of conduct. We also note (4) that in *Gordon*[14] and
> *NASD*[15] the possible conflict affected practices that lie
> squarely within an area of financial market activity that
> the securities law seeks to regulate.

Here, the joint underwriting activities at issue were clearly
central to the running of a well functioning capital market. Further,

> The IPO process supports new firms that seek to raise
> capital; it helps to spread ownership of those firms broadly
> among investors; it directs capital flows in ways that better
> correspond to the public's demand for goods and services.
> Moreover, financial experts, including the securities
> regulators, consider the general kind of joint underwriting
> activity at issue in this case, including road shows and book-
> building efforts essential to the successful marketing of an
> IPO.[16]

More importantly, all of the challenged activities were within the
regulatory jurisdiction of the SEC, which possessed considerable

---

[13]   See United States v. Morgan, 118 F.Supp. 621, 635 (S.D.N.Y. 1953) (rejecting
government's claim that syndicated underwriting was inherently collusive).

[14]   See *supra*, 422 U.S. 659.

[15]   Referring to United States v. National Assn. of Securities Dealers (NASD), 422
U.S. 694, 95 S.Ct. 2427 (1975) (granting immunity from challenges to alleged resale
price maintenance and limitations on inter-dealer sales).

[16]   Ibid.

power to oversee them and prevent misconduct. Further, there was nothing to suggest that the SEC was not carrying out this regulatory mandate faithfully. In this particular area "securities law and antitrust law are clearly incompatible."

The Court was particularly concerned about the problem of multiple tribunals evaluating the same conduct and coming to potentially inconsistent conclusions, and the generalist nature of antitrust proceedings would exacerbate these results.[17]

16.1c.   Requisite Regulatory Oversight; "State Action" Compared

How much regulatory oversight is necessary to make particular conduct immune from antitrust scrutiny? The Supreme Court has had little to say on that question in the context of federally regulated industries. However, as the following chapter notes, the Court has said a great deal concerning the amount of "active supervision" that a *state* regulatory agency must engage in before private activity qualifies for the state action exemption. There is no obvious reason why the standard should be any different. That is, once we have concluded that the regulatory regime itself has been properly authorized and is operating within its jurisdiction, we want to assure ourselves that private conduct has been reviewed with the suitable degree of attentiveness. This question should be about the same for both federal and state agencies.[18] In the context of state action, the Supreme Court's 2015 decision in the *North Carolina Dental* case, discussed in the next chapter, re-emphasized the need for independent supervision by a sufficiently disinterested government official.[19]

A few decisions have looked to the Supreme Court's "state action" decisions in determining the degree of scrutiny that is appropriate when federal regulation is in question. For example, in *American Agriculture Movement*[20] the Seventh Circuit relied on *Ticor Title Insurance*,[21] a state action decision involving state regulatory agencies, to query into the degree of supervision required of a federal agency:

---

[17]   Credit Suisse, 551 U.S. at 282–283, 127 S.Ct. at 2395–2396.

[18]   On the "active supervision" requirement of the state action doctrine, see § 20.5.

[19]   N.C. State Board of Dental Examiners v. FTC, 574 U.S. 494, 135 S.Ct. 1101 (2015). See § 20.5a.

[20]   American Agriculture Movement v. Board of Trade, City of Chicago, 977 F.2d 1147 (7th Cir. 1992).

[21]   FTC v. Ticor Title Ins. Co., 504 U.S. 621, 112 S.Ct. 2169 (1992), on remand, 998 F.2d 1129 (3d Cir. 1993). See § 20.5b.

[I]mmunity is proper when the relevant agency's scrutiny and approval of the challenged practice is active, intrusive and appropriately deliberative. Put another way, an antitrust court, before relinquishing jurisdiction over allegedly anticompetitive activities, must be convinced that the agency has exercised its independent judgment in reflecting upon and approving the activity at issue.[22]

This required a level of scrutiny that "focuses on the extent to which an administrative agency has actually exercised its supervisory powers over the particular practices at issue."[23] In sum, that inquiry is essentially the same, whether the source of the regulation is the federal government or the states or their properly authorized subdivisions.

The Supreme Court's 2004 *Trinko* decision revisited these issues in a dispute not implicating regulatory immunity as such.[24] The case involved an incumbent telephone carrier's obligation to "interconnect" with rivals so that they could have effective access to the telecommunications system. The 1996 Telecommunications Act, which imposed the interconnection requirement, also contained an antitrust savings clause that the Court read as precluding regulatory immunity.[25] The issue was whether a failure to interconnect in violation of the Telecommunications Act also created liability under § 2 of the Sherman Act. The Supreme Court held that the antitrust laws should not be applied. In this case both federal and state agencies had oversight over interconnection disputes, and they had already responded to the same complaints by disciplining the defendant through the regulatory process. In such a setting, "regulation significantly diminishes the likelihood of major antitrust harm."[26] In addition, the claim of unlawful refusal to deal that the plaintiffs were asserting was extremely complex and the error rate was very high.[27] In this setting, the Court concluded, the antitrust

---

[22]   *American Agriculture Movement*, 977 F.2d at 1166, relying on *Ticor Title*, 504 U.S. at 633–634, 112 S.Ct. at 2177. The court found the scrutiny inadequate.

[23]   *American Agriculture Movement*, 977 F.2d at 1158.

[24]   Verizon Communications, Inc. v. Law Offices of Curtis V. Trinko, LLP, 540 U.S. 398, 124 S.Ct. 872 (2004).

[25]   47 U.S.C. § 152: "... nothing in this Act ... shall be construed to modify, impair, or supersede the applicability of any of the antitrust laws." On antitrust in the regulatory regime for telecommunications see Herbert Hovenkamp, Antitrust and the Regulatory Enterprise, 2004 Col.Bus.L.Rev. 335, 366–377; Howard A. Shelanski, The Case for Rebalancing Antitrust and Regulation, 100 Mich. L. Rev. 683 (2011).

[26]   *Trinko*, 540 U.S. at 412–413, 124 S.Ct. at 881, quoting Concord v. Boston Edison Co., 915 F.2d 17, 25 (1st Cir. 1990).

[27]   *Trinko*, 540 U.S. at 412–414, 124 S.Ct. at 882–883. On unilateral refusal to deal claims, see §§ 7.5–7.7.

laws could not realistically add anything to the discipline that the regulatory agencies already provided.

§ 16.2   Procedure in Areas of Divided Authority; "Primary Jurisdiction"

The "primary jurisdiction" doctrine, as its name implies, is not an antitrust exemption but a mechanism for proceeding with a case that may involve an antitrust claim in an agency regulated industry. When a regulatory regime completely ousts the antitrust court, the regulatory agency's jurisdiction over the claim is said to be "exclusive."

Even when courts have some jurisdiction to resolve antitrust disputes in a regulated market, some deference to the regulatory agency may be in order. This is particularly true of cases where the agency is better situated than the court to make complex factual determinations. Further, the agency may be in a much better position than the court to evaluate how the antitrust claim fits into the entire regulatory picture.

In Ricci v. Chicago Mercantile Exchange, the Supreme Court elaborated on the rationale and process of the primary jurisdiction doctrine.[28] Ricci, a broker, claimed that he had been denied a seat on the Exchange as a result of a concerted refusal to deal involving the Exchange itself and at least one Exchange member. The Commodity Exchange Commission had oversight of the exchange and its rule making, and the plaintiff was alleging violations of the Commodity Exchange Act as well as the Sherman Act. The Supreme Court held that the antitrust court should stay its hand until the Commission had had a chance to decide. Importantly, this was not an exclusive jurisdiction case: the Commission did not have the power to confer antitrust immunity. Rather, it was to determine what the Exchange policies were and whether they had been violated in this case. If the rule had been violated, then there was nothing to prevent the antitrust litigation from proceeding. If the rule had not been violated, then perhaps the antitrust dispute could proceed in any event, but first the court would have to determine whether use of the antitrust laws to condemn conduct permitted under a rule approved by the Commission created a fundamental inconsistency justifying a limited antitrust exemption.[29]

Where the primary jurisdiction doctrine operates, it can have two effects. In some cases a federal court will simply stay its

---

[28]   409 U.S. 289, 93 S.Ct. 573 (1973).

[29]   Id. at 307, 93 S.Ct. at 583.

proceedings pending an agency resolution of a particular issue.[30] In other cases the antitrust suit will be dismissed without prejudice and the antitrust plaintiff effectively told to take its case to the agency first.[31] If the plaintiff files its antitrust claim in court on time, and the court defers to the regulatory agency, then the statute of limitation has been tolled even though agency resolution will run beyond the four year limit.

Also problematic is the weight that the antitrust court must give to the fact findings made by the regulatory agency. In *Ricci*, the Supreme Court suggested that issues actually determined in the agency proceeding would not have to be relitigated in the subsequent judicial proceeding—that is, there should be a kind of collateral estoppel, or issue preclusion, as between the agency and the court.[32] Often this could be a peculiar outcome to say the least, because very likely the antitrust plaintiff was not a party in the agency proceeding. Often, when a competitor, consumer or other aggrieved person complains to a regulatory agency, the parties to the inquiry that results are the agency and the firm against which the complaint is brought. The complainant itself is merely a witness. To bind a non-party to an adverse judgment of the agency might violate due process. Of course, if the complainant is a party, collateral estoppel or res judicata could apply.[33] A better way to view the matter in such cases is that the court should give some deference to the agency's expertise, but cannot consider itself bound by the judgment. By contrast, if the complainant wins in the regulatory agency, then there may be a good case for nonmutual, or "offensive" collateral estoppel. The antitrust defendant, or the firm that lost in the regulatory proceeding, *was* a party there, and could be bound to the extent that an issue was the same, was fully and fairly litigated and essential to the outcome.[34] Even then, courts may refuse to apply offensive collateral estoppel if the agency had different burdens of proof than the court, used

---

[30]   Segal v. AT & T, 606 F.2d 842 (9th Cir. 1979) (staying proceeding pending FCC resolution of administrative claims).

[31]   For example, Sea-Land Serv. v. Alaska R.R., 1980–2 Trade Cas. (CCH) ¶ 63481 at 76527, 1980 WL 1881 (D.D.C. 1980), affirmed on other grounds, 659 F.2d 243 (D.C.Cir. 1981), cert. denied, 455 U.S. 919, 102 S.Ct. 1274 (1982).

[32]   *Ricci*, 409 U.S. at 305, 93 S.Ct. at 582.

[33]   See Aunyx Corp. v. Canon U.S.A., 978 F.2d 3 (1st Cir. 1992), cert. denied, 507 U.S. 973, 113 S.Ct. 1416 (1993) (dealer who was a party, and who lost conspiracy claim before International Trade Commission, could not bring subsequent federal court antitrust suit).

[34]   City of Anaheim v. Southern Cal. Edison Co., 1990–2 Trade Cas. ¶ 69246, 1990 WL 209261 (C.D.Cal. 1990) (no offensive collateral estoppel where price/cost issues addressed by agency did not include all elements of an attempt to monopolize claim).

different rules of evidence, or had substantially different procedures.[35]

§ 16.3   Particular Exemptions

A detailed survey of the voluminous regulatory exemptions accorded under federal law is beyond the scope of this volume. What is offered here is a brief description of the most important antitrust exemptions, with particular attention to the labor exemption and the insurance exemption.

16.3a.   Miscellaneous Express Exemptions

Agricultural cooperatives are granted an antitrust exemption in § 6 of the Clayton Act[36] and the Capper-Volstead Act.[37] The statutes permit agricultural producers to agree with each other to set price and output, but in *Borden* the Supreme Court held that agreements between producers and non-producers were not exempt.[38] Likewise, although the exemption applies to price-fixing, it does not apply to exclusionary practices such as predatory pricing.[39]

Today ocean common carriers are regulated by the Federal Maritime Commission (FMC) under the Shipping Act of 1984.[40] Under that Act ocean shippers may file a common tariff, or rate, with the FMC. The rates are then presumptively exempt from the antitrust laws. If part of the conduct is alleged to fall outside the broad 1984 Shipping Act exemptions and is claimed to violate the antitrust laws, the private plaintiff may bring a court action for the non-exempt part.[41] The Airline Deregulation Act of 1978 creates at least an implied immunity from state antitrust law which might

---

[35]   See, for example, Borough of Ellwood City v. Pennsylvania Power Co., 570 F.Supp. 553, 560 (W.D.Pa. 1983) (declining to apply offensive collateral estoppel because agency did not have jurisdiction over federal antitrust claims, could not give the relief requested, and was willing to accept defenses that would not have been accepted to an antitrust claim).

[36]   15 U.S.C.A. § 17.

[37]   7 U.S.C.A. §§ 291–292.

[38]   United States v. Borden Co., 308 U.S. 188, 60 S.Ct. 182 (1939) (denying exemption for dairy price fixing agreement involving dairy cooperative, processors, distributors and a labor union). Compare National Broiler Marketing Association v. United States, 436 U.S. 816, 98 S.Ct. 2122 (1978), refusing to extend the exemption to non-farmer processors of agricultural products.

[39]   Maryland & Virginia Milk Producers Assn. v. United States, 362 U.S. 458, 80 S.Ct. 847 (1960).

[40]   49 U.S.C.A. App. §§ 1701–1720.

[41]   See American Assn. of Cruise Passengers v. Carnival Cruise Lines, 31 F.3d 1184 (D.C.Cir. 1994).

threaten to impose a type of regulation inconsistent with federal intent. [42]

Although banking does not enjoy a general antitrust exemption, several federal statutes provide antitrust-like regulations. These standards may take precedence over antitrust standards when a violation is alleged. For example, the Bank Merger Act of 1960 (amended in 1966), provides for special procedures to be used in evaluating bank mergers, although the substantive standard to be applied mimics that of Clayton Act § 7.[43] Likewise, bank tying arrangements requiring loans to be joined with insurance, title examination fees, legal services, or other services, are governed by a variety of federal statutes.[44] These provisions can be more aggressive than the law of tie-ins generally, for they do not require a showing of the bank's market power in the tying product or of anticompetitive effects in the tied product market.[45]

Amateur athletic associations receive a partial antitrust exemption through the Amateur Sports Act,[46] when they regulate amateur status. Further, the Sports Broadcasting Act, permits football, baseball, basketball, or hockey leagues to deal for all league members in selling television rights, provided that telecasting is not limited in any city other than "the home territory of a member club of the league on a day when such club is playing a game at home."[47] In *Chicago Professional Sports* the Seventh Circuit held that this statute did not justify a National Basketball Association rule limiting the number of times individual teams could sell television rights to certain stations—that is, the statute authorizes teams to make joint sales, but not to prevent their members from making individual

---

[42]   49 U.S.C. § 40102(2), 41713(b)(1). See Korean Air Lines Co., Ltd. Antitrust Litig., 642 F.3d 685 (9th Cir. 2011) (Airline Deregulation Act preempted state regulation of foreign and domestic air carriers and thus precluded state indirect purchaser antitrust challenge;; the purpose of the ADA's preemption provision was "to ensure that the [s]tates would not undo federal deregulation with regulation of their own.").

[43]   12 U.S.C.A. § 1828(c). The FDIC once promulgated its own set of "merger guidelines" for mergers within its jurisdiction. See 53 Fed. Reg. 39,803, 1988 WL 257396 (1988).

[44]   The principal statute is the Bank Holding Company Act of 1970. 12 U.S.C.A. §§ 1971–1978.

[45]   For example, Dibidale of Louisiana, Inc. v. American Bank & Trust Co., 916 F.2d 300, 305–306 (5th Cir. 1990), opinion amended and reinstated on rehearing, 941 F.2d 308 (5th Cir. 1991); Parsons Steel, Inc. v. First Ala. Bank, 679 F.2d 242, 245 (11th Cir. 1982).

[46]   36 U.S.C.A. §§ 371 et seq. See Gold Medal LLC v. USA Track & Field, 899 F.3d 712 (9th Cir. 2018) (Amateur Sports Act immunized U.S. Olympic Committee and related organizations from antitrust challenge to Committee rule barring athletes from wearing apparel bearing compensated product advertising).

[47]   15 U.S.C.A. §§ 1291–1295.

sales.[48] Finally, baseball enjoys its own very broad judge made immunity that dates from the early twentieth century. The immunity was based on a premise that clearly no longer obtains—namely, that baseball is purely recreational and thus not "commerce" within the jurisdiction of the antitrust laws.[49]

16.3b. Antitrust and Federal Labor Policy

One of the unexpected results of passage of the Sherman Act was its aggressive use against labor unions.[50] Indeed, in the early years of antitrust enforcement the Sherman Act was employed much more effectively against labor than against restraints in product markets. Of the first thirteen antitrust violations found by American courts during the period 1890–1897, twelve were challenges to labor strikes, while only one was a challenge to an agreement among manufacturers.[51] Although labor leaders argued that the framers of the Sherman Act never intended it to cover labor strikes as a form of "price-fixing," there is very little in the legislative history of that statute to support their claims. However, in 1914 a Progressive Congress responded by enacting § 6 of the Clayton Act, which provided that "[t]he labor of a human being is not a commodity or article of commerce," and that the Sherman Act should not be interpreted to forbid the organization and legitimate operation of labor unions.[52] Section 6 proved to be a weak instrument, and the Supreme Court continued to permit Sherman Act injunctions against labor boycotts;[53] so in 1932 Congress passed the Norris-LaGuardia Act, which deprives the federal courts of jurisdiction to issue

---

[48]   Chicago Professional Sports Limited Partnership v. NBA, 961 F.2d 667, 670 (7th Cir.), cert. denied, 506 U.S. 954, 113 S.Ct. 409 (1992).

[49]   Federal Baseball Club v. National League, 259 U.S. 200 (1922); Flood v. Kuhn, 407 U.S. 258 (1972). See also Miranda v. Selig, 860 F.3d 1237 (9th Cir.), cert. denied, 138 S.Ct. 507 (2017) (baseball exemption immunized minor league baseball from claim that inter-team uniform salary restrictions were unlawful price fixing); Right Field Rooftops, LLC v. Chicago Cubs Baseball Club, LLC, 870 F.3d 682 (7th Cir. 2017), cert. denied, 138 S.Ct. 2621 (2018) (baseball exemption precluded antitrust claim against Chicago Cubs for installing a wind shield that obstructed rooftop owners' view, thus ruining its business of selling rooftop viewing access to games). See also Major League Baseball v. Crist, 331 F.3d 1177 (11th Cir. 2003) (federal antitrust exemption for baseball also applied to state antitrust law). See 1B Antitrust Law ¶ 251h2 (5th ed. 2020).

[50]   For example, Loewe v. Lawlor (Danbury Hatters case), 208 U.S. 274, 28 S.Ct. 301 (1908) (union organized secondary boycott violated Sherman Act).

[51]   See Herbert Hovenkamp, Enterprise and American Law, 1836–1937 at 229 (1991).

[52]   15 U.S.C.A. § 17. Section 20 of the Clayton Act, passed at the same time, was designed to prevent the issuance of federal injunctions against strikes or labor boycotts. 29 U.S.C.A. § 52.

[53]   See Duplex Printing Press Co. v. Deering, 254 U.S. 443, 41 S.Ct. 172 (1921); and see Hovenkamp, *Enterprise*, at 229–238.

injunctions in labor disputes, unless independently unlawful acts are threatened or committed.[54]

In order to claim this so-called "statutory" exemption from the labor laws, a labor union must act "in its self-interest" and it may not "combine with non-labor groups."[55] The question of when an agreement is with a "non-labor" group has generated some dispute. Some cases are clear. For example, building contractors organizing a boycott could not ordinarily claim the labor exemption, because their interests are normally aligned with employers rather than employees.[56] However, the Supreme Court has generally interpreted the concept of "labor group," or labor organization broadly. For example, it has held that orchestra leaders, who are in a position to select individual musicians, were a labor group rather than an employer group, particularly since orchestra leaders and musicians often competed with each other in the same labor market.[57] And in *H.A. Artists* the Supreme Court held that an agreement between actors and independent theatrical agents who represented them was not a combination with a non-labor group.[58] Although the agents were self-employed, they were an essential part of the mechanism by which the actors obtained their employment; as a result, they should be considered a labor organization.

But even some agreements between labor organizations and non-labor groups are exempt under the so-called "nonstatutory exemption." The nonstatutory exemption generally applies in a collective bargaining situation where the union has entered into a contract with an employer that imposes potentially anticompetitive limitations on other contractors, competitors or suppliers in the employers' market. These latter are not labor groups; so the statutory exemption itself would not ordinarily apply. In *Jewel Tea,* the Supreme Court exempted an agreement between a butchers' union and an association of grocers limiting the butchers' working hours.[59]

---

[54]   29 U.S.C.A. §§ 101 et seq. See Brady v. NFL, 644 F.3d 661 (8th Cir. 2011) (Norris-LaGuardia Act deprived district court of jurisdiction to enjoin a lockout; staying injunction pending appeal).

[55]   United States v. Hutcheson, 312 U.S. 219, 232, 61 S.Ct. 463, 466 (1941).

[56]   Altemose Construction Co. v. Building & Constr. Trades Council, 751 F.2d 653, 657 (3d Cir. 1985), cert. denied, 475 U.S. 1107, 106 S.Ct. 1513 (1986).

[57]   American Federation of Musicians v. Carroll, 391 U.S. 99, 88 S.Ct. 1562, rehearing denied, 393 U.S. 902, 89 S.Ct. 64 (1968).

[58]   H.A. Artists & Assocs. v. Actors' Equity Ass'n, 451 U.S. 704, 101 S.Ct. 2102 (1981).

[59]   Local 189, Amalgamated Meat Cutters v. Jewel Tea Co., 381 U.S. 676, 85 S.Ct. 1596 (1965). See also Clarett v. NFL, 369 F.3d 124 (2d Cir. 2004) (NFL rule requiring entry draft player to be at least three full college seasons beyond high school addressed a mandatory subject of collective bargaining and qualified for nonstatutory exemption); Connecticut Ironworkers Emp'rs Ass'n, Inc. v. New England Reg'l Council

The lower court had refused an exemption, noting that the association of grocers was not a labor organization, and that the agreement interfered with the natural competition that would otherwise occur among grocers to offer increased services.[60] In reversing, a deeply divided Supreme Court seemed to find the fact of an agreement with a non-labor group relatively unimportant. More important, the heart of the agreement at issue went to working conditions, which are a legitimate subject of collective bargaining.

The Supreme Court's important decision in Connell Construction Co. v. Plumbers & Steamfitters Local Union No. 100[61] suggests the limits of the nonstatutory exemption. A union picketed a general contractor in order to win an agreement that the general contractor would give subcontracting jobs for plumbing and other work only to firms represented by that union. The picketing union was not seeking to organize the general contractor itself. A divided (5–4) Supreme Court found the conduct not to be exempt. The principal impact of the solicited agreement was not on wages and hours, but on entitlement to bid to be a subcontractor—that is, the sought for agreement would have limited competition among plumbing subcontractors to those that had a particular union contract. To put it another way, the union was not attempting to regulate the wages and working conditions of the affected subcontractors, but rather was seeking to exclude them from the market altogether. The distinction is quite subtle, since the principal way a union gets what it wants is by striking and boycotting.

In the wake of *Connell* courts have attempted to craft an exemption that incorporates the concerns of earlier decisions, without permitting labor unions to go too far in limiting competition in nonlabor markets. They generally require three things before the nonstatutory exemption can be claimed: (1) the restraint on trade contained in the agreement must be one that affects primarily the parties; (2) the subject matter of the agreement must be what is normally considered a mandatory subject of collective bargaining— that is, wages, hours, and working conditions; and (3) the provision must be the subject of arm's length bargaining. The *Connell* boycott violated at least (1) and (2). First, it seriously affected subcontractors who were not bargaining with the union at all. Second, the primary

---

of Carpenters, 869 F.3d 92 (2d Cir. 2017), cert. denied, 138 S.Ct. 1547 (2018) (subcontracting clause forbidding primary contractors from subcontracting with non-signatories was protected by nonstatutory exemption, provided that it was being used for work preservation; remanding on that issue).

[60]   Jewel Tea Co. v. Associated Food Retailers of Greater Chicago, Inc., 331 F.2d 547 (7th Cir. 1964).

[61]   421 U.S. 616, 95 S.Ct. 1830 (1975).

issue was not wages, hours and working conditions, but the basic right to bid as a subcontractor.

Although the post-*Connell* cases are often difficult to parse, they contain the germ of an important principle: unions should not be permitted to "monopolize" a market any more than capitalists. A union of, say, electrical subcontractors may have a legitimate interest in ensuring that employees of other subcontractors are paid the same wages that the union members are paid. Their motive is not so much to protect these other employees as to ensure that the other subcontractors do not have a cost advantage over their own employer. But the union is not entitled to insist that organization by that particular union be a prerequisite for a particular subcontractor's right to be a market participant.

The courts have generally declined to apply the nonstatutory exemption to agreements occurring outside the context of bargaining between a union and an employer. For example, in *Detroit Auto Dealers* the court found no exemption for an agreement among car dealers to restrict showroom hours.[62] Although employees wanted the agreement, the agreement itself was not a direct result of collective bargaining by employees. By contrast, Powell v. NFL[63] applied the nonstatutory exemption to an agreement among NFL players and NFL teams that limited a player's ability to be a "free agent," or to sign freely with a different team than his current one.

Finally, in a significant expansion of the non-statutory exemption, in 1996 the Supreme Court immunized an agreement among employers (NFL football teams) to set the maximum wage they would pay to a certain class of employees.[64] While the union and the teams had bargained after the collective bargaining agreement expired, the bargaining had reached a technical impasse, or situation where the parties had presumably bargained in good faith, but irreconcilable differences remained.[65] The Supreme Court found this agreement reasonable, but only because the employers (the teams) had reached it in the context of collective bargaining with the players' union. As the Court pointed out, the logic of multi-employer collective bargaining demanded that *both* sides be able to agree about the various issues that would be brought to the bargaining table. Further, the National Labor Relations Board supervised the entire collective bargaining process, and the principal card that the players

---

[62]   Detroit Auto Dealers Assn. v. FTC, 955 F.2d 457, 467 (6th Cir.), cert. denied, 506 U.S. 973, 113 S.Ct. 461 (1992).

[63]   888 F.2d 559 (8th Cir. 1989), cert. denied, 498 U.S. 1040, 111 S.Ct. 711 (1991). Accord Wood v. NBA, 809 F.2d 954 (2d Cir. 1987).

[64]   Brown v. Pro Football, 518 U.S. 231, 116 S.Ct. 2116 (1996).

[65]   See 1A Antitrust Law ¶ 257b2 (5th ed. 2020).

held was their ability to strike if the teams did something that injured them excessively. But this was all part of the give-and-take of collective bargaining—a process into which antitrust courts must be loath to interfere.[66]

16.3c.   The McCarran-Ferguson Act and the Insurance Exemption

The federally created exemption for insurance is unique in one important respect: although the exemption is created by federal law, the source of the regulation at issue is the states. However, the federal source of the exemption makes it different from and more expansive than the more limited immunity for "state action" discussed in the following chapter.

Most of the litigation concerning the insurance exemption has involved three different questions: what kinds of activities are encompassed within the "business of insurance?" When is the business of insurance effectively "regulated" by state law, and thus exempt? and When does coercive activity amount to a "boycott, coercion, or intimidation," and thus fall outside of the exemption?

16.3c1.   "Business of Insurance"[67]

The McCarran exemption applies only to activities that constitute the "business of insurance." Ordinary rate setting, even if collusive, falls into this category.[68] Often insurance companies perform a variety of services, however. For example, title insurance companies do title searches and prepare title reports as well as writing title insurance.[69] Many health insurers are heavily involved in the direct provision of health care or pharmaceuticals through prepaid health plans. Some life insurance companies are in the business of selling other kinds of investments or perhaps even lending money or drafting legal documents.[70] When an insurance company has its thumbs in many pies, the antitrust tribunal may have to consider whether the challenged activity constitutes the "business of insurance." The Supreme Court has identified three

---

[66]   Id. at 242–243, 116 S.Ct. at 2123.

[67]   See 1 Antitrust Law ¶ 219b (5th ed. 2020).

[68]   E.g., Katz v. Fidelity Nat. Title Ins. Co., 685 F.3d 588 (6th Cir. 2012).

[69]   See Ticor Title Ins. Co., 5 Trade Reg. Rep. ¶ 22744 (FTC 1989) (title searching by title insurance companies, as opposed to the issuance of the title policy itself, not part of the business of insurance).

[70]   See Perry v. Fidelity Union Life Ins. Co., 606 F.2d 468 (5th Cir. 1979), cert. denied, 446 U.S. 987, 100 S.Ct. 2973 (1980) (lending money not part of business of insurance). See also Insurance Brokerage Antitrust Litigation, 618 F.3d 300 (3d Cir. 2010) (payments to brokers beyond usual commissions and intended to steer brokers to favored insurers not part of business of insurance).

criteria for making that determination. First, the practice must have "the effect of transferring or spreading a policy holder's risk. * * *" Second, the practice must be "an integral part of the policy relationship between the insurer and the insured." Third, the practice should be "limited to entities within the insurance industry." The Court then added that "[n]one of these criteria is necessarily determinative in itself. * * *"[71]

Applying these criteria, the courts have had little difficulty in concluding the following: reinsurance—or insurance purchased by insurance companies to protect themselves from catastrophic events—is part of the business of insurance.[72] By contrast, a divided Supreme Court held that a health insurer's agreement with pharmacies for filling the prescriptions of its insureds was not part of the business of insurance; first, the pharmacies were not parties to the insurance policy; further, these agreements did not serve to spread risk, in the way that an insurance policy does.[73] Likewise, in *Pireno*[74] the Court held that peer review of medical claims for reasonableness does not fall within the business of insurance. In that case the insurer asked one set of chiropractors to assess the reasonableness of the plaintiff chiropractors' treatments of the insured patients. The Court found this activity not to be part of the transfer of risk inherent in insurance, but merely a mechanism by which the insurance company attempted to reduce its costs. For largely analogous reasons, some lower courts have found that insurer limitations to specific kinds of providers are not part of the business of insurance. For example, a health policy might provide that only psychiatrists with M.D. degrees, not psychologists, may give covered treatment for mental or nervous conditions.[75] Likewise, a health insurer may exclude coverage for services provided by chiropractors or other health care professionals who do not have M.D. degrees, and these exclusions may not be part of the business of insurance.

One might dispute the wisdom of such policy limitations and even suspect that they are sometimes anticompetitive. Nevertheless,

---

[71]   Union Labor Life Ins. Co. v. Pireno, 458 U.S. 119, 129, 102 S.Ct. 3002, 3008 (1982), following Group Life & Health Ins. Co. v. Royal Drug Co., 440 U.S. 205, 99 S.Ct. 1067 (1979).

[72]   In re Insurance Antitrust Litigation, 723 F.Supp. 464 (N.D.Cal. 1989), reversed on other grounds, 938 F.2d 919 (9th Cir. 1991), affirmed in part, reversed in part sub nom. Hartford Fire Insurance v. California, 509 U.S. 764, 113 S.Ct. 2891 (1993).

[73]   Royal Drug, 440 U.S. 205.

[74]   *Supra*, 458 U.S. 119.

[75]   Virginia Academy of Clinical Psychologists v. Blue Shield of Virginia, 624 F.2d 476 (4th Cir. 1980), cert. denied, 450 U.S. 916, 101 S.Ct. 1360 (1981) (finding that the decision to exclude was not part of the business of insurance).

the conclusion that they are not part of the "business of insurance" is strained at best. Supposedly, if one wishes to have coverage for psychologists' services, he can obtain it by purchasing a different health insurance policy and perhaps paying more. Inherent in the business of insurance is the underwriter's determination of which risks it will insure for a certain premium. For example, the home insurer's decision not to include flood insurance for homes within flood plains is unquestionably part of the "business of insurance."

The efficient provision of insurance requires joint activity. For example, risk data are more reliable as the "pool" of people from whom the data are taken grows larger. As a result, insurers can compute risks more accurately if they can share data about specific risks. Indeed, many insurers cannot write certain kinds of coverage at all if they cannot use data collected by other insurers in computing their premiums. Likewise, agreements about the content of the insurance policy performs a kind of product standardization that often works to consumers' best interests. In most states so-called "forms development" is a process in which all insurers in the affected market participate. One result is that the consumer shopping for, say, automobile insurance compares products that are in most respects identical, and is not mired in numerous technical variations in coverage that make price comparison all but impossible.

But once the data have been gathered and the forms produced, should insurers be able to agree about premiums—that is, should they be permitted to fix prices? The courts agree that if the state regulation contemplates joint rate-making, such rate-making is clearly within the "business of insurance" and thus antitrust exempt.[76] So the legality of joint rate making is generally left up to the state regulators, whose policy varies greatly from state to state and depending on the type of insurance.

16.3c2. "Regulated by State Law"

McCarran also exempts the business of insurance only "to the extent" that the business is "regulated by state law." Importantly, "regulated by state law" for McCarran purposes means much less than the kind of state regulation necessary to qualify for the "state action" immunity, discussed in the next chapter. If that were not the case, the McCarran exemption would become superfluous. Indeed, the state need not actively "regulate" at all; it need only pass a statute that purports to regulate. It makes no difference that the state

---

[76]   Owens v. Aetna Life & Casualty Co., 654 F.2d 218 (3d Cir.), cert. denied, 454 U.S. 1092, 102 S.Ct. 657 (1981); In re Workers' Compensation Insurance Antitrust Litigation, 867 F.2d 1552 (8th Cir.), cert. denied, 492 U.S. 920, 109 S.Ct. 3247 (1989).

regulation is not actively enforced, or that the state agency simply rubber stamps the insurance companies' requests.[77]

One important exception is that if a certain activity is not within the jurisdictional reach of the states, then it cannot be "regulated by the states" under McCarran. Accordingly, it loses its exemption. In *Hartford*, the Supreme Court suggested that foreign reinsurers might be out of the jurisdictional reach of state regulation. If that were so, then they would not be "regulated" for McCarran purposes.[78] The Court remanded to the Ninth Circuit for that determination.

16.3c3. *Acts of Boycott, Coercion or Intimidation*

The McCarran antitrust exemption does not apply to acts of boycott, coercion or intimidation.[79] The Supreme Court has generally held that the term "boycott" must be understood in its Sherman Act sense, which includes a wide variety of refusals to deal, both absolute and conditional.[80]

In *Hartford*, the Supreme Court found that the McCarran-Ferguson Act did not exempt alleged agreements among primary insurers to reduce their policy coverages so as to eliminate losses that occurred outside the policy period, or upon which claims were made outside the policy period, and losses caused by certain forms of "sudden and accidental" pollution.[81] Although a simple agreement to develop a new insurance form with reduced coverage was exempt "business of insurance," the plaintiffs[82] alleged that the defendants entered collateral agreements with two other entities. The first was an agreement with Insurance Services Office (ISO) that the latter would not supply risk data for risks that the conspirators no longer wished to cover. Several non-conspiring insurers would have continued to write the larger risks, but they could not do so without adequate risk data. Secondly, the defendant insurers allegedly agreed with foreign sellers of *re*insurance that the reinsurers would not provide their services to the non-conspiring insurers either. In finding a boycott the Court noted:

---

77   See FTC v. National Casualty Co., 357 U.S. 560, 78 S.Ct. 1260 (1958) (mere enactment of standard sufficient; no administrative supervision needed); Seasongood v. K & K Ins. Agency, 548 F.2d 729 (8th Cir. 1977); Ohio AFL-CIO v. Insurance Rating Bd., 451 F.2d 1178, 1184 (6th Cir. 1971), cert. denied, 409 U.S. 917, 93 S.Ct. 215 (1972).

78   *Hartford*, 509 U.S. at 784 n. 12, 113 S.Ct. at 2902 n. 12.

79   15 U.S.C.A. § 1013(b); see 1 Antitrust Law ¶ 220 (5th ed. 2020).

80   In *Hartford* the Supreme Court rejected the argument that only absolute refusals to deal "on any terms" qualified as boycotts. Rather, "[t]he refusal to deal may * * * be conditional, offering its target the incentive of renewed dealing if and when he mends his ways." 509 U.S. at 801, 113 S.Ct. at 2911.

81   *Hartford*, 509 U.S. 764.

82   Several states' attorneys general, in addition to private plaintiffs.

It is * * * important * * * to distinguish between a conditional boycott and a concerted agreement to seek particular terms in particular transactions. A concerted agreement to terms (a "cartelization") is "a way of obtaining and exercising market power by concertedly exacting terms like those which a monopolist might exact." The parties to such an agreement (the members of a cartel) are not engaging in a boycott, because: "They are not coercing anyone, at least in the usual sense of that word; they are merely (though concertedly) saying 'we will deal with you only on the following trade terms.' "[83]

The critical distinction for the Court was whether the agreement at hand covered only the terms of the contract under negotiation, or whether it reached further. For example, if a group of tenants agreed with each other that they would not renew their leases unless they received lower rents from the landlord, they would be negotiating the contract at hand. They would not be "boycotting" anyone. However, if the tenants also refused to engage in unrelated transactions—for example, if they refused to sell their landlord food or other supplies until he lowered the rents—this latter agreement would be a boycott.[84] "[T]his expansion of the refusal to deal beyond the targeted transaction * * * gives great coercive force to a commercial boycott: unrelated transactions are used as leverage to achieve the terms desired."[85] Applying this definition, the Court found that the plaintiffs' allegations contained several qualifying "boycotts." For example, the reinsurers allegedly refused to write reinsurance on any policy given by a firm that also wrote policies containing the coverages that the defendants wanted removed from the market.

---

[83]   509 U.S. at 802, 113 S.Ct. at 2912.

[84]   The *Hartford* dissenters—Justice Souter, joined by Justices White, Blackmun and Stevens—would have interpreted "boycott" somewhat more broadly to include a cartel's enforcement activities generally. For example, if the reinsurers agreed with each other not to write reinsurance for certain risks, that would not be a boycott. But if the reinsurers and the defendant insurers agreed among themselves that the reinsurers would not write reinsurance for the non-conspiring insurers, then the term "boycott" was appropriate. 509 U.S. at 785, 113 S.Ct. at 2903.

[85]   Compare Eastern States Retail Lumber Dealers' Ass'n v. United States, 234 U.S. 600, 34 S.Ct. 951 (1914), a Sherman Act case not involving insurance, where lumber retailers agreed with each other that they would not purchase lumber from wholesalers that also engaged directly in retailing. The *Hartford* Court noted that the *Eastern States* agreement was "a boycott because [the defendants] sought an objective—the wholesale dealers' forbearance from retail trade—that was collateral to their transactions with the wholesalers." 509 U.S. at 803, 113 S.Ct. at 2912.

Chapter 17

ANTITRUST FEDERALISM AND THE "STATE ACTION" DOCTRINE

Table of Sections

§ 17.1   Introduction; Preemption

In the United States, individual states and even local governments make regulatory policy. Under the Supremacy Clause of the Federal Constitution,[1] the federal government undoubtedly has the power to preempt much of this state and local regulation. In some markets, such as the regulation of labor relations or most intellectual property rights, it has chosen to do so. But nothing in the federal *antitrust* laws even hints that Congress intended to preempt internally applied state and local economic law simply because that law interferes with competitive markets.

State and local governments are not free to regulate without any restraint whatsoever. Nevertheless, the mere fact that state law differs from federal antitrust policy is generally not enough to preempt the state or local law. This is often the case where the state or local law regulates more intensively than federal antitrust law does. For example, *Exxon* upheld a state statute forbidding vertical integration by petroleum refiners into retailing, notwithstanding that federal antitrust law generally permits vertical ownership and

---

[1]   U.S. Const. Art. VI, § 2.

regards most of it as efficient.[2] In addition, state antitrust laws that permit indirect purchasers to sue for damages have been upheld, notwithstanding that federal law limits damage recoveries to direct purchasers.[3] In its *Oneok* decision, the Supreme Court held that the federal Natural Gas Act did not preclude the application of state antitrust law to alleged price fixing, mainly because the statutory language made clear that Congress had intended to complement rather than replace state law.[4]

Where state law permits or in some cases compels something that the federal antitrust laws prohibit, the preemption question becomes more complex. Mere inconsistency is not enough. Federal decisions considering preemption have generally focused on two issues: *first*, does the state statute under challenge compel what amounts to a *per se* violation of the federal antitrust laws, or merely something that is arguably a violation under the rule of reason? *second*, to what extent does the challenged statute vest discretion to make anticompetitive decisions in private parties who are not adequately supervised by the state itself? That is, the federal antitrust laws are generally concerned with *privately* initiated restraints, not those compelled by or effectively controlled by the government.

The statute at issue in the *Midcal Aluminum* case failed this test.[5] It required producers and wholesalers of alcoholic beverages to publish resale price schedules, and then required dealers to sell at these prices. This appeared to establish resale price maintenance that was illegal per se at the time, and left the determination of resale prices to the unsupervised discretion of the producers and wholesalers. As a result, the Sherman Act preempted the state statute.

One essential element of illegal RPM was missing in *Midcal*: there was no "agreement" between the manufacturer/wholesalers and the retailers to charge a specific set of resale prices. Rather, the

---

    2   Exxon Corp. v. Governor of Maryland, 437 U.S. 117, 98 S.Ct. 2207 (1978). Contrast, State ex rel. Van de Kamp v. Texaco, Inc., 193 Cal.App.3d 8, 219 Cal.Rptr. 824 (1985), affirmed, 46 Cal.3d 1147, 252 Cal.Rptr. 221, 762 P.2d 385 (1988), which held that a federal consent decree permitting a merger prevented condemnation of the merger under California antitrust law, because the federal consent decree "occupied the field," in this case regulating the details of the merger.

    3   California v. ARC America Corp., 490 U.S. 93, 109 S.Ct. 1661 (1989), on remand, 940 F.2d 1583 (9th Cir. 1991). On indirect purchasers under federal law, see § 16.6. State antitrust laws and their indirect purchaser provisions are discussed more fully in § 20.8.

    4   Oneok, Inc. v. Learjet, Inc., 575 U.S. 373, 135 S.Ct. 1591 (2015).

    5   California Retail Liquor Dealers Assn. v. Midcal Aluminum (Midcal), 445 U.S. 97, 100 S.Ct. 937 (1980).

statute ordered retailers to charge the prices specified by the manufacturers and wholesalers. The Court simply noted that the statute brought about a result that precisely duplicated the result of a resale price maintenance agreement.

If the challenged statute does not compel what amounts to a *per se* violation, then it is usually not preempted. In *Rice v. Norman Williams Co.*[6] the Supreme Court upheld a California statute permitting manufacturers of liquor to "authorize" particular importers of liquor to bring their brands into the state, but exclude others. The Court treated this arrangement as giving state sanction to vertical territorial division, which is analyzed under the rule of reason and only rarely illegal. It then held that, when a state statute is challenged on its face, it "may be condemned under the antitrust laws only if it mandates or authorizes conduct that necessarily constitutes a violation of the antitrust laws in all cases, or if it places irresistible pressure on a private party to violate the antitrust laws in order to comply with the statute."[7]

Subsequent to *324 Liquor* and *Rice* the Supreme Court adopted a rule of reason for resale price maintenance.[8] Does this mean that liquor price maintenance and posting statutes will be treated like the territorial restraints in *Rice*, which were not preempted? One question is whether the arrangement should be regarded as fundamentally vertical or horizontal. Some state provisions, such as those in *324 Liquor*, seem to resemble vertical resale price maintenance. Accordingly, they will not be preempted, as the majority held in *Connecticut Fine Wine*.[9] Others, as in the post-and-hold cases, look more like horizontal restraints and *Leegin*'s rule of reason for resale price maintenance did not apply to them. These statutes require liquor resellers to "post," or publish, their resale prices and then promise not to deviate from those prices for a defined time period such as thirty days. That kind of activity looks more like a horizontal price fix than an act of resale price maintenance.[10]

6　　458 U.S. 654, 102 S.Ct. 3294 (1982).

7　　*Rice*, 458 U.S. at 661, 102 S.Ct. at 3300.

8　　See § 11.5; and Leegin Creative Leather Prods., Inc. v. PSKS, Inc., 551 U.S. 877, 127 S.Ct. 2705 (2007).

9　　See, e.g., Connecticut Fine Wine and Spirits, LLC v. Seagull, 916 F.3d 160 (2d Cir. 2019), cert. denied, 2020 WL 1668298 (April 6, 2020) (given that resale price maintenance is no longer per se unlawful, a statute compelling it is no longer preempted by the Sherman Act).

10　　E.g., TFWS, Inc. v. Schaefer, 2007 WL 2917025 (D. Md. 2007), aff'd, 572 F.3d 186 (4th Cir. 2009), finding antitrust preemption of a statute under which wholesalers were required to post their price schedules with the Comptroller by the fifth of each month. These prices were: (1) made available to all other wholesalers; and (2) locked in for the following month. Under the volume-discount ban, a wholesaler must offer

Dissenters from the denial of rehearing in *Connecticut Fine Wine* observed that the posting requirements in that statute actually facilitated horizontal collusion, and they would have found preemption.[11]

§ 17.2 Federalism and the Policy of the "State Action" Doctrine

The "State Action" doctrine exempts qualifying state and local government regulation from federal antitrust, even if the regulation at issue compels an otherwise clear violation of the federal antitrust laws. The term "state action" should not be confused with the same term as it is used in Constitutional cases interpreting the Fourteenth Amendment and the Bill of Rights. In such cases, the term "state action" is interpreted broadly. Many actions that would be constitutional "state action" for Fourteenth Amendment purposes would not qualify for the "state action" antitrust exemption because they were insufficiently articulated as state policy or insufficiently supervised by a state agency. For example, a state regulatory agency that simply authorized private collusion in violation of its own statutory mandate would certainly be engaged in "state action" for Fourteenth Amendment purposes. But such an agency rule would not qualify for the "state action" antitrust exemption because the rule was not articulated in the state's policy and the private conduct that resulted was unsupervised. In the balance of this chapter, the term "state action" refers only to the antitrust doctrine. The term *"Parker"* doctrine or immunity also refers to the antitrust state action doctrine.[12]

The "state action" doctrine itself rests on a fictional reading of the legislative history of the antitrust laws. In Parker v. Brown, which first recognized the doctrine, the Supreme Court upheld a California statute that limited the production of raisins by California farmers, with allocation decisions made by private participants in the industry, supervised by state officials.[13] The Court found that when Congress passed the Sherman Act in 1890 it never intended the statute to undermine the regulatory power of state and local governments. But the prevailing view of federal power under the Commerce Clause in 1890 was that Congress could not have done

---

every retailer the same price for a given product, thus preventing wholesalers from cutting prices to large retailers. See also 1 Antitrust Law ¶ 217 (5th ed. 2020).

[11]   Connecticut Fine Wine and Spirits, LLC v. Seagull, 936 F.3d 119 (2d Cir. 2019), cert. denied, 2020 WL 1668298 (April 6, 2020).

[12]   The term comes from Parker v. Brown, 317 U.S. 341, 63 S.Ct. 307 (1943).

[13]   Parker v. Brown, 317 U.S. 341, 350–352, 63 S.Ct. 307, 313–315 (1943). See 1 Antitrust Law ¶ 221 (5th ed. 2020).

this even had it wished to. Under that view, which the Supreme Court confirmed in its 1895 *E. C. Knight* decision, the federal government had no power to regulate markets that were perceived to be purely intrastate.[14] By the same token, extraterritorial state regulation was unconstitutional.[15] Under this regime of "dual federalism," any form of regulation that was within the regulatory power of state and local government was outside the reach of the federal antitrust laws. Small wonder that the Supreme Court could find no evidence that the Sherman Act's framers intended to control state and local regulation.

The "state action" exemption thus stands for the proposition that federal antitrust should not be used to intrude too deeply into state regulatory process. For example, if the state decides to regulate intrastate trucking rates or a city grants an exclusive right to operate a cable television system, these acts should not be challengeable as price fixing or monopolization under federal law.

§ 17.3   Basic Qualifications for Exemption

Federal antitrust immunizes state and local regulation from its prohibitions, without inquiring into competitive effects, provided that:

1.   The challenged activity is authorized by a "clearly articulated" state regulatory policy ("authorization"); and

2.   Any private conduct authorized by the state policy is "actively supervised" by an appropriate governmental agency ("supervision").

The state is free to regulate in as anticompetitive a manner as it pleases, provided that it ensures that private firms act consistently with the stated policy. About the only qualification to attach is that the active supervision requirement does not permit the state to have a "regulatory policy" of permitting private actors to do whatever they please.

Although this two-part test was first articulated in full bloom in the *Midcal* decision,[16] it developed through several earlier decisions.

---

[14]   See United States v. E.C. Knight Co., 156 U.S. 1, 15 S.Ct. 249 (1895); Herbert Hovenkamp, Enterprise and American Law, 1836–1937, ch. 20 (1991).

[15]   See Wabash, St. Louis & Pacific Ry. Co. v. Illinois, 118 U.S. 557, 7 S.Ct. 4 (1886) (state has no power to regulate interstate railroad shipment). See Hovenkamp, *Enterprise*, ch. 13.

[16]   California Retail Liquor Dealers Assn. v. Midcal Aluminum, Inc., 445 U.S. 97, 105, 100 S.Ct. 937, 943 (1980). It was initially proposed in 1 Phillip Areeda & Donald F. Turner, Antitrust Law ¶ 213 (supervision), ¶ 214 (authorization) (1978).

In *Goldfarb*[17] the Supreme Court held that the adoption and enforcement of minimum fee schedules for lawyers was not immune from antitrust attack because the scheme amounted to "essentially ... private anticompetitive activity," in contrast to the publicly created quota program at issue in *Parker*. Although a state statute gave the state supreme court power to regulate the practice of law, and the court in turn carried this function out through the local bar associations, nothing in the authorizing scheme compelled the setting of minimum fees. The Court reiterated that view in Cantor v. Detroit Edison Co., denying immunity to a regulated utility's policy of providing "free" light bulbs to customers.[18] The mere fact that the state's public utility commission had approved a tariff[19] including the policy was insufficient.

However, the Supreme Court subsequently rejected any compulsion requirement. In *Hallie* the Supreme Court unanimously held that conduct need not be compelled when the relevant actor is a municipality rather than a private party; authorization is sufficient.[20] In *Southern Motor Carriers* the Court extended this holding to private actors.[21] The decision involved so-called "rate bureaus," or joint rate-making by price regulated firms, challenged as simple price fixing. Under the state statutory scheme in question, a trucking company could choose either to participate in a rate bureau and submit a joint rate proposal with competitors, or else it could propose its own rate tariff individually to the regulatory agency. The Court concluded that "[a]s long as the State clearly articulates its intent to adopt a permissive policy, the first prong of the *Midcal* test [clear authorization] is satisfied."[22] Indeed, under the circumstances a mere authorization requirement would be more competitive than a compulsion requirement. Under compulsion, trucking firms would be *required* to collude—that is, to agree in advance on rates before submitting a joint proposal to the regulatory agency. But under the permissive policy, any firm that wanted to

---

[17]   Goldfarb v. Virginia State Bar, 421 U.S. 773, 791–792, 95 S.Ct. 2004, 2015–2016 (1975).

[18]   Cantor v. Detroit Edison Co., 428 U.S. 579, 96 S.Ct. 3110 (1976).

[19]   A "tariff" is a document that a regulated firm files with its regulatory agency, requesting that it be required to charge certain prices, offer certain packages of services, have certain policies respecting treatment of customers, and the like. Once the tariff has been approved by the agency, the firm is legally obliged to follow the tariff.

[20]   Town of Hallie v. City of Eau Claire, 471 U.S. 34, 105 S.Ct. 1713 (1985). See § 20.6.

[21]   Southern Motor Carriers Rate Conference, Inc. v. United States, 471 U.S. 48, 105 S.Ct. 1721 (1985). Accord Snake River Valley Electric Assn. v. PacifiCorp., 238 F.3d 1189 (9th Cir. 2001).

[22]   Id. at 60, 105 S.Ct. at 1728.

deviate downward was free to file its own separate tariff request. That tended to make the filed tariffs more competitive.

The *Southern Motor Carriers* Court emphasized that compulsion could be evidence of authorization.[23] Nevertheless, it now seems clear that the effective requirement is *authorization*, not compulsion.

§ 17.4   Authorization

In applying the "state action" exemption, the court must first consider whether the challenged conduct has been properly authorized by the state. Then it must consider whether any private decision-making under the authorized scheme is adequately supervised by public officials. These two requirements are taken up in this and the following sections.

Authorization must come from the state itself, not from a municipality or other governmental subdivision, and not from a subordinate agency of the state. In *Lafayette*, four members of a deeply divided Supreme Court agreed that a municipality could not authorize anticompetitive conduct, even if the conduct was legal under state law.[24] The Court later clarified its meaning in the *Boulder* decision.[25] The City of Boulder, Colorado, attempted to justify its ordinance restricting the expansion of a private cable television company by noting that the city was a "home rule" municipality, having essentially all the regulatory power of the state. Home rule provisions are created by state law and designed to increase the regulatory power of designated municipalities. Sometimes they appear in state constitutions, but they may also be statutory. The Supreme Court found home rule to be inadequate state authorization for *Parker* purposes, noting that although the home rule provision itself came from the state, the substance of the provision did not authorize any particular ordinance that the municipality might pass. Rather, it was merely neutral, effectively giving the City of Boulder carte blanche to regulate its CATV system as it pleased.

Likewise, *Southern Motor* concluded that joint rate making would not be found exempt merely because a *regulatory agency* authorized it. The authorization had to appear in some fashion in the *state* statutory scheme creating the agency and enumerating its

---

[23]   471 U.S. at 61–62, 105 S.Ct. at 1729.

[24]   City of Lafayette v. Louisiana Power & Light Co., 435 U.S. 389, 98 S.Ct. 1123 (1978).

[25]   Community Communications Co. v. City of Boulder, 455 U.S. 40, 102 S.Ct. 835 (1982).

powers.[26] But this analysis creates some problems in identifying exactly who the state is. The state acts only through its agencies and officials. A legislature is an "agency" of the state, but so is an administrative agency charged with regulating trucking. Today it seems quite clear that the legislature and the state's supreme court are the "state itself" for *Parker* authorization purposes.[27] Most, but not all, regulatory agencies are part of the executive branch; but decisions such as *Southern Motor Carriers* should not be read for the proposition that the Governor's Office is not part of the state for *Parker* purposes. Rather, one must distinguish between primary and subordinate government agencies. But even here is considerable ambiguity. For example, the Ninth Circuit has found that the state Director of the Department of Transportation should be treated as the "state itself" for *Parker* purposes.[28]

Assuming that the authorization has come from the appropriate source, exactly what must be authorized and how unambiguous must the authorization be? As the *Boulder* decision noted, mere neutrality is not "authorization." Those defending the regulatory regime being challenged must point to something suggesting that the state contemplated the activity being challenged and decided to permit it. At the same time, most of the details of the regulatory scheme itself may be left to the state agency or governmental subdivision that carries it out. In the context of municipal regulation, it is sufficient that the challenged effects "logically would result" from the authorizing language in the statute. Thus, if state legislation authorizes a city to provide sewage treatment services, and permits it to decline service to areas outside the city, it is reasonably foreseeable that the city would insist on annexation before agreeing to supply sewage treatment services to adjacent areas.[29]

In *Southern Motor*, the Court made clear that authorization does not require that the state engage in micro-management of the regulatory agency's decision-making.[30] In that case, a general statute

---

[26] Southern Motor Carriers Rate Conference, Inc. v. United States, 471 U.S. 48, 105 S.Ct. 1721, on remand, 764 F.2d 748 (11th Cir. 1985).

[27] Cases finding that a state's highest court is part of the state itself are Bates v. State Bar of Arizona, 433 U.S. 350, 97 S.Ct. 2691 (1977); Hoover v. Ronwin, 466 U.S. 558, 104 S.Ct. 1989 (1984). See Grand River Enters. Six Nations, Ltd. v. Beebe, 574 F.3d 929 (8th Cir. 2009) (where the state legislature had entered cigarette settlement agreement and enacted the market share allocation provisions under challenge the "state itself" had approved the agreement).

[28] Charley's Taxi Radio Dispatch v. SIDA of Haw., Inc., 810 F.2d 869, 875 (9th Cir. 1987).

[29] Town of Hallie v. City of Eau Claire, 471 U.S. 34, 105 S.Ct. 1713 (1985).

[30] Southern Motor Carriers Rate Conference, Inc. v. United States, 471 U.S. 48, 63–64, 105 S.Ct. 1721, 1729–1731 (1985).

enabling the agency to supervise the rate-making process was all that was needed for authorization of joint rate-making.

Plaintiffs have often argued that, even though a state statute supplies a kind of general authorization, the particular conduct in the case at hand could not have been authorized. For example, suppose that the complaint alleges that a government official entered into a "conspiracy" with one or more private persons to deny market access to the plaintiff. Surely, no state authorizing statute should be construed to authorize its agencies or subdivisions to engage in conspiracies. True enough. But upon inspection, nearly all the conspiracy claims amount to petitioning and governmental response. Uniformly, the courts hold that a private citizen's request that a government agency undertake a certain action, and the agency's affirmative response, cannot be construed as a "conspiracy."[31] Further, such a holding would undermine the constitutional right to petition the government, embodied in antitrust's *Noerr-Pennington* doctrine.[32]

In other cases the claim is that, although certain conduct was authorized, the state officials went beyond that point and engaged in unauthorized conduct as well.[33] Some of these cases fall in the area of individual conduct that was probably not part of the official policy of either the state or the agency carrying it out. Some of the cases involve state or local government agencies that violated the state authorizing statutes under which they operated.[34]

Should such situations become antitrust violations, simply because they may have anticompetitive consequences? Many state law violations, it is worth noting, have consequences for competition. The trend in decisions is that state law irregularities should not be

---

[31] See City of Columbia & Columbia Outdoor Advertising v. Omni Outdoor Advertising, Inc., 499 U.S. 365, 383–384, 111 S.Ct. 1344, 1356 (1991), on remand, 974 F.2d 502 (4th Cir. 1992). See § 20.6; and 1 Antitrust Law ¶ 224d (5th ed. 2020).

[32] See Ch. 18.

[33] Surgical Care Center of Hammond v. Hospital Service Dist., 171 F.3d 231 (5th Cir. 1999), cert. denied, 528 U.S. 964, 120 S.Ct. 398 (1999), on remand, 2001 WL 8586 (E.D.La.2001), affirmed, 309 F.3d 836 (5th Cir. 2002) (state statute authorized hospital district to enter into joint ventures, but this did not include an anticompetitive concerted refusal to deal; "Not all joint ventures are anticompetitive. Thus, it is not the foreseeable result of allowing a hospital service district to form joint ventures that it will engage in anticompetitive conduct.").

[34] For example, First Am. Title Co. v. DeVaugh, 480 F.3d 438 (6th Cir. 2007) (fact that country registry of deeds had authority to accept and record title documents and supply copies to third parties did not empower it to impose restraints on the resale of such documents).

turned into federal antitrust violations, particularly where the state law itself provides a remedy.[35]

This conclusion seems unescapable. When a state regulates, it naturally contemplates that agencies or private actors will make mistakes or even engage in willful violations of the regulatory scheme. The relevant question is then whether state law can be brought to bear so as to correct or punish these violations. If every imperfection in compliance with a state regulatory scheme instantly becomes a federal antitrust violation, then the state scheme loses its integrity. For example, suppose that a state statute authorizes an agency to regulate, but the agency official makes secret deals favoring one firm at the expense of others. The first question that the federal antitrust tribunal should ask is whether state law creates an effective remedy for those victimized by this official's illegal act. If so, federal antitrust has no place.

In the context of private action, the authorization question becomes a little easier. Private firms are inherently self-interested actors, and with respect to them the exemption should be fairly strictly construed.[36] The courts are generally less willing to infer that the state intended to displace competition when the authorized parties are private actors.

In general, a grant of ordinary corporate power should not be interpreted to authorize anticompetitive actions. For example, the mere fact that a hospital or other actor has been granted the power to make all contracts needed to carry out its business does not suggest that the hospital has been authorized to enter anticompetitive agreements. In its *Phoebe-Putney* decision the Supreme Court confirmed this proposition, holding that a state law authorization of hospital mergers should not be construed to authorize a merger to monopoly.[37] Writing for a unanimous Court, Justice Sotomayor stated the issue as "whether a Georgia law that creates special-purpose public entities called hospital authorities and gives those entities general corporate powers, including the power to acquire hospitals, clearly articulates and affirmatively expresses a state policy to permit acquisitions that substantially lessen

---

[35]   For example, Kern-Tulare Water Dist. v. City of Bakersfield, 828 F.2d 514, 522 (9th Cir. 1987), cert. denied, 486 U.S. 1015, 108 S.Ct. 1752 (1988) (Federalist notion of respect for states as sovereigns entails that "[w]here ordinary errors or abuses in exercise of state law * * * serves to strip the city of state authorization, aggrieved parties should not forego customary state corrective processes.").

[36]   E.g., In re Insurance Antitrust Litigation, 938 F.2d 919, 931 (9th Cir. 1991), affirmed in part, reversed in part on other grounds, 509 U.S. 764, 113 S.Ct. 2891 (1993) (state insurance regulations did not authorize private conspiracies).

[37]   FTC v. Phoebe Putney Health Sys., Inc., 568 U.S. 216, 227, 133 S.Ct. 1003, 1011 (2013). See 1 Antitrust Law ¶ 225b4 (5th ed. 2020).

competition."[38] In order to qualify as "clear articulation" the state legislature need not "expressly state in a statute or its legislative history" that it intends specific anticompetitive effects. Rather, as *Hallie* directed, it was enough that the effects be the "foreseeable result" of what was authorized.[39] In this case, however, the ordinary acquisition and leasing powers "mirror general powers routinely conferred by state law upon private corporations."[40] That last point was critical. Virtually every state corporation act authorizes corporations to acquire the shares or assets of other corporations. The lower court's interpretation would have completely undermined federal antitrust policy toward corporate mergers.

§ 17.5 Active Supervision

In *Midcal* the Supreme Court held that the state could not simply authorize private actors to create and implement what was at the time *per se* illegal resale price maintenance without effective state oversight.[41] If the state's policy is to permit private actors to do anticompetitive things, so be it; but the state must ensure that private decision makers are acting in accordance with state policy and not engaged in additional anticompetitive actions that fall outside the scope of state authorization. In *324 Liquor* the Court clarified that holding, striking down a statute that required liquor retailers to resell liquor at a price 12% above a price posted by the wholesaler, but with no agency supervision of the prices that wholesalers posted.[42] Effectively, the statute gave wholesalers the unsupervised discretion to set retail prices.

The law of active supervision has focused on three issues. Two have been addressed, although not conclusively settled, by Supreme Court decisions. The three issues are (1) When is supervision required? (2) What kind of supervision is required? and (3) Who must do the supervising?

---

[38]   Id. at 219–220, 133 S.Ct. at 1007.

[39]   Id. at 227, 133 S.Ct. at 1011, quoting *Hallie*, 471 U.S. at 42, 43.

[40]   Id. at 227, 133 S.Ct. at 1011.

[41]   California Retail Liquor Dealers Assn. v. Midcal Aluminum (Midcal), 445 U.S. 97, 100 S.Ct. 937 (1980).

[42]   324 Liquor Corp. v. Duffy, 479 U.S. 335, 107 S.Ct. 720, on remand, 69 N.Y.2d 891, 515 N.Y.S.2d 231, 507 N.E.2d 1087 (1987). See also A.D. Bedell Wholesale Co. v. Philip Morris, Inc., 263 F.3d 239 (3d Cir. 2001), cert. denied, 534 U.S. 1081, 122 S.Ct. 813 (2002) (multistate tobacco settlement agreement did not qualify for state action immunity because it gave the cigarette companies significant private power to collude on their output); Accord Freedom Holdings, Inc. v. Spitzer, 357 F.3d 205, 223 (2d Cir. 2004).

17.5a. When Is Supervision Required?

Active supervision is required whenever the conduct being challenged is that of a private party.[43] The Supreme Court's principal concern in establishing the requirement was that states not simply use *Parker* to give parties carte blanche to do what they wish. When the State itself is the relevant actor, then "supervision" is clearly not required, because there is no relevant entity above the state to do the supervising.

In the *Hallie* case the Supreme Court also held that state supervision is not required when the conduct being challenged is that of a governmental subdivision such as a municipality operating under state authority.[44] That is, the *Parker* doctrine does not require a state both to authorize municipal regulation and to supervise, or review, that regulation once it is in place; municipal governments are trusted to doing their own supervising. This rule is not limited to situations when municipalities are engaged in traditional "governmental" functions, but also applies when they act as entrepreneurs in private markets, in competition with private sellers.[45] Thus, if the actor is "governmental," supervision is not required.

As a principle of government, federalism is concerned with protecting the sovereignty of states, not with protecting individual rights—and particularly not a "right" to engage in anticompetitive conduct in economic markets. Thus before a body can qualify as part of the "state itself," and not be in need of supervision, the effective decision makers must be economically independent of the conduct that they are regulating. A municipal government generally (although perhaps not always) meets such criteria, as perhaps does a regulatory agency containing salary-paid officials. To be sure, both regulatory officials and local politicians can be "captured," even though they are not individual participants in the private market at issue. But capture is still not the same thing as direct economic interest. Different interest groups can vie with each other to capture the employee official. "Capture" is not a foregone conclusion, and we presume that most government officials do their jobs well. Most

---

[43] *Midcal*, 445 U.S. at 105–106, 100 S.Ct. at 943–944; Southern Motor Carriers Rate Conference v. United States, 471 U.S. 48, 58–59, 105 S.Ct. 1721, 1727–1728 (1985).

[44] Town of Hallie v. City of Eau Claire, 471 U.S. 34, 47, 105 S.Ct. 1713, 1720 (1985).

[45] See Danner Construction Co., Inc. v. Hillsborough County, Fla., 608 F.3d 809 (11th Cir. 2010) (waste collection franchises by municipalities; authorization required and found; active supervision not required where the municipality itself is the relevant actor).

importantly, capture itself is ultimately not an antitrust problem but a political one.[46]

In any event, state agencies stand on a different footing than municipalities. Unlike municipalities, they may have power that extends over the entire state, and thus may carry out the state's own functions. On the other hand, they very often operate in a single market. As a result, they are more likely to be controlled by the very interests that they should be regulating. The *North Carolina Dental* decision involved a professional association of dentists that had been designated an "agency" by the state and given the power to regulate the statewide practice of dentistry.[47] But the association was controlled by practicing dentists who were thus in a position to profit from the agency's own anticompetitive decision making. It passed a rule that prohibited anyone except a licensed dentist from providing teeth whitening services in North Carolina. No independent state official reviewed this conduct. The FTC challenged and condemned the rule, the Fourth Circuit affirmed, and a divided Supreme Court agreed that such an agency, unlike a municipality, required supervision by an independent state actor with power to pass judgment on the merits. As the Court observed:

> Limits on state-action immunity are most essential when the State seeks to delegate its regulatory power to active market participants, for established ethical standards may blend with private anticompetitive motives in a way difficult even for market participants to discern. Dual allegiances are not always apparent to an actor. In consequence, active market participants cannot be allowed to regulate their own markets free from antitrust accountability. . . . So it follows that, under *Parker* and the Supremacy Clause, the States' greater power to attain an end does not include the lesser power to negate the congressional judgment embodied in the Sherman Act through unsupervised delegations to active market participants.
>
> . . . *Parker* immunity requires that the anticompetitive conduct of nonsovereign actors, especially those authorized

---

[46]   On this point, see Einer Elhauge, The Scope of Antitrust Process, 104 Harv. L. Rev. 667 (1991).

[47]   N.C. State Board of Dental Examiners v. FTC, 574 U.S. 494, 135 S.Ct. 1101 (2015). See Herbert Hovenkamp, Rediscovering Capture: Antitrust Federalism and the *North Carolina Dental* Case, CPI Antitrust Chronicle 1 (April 2015); Aaron Edlin & Rebecca Haw, Cartels by Another Name: Should Licensed Occupations Face Antitrust Scrutiny, 162 Univ. Pa. L. Rev. 1093 (2014); Ingram Weber, The Antitrust State Action Doctrine and State Licensing Boards, 79 Univ. Chi. L. Rev. 737 (2012).

by the State to regulate their own profession, result from procedures that suffice to make it the State's own.[48]

Further,

> The similarities between agencies controlled by active market participants and private trade associations are not eliminated simply because the former are given a formal designation by the State, vested with a measure of government power, and required to follow some procedural rules. *Parker* immunity does not derive from nomenclature alone. When a State empowers a group of active market participants to decide who can participate in its market, and on what terms, the need for supervision is manifest. The Court holds today that a state board on which a controlling number of decision makers are active market participants in the occupation the board regulates must satisfy *Midcal*'s active supervision requirement in order to invoke state-action antitrust immunity.[49]

Dissenting, Justice Alito protested that this was too much interference in the state's prerogative to regulate its own professions, even if they decided to regulate by doing nothing. For him, if the state acting as sovereign had declared the dental board to be an "agency," then "that is the end of the matter," and it should be irrelevant that "the Board is not structured in a way that merits a good-government seal of approval."[50]

Under *North Carolina Dental* municipalities, with their diverse economic activities and largely elected officials, require authorization but not supervision. By contrast, state "agencies" need supervision as well whenever the decision maker is a direct market participant or perhaps other interested private actor rather than a disinterested state official.

One key to solving the supervision problem is to make the analysis specific to the conduct being challenged. The antitrust tribunal should look at the challenged conduct and determine first whether the person engaged in the conduct is a private party. If not, supervision is not required. If the actor is private, then the court must consider whether the act was a matter over which the private actor had some discretion. If the answer is no—if the private actor

---

[48]   Id. at 1111, citing 1A ANTITRUST LAW ¶ 226; Einer Elhauge, The Scope of Antitrust Process, 104 Harv. L. Rev. 667, 672 (1991); and Merrick B. Garland, Antitrust and State Action: Economic Efficiency and the Political Process, 96 Yale L. J. 486, 500 (1986).

[49]   *N.C. Dental*, 135 S.Ct. at 1114, citing 1A ANTITRUST LAW ¶ 227.

[50]   Id. at 1117–1118.

was simply following a statutory mandate that compelled a certain outcome—then there is nothing to supervise. But if the act was one about which the private actor had choices, then the choice selected must be effectively supervised by a qualified state official.

17.5b.　What Kind of Supervision Is Required?

Governmental supervision comes in many types and levels of scrutiny. For example, an appellate court "supervises" lower courts by reviewing substantive rulings for legal errors and reversing incorrect decisions. By contrast, an understaffed licensing agency might routinely grant licenses to do business upon application, "rubber-stamping" them without making any substantive investigation into their truthfulness, and reviewing them only when a complaint brings some problem to light, or perhaps not even then. Further, some agencies may not even be empowered to second-guess the merits of private conduct; they can object only to procedural deviations. Indeed, with respect to some activities, the agency may have jurisdiction only to accept reports. For example, in some markets sellers are required to report the prices they charge or the quantities they sell. But the agency that receives the report has no authority to regulate either price or output.

Today it is clear that mere reporting, or agency supervision that extends only to process, does not satisfy the "active supervision" requirement. The Supreme Court so held in Patrick v. Burget, which refused to find adequate supervision in a state-authorized medical peer review scheme.[51] The plaintiff was a physician who had been disciplined by the physician-controlled peer review board of a public hospital. Under state law a public agency had the power to require reports of staff terminations, and to review denials of hospital staff privileges for procedural irregularities, but it had no power to review the substantive decisions themselves. The Court held that active supervision "requires that state officials have and exercise power to review particular anticompetitive acts of private parties and disapprove those that fail to accord with state policy."[52] It reiterated this requirement in North Carolina Dental: "The supervisor must review the substance of the anticompetitive decision, not merely the procedures followed to produce it. . ."[53]

The decisions leave open the possibility that judicial review in the state courts can satisfy the active supervision requirement, but the court's decision-making power would have to extend to the merits

---

[51]　Patrick v. Burget, 486 U.S. 94, 108 S.Ct. 1658, rehearing denied, 487 U.S. 1243, 108 S.Ct. 2921 (1988).

[52]　Id. at 101, 108 S.Ct. at 1663.

[53]　North Carolina Dental, 135 S.Ct. at 1116.

of the private decision itself. It is unclear, however, whether the standard of review in such a case need be no higher than the standard often applied to court review of public agency actions—that is, whether the decision is supported by evidence in the record—or whether some stricter standard of review is required.[54]

Supervision involves two quite different questions: what the supervising agency or court is *empowered* to do, and what it does in fact. For example, suppose a rate regulating agency is authorized to review requests for rate increases, determine whether they are reasonably based on increased costs, and approve or disapprove the request depending on what it finds. Such a scheme would certainly qualify as active supervision. But suppose that in fact the agency is underfunded and simply lacks the resources to investigate such requests. Suppose further that for an extended period of time it has followed a practice of simply rubber-stamping all such requests. Alternatively, the regulatory statute may state that the requested rate will go into effect, say, thirty days after the application unless the agency raises an objection; but in fact the agency never objects. Is "active supervision" for federal antitrust purposes established by the fact that the agency has the authority to supervise, or must it be "actively" supervising as well?

In *New England Motor* the First Circuit essentially found the former, holding that state agencies regulating trucking rates met the supervision requirement simply by virtue of the fact that they were *authorized* to review rates and that they were "staffed and funded" to some degree. In one particular case the state agency had never in its history rejected a rate request, and had never even "requested financial information to support collectively set rates."[55]

But in *Ticor Title* the Supreme Court disagreed with *New England Motor* and found supervision inadequate in a similar situation.[56] The defendants were firms that performed title searches of real property, prepared escrow documents, and sold title insurance. They jointly proposed rates to state insurance regulators through rate bureaus.[57] The state regulatory schemes included a "negative option" provision—that is, proposed rates became effective automatically after a specified time period, commonly thirty days, unless the agency voiced an objection. But the history of

---

[54]   One court found that judicial review was not adequate when the review standard was merely whether the private peer review decision had been arbitrary and capricious. Shahawy v. Harrison, 875 F.2d 1529 (11th Cir. 1989).

[55]   New England Motor Rate Bureau, Inc. v. FTC, 908 F.2d 1064 (1st Cir. 1990).

[56]   FTC v. Ticor Title Ins. Co., 504 U.S. 621, 112 S.Ct. 2169 (1992), on remand, 998 F.2d 1129 (3d Cir. 1993).

[57]   For the definition of a rate bureau, see § 20.3.

attentiveness of the regulatory agencies was quite embarrassing. Some of them checked the arithmetic for accuracy, but some did not even do that. The agencies only infrequently requested additional data in support of a rate increase proposal. Although the agencies were required by law to audit the insurers' costs periodically, very few of the audits were performed. In sum, regulation amounted to little more than a legalized cartel.

In rejecting the *New England Motor* test[58] the Court observed:

Where prices or rates are set as an initial matter by private parties, subject only to a veto if the State chooses to exercise it, the party claiming the immunity must show that state officials have undertaken the necessary steps to determine the specifics of the price-fixing or rate-setting scheme. The mere potential for state supervision is not an adequate substitute for a decision by the State.[59]

In dissent, Chief Justice Rehnquist complained that the majority's position would necessitate substantive review of the quality of state regulation. He predicted that joint rate making could become so dangerous that many regulated firms would abandon it.[60] In that case, the workload on agencies would become even greater. More tariff applications would have to be reviewed, since each firm would be submitting its own. Of course, that result is not necessarily bad. It all depends on what one thinks of the entire enterprise of joint rate proposals. The higher costs of making and supervising individual tariffs may be more than offset by the increased rate competition that results.[61]

Of course, a fundamental problem is that joint tariffs are necessary only in markets where otherwise competing firms operate—thus suggesting that prices should be set by competition rather than regulation in the first place. As the previous chapter notes, many industries of this sort have gone through deregulation, which gives individual firms much greater discretion to set competitive prices.[62]

---

[58] New England Motor, 908 F.2d 1064 (1st Cir. 1990).

[59] *Ticor*, 504 U.S. at 638, 112 S.Ct. at 2179.

[60] *Ticor*, 504 U.S. at 643–644, 112 S.Ct. at 2182.

[61] The more fundamental question, of course, is whether groups of otherwise competing firms in a position to submit joint rate proposals need to be price regulated in the first place; or is price regulation of such markets simply a consequence of regulatory capture?

[62] See §§ 16.1–16.2.

17.5c. Who Must Supervise?

The Supreme Court has generally spoken of supervision of private conduct as coming from the state itself. But in those cases, such as *Midcal*[63] and *Patrick*,[64] the state was the relevant party and the source of the supervision was not an issue.[65] The better rule is that the level of government imposing the regulation is also the one that should do the supervising. If the regulation at issue is from the state, then supervision is ordinarily carried out by the state agency charged with enforcing the regulatory regime. By contrast, if the regulation is municipal, then the municipality should supervise, either through its city council directly or perhaps by a commission or agency.

For example, suppose a city regulates taxicab fares through a scheme in which taxicab companies present evidence of cost increases and request corresponding rate increases. No purpose would be served by a federal antitrust policy that required a state agency, rather than a municipal agency, to review these requests and pass judgment on them. Such a regulatory regime could be very cumbersome, and could put the state in the peculiar position of having to carry out the various, perhaps inconsistent regulatory policies of its many municipalities and other political subdivisions. Indeed, in many instances it would result in a situation where the government entity doing the supervision is less accountable politically to those affected, and this certainly is not the goal of antitrust's "state action" doctrine. Many lower court decisions have suggested that, in assessing supervision, one looks primarily to the supervision applied by the governmental entity imposing the regulation.[66]

§ 17.6 The Special but Shrinking Problem of Municipal Antitrust Liability

The Local Government Antitrust Act (LGAA), passed in 1984, provides that "no damages, interest on damages, costs, or attorney's

---

[63]   445 U.S. 97, 100 S.Ct. 937 (1980).

[64]   486 U.S. 94, 108 S.Ct. 1658, rehearing denied, 487 U.S. 1243, 108 S.Ct. 2921 (1988).

[65]   See also *Hallie*, 471 U.S. at 46 n. 10, 105 S.Ct. at 1720 n. 10, stating that "where state or municipal regulation of a private party is involved * * * active state supervision must be shown. * * *"

[66]   Tri-State Rubbish, Inc. v. Waste Management, Inc., 998 F.2d 1073 (1st Cir. 1993) (municipal, as opposed to state, supervision, is permissible); contrast Chamber of Commerce of USA v. City of Seattle, 890 F.3d 769 (9th Cir. 2018) (municipal ordinance providing for collective bargaining by self-employed drivers required supervision by the state, not the municipality). Other cases are discussed in 1 Antitrust Law ¶ 226d (5th ed. 2020).

fees may be recovered * * * from any local government, or official or employee thereof acting in an official capacity."[67] The right to an injunction is not restricted, and a prevailing plaintiff in an injunction action may recover attorneys fees.[68] The statute gives similar protection for suits "against a person based on any official action directed by a local government, or official or employee thereof acting in an official capacity."[69]

The LGAA removes the most severe antitrust remedies but leaves unanswered the underlying question of when a municipality may claim the *Parker* exemption. In two subsequent cases the Supreme Court addressed that question, and in the process has almost entirely removed the spectre of municipal antitrust liability.

In *Hallie*, the Supreme Court came to two important conclusions that it had resisted earlier.[70] First, although municipal conduct qualifies for *Parker* immunity only if it meets the authorization, or "clear articulation," requirement, no legislature could "be expected to catalog all of the anticipated effects" of its delegation of regulatory authority. The true test should be whether the challenged activity "logically would result" from or be a "foreseeable result" of the state delegation.[71] In this case the city had proposed to annex four adjacent towns, and then give the residents of those towns access to its sewage treatment facility only if they agreed to use the city's entire sewage system. Such a decision was found to be a foreseeable consequence of a state grant of authority to the city to operate a sewage treatment facility and sewage system. Indeed, most post-*Hallie* decisions have found that municipal creation of a monopoly is a foreseeable consequence of a state grant of authority to regulate in a particular market.[72]

---

[67]   15 U.S.C.A. §§ 34–36. See Thatcher Enters. v. Cache County Corp., 902 F.2d 1472, 1477–1478 (10th Cir. 1990) (barring damage award against municipality and its officials).

[68]   See Lancaster Community Hosp. v. Antelope Valley Hosp. Dist., 940 F.2d 397, 404 n. 14 (9th Cir. 1991), cert. denied, 502 U.S. 1094, 112 S.Ct. 1168 (1992).

[69]   See Wee Child Ctr., Inc. v. Lumpkin, 680 F.3d 841 (6th Cir. 2012) (LCGA barred claims against employees of family services agency that allegedly excluded the plaintiffs).

[70]   Town of Hallie v. City of Eau Claire, 471 U.S. 34, 105 S.Ct. 1713 (1985).

[71]   471 U.S. at 42, 105 S.Ct. at 1718.

[72]   For example, City of Columbia & Columbia Outdoor Advertising v. Omni Outdoor Advertising, Inc., 499 U.S. 365, 111 S.Ct. 1344, 1350 (1991) (grant of power to zone foreseeably led to municipal creation of de facto billboard monopoly); Diverse Power, Inc. v. City of LaGrange, Ga., 934 F.3d 1270 (11th Cir. 2019) (state statute permitting city to provide water service did not contemplate, and thus did not authorize, the city's statute tying gas service to water service); AmeriCare MedServices, Inc. v. City of Anaheim, 735 Fed. Appx. 473, 2019-1 Trade Cas. ¶ 80,640 (9th Cir. Aug. 27, 2018), cert. denied, 139 S.Ct. 1338 (2019) (municipality's exclusive contract for emergency medical services was authorized and thus immune under *Parker*).

Of course, this foreseeability test can be pushed only so far. A home rule provision, such as the one at issue in the *Boulder* case, permits a municipality to regulate all of its local markets. It is thus certainly "foreseeable" that a home rule city would regulate land use, cable television, taxicabs, or all the numerous and diverse markets that large municipalities ordinarily regulate. But *Hallie* did not purport to overrule *Boulder*'s conclusion that a home rule provision does not effectively "authorize" anything.

Under *Boulder*, before a municipality can meet the authorization requirement the state must have given a *market specific* grant of regulatory power. A generic power to regulate, such as is contained in a home rule provision, is insufficient. However, once a city enjoys such a market specific grant, the regulatory decisions that arguably flow from regulation in the area meet the test. One apparent exception is if the local government's regulatory action is manifestly contrary to the state grant of regulatory authority. For example, a few courts have held that a state grant of authority to regulate did not authorize the municipality to engage in anticompetitive or unfair exclusionary practices.[73] As a general matter, however, questions about whether a municipality goes beyond its regulatory authority, or violates its regulatory mandate, should be addressed under state law. The source of municipal power to regulate comes from the state, and the state courts are the best forums for deciding when a municipality has overstepped. A contrary result would turn every municipal violation of its regulatory power into the basis for a federal antitrust challenge.[74]

As noted previously,[75] the *Hallie* decision also established that, with respect to the municipality's own actions, "active supervision" was not required. The Supreme Court returned to this point in its *North Carolina Dental* decision, noting that, unlike agencies, municipalities have "powers across different economic spheres, substantially reducing the risk that [they] would pursue private interests while regulating any single field." Further, they have elected leaders accountable in the political process.[76] The dentists who formed the "agency" in this case did not.

---

[73]   Surgical Care Center of Hammond v. Hospital Service Dist., 171 F.3d 231 (5th Cir. 1999), cert. denied, 528 U.S. 964, 120 S.Ct. 398 (1999), on remand, 2001 WL 8586 (E.D.La.2001), affirmed, 309 F.3d 836 (5th Cir. 2002) (statute permitting joint ventures did not authorize anticompetitive exclusion).

[74]   On this point, see § 20.4.

[75]   See § 20.5a.

[76]   North Carolina State Bd. of Dental Examiners v. FTC, 574 U.S. 494, 508, 135 S.Ct. 1101, 1112–1113 (2015).

Table of Cases

Table of Statutes

Table of Regulations

Table of Rules

Index

References are to Sections